Books by Roy Hoopes

RALPH INGERSOLL

A Biography

RALPH INGERSOLL

A Biography
ROY HOOPES

FOREWORD BY MAX LERNER

NEW YORK *Atheneum* 1985

Library of Congress Cataloging in Publication Data

Hoopes, Roy,———
    Ralph Ingersoll.

    Bibliography: p.
    Includes index.
    1. Ingersoll, Ralph, 1900-   2. Journalists —
United States —Biography.   I. Title.
PN4874.I5H66 1985   070'.92'4 [B]   84-45624
ISBN 0-689-11554-7

Published simultaneously in Canada by Collier Macmillan Canada, Inc.
Composition by Westchester Book Composition, Inc., Yorktown Heights, New York
Printed and bound by Fairfield Graphics, Fairfield, Pennsylvania
Designed by Kathleen Carey
First Edition

For Robert Yoakum,

who, in the best Ingersoll tradition, made it happen

Foreword

"It is harder to write a good life than to live one," said Lytton Strachey. Ralph Ingersoll's was a tempestuous life, and he was lucky in finding—in Roy Hoopes—a biographer who has restored to their rightful place in the history of the print media a personality and career that stirred considerable tumult in their day. The history of journalism has paid attention to the press barons but too little to the men who have charged the imagination of journalism.

Ingersoll never had the piratical energy and empire-building will of a Bennett, Hearst, Pulitzer, Beaverbrook. He was more formative in Henry Luce's developing press empire than is usually recognized—which is part of Roy Hoopes' story. But his great journalistic craft was in vision, whose payoffs are hard to trace.

He was prolific in starting innovations but spotty as an enterpriser in running or finishing them. Always he was hypnotic in his face-to-face encounters, but also neurotic, contumacious, abrasive—which cost him heavily in the enemies he made and the sense of wreckage he left behind. So much of his achievement was taken over by others, without acknowledgment, that—like many rebellious spirits—he was buried in the ruins he had made.

There are three major stories in his life—his role on the *New Yorker* staff and later in the Luce magazine empire; his trials, triumphs, and disasters with his own path-breaking daily newspaper, *PM*; and his war adventures as adviser to generals and as combat correspondent. I was a fascinated observer of the first, very much a participant in the second, and marginally involved in the third.

But the *PM* episode is the central one for me, as it was indeed for Ingersoll himself. *Fortune*, *Time*, and *Life* were his training grounds, but *PM* was his battlefield; and it was his *PM* fame that led to his war career and writing. Although he was away from *PM*, on war duty, as long as he was running it, it was his *PM*. It took its character from him. It was his glory and doom as well as his dream, and for the rest of his life he carried its scars.

I was two years younger than Ingersoll, and younger also than Henry Luce and Briton Hadden, who were seniors at Yale when I was a freshman in 1919. Reading this book, I was reminded again of how different the America of the 1920s was for me and for this little elite band who belonged to the same clubs, drank and partied together, danced and slept with—and perhaps married and divorced—the same girls, competed with each other in the same corporate board rooms or editorial offices. My family were Russian immigrant Jews, I was at Yale only because of a Hillhouse High School scholarship, and I "heeled" the *Yale Daily News* of Luce and Hadden without success. So I taught at Sarah Lawrence and Harvard in the 1930s, with a three-year stint as political editor of the *Nation* before I resumed teaching constitutional history and presidential politics at Williams College. It was from Williams that I joined *PM* in 1943.

I say this to underscore the gulf between Ingersoll's world and mine, which is essential in understanding what happened to both of us at *PM* and to *PM* itself. It was a social and class difference between two groups of writers and in fact two Americas. The common ground we had was Adolf Hitler and Franklin Roosevelt, one the serpent to be slain, the other the hero to slay him. But there was a ground of experience we didn't share.

Pearl Harbor emptied colleges like Williams of their students, and when Ralph Ingersoll was called off to war and I was exempt as a man with a family, I figured there might be editorial room for me on the page and took the chance of calling him. He wasn't eager but suggested I do some sample editorials. I wrote two and met him under the clock at the Waldorf—a big, hulking figure who had the look of a balding eagle very much in a hurry. He stopped for a moment, swept his formidable eyes over my two pieces, thrust them back with a magisterial "You'll never be a journalist"—and was gone by the time my stomach started to knot and my heart to break.

A month or so later, when Ingersoll was in the army and John P. Lewis was his managing editor in charge, Lewis invited me to lunch; I brought two or three editorials again, and he said "Fine, will do." Within a few days, after an editorial meeting on the news of the Casablanca Conference, Lewis said, "The Professor will do the editorial. It either will or won't run." It did, and brashly

I took leave from my college post and became part of *PM*.

There I was, writing and signing the editorial page that Ingersoll had written and signed before. When he returned I continued to write it, and was part of the governing board of *PM*. Yet looking back from these pages, I see the gaps in my knowledge of him.

I knew little about his relation with his parents, the battles with Ross at the *New Yorker*, the lethal mayhems and murders inflicted in the Florentine corridors of power at Time Inc., the love-hate relationship with Henry Luce, the "million-dollar lunch" that Luce gave Ingersoll to keep from losing him.

In short, while we all gossiped a good deal about Ingersoll—especially during the late hours when the night staff was putting the paper to bed and I was waiting to correct my page proofs—we didn't get much beyond the routine scuttlebutt. It was mostly about his legendary affairs with Lillian Hellman and with Laura Hobson, his psychoanalysis with Gregory Zilboorg, his difficult relations with Marshall Field, and his handling or mishandling of the raging pro-Communist and anti-Communist bands that had ravaged the morale and diverted much of the energy of the staff.

This is why Roy Hoopes' account is bound to be absorbing reading, especially for the generations that didn't live through these fiery decades of journalistic rivalries.

But I also wonder how well Ingersoll knew us—the staff and readers of the paper whom he left behind when he went off to the wars. His battles in the Time Inc. empire had been managerial and power battles, at which he wasn't much good. He was one of the great memorandum writers of our age and his prospectus for *PM* has become a classic of promise and commitment. But in the ideological staff battles his style, so effective in Time Inc.'s war of memoranda, was of little avail. Neither of the two camps thought much of Ingersoll's sophistication with ideas.

His war experiences were happy ones and released his energies, giving him a new domain to conquer, which he did with his old zest for hypnotic one-on-one persuasion. Generals succumbed to it, all the way to Omar Bradley, who became his military hero. Ingersoll was again able to display his talent for infighting. But he showed a new one as well—the talent for deception, to divert the attention of the German enemy from the actual Channel crossing. He also developed his writing talents in his vivid and popular war books. His war dispatches, especially those on his D-Day experiences, owe more to Hemingway than he admitted but belong in any anthology of World War II correspondents.

His return to *PM* must have been a letdown, like Ulysses' return from his glamorous world travels to the little closed-in world of Ithaca. This was when I came to know him best, and I fear now that it was a muted, embittered man I knew, who had come home where he no longer felt at home.

I had experienced his generosity during a spell in the war years, when I was waiting in Paris for an assignment to the front as a war correspondent, in the meantime sending overlong dispatches to *PM* on the French political struggles, which ran as *The Third Battle for France*. Ingersoll knew exactly how to break through the bureaucratic logjam, got me my assignments, arranged for my quartering in a succession of press camps on the front, and showed extraordinary kindness to one whose amateurism at the craft he had predicted.

But after his return to take over the reins of power at *PM*, I found him suspicious of me as of others. He seemed to have projected his own talent for intrigue onto us, seeing me as part of a cabal against him and even convincing himself that I wanted to take over the paper for myself. I quickly disabused him of that.

I have in fact always been disastrously deficient in the power drive and in bureaucratic intrigue. I worked with John P. Lewis, whose tough-minded talents as editor made *PM* function effectively while he headed it, and with Louis Weiss, Marshall Field's shrewd and subtle adviser on the directing board. Yet there were times when Field, the publisher and patron, would write on some cherished topic and I would answer him publicly and too brashly.

My energies went into the Opinion page where my signed editorials became my columns, as happened also with I. F. Stone and Saul K. Padover, who often shared the page with me. Together we developed a *PM* audience who joined us in our pretty radical beliefs and illusions, even though they could never make the paper pay. It was that kind of paper.

There was a tragic element in it for Ingersoll, who had to leave the paper he had founded, in midstream, and who thus cut himself off from its editors and staffers and its new postwar audience. He had always depended on the magic, not only of his magnetism but also of being in tune with the deep tides of history, and now the magic seemed to have deserted him. So he lost or left *PM*, or both, and was never the same again.

I met him again, long after, with his business partner Charles Marsh at the Jamaica Inn, which they had a stake in. He had made millions in a chain of small-town papers, to which he sometimes gave a conservative touch. "I wanted to show the S.O.B.'s," he said with his old flair, "that I could beat them at their own game." He was still self-assertive, adversarial. His governing life paradigm was still Ralph Ingersoll against the world.

But the earlier Ingersoll, that of *PM*, had done something with journalism that no one had done before, and American journalism was never the same after he did it. We owe a debt to Roy Hoopes for giving us the richly detailed story of what he did and how he did it and where he succeeded as well as failed.

In the current evaluations of Ingersoll, using the metaphors of Gestalt psychology, the failures have been the figure, the success has been the ground. But the long-range Gestalt is likely to show the failures as ground and the success as figure. The American media today, both print and electronic, carry his image somewhere within them. For Ingersoll dreamt the impossible dream of a fiercely independent daily that would have clarity, judgment, patterned structure, beauty, would draw talent to it like a magnet, and would always be in the thick of the fight, living dangerously so that people could live more fully.

It was indeed an impossible dream. But, with all his acerbities, he had passion and vision; and the dream will live on, long after he and I are dead.

M AX LERNER
March 4, 1985

Preface

The death of Ralph Ingersoll on March 8, 1985, as this book was going to press, prompts me to present a bit of background on the origins and writing of his biography. In the winter of 1981, Robert and Alice Yoakum were visiting the Ingersolls in what was then their winter home in St. Croix, U.S. Virgin Islands. The Yoakums live in Lakeville, Connecticut, a few miles from the Ingersoll home in Cornwall Bridge, and have been, for years, friends of Ralph and Toby, as everyone calls Thelma, Ingersoll's fourth wife. Yoakum is a writer and syndicated humor columnist, and while they were in St. Croix that winter, the idea that he might write a biography of Ingersoll came up and the project was initiated with enthusiasm. The Yoakums taped several interviews with Ralph and one with Toby, and when they left the island, plans were made to continue the book when the Ingersolls returned to Cornwall Bridge in the spring. Yoakum anticipated a project of two or three years, with him interviewing Ralph and others and doing the necessary research in between the deadlines for his twice-a-week column. As the months went by, however, he was able to do very little work on the biography, and Yoakum decided to look around for someone who might share the burden.

About this time, I had just completed my biography of the American novelist, James M. Cain, and Yoakum, a long-time friend, knew about it; in fact he had heard nothing from me but James M. Cain for about three years. He was also beginning to realize what a huge and demanding undertaking a biography is. So he asked me if I would join him as co-biographer, assuming that Ralph would approve. This was to be an authorized biography, with full access to all the Ingersoll papers. After reading *Cain*, looking over my professional résumé, and inviting me to Cornwall Bridge for a personal meeting, Ingersoll approved Yoakum's co-author.

The next step was to survey the raw material contained in 191 standard library manuscript boxes, plus 9 huge transfiles of material not yet processed but on deposit in the Boston University Library. There were also several file cabinets full of manuscripts and correspondence still in Ingersoll's office in Cornwall Bridge. The most important of these papers were the three unpublished manuscripts of Ingersoll's autobiography—*The Years with Luce, The Story of PM,* and *Time Out for A War.* The first thing I did was read these books, and soon I was turning the pages with all the excitement of a journalist who has stumbled upon a major story that has never been told.

After we had made a full survey of the material, Yoakum realized that even with the help of another author, the book would still put a tremendous demand on his time, so he inquired whether I might be interested in taking on the entire project. I said I would be delighted.

We already had an understanding from Ingersoll that we would have complete freedom in writing the book, but I wanted this spelled out in writing, and Ingersoll had no objection. He was the ultimate professional. He saw each chapter as it emerged from the typewriter and he always confined his comments to questions of fact and rarely questioned my judgment or interpretation. When he did, he backed up his comments with additional facts. But he never insisted that I change anything simply because it did not paint him in the best of colors. Once, Toby says, when he was reading the chapter on his life in the 1920's, he looked up from the manuscript and said, "What a fool I was."

The book took approximately one year to research, another to write, and a third to polish, proof, and illustrate. Every moment was fascinating for me and my only regret is that Ralph did not live to see its publication. Although he had read the manuscript, he did not see the finished book, which saddened all of us who were close to him at the end. We knew how much this book meant to him and how anxious he was to see it published and to measure the reaction.

The book is written in the present tense because during its evolution, Ralph Ingersoll was very much alive. Hence, when I quote from his autobiography or from a personal interview, I inevitably use the citation "Ingersoll says." His presence will be felt for some time and I am pleased that it lingers on in the pages of this biography.

ROY HOOPES
Bethesda, Maryland
March, 1985

Contents

Illustrations

*A Time Inc. executive, circa 1935, on the move—Ralph Ingersoll,
managing editor of* Fortune

1: The Million-Dollar Lunch

In 1937 the Ritz Carlton Hotel occupied a whole block along the west side of Manhattan's Madison Avenue, from Forty-sixth Street to Forty-seventh. It had been built in 1910 and would be torn down in 1951, because the property on which it stood had become too valuable to support a hotel of the nineteenth-century type, even one that had been immortalized by Ludwig Bemelmans as the Hotel Splendide. But in the 1930s it was in its prime, a landmark of the New York Establishment where at night beautiful people gathered to drink champagne and dance at Society balls, while by day Very Important Persons made their way past the potted palms in the lobby to one of the hotel's many restaurants to eat lunch and talk business—and, as often happened, to cut some Very Big deals.

It was fall, the air was crisp and alive but still warm, and two familiar figures in the city's exciting world of mass communications were waiting to be seated in the Ritz's big oval restaurant. Both were in their late thirties, obviously prosperous, and prematurely balding. The shorter and better known of the two was serious, shy, articulate, but, as most of his associates knew, given to stammering, especially when excited. His name was Henry Robinson Luce. He was president of Time Inc. and editor in chief of *Time*, *Fortune*, and *Life*. Only the year before, he had been characterized by a now-famous *New Yorker* profile as an "ambitious, gimlet-eyed baby tycoon."

The other man had also been etched in Wolcott Gibbs's acid prose: "a burly, able, tumbledown Yaleman . . . former Fortune editor, . . . descendant of 400-famed Ward McAllister . . . *Time*'s No. 1 hypochondriac littered his desk with pills, unguents, Kleenex." Gibbs had had first-hand experience with his hypochondria; for two years, at the *New Yorker*, he had shared office space with McAllister's descendant. He was, of course, not as recognizable as Luce but was enough of a celebrity for it to have been reported on the radio the previous spring that he was among those who had been killed when the German dirigible *Hindenburg* burst into flames while landing at Lakehurst, New Jersey. (The fact was that he had been booked on the *return* trip of the *Hindenburg*, headed for a secret interview with Adolf Hitler. The radio station had based its casualties report on the wrong list.) He was six feet two and slightly stooped, with a brown mustache and wide, sparkling eyes that radiated vitality and nervous energy. He was also, as most of his associates knew, a compulsive writer, especially of memos signed "Ralph McAllister Ingersoll." He was general manager of Time Inc. and publisher of its flagship, *Time*.

Luce and Ingersoll were probably the most talented and successful editors in New York in 1937—and they had a lot to talk about on that crisp autumn day. Less than a year earlier, on an exhilarating, emotional morning in November, when everyone at Time Inc. knew the recently launched magazine called *Life* was an incredible success, Luce had shocked Ingersoll with the announcement that he (Luce) would be taking over management of the new magazine, which Ingersoll had considered his baby. Ingersoll, as general manager of the company during a period when Luce, for personal reasons, was absent from the office a great deal, had been the one to move the idea for a picture magazine out of mothballs and onto the drawing boards. When Luce returned from his honeymoon, he became more active in its creation. Then, when *Life* was finally published, and its success, combined with a ridiculously low first-year guaranteed advertising rate, threatened to bankrupt the company if it fulfilled the obvious demand, Luce felt it was his responsibility to nurse the new magazine through its expensive growing pains. At the same time, he knew the company would need a healthy flagship, and *Time* was beginning to have problems of its own; so he decided to make "the best man I could find," as he later described his choice in a memo, publisher of *Time*. It would be Ingersoll's job to see that *Time* made the money necessary to support *Life*. Ingersoll had been stunned, far more than the often insensitive Luce appreciated then, and furthermore, he did not like *Time*. But he was a loyal lieutenant and could not, of course, refuse such a request. He agreed to take the new assignment and to stay with the company five more years, or until *Life* was in the black, then he would leave Time Inc. He had told Luce this. "Good," said Luce. "Five years is a long time, Mac" (everyone called Ingersoll "Mac" in those days).

What Ingersoll did not tell Luce was that by the time he returned to his office that morning, he had resolved never again to give his soul to a publication that was not his own. Now, late in 1937, Ingersoll knew the day was approaching when his pledge to Luce of the year before would be fulfilled. Luce, on the other hand, had come to realize the depth of Ingersoll's disappointment at having *Life* taken away from him, and he certainly appreciated the contribution Ingersoll had made to Time Inc. Furthermore, Luce was now aware that Ingersoll had meant what he had said from time to time in earlier luncheon conversations, about leaving the company to start a publication of his own. That spring Ingersoll and his secretary, Veronica Keating, had taken simultaneous vacations and retreated to Ingersoll's Shadow Rock Farm in Lakeville, Connecticut, where Ingersoll dictated a sixty-one-page (long even for him) memorandum outlining his first thoughts about a "new form of newspaper." He had mentioned it to Luce and had, in fact, begun making overtures around town to see if the climate might be right for financing a new newspaper.

So the two men had a lot to discuss. Luce, especially, seemed anxious to talk, and Ingersoll knew it. "When Harry had something important to say," Ingersoll recalled, "he liked to make an occasion of it, and that day he asked the captain to get us one of the front-row terrace tables."

Henry Luce was not much of a man for small talk. As soon as they were seated and had ordered drinks, he launched into "his speech," as Ingersoll described it. And Ingersoll, who was gregarious and given to interrupting conversations with his own ideas and observations, was, for once, conspicuously silent. In fact, as Luce's proposal began to unfold, Ingersoll became "spellbound."

Many years later, in his unpublished memoirs, Ingersoll reconstructed the speech, which was not so difficult a task because the imagery was so strong and uncomplicated.

"Mac," Luce began, "we are like farmers, you and I, and there are seasons in our lives. First there is the planting and then the tough, hard work of cultivating, and finally the crop grows. Then comes the rich experience of harvesting it. At Time Inc. we planted good crops and we have cultivated them well. Now they are ready to harvest. You have done well with *Time* in the last year and a half, and *Life* will make a very great deal of money next year.

"So we have come to the time of harvest. We have the young men to bring in the harvest for us. We are not young men anymore. [Luce was hardly thirty-nine and Ingersoll was two years younger.] So it is a good thing for us to let them harvest our crops for us. No one begrudges our share, because they are *our* crops, grown with the sweat of our labor. I want you to think in these terms. I want you to see what a happy life we would have and how much satisfaction we would get out of it, and how right it would be for us—I say 'us' because we are a very good team together, we understand each other."

Suddenly, switching the subject, as Luce often did, from poetic imagery to dollars, he continued: "Here is what I think is right, Mac: If you say you'll stay for five more years, I will give you—today—a million dollars in Time stock. After five years—well, you can make up your mind."

Then, in what seems to Ingersoll a characteristic Lucian aside, he added: "A million dollars is a good thing to have."

It was easy to see why Ingersoll was spellbound. A million dollars was, indeed, a good thing to have—then or now. But there was something else. For some time Ingersoll had felt a definite hostility from his boss. Ingersoll was, in fact, engaged in an inner-office struggle to remake *Time*'s image and was meeting considerable resistance from most of Time Inc.'s brass, including Luce. But now Luce was replacing "that hostility with love," and Ingersoll was admittedly "numbed."

The story behind Henry Luce's unusual offer that day is a long one, which will be told in due time. But to understand Ingersoll's reaction it is necessary to know something about the relationship these men shared in 1937. The two editors were a very good team, which was formed in 1930 when Luce lured Ingersoll away from the *New Yorker* to manage his fledgling magazine *Fortune*. In five years Ingersoll boosted *Fortune*'s circulation to 130,000, from 30,000, and in his last year as managing editor the magazine had shown a profit of half a million dollars. It sold for one dollar a copy in the depths of the depression; its readers, mostly corporate executives, felt they had to have it. Luce rewarded Ingersoll by making him vice president and general manager, and Ingersoll in turn rewarded Luce by providing the moving force that led to the creation of *Life*. During this period the two men also drew together personally; Ingersoll was one of the first two Time Inc. staffers (the other was *Fortune* writer Archibald MacLeish) whom Luce told about his plans to divorce his wife, Lila, and marry Clare Brokaw. And it was Ingersoll whom he had called one night at the height of the divorce crisis, frightened and stammering that he was alone in a hotel room and afraid he might jump out of the window. Ingersoll rushed over to the hotel with his doctor friend Louis Bishop, and the two of them calmed Luce down.

But most important, Luce admired Ingersoll's ability and is known to have told at least one Time Inc. staffer in the 1930s that Ingersoll was the only man in the company who had the right stuff to be a publisher. He valued Ingersoll as a great editor, innovator, and generator of a constant stream of editorial and publishing ideas.

What Luce did not know, however, was the extent to which his impressionable, quick-learning alter ego had been influenced by the ideas and emotions prevalent in the thirties. It was a time when the very foundations of the capitalist system were being questioned by intellectuals everywhere, and many, in their disappointment at the failure of the system to cope with the depression, had begun a flirtation with communism. In fact, *Fortune* magazine in the early 1930s (under the editorship of Ralph Ingersoll) had led the way in examining the morals, ethics, and practices of American business and had run at least two major articles on the communist system and the Russian economy. Ingersoll was not immune to the political, economic, and social ferment of that period. He had come to Time Inc. remarkably apolitical and naive, but through the friends he had met during his early *Fortune* days—Archibald MacLeish, Lillian Hellman, Ernest Hemingway and John Dos Passos, to mention the best known—he had begun to question the values of the capitalist system and to consider communist doctrine, at least with an open mind.

By 1937 Ingersoll was in something of an intellectual turmoil as his intensifying political, economic, and social liberalism came increasingly into conflict with the conservative philosophy of his boss. And the conflict was aggravated by the fact that *Time*, the magazine he published, was uncomfortably tolerant of the winds of fascism blowing in Europe. Ingersoll was struggling not only to change this situation but to improve the caliber of the writing in *Time*. He was making progress, but the difficulty only reaffirmed his conviction that the day was approaching when he would have to seek his freedom. In college he had decided it would be words that set him free; by 1937 he knew it would take a publication of his own. But there was another thing bothering Ralph Ingersoll: As he would later put it to Wolcott Gibbs, he was "an editor making $45,000 a year, but practically unknown." By 1937, having played critical roles in the evolution of three major American magazines—the *New Yorker*, *Fortune*, and *Life*—and having long since decided that Harold Ross, although an eccentric genius, was not his equal as an editor, Ingersoll, after running Time Inc. for two years, had come to the conclusion (expressed in a curious self-analysis written in the 1950s) that he was "genuinely Henry Luce's superior." He also knew, and had known for some time, that the only way he could establish the kind of reputation he wanted was as editor and publisher of his own magazine— or newspaper. And he had already taken some concrete steps in that direction. His preliminary explorations had provided him with a glimpse of his publishing future as his own boss—and he had liked it.

Ingersoll could not, of course, announce at that luncheon that he was leaving Henry Luce. For one thing, *Life* was still in the red; for another, he had not yet done enough groundwork on his new publication to know if it was feasible, how much it would cost, or whether he could raise the money. After Luce made his surprising offer, there was, Ingersoll recalls, a long, awkward silence, during which they both felt slightly embarrassed. Then Luce said briskly, "Well, that was what I had to say to you, Mac. Let it sink in, then let me know sometime— I'll put the stock through at the next directors' meeting after you tell me." Then he abruptly changed the subject.

Ingersoll does not remember how long he agonized over the offer before giving Luce his answer. He says, "I was moved—and I damned well should have been." But he also recalls his rather cavalier decision: "What the hell do I want with a million dollars?"

He was also struck by another thing: Luce's feeling that he was getting old and that it was time to let the young men do the harvesting. Ingersoll at thirty-six did not think he was getting too old to keep on planting—if it was his own crop. He believed he had at least five more years of high energy left—which turned out to be one of the worst estimates of human talent he ever made (he was still going strong in his late seventies).

Accompanying his professional development as an editor was a personal, emotional drive that was to play an equally significant role in the evolution of the new and different newspaper forming in his mind. Ever since he began to rebel against his father's desire that his son follow in his footsteps as an engineer, Ralph Ingersoll had been possessed by a desire to achieve—to prove that he was every bit as capable as his father and that he could do just as well, maybe even better, as a writer or editor.

He also needed to demonstrate his ability to women—or at least one woman. When Ingersoll was rejected by a girl he had fallen madly in love with, it took him two days of crying and five years of emotional turmoil to get over it. In 1925, when he had decided it was time to marry, the girl he proposed to surprised him by saying no. He soon married another girl, Elizabeth "Tommy" Carden, but that marriage was doomed, primarily because Tommy developed tuberculosis and could not have normal sexual relations. In 1935, on his last assignment as managing editor of *Fortune*, he had met and fallen in love with a talented emerging playwright named Lillian Hellman. The affair was brief and stormy, ending one Sunday on an island in the Long Island Sound, near the Connecticut side, where Lillian owned a small house. Ingersoll had been invited to spend a weekend with Lillian, the producer of her current play (Herman Shumlin), her ex-husband (Arthur Kober), and her reappearing ex-lover (Dashiell Hammett). The conversation at dinner was gay, witty, and relaxed, but Ingersoll was not; Lillian's companions were, as he wrote in his unpublished memoirs, "wittier than I," and he reacted violently. "I couldn't even sleep with her in this ménage, which would have been the only method by which I could have reassured myself. So when the pain became intolerable, I went down to the dock and untied a canoe and I paddled until the island was no more than a skyline. There I experienced an almost overwhelming emotional crisis in which . . . I was again a small boy defeated by the woman I loved, full of passions I did not understand. . . . I saved my soul by my resolve. . . . I would be a Man. I would take no man's ideas. I would work for no other man, except as a means to acquire my own ends. . . . I would prove my manhood by creating a publication of my own."

He would show them; he would show the world! An old story, perhaps, but Ingersoll says, quite candidly, that is the way it happened. He also says that if Henry Luce had allowed him to take charge of *Life* in a way that made it clear to the world that it was his, he would have been satisfied and probably would have stayed on at Time Inc. But he understood why Luce could not permit this. So he had to leave the company and carry out his resolve, made that day in a canoe on Long Island Sound.

Although his professional life had been remarkably successful, Ingersoll, in his personal relationships, especially with women, was "startlingly ineffective—almost an imbecile, a total failure." He could not seem to have the women he loved and wanted, and he rejected those (and there were many) who wanted and loved him. Finally he decided to seek psychiatric advice. The Hellman affair had led to the breakup of Ingersoll's marriage, and he was now dating another woman: Laura Hobson, then a promotion executive at Time Inc., who would go on to establish her own reputation as a novelist with the publication in 1947 of the widely admired and much-discussed best-seller *Gentleman's Agreement*. Through Laura, Ingersoll was introduced to Dr. Gregory Zilboorg, a prototype of the Park Avenue psychiatrist, whose wealthy and famous patients included, at one time, the millionaire playboy Marshall Field. That Field was an earlier patient of Zilboorg's would eventually cause problems for both Field and Ingersoll when the two became associated in the publication of Ingersoll's new kind of newspaper. Meanwhile, Zilboorg did have a profound impact on Ingersoll's life. After their very first session, the doctor said, "I will take you as a patient. . . . I think you are very ill, much more ill than you have any idea. But I believe you will have a very successful analysis because you are intensely curious . . . also, you have great energy, drive and obviously react positively to life."

Ingersoll was, as Zilboorg perceived, intensely curious, and this curiosity led him into another significant adventure. Ever since the early 1930s, when he had initiated stories about Russia and communism in *Fortune*, Ingersoll had been intrigued by the dedication of the Communists and curious about what communism really stood for. This interest led in 1938 to his joining a Communist party study group that met at the apartment of a friend. "It was very, very secret at the time," says Ingersoll, "and a damn foolish and dangerous thing for me to do . . . exposure could have ruined me over night." The only true-believing Communists in the group were the lecturers, who were introduced with pseudonyms. The rest were, like Ingersoll, "the most recent of silk-stocking recruits." Ingersoll remained a member of the group for less than a year and then made an open break with Russia over its foreign policy. But there is no question that he was receptive to Communist economics and always reluctant to reject an idea simply because it was supported by the Communists.

* * *

A few days later Ingersoll gave Luce his answer: He would stay at Time Inc. as long as Luce felt he was needed, but he would not commit himself for five years. When *Life* was in the black, he wanted to be relieved of his responsibilities so that he would have more time to explore the possibilities for his new publication.

Luce's response was surprisingly generous, very much in the manner of a kindly uncle to a younger nephew: "OK, if you must, get it out of your system: Go ahead and work up your ideas. When you get to where it needs all your time, take a sabbatical year—with pay—and see whether it is as good as you think it is. If it isn't, come back here; if it is maybe I'll go along with you."

The following year, having committed himself to his new publication and having taken the first step toward cutting himself free from Time Inc., Ingersoll began to do what he did best: put things in motion for publishing a new form of newspaper. The origins of his paper went back to 1924, when the pressmen who produced the New York metropolitan newspapers went on strike the very day Ingersoll was supposed to start as a cub reporter on Hearst's *New York American*. During the strike the New York papers published an eight-page summary of the news, which was easy to read and to hold, devoid of advertising and sensationalism. Over the years Ingersoll had reflected on the various criteria of the ideal newspaper. Then, as a participant in the journalistic revolution taking place at Time Inc., he began to visualize how the innovations made by the editors of *Time*, *Fortune*, and *Life* might be translated to a daily newspaper.

After Ingersoll told Luce that he was definitely going ahead with his plans to publish his own newspaper, Luce was very encouraging, even sounding as if Time Inc., might become involved in Ingersoll's project. At later lunches they began to talk about an independent, but joint, venture, which would make it possible for them to establish a world press association that would be closer to what they thought press associations should be—"alert, informed, and aggressive." Luce also implied that when Time Inc. could afford it, he would come into Ingersoll's company as a minority stockholder. Ingersoll was now estimating that it would take several million dollars to launch his publication, but Luce did not think that was a problem. "With Time Inc.'s endorsement," he said, "you won't even have to look; the money will come and find you."

Ingersoll was confident he could raise the money. He was descended from two well-known families and had impeccable credentials as a fund-raiser. The Very Rich did not awe Ralph McAllister Ingersoll. As a young man-about-town he had dated their daughters and had been invited to their mansions on Park Avenue, on Long Island, and in Newport. And as managing editor of *Fortune* he had met many of the nation's industrial leaders in their boardrooms and at luncheon or cocktail parties. His success at the *New Yorker* and Time Inc., moreover, gave credence to his enthusiastic upbeat promotional flare. Ingersoll knew he could sell the Very Rich anything he believed in, and in 1937 the two things he believed in most were (1) Ralph Ingersoll and (2) his idea for a new publication.

But as infectious as Ingersoll's salesmanship was, the money did not come looking for him. For one thing, not long after the lunch at which Luce had hinted that the new newspaper might have Time Inc. support, he began to back away. "I've been talking to . . . to two or three people—associates," Luce told Ingersoll. "It wouldn't be quite fair to put the finger on them, Mac. They've told me that Time Inc. shouldn't sponsor anything it doesn't control, and this is your show. Maybe later I can come in myself."

Later, Luce did talk about putting in a hundred thousand dollars, but then he backed away from that too.

Ingersoll did not know who these "associates" at Time Inc. were, but he had an idea: Clare Luce. He knew she disliked him, and he knew why. Back in 1936, several months before the first issue of *Life* was published, there had been a legendary confrontation between Clare Luce and Ralph Ingersoll, so legendary, in fact, that there are several accounts of what happened. Clare's version is that Ingersoll and Dan Longwell, a *Time* editor assigned to the *Life* task force, had invited the Luces to dinner one evening for the express purpose, Luce hinted, of asking her to take an editorial post at *Life* (she had at one time been an editor at *Vanity Fair*, where, among other things, she had proposed that Condé Nast publish a picture magazine). After the dinner they all retired to the Luce apartment for drinks, but instead of offering Clare a job, Ingersoll launched into a long tirade (seconded by Longwell) about how the planning of *Life* was suffering because Luce was spending too much time away from the office. "I don't like to have to put this bluntly," Ingersoll said to Luce, "but, Harry, you just can't make a success of *Life* with one hand tied behind Clare's back."

It was Clare who answered: "Harry Luce," she remembers saying, "could publish a better magazine than Ingersoll or Longwell with both hands tied behind his back." She then went to her bedroom, had a good cry—and resolved never again to set foot in her husband's office. She would devote herself to writing (the most immediate result of which, she says, was her play *The Women*).

Ingersoll's version is slightly different and will be told in due course. But years later Clare Luce said that what had really made her mad was that her husband had agreed with Ingersoll, saying "You are absolutely right." She also said, however, that she "never forgave Ingersoll for that remark."

She also flatly denies having had anything to do with Time Inc.'s decision not to back Ingersoll in starting a new publication. And whether she did or did not support Ingersoll's newspaper is irrelevant, because it would probably have been impossible to find anyone at Time Inc. in 1938 who was enthusiastic about the company's becoming involved in the publication of a major newspaper. Furthermore, it is safe to say that it would have been difficult to find a single executive at Time Inc. ready to endorse Henry Luce's involving the company in anything Ralph Ingersoll was running. By 1938 only a handful of people at Time Inc. were not waiting anxiously for Ingersoll to leave, and probably even a few of his colleagues had been disappointed to learn that he had *not* burned up with the *Hindenburg*. Eric Hodgins, who succeeded Ingersoll as managing editor of *Fortune*, thought it was Ingersoll who initiated the inner-office politics for which Time Inc. would later become famous. "The feeling was widespread among the staff," Hodgins wrote in his memoirs, "that Ingersoll was a tricky customer. It was often said of him, with variations: 'If there were two equally effective ways of reaching the same objective, and one of them was straight and above board and the other underground and devious, Mac Ingersoll would in-stinctively take the latter!'" And T. S. Matthews, who was picked by Ingersoll to be *Time*'s "Back-of-the-Book" editor (a promotion that subsequently led to his long career as managing editor), wrote in his memoirs that Ingersoll liked power, enjoyed exercising it, and was "a natural conspirator . . . to such an extent that his own allegiance became intolerable to him." Manfred Gottfried, whom Ingersoll made managing editor of *Time* in 1937, said that when Ingersoll finally did leave Time Inc., "I think I was the only one who was not stone-cold hostile to him."

Ingersoll, of course, knew he aroused hostility in the office, but he did not let that bother him. General managers do not as a rule win popularity contests, and Ingersoll could always (and with considerable justification) attribute the hostility to jealousy or misunderstanding. But there was no denying that he could be overbearing, and he did have a tendency to call erring managing editors on the carpet as if they were office boys, as T. S. Matthews once said.

This, then, was the situation in 1938 when Ingersoll, still the publisher of *Time*, began to think seriously about starting his own publication: He had turned down a million-dollar offer to remain at Time Inc., but was still being urged by his boss to stay, despite the fact that he was involved in a struggle to alter *Time*'s style and editorial policies and was disliked by most of his colleagues. He was seeking a divorce from his wife, involved in an emotional affair with Laura Hobson, and had been diagnosed as emotionally ill by a psychiatrist. He was also a secret, dues-paying member of a Communist party study group, which, if it became known, would probably cost him his job and make it virtually impossible for him to go among Wall Street's money men, as he would soon be doing, to raise the capital he needed to start his publication.

That Ingersoll in 1938 was very much concerned about the common man could be seen from the curious memorandum he had written the previous spring outlining his thoughts for the "new form of newspaper." Of sixty-one pages, eleven were devoted to "Principles," and Ingersoll made it perfectly clear that he believed newspapers were for crusading. The first crusade, of course, was to improve the miserable conditions of the U.S. press in general; but he also said, "I hasten to set down the basic fundamental conception that journalism is more than these things, more than simply the sale of a news service for profit." A journal such as the one he was contemplating, and the journalists he planned to hire, must "serve two things larger than themselves. The first is the truth as it exists. The second is the idea of a better mankind."

It is not difficult to see why the proposals Ingersoll would soon be circulating around New York had an overwhelming appeal to the idealistic men and women who populated the nation's intellectual and journalistic fraternity. The memorandum on which Ingersoll would eventually base his "Prospectus for a New Kind of Newspaper" was built on a very simple premise: That the American newspaper, as first conceived by James Gordon Bennett, Joseph Pulitzer, and others in the nineteenth century had not changed significantly in fifty years— despite the journalistic revolution that had been taking place at Time Inc. since 1923. The departmentalization of news, better paper, improved writing and photography, the importance of pictures and layout, and extensive research had all been pioneered by *Time*, *Fortune*, and *Life*, all three of which were mentioned repeatedly in Ingersoll's first memorandum. The time had come, he was convinced, to transmit the ideas that had revolutionized magazine journalism to the newspaper business. As Wolcott Gibbs would say of him in his *New Yorker* profile four years later, Ralph Ingersoll was "ripe for the great apocalypse."

At the age of 5 in Lakeville, Connecticut

2: Life With Father— and Without Mother

Ralph McAllister Ingersoll is, indeed, descended from two illustrious families, with the Ingersoll branch considerably more distinguished than the McAllister. He was born in a yellow brick house at 475 Whitney Avenue in New Haven, Connecticut, on December 8, 1900, making it, as he says, "always easy to tell my age." His parents were "ancestor worshipers," which meant he heard a lot about his forebears when he was growing up. Colin Macrae Ingersoll, Jr., his father, inherited a family name that could be traced back to one John Ingersoll in Bedfordshire, England, who started it all in 1615. His son, Johnathan, migrated to Connecticut and, before dying in 1760, had two sons, the Reverend Johnathan Ingersoll, Jr., a chaplain for the colonial troops in the French and Indian Wars, and Jared Ingersoll, stamp master general and an admiralty judge for the New England colonies. Johnathan, in turn, sired Johnathan III, a lawyer and judge who became lieutenant governor of Connecticut, and Jared sired Jared junior, a delegate to the Constitutional Convention, an attorney general of Pennsylvania, and the Federalist party's nominee for vice president in 1812.

A young country needed energetic, ambitious men to lead it, and the Ingersolls furnished their share: Jared's branch produced Charles Jared Ingersoll

(1782–1862), a Pennsylvania district attorney, congressman, and U.S. minister to England for President Millard Fillmore. Johnathan's branch gave us Charles Anthony Ingersoll (1796–1860), an attorney general of Connecticut and a U.S. district court judge; and the person for whom young Ralph was named, Ralph Isaacs Ingersoll (1789–1872), an attorney general of Connecticut, a member of Congress, a U.S. minister to Russia under President James Polk. The Russian ambassador's sons were Charles Roberts Ingersoll (1821–1903), who served three times as governor of Connecticut, and Colin Macrae Ingersoll (1819–1904), a member of Congress who was appointed chargé d'affaires of the U.S. legation to Russia in 1840. The family also produced Robert Ingersoll, the famous nineteenth-century orator and agnostic who nominated James G. Blaine— whom he dubbed "the plumed knight"—for president at the Republican National Convention in 1876.

As far as young Ralph was concerned, the most important thing Colin Macrae Ingersoll did was to marry Julia Pratt, the daughter of old Zadoc Pratt. The Ingersolls were lawyers and politicians who, for the most part, made their names by getting elected or—with work and money—helping others win office, for which they were rewarded by appointments to important jobs. But Zadoc was different. He was a working man, a doer, a builder—the kind of man who, until well into his seventies, liked to swim across the Hudson River every spring when the ice went out, just to prove he could do it. In the 1780s his father had moved from Connecticut west to New York, where he opened a tannery. Zadoc was born in 1790, and at the age of twenty-one he was a journeyman sadler making ten dollars a month. By the middle of the century he had come to own a thriving leather business, had built the town of Prattsville, which he also, naturally, represented in Congress; and to defend his holdings, he joined the local regiment and eventually became a colonel.

As a nineteenth-century tycoon, Zadoc had his own bank, which was attached to his house and printed notes with his picture on them. He thought that any banker who insisted on collateral should not be allowed to lend money. He was married four times and had three children: a son who was killed in the Battle of Manassas in the Civil War, one daughter who died in infancy, and another, Julia, who survived. Julia married Ralph's grandfather, who had two sons: George Pratt Ingersoll, whom President Woodrow Wilson appointed ambassador to Siam in 1917; and Colin Macrae Ingersoll, Jr., Ralph's father, who was born in Hartford, Connecticut, in 1858, and who must have shocked his family by choosing engineering as a career instead of the law and politics.

Colin graduated from the Sheffield Scientific School at Yale in 1880 and worked a year for the Missouri Pacific Railroad in Saint Louis before taking a job as an engineer with the New York, New Haven and Hartford Railroad. By the age of twenty-six he had become chief engineer for the NYNH&H and was responsible for double tracking the line from Boston to the Harlem River where it enters Manhattan.

In 1906 he moved to New York as chief engineer of the city's Bridge

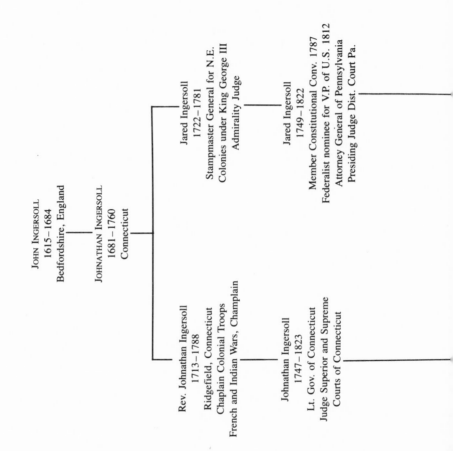

It is apparent why young Ralph was both impressed with and proud of his "Family Tree"

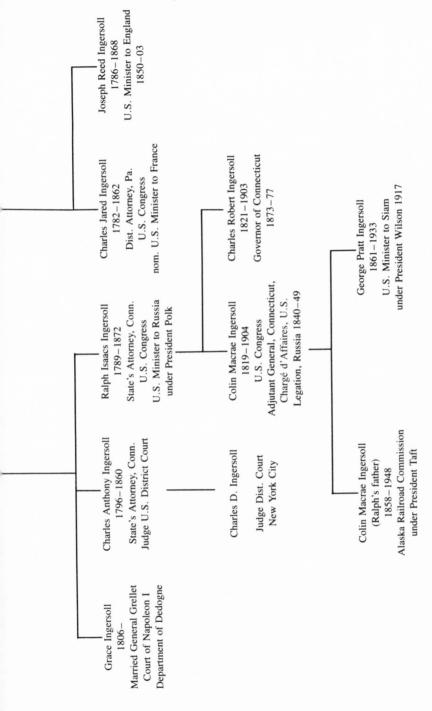

Joseph Reed Ingersoll
1786–1868
U.S. Minister to England
1850–03

Charles Jared Ingersoll
1782–1862
Dist. Attorney, Pa.
U.S. Congress
nom. U.S. Minister to France

Charles Robert Ingersoll
1821–1903
Governor of Connecticut
1873–77

Ralph Isaacs Ingersoll
1789–1872
State's Attorney, Conn.
U.S. Congress
U.S. Minister to Russia
under President Polk

Colin Macrae Ingersoll
1819–1904
U.S. Congress
Adjutant General, Connecticut,
Chargé d'Affaires, U.S.
Legation, Russia 1840–49

George Pratt Ingersoll
1861–1933
U.S. Minister to Siam
under President Wilson 1917

Charles Anthony Ingersoll
1796–1860
State's Attorney, Conn.
Judge U.S. District Court

Charles D. Ingersoll

Judge Dist. Court
New York City

Colin Macrae Ingersoll
(Ralph's father)
1858–1948
Alaska Railroad Commission
under President Taft

Grace Ingersoll
1806–
Married General Grellet
Court of Napoleon I
Department of Dedogne

Department, which was then building the Queensboro and Manhattan bridges. Years later, after he had served on the Alaskan Railroad Commission, Colin was offered the most important job of his life—to modernize the six-thousand-mile Trans-Siberian Railway—but he turned the czar down because he did not want to raise his children in Russia.

Colin Ingersoll was a classic nineteenth-century gentleman who considered himself first and foremost "an Ingersoll"; more specifically, a "Connecticut Ingersoll, Connecticut born and Connecticut bred." He was tall and handsome and had the kind of New England reserve and bearing that kept people, including his children, at a respectful distance. His manner was always proper, and "damn (never God damn) was his strongest profanity," said his son, "although he did occasionally allow himself a scornful 'Hell, no,' if some course that outraged him was proposed."

Ralph's father was also a fine draftsman and a skillful portraitist, but he did not take up painting seriously until he was seventy. And he had one quirk about which he was quite frank, says his son: "He never cared to draw anything except pretty girls"—which might explain why he was attracted to Theresa McAllister of New York City. To this day, Colin's son has never been able to understand how such a proper, reserved New England gentleman ever met the glamorous, fun-loving niece of the notorious Ward McAllister, whose name in the late nineteenth century was synonymous with the kind of glittering life his father disdained. In fact, "my father loathed him," says Ralph.

The McAllisters originally settled in Georgia where they were an established, respected family. But for some reason all the male McAllisters uprooted themselves and went west in the mid-nineteenth century. It could have been the gold rush of 1849 that prompted them to leave Georgia, but Ingersoll thinks some kind of family trouble might have caused them to make the move. Theresa McAllister was born in California; her parents died when she was very young, so she was raised by an uncle, an army officer stationed on what was then the frontier at Sausalito. By the turn of the century the McAllisters had become "established" in California—especially Hall and Ward McAllister and their father, who had opened a thriving San Francisco law firm. But Ward, born and raised in Georgia, was not really cut out for the frontier life; in fact, he was something of a sissy from childhood and an embarrassment. An old family letter reads: "little Wardy wants a tea set for Christmas."

When little Wardy's father's law firm struck it rich, what he wanted most was to leave the uncouth West for some place where a refined gentleman would be treated with more respect. So Ward went back east and supplemented his fortune by marrying the daughter of a Georgia millionaire. They settled in Newport, Rhode Island, where Ward bought a large estate; then they spent several years in Europe learning the social arts, before returning to New York, where McAllister planned to become the social arbiter. By 1872 he had organized a Ball Committee which would determine who would be invited to "Society's" functions. Then he decided that he alone would be responsible for making a list of *all* Society, and it would, of course, consist of no more than four hundred people because that was all Mrs. John Jacob Astor's ballroom at Fifth Avenue and Thirty-fourth Street would hold anyway.

Once reestablished in New York, McAllister invited his niece, Theresa, then in California, to come and live with them in New York. Theresa was an immediate social hit and made many conquests before she finally met Colin Ingersoll and accepted his proposal of marriage.

Colin and Theresa settled in New Haven and had four children: Theresa, Marion (who died of a ruptured appendix at the age of six), Coline, and Ralph, who was, naturally, groomed early to be an engineer. With so many illustrious and successful relatives, young Ralph also became very "family conscious."

But he was also suspicious about his familial purity: "Culturally, they told me, I am a half breed," the result of crossing Puritan New England blood with his mother's strain from Savannah. Nevertheless, with so many ambassadors, governors, congressmen, successful lawyers, and a businessman (Zadoc) in the family tree, he came to associate prominence with achievement. Even Ward McAllister's frivolity resulted in an achievement of a sort, although of a kind Ralph's father looked down on. "Whenever I showed any ambition," Ingersoll

(LEFT) The last photograph of Ralph's mother, Theresa McAllister Ingersoll; (RIGHT) "Connecticut born and Connecticut bred," Ralph's father, Colin Macrae Ingersoll. When asked what the Ingersolls did, he would invariably reply: "They are gentlemen"

says of his childhood, "Zadoc got the credit; whenever I stayed out late, Ward McAllister took the blame." The two strains—achievement and social success— were always at war within him, a condition compounded by the fact that both his father and his mother (until her early and untimely death) continually pros- elytized their son to the virtues of their particular tribe.

Ralph does not remember much about his New Haven childhood, except that his parents were very social and that a good deal of the time he was left in the care of an Irish girl who had been converted into his mother's alter ego. Her name was Annie McCabe, and everyone called her Arny. She spent her whole life in service to the Ingersolls, and after Ralph buried her in the late 1940s, he said, "I have never known a purer love than hers. It was mother's genius to inspire that kind of loyalty."

For most of his early years and well into his professional life, Ralph Ingersoll was called Mac—not, as it has often been presumed, to capitalize on the McAllister in his name, but because his father's middle name was Macrae and his intimates called him Mac. Ralph insisted on being called Mac as a protest against what he considered the theft of his birthright; when a third girl arrived in the family, the Ingersolls had already resigned themselves to never having a boy, so they added an *e* to Colin and christened her Coline.

When Ralph was six, the family closed up their glamorous Whitney Avenue house in New Haven and moved to New York where they rented a brownstone at 44 East Seventieth Street, across from the old Presbyterian Hospital. And now the merry Theresa—who, halfway through unpacking in a new house, would get bored and say, "Let's have a party"—was in her element. She had returned to the scene of her glamorous Society days married to a very successful man who was in charge of building the bridges into and out of New York and with three children of her own to introduce to Society. For young Ralph there were exciting days ahead, and he remembers this period well; in fact, twenty- eight years later his only bylined piece ever to appear in the *New Yorker* would be titled "A New York Childhood." One of his earliest New York memories was that of being the first boy to walk daringly across the high catwalk of the Queensboro Bridge, an honor naturally accorded to the son of the builder.

Little Ralph was very proud of Colin Ingersoll. But he was also developing a fear, and even hatred, of his father that he did not fully understand until years later, when he was in psychoanalysis. He loved his mother, but in his eyes she seemed to ignore him, obviously preferring his father. Years later he recalled one childhood incident that seemed to symbolize the first nine years of his life: Once, when he was approximately six, he was standing at the bottom of a stairwell, and his mother was a few steps above him, dressed for a party and looking very beautiful. Ralph wanted her to stay home, and she turned to look down at him, then laughed and said, "Oh, you silly child; you *know* I can't stay." A great rage came over Ralph, and he screamed at her, "Damn you, damn you, damn you!"

At that moment Ralph's father suddenly appeared in the darkened stairway, towering over him at six feet two. His cold blue eyes were hard and angry. He did not touch Ralph but stood there, and then his voice came like a cold steel knife: "Don't you *dare* ever to talk to your mother again like that."

Ralph remembers his early childhood as "Life with Father," just as it was in the 1935 play by Clarence Day. "Until he retired," said Ralph, "he led a life which made him available to his family only at breakfast and in the evenings— when he was my mother and my older sisters' possession."

Ralph was a discontented, whining child, who, to the horror of his relatives, clung to his nursing bottle until he was ten. He was obnoxious, fat, and spoiled (mostly by Arny), an introvert who liked to come up from behind and hit people with rolled-up newspapers and who stuffed platefuls of butterballs into his mouth like marbles. In grade school he was known as Fat or Stinky, and one relative who visited the Ingersolls during this period wrote a few years later, "Is little Ralph as disagreeable as ever?"

Within three years of their move to New York, Ralph's mother became ill, and it developed that she had cancer. She lingered for a year, her pain eased by opiates prescribed by her doctors which her husband and Arny ground up and administered to her. She was forty-nine years old and "spent her last months," says Ingersoll, "organizing, to the last minute detail, the lives that her husband and children should lead after she was dead."

Although it would be many years before he fully understood what had happened, the loss of his mother affected him profoundly. "From the date of her death," he said, "until well into my analysis, twenty-seven years later, I was under the absolute conviction that I had no memories whatever of her and actually no valid memories of anything that happened to me before the date of her death." For the next three years, on the anniversary of her death, he became ill with either rheumatic or scarlet fever, and, in each case, almost died. Yet during these same years Ralph's personality and physique changed dramatically. The fat little introvert became a tall, lean extrovert, a natural leader of organized sports at school and of his own gang—the XXX Club—after school. The club, which met weekly in a closet on the roof of the Ingersolls' brownstone, "followed me," said Ingersoll, "to a man," mostly in dropping water bombs on the East Side pedestrians below.

Ralph seems to remember most of his childhood in New York as having been spent on roller skates. Every afternoon he had to go from the East Sixties, where he went to school, up Fifth Avenue to the East Nineties, where the school rented a playground. The prescribed way to make this trip was to hitch oneself to the back of a beer truck and roll along up the avenue on one's roller skates. Ralph also discovered sex—or thought he did. He had been taught that masturbation was a sin, "punishable in this world by prison," he recalled, but he did not let that deter him. Then one day he made a nervous visit to an art museum to examine the opposite sex, only to find that sculptors had eliminated the thing from their female figures altogether! But there must be *something* there, and when he finally saw (peeping through the bathroom keyhole at an undressed maid) "that great black triangle . . . it *really* terrified" him.

Young Ralph also had his spiritual side—at least for a year or two. His mother was an Episcopalian who was able to persuade his father to attend church on Easter Sunday and maybe at Christmas. After her death the family continued to make certain young Ralph's religious education was not neglected. He attended Sunday school at Saint James Church at Madison Avenue and Seventy-first Street, and when he was being prepared for confirmation, he was so deeply moved by the experience that the bishop who confirmed him wrote his father asking if he would consider letting Ralph train for the ministry. His father was appalled, and the family decided that Ralph had "gone much too far" in his devotion to the cross. Ralph was going to be an engineer—in fact, according to Ralph, his father considered it immoral to be anything else. Within a year Ralph's variety of the religious experience was over, and he remained an agnostic most of his life. "But it is easier to believe in a God," he said years later, "so I'm willing to think there is one. But I'm anticlerical."

When his mother died, responsibility for the raising of young Ralph was passed along to his two sisters and to Arny—"the Board of Lady Managers," as Ralph's father called the matriarchy that dominated the Ingersoll household. Theresa and Coline were nineteen and fourteen respectively, when they inherited young Ralph, and unfortunately the age difference was too great for them ever to become close as children, something that Ralph has regretted all his life. "Coline," said Ingersoll, "was a gentle girl anxious to be loved, and easily hurt, just grown up enough to take the mission of civilizing me very seriously. But Te [Theresa] was something else again. She was smarter than Coline, and gifted with an uncanny instinct for knowing the vulnerable points in a small boy's armor. She knew, for instance, that the confiscation of prized possessions could hurt more than any lecture. And she was a natural born disciplinarian."

"As a boy," he said, "I liked Coline better but admired Theresa more." But, he concluded, "sisters—schmisters! Mine were shadowy characters to me when I was a boy." He was really raised by Arny.

Annie McCabe came from the Irish tradition that really believed in an aristocracy—and if a young man was born an aristocrat, he could do no wrong. He could, of course, do silly things, especially when he was young, but they could be ignored if he was truly bred. Clearly, in Annie McCabe's eyes, the Ingersolls were genuine aristocrats and Ralph was the crown prince. She spoiled him rotten, letting him eat or do anything (within the code for young gentlemen). He was the master and she his "body servant and slave," as Ralph's mother once described her. When he was in his teens, the first night he came home really drunk, Arny put him tenderly to bed sighing happily, for her young master was "drunk as a lord, drunk as a real lord."

But if Arny spoiled the young lord, she also gave him something he would treasure all his life: unwavering confidence in himself. Arny's conviction of his superiority rubbed off on her young master, and it was so deep, says Ingersoll, "that it never occurred to me that I could be really hurt by anyone's acts but my own." Many years later, he wrote: "I was Arny's boy, not Theresa McAllister's, when I was a child. I still am Arny's boy."

When the Ingersolls moved to New York, young Ralph attended Miss Keller's Day School at 35–37 East Sixty-second Street, and an early report card shows that he did very well, earning mostly A's and B's. After his mother's death the family moved to 167 East Seventy-first Street, a five-story brownstone where Ralph was given two connected maid's quarters on the fifth floor as his bedroom and "study." He was soon attending Mr. Kirmayer's classes (at 34 East Sixtieth Street) where he was also a good student. And that Arny was bringing him up as a young lord did not in any way dampen his instincts for self-improvement. At twelve he began to doubt that he was receiving a proper education. So he set aside the period from four to seven every day and opened up a school of his own at home.

Although there was never any discussion in the Ingersoll family to suggest that Ralph go into something other than engineering — even into that traditional career, the law — it gradually became obvious that the boy had instincts for the military and communications. At twelve, he joined the local drill team, the Knickerbocker Grays, and his self-taught courses included typing, shorthand, radio, and telegraphy. But Ralph's fascination with communications did not stop there. At eleven he was distributing handouts for the Barnum and Bailey Circus, and it was then that he acquired an early skepticism about advertising. He also acquired an early interest in photography, and with his 3-A Kodak, purchased with the first money he ever earned, he took pictures of everything and everybody, as the voluminous photo albums in his Boston University papers testify. His early instincts as a picture editor are also demonstrated in these albums, where his trips out west to visit relatives, to Maine on his first summer job, to summer camp at Lake Winnipesaukee, and, later, across Europe in a small plane in pursuit of a girl are all laid out as photo stories. After World War I broke out in Europe, he made huge scrapbooks about the war consisting mostly of photographs from the *New York Times* and the *London Illustrated News*, further testimony not only to his early preoccupation with photo journalism, but to a fascination with war that lasted all his life.

His literary bent also emerged early. Not only was he the publisher of, and a contributor to, his school paper, the *Kirmayer Echo*, but he spent hour after hour, while teaching himself to type, making up stories, single-spaced, on legal-size paper. These stories were heroic and adventurous, with such titles as "About a Castle," "A Case of the Mistaken Bank Account," "The "Motor Bandits," "Four Boys in Boats," and "Four Boys on a House Party." He was usually the hero, and in one story a young army officer saves New York from a German invasion by decoying the Huns into the Park Avenue railroad tunnel and blowing them up. He also wrote narrative accounts of trips and other personal adventures, some of which appeared in the *Echo*. His writing was not particularly original or artistic, but even then his reporting was good, and his narrative technique clear and concise.

Around 1912 he also started writing book reviews, for which his father paid him a penny a word; engineers, his father believed, should be able to write good, clear reports.

And it was in 1912 that he began the first volume of his diary. For the next thirteen years he would faithfully jot down each day's events, in ink, in a clear, precise handwriting. In 1925, when he went to work for the *New Yorker*, he stopped keeping a diary, but he never stopped writing, in one way or the other, about the life he lived. In fact, "whether life is more fun to live or write about" is something he has always found difficult to decide.

When he was about twelve, he also had a brief career as a stagestruck playwright. He saved his allowance to buy seats in the second balcony of Broadway theaters, where he saw most of the productions of 1912, 1913, and 1914. One play, his favorite *Misleading Lady*, he saw eleven times. He also began writing to actors, actresses, and other artists, requesting their autographs, and even struck up a correspondence with a few. Caruso and Maude Adams were two he remembered.

After his wife's death Colin Ingersoll was encouraged (mostly by his daughters and Amy) to avoid New York's glittering social life, which might lead him into the hands of "some woman," whose influence, as Ingersoll put it, "might threaten the sanctity of Mother's memory." All went well for about four years, during which time Colin devoted all his energies to building bridges. Then he met Marie Harrison, an aggressive, handsome, and unusual woman of forty. For a brief period she had been editor of *Vogue*, when its founder and editor, the husband of Marie's sister, died. Colin, obviously very much attracted to her, suddenly came out of mourning and began to escort Marie around town. "You will like her," he told his son. "She thinks like a man."

The Ingersoll women, however, did not think she was the right woman for Colin, and for two years they waged guerrilla warfare against her. But in 1916 they lost the battle when Colin married Marie (whom Ralph called Tante all his life).

As the obnoxious, spoiled fat kid began to grow tall, exchange his fat for muscle, gain the confidence Annie McCabe was instilling in him, and outgrow his contemporaries, the time inevitably came for his first revolt. The cause can be traced to several factors that converged after his mother's death. The Puritan in his father had replaced his mother's cavalier streak in determining the family budget; economy was now the word, and for the heir apparent this meant eliminating his music lessons, buying him cheap clothes instead of dressing him "in fashion," and economizing on tuition by keeping him at Kirmayer's, where he could live at home, instead of sending him to St. Paul's in New Hampshire, where all his friends went and where Ralph himself had been enrolled from the time he was christened. The arrival of Tante also contributed to the rebellion: "I surveyed my life," he says, "and found it seriously wanting. So with the household still preoccupied with the problems of its readjustment [to his father's marriage], I hit my father with my big idea: I was through with schools of any kind. I announced that come spring I was leaving home."

It is not clear whether Ralph's father was caught in a weak moment and grateful to his son for supporting his marriage, or whether he simply did not take the boy seriously. But Ingersoll's reaction to his son's announcement that he was finished with school was "Certainly! I'll start lining up a job for you"— which he did.

So in the spring of his fifteenth year Ralph McAllister Ingersoll quit school and went to work for forty dollars a month as a rodman for a group of Maine Central Railroad surveyors in Fairfield, Maine. Their job was to survey for the erection of a bridge over the Kennebec River, and the surveyors thought it was a fine thing having a fifteen-year-old rich kid from New York sharing a bunk with them in their house—a condemned building along the railroad right-of-way. They kidded him unmercifully, answered his questions about building bridges with questions about his private life and bodily functions, and kept him continually on his feet running errands for them. It took Ralph only a week to learn that holding a rod for another man not only was no life for him but would never pay any more than forty dollars a week. He was also crushed to learn that the beautiful bridge they were building would be ordered from a catalog.

It was a long summer, and in September when his father and Tante drove up in their new Maxwell to take him home, he was ready to go back to school. By now it had become obvious to Mr. Kirmayer that he had a young prodigy on his hands. By the time he was fifteen, Ralph had passed all but one or two of his college board examinations, and with further tutoring he could complete the examinations and be ready to enter Yale—which it was always assumed he would attend—before he was sixteen. Colin Ingersoll knew his son was exceptionally bright, and he was very proud of him, but when Ralph's sisters learned that their young brother would be taking a three-year course at the Yale Sheffield Scientific School and *graduating* when he was eighteen, thereby finishing college when most proper young men were entering it, they were horrified. Theresa was now about to be married, and one of her last acts before departing for the suburb of Boston that would be her new home was to convince her father to "hold the boy back until he was old enough to get something out of college."

After another year at Kirmayer's and a summer working for the Boston and Maine Railroad, Ralph was ready for prep school. Because his stepmother owned a farm in Lakeville, Connecticut, Ralph was eligible to attend Hotchkiss tuition-free.

As outsiders and outcasts, "townies" were tolerated at the school only because of the provision in Maria Hotchkiss's will that said the school must be open to local boys, free. But there was usually room in the dormitories only for the boarding students, so in the first semester Ralph lived at Farnham's Tavern in Lakeville and walked up the hill to school; later, when someone left school, he was permitted to move into Bissell Hall, the senior dormitory. But Ingersoll,

Growing up: (TOP) At the Kirmayer School, Ingersoll is in the first row, the fat little boy on the right; (BELOW, LEFT) Age 12 in the Knickerbocker Grays, a New York social club; (BELOW, RIGHT) at Hotchkiss

"from the Village" with his scholarship and outgrown ready-made clothes, was clearly of the lower classes, and his schoolmates treated him accordingly. In a class vote, recorded in the yearbook, Ingersoll got one vote for "Most Brass."

Ingersoll did not think much of his fellow students either, with their snobbish airs, plus fours, three-button herringbone jackets, and ritualistic conformity. "It was the Hotchkiss," he wrote later, "in which upperclassmen disciplined lower by bringing them to trial for offenses against The Code, and administered punishment to those found guilty by making them run the gauntlet, naked and prickly with goose flesh after a cold shower, their executioners whipping them with knotted towels. It was a Hotchkiss costumed—uniformed, rather—by the New Haven tailors who came each fall and spring to set up shop in Lakeville. One earned one's H for success in Competitive Dressing."

He said he did not make a single friend at Hotchkiss and hated every minute of the year he spent there. Although he does not remember debating anyone, he was a member of the Debating Society, and a local paper reported that he was on the team that took the affirmative on the question: "The Policy of a Closed Shop in Unions Is Justifiable." The affirmative lost.

If his Hotchkiss classmates had their arrogance of privilege, Ingersoll had his own arrogance of pride, which did not go unnoticed. The quote used in the yearbook to describe "Ingy" is "None but himself can be his parallel."

But on graduation day he was still not ready for Yale. Although he had high marks in most of his courses, he failed French and would not receive his diploma until he had special tutoring and passed the course. Then Uncle Sam intervened. America was now at war, and both Hotchkiss and Yale agreed to waive his failure in French if he would enlist in the U.S. Army's Student Training Course at Yale. The romantic Ingersoll, eager to join the war, which he had been following in the papers, had planned to enlist anyway. In fact, he very nearly went to France before he could get to Yale.

In the summer of 1918 Ralph was so grown-up that he had to carry his birth certificate to prove he was not a draft dodger, which was ironic, considering how desperately he wanted to go off to war and become a hero. He did not know what to do with himself, and neither did anyone else—until one day he received a letter from "Cousin" Alida in Stony Brook on Long Island asking if he would like to spend the summer visiting the Emmet family. Alida Emmet was not really a cousin, but had been such a close friend of Ralph's mother that she seemed like family. And what a family! By 1918 Alida was well on her way to achieving her ambition to have twelve children, and the oldest, Libba, was so classic in beauty and figure that, even forty years later, Ingersoll remembered her as the most beautiful woman he had ever seen. She died in her early twenties of a strange malady, but there was nothing about her then to suggest illness. In fact, she was so beautiful and vivacious that she attracted the young men from miles around—including members of the British Royal Flying Corps, which trained at the airfield at Garden City.

Ralph was enlisted to distract the swarming airmen, who, in turn, assigned a group captain to get rid of the young pest by inviting him for a ride in a fighter plane. The squadron dressed him in overalls, helmet, and goggles and waved him on his way. The plane went to ten thousand feet, twisted and turned and dived and looped and spun, then dropped the last three thousand feet, slid over the tops of the trees, and came bumping to a stop. The squadron was lined up to greet Ralph, and a few men helped him from the plane. His world was still spinning, and he had to hold on to the wing to stand up. When he got his breath, he said, "Gee, but I loved that." Then he took two steps forward, fell flat on his face, and passed out. When the men had revived him with pink ladies in a nearby bar, they proclaimed him "a bit of all right," and the young hero announced that he was ready there and then to enlist in the Royal Air Force. As a result, when the flyers sent him home, Ingersoll had with him a letter of introduction from the group captain to Air Marshal Hoare in Montreal. In Canada one could enlist at age seventeen.

Ralph had another reason for wanting to leave Stony Brook: He had fallen in love with another Emmet girl, Marga. Although Marga was the thing he desired most in the world, he also knew she was the "most unalterably forbidden." He did not know why he knew this; that's just the way it was then with properly raised young men and women. So Ralph and another cousin—Chandler Chapman, whose older brother had enlisted in the Lafayette Escadrille and was killed flying for the French—concocted a daring scheme to run away together to Montreal. The final details were worked out in a New York saloon; then they both went to their respective homes to get their clothes because it was agreed they would be apprehended on the train if they did not have luggage. Arriving at 167 East Seventy-first Street where the Ingersolls still had a house, Ralph, reeking of beer, was not hard to detect packing his gear, and his father sat him down for a "Now, what's this all about?" talk. Cousin Chandler was also apprehended by his parents, who did not want another young son to be lost fighting for a foreign country. Both boys went back to school that fall.

The seventeen-year-old Ingersoll who went off to the Yale Sheffield Scientific School in 1918 was an impressive young man, tall and skinny, with long hair, bright, shining eyes, a photographic memory, and a flair for learning fast. Even the humiliating year at Hotchkiss had not destroyed the self-confidence instilled in him by Arny. He still had some deep psychological scars stemming from his emotional involvement with his mother and the relationship with his father, but their only visible effect at this age was an already driving ambition to succeed—so as to free himself from his father's grip. By now he had started his practice of writing letters to his father on his father's birthday, which he continued well into his early thirties. They were long, emotional letters, said Ingersoll, "telling him how great a man I considered him to be. They were deeply sincere—and sickening."

In 1918 Yale Sheffield was still a three-year school, and even that curriculum was curtailed, because for Ingersoll's first fall semester in New Haven all of Yale was essentially a military base for the Student Army Training Corps, or

SATC. But by Feburary of 1919 Yale was struggling to return to a peacetime routine, and Ingersoll was ready for his only semester as a freshman. He had renewed his friendship with Louis Bishop, whom he had first met at the Emmets, and now they were rooming together in Van Sheff dormitory. With spring came Calling Week when the freshmen were invited to visit the fraternities and be inspected for possible membership. Ingersoll's father had been a member of Delta Psi and Bishop's had belonged to St. Elmo, so both boys expected that these fraternities would follow the tradition of "heritage" and invite the sons to join. But at the end of the week, said Ingersoll, he and Bishop "sat together in our rooms, like spinsters waiting for a telephone call that we hoped against hope would come but knew in our hearts would not. For we must have cast the die ourselves, months earlier—serious-minded Bishop by leaving his classmates behind him at St. Paul's (he had skipped the sixth form), and I by bringing my own private claque of detractors with me from Hotchkiss."

The calls never came, and their rejection by the fraternities drew Ingersoll and Bishop into a friendship that still lasts with both men well into their eighties. The following year they formed a club of their own.

Ingersoll remembers the spring of 1919 as the time when he was introduced to women and sex, New Haven style. As alumni of that period will recall, the action usually began with the meeting of local girls on Chapel Street or in the movie house at Church and Chapel. And if you got lucky, the young lady might accompany you to one of the dingy former rooming houses that had been re-modeled, making them convenient places to take a young lady for a drink while you worked up enough courage to ask her if she would go upstairs with you to a rented room. "The most vivid memory I have," says Ingersoll, "is the number of cigarettes my young lady had to light and smoke down to a stub that burned her before she would condescend to begin."

During the summer of 1919 Ingersoll convinced his father that he did not want to be an engineer who built bridges ordered from a catalog. This led to consultation in New York with a cousin he called Uncle who convinced both Ralph and his father that a mining career would be the best thing for the embryonic engineer. So Ingersoll went back to Yale in the fall to enroll in the new mining branch of the Sheffield School. Because Sheffield was a three-year school he and Bishop were now accorded the privileges of juniors, which meant that they could arrange for their own housing off campus. And what they found was a large, white clapboard house at 360 Temple Street, where it crossed Grove. Ingersoll and Bishop invited some other rejects to join them and formed their own fraternity, which they called the 360 Club. Because this was the year of the Volstead Act, they decided their fraternity "pin" would be a small gold replica of a pocket flask. Three sixty Temple was, in fact, a landmark, renowned as the house in which Noah Webster wrote his famous dictionary in the 1820s. In 1937 Henry Ford bought the house and had it moved to Dearborn, Michigan, where he restored it as a historic landmark. But in the early 1920s it was famous primarily as a gambling house and speakeasy.

Despite his reveling, Ingersoll was also doing a lot of thinking, much of which he set down in what he has called his "very peculiar kind of journal." Its object, he wrote, was "generally to let off surplus thinking matter and to try and establish a basis for whatever philosophy I have. I am doing much miscellaneous thinking and it would be well to find out, approximately, just what are the results of this waste energy."

The result was a philosophy derived almost solely, he said, from Mark Twain's essay *What Is Man?* As Ingersoll summed it up, it was, "of course, very complicated, but can briefly be stated as FATALISTIC. Not the mere idea that what is to be will be, but rather the same thing in another light. That is, I believe in the all powerful domination of CAUSE AND EFFECT. That man is the result of two influences, the character he was born with and the environment he goes thru, and is therefore, strictly speaking, quite a helpless machine who works solely with one motive, self-satisfaction."

Not a very deep or original philosophy of life, but at least he was thinking. It was also during this period, when he was convinced he was a helpless machine seeking self-satisfaction, that Ralph McAllister Ingersoll's vastly overrated reputation as a socialite began to develop. He may have been considered an oaf at Hotchkiss and ostracized by the fraternity men at Yale, but in New York City, only an hour and a half from New Haven, he was a registered member of the aristocracy. As both an Ingersoll and a McAllister, he was in great demand at the parties on which fawning mothers spent thousands of their husband's newly earned dollars to introduce their daughters to the "right boys." Because of his name and debonair manner, Ingersoll was considered a catch, despite the fact that he had no money and no special prospects for the future, as he was surely headed for the bottom of a mine somewhere out west when he graduated. During the Christmas season Ingersoll never had fewer than a half dozen invitations on any night. Most of the parties were "deadly dull," but when one looked promising, Ingersoll would drop by, condescending to spend a half hour or so, as, of course, he had to be off to the next party. Ingersoll was known among the girls as a "dancing fool." Although the style of the day was, as he put it, "to hold a girl with one arm limp, looking down on her as if she were something slightly distasteful," his own style was to grab his partners and with a vigorous pushing motion, mostly from the waist down, propel them across the room.

One girl he remembered from these days, although he never really knew or dated her, was Clare Boothe, "a party girl from Greenwich, Connecticut, of whom other men talked . . . a very pretty girl who 'got about'—blonde, good figure, could dance, would neck, but look out."

Although at Yale there was still never any question of his doing anything but following in his father's proper engineering footsteps, Ralph continued to demonstrate his literary and editorial flair. He liked to write, and he was very good at it. He could tell a story, and his prose was always lucid and well organized. He also wrote fast, which sometimes produced a rather breathless style. And his talent was recognized by at least one of his professors: On the first day of his freshman English composition class, the instructor asked each student to write an essay, which would help him assess the student's natural ability as a writer. Ingersoll went back to his room, wrote a three-thousand-word essay entitled "The Application of the Darwinian Theory to the Institution of the Stag Line," and turned it in that evening.

He actually did believe that only the fittest survived a New York party, but he felt that the subject was too frivolous and that he would not get a good mark on his paper. Consequently he was amazed the next morning when the professor not only gave him an A-plus but said: "Ingersoll, you have a fine feeling for satire. I don't want to spoil it with academic teaching. So I'll tell you what I'll do; you stay away from classes in composition from now on and I'll give you an A-plus for the year." And he did! Curiously, that was the last satire Ingersoll ever wrote.

Ingersoll's fame as a writer who was so good he did not have to attend freshman comp began to spread, and soon his own literary ethics were challenged. He was approached by several classmates who asked him to "edit" their composition papers—for which they offered cash in return. Ingersoll finally decided to hell with the ethics and before long had so much business that he had to standardize his rates: fifteen dollars for an A; ten dollars for a B; five dollars for a C—and nothing if the paper failed. He salved his conscience by honorably refusing to write a better paper than the student deserved; if he was a C student, he got a C paper, even though it cost Ingersoll money to keep his editing "honest." In the long run, he said, he made almost as much money "editing" as he did playing poker, at which he became quite skilled. More important, he had a very practical course in helping writers improve their copy without changing the essential quality of their own style—which is the trademark of a good editor.

If there is one thing for which Ralph Ingersoll is remembered as a journalist it is his talent as a polemicist. And his flair for crusading polemics was clearly foreshadowed in his Yale days by an incident that produced his first contact with Henry Robinson Luce.* The incident that brought Ingersoll and Luce together occurred when the biology department decided not to renew the contract of a very popular young biology instructor. The students were convinced that the instructor was fired not because he was incompetent but because the biology department was pro-German and the instructor was not. This produced a petition of protest signed by two hundred students, and Ingersoll was drafted to write an inflammatory letter to the *Yale Daily News* denouncing the biology department and declaring the matter one "which, beyond all doubt, we should not let rest in its present unpleasant grave." Although the letter was signed by three students, including Ingersoll's friend Louis Bishop, everyone knew it was Ingersoll's

---

*Ingersoll never actually met or knew Luce at Yale; the future founder of *Time* magazine graduated a year ahead of Ingersoll, and furthermore, at about the time Ingersoll was beginning to be noticed for his peculiar literary talents and emerging as a rebel socialite, Luce was already a big man on campus, so big that as his friend and future co-publisher of *Time* Briton Hadden once remarked when he saw Luce striding across the campus with the worries of the world clearly weighing down his bent shoulders, "Look out, Harry, you'll drop the college."

creation. The *Daily News* published the letter but also printed an editorial that sided with the university and called for a committee of investigation. Although Ingersoll recalls that it was Briton Hadden, Henry Luce, and their board of editors who really decided to print the letter, it must have been one of Luce's last acts. The incident occurred in the spring of 1920; Luce graduated in May of that year, and in their last years Hadden and Luce were chairman and managing editor, respectively, of the *News*. But the Ingersoll letter appeared in the June 9 issue, and by that time Hadden and Luce were no longer on the masthead.

At any rate, after the letter was reprinted in the *News* it immediately made headlines in the New York press: "STUDENTS ACCUSE YALE FACULTY OF PRO GERMAN LEANING."

This put everyone in trouble, and when Ingersoll was called on the carpet by Yale president Arthur Twining Hadley, who stuttered slightly, the president said, "Ingersoll, I would like you to give me one single r-r-r-reason why I should not expel you h-h-here and now."

Ingersoll had not left his brashness at Hotchkiss. He replied, "Because you don't dare."

Later he would consider his remark "appalling," but he knew his expulsion would only aggravate an already incendiary situation, and he said as much, bluntly, to Hadley. The university finally put out the fire by ordering a formal investigation; then, when the students had already left campus for the summer, the biology instructor was notified that he would not be rehired that fall.

When Ingersoll returned to New Haven in the fall of 1920 as a senior, he began the semester doing very well. He was one of a half dozen students selected for a special class in advanced calculus, and it seemed assured that he would graduate with honors in the spring. Then, as it has to many a young student, it happened! He met the love of his life—or at least of the next five years.

Until November of 1920 Ingersoll played the field. Despite the rejection by most of his schoolmates at Hotchkiss and Yale, Arny's young lord had grown up with a self-assurance bordering on arrogance. He had a tremendous, infectious vitality, and most girls, from the debutantes he met at the fancy coming-out balls on Park Avenue to the New Haven townies he met on Chapel Street, liked him. One, Nan Moran, had become his special friend; for a while Ralph even thought he was "in love" with her. Nan was one of the fastest of the New Haven girls, with a reputation that scared even the mighty seniors. But not Ingersoll, who took a dare from his classmates, picked her up in the movie theater, and struck up a warm friendship. "The malicious magic that had fashioned her reputation as a *femme fatale* fascinated me then and still fascinates me," Ingersoll said years later. "It was my first lesson in being skeptical of anybody's reputation, whether evil or good."

Ralph and Nan talked for hours, and he learned that her reputation was really built on withholding favors, not granting them. The year before, Nan's Yale boyfriend, with whom she had been deeply in love and willing, graduated, leaving her with a broken heart and a reputation. Now, when she went out with the Yale boys, she would usually go home from Savin Rock alone and unmolested, and the boys would protect *their* reputations by hinting at what a great lay she had been. Ralph remembers her as his best friend at school, male or female—"one of the nicest human beings I have ever known."

Nan's importance to Ingersoll is that she helped give him the emotional assurance to fall in love—with Harriet Camac. One November evening at a few minutes to eight, Ingersoll was standing in the doorway of an apartment in Manhattan's East Sixties, dressed in white tie and tails. The door opened to reveal a young girl in a blue evening gown cut too low for her eighteen years, with platinum-blond hair, clear, wide-set blue eyes, and finely chiseled features; and "from the waist up, her body was for a Titian to imitate—something perfect." Ingersoll instantly suspected other traits, which he later confirmed: "She was as arrogant and as self-assured as I, as ambitious and as brash. She was not very bright; she was wholly self-centered. She was strong willed and unsubtle, considerable of a bully." He fell in love immediately, despite the fact that he knew— and also confirmed later—that he did not really like her. It happens that way.

Harriet Camac would be the first of several loves who would prove Ingersoll's almost total inability to sustain an emotional relationship with a woman. Not until after psychoanalysis fifteen years later and his second marriage in 1945 would Ingersoll be able to deal emotionally with love. He may not have remembered much about his mother in 1920, but he was still feeling her impact.

There was an immediate physical attraction between Ingersoll and Harriet Camac, but it was never consummated. The code was never violated; Ingersoll knew he was in love with a "good" woman, and good women do not enjoy premarital sex. They met during the Thanksgiving holidays, and at the end of the Christmas vacation they were engaged and planning to be married as soon as Ingersoll could support a wife. Cupid had ruined another honor student. Not only was Ingersoll dropped from the special calculus class, he was put in with a group of "the morons," as he put it. He wanted to graduate with honors and worked very hard at it, but suddenly he had lost the easy understanding and talent for quick learning that he had always had—and that he would regain. For now, he said, "I just plain knew that I could not understand things today that I knew I had understood yesterday. It was very, very disconcerting and I thought seriously that I might be losing my mind." Unconsummated love was taking its toll, although it is quite possible that something more complex involving his mother was producing his temporary intellectual decline.

Despite his emotional condition in the spring of 1921, Ingersoll did graduate from Yale Sheffield School. And luckily he had a job to go to that fall. A rather nasty recession was in progress three years after the war, and it was hitting especially hard the markets for copper, lead, and zinc. But a cousin, George Haven, had found him a job in a gold mine owned by the North Star Mining and Development Company in Grass Valley, California. Ralph agreed to go west because he was still not ready to defy his father. But "switching goals from my father's kind of engineering to my uncle's," he said, "was simply postponing an

inevitable showdown between my father's creed and one that I felt desperately
I must work out for myself to fit my own strange pattern. It was *words*, not
figures, I have always felt would one day set me free."

When Ingersoll graduated in 1921 it was, however, not words but a figure—
Harriet's—that he hoped would set him free. He was not sure what he was going
to do that summer, while he waited for the job that would enable him to marry
Harriet. Then, suddenly, an unusual opportunity developed. Poly Hooker, a
member of the 360 Club, was given, as a graduation present, a tour of the
Continent. And Poly's mother thought his college friend Ralph Ingersoll, who
seemed to have all his wits about him, would make a good traveling companion;
at least he might keep Poly from losing his tickets.

So, encouraged by Harriet who thought the trip would be beneficial, and
with her promise to marry him in the fall, Ralph was persuaded to leave his true
love for a few weeks to accompany Poly Hooker to Europe. The nature of the
trip was determined as they were boarding the S.S. *Lorraine*, the small French
liner that would take them across the Atlantic. Hooker was not a very serious
young man and had never shown much interest in "nice girls," but as they went
up the gangplank he announced to Ingersoll that he had decided to get married.
"Who to?" Ralph asked, and Hooker pointed to an attractive young lady in a
large straw hat, who was leaning on the rail just above them. Neither of them

*The 360 Club. Ingersoll in top row, fourth from the right; Poly Hooker is to his right;
Louis Bishop is third from left in bottom row*

had ever seen her before—but she was good-looking. The grand tour was spent almost entirely in pursuit of Betty Holland, who was traveling to Rome with her mother. The chase took them first to Paris, then, in a dramatic airplane flight, to Dijon, to Lyons, over the Alps to Nice, down the coast to Pisa, and to Rome, where, instead of being met at the airport by Betty, who they had presumed would lead a triumphant motorcade into the ancient city, the reception committee was composed of two grumpy mechanics, who at least helped the heroes find their way to the trolley that would take them into Rome. Ingersoll had his 3-A Kodak with him and recorded the whole romantic flight in photographs.

Hooker's romance with Betty eventually had a happy ending, but Ingersoll's romance with Harriet was a sadder story. He had planned to spend a happy month with her at Murray Bay before leaving for California, and the train ride up was mostly devoted to daydreaming about Harriet and planning their future life together—after he had carved out a career as a mining engineer. But on the first night, after dinner, Ingersoll was given the news: Harriet had had time to "think it over" while he was in Europe, and had decided to marry someone else. Ingersoll was on the night train back to New York, a crushed young man. He said that he cried for two solid days and that it took him five years to recover from Harriet's rejection.

Ingersoll spent his last month before going west at Tante's farm in Lakeville and was saved from despair by what he said was "my first adventure in having someone fall in love with me before I fell in love with her." His father rewarded him for furiously chopping wood all day by letting "the boy" (that was what his father called him until he died; the boy was then almost fifty) take the family's 1920 Dodge in the evenings. One night he ended up at a dance in Lakeville where he met Jeannine, who was dark, very pretty, and a little older than the rest of the girls. Later, when they drove out into the country in the Dodge, Jeannine, aware of Ralph's blank stare and silence, finally said, "You're carrying a torch, aren't you? Tell me about it."

Ralph proceeded to do just that for most of a month, and in the process Jeannine, whose last name he could not recall years later, fell in love with him, which made him even more mixed up. The result was that he came to some conclusions about love that stuck with him for many years. He was in love with Harriet, but the more deeply he fell in love with her, the less impressed she was. Conversely, Jeannine was falling deeply in love with him, and all he felt was gratitude and pity. Conclusion: "To be loved one must withhold love, but to love intensely without reservations of any kind was to make oneself undesirable." So, Ingersoll "wrote the whole equation off as insoluble and saw no future in it." Years later, after he had been through psychoanalysis, he wrote: "The psychiatrist will recognize the pattern easily enough. I was arranging my life to protect myself from the one relationship I could not bear to face: fulfilled love. Fulfilled love could remind me only of what I had so desperately wanted as a child and yet known was forbidden: fulfillment of my love for my mother."

(ABOVE LEFT) At a railroad station in France during the trip Ingersoll took to Europe in the summer of 1921; (ABOVE RIGHT) Returning on the boat, with two unidentified ladies; (LEFT) At his mining camp in Mexico, 1923

For years after Jeannine there was, for Ingersoll, no sex with love—but there was one night with Jeannine, and he carried the memory of it in and out of the mines of California for several months. As the day approached for his departure, Jeannine asked if his family would be taking him to New York to catch the train. "Good lord, no," said Ingersoll. "They will drive me as far as the station in Millerton, and be so embarrassed about saying good-bye that they won't even wait for the train to come in."

"You will be leaving for the train a little before three, won't you?" asked Jeannine.

"Let's see, the train leaves at three twenty and the station is a good seven miles from the farm. My father will want the baggage in the car by two thirty and the oil and gas checked—and his formal farewell speech finished—by two forty-five. So we will start for the station at exactly two fifty. I can see that you haven't been around my family much. We run automobiles like railways where I come from."

On his last day in Lakeville, when they were packing for the ride to Millerton, the phone rang in Ralph's house. It was a person-to-person call for Ralph from New York. It was Jeannine, and she spoke quickly and to the point: "I don't want to talk on the telephone. When you get to New York, walk right on through the station and go into the Commodore Hotel. Just ask the man at the desk there for the key to Mrs. Rogers's suite. That's all you have to do. Can you remember?"

Then she hung up. Ralph, remarkably innocent despite his size, appearance, and sophistication, spent most of the trip into New York wondering about this Mrs. Rogers with whom Jeannine was staying. There was no Mrs. Rogers, of course, and the next day Ralph just barely caught his train for the West. The day before, as predicted, his father had made his speech, which was over at two forty-four. Among other things, he had said, "You are going out to California to start your career at the bottom of the ladder, boy. I envy you. Remember as you climb, boy, that there is always room at the top."

Ralph always thought this a very appropriate speech for a young man about to go down to the bottom of a mine.

* * *

The young man who headed west for Grass Valley, California, in the late summer of 1921 had graduated from Hotchkiss and Yale but was far from being a preppie or Yalie. These credentials, which would someday help persuade both Harold Ross and Henry Luce to hire him, were not really authentic, and the only valid aspect of his reputed social status were the names McAllister and Ingersoll, which he proudly proclaimed whenever he had the chance. He had only modest prospects as an engineer, having done rather poorly in his senior year at college. But he showed great promise as an editor and writer, although he was still not ready to defy his father, who was, as Wolcott Gibbs later put it in his *New Yorker* profile, "probably the first member of the vast conspiracy to keep Ingersoll from getting his words on paper." But the conspiracy could not succeed even when Ingersoll was three thousand miles away from New York and exhausting himself six days a week in heavy manual labor. There was time to write on Sundays, and he still thought that words would someday set him free. Since he could not decide whether it was more fun to live life or to write about it, it was his plan to do both.

Ingersoll started his career in mining engineering as a mucker—the brute who shovels up the ore after the miner has drilled or dynamited. At the beginning he was paid $3.75 for every eight-hour day, and for the first few weeks he could never work more than three or four days in succession without collapsing from sheer fatigue or a variety of bronchial ailments. But he was determined to prove to his father and also to himself that he could do it. And gradually he began to toughen up enough to work a full week. Before long he was 175 pounds of muscle and bone and competing feverishly with the Cousin Jacks, as the Cornish miners in California were called. Eventually he would be setting records for his mine: fifty-six tons of ore mucked into the dump cars in an eight-hour shift.

As his health, conditioning, and confidence improved, not only did he become proud of his work, but his inherent romanticism inspired him to look at the dreary mines with different eyes. Deep down in the shaft, he could see how beautiful the timbers and the men appeared in the peculiar lights and shadows painted by the carbine lamps the miners wore on their helmets: "Often the newly broken quartz reflected the light and made its own patterns. The exhaust from the big drills, which I found so hard to breathe, condensed as it erupted and made weird fog effects. And the miners working their drills I found beautiful, too, silhouetted against the rock. They were always in movement, for the great drills had to be wrestled into the holes they cut."

For a while, at least, Ingersoll enjoyed the underground work. The Cornishmen loved to tell stories, and when they heard a good one, the custom was to retell it, usually during the underground lunch breaks, embellishing it each time. Ingersoll became a master at telling tales and improving stories, a talent he never lost.

Gradually the miners began to respect and like the green college kid from the East. But they were also aware that he had a short temper, another characteristic that would mark him the rest of his life. Once, down in the mine, his quick fuse very nearly got him in serious trouble. After being given a drilling machine of his own and promoted to miner (at $4.50 a day), he was put under a foreman named Harry, a mean little cockney who hated the world, especially big bright American college boys. Harry spent most of his time screaming at Ingersoll in the vilest language, criticizing everything he did. Ingersoll knew that he wasn't handling his 180-pound drill right, but he also knew that Harry was not going to show him how and, furthermore, that Harry was out to see him fired. So Ingersoll made one last effort to impress Harry by drilling so dramatically better than anyone else that he could not ignore it. "I used my brain instead of my brawn," ingersoll said. "I tore down my big one-hundred-eighty-pound drill setup and I got hold of a little eighty-pound plugger drill. From the storeroom I requisitioned a block and tackle. Then I rigged the tackle to suspend my plugger from the timber overhead. It worked: I could run my contraption with one hand, pick the soft spots, sideslip the hard. It was a piece of cake. In the first hour I got more ore blocked out to blast than I'd done all the day before. I went up to the showers singing. It took two muckers the whole night shift to clean up the ore I'd broken, and I came to work next morning prepared to burn up the track."

But the next morning, when Harry's lamp-lit head came poking up through the opening in the planked floor, Ingersoll sensed trouble. Harry stood up, took a position next to the eighteen-inch oak post that supported the ceiling, then pointed his hand-held lantern at Ingersoll's rig. After studying it a moment, he snorted, "'Ere boy, take 'er down!"

"Take what down?" Ingersoll replied.

"Take that fuckin' nonsense down . . . and be quick about it. This 'ere's no fuckin' playpen."

Ingersoll could still recall his reaction years later: "It doesn't take a lot of seconds to live the sensations of a lifetime. Harry and I relived our whole relationship from our first glimpse of each other in the few seconds in which we stood there, the light from his lamp on my face, the light from mine on his. Every fiber in my being drew together in self-preservation, against the threat that Harry stood for—the threat to truth and reason, the threat to me as an individual. This was it. No conscious thoughts went through my mind. I felt my fingers tightening around the pick handle in my hand and my arm draw back and rise. There was in me, suddenly, nothing but pure and unadulterated hatred. The pickhead swung in its slow arc backward, paused, lined itself up—and came forward fast. In midair I saw it, flying fast and true, its newly sharpened point aimed straight for Harry's forehead.

"Then, suddenly and without warning, my mind turned itself on. It thought, and thought clearly, and at fantastic speed. And it simply said: If you kill him there will be messy consequences. Frightening him will do just as well. Leave it at that."

The mind caused the wrist to twist, and the pick whistled by Harry's left ear, missing it by an inch, and embedding itself six inches in the oak timber. For the first time in his life Ingersoll's uncontrollable temper had almost led to murder. There was no word spoken. Harry turned, went down the ladder, and disappeared. Ingersoll was not reported, and within twenty-four hours it was obvious that neither Harry nor Ingersoll wanted to acknowledge that the incident had ever happened. The next month Harry was transferred, and Ingersoll could not resist going by the office to inquire about what had happened. "I have reasons for wanting to know if he asked to be transferred," Ingersoll said to his boss. "We had a little difference once."

The boss replied, "No, he didn't. If you had a run-in with him, you know that he used to be pretty hard to get along with. Think this over for your own guidance when you get to be a boss. Some way or other he cured himself—and just as soon as he got to be a reasonable fellow, we gave him a whole shift to look out for. So you see a man can *cure* his own weaknesses—all by himself, son, all by himself!"

The boss paused.

"And by the way," he concluded, "Harry put you in for his old job. I may even give it to you someday—if you'll learn to control that temper of yours."

But the promotion to foreman never came. So, in the spring of 1922, Ingersoll, now chafing with characteristic impatience to keep moving up the ladder, tried a different tactic: using his typewriter instead of a drill. The year before, after his cousin had arranged for his job through a friend who was a director of the company, Ingersoll had gone down to New York to thank the man. During the course of the conversation the director had said, "Let me know what you think of the mine after you get there."

The director obviously did not know that he was dealing with a man who would eventually become one of the most prolific memorandum writers in the publishing industry. After it was clear to Ingersoll that he had gone about as far as he could go with his drill, he began inundating the New York director with letters—sometimes thousands of words long—describing every aspect of the operation. He devoted one entire report to labor relations, recommending, among other things, an incentive system based on production. This particular letter impressed the director, and he passed it along to the company president. The letter eventually came back to Ingersoll with the president's penciled comment at the top: "Your young man will go far in this company—if his patience with us holds out."

But Ingersoll's patience was not holding out. By spring he not only felt that he had learned as much as he could as a drilling miner, but he had had just enough success writing stories on Sundays to make him start thinking again about a literary career. Most of his submissions came back from the magazines he sent them to, but he did sell one to *Vogue*—an account of his romantic airplane trip over the Alps with Poly Hooker, which he signed "Ralph McAllister." It was just a short, back-of-the-book filler, but *Vogue* paid him $40—for a Sunday morning's work! Ingersoll could not help contrasting this with the $4.50 he earned for one hard day's work in the mines.

In addition, Ingersoll now had some money of his own. When his mother died, she left the New Haven house to the three children. His father had sold it, and on Ralph's twenty-first birthday—December 8, 1921—he came into his share of his inheritance: five thousand dollars. There was also Aunt Emily Watson. She was in her eighties and lived alone in White Plains, New York, with her parrots, cats, and Rolls-Royce. The Colin Ingersolls were her closest relatives; they called on her at least once a year, and little Ralph had always been one of her favorites. She had inherited her fortune from old Zadoc Pratt when she was a little girl, and everyone was sure it had been at least a half million dollars. All reports from the East indicated, tastefully, of course, that Aunt Em was growing more feeble every day.

So, when the letter came from the company president, Ingersoll announced to his boss that he was "deep enough," a miner's way of saying he quits. He decided to go back east and request a promotion or persuade his father to find him a new job as an engineer or—better still—convince his father that he was really cut out for the literary life.

In New York, with Bishop, Arny, and a variety of girl friends, he was happy for a few days, but then it became obvious that it was going to be a long, disappointing summer. None of his new girl friends could make him forget Harriet, and he soon found that he could not persuade the top brass of North Star Mining to make him an engineer. His father was very disappointed that he had come home, and would "not even discuss the proposition of a career in literature," says Ingersoll. Ralph's savings were running out, and his father repeatedly stressed that New Englanders invested inherited capital, they did not spend it, especially on such frivolous things as a literary career. His prospects with regard to Aunt Emily did not look good either. When the Ingersolls went to visit her, it was obvious that she was no longer in complete control of her senses. Once Ralph caught her eye: "You're a very large man, whoever you are. I have a nephew as big as you. His name is Ralph. He's the only one in the family who amounts to anything; he's out west earning his living with a pick and shovel."

That summer Ralph's father and Tante went to live permanently on the farm in Lakeville, and Ralph moved in with Louis Bishop, now in medical school and living with his family on East Sixtieth Street. And Ralph commuted to Columbia University, where he took two courses: one in psychology and one in short-story writing, taught by Blanche Williams. He does not recall learning much in the course, except to be vigilantly on guard against clichés, a vigil some literary critics would say he failed miserably to maintain.

When the summer was over, Ingersoll was on the train west again, headed this time for the Phelps Dodge mine in Bisbee, Arizona. Despite the fact that he was twenty-one years old, six feet two, strong as an ox, obviously unenthusiastic about a mining career, and possessed of a natural talent for organizing words and photographs on paper, he still could not defy his father and do what he wanted to do in his life. He was really no longer Arny's boy, but papa's, a fact that is reflected in the annual "Happy Birthday" letter he wrote from Bisbee in November of 1922. "You have been so darn good to me always," Ralph wrote his father, "that it is so futile to try and thank you or repay you—all I can do is tell you and tell you again that I appreciate—only with a feeling that is so much more than appreciate it doesn't go in words—it is just too big and means so much to me and I have always tried (perhaps with not too great success) and I shall go on trying to show it with what I can make out of my life for you."

In Bisbee Ingersoll went back to work operating a compressed drill underground, but this time he mined copper rather than gold. And instead of living in the mine's boardinghouse, as he had done in California, he lived with William Osborn, his then wife, Peggy LaFarge, and their two small boys. Osborn's father was one of the principal owners of Phelps Dodge, which owned the Copper Queen mine, and Osborn was also doing his apprenticeship. Most of Ingersoll's off-hours in Bisbee were spent socializing with the Osborns, and through them he finally managed to get an engineering job—with the company's copper mine in Sonora, Mexico, about eighty miles south of the border.

So, on January 1, 1923, Ingersoll set out on his big adventure, which he describes in detail in his book *In and Under Mexico*. The first leg of the journey began with Ingersoll sitting on top of his luggage in the rear of the little Ford truck that took him to the company railroad depot, five hundred yards south of the border, and ended up, after a precarious ascent on a small train and then an elevator, on top of a mountain near Sonora. Ingersoll was a combination of engineer and paymaster, and as a romantic who played hero in all the stories he wrote, he found it exciting. To him, all the young engineers "looked like characters from a novel by Richard Harding Davis. As they came out [of the mine] each threw his lamp to the little Mexican helper trotting at his heels, who took it away to clean it. I felt a great longing to become one of these swashbuckling characters."

Ingersoll was apprenticed to a young swashbuckler from Arizona University named Michael Leary, and soon he learned that in the mines all Mexicans were children and had to be treated accordingly. "The engineer has to be sort of amateur god," a role Ingersoll eventually found he could handle rather well. But on the first day he got lost, a terrifying experience: "My footsteps echoed with hard, hollow sounds as I strode over track ties or sank into an empty nothing when I struck long stretches of mud beneath my feet. My light seemed to grow smaller and illuminated only the little circle in front of my feet. It was impossible to preserve a sense of direction. . . . I went on faster and faster, stumbling over debris and striking my head on low spots . . . my doubling tracks leading nowhere." Finally he came on a group of miners and explained his predicament very slowly—in English. After he had finished, they began a debate among themselves about what he had said. Ingersoll finally solved the problem by improvising a marionette with his plumb bob, which was attached to a string. Bouncing it around in his lamplight, he showed the men that he was lost. They roared with laughter and escorted him to the ladder, which was only a hundred feet away.

Life in the mine was dangerous, and Ingersoll had several brushes with death in the dark depths. But despite the risks and the exciting stories they produced, which no doubt became more exciting with each retelling at the bar, Ingersoll enjoyed life in the mines. It gave him the thrill of being "on the firing line," like the stoker in Eugene O'Neill's *Hairy Ape*. And he could hardly have picked a better place to learn about life in the raw. Every Mexican in camp was so drunk at least one day in five that he could not work and, by Ingersoll's count, there was a murder in camp every ten days. He discovered that Mexican funerals rivaled Irish wakes in their drunken gaiety and open sentimentality. He also studied the American colony and its rigid social system "that would have delighted old Ward McAllister." He never turned down an invitation to a dance but went reluctantly to the bridge parties that were a "mild form of torture instituted by a kindly god to prepare suffering humanity for the burden of Mah Jong [sic]."

Ingersoll was intrigued by the engineers, most of whom would say over and over, "We're here only for a while you know." He drank with them at the bars and viewed them all with a reporter's eye: "the young engineer" who would end up either a wizened veteran of the mines or behind a desk in Brooklyn; the "heavy drinking clerk" who had worked in mines all over the world on jobs that always came to the same ending—alcohol and ennui; "Harry, the Englishman," the youngest son of an established British family, a fixture. But the most intriguing types were the veteran engineers who lived in the wilderness "mainly," as one of them told Ingersoll, "to get back to civilization."

Most of these men were single and, as Ingersoll pointed out to one of them, could have lived anywhere they wished. But the engineer said it was not living in the crowded places but getting back to them that he looked forward to. "The thrill of going out after you have been in here a year is worth every second of the three hundred and sixty-five days—to feel the world around you and to jingle new money in your pocket and have nothing before you but one grand, glorious bat." Then it was time to go back to the wilderness, before your "illusions of the gaiety of the city began to totter. If those illusions ever went, then I don't believe I'd have a thing left to live for."

For three months Ingersoll soaked up the life in a Mexican mine and recorded it in his diary. The people he met also inspired more short stories, such as the one titled "The School Marm with a Past in Mexico." But they were not very good, and none of them sold. On those evenings when he drank with the cynical engineers at the bars, he listened as they talked about their disillusionment with the city; but Ingersoll himself had no illusions about where he wanted to be: "I thought of a flaming sunset seen at the end of a brown-stone canyon in a far-off city and the smell of gasoline and hot asphalt seemed to saturate the air. The roar of the shops turned into the dull vibrations of the city's traffic; the gleam of the sun in the windows of the houses opposite were only the electric signs on Broadway twinkling an invitation to see the greatest hit of the year."

His diaries reveal a change in late March; he had become preoccupied with his personal unrest. He was obviously unhappy, and during one week, spent mostly in bed with a cold, he came to a decision: He would leave the mine for good in April and return to New York. He was, finally, ready to defy his father! He did not know exactly what he wanted to do next, but he hoped to begin his "career in literature" with a job on *Vogue* or *Vanity Fair*—or at least somewhere in publishing.

So, in April of 1923, Ingersoll once again told his boss he was deep enough. The miners gave him a good-bye dinner, which they dedicated to the "Departure of the Reckless Dancer," and Ingersoll returned to Bisbee, Arizona—not exactly the heart of Western civilization as we know it. But on his first full week back from the mines he could say, "New York never afforded the thrills that the border cabarets gave me." When he finally arrived in New York on April 29, though, he was almost overcome with emotion. "As the city grew up about me I became incoherent with excitement." The next day he went up to his family's farm in Lakeville to learn that his father had still not recovered from the shock and disappointment of his coming home. It was a very painful meeting. "In Father's presence," he said, "I lost all the swagger I had acquired as a division engineer in Mexico. We sat under the big maple on the lawn and talked and talked. And the longer we talked, the less convincing I sounded, even to myself—and Father was totally unmoved toward my point of view. His face, which had lines in it now, grew longer and longer, until even his ferocious white mustaches seemed to droop. If he had become angry, my courage might have been rekindled by a spark; but he seemed only depressed and humiliated by this final evidence that he had a fool for a son."

What troubled Ingersoll most was the conviction that his father thought of him as an inherent fool, not merely a foolish, immature child. He was too big and worldly now to be considered immature, although that was closer to the fact. But Ingersoll was convinced his character was at fault.

The result of this conversation with his father was that the son went back to New York having lost most of the confidence that Arny and his success as an engineer had given him. He was determined more than ever now to show his father that a career dealing with words had been his destiny from the beginning.

On board the S.S. Southern Cross

3: Adventures in the Jazz Age

On the platform in Millerton, waiting for the train after the discouraging talk with his father, Ingersoll met a young man he had known before, although he could not recall his name. He turned out to be Charles Greenwood who immediately took pity on the forlorn aspiring author who was heading for New York to look for a job. As Ingersoll had no place to stay, Greenwood offered him a room in the cellar of his family's house in Brooklyn Heights, where he also lived. One phone call from his father, Ingersoll thought, would probably have brought him scurrying home to repent, apologize, and resume his mining career. But the call never came, and he plunged into his new life in the city, full of anxiety. For one thing, the money he had saved while working in the mines would soon be exhausted, and his father had insisted, again, that New Englanders did not spend inherited capital. He also felt he was living in sin because he enjoyed New York social life so much.

Ingersoll, Greenwood, and Louis Bishop soon became a familiar threesome around town, and once, at a bar, they vowed that whoever achieved his professional goal first would throw a big dinner. Bishop knew his goal, which was to finish medical school; Greenwood's ambition was to become an officer in the bank where he clerked. Ingersoll did not know exactly what the proper objective should be in his vaguely defined career, so he decided that his celebratory dinner would be given when he published his first book. He was sure he had them in a sucker bet.

Through Greenwood Ingersoll met a girl, Mary Smith, let us call her, and before long they were sitting until dawn in a tiny Russian restaurant nursing the drinks that came with the two-dollar cover charge, riding the double-decker buses on Fifth Avenue or the open trolley cars on Lexington, going to cocktail parties and dances uptown and downtown, although Ingersoll considered the Village kid stuff and touristy. He still went out with other girls, of course, but he liked Mary very much. Even at 1923 prices, however, courting girls cost money, and his savings began to disappear a little faster. The life of a New York playboy was appealing, and Ingersoll took to it instinctively. But he also needed to work.

As credentials for launching his new career, he had only his brief article in *Vogue* and the short-story course with Blanche Williams at Columbia. And he quickly found that there were no jobs for him at *Vogue* or *Vanity Fair*. So he decided that the only way to begin the literary life was to approach it as an engineer would. And in the process he demonstrated very early two characteristics that would mark him for the rest of his years: a methodical determination (to the point of ruthlessness, his critics said) to succeed at whatever he set out to do and an instinctive flair for the dramatic. He copied the name of every news-paper, magazine, and book publisher in the phone book, then, using a map of Manhattan to group them, organized a campaign that enabled him to call on as many as sixteen potential employers a day. For six straight weeks, he said, "I made these solemn rounds—and never, in but a single instance, got past the receptionist. I was all dressed up and my hair was cut and my shoes shined, the way the book says, but it didn't help. The single exception was the *New York Tribune*'s office, where, on my third visit, a city editor named Stanley Walker did me the honor of looking me over. He was not impressed."

Soon Ingersoll was, in some cases, on his second and third round of calls, and one day, when he went back to the office of the Century Book Company and Magazine on Fourth Avenue, he found a new receptionist. Rather than asking if he could see Mr. Frank, he blurted out, "Is Glenn Frank in?" She waved him past her desk, and he was soon in the inner sanctum of the famous editor. It was a scorching August day, and an irritated and harassed Frank said, "Well, what do you want?"

Ingersoll lost his nerve, and instead of asking him for a job, he mumbled, "I want to write a book."

"About what?"

"A mine in Mexico."

"Then why don't you write it?"

"I don't know how," Ingersoll replied.

Something about Ingersoll's candor must have caught Frank's attention, and instead of ushering him out the door, he replied with heavy sarcasm, "It's really very easy, you know. You just decide how many chapters it is going to have and give each one of them a name. Then under each chapter's name you set down what you're going to put in it. Now that's your outline. You just go ahead and write chapter one—and get the hell out!"

A week later Ingersoll was back with his outline, and Frank liked it. He urged Ingersoll to write four chapters and said they then might talk about a contract. Three weeks later Ingersoll returned to the Century office and gave the four chapters to Frank, who read the first page and said, "I'll let you know."

He had not shown his book to Mary while writing the first four chapters, despite the fact that his new girl friend worked for a magazine and had a fine instinct for words. But now she became his "school mistress" as well as his lover. Most of his days were spent in Mary's apartment while she was at work. In the evening, page by page, she criticized and improved his manuscript until finally he came to feel it was as much her book as his. The experience drew them even closer, and they talked about sailing for the South Pacific after the book was finished. He also resolved to sleep only with Mary. By now he was beginning to think he might be in love.

The first draft of the book was completed within a month, at about the same time he received a letter from Century saying they liked the first four chapters but wanted to see the rest. He immediately delivered it to the Century office—then steeled himself for the final decision, which would be much longer in coming than he imagined. Things were made worse when he learned that a friend had also been carrying on an affair with Mary. Puzzled and hurt (and also running out of funds), he told her he did not want to go to the South Pacific. So Mary, infuriated, went off by herself, and Ingersoll became a little more cynical about women and love.

Bishop's mother had given Ralph a letter to one of Hearst's "$30,000-a-year men," who offered him a job as a cub reporter on the *New York American*; he was to start in a month, at fifteen dollars a week. Ingersoll was in something of a turmoil, convinced now that he was at a crossroads in his career, and still not confident he had done the right thing when he told his father he was going to live his life the way he wanted. Since then he had been writing stories continuously, and they were regularly rejected by the magazines. He had, however, one sale, a fictionalized version of an incident that took place in the Mexican mine. The magazine was *Our World* and it paid him fifty dollars.

In a terribly glum mood, he went to Lakeville for a weekend to do a little soul-searching, but he felt even worse at the farm. He had impressed everyone with his uncontrollable urge to put words on paper—but he had not convinced himself. "There is something peculiarly insecure in my desire to write that I can't fathom," he noted in his diary while at the farm. He returned to New York vowing to start over and make something of himself as a newspaperman. But, as he had to admit frankly, "I was lonely and I was scared." There was, he realized, a price to be paid for living a self-centered, independent life. Later he would feel this realization marked the end of his childhood.

Ingersoll was scheduled to start his new job on the *New York American* on September 18, and perhaps the most significant event of his *American* career, such as it was, occurred on what was to have been his first day: The pressmen went on strike. The New York newspapers immediately combined to publish an eight-page daily that printed the news in capsule form. It carried no advertising and did not cater to the morbid tastes and interests editors then presumed the masses possessed. Ingersoll noted in his diary how easy and convenient the eight-page summary was to read, and from that day on, the idea of a newspaper that did not pander to a mass audience, that printed only the essential news and carried no advertising, was to remain in the back of his mind.

The strike lasted three weeks, during which Ingersoll tried to sell short stories to the romance and confession magazines. One, "The Girl on the Night Boat," went to most of the pulp magazines in Manhattan but never did sell. Another, "Kiss Me Again—A Man Confesses," sold to *Confess* (for twenty-seven dollars). But the real boost to his sagging literary career came from Century. His book had finally been accepted! Ingersoll was almost delirious with excitement when he went to the Century office to discuss the contract, illustrations, and publicity. Century decided on a somewhat awkward title, *In and Under Mexico*, and suggested a few changes in the manuscript. All in all, the people at the publishing house seemed genuinely excited about the book, and this was no small achievement for a young, ambitious writer. After groping around on the bottom rungs of the engineering ladder for two years, in less than six months he was starting a new career at what must be the top—his own book published by a major house, something most writers do not achieve for years, if ever.

During the pressmen's strike his friend's mother tried to talk Ingersoll out of taking the job with the *American*, arguing that Hearst's brand of journalism was too specialized for the would-be author. But Ingersoll said he had resolved to make good as a reporter, and a few days later a telegram arrived from his friend's mother saying he definitely had an appointment with Victor Watson, the assistant publisher of the *American*. Watson was a harassed, rotund little man who told Ingersoll that seventeen years before, he himself had started as a cub reporter, exactly as Ingersoll was doing, and that he should report to work the following day at two P.M. There would be a one-month trial, and if he passed that test, he would have a six-month job; then they would make another assessment. Ingersoll went home "shaking with nervousness," as he noted in his diary, and very much aware of his "acid stomach," which was becoming a serious problem.

The nervousness and excitement continued to plague him during his first days on the paper, but before long he was convinced: "I had found my calling." The city room made an immediate impression on the twenty-two-year-old Ingersoll, and he liked it: "the forest of hanging lights, the underbrush of crumpled paper and the nervous tension broken by the cries of 'Boy [copy boy]!'" He was, at last, "a gentleman of the press."

Ingersoll also made an immediate impression on the men and women who put out the *American*. He was tall and had a striking face dominated by wide round eyes that gleamed and a wide smile. Because he was in the Social Register, everyone presumed he was rich, although he worked a twenty-six-hour, seven-day week. He came to work in Poly Hooker's cast-off coonskin coat, which quickly led to his becoming known around town as the "Park Avenue playboy reporter," although the *American* staff also knew that he had written a book scheduled to be published the next year.

His first assignment concerned a young lady who thought she had concocted a serum that would make her immune to the bite of the lovebug. Ingersoll was almost too nervous to type up the story, but he finally finished it and turned it in. Then the thrill that comes once in a lifetime: seeing your first story in print, only two hours after you have written it. Three days later he had his first headline story, about a "wealthy widow" who had been dating a man who was found shot in the widow's Sound Beach house. Ingersoll's scrapbook of frayed, yellow clippings contains stories with such headlines as "Hamlet Backer Lands in Cell" and "Ingrate Son Beats Mother Over a Dollar." His magazine-fiction style helped him write light, breezy leads, as he did for his story about a minister who was preaching that too many Americans were committing the "new sin of 'social trespass'": "Are you one of the kind that steps on a man's toe in the subway and then bellows across the car to a friend so that the little stenographer hanging on a strap next to you loses her place in 'Life Stories' and rides past her station trying to find it again?"

Gradually he overcame his nervousness, and his stomach calmed down enough to enable him to type his stories with a minimum of agony. Still, he knew he was not progressing in the eyes of Martin Dunn, the city editor. In little ways he always seemed to make an ass of himself in front of the boss. He hated Dunn for it and was always resisting an urge to punch him in the nose. One of the men he worked for thought Ingersoll was "very successful," and said he had put in a good word for him with Dunn. But when Ingersoll went in after one month on the job to ask the city editor for a raise, Dunn said he wasn't sure yet, that Ingersoll had done some good stories and some bad ones: "Let's wait awhile."

But Ingersoll was learning. One day he went out with Jim Whittaker, who everyone agreed was the *American*'s star reporter, to work with him on an assignment. Whittaker went after the story, Ingersoll noted, "never missing a trick, but all the time laughing at the whole thing—the story, the newspaper, himself, life—in a most charming, smooth, flowing way."

He was, however, still dissatisfied with his own writing, especially his efforts to keep his copy breezy. "My light humor," he complained, "is always on the verge of being ponderously asinine." By the end of 1923 he had become convinced that he was not doing very well as a Hearst reporter. The "times were out of joint," and the only good thing to come out of the year was his book. Early in 1924 he applied for a job with the *Herald-Tribune* but was turned down.

Ingersoll, as a former engineer and a socialite, had not yet developed much of a social consciousness. Everyone in the office was talking about a big scandal breaking in Washington, something to do with oil and a place called Teapot Dome; yet he noted in his diary, "it doesn't excite me." At the same time he had also heard a speech given at the Commodore Hotel by William Jennings Bryan, which, he said, made him eager to learn more about politics. He was not totally unaware of the social, political, and economic issues of the day, and gradually he was becoming convinced that every newspaperman in the business was being exploited by the capitalist system that produced the American newspaper. His stint on the *American* also gave him a chance to see firsthand just how sleazy and corrupt American newspapers of the 1920s were, especially the ones published by Hearst. And, as in Mexico, he was a quick learner. In less than six months on the newspaper he had absorbed enough to put together an impressive outline for a book (which was never written) to be called "The Adventures of an Amateur Reporter in New York."

Although Ingersoll's *American* career was brief, it was not forgotten. He established a reputation for being ingenious, aggressive, persistent, persuasive— and unbelievably naïve. And it was his naïveté that led to the assignment that eventually had everyone in New York's cynical and gossipy newspaper crowd talking—and laughing.

One morning, in mid-February 1924, the city editor called him into his office: "I'm sending you on a big story. The United States Veterans Bureau has been getting a great deal of unpleasant notoriety [much of it from the Hearst press] and Mr. Hearst feels that it has hurt the chances of veterans getting jobs. I want you to go to their headquarters. They are doing great work—and I want you to get me the whole story. I'm sending the best photographer in the shop with you. I want pictures of all these men and their work." Martin Dunn handed Ingersoll two pieces of paper, one of which was a letter from the bureau's employment agent asking for publicity on the trained veterans who were out of jobs. Across the bottom Victor Watson had written: "Make into a big Sunday story for the veterans."

The photographer's name was Helen Kanaga, whom Ingersoll described in his diary as a regular girl and most interesting. They set off for the local office of the Veterans Bureau convinced they were on a "big story" and laughing at Hearst's change of attitude, although it was not the first time he had come around to supporting some institution or person he had previously attacked. It took Ingersoll and Kanaga more than an hour to convince the bureau officials that Hearst really wanted to do an upbeat story, but then they were given complete cooperation. They did the story and took the photographs in two days, then returned to Dunn's office and triumphantly laid the whole package on his desk. A delighted Dunn said, "Take the week off."

As Ingersoll was leaving the building he ran into a reporter named Mefford and could not help telling him about his big story. Mefford was amazed and said he and another *American* reporter had just come back from the West Coast where they had been "digging up some dirt for the Old Man's peeve on the Veterans Bureau." According to Mefford, the *American* was about to break a big story on scandal in the bureau.

The next morning, Feburary 15, Ingersoll's worst fears were confirmed. The *American* ran a huge spread with photographs, under a banner headline announcing widespread corruption in the New York office of the Veterans Bureau. It was Ingersoll's day off, but he went storming into the office in a rage, his coonskin coat billowing out behind him. All he could think of was punching Dunn in the nose for having made such fools of him and Kanaga. When Dunn admitted they had been duped, Ingersoll shouted that he did not think it was fair to send him up there, using his good name, to gain the bureau's confidence. He said that if he had known there was scandal in the bureau and had been told to go after it, he might have done so, possibly using the same technique he and Kanaga had used. But as it was, he had been tricked, used, pure and simple.

"Well, what do you want to do about it," Dunn shot back, "fight a duel?"

Missing the opportunity to smash Dunn in the nose, which he would regret the rest of his life, Ingersoll pushed him back into a large wastebasket behind his desk and said, "No, I want to offer my resignation."

"Wait a minute, now," replied Dunn. "We got the story the only way we could have gotten it. Besides, you did a patriotic thing. That Veterans Bureau's full of graft and you're helping to clean it out."

"That's not the question," Ingersoll replied, still seething. "I saw many things yesterday I didn't like, and practically every executive in the bureau opened up to me and told me what was going on and what they were trying to do about it. But I was double-crossed by my own employer, and no man could go on working like that and keep his self-respect."

"I had to," said Dunn. "I had to get your enthusiasm."

"Didn't you give me this letter with Mr. Watson's notation on it?" he asked, showing Dunn the letter.

"By God, give me that letter," said Dunn, snatching it from Ingersoll. Then he shrugged his shoulders and said Ingersoll was a "damn fool to resign."

Ingersoll went home humiliated and angry. Photographer Kanaga said she was resigning too, and Ingersoll's friends applauded his stand on principle, many of them offering him money to tide him over until he found another job. That night he closed his diary entry for the day with the line "But, God Almighty, I wish I had hit Martin Dunn."

The following Tuesday he returned to the *American* to pick up his last paycheck. He also stopped in Dunn's office to retrieve the letter with Watson's notation on it, secretly hoping to find another opportunity to smash Dunn's face. Dunn would not return the note and tried to make peace—all the while remaining seated and wearing eyeglasses. Shaking with rage, Ingersoll stammered through a long litany of insults, concluding, "Mr. Dunn, if it takes fifty years, I'll get

back at you for what you did." But the words gave him no satisfaction, and he
spent the rest of his life regretting that he had not smacked Dunn in the nose.*

Ingersoll was soon making the rounds again, but he quickly discovered that
although he might be a hero in the bars (where other Hearst reporters cried in
their beers telling him how much they hated their jobs and admired him for what
he had done), he was virtually *persona non grata* in the city rooms of New
York's newspapers. As a result, he did what most unemployed newspapermen
do: He became a free-lance writer, which was fortuitous. Being a struggling,
unemployed author in New York in the 1920s was perhaps the most glamorous
career a young man could pursue.

The literary life in this country has probably never known a more exciting
place and time than New York in the 1920s. After the war the young men
returning from Europe led America's rebellion against Victorian traditions, and
a host of poets, writers, artists, and editors took their rebellion into the newspapers. Most of these intellectuals were working or writing in New York, and
almost every writer among them wanted to produce the Great American Novel.
"In those days," one commentator wrote, "people talked of the great American
novel as ministers spoke of the second coming." Franklin P. Adams (known as
F.P.A.), who was writing the most widely read literary column in the country—
which appeared in the *New York World* under the title "The Conning Tower"—
referred so often to the Great American Novel that he finally assigned it an
acronym, *G.A.N.* In 1924, when Ingersoll left the *American*, everyone was
working on a novel—and the following year, 1925, has gone down as probably
the most extraordinary in American publishing history, with the publication of
An American Tragedy, by Theodore Dreiser; *Dark Laughter*, by Sherwood Anderson; *In Our Time*, by Ernest Hemingway; *Soldier's Pay*, by William Faulkner;
Gentlemen Prefer Blondes, by Anita Loos; *The Great Gatsby*, by F. Scott Fitzgerald; *Arrowsmith*, by Sinclair Lewis; *Barren Ground*, by Ellen Glasgow; *The
Professor's House*, by Willa Cather; *Death in Venice*, by Thomas Mann; *Manhattan Transfer*, by John Dos Passos; *Those Barren Leaves*, by Aldous Huxley;
Mrs. Dalloway, by Virginia Woolf; *Thunder on the Left*, by Christopher Morley;
as well as books by Van Wyck Brooks, Amy Lowell, Elinor Wylie, Lewis
Mumford, Sigmund Spaeth, T. S. Eliot, Edgar Lee Masters, Ezra Pound, and
Robinson Jeffers. Writing and books were everywhere in the air, and it would
have been impossible for such an intensely ambitious and perceptive young man
as Ralph Ingersoll not to be caught up in the literary excitement.

Even before he resigned from the *American*, Ingersoll had been thinking
about a novel based on what he called "Rosalie's plot," suggested to him by one
of his friends. It was to be the story of a conflict between two women, one of
whom had given birth to a child because the other wanted a baby. "God knows

---

*Years later, in fact, when the *New Yorker* did its profile on Ingersoll, he told Wolcott Gibbs
that he had hit Dunn in the midsection, knocking him down, and he repeated the story in his
autobiography, *Point of Departure*. Obviously, in his mining days, sitting around the fire with his
Cornish colleagues, he had learned the fine art of embellishing a tale each time it is retold.

where I ever acquired . . . the mistaken confidence that I could give reality to a wholly imagined fable," Ingersoll wondered years later, and he was not alone. His editor at Century rejected the idea, saying politely that the ending was too tragic. And Mary Smith, his most important literary collaborator (now back from the South Pacific, and no longer angry that Ingersoll had not gone with her), said that although she liked the plot, she doubted that Ralph had the ability to bring it off with conviction. But he could not put it out of his mind.

* * *

Ingersoll never denied that one of the main reasons he had returned to New York from the West was that he missed the glittering Park Avenue social life he had learned to love while he was at Yale. His diaries for the years 1923, 1924, and 1925 read like a chronicle of the Jazz Age. He and his friends seemed determined to drink all the whiskey in town and sleep with all the girls, and most of their waking hours were spent planning parties, dances, and football weekends.

Despite his chronic indigestion and recurring headaches, Ingersoll's life in the early 1920s was one long pursuit of a hangover. Most of his drinking was connected with the conquest of women, and each success (or failure) was duly recorded in his diary. At the end of the year he summarized his records. In 1924 his girl friends decreased to nineteen, from twenty-six, but his total triumphant scores (or parties as he called them) increased from sixteen to twenty-seven. He frankly recognized that his intense heat, as he called it, could come on at any time—at the typewriter, at a party, or at dinner.

Although he was dining, dancing, and sleeping with as many girls as he could, by early 1924 his interests had focused on three: Mary Smith, Eleanor Peabody, and Katherine Spaeth. Mary was his main intellectual companion and literary mentor. An English major, she had graduated *magna cum laude* from college, and considered Ingersoll bright but a "literary ignoramus." After she returned from the South Pacific, she confessed to Ralph that she had been in love with him, and one night at a bridge party when everyone had been drinking a lot, Mary said quite seriously, "You know, Ralph, I'd marry you any day in the week." Ingersoll declined, saying that when he talked about such a serious subject, he did not want to be drinking so much gin. But the proposal rocked him a little and started him thinking about marriage and love. Although he genuinely liked Mary, she did not fit in with his "social ambitions," as he outlined them in his diary: "that pre-conceived life in which I take up a career, marry an equal in my class and become a conservative, upper-class head of household."

In his class, of course, one did not make serious advances to a "marrying kind" of girl, a girl like Eleanor Emmet Peabody, whom he had known since his prep school days. Eleanor came from fine families on both sides, and although her branch was not wealthy, she had the kind of quality Ingersoll appreciated. He dated her off and on, always finding her exciting to be with. Then, suddenly, Eleanor announced that she was going on an around-the-world trip as a traveling companion to a rich friend of Ralph's father, a legendary woman from Chicago whom everyone called Ri-Ti. The difference between Mary and Eleanor can be seen in Ralph's record of conquests for 1924 (noted in his diary): There are twelve assorted entries for "heavy necking" and "parties" under Mary's name and only one kiss and "heavy necking" under Eleanor's.

The more Ingersoll thought about it, the more he became convinced that it would be exceedingly proper for him to marry a Peabody, even if he knew he did not love her. But, of course, one did not marry a girl like Eleanor Peabody unless one was established in a business or profession or had come into a fortune. In early 1924 Ralph's aunt Emily died. Although she left eleven million dollars, not one penny went to her favorite nephew. She bequeathed most of her money to eighteen charities, all of which were listed in her will before any bequests to a relative. Ingersoll's father was left fifty thousand dollars. And it was now clear that Ralph Ingersoll would not inherit a fortune. So he could only propose to a girl such as Eleanor Peabody with the qualification "If I make good," which looked none too promising in 1924. Eleanor went off on her round-the-world trip with Ri-Ti, and Ralph made plans to meet her the following spring when she reached Europe.

Katherine Spaeth was married to the musicologist Sigmund Spaeth, whose book *The Common Sense of Music* had been published just before Ingersoll met the couple. Katie was primarily a hostess who supported the arts and artists, often with love and affection. She had the kind of bohemian arrangement with her husband that permitted freedom of action and attachments on both sides, and Katie had a series of lovers, including, eventually, Ralph Ingersoll. The Spaeths lived on the top floor of the old brownstone building that housed the Fifth Avenue Bank at Forty-fourth and Fifth. They gave fabulous parties, which sometimes went on for days, with most of the literary lights of the 1920s coming and going, including the hard-drinking crowd of wits and intellectuals who hung out at the nearby Algonquin Hotel. According to his diary, Ingersoll first met a strange, shy young man named Harold Ross at one of Katherine's parties. The date was May 16, 1924. He did not comment about meeting Ross; of that occasion he only remembered "getting tight without noticing it and trying to be nice to everyone and becoming a little silly." On another occasion he met a young lady named Edna Ferber, but he was too drunk to do much about it, which was too bad, he thought, because Miss Ferber intrigued him. His main interest, however, was the older, sophisticated Katie, whom he was gradually coming to regard as the epitome of the glamorous, seductive New York hostess at the center of the kind of life that had drawn him back east.

It was during this period that Ingersoll evolved what he always called his "career in both camps": Park Avenue Society and bohemia. It is obvious, reading his diary, that he was at home in both groups and enjoyed the hard-drinking parties and conversations with his bohemian friends as much as he did the Society dances and Yale weekends. And he cut an impressive figure around town. In addition to the coonskin coat he wore in the winter, he would, on occasion, wear spats and carry a cane. But his favorite attire was formal party clothes: "Ah, what magnificence," he recorded in his diary one morning after trying on his new cutaway in front of a mirror. "I could feel the change in personality a girl is said to undergo under the influence of a new dress. But mainly I was a little awed by myself and instead of rising to my own splendor as a girl seems to do, I subsided into a stifling glow of self-satisfaction."

He was also satisfied with the number of people he knew around town. One day, transferring names from an old address book to a new one he had received for Christmas, he counted ninety-eight prominent or up-and-coming people and estimated, smugly, that he must know at least five hundred people he could converse with without having to be introduced.

To know that many people one had to travel in at least two worlds, and Ingersoll kept one foot firmly in Katie Spaeth's Fifth Avenue bohemia and the other solidly planted in the Yale Club on Vanderbilt Avenue. Ingersoll had never been a Yalie at New Haven, but now that he was a young man about New York, the post-Yale life became as much a part of his day-to-day existence as the parties at the Spaeths or with Mary and his other girls. The common denominator of the two worlds he lived in was whiskey. It is hard to tell which of the two camps drank the most scotch and gin in the 1920s, but he drank more than his share of both.

Ingersoll could be found any time of the day or night at the Yale Club— for breakfast, lunch, or dinner. The center of this life, of course, was the football weekend, a ritual that included trips to New Haven, Princeton, Cambridge, or wherever Yale was playing, with non-stop drinking and gambling coming and going. On one memorable return trip from New Haven, Ingersoll won four hundred dollars in a crap game on the train. At a celebration after Yale won the big game with Princeton in 1923, Ingersoll was so exalted he told one girl, "I would never marry a girl who didn't like Yale." The following week, as the Harvard game approached, he recorded in his diary that the excitement was now "almost unendurable," so much so that he could not sleep. The Saturday Yale beat Harvard 13–0 is recorded in his diary in huge block letters, and he called it "The Biggest Day of My Existence!" "Football games are to men," he wrote, "what anniversaries are to women—of prodigious importance, which can't possibly be realized by the other sex."

Football weekends, Society parties, promiscuous women, proper debutantes, and whiskey—these were the ingredients of Ingersoll's personal life during the 1920s, and he indulged in them so intensely and passionately that it is a wonder he did any writing at all. But the literary explosion of the 1920s is testimony to the fact that the hard-drinking, late-partying intellectuals in New York also did their thousand or two thousand words a day, and Ingersoll was no exception. His main problem was that he simply did not write as well as most of the other young men and women caught up in the literary revolution. But his compulsion to put words on paper could rival anyone's. As soon as he left the *American*, he settled into his little apartment at 111 East Thirty-fifth Street to start to write, occasionally pursuing an interesting job lead. One of his efforts was a story called "The Wages of Mismanagement," which begins: "We are all of us strange people on the island of Andalini. We are drunk almost every night and each one of us drinks for a different reason." The narrator is there because he had made an employee in the bank where he worked pregnant, then let her have an abortion, which killed her. No one knew he was the father. He was promoted—then had a nervous breakdown and took his secret to Andalini.

Ingersoll sent "Wages" and a few other stories on their rounds to the magazines (they did not sell) and then began work on the novel based on Rosalie's plot. When he found it was not going well, he retreated to the family's farm in Lakeville but discovered he could not write there, either. Searching for the reasons, he recalled that when he was working on *In and Under Mexico*, he lived in the city, wrote by day, and drank and made love to Mary—when not reading her the manuscript and listening to her suggestions—by night. He decided that was what he needed, so he abruptly returned to New York, which he called "my mistress"—as he noted in his diary, "I shall never be quite happy away from my city." As for Mary: "Even if we can't work, we can still make love."

Back in the bosom of his two mistresses, he was surprised to find that his novel still would not develop. But this discouragement was almost relieved at a lunch with Century editor Bob Wise, who presented him with the first bound copy of *In and Under Mexico*. It was, he said, "splattered with my name," and he was thrilled just to hold it in his hand. He and Wise agreed that what Ingersoll did best was reporting and that he needed to find another subject similar to Mexico. But where to go?

What about doing the romantic thing all his bohemian friends talked about: shipping out as a steward on a passenger ship, then writing a book about the experience? His Century editor liked the idea, and they agreed that South America would be the place to go, not only because he had had such success with Central America, but because people knew so little about the region.

Excited again about writing, Ingersoll made arrangements with the Munson line to work as a steward aboard the S.S. *Southern Cross* on a six-week round trip to South America. It was the spring of 1924 when he went over to Hoboken to sail for Buenos Aires, bolstered by two events that helped confirm his feeling that he had finally arrived as one of New York's most successful and promising young men.

Just before the S.S. *Southern Cross* sailed for South America, the early reviews of *In and Under Mexico* began appearing, and they were very favorable. The book clearly established him as a superb reporter and an accomplished writer. "Mr. Ingersoll is a born raconteur," said the *Literary Review*, "possessor of something of the magic of 'the teller of tales,' that elusive, undefinable something that cannot be taught." He "tells his story simply and strongly," said the all-important review in the *New York World*; "we did not feel there was anything in *In and Under Mexico* to interest a newspaper reader who never found much joy in Mexican stories, but Mr. Ingersoll proves a delightful entertainer. His story reads like the best letters an amusing and intelligent friend might write." Ingersoll must have loved the *New York Herald-Tribune*'s comment, knowing that his father would be sure to see it: "Mr. Ingersoll is probably a rotten miner," said the *Tribune* reviewer Frederick F. Van de Water. "He's so good a writer. He has not only a gift for words, but also a gift for sight and the rare ability to put things he has witnessed into words."

Ingersoll could not have been happier about the publication of his book, though he observed, "I was certainly under no illusion that *In and Under Mexico* was literature—and I was anything but sure that I could ever write another even as good as that. As a literary discovery, I knew *I* was a fraud." But the publication of *In and Under Mexico* was a major occurrence in Ingersoll's coming of age, as was the second event that occurred on the eve of his sailing for South America: a secret assignation with Katie Spaeth. The meeting took place in Katie's bedroom, where she had confined herself with a mild case of bronchitis. After being shown where the back stairs were—just in case—he slipped into her husband's pajamas, and he and Katie lay in bed, her long golden hair glistening in the moonlight, all of which was breathlessly recorded in his diary: "Even in the sublime intimacy, I am in awe of her. It was a soft, gentle night, the most glamorous, romantic night I have ever spent. We got up and knelt in the open window and looked out over the sleeping city bathed in moonlight with soft Jupiter shining. . . . The realization that I had slept with Katie Spaeth came to me and it put a new premium upon my self-respect. It alternated with a joy and physical delight."

The next day he saw Katie again and tried to tell her all the beautiful things he was thinking, but he was inarticulate. The following morning he sailed out of the harbor on the *Southern Cross*. He was seasick all day, and only his rhapsodic thoughts of Katie kept him from "sinking." He knew he would marry her in a minute if he had the chance.

Ingersoll had not been at sea ten days before he realized that shipping out as a ship's steward, although the romantic thing to do in the 1920s, was not going to provide him much material. He was having difficulty making it dramatic. Although he rubbed shoulders with larceny, homosexuality, smuggling, shipboard and shore-leave sex, rum-running, and crooked bookkeeping in the steward's office, writing about it would be difficult; the last man to be indiscreet, he was told, had been found wedged between a ship and the pier in Hoboken. The most interesting passengers were his fellow crewmen, particularly one little Irish bellboy. "Although he came from the city I call my mistress," Ingersoll wrote, "it is difficult for me to understand what he says." But he kept Ingersoll riveted with stories of "gang rapes" and other East Side games.

But if the trip was a literary disappointment, it at least gave him a chance to get away from the social whirl for a while and to think. He decided that what he really worried about most was money. Through his shipmates he had seen the other side of New York; "now that I have been in contact with the penniless," he said, "it has frightened me instead of being reassuring." The "money all around" him, and the thought of Aunt Emily's fortune, had given him a false sense of security and the illusion of being wealthy himself. And now, he told his diary, "here alone, half sick [with recurring headaches and nausea] I have felt quite helpless."

Although he felt much better after visits to the whorehouses in Rio and Buenos Aires, he was vaguely ill during most of the trip. He was glad to return to New York in mid-July. He went immediately to the Yale Club to find a collection of reviews of his book, which his father had sent down from Connecticut. They were almost all favorable, and he was delirious with joy. Then he went up to the farm and was struck by his father's change of attitude. The elder Ingersoll had even dressed up to meet his illustrious son. "The very traits he had most criticized in me, he now admired," Ralph wrote. "My reliance on my own judgment, my 'idealism' (in not resigning myself to a career I thought 'second best'), and—of all things—my perseverance! By my stubbornness about having my own way, I had proved my 'stick-to-itiveness.' And the thing of which he was suddenly proudest was the way in which I had stood up to him, defied his threat of disinheritance and challenged his will with my own—the very same behavior that had once hurt him most. Father remained in a kind of trance about me for the rest of his long, long life. Even the most appalling of scrapes I got into, he forgave and tried hard to understand. I could marry women he did not like, vote for Presidents he abhorred—and even lose all my money gambling in the stock market on margin—but still he was for me and against any detractor." But his father's reaction also disillusioned him because he still felt he was something of a fraud as an author. "And so my father seemed suddenly revealed as a fraud himself. From an august symbol of righteous wisdom he was suddenly shrunk to the dimensions of a mortal; he was not a god after all, but simply a nice old gentleman gone silly about his son."

But, Ingersoll says, "eventually I got over my embarrassment and came to love him very dearly."

Ingersoll returned to New York after the homecoming weekend feeling on top of the world. He was both a successful author with a new book to work on and a glamorous young bachelor who was beginning an affair with one of bohemia's most intriguing women. Katie had planned to wait for the *Southern Cross* to return from South America before departing on a European trip, but when Ingersoll's ship was delayed, she had to sail without seeing him, leaving her husband and Ingersoll in New York, and she had insisted that while she was gone, Ralph move in with Sigmund. It gave him a "strange sensation."

Before long, however, Ingersoll's self-image as the enviable, glamorous, promising young author-about-town would be as flawed as the picture of Dorian Gray. He went to lunch to discuss his South American experiences with his Century editor, who decided that his few days ashore in Argentina and Brazil were not enough to provide material for a book. Furthermore, he still did not like Ingersoll's idea for a novel, and he was pessimistic about the prospects for

In and Under Mexico. Despite the excellent reviews, it was not selling. Ingersoll went back to the Spaeth apartment deflated and depressed and spent the evening trying to drown his discouragement in scotch.

He had, however, not been completely discouraged from writing the South American book, and the next morning, despite a hangover, he started his story. His first day produced five thousand words, which he thought was a good sign. But then the writing began to flag, and he realized his material was not very good. When it did not improve, he went up to the family farm to work on the book; he could not write there either and confessed to his diary, "There is a great need in me to accomplish."

He returned to New York about the time Katie finally returned from Europe, and she was obviously not well. Although it had been rumored that she had cancer, that did not appear to be the case; she seemed to be suffering primarily from a gradually worsening depression, combined with some vague physical illness. But Ingersoll still wanted her—or at least her help in his career. He gave Katie four chapters of his steward book, which she liked and promised to show to Thomas Costain, a *Saturday Evening Post* editor. Despite her illness, she and Ingersoll drifted into what he called an "unofficial marriage," which was public enough to permit them to spend a few weekends at the farm in Lakeville. Katie charmed his parents so much that even his father accepted the fact that his son was having an affair with a married woman—although at the farm he continued to treat Ralph, despite his literary success, like a twelve-year-old boy, which amused Katie who commented that he really ought to be dating debutantes.

With Katie's encouragement he became once more enthusiastic about his book (now titled "Thank You, Steward"), and his new "fever of success" rose a few degrees when he learned the *Post* was definitely interested in an article based on the material. This was all he needed to make a commitment to stay in New York and pursue a career as an author. Swallowing his self-doubts, he signed a lease for a penthouse apartment at 135 East Fiftieth. It was small but gave him a glamorous view of his city. He called it the Eagle's Nest, and when Katie went to the country for a while to regain her health, it proved the perfect nest for parties of all kinds. Before long, Mary would be back in his life, too, although he had not forgotten Eleanor Peabody and still planned to meet her in Europe in the spring of 1925.

The truth is, he was more confused than ever about women, love, and marriage. He still had not overcome his distrust of love, and although he wanted to marry someone "in his class," he did not enjoy socialites or debutantes and much preferred the women in Katie's bohemian circle.

As for Katie, she seemed to be drifting away from him in her depression and illness, although Ingersoll was determined to stick by her—partly out of loyalty, but also, as he frankly admitted to himself, to further his career. A fascinating description of his affair with Katie Spaeth appears in his diary in the form of a plot summary for a "fine tale" written from his point of view. Not only does it provide insight into his relationship with Katie, but it shows his instinct for dramatizing life situations as plots for stories:

"Behold, the young writer . . . begins the conquest of New York. He picks out the older woman just on the far side of her prime, who is the center of a circle which includes the critics and writers whom he must know to get on. She is charming—beautiful and full of wit. He makes an impression and under her guidance, his writings begin to get published, to be known. Then he finds that he has a glamorous attraction for her; he becomes her lover. With him, it is romance with the sanction of the intellect. They become caught up in one another and their affair is full of fire; all is perfect. With such a woman as his mistress, he will become perfect. Then she falls ill. She can no longer have the circle about her; her guidance of his work is spasmodic. He is thrown on his own. He finds it good for him; he can continue to make headway but his hold is tenuous. . . . He realizes now that she is a human being and that she needs him very much. . . . The young writer's hands are tied. He can't dominate the situation, but his idealism has come to the fore and he cannot leave her. Once his mistress and his work were one; now they are two masters. He struggles to master both and the logical end would seem failure to succeed in either—or destruction of his career for the woman who is now a petulant invalid."

"How will it come out?" Ingersoll is not sure, but he speculates: "Perhaps I shall fail and this plot [for the novel] will, in the end, make me!"

Of one thing he was certain: His work remained "the only real thing in these women infested times." Suddenly, his doubts were gone again, and he felt himself once more "in stride, young, ambitious and capable." He was, however, aware that his writing was suffering from his reading too much Michael Arlen, whose phenomenally successful *The Green Hat* was then the most-talked-about novel in the country. Most critics, however, agreed with George Jean Nathan who called Arlen a "purveyor of . . . rented dress-suit literature . . . to the manor born," which would not have been a bad critique of Ingersoll's writing in 1924.

Ingersoll's archaic style, however, did not discourage him, and by the end of 1924 he had finished "Thank You, Steward" and sent it on its rounds to the publishers. Then, rereading what he had written on his novel in the spring, he decided to finish that, too, giving it the tentative title "Beryl and Anne." He went to Boston for a family Christmas, then back to the city by way of Schenectady, where he gave a radio talk about Mexico over station WGY. On the train, heading for New York and a series of New Year's Eve parties, he had a "peculiar feeling of accomplishment." Not only had the article about his South American trip been published in the *Saturday Evening Post* that week, but reaching "the broadcast stage" in his career was, he felt, also significant. That night, in a howling blizzard, as he made the round of parties—including one at the Heywood Brouns' ("literati, dull and slopping around in bad bathtub gin") and another at the Rube Goldbergs' ("a celebrity hunt")—he had "the distinct impression that something had happened—that a new leaf had been turned." At one party he saw Katie, who was back from the country after a long rest. But they were "terribly distant."

Ingersoll's instinctive feeling that a new leaf had been turned was correct: The new year, 1925, would be the turning point in his uncertain "literary career," as well as in his turbulent personal life. Although the *Post* had taken the article about his experience as a steward, and had also commissioned another on the new phenomenon of radio (based on his fifteen-minute talk over WGY), the book about his South American trip had still not found a publisher. He had also finished his novel (now titled "Fair Exchange") but his new agent, Brandt and Brandt, had not yet placed it. He did have a conference with an editor at Alfred A. Knopf, and although she was very encouraging—he had managed, she said, to make at least one minor character come alive—she suggested gently, "Mr. Ingersoll, I do think it would be better if we don't let anyone see this *particular* manuscript."

Ingersoll also signed up with the pulp magazine *Art Lovers* to do articles for a series called "Confessions of a Society Girl," but after the first installment *Art Lovers* went out of business. By spring he was again in turmoil. His agent was urging him to do more magazine articles, but he wanted to rewrite "Fair Exchange" based on the advice some of his readers had given him about what was wrong with it. He had also spent half of his inheritance supporting himself as a writer and speculating in the stock market. And he had now decided that he definitely wanted to marry Eleanor Peabody. So he told his father that he was cashing in the last of his inheritance to finance a trip to Europe to propose to her. His father must have approved, because he invested five hundred dollars in the project.

On March 24, 1925, Ralph McAllister Ingersoll, the glamorous young author and man-about-New York, sailed on *La Bourdemais* for France, where he planned to meet his true love in Nice, propose to her, then settle down in marital bliss in a rented villa on the Riviera, rewriting "Fair Exchange" by day and dancing, gambling, and drinking champagne in the romantic cafés of Monte Carlo by night. It did not, however, work out quite that way. Ralph and Eleanor on the Riviera turned out to be a parody of Scott and Zelda in Europe during the year Fitzgerald wrote *The Great Gatsby*. It is questionable whether Ingersoll ever rewrote one line of "Fair Exchange" while he was an expatriate. And he never did marry Eleanor, who said she had always been in love with another man and would only make Ralph's life "hell."

Ingersoll, demonstrating that he, too, knew all the clichés of the 1920s romance magazines, replied, "I don't care. I want to marry you anyway"; and continued the pursuit until, finally, the endless bickering, gambling, and partying began to pall and the money ran out. After that there was no choice but to board a ship for home; in fact, he could hardly wait to return to New York. But even his beloved Manhattan looked brown and dreary. He still continued to see Eleanor, who had come back on the ship with him, and he saw Katie occasionally, but that affair was also dead. And his closest friend, Louis Bishop, was getting married. It was, in fact, the end of an era, although at the time Ingersoll did not accept or understand it. All he knew was that he felt miserable—especially when alone.

Nor did his agents give him much to cheer about. Neither "Thank You, Steward" nor "Fair Exchange" had found a publisher. But one young lady, who worked for Brandt and Brandt, had heard that Harold Ross was desperately looking for staffers to help save his new magazine, the *New Yorker*, and suggested Ingersoll talk to him.

Ingersoll knew all about Harold Ross, the strange young man with the rubbery face, gappy front teeth, and bushy black hair that looked like a shaving brush. Ross, a provincial born in Salt Lake City, had had a few newspaper jobs before editing the *Stars and Stripes* in Europe during World War I. After the war Ross and Alexander Woollcott, who had also worked on *Stars and Stripes*, became the center of a corps of fast-talking wits who gathered for lunch at the Algonquin Hotel to debunk everything and everybody. In the evenings they usually played poker at somebody's apartment. Ross was shy and inarticulate and mostly in awe of the Algonquin wits who, in 1924, included Woollcott, Marc Connelly, Dorothy Parker, and George S. Kaufman, to mention the ones most closely associated with the early days of the *New Yorker*. But Ross also sensed that a gold mine was waiting to be tapped in the irreverent, debunking wit of the writers, artists, and intellectuals who made up this tight-knit little group—if only he could capture it in print.

But launching a magazine cost money, and Ross was not wealthy. Then one day at the poker table he met Raoul Fleischmann, an heir to the Fleischmann's yeast fortune. Fleischmann agreed to launch Ross's magazine, and by Feburary 1925, when Ingersoll was just finishing the first draft of the book he hoped would prompt F.P.A. to announce that, finally, G.A.N. had been written, Fleischmann, Ross, and his gang of wits were ready with their prospectus announcing a magazine that would definitely *not* be "edited for the old lady in Dubuque."

Ingersoll had seen the first few issues of the *New Yorker* before he had sailed for Europe that spring, and he had not been impressed. All the Algonquin wits were on the masthead, but unfortunately, their printed product did not have the sparkle and bite of their luncheon and poker-table banter. Ingersoll also knew that in April, while he was in Europe, the F-R (for Fleischmann and Ross) Publishing Company had almost failed. In fact, at a luncheon meeting one Friday Ross, Fleischmann and two other members of the F-R Company, John Hanrahan and Hawley Truax, had decided to kill the magazine, whose circulation had decreased to eight thousand, which was the number of dollars it was losing every week. But by the time Fleischmann returned to his office, he had decided to put up enough additional money to give the magazine one more chance, and the *New Yorker* was now on a sort of probation until the fall. Ross was looking for new blood for his continually rotating staff. When Ingersoll returned from Europe, he was surprised to see that the *New Yorker* was still being published. He did not think it had improved very much since the early issues, but he was thoroughly broke now and needed a job.

The *New Yorker* offices were on the sixth floor of an office building at 25 West Forty-fifth Street. The quarters, which were unusually dreary, did nothing to improve Ingersoll's mood or disposition when he was ushered into Ross's cubicle. During the interview he felt dull and listless, which did not go unnoticed by Ross, who commented, "You look a little vague about the whole thing." Ingersoll liked Ross for saying that, and for the first time found him oddly appealing. There was no job offer, but Ross did suggest that Ingersoll work up a package of short sketches, then come back for another meeting.

When Ingersoll returned with his package, they discussed the possibility of his working on the front of the book section, called "Talk of the Town." Ingersoll was dressed in a new white Palm Beach suit, and at one point Ross was waving his arms to emphasize a point when he hit a bottle of ink and it splattered all over Ingersoll's white suit. When they finally returned to the subject at hand, Ross said the man he was really looking for probably did not exist. He would have to be a combination of Richard Harding Davis and Ward McAllister.

"Well," Ingersoll said, "I've been a reporter, and Ward was my mother's uncle."

"Jeeeesus," said Ross, registering complete disgust, as Ingersoll interpreted it, at having given him an opening. Then he sighed and said, "OK, you're hired."

As Ingersoll was leaving the office, he heard Ross tell his secretary, "Hell, I'll hire anybody!"

But Ingersoll still was not sure he had been hired. Then, a few days later, after Ross had read his sketches, Ingersoll went back to see the editor, and this time he was offered a firm job—at fifty dollars a week.

So Ralph McAllister Ingersoll, who had failed not only as a novelist but at his second attempt to write a nonfiction book (neither "Fair Exchange" nor "Thank You, Steward" was ever published), who had shown little promise as a Hearst reporter, who had not even been a success writing stories for the pulps at three cents a word, and whose light humor, by his own admission, bordered on the ponderously asinine, went to work for the man and the magazine that would soon become synonymous with literate, sophisticated journalism.

Sketch made by Carila Spaeth in 1925 in Katie Spaeth's salon, where Ingersoll first met an unusual young man named Harold Ross

4: "Talk of the Town"

The story of Harold Ross and the first years of the *New Yorker* has been told many times, but the role played by Ralph Ingersoll has generally been overlooked. Curiously, Ingersoll himself was partly responsible for the oversight. In 1934 he wrote an article about the *New Yorker* for *Fortune* and did not once mention that he had been its managing editor for five years. He did this not only to keep the article "pure," as he said, but to prevent Ross from laughing at or criticizing his interpretation of his role. For years this article was the primary source of information about the *New Yorker*'s formative period, and researchers could be forgiven if they came to the conclusion that Ralph Ingersoll had never even worked for the magazine.

Others, for reasons of their own, have minimized Ingersoll's part in the evolution of the *New Yorker*. Jane Grant, Harold Ross's wife at the time he started the magazine, clearly did not appreciate Ingersoll, and her feelings were reflected in the book she wrote about those days. Grant's disenchantment with Ingersoll may in fact have been a reaction to Ingersoll's dislike for her. She was a Lucy Stone Leaguer, which meant she believed that a wife should keep her own name and lead a life independent of her husband's. Ingersoll occasionally took her dancing, and after one such evening, about the time he went to work for Ross, he entered in his diary: "Jane is a shy little soul but I cannot get to like her."

Wolcott Gibbs, who came to the *New Yorker* near the end of Ingersoll's time there, also played down Ingersoll's role in the *New Yorker* profile he wrote in 1942. "Ingersoll worked on the magazine for nearly five years," Gibbs reported, "winding up as managing editor. He is remembered by pioneer members of the staff as an untidy man of formidable energy—the creator of elaborate systems for simplifying office routine, the author of prodigious memoranda on every subject under the sun, a valuable authority on the fashionable doings of Park Avenue and Long Island. His desk was a pharmacist's treasury of pills, disinfectants, and hair-restorers, for he was convinced that his health was precarious and it was obvious that his hair was getting thin. He was not always easy to understand, because he had a tendency to lisp and some of his other consonants were rather blurred."

Gradually, however, the record is being corrected. James Thurber, in his *The Years with Ross* (1957), revealed the importance of Ingersoll's contribution to the early development of the magazine and described how Ross, characteristically, built Ingersoll up as the indispensable man, then turned against him. And in 1962 Ingersoll himself discussed in more detail his role on the magazine in the first and only published volume of his autobiography.

When Ingersoll reported to work in June of 1925, the *New Yorker* had been on the newsstands for only four months, and the great majority of sophisticated New York readers frankly did not give it much of a chance to succeed. One weekend at the farm in Connecticut he had a conversation with his family that reflected the general opinion of New Yorkers about the magazine: the *New Yorker* is simply not "smart," they concluded, which should have surprised no one. How could a staff so rooted in "middle westernness" edit a magazine about sophisticated New York?

After an initial splash, produced in part by the promotional power and zest of its witty sponsors, the magazine's circulation began declining steadily, and in August 1925 it would reach an all-time low of 2,719. By the time Ross hired Ingersoll, the *New Yorker* editor had come to an important conclusion: The Algonquin wits who had encouraged him to publish his magazine, and assured him they would have no trouble supplying the manuscripts to sustain it, had let him down. To Ross this was as puzzling as it was disappointing because the men and women who had signed the famous "old lady in Dubuque" prospectus as the magazine's "advisory editors" were the city's most sparkling wits and intellectuals: Ralph Barton, Heywood Broun, Marc Connelly, Edna Ferber, Rea Irwin, George S. Kaufman, Alice Duer Miller, Dorothy Parker, Laurence Stallings, and Alexander Woollcott. Obviously a talented group destined to play significant roles in American letters for the next few decades. But only Rea Irwin (as art editor) and Dorothy Parker (as a book reviewer) were making significant contributions to the magazine. Most of the others had retrieved old, unsold manuscripts from their desk drawers, offered them to Ross, and, when he rejected them, gone about the business of making a living and promoting their own careers. Alexander Woollcott was eventually to be hired as a theater critic, but Ross was not very enthusiastic about the arrangement even though Woollcott was a personal friend.

In 1925 the regular staff of the *New Yorker* consisted of Ross, James Kevin McGuinness, a temperamental Irishman who edited the "Talk of the Town" department, Joseph Moncure March (the closest thing the magazine had to a managing editor), a secretary, and an office boy. There were plenty of future big-name bylines appearing at the ends of articles and stories, but they were all "contributors" and unknown then. Ingersoll was the first staffer Ross hired after coming to the realization that he could not rely on his advisory editors to get out the magazine.

It is a curious fact that Harold Ross, founder of the most literate magazine ever produced in America, had only a high school education. He was, however, a grammarian and a purist when it came to the English language, even though he could not, as Ingersoll says, "express himself in any but the simplest words in the simplest of sentences, often run together in rambling incoherence." But when he read a manuscript, he knew what he wanted. Ross did not like to have women around because he cursed freely in the office and was, he frankly admitted, hard on his employees. Women were given to bursting into tears, and Ross felt they restricted him. Consequently, it was most unlikely that shortly after hiring Ingersoll, Ross took on a young lady, just long enough out of Bryn Mawr to have married a Boston lawyer and written a few articles for the *New Republic*, *Atlantic*, and *Harper's*. Her job was to read incoming manuscripts. Her name was Katherine Sergeant Angell, and she impressed Ross because when it came to the English language, she was just as much a purist as he. Furthermore, he said, "she knows the Bible and literature and foreign languages. She has taste."

The other key staff member was also a woman, Lois Long, who had been lured away from *Vanity Fair*. Soon she would be writing the two departments that would make her famous: "Table for Two" (signed at first by "Lipstick") and "On and Off the Avenue" (first appearing as "Fifth Avenue" and signed "L.L.").

The truth is, despite Ross's fame as an editor, it was his shrewd perception of advertisers and their needs that really made the *New Yorker* the publishing success it came to be. Ross knew that New York merchants, especially proprietors of the smart boutiques, little shops, and big department stores catering to the affluent few, resented the advertising rates they had to pay New York newspapers, which were directed to a mass audience. Ross also knew that if he could attract the wealthy, fashionable New Yorkers who patronized the smart shops, the managers of those shops would transfer their advertising from the mass publications to his exclusive magazine.

At the same time, Ross believed that advertising corrupted the English language and he was also aware of the influence the advertising dollar could have on editorial policy. Ingersoll's files contain one memo Ross wrote to the *New Yorker*'s general manager Eugene Spaulding in which Ross said, "We should not use any endorsement advertising containing a palpable lie, or a statement we are morally certain is a lie." Then he elaborated: "I urge this policy not as an idealistic measure in any way. I may be idealistic in it, but I would point out also that it is not good business to print palpable lies. It is not bright to do so. Our readers . . . are intelligent enough to know that this stuff is bunk. We are being shortsighted running it. We have an opportunity to live honestly. We have also the great privilege now of being in a position to lead the advertising industry. For Christ's sake, let us no longer pussyfoot. Let us be really honest and not just slick."

In reference to this memo Ingersoll has said, "[Anyone] seeking the point of origin of my own ideas which grew into the concept of the advertisingless *PM* could well start here."

As Ross once told James Thurber, Ingersoll was hired "because he knows the clubs Percy R. Pyne belongs to and everybody else. He has entrée in the right places. He knows who owns private Pullman cars and he can have tea with all the little old women that still have coachmen or footmen or drive electric runabouts. It's damned important for a magazine called *The New Yorker* to have such a man around." Ross was convinced that Ingersoll's background as a New York socialite would open doors in the world the *New Yorker* intended to dissect in its "Talk of the Town" department. So Ingersoll began as a "Talk" reporter and contributed several pieces to the mid-1925 issues. He did not keep a scrapbook of these pieces, and they are unsigned, so most of his contributions remain unidentified. But in his diary references do supply some clues, and with a little detective work, it is not hard to identify a few of his "Talk" pieces. One was on the actress Julia Lydig Hoyt's endorsements of cosmetics and dress designs, and another on the novelist Maxwell Bodenheim and his social eccentricities. They were 750 to 1,000 words long (lengthy for a "Talk" piece then) and written in a detached sardonic tone that over the years would be refined and perfected into the characteristic *New Yorker* style.

Ingersoll's prose had clearly improved in the little more than a year since he had left the *New York American*, and soon he was sharing with James Kevin McGuinness the task of organizing and editing the "Talk" department. This inevitably led to a conflict with McGuinness, and at first Ingersoll was convinced he would not survive as a *New Yorker* editor. He confessed to his diary that he was "not in gear on the job," and in another entry said that Ross had "hit the ceiling" and ordered an entire "Talk" section rewritten. A few days later he concluded again that he could not "wing" this job, and was understandably depressed that the copy desk had found twenty-seven misspelled words in "Talk." He was amazed that he had not been fired.

But suddenly the situation began to change, and his diary entries reported, optimistically, that there had been hints of making him a permanent member of the staff. He was given more responsibility for editing "Talk," until finally, in August, McGuinness rebelled, telling Ross that Ingersoll was "not competent" to edit his copy. Ross took them both out for drinks, pacified McGuinness and, after the disgruntled Irishman had departed, took Ingersoll up to his apartment. Ross expressed his confidence in Ingersoll, who felt the editor had clearly sided with him in the conflict. This appeared to be the turning point in Ingersoll's relationship with Ross.

Also approaching was the moment of truth in the Fleischmann plan to save the magazine. It involved a major promotion campaign and they were saving their best material for the issue of September 12, 1925, and those following. But September and October came and went without the *New Yorker*'s causing much excitement or comment. Then in November they had the break that Ingersoll and others have always believed was responsible for saving the magazine. Jane Grant had come across an article written by a young debutante named Ellin Mackay, a cousin of Alice Duer Miller and the daughter of Charles Mackay, a wealthy New York socialite who had spent a considerable amount of money introducing his daughter to Society. Ellin had rebelled, however, and decided to tell why in an article she titled "Why We Go to Cabarets—A Post-Debutante Explains." Grant began pushing the article with Ross, who showed little interest. Then one morning it turned up on Ingersoll's desk, bound in leather and with a covering note from Ross: "What think?"

Ingersoll's reaction, which he considered "a historic moment" in his embryonic career at the *New Yorker*, was immediate: "It's a must," he wrote Ross.

The theme of the piece was that nice young New York girls were being driven into the wicked cabarets where they listened to jazz and danced with almost anyone because they resented being put on the auction blocks at debutante parties and because the eligible young men they met at these balls were all bores. Ingersoll thought the article struck just the right note for a magazine "advertising itself as a sophisticated social critic." And Ross must have decided that if Ingersoll, a veteran of hundreds of debutante balls, thought the article significant, it must be so. According to Thurber, who was not yet a member of the staff, it was Ingersoll's endorsement that convinced Ross to run the Mackay piece. But Jane Grant (who had worked for the *New York Times* and was well connected in New York journalism) was responsible for the story's making such a splash. She convinced the editors of the *Times*, the *Tribune*, and the *World* not only that Mackay's revelations were "news" but that each paper had an exclusive. So all three ran a front-page story about the article the morning the *New Yorker* issue carrying Mackay's piece hit the newsstands.

If there was one article that could be said to have turned the *New Yorker* around, this was it.* By the end of 1925 the magazine's circulation had soared to nearly thirty thousand, and its fifty-six pages were fat with advertising, which Ross, groaning all the way to the bank, had accepted.

---

*James Thurber, then in France, read about the article in the Paris edition of the *Herald* and decided that the *New Yorker* sounded like the kind of magazine he would like to write for.

With the *New Yorker*'s financial position thus assured, at least for the immediate future, Ingersoll gradually began to emerge as Ross's right-hand man—mostly through staff attrition. And when, near the end of the year, the *New Yorker* was required by law to print its "Statement of Ownership," Ross listed Ingersoll as managing editor, although with typical Rossian glee he insisted that Ingersoll was no more qualified to be managing editor than an office boy and that he was thinking of listing his butler in that position the next time around.

The fact was that Ross really did not know what kind of managing editor he wanted or how to organize a magazine. His endless search for just the right man is now lengendary, and James Thurber probably came closest of anyone to describing Ross's dilemma: "From the beginning," he wrote in *The Years with Ross*, "Ross cherished his dream of a Central Desk at which infallible omniscience would sit, a dedicated genius, out of Technology by Mysticism, effortlessly controlling and coordinating editorial personnel, contributors, office boys, cranks and other visitors, manuscripts, proofs, cartoons, captions, covers, fiction, poetry and facts, bringing forth each Thursday a magazine at once funny, journalistically sound, and flawless . . . a dehumanized figure, disguised as a man."

The man who sat at this central desk eventually came to be known as Jesus, and Ross continued hiring and firing young men in search of the right stuff. When one who had been tried, found wanting, and then fired asked plaintively why, Ross replied, "Because you're no God damn genius."

Ingersoll, at least at first, was the genius. Young, ambitious, and well organized, he managed to keep his job while all about him were losing theirs. Within five months of going to work for the *New Yorker*, Ingersoll was the senior staffer, and more and more Ross and the business department, under Fleischmann, turned to him to keep the magazine functioning. He also inherited the "Talk" department from McGuinness, who finally fled to Hollywood to pursue what would prove to be a successful screenwriting career (his most notable achievement was the original script for the Marx brothers' *A Night at the Opera*). Within six months Ingersoll had created "the magazine within a magazine," as he called "Talk of the Town." "It was I," he wrote Thurber many years later, "who invented,—literally—the form of the Talk department. Not the style, God forbid, nor the polish—just the form: of alternating short essays with anecdotes; inventing the several different essay forms—literary vehicles—consisting of 'visit pieces,' miniature Profiles, dope stories (background pieces . . .), etc., the whole anecdotal warp and short essay woof to be woven into a disguised but discernible pattern to cover those fields of Metropolitan endeavor and interest which were our special province; each of the arts, Park Avenue and a touch of Wall Street, the beginnings of what's now known as Café Society." It was also his idea that the department be put together with a mix of spot news and visits so that if "done right, the whole would give the reader—unobtrusively—the feeling that he had been everywhere, knew everyone, was up on everything. And each week, a different locale and subject pattern, so that every, say, month or six weeks with Talk, a reader really did get around."

During the years that he was editing "Talk" for the *New Yorker* Ralph Ingersoll really did get around town. His method of covering the city was suggested by a young public relations man named Edward L. Bernays, who told Ingersoll: "In each world there's always one gossipy individual who makes it his or her business to know everything. Sometimes they're the biggest people in the business, but more likely they're frustrated second-stringers or some boss's secretary. You go find them and offer each this trade: the low-down in *his* field for what you know about what's going on elsewhere in town. Part of the trade is that you buy him lunch once a month. But don't rely on the lunch—or your charm—to get you what you want; you must pay off in sound money—in a world in which gossip is legal tender." Within a few months Ingersoll had a network feeding him gossip, and one of his most valuable contributors was a young columnist named Walter Winchell, whom he regularly met for lunch at the Yale Club.

During the first two years of the *New Yorker*'s life Ingersoll was extremely close to Ross, and despite the editor's continual ribbing and ridiculing, he obviously had confidence in his Jesus. Ingersoll worked sixteen-hour days, and most of his meals were shared with Ross. During these meals—and at the office—they talked incessantly about the *New Yorker* in particular, magazine publishing in general, and ideas for new magazines. Ingersoll seemed to possess traits that Ross had to lean on in order to function—"a man at once sensitive enough to understand him and practical enough to get some fraction of what he wanted accomplished" was the way Ingersoll interpreted it, and he added to that, someone with "a skin thick enough to stand working, really working with him, for he was a tyrant and sadist, as illogical as he was demanding."

Ingersoll said he would have fought a duel with any man who claimed that Harold Ross was not the sole creator and proprietor of the *New Yorker*, but, at the same time, he came to identify with it completely. The magazine was, he has said, "my baby. To me, Ross was the father of the *New Yorker* and I was the mother. It came out of my loins, with all the pain and agony of childbirth and it was my child by an exasperating unholy ghost whose materialization looked like a gargoyle with crew-cut hair."

By early 1926 the *New Yorker*'s young staff was gradually bringing a semblance of order to what had been chaos: Ross was the guiding genius who rarely could find or define what he liked in a manuscript, but who knew what he did *not* like. Agonizing through each week, he reluctantly printed the things he disliked least, convinced that there really was not enough good writing in America to sustain a weekly magazine. The "managing editor of facts," as he called Ingersoll, was responsible for "Talk," for most of the nonfiction and reporting, and for seeing to it that the "book" went to the printer on time every week. Katherine Angell, "the managing editor of fiction," handled everything literary: the casuals, long profiles, and fiction. Lois Long was writing her columns; an ex-*New York World* reporter named Morris Markey was writing "Reporter at Large," and a variety of continually changing contributors were doing signed columns, the best known then being Dorothy Parker, Robert Benchley (who sometimes wrote under the byline Guy Fawkes), and Janet Flanner, who signed her "Letter from Paris" with the name Genêt.

The cartoons, layout, and artwork were entrusted to Rea Irwin, who, next to Ross, was probably the most important editor on the staff. Older than Ross, he had enjoyed a distinguished career as a cartoonist for the *San Francisco Examiner*, a comic-strip artist, and an art editor of the old *Life*, before he met the *New Yorker* editor. He managed to keep his distance from Ross and his sanity by coming to the office only once a week—for the regular Tuesday afternoon art meeting, during which all the cartoons and art submitted in the previous week were considered and then rejected, accepted, or sent back for revisions. The panel that made these decisions consisted of Ross, Irwin, Ingersoll, and Katherine Angell, all of whom sat on one side of a long table. On the other side sat Ross's secretary, who would hold up each piece of artwork, then take notes on the panel's decision and, if more work was needed, on what was to be said to the artist.

Almost everyone had a hand in writing or rewriting captions until, midway in the year, another unlikely candidate was hired. Elwyn Brooks White, known as Andy since his days at Cornell where a former president's name was Andrew White, was a mild, gentle man who spoke so softly one could barely understand him. But he wrote perhaps the closest thing to perfect prose of anyone in America and had been wasting this talent as a reporter for the United Press and a copywriter in an advertising agency. He, of course, hated the advertising business even more than Ross, and within a few months of joining the *New Yorker* staff he was writing almost everything and anything: "Notes and Comments," casuals, the one-line comments under the "newsbreaks," and cartoon captions. Ross had finally found his literary voice; in fact, says Ingersoll, "I can't remember any piece by anyone but E. B. White that Ross ever really thought was just right."

By 1926 Ingersoll was doing virtually no writing for the *New Yorker*; not only was he too busy, but Ross had become convinced that he could not write and, furthermore, that good editors should not waste their time trying to write. ("Writers are a dime a dozen," he said. Ingersoll's job was more important.) And Ross trusted him. For a period of about a month, when Katherine Angell was vacationing in Europe and Ross had to go into the hospital because of an infected tooth, Ingersoll put out the *New Yorker* single-handedly, working as many as twenty hours a day and going on a diet of coffee, tomato juice, and gin—"the only substances," as he put it, "I could digest and still work at the pace I was setting for myself and everyone else." When Ross came back, he was at once amazed and resentful at what Ingersoll had achieved. Ingersoll's reaction was total collapse—a nervous breakdown that sent him to his father's farm for rest and recovery.

Actually, the close relationship between Ross and Ingersoll had become strained even before Ross was hospitalized, and the focal point of their friction was Ingersoll's determination that he be married to someone other than the *New*

Ingersoll called the New Yorker *writers "gentlemen pranksters" who would do anything and go anywhere for a "Talk" piece. (ABOVE) E. B. White, in rear of canoe wearing wig, prepares to shove off for the Bronx River caper. A dummy is in the front of the canoe; Ingersoll took the photo; (BELOW) Ingersoll (left) with unidentified companions, taking a locomotive ride from Albany to New York for the magazine*

Yorker. He wanted a real wife. He still saw some of his bohemian friends occasionally, but now his social life revolved almost exclusively around the business of the magazine, which, around five or six P.M. every evening would be transferred from 25 West Forty-fifth Street to the currently favored bar. At one time Ross even tried to recreate the famous *Punch* literary saloon, where editors drank and fraternized with contributors, from whom new editors would occasionally be selected. But this experiment ended abruptly one morning when Ross was informed that two naked (male and female) contributors were out cold on the saloon couch locked arm in arm.

Ross's response was, "God damn it, Ingersoll, you ought to know better than to let something like this happen."

The drinking and talking shop went on night after night, every night of the week, until finally, as Ingersoll has said, "in my furious functioning I was more machine than human being." So one night, with a vague idea, perhaps, of meeting a girl, he went to the kind of function he had not attended for years: a coming-out party, this one for someone he did not know. He convinced himself that he was going as a reporter, intent on learning whether such parties were the same as he remembered. To pass the time, he cut in on a young lady named Mary Elizabeth "Tommy" Carden. She was the daughter of "Judge" George Alexander Carden, a Wall Street speculator who had recently made headlines in the New York press by losing several million dollars in a stock venture.

Tommy Carden was not the prettiest girl at the ball, but Ingersoll liked her and enjoyed talking to her. Obviously she was "the marrying kind." One night

Ingersoll in 1924, the year before he met Elizabeth "Tommy" Carden, whom he married in 1926

when they were in New London, Connecticut, where Ingersoll was covering a boat race for "Talk," he proposed to Tommy. She accepted—but Ross did not.

The first word the *New Yorker* editor had about his managing editor's engagement came from the press, and he was furious. His own marriage was now virtually nonexistent. He was totally wedded to the magazine and believed that Ingersoll should be too. As Ingersoll recalled Ross's reaction: "I had no right to take such a step without consulting him. I was crazy. I was going to ruin a life he thought might have promise. It was even worse than that. It was— God damn it, there wasn't any other way of putting it—just plain *disloyal!*"

Ross's tirades about the engagement started before he went into the hospital and continued when he came out, contributing significantly to the emotional turmoil that led to Ingersoll's breakdown. Ross's effort to influence his personal life led Ingersoll, in his nervous, exhausted state, to confuse his boss with his real father, who had also tried to dictate his life. So Ingersoll fled to the farm and regained his sanity by chopping wood for thirty days as he chanted over and over, "I don't ever have to go back. I don't ever have to go back." When he wasn't chopping wood, he was fantasizing about "how to dispense with Ross once and for all—by garroting, disemboweling or simply shooting in the head with a .45."

After a month in Lakeville, Ingersoll recovered and decided he would go back. He took the train to New York and walked abruptly into Ross's office. "Well ... I'm glad you're back" was the editor's only comment.

Ingersoll replied, "I'm back, but I'm darned if I know if I'm the same guy who left here." He went on to say that if Ross wanted him, he would return at half salary until he knew whether he could resume his usual responsibilities. After six weeks he wrote Ross a note: "I'm not merely as good as I was; I'm better. I'll take back my salary and a raise." Ross restored his salary, but it was several months before Ingersoll had a raise—to $150 a week.

Ingersoll's nervous breakdown had also delayed his marriage to Tommy, but now that he was back at work and functioning again, they went ahead with their plans. On November 18, 1926, they were married in Grace Church in New York, in the chapel where Ingersoll's mother and father had been married in the 1880s. The press covered the wedding as a Society event. The faded newspaper photographs in his album show a tall, debonair Ingersoll, in top hat, white tie, chesterfield, and white scarf, escorting a handsome Tommy wearing "a *robe de style* of old ivory velvet, embroidered in pearls under an ermine wrap." Afterward there was a huge party interrupted temporarily by Ross who could not control his laughter at being introduced in the receiving line by the Carden butler. Soon everyone was laughing with him—even the starched bridesmaids and Ingersoll's ushers. Ross gave the bride and groom a six-day honeymoon, which they spent at Goshen, New York. Then they returned to settle into Ingersoll's little apartment on Thirty-fifth Street. But in less than two months Tommy fell ill with an infection resulting from the incompetent installation of a contraceptive device. She was hospitalized for several months, and Ingersoll spent most of the first year of their marriage trying to prevent a series of doctors from performing a hysterectomy. Tommy finally recovered without surgery, but a few months later she developed a much more serious illness—pulmonary tuberculosis. In those days the treatment for TB was immobilization, and "that was the end of the ball game," Ingersoll wrote later. "Together we fought something much more real than potential triangles and the servant problem. We fought death, living with us and accepted as a member of the household."

It also meant living an unnatural life: Tommy was hospitalized at Saranac Lake, New York, and Ingersoll would commute there on weekends; he spent most of his time there telling Tommy tales of the real world, omitting anything that might get her excited. When her lesion healed, Tommy was permitted to return to New York, where they would enjoy a few months of cautious normality. "But these happy interludes," Ingersoll says, "would always end with another lesion." Even during the happy interludes Tommy was not permitted to have sexual relations, and for the emotional, virile Ingersoll, this would eventually prove to be a considerable problem—which he solved in his own way, until it inevitably destroyed his relationship with Tommy.

Ingersoll's marriage also involved him in a brief but disastrous career as a stock-market speculator. Several of his friends were making incredible amounts of money playing the bull market of 1927, and as Ingersoll's medical bills began to rise, he decided he ought to buy some stock. As a wedding present, Judge Carden had given the bride and groom a thousand-dollar bill to buy "a little something for the apartment." But they had never spent it, so Ingersoll used it to buy, on margin, fifty-six hundred dollars worth of Manhattan Electrical Supply Company stock, which he knew from dinner-table conversation at the Cardens was one his father-in-law not only thought a good buy but had invested in heavily himself. By the summer of 1927 Ingersoll's thousand was worth thirty thousand, and in 1927 his total income from stock-market earnings was fourteen thousand dollars—compared with the six thousand he earned from his job. But, he says, "I found myself in bed with two hitherto total strangers, Fear and Greed." The instant fortune also confused him: "Six-day weeks of sixteen-hours-a-day on the *New Yorker* netted me no more than a point and a half on a hundred shares!" In addition, he was being called every hour on the hour by his broker, until Ross was becoming annoyed. Finally Ingersoll knew he had to make a choice. "It was the magazine not the market that I respected; I knew how to make my living on the *New Yorker* and I knew just as clearly that I didn't know one darned thing about what Manhattan Electrical Supply stock was really worth."

So he sold his thirty thousand dollars' worth of stock—at a time, just by chance, when his father-in-law was getting ready to lay several million dollars' worth of Manhattan Electrical on the line in one of those classic bulls-versus-bears showdowns. Within a week the bears would come selling into the market, and the bulls (commanded by the Judge) would retreat, then start buying. When Ingersoll told his father-in-law he had decided to sell his stock, the Judge replied: "It's not a good market for you now, but you might put in an order for a thousand shares at some price—oh, say, twenty points below the market—just in case it should sell off." Why not, Ingersoll thought. But playing it safe, he put in an order to buy a thousand shares at thirty points below the market, then forgot about it. On August 11, 1927, the bulls and the bears met in mortal combat. The night before the confrontation the Judge knew he would probably lose and, recalling the advice he had given his son-in-law, sent him a telegram (rather than using his telephone, which he suspected was tapped by the bears) warning him to get out of the market early the next day. He sent the wire to the *New Yorker* office. But Ingersoll had decided to work at home that day, the same day his secretary had chosen "to have her hair done," so the frantic calls from his broker never reached him; the telegram from the Judge lay unopened on the desk, and on the last hour before trading stopped, Manhattan Electrical fell from 121 to the mid-fifties. On the way, Ingersoll's thousand shares were bought, as ordered, and forty-five points down, they were sold again. Ingersoll had lost his thirty thousand dollars plus fifteen thousand more—just one week after he and Tommy had celebrated one of her periodic returns to New York by signing a five-year lease on a penthouse apartment at 57 East Eighty-eighth Street.

The crash of Manhattan Electrical was a big story, covered by the *Times* and the financial press. Judge Carden had to make a statement to the press (which Ingersoll helped draft) defending his position and trying to explain what was happening. When it was all over, the Judge had lost seven or eight million dollars and one of his friends had committed suicide.

Ingersoll was bankrupt, and to pay off his debts he had to borrow from the banks, using collateral put up by his father. It took him five years to repay his loan, and it would have taken him sixty years, he said, except for his father-in-law. Shortly after the crash, the Judge came to him and said that a friend for whom he once had done a financial favor had given his wife a sealed envelope with instructions not to open it until the Judge needed help. When he opened it, the Judge found that the envelope contained three $10,000 bills, which he now wanted Ingersoll to invest for him because he no longer had credit in the market. If the money was lost, that would be that; if they made a profit, Ingersoll would keep ten percent. Within five years, the Judge had pyramided the $30,000 into $1.5 million; Ingersoll paid off his debts and Tommy's medical bills, then turned the business back to the Judge and got out of the market forever—just in time. A year later Carden became convinced there would be a wheat shortage and put all his money into that commodity. The Judge was right: There was a wheat shortage throughout most of the world—but not in Russia. For the first time in years the Russians had an excess of wheat, which they dumped on the world market, and the Judge was ruined, this time for good.

* * *

After Ingersoll's nervous breakdown and marriage he settled into something of a new routine at the *New Yorker* as the senior editor, a sort of "Jesus emeritus," as Ingersoll puts it. But his relationship with Ross was never quite the same. And things were changing at the magazine. In early 1927 Ross hired another unlikely candidate, a young writer named James Thurber who had been trying ever since he returned from Paris (where he had been a code clerk in the American embassy, worked briefly for the Paris edition of the *Chicago Tribune*, and tried to write a novel) to sell the *New Yorker* one of his unusual little satires. Ross finally hired him, then tried to make a Jesus out of him, until Ingersoll convinced Ross of Thurber's obvious ineptitude. So, Thurber was freed from his editorial duties to write—when he wasn't sketching animals and people on every piece of empty scratch paper in the office. E. B. White tried to convince Ross that Thurber's drawings ought to be used in the magazine, but Ross resisted—until White insisted they be used to illustrate *Is Sex Necessary?*, the book he and Thurber were to write together. After its success Ross consented. Soon Thurber and White were collaborating to give the *New Yorker* the unique tone of sardonic detachment for which it became famous. The following year Wolcott Gibbs, another talented young writer and editor, and probably the best parodist the country has ever produced, would join the staff, completing the quintet of editors (with Ross, Katherine Angell, E. B. White, and Thurber) often credited with

When Ingersoll was managing editor at the New Yorker, *he kept a note pad on his desk for people to leave messages. When James Thurber waited at his desk, says Ingersoll, "he'd literally fill the pad with crazy sketches—the idea being that when I tore off the top one to get a blank page, there wouldn't be one. So I'd go on tearing off page after page." Ingersoll saved the doodles, of which these are samples.*

creating the *New Yorker*, as we know it. They were brilliant, witty, and talented, but it is questionable whether any of them (with the exception of Angell) could ever have put their minds to getting out a magazine on a weekly basis. That job was left to Ingersoll.

The trouble was that Ingersoll was now on the down side of what Thurber has termed Ross's "almost pathological cycle of admiration and disillusionment." And this was ironic, because in Thurber's opinion Ingersoll was "the best of all the Central Desk men, the very administrative expert Ross spent his life looking for." Thurber also believed that Ross knew this subconsciously but, through some strange Rossian quirk of the mind, would not admit it, even to himself. At the weekly "Talk" meetings, over which Ross usually presided, the editor would inevitably ridicule Ingersoll or jump on him for some trivial mistake. "When Ingersoll suggested a dope piece about the enormous ball that surmounts the Paramount building," Thurber recalled, "Ross glared at him and snarled: 'I wouldn't print a piece about that ball if Lord Louis Mountbatten were living in it.' On another Wednesday, when Ingersoll told him: 'I have the stuff you wanted on Thaw,'* Ross's eyes brightened darkly. Ingersoll always pronounced Thaw as if it were Thor and Ross knew this, but he said: 'I don't want a piece about Thor, or Mercury or *any* of the other Greek Gods.'"

By 1928 it had become clear that Ross thought Ingersoll had failed him by having a nervous breakdown and then taking a wife. And as Ross made life more and more miserable for his managing editor, Ingersoll began to hate the editor and to look on him even more as a father image to be scorned. He also had the urge to write again, which did not impress Ross. The year before, Ingersoll had written a piece about Gene Tunney for *Liberty*, a nicely done, well-reported account of the gentleman boxer's sudden emergence as a celebrity—1920s style—after he had defeated Jack Dempsey for the world championship. Ingersoll had met Tunney at the Yale Club long before he emerged as a national hero, and had followed his career, both in the ring and in Long Island–Park Avenue Society, with intense interest. It was a good piece, but Ross was opposed to the *New Yorker* staff's writing for other magazines and Ingersoll had to sign the article "Robert Ingerley."

Ingersoll also wanted to do more writing for the *New Yorker*, but Ross was against that too. "He thinks he's a writer," Ross once said to Thurber. "He wrote a book called *In and Under Mexico*. I haven't read it, and don't want to, but it can't be good." On another occasion, when Thurber was acting as Jesus, Ross said, "Don't let him write anything. He did the captions on covering art [two-page illustrations accompanying various departments] this week. That's your fault. Change them."

Ingersoll finally did do some writing for the magazine, but it was not easy, and then Ross was reluctant to pay him for it. His first and only signed article

*Referring, no doubt, to Harry K. Thaw, who shot and killed architect Stanford White in a jealous rage over the former chorus girl Evelyn Nesbit. Thaw died in 1924, after spending years in and out of insane asylums.

for the *New Yorker* was titled "A New York Childhood," and an Ingersoll memo to Ross after the piece had been accepted illustrates not only Ross's disenchantment with him but Ingersoll's growing impatience with his boss:

> This is one of those unpleasant memos. Mrs. White tells me that you vetoed payment on the N.Y. Childhood I wrote on the grounds that I am an editor and an old member of the family.
>
> Since when, let us consider, have editorial salaries been so princely or hours so inviting that any member of the staff could afford to give the magazine work done "on his own time." The compliment implied in the "member of the family" title is pleasant but does not analyze well. For I would be stupid indeed if I thought myself more valuable to *The New Yorker* than White or Thurber. Ideas, talk stories, etc.—it is logical that these should be included in my salary. But I can see no difference between my contributing a longer piece and John Smith or Jim Thurber sending in the same. Nor did the piece, I am sure, receive any special attention because I am "one of us." In fact, I suspect the contrary. For I heard no word for months, not even news of its progress, and you have never even mentioned it. The fact that I did not put a price tag on it when I sent it in, you can put down to the fact that I thought it more gracious to let you make the gesture.
>
> Frankly, your attitude seems to me shabby. Nor have I the consolation of the Rolls Royce Mr. Fleischmann once promised "members of the family" the day *The New Yorker* got out of the red. Neither that nor, with your mercurial temperament, the assurance that someday you will not go out to lunch once too often and I be out of a job when you return. Have any of us?

Ingersoll was eventually paid for his article, a gracefully written piece about growing up on the East Side of New York just after the turn of the century. But Ross held it four years before finally publishing it. In his last year on the magazine Ingersoll was even permitted to write a regular column on football, which was signed "Linesman." Wolcott Gibbs describes the column with typical Gibbsian venom: "He took this seriously, bustling off to Yale, Harvard and Princeton (the power football played by the big, tough schools didn't interest him) as picturesquely draped with blankets, flasks, binoculars, and assorted pelts as a man in *Esquire*. Later, he watched in agony as the hired assassin on the copy desk mutilated a prose chiefly remarkable for its patient struggle to find a synonym for 'football' and its rather frantic admiration for a young man named Albie Booth."

Of Ingersoll's dedication to Ivy League football, one can only say that it was deep, genuine, and long-lasting: Well into his eighties, he still listens to Ivy League games on the radio or watches them on television, carefully plotting each play up and down the field on his game chart.

Although Ross had turned against him, most of Ingersoll's colleagues liked him, not only for the flair he demonstrated in wearing a coonskin coat to football games, but because they knew they would probably never see again, as Gibbs put it, a "Talk" reporter "who put on striped trousers and a top hat as a matter of course when he went out to report the Easter parade." Ingersoll became especially good friends with Andy White, who considered him "ingenious" at dreaming up "Talk" ideas, and with Thurber. The three of them were continually staging pranks—such as the time they decided to explore the headwaters of the Bronx River. Ingersoll and White rented a canoe, dressed up a department-store dummy as an Indian guide, and timed their charade to coincide with the evening rush hour so that passengers on the commuter trains could sight the expedition (which was finally terminated by the state police).

On the other hand, he did not particularly like Wolcott Gibbs, especially after a tragic incident that occurred in the late 1920s. Gibbs's wife, Elizabeth, wanted to write, but Gibbs was scornful of her ambition and ridiculed her writing. So she wrote a piece for the *New Yorker* and turned it in under an assumed name. Gibbs bought it and became enraged when he was told at dinner one night what had happened. Ingersoll and Tommy happened to be at the dinner and were very upset at the cruel tongue-lashing Elizabeth Gibbs received from her husband. That night, after everyone had gone home, Elizabeth Gibbs committed suicide by jumping out the window. Whether or not the abuse she had taken from Gibbs about her writing had anything to do with her suicide, Ingersoll was never sure; but the tragedy ended his relationship with Gibbs.

In the late 1920s Ingersoll was approved by, and very much a part of, the *New Yorker* clique of arrogant wits who did not like or approve of anyone else. Years later, after he had left the *New Yorker*, Ingersoll ran into one former "Talk" writer, who said, "Why, you're almost human now. On *The New Yorker* you were disgusted with yourself if you ever said anything nice to anybody. All of you were."

Ingersoll's five years on the *New Yorker* staff was a stepping stone to big-league journalism. During this period he gained the experience and confidence he would need in the years ahead. Also he met most of the writers of the 1920s. Many of them would go on to dominate American letters for several decades to come, and some would write for him when he eventually published his own periodical.

But the years did not make him rich—although they could have. At one point Fleischmann had agreed to let Ingersoll buy ten thousand dollars' worth of *New Yorker* stock at a favorable price. But Ingersoll consulted with Uncle George Ingersoll (a corporation lawyer), who advised against it. Part of the agreement was that if Ingersoll left the magazine, he would have to sell the stock back at its original price, and Uncle George argued that if the *New Yorker* was successful, Fleischmann would have a good incentive to fire him—in order to get the stock back at the original price. Ingersoll thought his uncle was being unduly suspicious, but since he would have had to borrow the money from his father, he decided he could not do so over his uncle's opposition, so he declined. Within a few years of his departure from the *New Yorker*, the stock he did not buy was worth one million dollars.

By the end of the 1920s Ingersoll and the country were beginning to grow up; the fun and games had gone sour, along with the stock market, and the arrogant pranks and biting wit of the Algonquinites had begun to pall. Their humor was too often malicious, and Ingersoll did not like to hurt people. As Gibbs later reported, Ingersoll's desk did look like a prescription pharmacy— with good reason. The nervous stomach of his bohemian days had turned into a full-fledged gastric ulcer, the result of a hyperacidic system confronting a slightly mad editor named Harold Ross, who now began to include among his reasons for disliking Ingersoll the one that he had hired him for in the first place: "He brought Hush-a-phones into the office," Ross complained to Thurber, "he talked . . . to people like Cornelius Vanderbilt. He knew too many people."

Ross was becoming more than an irritant: In Ingersoll's view, his own stature was shrinking as the success of the *New Yorker* was established and Ross's anxiety to maintain its prosperity and reputation increased. He and Ross no longer talked with great excitement about the new magazines they were going to publish as soon as Ross could overcome "that God damned Fleischmann . . . those God damned incompetent bastards that are all we have to get out this magazine with. Women and children!" In Ingersoll's view, Ross's "future was already behind him."

So, in 1929, when his friend Charles Stillman told him that Henry Luce, publisher of *Time* and a new magazine called *Fortune*, wanted to talk with him, Ingersoll was intrigued. Time Inc.'s chairman of the board at that time was William Griffin (whose wife was the half sister of Ingersoll's wife), and Griffin had helped convince Luce to make Stillman, a genius with figures, his treasurer. That Ingersoll, like Stillman and almost everyone else in the upper echelons of Time Inc., had gone to Yale did not hurt his chances.

Stillman had urged Luce to talk to Ingersoll because Stillman was not happy with the way things were going at *Fortune*, which had a brilliant young editor named Parker Lloyd-Smith whose literary talents were offset by his managerial ineptitude. Stillman was aware of Ingersoll's reputation as the man who kept the *New Yorker* running, and believed that this kind of talent was desperately needed on *Fortune*. Stillman's conversations with Luce dragged on for nearly a year, and Ingersoll guesses that one reason things were slow in coming to a head was Griffin's lack of enthusiasm. Shortly after Ingersoll married Tommy Carden, he spent a weekend at the Griffin estate in Peapack, New Jersey, where riding to the hounds was the principal recreation. When Ingersoll subsequently returned to the *New Yorker* office, he regaled the staff, as only Ingersoll the storyteller could do, with tales of the absurdities of the fox hunt. The stories inspired Andy White to write a poem from the viewpoint of the fox, the refrain of which ran:

> He smelled the hounds
> He smelled the horse
> He smelled the Peapack store
> and steeple
> And lastly, as a matter of course,
> He smelled the Peapack people.

Ross thought the poem was hilarious, and printed it; and Griffin was enraged. Within twenty-four hours Ingersoll was called to a family meeting at his father-in-law's suite in the St. Regis Hotel, where Griffin lectured him for having betrayed the family, shown bad taste, and inspired misinformation: "God damn it, Ingersoll," Griffin yelled, "the Peapack people just don't smell."

Whether or not Griffin was still angry, Stillman eventually prevailed, and it was finally agreed that Luce would at least meet with Ingersoll. They did not want New York's gossipy media clique to know they were talking, so they rendezvoused, in secret, at the Ritz Carlton, taking lunch in the little bar on the Madison Avenue side of the hotel. It was an exciting moment for Ingersoll, and forty years later he said he could still "actually feel that first time I ever met Henry Luce—the intensity of my curiosity about him—the excitement of impending adventure."

During that lunch Luce proposed to Ingersoll that he join the staff of *Fortune*. Ingersoll said he would not leave the *New Yorker* unless he was made managing editor of the new magazine. But Luce did not want to fire Lloyd-Smith, so they worked out a rather peculiar compromise in which Ingersoll would be hired without title and assigned one-half of the *Fortune* staff and budget to produce as many articles as he could, none of which would be published for one year. Lloyd-Smith would continue to get out the magazine with half of the staff and budget formerly at his disposal. At the end of the year, if Luce approved of Ingersoll's work, he would become managing editor and have several articles ready to go. There was no contract, just a handshake and an agreement that Ingersoll would get fifteen thousand dollars a year (nearly twice what he was making at the *New Yorker*) and another fifteen thousand at the end of the year if Luce did not like his work and the arrangement was terminated.

Ingersoll's decision to leave the *New Yorker* came as shocking news to most of the magazine's staff: Fleischmann knew the extent of his contribution and years later wrote him: "You are the only man we had who did an honest day's work, or maybe two honest day's work in one." Katherine Angell (later Mrs. E. B. White) spent several lunches trying to persuade him to stay, and Thurber, who was appalled, bawled Ross out for letting Ingersoll get away. "After Ingersoll left," Thurber said, "Ross realized, but never said so, that he had left behind an empty space that it would take at least two men to fill."

The actual parting with Ross was, to Ingersoll, as surprising and unexpected as his meeting with Luce. Ingersoll knew Ross thought Luce's crime against the English language, namely, the writing in *Time*, was even worse than what advertising copywriters were doing to it, and so he expected a reproach. Instead, when he told his boss he was going to work for Henry Luce, Ross just stared at him moodily until finally Ingersoll had to say "Well?"

Ross sighed and, with his usual perception when it came to editorial matters, said, "Hell, Ingersoll, *Fortune* was invented for you to edit."

Then there was another long pause and he said simply, "G'bye."

Lecturing his Fortune *staff in the early 1930s*

5: Camelot on East Forty-second Street

When Ralph McAllister Ingersoll went to work for Time Inc. in the summer of 1930, *Fortune* was still suffering growing pains and the company itself had not yet recovered from the shock of Briton Hadden's sudden death in February of 1929. Hadden and Luce had been friends since prep school, and within eighteen months of their graduation from Yale they had started *Time* magazine. It was their belief that while professional newsmen may know how to gather news, they did not know how to make it interesting and readable. There was, they decided, room for a weekly magazine that would make the news more digestible, a service they felt could best be performed by gifted amateurs (such as themselves) rather than seasoned, undertalented (because newspaper salaries did not attract talent), sometimes cynical professionals. It had been agreed that the task of editing *Time* would be taken in turns, first by Hadden, then by Luce. But the early years were so difficult, and so much time was spent on the brink of financial disaster, that they soon decided that, in the beginning at least, each one would stick to what he did best, with Hadden editing and Luce running the business side of the operation. It was not until 1928, five years after the first issue, that Luce had his year to edit and Hadden his year to operate the business. Although

Luce did well enough as an editor, Hadden, by unanimous agreement, was a disaster as a businessman. By the end of Hadden's year as publisher, just before his death from a streptococcus infection, friction had clearly developed between the two founders of *Time*. As Ingersoll diagnosed it, based on later conversation with his new boss, Luce was jealous of Hadden for preempting the editorial side of the operation (which, as anyone who has ever worked on a magazine knows, is the most interesting and glamorous phase of publishing), and Hadden, in turn, was contemptuous of Luce's obvious superiority as a businessman. Many thought Luce was cold-blooded in his response to Hadden's death. But Luce, says Ingersoll, truly loved Hadden and felt they had resolved all their differences on Hadden's deathbed. The conflict, however, had been open enough, so that by 1930 the company had two factions: "Luce men" and "Hadden men." Ingersoll, hired by Luce, was clearly one of Luce's men. And there were still enough Hadden men around to account for what Ingersoll considers a "cool reception" when he reported to work at the young company's office on Forty-second Street.

Luce, certainly, did not make it easy for him. He told no one in the company that he had hired a new man, and had mentioned Ingersoll's arrival to Lloyd-Smith in only the most offhand manner: "By the way, I've hired a fellow named Ingersoll from *The New Yorker*. When he shows up find something for him to do." Luce had proposed his "Rube Goldberg," two-editor arrangement to Ingersoll at lunch, then had done nothing to implement it. But Lloyd-Smith made it worse. On being introduced to Ingersoll by his secretary, Nancy Osborne, he said, "I'm much too busy to talk to you now, you know."

"It's not necessary to talk," said Ingersoll, obviously annoyed, "just show me where my office is."

"Oh, we haven't any office space and we haven't any desks, but it's quite all right if you move in with Miss Osborne," said Lloyd-Smith, gesturing in the general direction of a little desk and stenographic chair with a plastic back support.

Robert Elson, in his official history of Time Inc., describes Lloyd-Smith as "a friendly, brilliant, witty young man," and Margaret Bourke-White, the photographer who worked with him in the planning stages of *Fortune*, remembered him as having "a headful of tight, short black curls, a profile of almost Grecian regularity, and a spirit of fun-loving, a delight in the ridiculous." Ingersoll liked Lloyd-Smith, calling him a "Byronesque character, the essence of a dilettante," the kind of executive who would let the mail pile up in his in box until it spilled over into the wastebasket, then answer the remaining letters, agree to meet half a dozen of the magazine's most important contacts from the business world at lunch in the Cloud Room of the nearby Chrysler Building (where *Fortune*'s staff would soon be moving), then go off to a movie.

He was, indeed, a charming, brilliant man, the kind of amateur Luce liked. But the abrupt treatment Ingersoll received from both Luce and Lloyd-Smith upon entering the company infuriated him. Ross might have been difficult to work with, but Ingersoll had had real responsibility at the *New Yorker*, which, as a magazine, was, he felt, eminently superior to both *Time* and *Fortune*. Who were Henry Luce and this young dilettante to treat Ralph Ingersoll as if he had just come out of journalism school? He would show them. With nothing else to do, he sat down at his little desk in his plastic-backed stenographer's chair and for the next two or three weeks, while the rest of the staff totally ignored him, studied the four or five issues of *Fortune*, article by article, page by page, and wrote a blistering memo (he was already a master of the art), criticizing every aspect of the magazine's editorial content. Luce, also, seemed too busy to talk; but Ingersoll planned to catch up with him and drop the memo on his desk: then "he could make up his own God-damned mind whether he wanted me to edit his God-damned magazine or whether he wanted to turn me loose—with a year's pay in my pocket. I couldn't care less."

The memo was an indictment of Lloyd-Smith's work. Not to let him see it first, and so give him an opportunity to defend himself, seemed "conduct unbecoming a gentleman"—the kind of thing Ingersoll had so often held against Ross. So, one morning, after Lloyd-Smith had wandered in, Ingersoll went to his cubbyhole and laid the memorandum on his desk: "This is about what's wrong with your magazine. Tomorrow I take it up with Luce. But I consider you are entitled to read it first." Thereupon he went home, had several drinks, and contemplated where he would look for another job.

The next morning, for the first time since his arrival, Lloyd-Smith stopped by Ingersoll's desk to ask if he would have lunch. They went to the Cloud Room and after drinks were ordered, Lloyd-Smith took the bulky memorandum from his briefcase, laid it on Ingersoll's plate, and said:

"Ingersoll, everything in this is true. It's a brilliant paper. So how are you and I going to fix what's wrong with *Fortune*?"

Ingersoll was astounded; then he realized that Lloyd-Smith had understood what was happening: Luce was unhappy with his handling of *Fortune* but had not had the heart to tell him or to replace him, so he had brought in an experienced editor to see what might be done to improve the situation.

In an hour of luncheon conversation Ingersoll and Lloyd-Smith reorganized the whole magazine operation, coming, as Ingersoll says, to "a personal understanding between us"—of their relationship, how they would divide responsibilities, and how they would work together to make *Fortune* the best magazine in the country. They took Luce's misbegotten plan and reworked it into their own formula, "dividing the magazine's staff in half," says Ingersoll. "But the halves were to be cooperative, and co-equal. Half of each issue's ideas were to be mine, half his; half the staff his to direct, half mine. While each was to have unquestioned final authority over each piece for which he was responsible, he was committed to submit it first to the other—for unbridled criticism. These critiques were to be secret, the ideas therein to be for taking or for leaving." Although it was an improvement over Luce's plan, it was still an unusual operating structure. But it worked: "Neither of us," says Ingersoll, "ever questioned it—for the brief fourteen months we were a team."

The idea of a magazine devoted to industrial America had first been discussed at Time Inc. in a Luce memorandum titled simply "Expansion: Business Mag." "It will be as beautiful a magazine as exists in the United States; . . . It will be authoritative to the last letter; It will be brilliantly written; . . . It will attempt, subtly, to 'take a position' particularly as regards what may be called the ethics of business; . . . the line can be drawn between the gentleman and the money-grubber."

Hadden, who was lukewarm to the idea, died shortly after the conception was proposed to the Time Inc. board, and Luce continued to argue for the magazine. Even before Hadden's death Luce had taken Lloyd-Smith from the staff of *Time*, and the two of them, with the aid of photographer Margaret Bourke-White, had started to develop dummy issues. Occasionally Luce even went along with them on a story. And Bourke-White was very much impressed by the editor: "His words tumbled out with such haste and emphasis," she recalled, "that I had the feeling he was thinking ten words for every one that managed to emerge, . . . tracing from one thought to the next, breaking off into short silences, then leaping again from point to point in a kind of verbal shorthand. He left such gaps that at first I had difficulty in following him."

In a 1929 speech, Luce said: "Business is essentially our civilization; for it is the essential characteristic of our times. . . . It is the life of the artist, the clergyman, the philosopher, the doctor, because it determines the condition and problems of life with which either artist or philosopher, let alone ordinary mortals, have to deal." And in the prospectus for his new publication he announced: "American business is worthy of a literature of its own. We propose to create it in a magazine called *Fortune*. American business has importance—even majesty—so the magazine in which we are able to interpret it will look and feel important—even majestic."

Luce, believing that photographs could often describe the power, excitement, and drama of the American factory better than words, planned to use the camera extensively to help tell the majestic story of American business. He also visualized high-quality paper and color illustrations by first-rate artists, all packaged in an attractive format designed by one of the country's most distinguished authorities on type, the artist Thomas Cleland. According to Ingersoll, the primary reason Cleland took the assignment was to install as art editor of *Fortune* his friend, a "wide-eyed, unsophisticated, hard-working, and extremely conscientious young girl" named Eleanor Treacy. After starting her in the job, Cleland "disappeared to Connecticut," as Miss Treacy puts it. She quickly won for herself a reputation as one of New York's most talented art directors and, in Ingersoll's words, "a hard-headed, ferocious defender of *Fortune*'s artistic integrity." (Later she married Eric Hodgins, after he became the magazine's managing editor.)

The new "Business Mag." would be "brilliantly written," said Luce, who was perhaps smarting from what the literati were already saying about *Time*'s breezy, flippant style. At first, they planned to have carefully edited articles written by experts, but it quickly became apparent that this would not work.

Luce decided "it was easier to transform poets into business journalists than bookkeepers into writers," so he began hiring sensitive, creative writers, a formula that eventually resulted in perhaps the most talented editorial staff ever assembled on the masthead of one magazine. The caliber of *Fortune*'s text can be seen in the men who had already been hired by the time Ingersoll joined the staff. The most talented, everyone agreed, was a young poet named Archibald MacLeish, who had graduated from Yale in 1915 and Harvard Law School in 1919 but had decided to devote his life to poetry. After a few years in France he returned to America in 1928 with three children and the need of a job to support him while he worked on a long epic poem about Cortés and Mexico. Before going to Paris, he wrote the "Education" department for *Time*, and when Luce approached him to write for *Fortune* MacLeish said, "I'm flattered, but I know absolutely nothing about business."

"That's why I want you," replied Luce. "You can work for *Fortune* as much of the time as you need to pay your bills and take the rest of the time off for poetry."

MacLeish accepted, and he would later say, "My essential education began on *Fortune*." He also came to believe, as the years went by, that *Fortune* would "stand out as the one great journalistic innovation of our time."

Another poet to join the *Fortune* staff was Russell "Mitch" Davenport (Yale, '23) who had worked for the *Spokane Spokesman* and *Time* before deciding to quit and write a long poem called "The Californian Spring." In 1929 he married Marcia Clarke; the daughter of the opera star Alma Gluck, she had worked for Ingersoll on the *New Yorker*. The following year, just about the time Ingersoll was joining *Fortune*, Davenport decided to approach Luce for a job. Luce called Lloyd-Smith to see if he had anything for Davenport, and the *Fortune* editor said yes—an article on the Atlantic and Pacific Tea Company, which had to be written in three weeks. Even Luce was uncertain about Davenport's qualifications for this assignment: "My God, Parker, don't you know that Russ doesn't even know how to read a Standard Statistics Card?"

As Davenport recalled it, "Lloyd-Smith's answer was that the cards were not very hard to read and that anyway somebody else could read the cards. So I got the story"—and the job.

There were also Dwight Macdonald (just out of Yale), "a rough diamond," as Luce described him, who planned "to make a lot of money rapidly and retire to write literary criticism," and Edward P. Kennedy, perhaps the one misfit among *Fortune*'s Ivy League literature majors. Kennedy had gone to the University of Cincinnati but did not have a degree because he did not show up for graduation. He wrote for *Time*'s "Business" department before joining *Fortune*, where he became perhaps the magazine's most prolific producer, dividing his time more or less equally between his typewriter and the local bar.

And soon to come were:

• Charles Wertenbaker from the University of Virginia, an extraordinarily good-looking Virginian, who, in Ingersoll's opinion, approximated F. Scott Fitzgerald in talent, looks, and approach to life. He also wrote for *Time*'s "Business" department before moving over to *Fortune*;

• Eric Hodgins, an engineer who had decided he was born to be a journalist, and swore after graduation from M.I.T. "never to use as much as a flint gun without professional assistance." A brilliant, eccentric personality who had emotional problems which he tried to solve with alcohol, he was an associate editor of *Redbook* when a *Time* staffer recommended him to Luce;

• Wilder Hobson, a talented wordsmith and a jazz fanatic who occasionally suffered from writer's block;

• James Agee, another young poet, from Harvard rather than Yale, whose first collection of verse, "Permit Me Voyage," was published the same year he went to work for *Fortune*. He was hired by Ingersoll.

This was essentially the group of writers Ingersoll would pass on to Eric Hodgins in 1935—"all in all," as Hodgins would later say, "I think the most brilliant magazine staff ever to exist in America." But he would also say the staff was "insane, unreliable and alcoholic." The writers were, in varying degree, temperamental and sensitive, and they sometimes needed to be encouraged, inspired, and prodded into producing. For example, Ingersoll remembers that Hobson once stared at a blank piece of paper for twenty-four consecutive working days, without writing a single word. And Agee sat in his office and sucked on the end of his pencil for so long after he was hired that MacLeish was afraid he would be fired.

There was also another problem: *Fortune* had been conceived as a magazine that would, in part at least, promote and glorify American business, thereby attracting corporation executives and aspiring company men as readers and prosperous industries as advertisers. But between its conception in early 1929 and Ingersoll's being hired in 1930, the stock market had crashed, the banks had closed, businesses had failed, and the country was slipping into the tragic depression from which it would not fully emerge until ten years later when its economy was revived by wartime production. Luce had correctly perceived that American business was something new and significant in the world, and that very few, including many of the businessmen who made the economy tick, understood or knew much about it. But by February of 1930, when the first issue of *Fortune* with its wheel-of-fortune cover appeared, the American business system had failed—at least temporarily—and there were those who said the collapse was permanent, and so were looking for a new and different system to replace it.

Luce, Lloyd-Smith, Ingersoll, and the *Fortune* staff still had faith in the system, but if they were going to give American industry a "literature," they would have to do more than promote it. They would have to investigate it to discover what made it work and what was wrong with it. To provide this literature, the magazine needed a form, and the men and women who were to do the investigating would have to be backed by a functioning organization that could translate their words and pictures into that form. It was up to Lloyd-Smith and

Ingersoll working as a team, and then to Ingersoll alone, to provide this organization.

The year he worked with Lloyd-Smith was crucial to Ingersoll's career because it enabled him to see Luce through the eyes of someone who, as the saying went around the office, had the "Indian sign" on him. "Parker seemed to understand Harry Luce so well," said Ingersoll, "that, as a problem in the making of the magazine, he simply ceased to exist." Lloyd-Smith knew, from the beginning, that *Fortune* had been his, not Luce's, and he knew he could handle Luce in any situation. Ingersoll recalls several meetings with Luce that should have been confrontations; but while he was building up his usual antagonism in the face of authority and marshaling his arguments against one of Luce's "Big Ideas," Lloyd-Smith just sat there calmly, with his Mona Lisa smile, listening. Luce would begin to wind down, and finally blurt out, "Well, wha—wha—what do you think of it?" Lloyd-Smith would reply gently and in a clear, quiet voice, "Harry, it stinks." Then, as Ingersoll describes it, "a moment of embarrassment. A stuttered apology. And Parker and I would leave—with no comment whatever from Parker even when we were back in the office."

Of course, many of Luce's Big Ideas were first-rate, even inspired, and they were accepted, but only with Lloyd-Smith's approval. This left the two editors almost complete freedom to develop their concept of how to create a literature for American business—a task Ingersoll likened to Harold Ross's attempt, in the early days of the *New Yorker*, to create a literature for New York City and a form for its presentation. Now Ingersoll, with the benefit of his five years with Ross and the confidence that he knew how to translate basic literary concepts into the periodical form, was in his element. In addition, he was even encouraged to write. Luce always felt that his editors should descend into the arena every now and then and do a story themselves, so Lloyd-Smith and Ingersoll agreed they would each try to write at least two *Fortune* pieces every year.

Ingersoll and Lloyd-Smith were never close socially. Their basic differences can be seen in a story about Lloyd-Smith during his Princeton days. He had called together a small group of classmates to read Greek classics aloud in his room—*during the Yale-Princeton game*! Hardly Ingersoll's type. But Ingersoll liked Lloyd-Smith and enjoyed working with him. He seemed to have found a home at *Fortune*. Then, on the morning of September 16, 1931, when Ingersoll came barging into the office preoccupied with the work ahead, banging the little swinging gate that separated the anteroom from the rest of the cubbyholes, Nancy Osborne met him, white-faced and tense: "I tried to catch you at home," she blurted out. "Parker killed himself this morning!"

The evening before, Lloyd-Smith had taken a Princeton classmate, whom he had not seen for some years, to dinner, to the theater, and later to a nightclub where they had stayed for a few hours. The classmate was not a close companion, and there had been no personal conversation. Parker left his friend in casual good humor and went directly to his apartment house on Eighty-sixth Street, just off Fifth Avenue, where he lived with his mother. He did not go to bed.

Sometime between his arrival at two A.M. and six A.M., he wrote three notes. One was to his closest friend on *Fortune*, Mitch Davenport; one was to his brother, Wilton; the third was to his mother, who was asleep in another room. Only the note to his mother was made public. It read simply: "Mother Charm. Heat is frightful—but this is a farewell—if this is waiting—I shall wait for you. My love and gratitude always. Parker."

At six A.M., stark naked, Lloyd-Smith climbed the service stairs to the top of his apartment house, ran from west to east across the flat roof, and, at the full speed of his sprint, dove over the low railing, his arms outstretched as in a perfect swan dive. (This was proved by the position of the body.) None of the endless theories that were advanced to explain Lloyd-Smith's suicide ever satisfied Ingersoll or any of his friends. "I remain today as mystified as I was that morning," Ingersoll said many years later. "Had he been a latent homosexual [as others, including Eleanor Treacy, thought too] tortured beyond endurance by the conflict? To many, he had seemed effeminate. But he had been engaged to an extremely good-looking young girl and . . . there had been other women in his life."

Ingersoll thought the suicide might have had something to do with Lloyd-Smith's purchase of the Time Inc. stock made available by the Hadden estate and offered by Luce to favored employees. Lloyd-Smith had borrowed ten thousand dollars, he thought, from his brother to buy the stock, only to learn later that his brother had kept the stock in his name. Ingersoll recalled that in the few months before his suicide, when *Fortune* was obviously beginning to prosper, Lloyd-Smith was depressed because he was aware the fruits of his labor were not really his. A few years later his brother also committed suicide.

Ingersoll realized he had never before had such a creative working relationship with anyone—and probably never would again. "I could damn him to hell for jumping off that roof!" He was now faced with getting out *Fortune* by himself and for a while it was questionable whether there would even be a next issue, because for at least a month before his death Lloyd-Smith had done nothing about developing his half of the magazine. But Ingersoll managed, and by the time he had put another issue to bed, the staff had begun to acknowledge that he was the sole managing editor. It was at least six months, however, before Luce would agree that the man he had brought over from the *New Yorker* could, in fact, do the job.

By 1932, which marked Ingersoll's first complete year as managing editor of *Fortune*, the magazine's editorial approach was being refined to a technique that would serve as a model for quality journalism around the world. The single most important component of the monthly table of contents was the *Fortune* "corporation story," which may have been a new literary form. "To *Fortune*," says Ingersoll, "the American corporation was eminently and distinctively the owners of stock. But in its search for ownership *Fortune* was the first, except for professors of economics, to come upon the fact that many important corporations in America were owned by so many people that they were not owned by anybody." *Fortune*'s writers had first to see the company whole, then take it apart to explain how it worked. This process necessitated writing about patents, raw materials, advertising, sales, everything from the original idea to the finished product, and steps taken by owners, managers, and workers.

Then came the industry story (on automobiles, for example) or a regional story, a city story, a state story, or a country story (during Ingersoll's time, one whole issue was devoted to Fascist Italy, another to the Japanese industrial empire). They also developed the "family story" which attempted to take the *New Yorker* profile and the *Time* cover story a step further and develop a complete biography in words and pictures of the builder of a company and his family. Then, to provide an outlet for striking color photography and lavish artistic conceptions, they had what might be called the "collections story," about the beautiful things on which rich men spend their money. After 1933, of course, with Franklin Roosevelt and his New Dealers in Washington intent on regulating American industry, there had to be stories on government in general and the regulatory agencies in particular.

Following Luce's wish that *Fortune* devote almost as much time, effort, and money to photographs and attractive layouts as it did to text, Ingersoll and his staff developed the technique, right at the beginning, of breaking every *Fortune* story into parts that could best be told in words and parts best told in photographs or art, then sending out the writers, photographers, and artists separately, with specific instructions as to what the editors were looking for. Margaret Bourke-White was the first *Fortune* photographer, but she was soon joined by others, including Dr. Eric Salomon, who coined the phrase "candid camera" to describe the photographic techniques he had developed in Europe, where he had pioneered the idea of taking a small sensitive camera into conference rooms and offices. When Salomon's work was brought to his attention, Ingersoll invited him to work for *Fortune*, and one hot July day Salomon appeared in New York, called Ingersoll, and asked him to join him at the Algonquin bar. When Ingersoll arrived, Salomon said he was taking the next ship back to Europe because of the heat. But he did agree to return to work for *Fortune*. And typically, says Ingersoll, Salomon's pictures, while a sensation in *Fortune*, were almost ignored by other journals and by the press. "It was several years before the fact that something new had happened in camera technique percolated in the skulls of American newspaper picture editors."

Although by 1940 highly paid public-relations men would spend hours and great quantities of money trying to interest the editors of *Fortune* in doing an article on their company or industry, at first many businessmen panicked when they were informed that *Fortune* wanted to write about them. "As late as the mid-thirties," says Ingersoll, "I had the bizarre experience of having the chairman of the board and principal owner of one of America's largest and already inter-nationally famous manufacturing companies break into tears in my presence when he realized I meant it when I said that *Fortune* was going to do an article about him and his company. There was no scandal of any kind in either his life or his company. The idea of being discussed in public was as shocking to him as if what I proposed was that he attend the opening of the opera with a top hat on and stark naked. He was such a nice man that I put off publishing the article for several months so that he could properly prepare himself for the ordeal."

Fortune's "charter" had always taken the position that American industry was "endowed with the public interest," not only because of its importance to the economy but because the stock of many of the country's largest corporations was so widely distributed as to make them virtually public-owned companies. It was Ingersoll's job to make the first overture to a company, letting it know *Fortune* planned an article and what the ground rules were. Ingersoll let it be known that the editors would prefer the company's cooperation, but that if it was not forthcoming, they would go ahead without it. If the corporation agreed to cooperate, the next step, in the formula developed by Ingersoll, was an offer from *Fortune* of a quid pro quo: to submit the final manuscript *before* publication, "it being agreed"—as the usual phrasing went—"that you shall have the right to correct all matters of fact and to discuss all matters of opinion, it being understood that in matters of opinion, the editors of *Fortune* shall be the final arbiters."

It was also Ingersoll's job to stand up to the big corporations who threatened to cancel their advertising in all Time Inc., magazines when they were unhappy with a *Fortune* story. In dealing with the offended crybabies, he was tough and abrasive—and had the complete support of Luce. To the Matson Line, which had objected to some things *Fortune* had said about one of its ships, and canceled a substantial advertising budget, Ingersoll wrote: "The Matson Line's policy on advertising is obviously no concern to the editorial department of *Fortune*. . . . We set for our goal the highest journalistic and literary standard, the production of a magazine worthy of its subject. . . . *Fortune*'s editorial department has neither the right nor the disposition to concern itself with whether the advertising executives of American industry consider its columns worthy of advertising or unworthy."

Ingersoll did not hesitate to use his name and good standing in the social world to reassure corporation presidents that their company would be treated fairly in the pages of his magazine and, when he thought it would do some good, he would also throw in his father, a former "chief engineer of the Bridge Department of New York City." But it was more than his family name and his connections that made Ingersoll, as editor of *Fortune*, clearly one of the most capable and promising of all the young men who worked for Henry Luce in the early thirties. Ralph Ingersoll was now completely confident as an editor. He had learned the hard way under Harold Ross and had inherited the Rossian belief that an editor's first obligation was to himself. "On this one facet, Ross was articulate," said Ingersoll. "An editor may pass for print only what pleases him. It is his own taste he must discover. If he then finds that other people share his taste and like or enjoy or approve of what his taste has chosen, then he is a successful editor. If they don't then he had better choose another trade, for no man can base his choice of what to print on what he imagines or reasons other people *might* like. If only a few readers respond, then the aspirant to editorship will make his choices for an esoteric quarterly, subsidized by someone who likes him or has nothing better to do with his money. If enough people like what he likes, he will become an honest professional whom society will support."

Another ingredient in Ingersoll's success at *Fortune* was Luce's policy of picking good men (for which he usually, but not always, had unerring instincts), and giving them complete confidence and support—until they failed him. Then, of course, they had to be removed from the job. When Luce put a man in charge, says Ingersoll, "he was in charge." And Luce was able to submerge his own ego in the interest of achieving the desired results.

After Lloyd-Smith died, and especially in the initial period when he was still on trial, Ingersoll came to know Luce well, and he learned to like and respect him. Luce was, Ingersoll said, a different man in the 1930s, so unlike the man he later became, and one of his main criticisms of W. A. Swanberg's monumental biography of Luce is that it is too harsh, failing to portray the talented, complex, and gentle man whom Ingersoll knew when he first went to *Fortune*. In one of his early unpublished memoirs dealing with his years with Luce, Ingersoll includes some remarkably sensitive passages about the editor: "One did most definitely never think of Harry as a brilliant man—or as a man who thought of himself as brilliant. His forte was not in having brilliant ideas but in recognizing them, and throwing the weight of his solid practicability behind them. And, he still had, in those years, a truly boyish enthusiasm—for his people, his publications, towards the world in general. . . . The nature of the man Luce was a nature of intense passion, so intense that he had all his life been terrified of it. I have speculated that this might be the intensity of what the psychologists call latent homosexuality. Harry was always clearly drawn towards certain men and affected emotionally by them; and just as clearly lived by denying the relationship. . . . Yet, none of these men were an intimate of Harry's. The fact is that Harry had no intimate friends among men. It was as if, when he came to a certain specific degree of warmth in his relationship with a man, Harry suddenly turned and fled from coming any closer. The men who 'had the Indian sign on Harry' rarely lunched with him or went to his home for dinner. The occasional convivial drink was not at any time part of Harry's working routine, as it is with most editors and publishers—and with most executives in general, I think. In the social sense, Harry was a 'loner.' And when you did have a meal with him outside the office—unless it be a very orthodox working luncheon— he was characteristically ill at ease, unsure of himself, more awkward than usual.

"Men were drawn to Harry and served him well, and Harry was drawn to them, and handled their capabilities with real and subtle perception and was generous in his rewards to them over and beyond necessity, because of real emotional rapport. . . . There was a strange intensity and such an equally strange impersonal quality to Harry's relations with the men who were most important to him as to seem unique. Luce's top executives always had, towards Luce himself, an ambivalent attitude that is at once patronizing and respectful. Writers who have been close to Luce seem to have always felt confident that in a showdown they could sway him—and to have been quite bewildered when they could not. And when one finally came to an intellectual breaking point, he was always more apt to write Harry into a complicated novel than to attack him with a direct public denunciation, as one intellectual usually attacks another when he has fallen out with him."

Parker Lloyd-Smith had treated Luce in such a cavalier manner and had been so contemptuous of him and his ideas that Ingersoll, when finally drawn into a closer relationship with Luce, was surprised to learn how much substance there was to the man. He not only knew a good idea for a *Fortune* story when he heard one, but was often an ingenious editor. Luce contributed many of the ideas for *Fortune* stories in the early 1930s, including several that Ingersoll would write himself.

So Luce's confidence in Ingersoll and Ingersoll's confidence in himself combined to enable Ingersoll to carry out his own credo that the ideal medium for seeking truth is the monthly magazine. Newspapers and weeklies are under too much daily pressure, and books take too long to write and read. But a monthly magazine, which can condense a year's work of research done by a trained staff into one piece by a creative writer who can give it life and make an art of communicating, provides the proper format for finding out "what the hell kind of a civilization we've gotten ourselves stuck with." Right or wrong, Ingersoll truly believe this, and it is what made him a great editor. Of course, he also had a natural flair and a driving energy. Eric Hodgins recalled that when he finished the first story Luce asked him to rewrite for *Fortune* (while he was still on the staff of *Redbook*) at about eleven P.M. one December evening, he called Ingersoll and asked when he would like to see it. Ingersoll replied, "Instantly!"

Hodgins was only five minutes away from the Chrysler Building, so he walked over, and when he arrived at the *Fortune* offices he was "flabbergasted to find every desk occupied and all lights blazing. It was editorial high noon." Hodgins, who later became something less than an Ingersoll admirer, was immediately impressed by his editorial ability. "As a magazine editor, he was swift, sure, incisive and decisive. . . . He knew precisely what he thought from sentence to sentence and paragraph to paragraph. Within a half hour he had read my draft and covered it with marginal scrawls—'Good'; 'Dull'; 'Hit it harder'; 'Kill'; etc. I asked Ingersoll when he wanted me to rework it. 'Right now, for Christ sake,' he said. So I sat down at a secretary's typewriter outside his office and went to work. I finished about 2:30 A.M."

Fortune's first year under Ingersoll's direction shows a good mix of stories, including many in the Ross-Ingersoll editorial tradition, reflecting his own interests: New York (his city) in its third winter of depression; Berkshire (his beloved Berkshires) Knitting Mills; Teletype (an enthusiasm of his youth); United

Aircraft (he would soon be taking flying lessons and has had a lifelong love affair with airplanes); beer brewing; Eastman Kodak (reflecting his early interest in photography); Long Island (summer playground of New York Society); bullfighting (violently opposed after his Mexican experience); the zipper (perhaps recalling its introduction during his bohemian days, when young ladies were awed by the speed with which young men were able to go into action); the common cold (from which he was a spectacular sufferer); Harry Sinclair (whom he had met through the Bishops); the Union Club (he was always an inveterate New York club man).

The year 1932 was also significant for *Fortune* and Ingersoll in another respect: In November there would be the first presidential election since the great crash and the depression. Politics and economic revolt were in the air, and the question was how a magazine devoted to the making of money would cover it. Neither Luce nor Ingersoll were at that time particularly interested in politics. Ingersoll was still operating under the Russian belief that all politics was humbug. Luce called himself a Republican but still had a wariness of Very Rich Men, some of whom had given him the runaround when he was trying to raise the money to start *Time*, while others were quite vocal in criticizing its new cheekiness. Luce, however, was convinced that the Russian Revolution was over and that the Soviet Union had to be taken seriously—and had, in fact, devoted nearly a whole issue of *Fortune* to Russia, with photographs by Margaret Bourke-White.

The first approach to a presidential year was an obvious one: a piece by Walter Lippmann, who was in the process of shifting from the Left to the Right in the political spectrum and beginning his long career as a *New York Herald-Tribune* columnist. Then Ingersoll came up with the idea of doing two separate stories on the fortunes behind the candidates, President Herbert Hoover and Franklin D. Roosevelt, governor of New York. The Hoover article was written by MacLeish, who became so angry with the lies Hoover told him (in contrast with evidence he had uncovered about his early career) that the resulting piece became an exposé and was widely quoted. The Roosevelt article was written by Wilder Hobson, and Ingersoll went up to Albany with him to go over the final manuscript. When Hobson read FDR the opening paragraph, which described him as a "country gentleman" millionaire, Roosevelt's reaction was simply "Balls!" which Ingersoll said echoed and reechoed through the governor's mansion, and Ingersoll became an instant FDR fan.

By election time, 1932, Ingersoll and most of his writers were for Roosevelt, although *Time*'s staff were split fifty-fifty, with most of the senior writers for Hoover. It was Luce's hope at the time that *Fortune* would gradually draw its writers from *Time* and that the two staffs would be one big family. Many *Time* writers were, in fact, carried on the *Fortune* masthead, although Ingersoll says they did very little work for him. The truth is, the two staffs were becoming increasingly hostile, with the intellectuals on *Fortune* looking down on the *Time* writers as hacks who had sold out to the conservatives. This hostility between the two camps would persist throughout most of the 1930s and eventually become open enough to make Walter Winchell's column.

After Roosevelt was inaugurated in March of 1933, there came the "One Hundred Days" and the New Deal's politicization of American business, from which it has never really recovered. That year *Fortune* ran several articles on the New Dealers ("The Wonder Boys"), including one on the Tennessee Valley Authority (which won its author James Agee high praise and an offer of a permanent job from Luce) and a surprisingly enthusiastic article about the National Industrial Recovery Act, which it called "pure socialism," but supported anyway. It closed the year with a long profile of FDR, written by MacLeish, in which he expressed *Fortune*'s support for the president. No man should be allowed to exploit the profit system to the injury of others, MacLeish said, adding: "Granted that Mr. Roosevelt, shaped as he is by nature and tradition . . . will attempt to preserve a profit system operating under the eye of a kind of public conscience, the regulations which he is obliged to impose to enforce that end will irk only those who are irked by any limitation upon sheer industrial banditry."

Before the article went to press, Luce and MacLeish visited the president, and Luce came away tremendously impressed: "What a man! What a man!" he exclaimed to MacLeish after they had left the Oval Office.

With the New Deal to explain to its readers, plus its obligation to dissect American industry, the organization Ingersoll had put together after Lloyd-Smith's death began to creak and strain, which prompted a battle of memos between Luce (a pretty good memorandum writer himself) and his managing editor. Luce argued that the whole operation needed reorganization; writers must act more like editors, taking complete responsibility for the stories assigned to them, although the managing editor, of course, would have ultimate responsibility; the research department must be abolished and a new, more professional staff developed.

Ingersoll countered. In his view *Fortune* was a "cross-breed" (between a "business magazine and parlor-table picture book"). "I honestly think that *Fortune* is lousy," he concluded, that it has succeeded "only because the fundamental idea was so sound," that it has gone over "despite imperfect execution." The solution was not reorganization but content and scheduling, "not how to get a story but what story to get."

The Battle of Memos was eventually won by Luce, and the reorganization was appropriately set forth in a memo to *Fortune* writers and researchers, drafted by Luce but sent out over Ingersoll's name and described by him as a "New Deal" for the editorial department. In it Luce creates a hypothetical assignment (one of twelve to eighteen such stories running ten thousand to twenty-five thousand words) made on May 1 and scheduled for the August issue, which gives us a nice glimpse of how *Fortune* functioned in the mid-thirties. In this illustration on May 8 the writer reports:

(a) The story idea is lousy for a variety of reasons or that he has no confidence that he can get it for the August issue, or

(b) That the story has possibilities; he doesn't guarantee it; but he proposes to attack it as follows.

Let us say he reports "b" and let us say the story is International Harvester. Managing Editor discusses his plan of attack. Responsibility for getting into Harvester is the Writer's. M.E. may or may not help with introductions. Writer may have certain wild notions about illustrations which M.E. turns down. M.E. sells him alternative notions.

About May 15th, Writer advises M.E. that he has *got* the story. Maybe many a missing link, many a looming quarrel, but there *is* a story. Writer has seen Economic Adviser and been told there *is* a story. This moment is the guarantee. M.E.'s peace of mind rests entirely on these guarantees.

From here on course of pictorial make-up and writing proceeds as usual—except that Writer knows what's going on about his story *every minute*. At some point, Writer and Treacy make up the pages. Writer naturally wants *twice* as many pages as M.E. can give him. Writer will battle for it. M.E. may step in and completely re-make the pages. M.E. is final judge. But what he does must every step of the way be sold to Writer.

At some later point, Draft One is finished. M.E. criticizes. Draft Two. *There are no more drafts*. Either M.E. likes or doesn't like. If he likes he "edits" and that's that. If he doesn't like, he rejects and Writer's name is M U D. The red light goes up. H. R. Luce is told about it. It is all very, very sad and dreadful. There is a crisis. We recognize it as such. Probably the Writer isn't going to be fired. He has done excellent work before. Somehow we pick up the pieces—of the story and of the utterly and quite properly heart-broken writer. It is a dreadful situation. But, my God, it isn't the *normal* situation. We don't say: "Well, that's how it is" and proceed to lose a dozen more battles!

Normality: the M.E. accepts the story, edits it, hands it back to the Writer, tells him to deliver proof complete with headlines, captions, boxes, etc.

The story is then checked *by* the Writer! He is personally responsible *for every single statement and implication*. In his checking process he is, of course, enormously aided by his Assistant. He tells his Assistant to verify every name and date and figure. He asks himself critically where he got this fact or that notion.

Incidentally, Writer is also completely responsible for relations with Harvester. He has all the rows and arguments with Harvester. He is free, of course, to consult and advise with M.E. and M.E. may often be willing to step in and help.

But the nuts of the whole thing is this: No story is scheduled, no story is anything more than an "ideer" until the M.E. has a Writer's guarantee and after the guarantee the M.E. doesn't have to do a damn thing except watch the wheels go round.

That the research department had to be improved was a point on which everyone agreed. Ingersoll himself had referred, in a letter, to the "unhappy repercussions of the first two years of *Fortune*, when we were accused of basing our interpretations of business on the opinions of flighty young ladies who popped in asking stupid questions."

The solution was to require that all researchers have college degrees, and a specialization in some branch of business or economics was welcomed. They were put under the general direction of Louise Wells, and soon *Fortune*'s "dusty little delvers," as Alexander Woollcott would describe them, were establishing new levels of factual accuracy for journalism. In addition, Luce brought in another typical amateur, a charming young man named Allen Grover, who just happened to have gone to Yale, but who also had had some practical experience on Wall Street. Grover was installed as Ingersoll's right-hand man and became the principal contact with the writers concerning the basic economics of business. In the hypothetical article above, Grover was the economic adviser who had to be convinced there was a story, and, as the memo put it, anything Grover said was "the same as from God."

Writers who came to *Fortune* in the mid-thirties recall that what impressed them most was the "electric excitement" about the place. The combination of Ingersoll's infectious enthusiasm and unflagging energy and the staff's response to the intellectual challenge flowing from Washington made *Fortune* the ideal place to work during the early days of the New Deal. And, according to Ingersoll, MacLeish was the "moving spirit," not only behind the magazine's preoccupation with the economic revolution taking place in the country, but behind the development of Ingersoll's own political consciousness as well. MacLeish, a graduate of Harvard Law School, knew many of the New Dealers and sympathized completely with their efforts to move the country toward a regulated welfare state. By 1934 Ingersoll had also come to see the inevitability of the business community's hostility to what was going on in Washington, and he summed up his position in one of his many memos to the staff: "For October, November and December we should have from two to three pieces an issue on—for want of a better word—New Dealing. . . . our function should be neither that of prophet nor of expounder but that of the stern complete factual authority giving the reader the material with which to answer the questions the politicians will be batting back and forth over his head. They will be talking about 'liberty lost' and 'the forgotten men.' We will be telling them what the hell's what."

But just what was what in that bleak period when many people in America, especially her young intellectuals, had turned sour on materialism? "The twenties," says Ingersoll, "had disillusioned my generation with world politics—with World War I's 'saving the world for democracy' and all that crap—but we had a century of success with materialism behind us to sustain our faith in it—until November of 1929. Sure all politics were crooked, and most presidents (like Coolidge and Harding) were dopes—and our Mid-West might be peopled by Babbitts—but it was still a world in which you could start a *New Yorker* magazine to make fun of it all—and write whatever you wanted (with the aid of four dots when you wanted to use a four-letter word and get it published). And then came that horrible day when everything the Menckens and the Sinclair Lewises had been saying about the world that supported them was so dramatically proved to be true: our best business brains *were* stupid, and so were the politicians they hired. We were never richer—and never flatter busted!"

Disillusioned young Americans began to look elsewhere for the answers, and one group in particular seemed to know what was wrong: the Communists. Ingersoll well remembers the first encounter he had with them. It was a Friday afternoon, in the summer of 1934, just about the time he wrote his "New Dealing" memo. He was driving alone in his big tan Lincoln convertible with green leather seats, toward the farm he had bought a little more than a year earlier in Lakeville, Connecticut. On Route 22 around Pawling, New York, a young girl standing by the side of the highway pulled up her skirt, showing a pretty leg, and motioned her thumb in Ingersoll's direction. It was the old trick; as soon as Ingersoll stopped, a young man appeared and they both climbed in. Then they started needling Ingersoll: "Jeez, whatta car! Who are you, comrade, J. P. Morgan?"

They were, in fact, nice kids, and Ingersoll played it straight, telling them he was the editor of a magazine called *Fortune* and one of Morgan's critics.

But the kids would not buy it: "What's the matter with J. P. Morgan? He's an honest man. You're probably one of those rich liberals—all for the working man as long as he sweats to see you don't miss a dividend check. Morgan's OK; he knows which side he is on."

Ingersoll was enjoying it, and his reporter's instinct told him he was hearing a viewpoint totally new to him. By the time they reached Wingdale, New York, where there was a Communist Youth Camp, Ingersoll had almost convinced the girl he was human, but not the young man. When they drove into the camp, he stood up and yelled, "Hey, look what we captured," and for a moment Ingersoll thought he was in real trouble. Then the girl shouted, "Shut up. He's a good guy and he gave us a lift; let him alone."

Ingersoll was permitted to leave unharmed, and he was genuinely impressed by the number and quality of the kids he had seen in the camp. The following Monday he ordered his *Fortune* researchers to begin looking into the American Communist party, and that September the magazine printed an extensive survey of the party's beliefs, activities, and strength. Its conclusion: "The Reds may be 'trouble makers,' and 'fomenters of rebellion,' but they can make trouble and riots only when the capitalist system has done gross injustice to some social group. By leading the oppressed classes and making their grievances articulate, the Communists force the capitalist system to adjust its more glaring inequalities. Whatever else it does or will do, the Communist Party in the U.S. provides a vigilant and persistent opposition."

By 1934 Ingersoll's curiosity about communism had been aroused, but during most of the thirties it remained, as he put it, "a drawing-room thing." He later said frankly that in many respects he was naive about what was going on in the Communist party, especially its struggle to take over the labor movement in the country. But labor had legitimate complaints against big business, and for the most part, they were given a fair hearing in *Fortune*. "Almost invariably," says Ingersoll, "wherever we touched on labor problems, we came out more sympathetic with labor than with management. It was in these contacts that we rich boys learned for the first time what a hell of a time the working people of America had had—and were still having—in the depression. It was a terrific shock to each writer and researcher in turn. Wilder Hobson, a very mild and generally conservative intellectual, went out to cover a strike in a company-owned coal mine town and came back completely horrified. Labor leaders made out a much better case for their side than the employers did. The great corporations of America claimed they were responsible for the American economy, but had proved themselves helpless or irresponsible or both when the heat had come."

The magazine's interest in the conflict between labor and industry led to one of its most ambitious and controversial projects of the mid-1930s: a four-part series on U.S. Steel. Dwight Macdonald and a new young writer named Robert Cantwell were to do the test. When the series was finished, Luce objected to the lead article and a none-too-flattering profile of Myron Taylor, the president of U.S. Steel, who, Macdonald said, had achieved his position not because he had any business acumen, but because he looked like a movie director's idea of the chairman of a big corporation. "I was looking for trouble and I got it," Macdonald said later. But when Luce ordered Ingersoll to rewrite it, Macdonald resigned.

Ingersoll maintained that Macdonald's piece was not wrong in its approach to U.S. Steel; it did, however, amount to an "editorial," which was not *Fortune*'s style. In rewriting the piece, he used Macdonald's material, which he said was "informed and intelligent." When he flew down to Florida to go over the manuscript with Taylor, Ingersoll was impressed by the impact the information had on him. He also thinks *Fortune*'s revelations about how U.S. Steel had failed the workingman played a major role in Taylor's surprise decision to meet with John L. Lewis and sign a labor agreement. He also recalls Luce telling *Fortune*'s staff during the U.S. Steel turmoil that there was a war going on between capital and labor, and that if they had to choose sides, there would be no question which side Time Inc. was on: the side of capital!

Another story that brought *Fortune* widespread attention in the mid-1930s was a piece on European munitions: "Arms and the Men," written by Eric Hodgins. Again Luce demonstrated that, in 1934 at least, his instincts as a journalist overrode his personal judgments. The article, whicn Ingersoll pushed for all the way, was an eyebrow-raising indictment of the profits European munitions manufacturers made from killing human beings. It created a worldwide sensation, especially coming from that "well-groomed organ of Big Business," as the *New Yorker* described *Fortune* when nominating it for the 1934 Pulitzer Prize for the armaments article. It was this compliment that Hodgins appreciated more than any other plaudit he received on the piece—except for Luce's own prepublication congratulations. Luce also said at the time, "Now don't get me wrong about any of this. It doesn't mean that *Fortune* might not want to turn around the next month and publish one hell of a fine story whooping it up for the biggest navy in the world."

Two months later *Fortune* caused another sensation with a whole issue devoted to Fascist Italy. Luce argued that because of the coverage the magazine had given to the Russian economic system in 1932, it was obligated to treat fascism similarly. But Luce gave a speech in Scranton that April in which he called fascism a "moral force" and sounded rather sympathetic to what Mussolini was trying to do with his corporation state. After the issue appeared, many people claimed *Fortune* had been a little too friendly, and pointed to a statement in the introduction, "the good journalist" it read, "must recognize in Fascism certain ancient virtues . . ."

As *Fortune* and its brilliant staff, led by Luce and Ingersoll, plunged into the most controversial issues of the day, the education of Ralph McAllister Ingersoll began to intensify. He had shown great promise as an editor at the *New Yorker*, and now that promise was fulfilled as he and his "Knights of the Round Table" (as he would later call his talented staff) created a literature of American business and society in turmoil. Even his severest critics conceded that Ralph Ingersoll was, as Eric Hodgins described him in his memoirs, "a brilliant journalist and a highly creative editor." And Hodgins had good reason to be indebted to Ingersoll: At the end of one two-month period in 1934, when he had been simultaneously assigned two stories, on unemployment and General Foods, for the October issue, Hodgins completed his assignment, then collapsed, overcome by excessive drinking and a nervous breakdown, which ended in a rather confused suicide attempt. But Ingersoll never once suggested to Luce that Hodgins had a problem. "I'm to blame," Ingersoll said, "I worked you too hard: I put too heavy loads on you and you just collapsed, that's all." When Hodgins came out of the hospital, Ingersoll said: "You're coming up to Lakeville with my wife and me for a couple of days of rest and country air and then next Monday we'll go back to the office together. This is an invitation but it's one that I'm prepared to back up with force if necessary."

What Hodgins remembered most was Ingersoll's insistence that they *go back to the office together*. As Hodgins explained, this meant that Ingersoll was "standing sturdily behind me and that as far as he and Time Inc. were concerned I was just an ordinary battle casualty." His professional reputation remained intact, and Hodgins was convinced that Luce would never have made him managing editor, as he later did, if Ingersoll had not covered up this incident so effectively.

James Agee gave Ingersoll problems of a different sort. "A real honey of an article idea popped into Ingersoll's mind," as one of his writers put it, in the summer of 1934 — a piece on the American roadside. The poetic Agee seemed the perfect writer to do the story. The poet spent sixty days traveling the highways and byways of America, and when he came back to the Chrysler Building it appeared that he was going to take another sixty days, or longer, to complete the story. When suddenly it turned up in galleys one day, a surprised Hodgins asked Ingersoll, "How come it wasn't late?"

"I had to go down one evening and take eight thousand words off the top of Jim's desk and send them to the printer," replied Ingersoll. "They were great."

"I don't think Jim knows that," Hodgins said. "He's still in his office writing like hell and I think it's still on 'The Great American Roadside.'"

Ingersoll said, "Will you be a good fellow and go down and tell Jim everything's fine," and Hodgins did. Agee just said "Oh," but that night, said Hodgins, "I am sure James Agee must have cursed Ingersoll in fifty languages"—which is what managing editors are for.

Ingersoll could be tough, even "brutal," as one staffer said, in such things as taking a story away from one man and giving it to another for rewrite. But he had a masterly way of letting down writers who did not measure up. "Your manuscript failed to convince us," he said to one writer he rejected but recommended to *Time*, "that you had the special and unique flair which we are hunting for—that flair which might have brought you to the top earning brackets of *Fortune* in a few years. There is nothing to reproach yourself about if you haven't got it. What we are looking for is not exclusively writing but a strange combination of talents which would be useful to no other magazine in the world . . . if you like, we are looking for a certain kind of freak to join our menagerie."

He also set very high standards for the magazine. After the May 1935 issue had been put to bed, he sent a memo to the staff saying that although it was one of the "best looking" and most factually accurate issues in recent months it was also "a new low" journalistically. "*Fortune*'s job is covering the contemporary industrial scene, but covering it not as a *National Geographic* magazine of industry, but as *Fortune*, the alert journalist writing about a living and exciting world."

Then he took the issue apart, article by article, as he had done in his first week at *Fortune*, and concluded with a warning: If the magazine did not rediscover the alertness and vitality it once had, it would simply degenerate into "a pretty text book."

Luce concurred, adding a covering memo in which he said, "Ingersoll has clearly articulated an unhappy feeling which I have had lately about *Fortune*." He thought *Fortune*'s writers had become too interested in their work and were ignoring their readers. But Ingersoll thought they were not preoccupied enough with *news*. To keep the magazine from degenerating into a pretty *National Geographic*, and to generate a little news of its own, he introduced, three months after the dissected May issue, a new feature called the *Fortune* Survey. The basic idea had come during a lunch he had arranged with Richardson Wood, a young copywriter for the market research firm of Cherington, Roper and Wood.* At the lunch Wood told Ingersoll about some market research his firm had been doing and said that their methods had proved to be accurate. Ingersoll inquired whether he might be permitted to reprint some of the surveys made for large corporations. Wood said he doubted it, and Ingersoll said, "Well, then, why can't we buy a survey of our own?"

"You can if you pay for it" was Wood's reply.

---

* In a seemingly continual effort to play down Ingersoll's contribution to the company, Robert Elson, in his official history of Time Inc., reported that the idea for the *Fortune* survey was Wood's and that it was refined to include public opinion research by Eric Hodgins. But Ingersoll did not remember it that way, and his memory was confirmed by Wood in two letters he later wrote to Ingersoll.

Ingersoll persuaded Luce to give him ten thousand dollars over his budget to pay for a survey. During the conversations in the office about what subjects they would survey first, Ingersoll decided that market research techniques would work just as well for sampling public opinion. He mentioned the idea to MacLeish, who became just as excited as Ingersoll. Ingersoll was especially intrigued because of his engineering background. He had told Wood that when he was working in the mines, they used weighted sampling techniques for assessing ore, and Wood had said that his research worked on exactly the same principle. The problem was: how did you translate this technique into public-opinion sampling? *Fortune*'s original survey divided Americans according to which parts of the country they lived in and how prosperous they were. Questions were asked of a group that represented in microcosm the geographic and economic divisions of the country and the distribution of population between large and small communities. "Geographically," says Ingersoll, "*Fortune* divided the country into five parts: Northeast, Southeast, Southwest, West and Pacific Coast. The ratio of total interviews to interviews in each of these sections paralleled the ratio of the population of the entire country to the population of the section in question. Similarly, people living in large, medium, and small cities, in towns and in rural areas were represented in the same proportion that these communities bore to the total population in the census of 1930. Lastly, people in each of five economic levels were interviewed in proportion to the total numbers at each level, as determined by a classification of homes by value or rental. This proportion was observed in every locality where interviews were made. All interviews would be made under uniform instructions on pretested questionnaires and the work of the interviewers would be checked by supervisors making follow-up calls."

MacLeish, however, felt the project still needed some heavyweight support, and he knew where to look for it. His old friend James Bryant Conant had just been made president of Harvard, and soon MacLeish and Ingersoll were having breakfast in the Harvard president's private dining room. When MacLeish and Ingersoll explained what they were planning, Conant jumped to his feet, exclaiming, "This concept is of enormous importance! It will revolutionize the functioning of democracy. And you have brought it to the right place—where academic disciplines can collaborate with pragmatic men of the world." Conant paused to walk the length of the room, then began talking again: "It is an exact parallel to the development of the steam engine! Watt was the pragmatic inventor who brought his ideas to the University of London, where they were able to understand what he had stumbled on. Their collaboration changed the world! Together, we will again! I'll turn the University loose. Statisticians we have by the bushel. No trouble getting sample percentages by sex (which you've ignored) and simple categories like that. But a truly representative sample would have to recognize the influence of glands on opinions. I've got a whole medical school to go into their effect. What makes people make up their minds, anyway? That's one for my psychologists and psychiatrists.

"My God, this is immense!"

Then, suddenly, the president came to a stop. "No! We can have nothing to do with it. *Nothing*, you understand, *nothing*. You haven't even discussed it with me!"

"But, Jim," MacLeish interrupted.

"Archie, we couldn't even begin before we'd be in politics. And this University is a privately endowed institution. The slightest breath of involvement would destroy it. No, no, no . . . please leave me and don't ever say you've been here."

So Ingersoll and MacLeish had to find other ways to make the *Fortune* poll credible. MacLeish wrote a brilliant introduction to the first survey in which he cited Walter Lippmann's thesis, developed in his book *Public Opinion* (1922), that knowledge of public opinion was essential in a democracy. "It is the hope of the editors," MacLeish wrote in his unsigned introduction, "that by experiment and correction the *Fortune* Survey may come in time to enjoy a certain authority as a barometer of that public opinion, the importance of which has been so well described—the nature of which has been so blankly ignored."

The first survey measured such controversial issues as sharing the wealth, and public services versus taxation. It had been decided to run the survey quarterly, and three issues later it measured public opinion on the right to inherit, taxing income, the treatment of labor, and modern architecture. Among other things, the surveys showed that over seventy-five percent of those polled thought the government had a responsibility to see that every man who wanted to work had a job; that there was a significant division of opinion in the country as to whether labor was fairly treated; that apathy about foreign affairs was widespread, but Americans did show discernible concern about German and Japanese intentions and an inclination to side with the British in international conflicts.

The surveys immediately began to attract attention, and one of their most avid readers was in Washington, at 1600 Pennsylvania Avenue. Just to make sure that President Roosevelt really read the survey, MacLeish suggested they withhold it from one issue, which prompted FDR's assistant Judge Samuel Rosenman to inquire, "Where's the report?" Richardson Wood has also said that from September 1939 to December 1941, each of Roosevelt's moves closer to war took place soon after a *Fortune* Survey had shown a clear majority for repeal of the Neutrality Act; for lend-lease; for the convoy of ships to Britain; and for resistance to Japanese moves in Southeast Asia. The survey also correctly predicted, within 1.2 percentage points, Roosevelt's margin of victory over Governor Alfred Landon in 1936. Luce supported the survey, but it was eventually killed by Ralph Paine, who became managing editor of *Fortune* in 1941.

Ingersoll has always thought that *Fortune* pioneered the public-opinion poll and that George Gallup copied it. But Wood's research showed that as far back as Andrew Jackson's day, newspapers conducted straw polls at election time; and that Gallup was working on his poll at the same time as the editors of *Fortune*, and when he heard about their work, he canceled a trip to Europe to speed up the development of his own poll. Ingersoll would eventually express serious doubts about the technique he helped pioneer, pointing specifically to its taking off "from its modest beginnings and turning into the national specter it now is—illegitimately dominating democracy's political process and affecting even international relations." Maybe James Bryant Conant's instincts were right.

By February of 1935 *Fortune* had achieved a circulation of one hundred thousand and was headed toward an annual profit of half a million dollars. Luce was incredulous—especially about the circulation. When he saw the projections, he called in Hodgins and *Fortune*'s business manager, P. I. Prentice (Ingersoll was in Key West fishing with Ernest Hemingway about this time), and asked, "What are you guys doing?"

Hodgins said "Nothing" and Luce went on: "I don't understand it. *Fortune* with a circulation of a hundred thousand? I don't understand it at all and I don't think I like it."

But he did like it, and would soon reward Ingersoll for what he had done with the magazine.

Later, in a memo to MacLeish, who had objected to some of *Fortune*'s advertising promotion, Luce defended the magazine's efforts to reach million-aires:

At 100,000 circulation, *Fortune* is far from being a millionaire's club—but the presence of the millionaires had a lot to do with paying our bills.

Fortune writers should not, I think, resent their presence. . . .

Maybe we should like to publish a magazine for intellectuals only, but I don't know how you do that except by getting *one* millionaire to pay the deficits! . . . I think *Fortune* writers (1) ought not to resent the millionaires in the audience, and (2) should cheerfully remember that *that* happens to be the audience to which they were invited to lecture.

Clearly Ingersoll's Knights were becoming restless performing for million-aires rather than for readers who really understood and/or were active in modern industry. And Luce's gradual swing toward a more open support of big business and capital in the 1930s put Ingersoll in a difficult position. Once again he found himself with his feet planted squarely in two camps: On the one hand, he was sympathetic to the social and economic revolution that MacLeish and most of the *Fortune* writers were caught up in, and he was upset when Luce had an-nounced during the U.S. Steel flap that, when it came to choosing sides, *Fortune* was on the side of capital. Furthermore, he did not think, then, that objective journalists should take sides (although *he* would later take sides on national and international issues when he produced his own publication). On the other hand, he was definitely attracted to men of power and influence in America, and his association with Luce and his burgeoning empire had advanced him much further in this world than Park Avenue Society or the *New Yorker* ever had. He was ambitious and liked the corporate world.

Despite his concern about Luce's moving *Fortune* toward the Right (or perhaps because of it), he would soon consider asking Luce to make him publisher of *Fortune*, which would have taken him even further into that world. Luce would promote him, all right, but not to the job of publisher.

By 1935 the unique education of Ralph Ingersoll was reaching a temporary peak. He was a staunch New Dealer and a Roosevelt supporter and was even sympathetic to some ideas held by the Communists. At the same time he liked meeting and getting to know men of power and wealth. It was Ingersoll who wrote the initial letter to corporation and government leaders announcing that they were to be the subject of a *Fortune* article, and it was usually Ingersoll who took the final manuscript around to headquarters to go over it with the boss. He also met many industrial leaders through Luce, and they were usually impressed with his quick intelligence, his articulateness, and the fact that Luce obviously placed great confidence in him. He presided over a brilliant, talented staff which respected him as an editor and kept him constantly alert with fresh viewpoints and new ideas about a country and an economy in transition. It is not surprising, then, that Ralph Ingersoll always considered his five years on *Fortune* his Camelot—the happiest days of his life. Even his ulcers had disappeared. And the truth is that professionally he would never be so happy again, even when he had his own publication—in fact, especially when he had his own publication.

In the cockpit of his Fairchild-24

6: "A Very Active Type Man" Makes His *Fortune*

Fortune was obviously an idea whose time had come. Ingersoll thought it was Luce who said that "in the 1920s it was bad taste to bring up business at the dinner table, but within a year after *Fortune*'s founding, you heard nothing else discussed." These were depression years, of course, which is why business was on everyone's mind. And as editor of the right magazine for the times, Ingersoll came out looking like the brightest and most capable of all the wunderkind who worked for Henry Luce in the 1930s. He could sit in his office high up on the northeast side of the Chrysler Building and look down on the Queensboro Bridge, which his father had built, and the streets of the East Side where he had grown up. "If my magazine dealt with American dreams," he recalls, "I could take satisfaction in my own snippet: an executive's corner office on the fiftieth floor, in my own home town."

Ingersoll had indeed come up in the world, and by 1942 he would have become enough of a celebrity to be the subject of a *New Yorker* profile in which Wolcott Gibbs would quote Ingersoll's chauffeur as saying his employer was "a very active type man." And active he was. In the mid-1930s Ingersoll, it seemed, was everywhere: Flying to Canada to do a *Fortune* story on gold mines; spending

a month with Bob Kleberg on the King Ranch in Texas; taking tea at the Ritz
in London with Randolph Churchill; fishing with Ernest Hemingway off Key
West; weekending (on a self-given assignment for *Fortune*) with William Randolph Hearst and Marian Davies at Wyntoon in southern California; driving his
big Lincoln convertible to visit his wife at Saranac Lake; having lunch, drinks,
or dinner at the Yale, Racquet, or Union clubs, or at Voisin or "21" with notables
from the corporate world or the *New Yorker* crowd; helping to stage the New
Year's Eve show at the Apollo burlesque theater; quietly waiting to be identified
at the door of Anna Swift's Massage Parlour; taking a stripper named "Jane"
out for a midnight snack at a little bar on the West Side; attending the theater
with Lillian Hellman; taking the Congressional to Washington to meet with Harry
Hopkins or Tommy Corcoran or even the president (Thurber says one reason
Harold Ross did not like FDR was that he called Ingersoll "Ralph").

Of course, it took money to lead such a life, but Ingersoll was making a
good salary—especially for the depression years: He started at *Fortune* at fifteen
thousand and by his last year there was making thirty thousand.

Another reason Ingersoll was able to lead such an active business and social
life was that for much of the time he was, as he wrote Katherine White, angling
for a dinner invitation, "a Monday-to-Friday bachelor." Tommy never did recover
from the tuberculosis developed a year after their marriage, and periodically she
had to return to Saranac Lake for rest and treatment. After 1932 she was hardly
ever in New York, spending most of her time in the fresher, crisper air at Shadow
Rock Farm in the northwestern corner of Connecticut. Shadow Rock, so named
because the small house stood in the shadow of a huge rock, was set on forty
acres of rolling countryside about one-half mile from the village of Lakeville.
Ingersoll paid under five thousand dollars for it and spent the next two decades
remodeling the farmhouse, including *lowering* the living-room floor so that he
could walk upright under the beamed ceiling. It eventually grew to twenty-seven
rooms, though the house, thus transformed, did not look one cubit larger as you
approached it—an accomplishment in which he took much pride. "It was from
the beginning," he says, "a place of great charm and into it my own roots were
to grow as surely as the root of the great oak had grown into the rock on
the lawn." Until he sold it in 1950, Ingersoll considered Shadow Rock his home.
His New York residences were "bachelor pads" of varying degrees of grandeur,
depending on his financial situation and mood. For a while, when Time Inc.,
was in the Chrysler Building, he lived at the Murray Hill Hotel, across the street;
later he had an apartment at 455 East Fifty-seventh, then a palace at 1035 Fifth
Avenue, a monastic room at the Union Club, and finally another apartment at
19 East Thirtieth.

He also started playing golf (mostly on weekends), and taking flying lessons
at Mitchell Field, Long Island. Eventually he bought his own Fairchild 24, which
he kept at the airport in Canaan. Learning to fly was, in his view, made up of
three great adventures: Your first flight around the field; your first solo flight,
and your first cross-country flight.

There were periods when Tommy was well enough to travel, and in 1933 Luce sent Ingersoll on a "cooked up" mission to London, to explore the possibility of a British edition of *Time*. But it was primarily a vacation, and on the first night out the steward announced at dinner that the champagne came with the "compliments of Mr. Luce." There would be a bottle every luncheon and dinner throughout the voyage. To carry out his charade, Ingersoll did schedule a meeting with Lord Beaverbrook, England's baron of the press, and in response to his inquiries as to what kind of man Beaverbrook was, Randolph Churchill told him what has since become one of Ingersoll's favorite stories. According to Churchill, there was a time when the *Daily Express* editor had a mistress he had grown tired of; he also had an ambitous young editor who was pressing him for promotion and otherwise making a nuisance of himself. So he called the young man in and convinced him that if he was going to rise in the Beaverbrook empire he needed a suitable wife, hinting that the perfect lady for this role would be his current mistress. The young man took the hint, eventually marrying the lady, who had also been given the word from the boss. The day after the wedding the young man was fired. When he finally gained an audience with the lord and pleaded his case, expressing astonishment at Beaverbrook's duplicity, the little publisher said, "Young man, the beginning of wisdom is when you learn to detect the note of irony in the human voice. Good day."

Otherwise the trip to England was uneventful. It was restful for Tommy, and they did take the opportunity to visit her relatives in Scotland. Another trip, the following year, led to a more exciting adventure. In late 1934 Ingersoll developed bronchitis, which turned into pneumonia, and to convalesce he went with Tommy to the west coast of Florida near Venice—just about the time the administration in Washington was trying to interest *Fortune* in doing an article about its renovation of Key West. With Ingersoll already in Florida, the administration offered a plan to fly *Fortune*'s managing editor over to Key West to see if the magazine might be interested in the story. Ingersoll was now well and bored with collecting shells on the beach, so he agreed to go. While he and Tommy were exploring Key West on their bikes, he decided to stop in at Sloppy Joe's Bar, well-known as Ernest Hemingway's favorite hangout. The interior was dark as a cave, but Ingersoll noticed that there was one man at the long curving bar. It was Hemingway, to whom MacLeish had sent Ingersoll a letter of introduction. For some reason, he decided not to give Hemingway MacLeish's letter, so he said nothing. But suddenly Tommy burst into the bar with a bloody shin she had hurt mounting her bike. Hemingway rushed over and took charge, ordering the bartender to break out the iodine and lecturing the Ingersolls on the danger of neglecting even a scratch in the subtropics.

When the shin was treated, Ingersoll ventured his name and said his friend Archie MacLeish had said to say hello. Then he told Hemingway he was headed for the docks to rent a boat for sailfishing. Hemingway would have none of it. There was not a single skipper in Key West who could navigate Ingersoll to a sailfish; only he could do it with the *Pilar*. But, damn it, he had to finish a story for *Redbook*. After a few more beers, however, Hemingway said, "To hell with it. You come down tomorrow to the *Pilar*'s dock, just after dawn, and I'll take a day off and you'll have a sailfish in the boat by eleven."

The next day, when he and Tommy went out with Hemingway on the *Pilar* they caught plenty of dolphin and barracuda—which was fine with Ingersoll, but not with Hemingway. So another outing was arranged, but still no sailfish. By now Hemingway's pride had been challenged, and he put aside the *Redbook* story and said they would go out every day until they caught a big one. Tommy dropped out after the third attempt, and mostly it was Hemingway and Ingersoll alone with the Cuban boatman, although Hemingway's wife, Pauline, did go on a couple of unsuccessful voyages. She took an immediate dislike to Ingersoll who, in the first days, before he had acquired a sufficient tan on his balding pate, wrapped a towel around his head to protect it from the sun. Once he heard Pauline tell her husband in disgust, "He just sits there like some God damned Buddha." The truth was, Ingersoll was suffering the humiliation of not measuring up as a sailfisher, by Hemingway's standards. "By the third day," he said, "getting a nod of approval from him—for doing a right thing at a right moment came to mean more to me than life itself. He had that quality. I remember once going forward to be alone with my tears of shame, when I'd made a clumsy or a stupid move."

Hemingway had mentioned casually that he was on the wagon. But each morning several cases of beer came aboard, and as they cast off he would duck below and come up with a very tall highball glass, balancing it carefully because it was filled to the brim with scotch. He carefully placed it on the coping over the control panel as he took the wheel; then, sipping from it as soon as they had cleared the dock, he said, grinning, "One drink—just one."

"Then there was the ritual," said Ingersoll, "of putting on the baits—needle-fish preferred, mouth-tied so that they trolled right—and hauling the lines up to the tips of the outriggers, the slender, tapering pieces of bamboo that now slanted out to port and starboard to spread the baits clear of the *Pilar*'s wake. After everything was in order, the boat slowed down to trolling speed and turned over to the silent Cuban boy, and Ernest and I in our fishing chairs in the stern, rods in lap, Ernest was ready to begin on the beer." They often played jazz on a tinny phonograph wound with a crank. Hemingway had a theory that fish were attracted by the sounds of brasses—particularly Louis Armstrong's. He had many superstitions about fishing, on which he would talk at length, half seriously, speculating on the factor of luck in everything man undertook. He also talked extensively, and with an infectious enthusiasm, about his writing and other writers, and Ingersoll frankly admits that his later fiction was influenced by Hemingway's style. But the thing he remembers most was the importance of doing everything absolutely right.

The increasingly obsessive effort to catch a sailfish went from days into weeks, until finally Ingersoll was beginning to worry about his absence from

Fortune. Hemingway himself was receiving telegrams from *Redbook* pleading for the story. Finally Hemingway said, "Mac, I just can't help it. We'll knock off a day and I'll finish the damn thing and get it off and we'll go back out and maybe the break will bring us luck."

The next day the *Pilar* stayed tied up. But now Ingersoll was also obsessed, so he and Tommy hired a fishing boat to take them out alone. And then, as Ingersoll describes it, it happened—"at the unlikely hour of noon on an oily sea, Tommy and I half dozing in our swivelled fishing chairs. Behind Tommy's bait, a blue-green sail broke through, slicing the mirror surface in fast sweeping arcs. 'Here, take it, take it,' she said, terrified, shoving the rod at me and I on my feet, my rod stored in its holster on the gunwale, as the great creature made his sharp slap at the bait and knocked its line free from the outrigger, so that the line lay slack on the water, as it should so that the bait fish stopped being pulled and lay still, appearing to have been stunned by the tap from the great fish's sword. The line came taut as I swept the rod back, the hook in the bait set itself—precariously, in the big fish's lip, it turned out. The magnificent creature leapt, arching high out of the still water, taking our breath away with the tense beauty of the flashing blue, standing now on his tail, shaking his great bill to free the hook—and crashing back. Now the reel in my hand is whirring, angry against its drag, as the fish sounds. And from the whir and the tension on the line, I knew I had him—so far. Again and again, my sailfish ran, sounded, rose and broke, now in a succession of leaps, now walking the water for foaming yards, held six feet high on his tail. An hour went by, and another—and I didn't plumber it and finally the boatman had a gaff in him, at the end of a long pole, and was pulling him close enough to beat a blunt club into his skull. Then he was finally still, stretched out on the cockpit's deck, almost filling it, magnificent even in death. It was a moment in memory, an elation of soul ranking with the sensation of a triumph that one's first solo flight gives."

But all the exhausted Ingersoll could think of was showing his beauty to Hemingway. With the big fish in his arms and Tommy trailing along behind, he walked immediately to Hemingway's house, where the writer, Pauline, and the boys were at dinner. "I can hear the clatter of exclamations," Ingersoll recalls, "then Ernest's roar—and I dropped the huge thing on the floor and he's hugging me and everyone's crowding around. The detailed memory has been confused but what has stayed with me all these years is the feeling in Ernest's response. He was happy and excited and pleased, and proud of his pupil."

With the sailfish caught, Ingersoll was now determined to drive to Miami and return to *Fortune* as soon as possible. Somehow, he obtained a Dodge, but by two A.M. both he and Hemingway were drunk and the question arose: Could Ingersoll make the trip? It was Hemingway who insisted he could. "This is the effect of alcohol on driving," he proclaimed, "it makes bad drivers worse and good drivers better. *Of course*, there is a high incidence of drunken accidents— because most drivers don't know how to drive when they're sober. But a *good* driver, whose reflexes are good and natural and well trained . . . he's better off with his top brain numb. His fuckin' brain's not there to get in the way of what's natural for him to do.

"And Mac here is A Man. I'll trust his fuckin' reflexes any time, anywhere, at anything. Today's the day he proved it!"

For the rest of his life Ingersoll, who always drove too fast, often with plenty of alcohol consumed, insisted that Hemingway was right "that there is a right amount of alcohol that makes a good driver better and anaesthetizes him from the cerebral contemplation of the possible consequences of the risks he is taking."

Drunk and happy, Ingersoll, with Tommy beside him, pulled out of Key West for the 160-mile, all-night ride to Miami—the high point of his rather unusual friendship with Hemingway having been reached. He would see the great man again in New York, but Hemingway would eventually turn against him, and they would never again enjoy the closeness and warmth of companionship they had shared in that month of sailfishing off Key West.

There was a period in Tommy's bout with tuberculosis when her doctor said they might consider having children. But Ingersoll had taken a test that led the doctor to conclude that he was sterile. The impact of this news—that he could not reproduce the Ingersoll name—was so shattering that his ulcer symptoms returned for nearly a month, and one memorable night when he was alone in his apartment he was overcome with an impulse: "What reason had I to go on living?" he wondered, and nearly jumped out the window before he could reject the urge. In the following days he managed to console himself with a rationalization: "I was a part of a human continuity, yes. But this continuity was the continuity of the whole, not of any one part. In the continuity of a single individual's life, flakes of his skin dry and blow away and are replaced by new living tissue. In the continuity of humanity, one individual's death is no more than a flaking off of a part of the whole. The role of each individual is to live for a little while and then be replaced."

Years later he would learn that the doctor was wrong. But now, as he had been convinced that he could not reproduce, it was agreed that there was no need to expose Tommy to the emotional responses of sexual intercourse simply for pleasure. Ingersoll truly loved Tommy and knew that if he slept with women in his own circle of friends whom he liked and admired, he would most likely fall in love, which would lead to conflict and probably divorce, and that would also produce an emotional crisis for Tommy. The solution was obvious: whorehouses and massage parlors, which he began visiting regularly long before he went to work for Henry Luce. The most famous house was Polly Adler's on West Fifty-fourth Street, but Ingersoll did not want a home away from home with the notoriety of Polly's. He chose, instead, the less-well-known house at 8 West Seventieth Street run by Anna Swift. Over the years he became a good friend of Anna and her staff and, with his reporter's inquiring mind, was soon an authority on massage parlors. And as a reporter Ingersoll describes the ritual: "Once admitted by Anna and shown up the stairs to a dim room with shades drawn, you were left alone to undress. Standing out from one wall, a high hospital-type massage table, two sheets thereon, the top one's corner neatly turned down below a single flattish pillow. In one corner, by the shaded light, a single grudgingly overstuffed chair with a clothes rack behind it. And, finally, along the walls, one made out an odd assortment of implements for exercising: barbells, a rowing machine, weights to be pulled up by pulleys."

The setting was like a doctor's examination room, and the single chair and clothes rack were for undressing, after which one proceeded to the massage table, covered one's nakedness, and waited. "Five or ten minutes were allowed for all this; then came a firm knock on the door. 'Come in'—and in came a very large and very muscular female masseuse, in spotless white uniform, short-sleeved for working purposes. Then this Amazon went to work, wordlessly administering as fine and as complete a therapeutic body massage as any male professional in an athletic club."

This part of the treatment was referred to at Miss Swift's as the Heavy Massage. After it, another stage pause—and then came the Light Massage. "Again, a tap on the door," Ingersoll recalls, "a 'come in,' and there stood another white-uniformed nurse—but this one smiling. By now one could see well enough to register that she had the kind of face one sees in hospitals only in one's dreams. Anna Swift's Light Operatives were damned good-looking, young—but not too young—women! The Light Operative's first duty was to give a Light Massage. Standing smiling, with a single gesture she slipped a single button and the uniform opened wide, and with another gesture she slipped it from her shoulders and laid it by. Almost ceremoniously, she lifted off the top sheet that covered her patient, to leave him as naked as she was. Then skillfully, mimickingly, she ran through her predecessor's motions of massage only this time not with muscles kneading but with fingertips caressing. And all the time smiling, but almost distantly. And on and on and on—until one couldn't stand it! What was your fantasy? Whatever it was, Anna Swift's Light Operatives knew how it was done and how to do it—and would do it if Miss Swift had set the price on it."

It took Ingersoll a long time to win Anna Swift's confidence—by minding his manners—and, as an old customer, to earn the right to stop off on his way upstairs to ask which Light Operative might be available and to express his preference. Of average height and with a head of graying red hair, Anna had the look of a woman of breeding. Her secret life, supported by her establishment, was lived for relatives' children whom she was putting through expensive private schools. "No one," Ingersoll says, "knew Anna Swift herself those days, but I did. Clients who felt it necessary to negotiate with her did so in a drawing room, second floor front, across an enormous round table littered with magazines and newspapers over which hung an equally enormous, round shade of multicolored

Tiffany glass enclosing a very few dim bulbs. Sitting across it, one saw of Anna only her corseted midriff and her fluttering hands; the top of her was cut off by the shade; the bottom by the table. From this impenetrable bastion came her voice, high, delicate, English accented, *very* genteel. Any question to which she didn't feel like replying, she answered with a teasing laugh that was almost a knowing giggle. She knew and did business with a very great many of New York's older elite in finance and politics, discussing business diffidently with sentences often left unfinished so as never to touch on the crude, the crass or unmentionable. She was a lady who dealt in the facts of life but always a lady— even when naming fees which were nonnegotiable."

From the late twenties into the mid-thirties, when Ingersoll regularly attended Miss Swift's, his main friend and source of information about the workings of a massage parlor was Miss Sinclair, "official hostess, executive, house mother and playing coach, instructing and maintaining discipline but also able and willing to fill in at any position, if called upon. She was tall, aquiline, handsome, red-headed, like Anna, and beautifully proportioned. She walked like an angel or, more accurately, the perfectly conditioned athlete she was—and her voice must have been trained, for it was perfectly modulated and accentless. To top it all, she had wit and the kind of sense of humor that made me think she had been around theatre people once—but I never knew because her past was the one subject Sinclair would never discuss."

Ingersoll soon became close friends with Miss Sinclair, and each visit would end with a coffee klatch in her room on the top floor, and together they would gossip about the day's work. During these sessions Ingersoll learned the secret of Anna Swift's success: an understanding of the unorthodox and what it was worth to those who could afford it. And the stories Miss Sinclair could tell were endless. Her favorite (and Ingersoll's): There was one small elderly pillar of the community who was willing to pay a hundred dollars (Ingersoll's sessions cost only fifteen) for what was, apparently, the only ritual to give him the satisfaction he desired. Before he undressed and seated himself in a chair, twelve custard pies had to be carefully placed between his chair and the door. When he was seated and ready, a naked girl entered the room, catching her client's eye and staring at him constantly. Then she moved slowly toward him, making certain that with each step her foot landed in a pie, hard enough so that the custard came oozing up between her toes. The client sat there with not even an erection, at least for the first few pies. Then it happened; and the whole thing was over in seconds. Immediately the girl had to freeze, turn around, and retreat from the room as fast as she could, trying to suppress her laughter or, sometimes, tears.

With his emotional life taken care of, Ingersoll was free to devote full time to the job he loved—and being managing editor of *Fortune* was more than a full-time occupation. In addition to presiding over the magazine's editorial operation, there were numerous luncheon and dinner speeches to be given, sometimes in New York, sometimes in nearby towns, at Rotary Clubs or trade associations. Ingersoll found that he not only enjoyed it but was a very effective, persuasive speaker. He also had to do a lot of traveling for the part of his job he enjoyed most: writing his own articles. It is hard to imagine a situation that would have made Ingersoll, with his compulsion to write, any happier: As managing editor, he could assign himself almost any subject he wanted (as long as it also interested Luce). There were, of course, a few staffers—Hodgins for one—who thought Ingersoll could "not write prose worth beans." But Luce was satisfied and, in fact, suggested several of the articles Ingersoll wrote. And if his prose was not as graceful as MacLeish's or Agee's or Wertenbaker's, he was a superb reporter and was confident, with some justification, that, with the exception of MacLeish, he could write as good a *Fortune* piece as any of his Knights.

His first few articles did not produce much excitement: the gold standard; Australia (which might have inspired an adventure or two if he had gone down under; but he wrote it in New York, interviewing four or five couples who had lived there); S. Klein's discount department store (in which he spent one day standing in as an interviewer whose job it was to lecture and frighten young shoplifters before sending them home to their parents); Canadian gold mines (which did produce a trip to Canada and some fine Ingersoll reporting on his specialty).

Ingersoll was at his best when he assigned himself a foreign subject or a complicated activity that people knew very little about. It was this skill, no doubt, that prompted Luce one day to suggest that Ingersoll do a *Fortune* article on the King Ranch in Texas. With 1.2 million acres on the border of Mexico, it was virtually a foreign country in itself, and everyone would be interested in the operation of a cattle ranch. Luce had read a story about the alleged mismanagement of the huge ranch, in which it was charged that thousands of dollars were wasted every year just shooting coyotes.

Ingersoll spent thirty days on the King Ranch, met its proprietor, Bob Kleberg, and his huge ranch family, and came back to New York with a hell of a story—and a lifelong habit of starting every morning, ranch style, with a brimming cup of steaming hot coffee before breakfast.

The story begins with some fine passages evoking the ranch's size:

> The King ranch is the biggest ranch of its kind in the world. It is so big that there is a full month's difference in seasons between the southernmost boundary and the northernmost tip. It is so big that five state game wardens spend their entire time protecting the wildlife on the game preserves that are leased to the state for ten-year periods. It is so big that King's grandson recently found the ruins of a village in a pasture corner. He'd ridden range every day of his life, yet he had not known of the village nor of its remains. It is so big that the cars carry compasses to navigate from pasture to pasture and always go out in pairs lest they have a breakdown fifty miles from nowhere. It is so big that a six-foot map of the U.S. hangs on the wall of one of the ranch houses and the King cowboys explain their geography by tracing thereon with blunt forefinger the boundaries of the ranch.

The article went on to tell a number of anecdotes about the ranch; then described, with the help of beautiful charts, the great movements of cattle to market; profiled the owners and managers, telling how much they made; and gave a brief history of the ranch. It concluded with an estimate of the ranch's profits and net worth: $18.5 million, not counting the oil reserves. There was also a special box on cattle breeding and many photographs, most of them taken by Ingersoll. It became something of a classic of the kind of story Luce wanted for *Fortune*.

Ingersoll's next story also caused something of a stir—but of a different kind. And it embroiled Time Inc. in a feud that lingered until the 1950s. Ingersoll had kept in touch with Ross and the *New Yorker* crowd and, in fact, had been instrumental in Ross's selling his *New Yorker* stock to Time Inc. When Ross told Phil Boyer, a Wall Street broker, that he wanted to unload his holdings, the first person Boyer approached for ideas was the well-connected Ingersoll. The reason Ross wanted to sell, Ingersoll had heard, was that he had finally become so annoyed with the *New Yorker*'s business office that he did not want to own stock in "Fleischmann's company," and also he could not really stand up to Fleischmann so long as they were partners. Ingersoll put Ross in touch with Luce; Luce decided against buying the stock personally but recommended to his treasurer Charles Stillman that Time Inc. buy the stock, which it did. Then Ross became upset about the commission he owed Ingersoll. Ross sent him a check for fifteen hundred dollars, which Ingersoll returned, saying he was a Time Inc. officer and did not want a commission. When he got the check back, Ross just frowned and kept walking back and forth in his office, snarling, "Son of a bitch, son of a bitch!",* apparently annoyed that his ex-employee could turn down $1500.

The year before the stock deal, Ingersoll had started thinking about an article on the *New Yorker*; it would be a typical *Fortune* corporation story, with profit and loss figures as well as detailed profiles on the people who ran the magazine. At one time he even speculated about a "collaboration" with Katherine and Andy White and "a touch of Thurber here and there." But it would have to be a labor of love, he wrote Katherine, because *"The New Yorker* is one piece I don't think I have to pay money to get,"* meaning he had enough material about the magazine to write a book. But he thought a collaboration would be fun; the *New Yorker* writers could chalk their time up to "promotion, for no matter what fun we poked, it would give your show a boost."

Mrs. White did not respond to the collaboration idea, so Ingersoll went ahead with the piece on his own, sending questionnaires to the *New Yorker*. He reassured its business manager, Eugene Spaulding, that the magazine would not regret its cooperation: "Really, we have been through the whole show with a great many corporations, and we have met all kinds of attitudes and all kinds

---

*The 2,190 shares of the F-R Publishing Company Ross sold Time Inc. in 1934 were sold in 1936 for a capital-gain profit of $61,315.

of arguments. One president took pencil from pocket and set out to prove that the publication of figures that we asked would cost him $1,000,000 cash. We finally persuaded him that we weren't the big bad wolf he feared and he was immensely pleased with our piece." Ingersoll also had tried to assure Mrs. White that he meant the *New Yorker* no harm in the article, but he added: "My point of view . . . is so different from yours I realize it must be difficult for you to understand. You go in for colored lights, plaintive music, charm. We work out in the unlovely sun, in sweaty factories, in graceless offices. The last quality *Fortune* should have is 'good taste.'"

The *New Yorker* article, written by Ingersoll, appeared in the August 1934 issue of *Fortune*, and it immediately caused a sensation—mostly in the cubicles at 25 West Forty-fifth Street. The lead paragraphs quickly developed the theme:

Harold Ross's father was not a Mormon. But his uncle joined the Church to get trade for his Salt Lake City grocery store. When Harold was fourteen he went to work in this store and, before he became sensitive about his eccentricites, he used to talk about his career there. He used to tell people he was so explosive a practical joker that his uncle remarked that no matter how well a business was founded, Harold could wreck it in two weeks. So just before the two weeks were up he was fired.

Ingersoll was instrumental in starting the feud between Henry Luce (in a "candid" photo taken with a camera Ingersoll kept hidden in the bookcase behind the desk in his Fortune *office) and Harold Ross*

Nephew Harold has run *The New Yorker* for nine years now, but its owner, Raoul Fleischmann, can still sympathize with the uncle. If you must have a reason why *The New Yorker* is able to make big business of frivolity, look to this effervescent quality in its genius, Harold Ross. To survive him at all it had early to acquire an organization and a technique which is not only foolproof but temperament-proof. For *The New Yorker* is fifteen cents' worth of commercialized temperament, distillate of bitter wit and frustrated humor—and these are explosive ingredients with which to devise a commercially stable formula.

The piece ran seventeen pages in *Fortune* and was a nuts-and-bolts description of how Fleischmann had built an organization (with help from Ingersoll between 1926 and 1930, which Ingersoll did not mention) that could survive Ross's temperamental shenanigans. It gave facts and figures about earnings and salaries and thumbnail sketches of Ross, Fleischmann, and the key staffers, with the role each played in the evolution and weekly operation of the magazine. And here is where Ingersoll may have ruffled some feathers: In addition to pointing out some of their eccentricities (which no one likes to see in print), he also stressed the importance of each staffer to the operation as a whole. It is very likely that Ross, for example, did not like the favorable treatment of Fleischmann, and Katherine White may have felt too much credit went to Ross; or *each* person may have felt that the whole show would have collapsed long since, were it not for his or her contribution, which Ingersoll had not adequately described.

Whatever the reasons, the sensitive *New Yorker* butterflies, who were making a good living satirizing others, did not like being written about themselves, despite the fact that the article, as James Thurber wrote several years later, "seems more like a bouquet of roses than anything else." Thurber said the staff was mostly peeved at the salary revelations, which were, in fact, "somewhat magnified." Ross was furious and pinned a note on the office bulletin board: "It is not true that I get $40,000 a year." And Andy White wrote in the *New Yorker*'s "Comment" section: "The editor of *Fortune* gets $30-a-week and carfare."

The immediate reaction at 25 West Forty-fifth was that the *New Yorker* should retaliate with a full-issue lampoon of *Time* or *Fortune*, but Ross vetoed that. ("Who reads *Fortune*? Dentists.") They decided the appropriate response would be a long profile of Luce, to be done by Gibbs and St. Clair McKelway, who was the one sent to do the interviews because they knew Gibbs's reputation as a satirist would arouse suspicion at Time Inc. They worked on the profile for over a year, then Ross held up publication of the finished piece until November of 1936, to coincide with a new magazine they heard Luce was planning to launch.

If the King Ranch and the F-R Publishing Company seemed like unusual candidates for a *Fortune* "corporation" story, Ingersoll's next subject—and especially the bare breasts that were a legitimate feature of some of the photographs accompanying it—really did raise a few eyebrows. One night he and Louis Bishop were having martinis and dinner at Luchow's when Bishop suggested they go over to a theater on Irving Place to see a young lady named Gypsy Rose Lee. Bishop argued that, as a journalist, Ingersoll would want to see how Miss Lee had transformed the removing of one's clothes into a fine art. Ingersoll agreed, and after the show they decided they must meet the artist. But how? Then Ingersoll had his inspiration: In the 1930s burlesque was big business, and any biz was *Fortune*'s business. So the two young men-about-town went around to the stage door and introduced themselves to Max Wilner, the king of burlesque. Wilner, unlike some executives Ingersoll had approached, was not averse to a story in the magazine, quite the contrary. Unfortunately, he had not heard of *Fortune*. But that problem was taken care of the next day when Ingersoll sent Wilner several copies and a formal letter making his usual pitch to do a *Fortune* corporation story. So almost every night for several weeks in the latter part of 1935, Ingersoll was a stage-door Johnny. He got to know most of the cast and became very good friends with a chorus girl named Jane.* Gypsy was delightful and very cooperative, although she did make one small demand when a Time Inc. attorney insisted that Ingersoll had to have a signed release to use the photographs of the cast taken on and off stage. Ingersoll took the papers and photographs to the Apollo and laid them out in front of Miss Lee. She liked most of the pictures, but then she came to one of her more or less in the nude and screamed, "For Christ's sake, haven't you got a decent retoucher in your shop. Get 'em to make 'em stand up," she shouted, penciling in a firm curve under her little breasts. "OK, if you do that, I'll sign the damn papers."

Gypsy Rose Lee recalled the *Fortune* piece as being primarily concerned with burlesque's "effect on real estate values." Ingersoll took her to dinner one night at Voisin, and all eyes in the restaurant were riveted on the queen of strippers as she made her regal entrance, and they were seated at a prominent table. Then, in a voice that could carry to the back row of most any theater in the country, she said, "Chee-rist, my dogs hurt!" Ingersoll would have taken her to dinner more often if Wilner had not informed him the next night that Miss Lee's boyfriend in the mob was jealous.

The mob, in fact, provided Ingersoll with one of the more moving experiences in his *Fortune* career. At the beginning of the burlesque research Wilner's producer, Allen Gilbert, had consented to the usual arrangement: In return for his cooperation, Gilbert would be shown the article before it went to press, and would be given a chance to argue about matters of opinion; but the *facts*, if correct, would stand. Gilbert was a twenty-five-year-old Broadway denizen of ageless appearance; emaciated and sharp-featured, he was a chain-smoker and heavy drinker—"the only man," Ingersoll says, "I ever knew, young or old, whose complexion actually had greenish tints to its flat pallor." Gilbert had started in the burlesque business in Cleveland when he was fourteen; but, despite

---

*That friendship ended one night about a year later, when she came to his apartment high over Manhattan, and kneeling in front of the picture window to look out at the sparkling lights, she said, "It's just too damn beautiful and I don't belong here"; she never came back.

his checkered background, he had clearly developed as a man of honor.

Once Ingersoll had dug into the basic structure of Wilner's burlesque business, he knew something was missing; but he did not know what. Then one night he and Gilbert got drunk together, and by dawn Gilbert had blurted out the whole story: How the mob moves in on a business and how it had taken over the Wilners' burlesque operation, leaving the Wilners only a minimum percentage of the profits for managing the business.

Ingersoll knew he had some solid news that would make the *Times*, so he put the whole story in his article, somewhat naively assuming it would not cause any problems because, of course, everyone in show biz must know the mob was involved. When he finished the article, he sent proofs to Gilbert and it was a week before he heard from him. Then one night Gilbert appeared at Ingersoll's apartment with two shabby suitcases; he just wanted to say good-bye to Ingersoll and "the doctor" (Bishop). It did not take long, or many bourbons, for Ingersoll to figure out what had happened; Gilbert had kept the proofs a week while making his decision—which was to leave town! In the time he knew it would take for the article to appear, he would have a chance to disappear before the mob could find him. When Ingersoll asked, "Why didn't you tell me?" Gilbert replied, "Well, we had a deal, didn't we? You didn't welsh: you showed me what you'd got out of me before you printed it and you didn't have to. And I didn't have to tell you nothin', either. I got no beef."

Ingersoll says this was the *only* time he ever cut essential information out of a *Fortune* article because one of the "executives" of the profiled firm objected to it. "But," he says in his defense, "I can't ever remember conduct as gallant from any tycoon threatened by a *Fortune* story." Actually, the burlesque "corporation story" did not need the mob connection to make news. With Ingersoll's characteristically thorough job of reporting—and, of course, the photographs of the bare (and, in some cases, retouched) breasts—the article created something of a sensation and helped make Gypsy Rose Lee's figure a national one. It also enhanced Ingersoll's reputation around the city's bars and lounges.

But despite his active social life Ingersoll was not neglecting his job; in fact, *Fortune* was at the center of most of his activity. Ingersoll was totally absorbed in his work and loved the rhythm of publishing a monthly magazine: Every thirty days the slate was wiped clean and you would start over with a new creative challenge. "For the first time, my New England conscience was at rest," he says. "The hours I spent purely for pleasure, I felt were justified because they rested me and helped me to concentrate on what was really important, the magazine."

Luce did not begrudge Ingersoll his good times or his emerging role as a man-about-town, and gradually he placed more and more confidence in him. Soon it would be Luce, not Ingersoll, who would be accused of neglecting his job. Luce's marriage to Lila Hotz, which had endured for eleven years and produced two sons, Henry III and Peter Paul, appeared, on the surface, to be solid. But it was not. Lila was a charming woman who loved music, art, gardening, and people, and who cared little for the world of wealth, power, and glamour that both Luce and Ingersoll were being drawn into. The marriage had drifted along in neutral for several years, until Luce met a woman who fascinated him totally. But not at first. Sometime in mid-1934 Luce and Lila dined at the house of New Haven classmate Thayer Hobson and his very attractive and talented wife, Laura. Hobson worked for the William Morrow publishing house; Laura wrote promotion copy for B. Altman's department store and was an aspiring fiction writer. And their marriage was apparently in about the same lukewarm state as Luce's. He was obviously impressed with Laura because it was about this time that she went to work for him at Time Inc. Ingersoll always speculated that Luce had seen more in Laura than her promotional talents (which were considerable) and had hired her and pursued a cautious fling at a time when his marriage, too, was beginning to sag. Whether there was anything to this theory will probably never be known (unless Laura Hobson chooses to confirm or deny it), and it is academic in any case because Luce would soon become involved with another woman whom he had met at dinner that night at the Hobsons. She was a friend of Laura's, an editor at *Vanity Fair* named Clare Brokaw. Over the next few months he met her at other dinner parties. Hostesses would later report to *New Yorker* profile writer Margaret Case Harriman that Clare Brokaw was a guest who knew how to operate, first "gazing speculatively around the table and silently deciding who is worth talking to. If she is not seated near that person (usually a man), she will seek him out afterward and give him what one hostess described as the full treatment. This consists of asking him endless questions about whatever subject temporarily interests her and which he is informed about."

In the early 1930s Clare Brokaw's subject was the picture magazine she had once tried to persuade Condé Nast to publish. Luce had something to say on this subject, because Time Inc. had also devoted some study to the idea. Luce impressed her—first as a bore, then as interesting but rude, because on more than one occasion he broke off conversation by abruptly looking at his watch and announcing that he had to leave. Then one night early in December, at about the time Ingersoll was researching burlesque in the West Side strip joints, Luce and Lila were across town at a party in the Waldorf Hotel given by Elsa Maxwell. There Luce met Clare again, had a long conversation with her over champagne, and invited her down to the lobby to give her some momentous news: "I think I must tell you, you are the one woman in my life."

The next morning an obviously unsettled Luce called Archibald MacLeish at the office and asked to meet him at the Commodore Hotel, in the ballroom off the mezzanine. When he arrived, a "shaken, overwhelmed and infatuated" Harry Luce, as MacLeish described his friend, told him that he was in love with another woman, wanted to marry her, and needed some advice.

That night there was another party at the Waldorf, this one attended by both Luce and Ingersoll. Before the festivities began, Luce seized Ingersoll's arm and took him into the men's room, where he looked under the stall doors to make certain there were no eavesdroppers. Then it came out: "I'm in love, Mac. With Clare Brokaw—*the* Clare Brokaw. I'm going to marry her. I've told Archie but no one else. Mac, you can't believe how wonderful she is. Oh, God, how wonderful she is! It's absolutely unbelievable."

Ingersoll was stunned. He remembered Clare Boothe as the rather wild young lady who had married one of his sister's rejected suitors. He had followed, with mild interest, her career as an editor at *Vanity Fair* and, as he puts it, "had her ticketed as a flashy bit, not to be taken seriously as a writer or an editor or a Social Figure." Now there was a real problem: Luce, the son of a minister and already emerging as a pillar of corporate America, was married and had a family. Clare Brokaw was, you might say, a "notorious woman—conspicuously a divorcée," says Ingersoll, "and too flashily pretty for her own, or anyone else's good."

Luce knew he had a problem, as he explained to Ingersoll the next day in his office. "My first question, Mac, was whether I had the *right*—the sheer Christian right. So I told Archie the whole story and put it to him and he gave me my answer: Love is all there is, Mac. I haven't any choice; I *have* to leave Lila because I *love* Clare.

"So now that that's settled, you tell me, Mac: how do I break the news... to Lila" and—after a pause—"to ... everybody."

If nothing else, Ingersoll now knew where he stood with the boss. When it came to morality and right or wrong, he turned to MacLeish; on practical matters of tactics and operation, he turned to his sophisticated strong right arm. In fact, Ingersoll was a little surprised that Luce had asked him for advice at all, because as far as he was concerned, despite his active social life, he was a faithful husband whose man-about-towning could be explained by his wife's poor health. The breakdown of the relationship between Henry and Lila Luce put Ingersoll in a terrible bind.

He did not particularly like Clare Brokaw, and he knew that if Luce divorced Lila and married her, it would hurt his own reputation and the company's. What is more, he also had a genuine fondness for Lila, which was shared by many Time Incers. "George S. Kaufman," Ingersoll said later, "wrote a play called *Dulcy* about a sweet idiot, lovable, pretty and childlike, who had such a flair for doing everything the wrong way that it broke your heart to laugh at her. It was such a good play that that year everybody knew what you meant when you said 'she's a Dulcy.' And that was Harry's Lila, to a T—the kind of a darling that could forget all about having asked a university president to dinner and, when he arrived in tails, answered the doorbell in her nightgown. The very nicest thing about Harry was his seeming understanding of this gentle creature and her innocent mismanagement of the role he had assigned her—as Great Man's Wife."

But he also knew Luce was totally and absolutely committed. "Any other course," he says, "was simply beyond his capacity. Thinking, as Harry always did, in the most grandiose of terms, his new emotion was one of The Great Loves of All Time—possibly *The* Greatest."

So Ingersoll's first reaction, when Luce asked him for his tactical advice, was: "For Christ's sake, Harry, get the hell out of here and go tell Lila right now—before someone else gets to her with the news and *really* breaks her heart."

Luce, however, did not act quickly enough, and soon Lila's case was being handled by a "competent lawyer" and she was demanding such a huge settlement that it appeared for a while as if there would be no divorce. Clare was balking too, but Luce told her he would press for a divorce no matter what she did. So she decided to go to Europe while Luce settled the whole mess, telling him, according to Ingersoll, that his family and the Time Inc. directors (all of whom were objecting to the divorce) were his problems, not hers, and that she would not be back until it was all settled.

It was that precipitate act, says Ingersoll, that brought about *his* break with Clare and marked the beginning of their famous feud. "When the going got tough and Lila's lawyers wouldn't agree to anything—just when it seemed to me that Harry most needed the woman he loved, she packed her bags and sailed for Europe."

Ingersoll says he heard that Clare Luce once said he was saying all the things about her that he did, because he was a disappointed suitor. This, according to Ingersoll, was laughingly untrue. "My 'case' against Clare was always an open one," he maintains. "She is not and never has been an adult woman and thus cannot be engaged with, pro or con, as such. For my money, she has always been a fascinating text book case of arrested development—the arrested emotional development of a precociously bright female child at or about early puberty. After her emotional nature developed to that point, her body continued to round out the form of a beautiful woman and her superior brain continued to store the purely factual content of life. But this she has never really understood. She has registered life only as does a child who observes everything—including her own effect on the people around her—but is unchanged by it because she is unaffected emotionally. . . . It is my position that one cannot—*I* cannot—truly engage emotionally with such a phenomenon and I never tried. Which may account for my singular lack of success in dealing with her."

The story of Henry Luce's prolonged courtship of Clare Brokaw and their eventual marriage and what it did to Time Inc. has been told elsewhere in detail, down to the internal dilemma in *Time*'s theater department over how to review Clare Boothe Luce's first play, *Abide With Me*, which opened on Broadway at about the time of their marriage. Mrs. Luce, of course, went on to become "one of America's most famous and controversial women," as a biography dust jacket announced—"playwright, actress, congresswoman, ambassador, friend or enemy of almost everyone worth knowing in our times." But her most immediate impact on Time Inc. was to make one of the most dedicated, hardworking editors in

New York, Henry Luce, a virtual stranger to the staffs of the magazines he loved so much—and that story has not been told in full. Others, of course, knew about, and have reported on, Luce's trancelike conduct in those days. As biographer W. A. Swanberg reported, *Time* editor John Shaw Billings remarked: "I'd go for weeks at a time during this domestic interlude without seeing him or hearing from him. At times, I'd find him listless or blue, as if he were sick."

But Billings probably did not learn until later what was causing Luce's turmoil, because for months only MacLeish and Ingersoll knew that this "domestic interlude" was in fact, the ugly breakup of his marriage. Gradually rumors were confirmed, and the word got around, but there was a prolonged period of near-total chaos when the top executives of Time Inc., were trying desperately and unsuccessfully to reach Luce and his secretary. "Within months," says Ingersoll, "*Time*'s once model organization was beginning to go to pieces. Star performers turned temperamental; they felt that God mustn't love them because God no longer answered his telephone—or cut them cold when they chanced to run into him in the elevator. Editors began feuding with advertising managers; business managers responsible for budgets began snapping at both. As the M.E. of only one show, I found that coordinating my work with the rest of the organization was becoming impossible."

The way the company was organized then, the managing editors and the advertising, circulation, and production directors of *Time*, *Fortune*, and *Architectural Forum* (which the company had bought in 1932) reported directly to Luce. The company had never really been organized as a modern corporation, a subject on which the managing editor of *Fortune* was now an expert. And unlike the other executives of Time Inc., Ingersoll not only knew what was preoccupying Luce but understood that the situation would probably persist for some time. He felt that something had to be done to save the company, and he thought he had the answer: Luce should reorganize the operation, appointing individual publishers for each magazine, who, in turn, would report to a general manager, responsible to Luce but free to make decisions in his absence.

In Ingersoll's view, there could be only one man for the number-two job: Roy Larsen, *Time*'s original circulation manager. Larsen was now running the movie feature *March of Time*, the first reel of which was shown at the Capital Theater on Broadway the same month Ingersoll's burlesque article appeared in *Fortune*. Although the conventional wisdom is that Ingersoll was bucking for the number-two job, and in doing so was knifing Larsen in the back, that is not the case. Ingersoll later became a master of internal political warfare waged quietly at lunch or openly in a broadside of memos fired from his huge corner office in the new Time-Life Building in Rockefeller Plaza. But in 1935 he was concerned primarily with *Fortune*, which he considered his magazine and which he believed to be threatened by Henry Luce. Consequently, if he had an ulterior motive in urging Luce to appoint a publisher of *Fortune* in 1935, it was to give him (Ingersoll) a freer hand with his magazine. His first candidate for the job of *Fortune* publisher was himself, although he envisioned an organization that would enable him to continue as managing editor, which he conceded would be difficult. The alternative would be to recommend a publisher whom he thought he could control, someone like P. I. Prentice, then *Fortune*'s business manager. Prentice had joined *Fortune*'s staff about the same time Ingersoll had—another friend of Luce's from school and a former staff member of the *Yale Daily News*.

As the paralyzing situation dragged on into the summer of 1935, Ingersoll sweated over tactics: How could he persuade Luce that he had to do something? "He was quite happy to talk with me any time," recalls Ingersoll, "about Clare, Lila, Lila's god-damn lawyers and the institution of divorce in general. But his eyes went blank whenever I mentioned anything to do with such trivia as the production of a magazine called *Fortune*."

Finally, one hot August morning, Ingersoll made his move: When Luce's secretary Corinne Thrasher signaled to Ingersoll that Luce had come in to pick up his mail, Ingersoll marched into his boss's office and said, "Get your hat and come with me."

The command was so abrupt that Luce didn't question it. He got up from behind his desk, followed Ingersoll meekly out and down the elevator and over to Park Avenue before he asked in bewilderment, "Where are we going, Mac?"

"To the Racquet Club" was all Ingersoll said. They were both members of the Racquet, and Ingersoll knew that its big card room on the southwest corner of Fifty-second and Park would, at eleven A.M., be deserted and totally private. Once they were seated in comfortable club chairs at a window overlooking the avenue, the dialogue was rapid and to the point. Ingersoll recalls it went something like this:

"Mac! What's this all about?"

"It's about what you're doing to the company," and Ingersoll proceeded to review all that had happened as a result of Luce's neglect.

"Okay, so what do I do about it?" asked Luce.

"Appoint a general manager and tell him how you want your company run when you're not there."

"Okay," Luce replied abruptly and without counter argument. "Who?"

Ingersoll maintains that even though Luce agreed with him about the need to appoint a general manager, he (Ingersoll) had not thought he would be asked to suggest the man. There was, however, only one qualified candidate and that was Larsen. So Ingersoll said, "Roy."

Luce's abrupt reply stunned Ingersoll: "No!"

There was a sudden silence. Ingersoll had no idea why Luce had rejected Larsen, but he could speculate: He knew the office gossip about Luce being annoyed when Larsen moved from the Chrysler Building to set up a separate *March of Time* office at Tenth Avenue and Fifty-fourth Street, and had heard hints of Luce's being more than a little jealous that *MOT* seemed to be considered more a Larsen success than a Time Inc. achievement. Furthermore, Larsen and his wife were both old friends of Lila's and might be expected to side with her in the current divorce proceedings.

If Ingersoll did not know the reason for Luce's response, he did not have time to speculate. Luce's next reaction came as even more of a shock. Suddenly sitting upright, he leaned forward and pointed his finger within an inch of Ingersoll's nose: "You!" he barked.*

Then, as Ingersoll recalls, Luce was suddenly on his feet; the conversation was over. He motioned Ingersoll to follow him back to the Chrysler Building, and Ingersoll never had a chance to propose his idea of having individual publishers for each magazine, which Luce later initiated.

Back in the office, Luce made no mention of the conversation, and Ingersoll says he didn't really believe he had been promoted until he read it in the *Times* the next morning. Luce had sent out a press release without showing it to Ingersoll, then felt compelled to apologize for some minor errors in the release: "I will take responsibility for big mistakes," Luce memoed Ingersoll. "If the company is ruined it's my fault. But I'll be goddamned if I will take responsibility for detailed mistakes, however attributable they may be to me. . . . What the hell are junior executives for?"

Luce decided that before Ingersoll assumed his new responsibilities, there was one more chore he had to undertake for *Fortune*. October was an important month for the magazine, the first of three when the bulk of *Fortune*'s subscriptions would be up for renewal. Luce wanted the October issue to be memorable, and he wanted to have at least one big, smashing article to carry it. One of Ingersoll's first assignments at *Fortune* had been to write the captions for a photographic essay by Eric Salomon on San Simeon, William Randolph Hearst's estate. Luce had liked the piece and now thought it was time for a major corporation story on Hearst and his empire, which was rumored to be having financial problems. Obviously Ingersoll was the man to do Hearst; it was his kind of story, and furthermore, he had once worked for a Hearst paper.

When Ingersoll arrived in San Francisco, the first man he sought out was a young Hearst lieutenant named Bartley Crum who, by one of those odd turn of events, would one day succeed Ingersoll as publisher of the newspaper he would start. Crum, in turn, introduced him to John Francis Neylan, a lawyer who had recently been hired by Hearst to untangle his tangled financial empire. And once again it was Ralph McAllister Ingersoll's name that helped him open the door. Not only was McAllister a big name in San Francisco, but Ingersoll was staying with his cousin Elliot McAllister, who was a very prominent San Franciscan about to become president of the Bank of California. McAllister lived

---

*According to the official history of Time Inc. by Robert Elson, Luce agreed that it was Ingersoll who had proposed a general manager, but said Ingersoll had suggested Ingersoll, rather than Larsen, as the man for the job. Ingersoll insists that that was not the case, that his version, told above, is correct. Later Larsen was vindicated by being named chairman of the executive committee of Time Inc. And one former Time Inc. executive says that Luce was so sensitive about what he had done to Larsen by promoting Ingersoll over him, that he tried in later years to make it up to him. Still another former Time Inc. staffer says that, in fact, Larsen played a critical role in Ingersoll's promotion: "He was at the *March of Time* then and bored with routine business affairs. He endorsed Ingersoll because he thought he could handle company affairs which liberated Larsen for other things."

in exclusive Woodside, and living next to him in the rather snobbish neighborhood was a newcomer who was having a difficult time getting himself invited into the community; his name was John Francis Neylan, and when Ingersoll, in his first interview at the Hearst office, told Neylan where he was staying, Neylan suddenly became cooperative.

The result was that Ingersoll was introduced to everyone and treated royally—even by Hearst himself (despite his lifelong feud with Time Inc.)—on a weekend at the publisher's hideout, Wyntoon, in northern California. Ingersoll had done his homework, and even before Neyland opened the doors, his head was full of facts and figures about Hearst's operation. There were, however, some critical missing links. He finally maneuvered Neylan into promising to fill the gaps and knew that, as a matter of honor, Neylan would have to produce; but he also knew that because of the nature of the figures and Hearst's instinctive secretiveness, Neylan would try to find a way to welsh on his promise. How would he do it?

The answer came one morning when Neylan called Ingersoll and said he would pick him up at nine A.M. and drive him to San Francisco on the first leg of his trip to Wyntoon. As the chauffeur-driven limousine took off at seventy miles an hour for the half-hour drive and the two men settled comfortably into the backseat, Neylan immediately began reeling off the figures he had promised. It was a neat trick: Ingersoll was unable to take notes because he was being told what he needed to know in a car traveling seventy miles an hour along a congested freeway.

But Neylan did not understand a peculiar quirk of Ingersoll's mind. When highly concentrated, his memory is superb; and when he can recall something—anything—that will suggest the general theme of what he is trying to remember, his mind works almost like a tape recorder on playback. After they reached Neylan's office, Ingersoll declined the chauffeur's offer to drive him to his next destination. Instead, he walked immediately to a nearby drugstore, sat down at the counter, and wrote out, almost verbatim, the entire twenty-five-minute recital given by Neylan on the drive from Woodside.

That was how Ingersoll "got the story," as they say in the trade. Hence, he was very pleased with himself and understandably euphoric as he boarded the DC-3 for the return flight to New York: He knew that he had a good story for his *Fortune* finale, and that he would be returning to exciting new challenges as general manager of one of the most prestigious and successful editorial operations in the country. It was Ingersoll's nature to be optimistic, and in his opinion, "euphoria is intensified optimism," therefore a state he entered into easily and often. "I can float up into euphoria without any awareness of the change," he says. He was mentally and literally floating up in the clouds on the trip back to New York, and therefore more than receptive to a chance meeting provided by a dust storm around Albuquerque, New Mexico, where the DC-2 was forced to land. He was walking on the tarmac between the plane and the hangar, his natural euphoria heightened by the champagne he had bought to celebrate a job well done; the champagne also intensified the alternating green-and-white beacon lights illuminating a young lady with blonde hair and a face, well, not especially pretty but very interesting. He asked her if the delay annoyed her, and she said:

"Not particularly; I'm on my way home from Hollywood."

Ingersoll said he was too, and asked what she had been doing there. "I'm a playwright," she replied.

"Oh, have you written any plays?"

"One. *The Children's Hour*."

Her name, of course, was Lillian Hellman, and when Ingersoll admitted that he had not heard of her or *The Children's Hour*, which had been running on Broadway since the previous fall and had created quite a sensation, she was clearly annoyed. On her part, she had never heard of Ralph McAllister Ingersoll, former managing editor of the *New Yorker*, managing editor of *Fortune*, and rising star in the Luce firmament. These two giant egos had a lot to talk about.

In the hangar they learned that they would have to spend the night in Albuquerque, so they took the bus into town to a hotel provided by the airline. While waiting for room assignments, they settled down in the restaurant to tell each other the story of their lives and what they were doing at the time—which in Hellman's case was writing screenplays for Samuel Goldwyn. In collaboration with Mordaunt Shairp, she had just finished working on *Dark Angel*, starring Fredric March and Merle Oberon, and the film was scheduled to be released the next month. She had two ongoing projects: a movie based on *The Children's Hour* and another play (to be called *Days to Come*). Ingersoll told her about the *New Yorker*, his efforts to write a novel, *Fortune*, and his rise at Time Inc., going into some detail about his last assignment for *Fortune*—the story on Hearst and his newspapers. Ingersoll always was an enthusiastic and rather loud conversationalist, and seated at the next table was Bernard Gimbel, proprietor of a New York department store. He could not help overhearing every word the boisterous Ingersoll said, and when the couple left the table, Gimbel got up and went immediately to a phone to call his associate in New York, instructing him to make a bid the next morning to acquire Hearst's fabulous art collection for Gimbel's, where it would then be sold. He had deduced from Ingersoll's conversation that Hearst was in such financial trouble that he would be receptive to an offer.*

Where Ingersoll and Hellman had gone, simply and without discussion, was up to her room, the number of which had just been announced over the loudspeaker. "We were starting to fall in love," says Ingersoll, "the violent physical part, and we simply took it for granted." So intense was this physical attraction that only when one of them noticed a face watching in open-mouthed wonder as they made love did they realize they had forgotten to close the hotel-room door.

*Gimbel told Ingersoll the story when the two men met years later.

Miss Hellman was at the time divorced from her husband, Arthur Kober, but was very much involved with Dashiell Hammett, although at that moment making one of several unsuccessful attempts to establish her independence. Tommy Ingersoll was enjoying one of her recurring periods of good health, so good, in fact, that she had been permitted to participate in an amateur theatrical production in Lakeville. "But by morning," Ingersoll says, "I knew I was in love and that I had no choice but to leave my wife for Lillian. Living an emotionally unfaithful life with Tommy was unthinkable."

So, less than eight months after the night Luce astounded Ingersoll by telling him he had fallen suddenly and hopelessly in love with Clare Brokaw, the general manager had gone out and done the same thing. Luce had still not obtained his divorce, which meant that in late 1935 the two top officers of Time Inc. were involved in messy, unsettling marital wars—just as the company was heading for its most tumultuous period. In the trying years ahead his Camelot at *Fortune* would, indeed, seem to Ingersoll to have been an all-too-brief shining moment.

General Manager of Time Inc. in Havana in 1935 to meet with his boss, who is on his honeymoon

7: What Happens When the Boss Takes Your *Life*?

In his press release announcing the appointment of Ralph Ingersoll as general manager of Time Inc., Luce stressed that his man was "largely responsible for the development of the scope, efficiency and literary standards of *Fortune*'s editorial organization," at the same time proving "himself to be one of those few able journalists who know business." There can be little doubt that in 1935 Luce had the utmost confidence in Ingersoll as an executive and editor. He advised Time Inc.'s board that, although the job of general manager would be "experimental," Ingersoll would be an "admirable choice." And he once told P. I. Prentice that Ingersoll was the only man on the payroll who "had publisher potential." Unfortunately, Luce was one of the few—if not the only executive—in the upper reaches of the Chrysler Building who saw Ingersoll that way. *Time* managing editor John Shaw Billings (who endorsed the appointment only after Luce assured him that Ingersoll would not interfere in editorial matters) said that when word spread around the building, "a great groan went up from the back benches"—which Ingersoll says was an understatement: "It wasn't a groan, it was a roar of anguish."

Ingersoll was, in fact, the prototype of the flamboyant, confident, and ambitious personality whose name could always be counted on to pick up a flagging office conversation. And it was not just his egocentricities—the mounted and proudly displayed sailfish; the office ant palace, introduced, says Wolcott Gibbs, "for study and emulation of employees," the camera hidden in a bookcase behind his desk to take candid snapshots of visiting dignitaries and staffers; his continuing "memo marathon," as one staffer put it; his famous hypochondria. A quick look through the company archives confirms that Ingersoll was not the only prolific Time Inc. memo writer, and after all, he did have a wife with infectious tuberculosis (which was something to worry about) and had once suffered from ulcers (which needed medication). More annoying was his impatience with anyone who was not so intensely devoted to achieving the objective at hand as he was. He could be insulting, abrasive, mean, and rude when dissatisfied with someone's performance; his mournful eyes "could freeze into a choleric stare," as a colleague says, when he disapproved. But his voice would often hold a "note of near apology," as one of his severest critics put it, which could be very attractive. And his secretary, Veronica Keating, says she always thought of her boss as being well liked and respected around the office. He would, however, resort to almost any strategy to achieve his goals, including the manipulation of other executives. Of Ingersoll's appointment, Eric Hodgins has said, "If a date could be set for the regrettable beginning of office politics in Time Inc. this was it."

But it takes two—or more—to politick, and in 1935 Time Inc. was primed for office politicking. In the twelve years since *Time* had been launched, Luce had hired a staff of extremely bright, talented, ambitious young men on the rise—now suddenly he disappeared into his personal life, leaving them in the hands of one of their peers. Ingersoll, trying some years later to describe what it had been like taking over Time Inc. said, "It felt as you would feel if a tamer of tigers handed you his chair and pushed you into the cage in which he kept half-tamed tigers, with the casual remark: 'Now, take over, boy.'" Probably the only man who could have tamed the tigers at Time Inc. during Luce's absence in 1935 and 1936 was Roy Larsen, and it is not certain that even the veteran Larsen could have handled the jealous, ambitious cats Luce had assembled in his cage on Forty-second Street. Most of the executives at Time Inc. agreed that Ingersoll was a good editor and had made *Fortune* a huge success. But envy can be a major factor in office rivalry and conspiracy.

Although bringing Ingersoll into the company to be managing editor of *Fortune* was one of Luce's most brilliant, intuitive moves, making him general manager in late 1935 was something less than inspired—and not just because Ingersoll's talents are primarily creative and editorial rather than managerial. At the time of the Ingersoll appointment the company was headed for its most difficult and tumultuous years; it would face serious problems made even worse by Luce's sudden distraction and preoccupation with personal affairs. Externally, the New Deal was forcing people to take sides between labor and capital, a regulated welfare state and a laissez-faire economy; in Europe Adolf Hitler's aggressions and the Spanish civil war were bringing to a head the basic conflict between fascism and communism that would lead to World War II, and the debate about communism that would drag on into the early 1950s. Internally, the intellectuals on Luce's magazines were caught up in these conflicts, and feuding between traditionally conservative *Time* writers and the more-often-than-not liberal *Fortune* writers would become intense and, at times, open. In addition, *Time* was coming under increasing fire for its flippant, smart-alecky style (which would culminate in the devastating 1936 *New Yorker* profile of Luce), and the company would soon be threatened with bankruptcy because of the surprising success of a new magazine. There would be times when Ingersoll seemed to be at the center of a hurricane—obviously not entirely of his own making. The only peaceful hours he would have during his tenure as general manager came in the first few weeks (after his return from the Hearst assignment). As he remembers that time: "I enjoyed the peace and tranquility of my new tower office, pacing back and forth trying to think out what I was doing there at all."

* * *

Ingersoll did not see Luce for a few days after his appointment, then one morning Luce appeared, in a good mood and seemingly at ease. He even had the mind for a little joke: "Mac, you're the boss now and your first decision's going to be your hardest. It's how much to pay yourself." Then Luce waited, grinning. But when Ingersoll said nothing and was obviously confused, Luce went on: "When you're boss you have to keep your salary down—because it's the lid on everybody else's salary. That's the way life is when you're the boss." Then he added sheepishly, "I pay myself fifty thousand dollars, Mac." Ingersoll set the new general manager's pay at a discreet forty-five thousand dollars, a fifteen-thousand-dollar increase over what he had been making at *Fortune*.

Luce's personal turmoil did not abate for some months. But he finally married Clare Brokaw on November 23, 1935, after which the newlyweds enjoyed a long honeymoon in Cuba. Ingersoll's personal travail was just beginning. Aware of his own emotional makeup, he had always known that if he was ever to become involved with a woman in his own walk of life, he would fall hopelessly in love and want a divorce from Tommy. And that is exactly what happened on the night he met Lillian Hellman, although his total commitment to Lillian came, perhaps, even faster than he would have imagined. "My falling in love," said Ingersoll many years later, "had caught me totally unprepared to make a sound decision between gratifying what every fibre of me seemed to demand—fulfilling my love for Lillian—and serving my need to care for Tommy. Both were masters whom I could not betray—so I ended by betraying both."

At first, it looked as if the conflict would be resolved in a civilized and painless manner. In the late summer of 1935 Tommy was—for the first time in their married life—in good health. When Ingersoll told her that he had fallen in love with another woman, she was sad but understanding, asking only that he not insist on her going to Reno until a little time had passed—time for him to make sure of his feelings for Lillian. Ingersoll agreed, but in a matter of weeks Tommy became an invalid again, with sudden new lesions on her lungs. Ingersoll, of course, could not bring himself to leave a dying woman of whom he was deeply fond. He had to tell Lillian the truth.

Then, as Ingersoll puts it, the second miracle happened. "I was only a few weeks back with Tommy, when she was pronounced cured again, with the healing just as plain in the X rays as the lesions had been! The irrefutable evidence bewildered the TB specialists as much as they bewildered me."

When she had recovered, he talked a somewhat skeptical Lillian into having him back and told Tommy, again, that he wanted a divorce.

Lillian was now living in a duplex apartment at 14 East Seventh Street, which Ingersoll remembers as having prints of early Picassos and a grand piano in the living room. George Gershwin used to play for assembled guests who considered it boring when his melodies drowned out their wisecracks. "That room," Ingersoll recalls, "was often filled with contemporary celebrities of the theater, to whom I must have seemed a Philistine, coming with such self-assurance from the world of Time Incorporated. I was amused, once, to overhear Lillian making a passionate defense of me to some one of them who was questioning my right to be present."

Ingersoll's recollections of Lillian are fond ones: "She had wit—not the quotable kind, like our friend Dotty Parker's, but subtler. She brought people out when she felt like it, with teasing provocativeness. And the rages into which she could be worked with the drop of a cliché had a comic quality which kept them from being frightening—she was so small, and so intense and she cherished her femininity so passionately. If she made you angry, she would not let you stay angry (unless she wanted to) but would be flirting again within moments. At the time, she seemed to me like a little girl pretending at being a serious woman but always asking you to remember that she was only pretending.

"The most buoyant of all the memories I have of Lillian's personality is of a woman with strong, rugged-handsome features, testifying to strength of will and precision of mind who, to herself, was nothing of the sort, being (who could question it) a delicate Princess, almost fluttery feminine. The contrast between such obvious fact and clearly played-out fantasy was the essence of a charm that was thereby made uniquely disconcerting—and to me, engaging."

His romance with Lillian Hellman was at its peak during the winter of 1935 and 1936—when Luce was marrying, and then honeymooning with, Clare. When Lillian went back to Hollywood to work on the movie *These Three*, they had a romantic rendezvous in the New Mexican desert where they had met. Once, he flew all the way to the coast and they drove through heavy fog to the top of the mountain that cradled Lake Arrowhead; and together they flew to Cuba for a fishing trip. Ingersoll also says that Hellman once told him she had secretly aborted his child. He did not believe it and remembers arguing violently at the time that he could not have a child, which is what the doctor had told him. Years later, long after he had learned he was capable of having children, he still did not believe her.

Although idyllic while it lasted, the Ingersoll-Hellman romance was doomed, primarily, says Ingersoll, because in the end he had his commitment to Tommy, and Hellman herself was really in love with and devoted to Dashiell Hammett. When Ingersoll returned to Lillian, Tommy's lesions returned and Ingersoll had to postpone his divorce again. Lillian became suspicious, deciding he was using Tommy's health to avoid entanglement and marriage; but Ingersoll saw it differently: "I was," he said, "the helpless victim of a neurosis [Tommy's] of which I was totally unconscious."

The neurosis was apparently quite cunning: When Ingersoll returned to Tommy, the lesions healed and she regained her health. When Ingersoll went back to Lillian (as he did do several times), Tommy's lesions reappeared. And eventually Ingersoll's ulcer returned, which not only made his life even more miserable but frightened him as well. So he broke the engagement with Lillian and told Tommy he wanted a divorce, not to marry Lillian Hellman but to gain his freedom. And this, according to Ingersoll, produced another miracle: An enduring cure for Tommy. If he was not leaving her for another woman, she could accept a divorce without its activating her tuberculosis. Ingersoll agreed to give Tommy ten thousand dollars a year and, when her health permitted, to set her up in the literary agency she operated for many years before her death in 1964.

By the summer of 1936 Dashiell Hammett had returned to Lillian's life, and she was renting a house on Tavern Island in Long Island Sound and working on another play, *Days to Come*. Ingersoll did not, however, stop seeing Lillian after their engagement was broken, and there was a period during which Hammett and Ingersoll were both involved with her, although Ingersoll insists he did not get to know Hammett well—then, or ever: "I knew Dash only as a rival for Lillian's commitment—with whom I could not compete because he wouldn't. I also knew him as a rival who raised in me no resentment, no hostility. He was too totally detached on the level of personal emotions. How he could have been so totally involved, as he was once assumed to be, in politics I don't understand. I can't see him taking orders that went against his grain—as the Communist party's must have. Years later, I was accused of having been under his leftish influence. What utter nonsense. I didn't even know whether he leaned left or right when I was slugging it out with Lillian."

Although Miss Hellman clearly loved Hammett, Ingersoll obviously ignited some kind of spark that kindled an intense attraction between them, even when they were raging mad in their own "private debating society," as Ingersoll described their relationship. Years later he said he fully appreciated Hammett's remark, quoted in Hellman's *An Unfinished Woman*: "All I ever wanted was a docile woman and look what I got."

Ingersoll and Hellman were both given to strong opinions and were very emotional in expressing them. The year 1936 was the beginning of the Spanish civil war; fascism was spreading in Europe; Hitler was on the rise; and the Communists were emerging as the only group seemingly willing to resist the Fascists anywhere. Socialism was in the air, and communism was not only accepted as a fact of life by most of the country's intellectuals but preferred by some to democratic capitalism, which could not solve its own economic problems and seemed all too willing to compromise with the Fascists. Hence, much of the debating during the brief and stormy romance concerned values, ideology, and what was wrong with capitalism and the world.* Ingersoll recalls Lillian screaming virtually one whole night that he was "an anti-Semitic son of a bitch," and he remembers another "slugging match" in which she listed all the sins of capitalism and socialism but said these were the only two choices available.

This enraged Ingersoll: "God damn it, no!"

"How can you say that," Hellman fired back in anger. "If there is no social system in which you can believe—"

"Then I'll invent one," he interrupted.

The angry debates finally culminated in the weekend (described in chapter one) Ingersoll spent at Lillian's place on Tavern Island when he vowed to *"show her!"* It was with Lillian Hellman that the political education of Ralph McAllister Ingersoll, begun by Archibald MacLeish and the intellectuals on *Fortune*, was made complete. He insists, years later, that *PM* grew out of his desire to show Lillian Hellman what he could do as an editor and, at the same time, to invent a social system that would take the best of capitalism and communism, while avoiding their faults. This passage in his much-quoted *PM* prospectus he attributes directly to the emotional and intellectual stimulus provided by Lillian Hellman: "We do not believe all mankind's problems are soluble in any existing social order, certainly not our own, and we propose to applaud those who seek constructively to improve the way men live together."

"It was Lillian," he says, "who shook me out of a monolithic complacency in what is now portentously called the 'value content of life.' It was her challenge to my values that left me no choice but to inquire into them. What debt I am in to her!"

Even after the island incident, they continued fighting, vowing never to see each other again, then getting back together. Once, Ingersoll says, he called Lillian and said, "Let's take a bisque."

"What's that?" said Lillian.

"A golf term. You get a free stroke that doesn't count in your score." Hellman got to laughing so hard she could hardly talk, but finally she said, "OK, let's take a bisque."

Ingersoll had invested five thousand dollars in her new play, and as the opening night approached, plans were made for a big party in his new "Kubla

---

*Ms. Hellman, because of ill health, her secretary said, declined to grant me an interview about her affair with Ingersoll. She also said virtually nothing about him in her autobiographical writings, so this account is essentially Ingersoll's. I had planned to send her the first draft of these pages, but she died before I could do so.

Khan apartment," as he called it, at 1035 Fifth Avenue. After he had formally separated from Tommy, Ingersoll decided he needed a grand bachelor's establishment befitting his new station as general manager of Time Inc. All the furniture and interior decor were designed by and built to order for an old girl friend—Eleanor Peabody, now married to Harding Scholle, the director of the Museum of the City of New York.

The living room, with windows overlooking Central Park, was done in three shades of gray. Mirrors ran along the walls beneath the windows; the window boxes contained living greens that blended with the green of the park beyond. The mantel over the fireplace was of molded glass, set against a mirrored wall. On either side were tall sconces made of leaves of opaque glass, with tapering blades delicately echoing the shapes of the live leaves in the window boxes. The centerpiece of the room was a great soft dark-gray rug on which rested a colossal sofa and groupings of chairs, comfortable to sit on and simple to look at—all in a medium-gray material that seemed rough surfaced but was in fact soft to the touch. The walls were light gray. In the dining room stood a striking rectangular table for ten made of jet-black Bakelite with copper-stripped edges. The straight-backed, straight-legged chairs were also jet black, except for their upholstered seats. Opening off the sweeping entrance was the most dramatic room, originally designed as a library. Ingersoll had planned, of course, to entertain people from Time Inc. as well as others in the corporate and communications worlds in which he traveled. He told Eleanor to put a bar in this room, a large one he could stand behind, because he liked talking with people at a bar. Eleanor's response was a room of cork and copper: cork floor and ceiling, with a high copper-sheathed bar across one corner in front of which were high padded stools with copper legs. There were also armless sofas and an overstuffed chair or two upholstered in a dark cocoa-bean material. The floor lamps were tall and substantial pillars of copper, with big shades that cast warm light. The whole apartment was a bachelor's dream, especially the bedroom, which contained a bed seven feet square opposite a wall of mirrors with windows overlooking the park and facing south toward the Plaza Hotel's romantic shimmer of lights. The carpeting was barefoot soft and wall to wall.

December 15, 1936, opening night at the Vanderbilt Theater for Hellman's new play, was also opening night for Ingersoll's grand apartment. And it was a disaster. *Days to Come* was about strikers and strikebreaking in a factory in a small town two hundred miles from Cleveland. It had a good cast, starring William Harrigan and Florence Eldridge, and the script was marked, as one critic put it, by the "burning intensity of her [Hellman's] utterance." Going into rehearsal, everyone, including Ingersoll and, more important, Hammett, thought it was going to be a hit. However, at the end of the first act, when William Randolph Hearst and his party of ten walked out, the play was obviously in trouble. Lillian, to ease the pain, had sent the doorman out for something to drink; later, when she had severe stomach cramps, she discovered he had bought a bottle of ninety-four-cent brandy. The critics tried to be sympathetic, but they could not help asking what the play was about. It closed in a week.

At the Ingersoll party after the show, Fanny Brice saved the night. She was the first to arrive, and after stretching herself out on the elegant sofa in the living room, she kicked off her shoes and took over. "By the time Lillian arrived," Ingersoll says, "two hours later, and alone—the party was in full swing, producer, cast and company well anesthetized. She stormed past them all and down tha hall and into my deserted bedroom, slamming, and locking, the door behind her. It was a graceful gesture. Who knew what to say to her in her agony."

Lillian stayed in the bedroom for over an hour, obviously not wanting to face the guests, especially while suffering from the effects of the cheap brandy— on top of which she had obviously added more alcohol. Ingersoll was beginning to worry when Lillian appeared in the doorway of the cork-and-copper barroom. The host was at his customary post, and Hammett, seated in front of the bar with his legs outstretched, was surrounded by guests who hung on his every word. Lillian pushed through the circle of admirers and stood over Hammett, finally blurting out, "You son of a bitch, you said it was good!"

Hammett took his time responding, then said, "OK, I did. I've changed my mind."

Ingersoll continued to see Lillian, even after that night, but by then he was involved in an affair with another woman that, if anything, was even more emotional and disconcerting than his romance with Lillian—and that would eventually lead to him to seek psychiatric help. He was also very much caught up in the turmoil at Time Inc. By now the event had occurred that marked the beginning of his parting with Luce—although perhaps the break was inevitable. After Hellman, Ingersoll was a man in search of new ways to reform not only the press but society—at a time when Luce was well on the way to developing his belief in a century dominated and saved by American capitalism.

* * *

In the immediate aftermath of Ingersoll's surprising appointment as general manager, it appeared that the company might be headed for a more productive, tranquil era. The idea of having business managers and managing editors reporting to Ingersoll, who, in turn, reported to Luce, worked so well that there were days when Ingersoll did not have much more to do than "sit back and admire Harry's judgment in picking men."

Harry's men, especially the editors, did not like having to report to Ingersoll but seemed to accept the arrangement as long as Ingersoll kept his nose out of their business. The only executive not reporting to Ingersoll was Roy Larsen, who was across town running "March of Time." There was no friction there; Ingersoll had immediately told Larsen that he should have had the new job and that he had recommended him to Luce, and the two men remained friends.

During this time Ingersoll also had time to develop his specialty: memorandum writing. In one marathon performance (the week before Luce's wedding) he fired off, in succession, three long memoranda. The first argued that *Time*'s "Business" department, if reorganized properly, could put *Business Week* out of business by telling the businessman everything he wanted to know about business each week and "pickling these answers in the *Time* acid bath." The second urged that no limit be placed on advertising in *Fortune*, even if it meant two-hundred-page issues (which some feared), making it impossible for the readers to hold the magazine in their hands. They should set it on a table for reading. "In the history of American publishing," said Ingersoll, "we have yet to find record of a publication dead—or even made ill by—too much advertising." (It should be noted, in light of what happened later, that Ralph Ingersoll was never really opposed to advertising.) And the third was a long report on *Fortune*'s art, which Luce had requested, and here Ingersoll revealed what was really on his mind, namely, photographs. The report included a summary of *Fortune*'s pioneering work in candid and color photography and argued that Time Inc. magazines had a real opportunity to develop photojournalism, although Ingersoll was aware that because of their established format (especially *Fortune*'s) there was a limit to how far they could go.

With the company's machinery, at least for the moment, running smoothly and profitably, Ingersoll had, for the first time in his journalistic career, the freedom to do some abstract thinking. And it is apparent from the memos quoted above what was preoccupying him. His line of thought was triggered by the hints already beginning to float through the trade that the *Literary Digest*, which had dominated public-affairs magazines in the 1920s, was in trouble, primarily because of the success of *Time*. The *Digest*'s formula was to run excerpts and quotes from people and other publications about things happening in the news; *Time*'s formula was to repackage the news—a brilliant, original idea, Ingersoll agreed, but was it the *ultimate* formula? Could not another idea come along to make *Time* obsolete, as *Time* had made the *Digest* obsolete?

Obviously the answer was yes. But what would the new formula be? Whatever it was, Ingersoll thought it was his responsibility, as general manager, and as perhaps the only top executive in the company with the leisure to think about the future, to make sure Time Inc. would be the publisher to introduce it. And it did not take much pacing back and forth to come up with the answer; it was right under his nose: The next idea to challenge *Time* would be a picture magazine.

It was, of course, not exactly an original notion. One of his *Fortune* staffers, Dwight Macdonald, had been part of a team (the other members were John Martin, temporarily relieved of his post as managing editor of *Time*, and a researcher named Natasha von Hoershelman) created by Luce in 1933 to look into the potential for a picture magazine. This Experimental Department, as it was called, produced several dummies, the third of which had excited Ingersoll, although it had left most Time Inc. executives cold. After being shown "Dummy

No. 3," he wrote Luce, "I am sold now"—not on a magazine designed for a sophisticated audience (like *Time*) or for a specialized audience (like *Fortune*), but on one designed for a mass audience—"the gum chewers," as he called them. After analyzing the dummy and criticizing parts he felt were "going smack-bang over a great many heads," he concluded: "I feel strongly that you have a magazine now. If a dummy as good as this can be produced three fortnights in succession, buy *Time* stock."

Luce, however, was still not persuaded, and after a little less than a year the project was abandoned because he decided that "the thinking and creative imagination had run into a dead-end. I was very dissatisfied with the whole procedure," he said later; "we just got off on the wrong track." As for photography, Luce felt the company should puts its creative efforts into transforming the radio version of "March of Time" into film.

But the idea of a picture magazine would not go away. "You would go to '21' and places like that," said Luce, "and people would buttonhole you and tell you what a natural it was." And Time Inc. was not the only publisher exploring the idea. In 1934, Ingersoll learned, H. E. North, the public relations director for A&P, had proposed that his company publish a picture magazine. And as early as 1931 Clare Brokaw, who was then an editor at *Vanity Fair*, had suggested that Condé Nast buy the failing humor magazine *Life* and remake it along the lines of the Parisian *Vu*: "It would be a weekly and would contain some of the editorial elements of *Time*, *Fortune* and even *Vanity Fair*, plus its own special angle . . . reporting . . . the most interesting and exciting news in photographs and interpreting it editorially through accompanying articles."

She had also discussed the magazine with Luce in their courtship days, and after first resisting the idea, he began to hint that if she married him he might start a picture magazine and make her editor. It is not exactly clear when Luce, in his own mind, finally became enthusiastic about a picture magazine, but by the time he went on his honeymoon in late November of 1935, he had at least been persuaded by Clare that the idea should be reconsidered.

The discovery that the idea for a picture magazine was everywhere in the air did not in any way discourage Ingersoll. Rather, the more he learned about how close other publishers were to publishing a picture magazine, the more he was determined "to make it happen"—his favorite phrase—at Time Inc. And after a long look at the record, it seems clear that Ralph Ingersoll was, in fact, the one primarily responsible for bringing *Life* magazine into existence. The original idea was not his, nor was he responsible for the finished product, which was eventually published on November 19, 1936; but it was Ingersoll who was the catalytic force that kept pushing everyone in the company, from Henry Luce to the "Old Bolsheviks" on *Time* and even Roy Larsen, to publish what he eventually came to call, and consider, "my magazine." But this is *not* the official version of how *Life* came into being. The conventional story has been told in varying detail by a number of sources:

• *Time Inc.*, an official history commissioned by Henry Luce and written by a Time Inc. staffer, Robert Elson;*
• Loudon Wainwright, a *Life* staffer, in a long article (from a still-unpublished book) that appeared in the May 1978 issue of the *Atlantic*;
• Clare Luce, who has given her version to a number of interviewers and biographers; and
• W. A. Swanberg in his biography *Luce and His Empire*.

All tell versions of *Life*'s creation that either play down or eliminate Ingersoll's role in its evolution, a curious omission in as much as Ingersoll, during the time it began to emerge, was virtually running the company. Considering the hostility for Ingersoll eventually developed by Clare Luce and her husband, one can safely discount her version, the official history, and perhaps Wainwright's version. One ex-Time Incer told me that before Luce died, he was talking with him at a small social gathering of the *Time* bureau in Canada and, knowing that Ingersoll had once worked for the company, happened to mention to Luce that he had just heard from Ralph Ingersoll. Luce responded with an icy stare, then said, "Never mention that name to me again"—and stalked to the other side of the room. Another time, in the 1950s, Ingersoll was having lunch with friends at the Racquet Club when someone told him that Henry Luce had been sitting about ten feet away for at least half an hour and then had gotten up and left the room without saying a word to Ingersoll. W. A. Swanberg is obviously not a partisan of Luce and his views, but, for some reason, he devoted very little space to the creation of *Life*.

The account set forth here of Ingersoll's role in the evolution of *Life* magazine is, of course, based primarily on his own story, but much of it is confirmed by research in the Time Inc. Archives, where I was given access to Ingersoll's memos and letters.† What one must keep in mind is that Luce, even after he returned from his honeymoon and resumed command of his company, did *not* remove Ingersoll as his general manager. Ingersoll retained his authority over the entire organization and could give any order he liked, subject only to a veto from Luce. "But the first six months after his return," says Ingersoll, "Harry

---

*Ingersoll states flatly that it is "inaccurate factually—and, I cannot escape the conclusion, knowingly. . . . the book is a kind of personal attack on me and the role I played during the ten most crucial years of Time Inc.'s development. . . . There are a curious mixture of the inclusion of things that aren't so, the omission of things that are, and the distortions inevitable from the writer's having to deify his hero Henry Robinson Luce who, after all, did assign him the job, and he an employee." P. I. Prentice also agrees that it is a "party line document." And Ingersoll's secretary, Veronica Keating, after rereading Elson's chapter on the creation of *Life*, agrees that it plays Ingersoll's role down to "making it almost sound like he was a casual participant. But his office was the center of everything then and he seemed to be more involved than anyone."

Elson declined to comment on Ingersoll's assessment of Time Inc.'s official history, except to say that "if he feels slighted in the creation of *Life*, so do many others." Ironically, Elson, who was a young editor in Vancouver struggling to keep a small newspaper alive at the time when Ingersoll was launching *PM*, has said, Ingersoll "was once a hero of mine."

†The archives would not, however, grant me permission to see Luce's letters to Ingersoll; these are reserved for Luce's official biographer.

was not in a vetoing mood." Ingersoll was closer to him than any man in or outside the organization, and Luce had complete confidence in him—"so much so," says Ingersoll, "that I knew instinctively that if I never backed him into a corner for a decision which he might not be prepared to make, one day my picture magazine would be a reality."

Only after Ingersoll's now famous—almost historic—confrontation with the Luces, in which he said Clare's husband could not remain on a perpetual honeymoon, did Luce resume anything approaching his old responsibilities. Ingersoll's abrupt remark may have enraged Clare, but it did have the effect of bringing her husband back into the company. Until then, any progress toward the development of a picture magazine was inspired by Ingersoll, operating on a mandate conferred on him by Luce. Finally, in mid-1936, Luce did take over its development, but his principal lieutenant continued to be Ingersoll, who was not only his general manager but the company's most enthusiastic promoter of a picture magazine.

* * *

In late 1935, when Ingersoll began seriously looking into the question of a picture magazine, there was only one other Time Inc. executive or staffer who shared his enthusiasm. Dan Longwell had been manager of trade books at Doubleday Doran, where he had edited a number of picture books. Luce had hired him in 1934, and in October of that year had made him assistant to John Shaw Billings on *Time*, with instructions "to introduce more pictures." Despite considerable resistance he had managed to increase the number and quality of pictures the magazine carried, and in the Feburary 25, 1935, issue he made a little journalistic history. In that issue *Time* had published three pages of remarkable candid photographs of President Roosevelt in his office taken by a young *Washington News* photographer named Thomas McAvoy. McAvoy had been shooting with available light, while the other photographers were using conventional equipment and kidding McAvoy: "In this light and with that box, boy, you won't get anything." McAvoy had prepared for the session by dipping his film in ammonia, making it especially sensitive. He was, of course, one of the first photographers hired for *Life*.

Ingersoll, a pioneer and champion of photojournalism even while he was still at *Fortune*, was naturally drawn to Longwell, and after he became general manager, they became good friends and Ingersoll encouraged Longwell in promoting the use of pictures, in *Time* specifically and at Time Inc. in general. In the hours he devoted to thinking about the use of pictures, he had come to the conclusion that the camera was ready for the next revolution in journalism— had, in fact, been ready for a few years years. The problem was paper and production. Good pictures needed large pages printed on coated stock, which were difficult to produce and expensive. He had convinced himself of the importance of size by taking photographs of the most gruesome Chinese beheading and the sexiest nude he could find, blowing them up and printing them on coated paper. At small newspaper size on rag paper, either could have been printed in the *New York Times* without causing too much comment; blown up and printed on coated stock, "one made you vomit and the other gave you a real thrill."

By late 1935 Ingersoll had become convinced—judging from the dozens of memos he was writing himself on the subject—that "the picture is the world's most powerful journalistic medium. The amazing fact that it has not been organized and presented [has been] almost entirely due to the mechanical limitations." Most of the mechanical problems, he felt, had now been licked (many by *Fortune*), and the time had come to start exploring ways and means of refining new techniques for producing a large magazine on coated stock, which would be devoted almost exclusively to photographs. He put some staffers quietly to work on the production problems and began talking with Longwell about the logistics of picture gathering. But for a project of this magnitude, he needed Luce's support. It would be expensive, and furthermore, most Time Inc. executives were still opposed to the idea of the company's publishing a picture magazine. Ingersoll, however, was one step ahead of them.

In December of 1935, while the Luces were honeymooning in Cuba, there were a number of things Ingersoll had to discuss with the boss—particularly the promotions and raises traditionally awarded at the end of the year. So when he was summoned, by phone, to Havana just before Christmas, he went primed to discuss the picture magazine. And when the review of the year and the raises and promotions were taken care of, Ingersoll brought up the subject that was now becoming almost an obsession. He made his case, told Luce about the exploratory moves he had made, and, in his enthusiasm, estimated that the magazine might have a circulation of one, three, even five million in three years.

Luce, in Ingersoll's words, was not buying it, but "he was giving it the old Harry try, beetle-browed and ear scratching, pacing around it. Harry was a word man and words had made his world; there wasn't enough substance in pictures to hold an audience. I guess there might be 5,000 newly taken photographs a week to choose from. 'OK, Mac, so maybe if you just took the 100 best you'd have something worth looking through in a dentist's office,' Luce said, 'but you can't make them tell stories.' 'But damn it, we've been doing just that on *Fortune*—for years,' Ingersoll argued.

"And Clare? She wasn't having Harry's argument," Ingersoll says, "and she wasn't quite sure she wanted to back me. But I do credit her with an assist that was vital. If the Empress' thumb didn't turn up, at least it stayed in her lap."

Then came Luce's final judgment, in a comment that has remained etched in Ingersoll's memory for more than forty years: "OK, Mac, go ahead and see if you can work it out. You're crazy about there being a million circulation in it; it's a hundred and fifty thousand slick paper carriage trade idea. But Time

Inc.'s rich enough now to afford a *succès d'estime*. It could be fun. Go ahead with it."

So Ingersoll returned from Cuba, not with a green light for his picture magazine, but with what he considered a cautious amber, backed by Luce's final remark: "Hell, Mac, we don't really have to burn any bridges; we can always call it off if the figures don't check out."

But Luce had been sold enough to let his key executives know that Ingersoll was operating with his complete authority. When he returned from Cuba in early February, he took Larsen, Billings, and Ingersoll to lunch in a private room at the Cloud Club to talk about the picture magazine. Larsen was doubtful and wanted more pictures in *Time*. Billings agreed with Larsen, but his attitude toward the picture magazine is unclear. His diary, however, recorded his distinct impression that Luce was for it.

Meanwhile, Ingersoll had already gone into action. As soon as he returned from a second trip to Cuba in mid-January, he had begun taking the first concrete steps to assure that Time Inc. would have a continuing flow of photographs to support the new magazine. Using *Time*'s new interest in pictures as a decoy, he quietly went around town buying up the right of first refusal to virtually all the photographs available from the picture agencies and news organizations. And it was in the process of negotiating the picture contract with Associated Press that he met a young man named Ed Stanley, who impressed him considerably and who would become the first employee he hired for his own venture. Ingersoll's success in engineering the Associated Press deal surprised him—first, because Time Inc.'s archenemy, Hearst, did not veto it; second, because Luce, who did not think much of the Associated Press, endorsed it. In fact, the only person really unhappy about the deal was Eleanor Treacy, the art editor of *Fortune*, who wrote Ingersoll a blistering memo saying he had double-crossed her and his old magazine by including *Fortune* in the deal—that is, *Fortune* photos had to be made available on a quid pro quo to the A.P.

Ingersoll responded with an apology for manipulating the deal in a clandestine manner and forgetting to tell her about it; but he also defended what he had done, concluding: "So please, Eleanor, don't go Margaret Bourke-White on me. Think these things over and just as soon as I get either (a) my health, or (b) my sanity (lost in the shuffle of these details) we will have a drink together and everything will be lovely."

Ingersoll tried to excuse his cavalier manner: "I have been carrying the details of ten or fifteen very complicated negotiations in my head for several months." This was in April. The following month, partly to restore his health, he took his secretary, Veronica Keating, with him to Shadow Rock Farm for a rest—and some memo writing. The result was a four-page single-spaced memorandum entitled "Notes on Picture Magazine," in which he pulled together all his earlier thoughts on the progress of magazine photography and offered this prediction: "Through the next decade the movement of pictures into journalism will be so rapid as possibly to revolutionize the journalistic machinery of the

In Decemer of 1935, Ingersoll went to Havana to discuss with Luce (who was on his honeymoon) the question of year-end promotions and raises for Time Inc. personnel. During most of their discussions, says Ingersoll, Luce's new wife, Clare, played on the sand with a ball. He took photographs of her and of the honeymooners running on the beach. (OPPOSITE PAGE) During his discussion with Luce, Ingersoll also brought up the idea of a picture magazine and was given the green light.

world," and Time Inc., through a magazine he called "PICTURES," would, he proclaimed, "play a leading—we hope *the* leading—part." And he still saw the picture magazine as not for the carriage trade but for a mass audience: "For the whole world . . . such pictures are for rich or poor, without regard for race, class, creed or prejudice, . . . you use one vernacular to a truck driver, another to a bank president but truck driver and bank president will stand shoulder-to-shoulder to watch a parade. . . . PICTURES' subject being the world we live in . . . plutocrat and filling station attendant will alike pay to sit in its rubber-neck wagon and ride around the world."*

When Ingersoll returned to New York, he immediately sent his memo to Luce, who made no effort to curb his general manager's enthusiasm. So the picture magazine continued to evolve, and Ingersoll says that "many years after *Life* was a reality, I used to chuckle over the historic oddity that *Life* got itself started without benefit, ever, of any formal decision to start it. This Time Inc.'s own book [by Robert Elson] makes perfectly clear. How it must have confused him, a researcher after the fact, to ruffle through Time Inc.'s interminable memoranda and the formal records of staff and even directors meetings and nowhere ever to find a flat statement: This is it! The decision has been made. . . . After Havana, the project, like Topsy, simply grew"—with Ingersoll playing the role of the proud father and taking part in every aspect of Topsy's growth. And this is why Ingersoll always looked on the project as his personal property. "At no stage did Harry contest this—in fact, it was not despite but because of my emotional involvement that he let the venture proceed. He never really believed in it . . . it was Mac's baby and he was having fun in his new role of backer of someone else's ideas, which were exciting even if they were impractical."

But, of course, with such an impractical and potentially expensive project growing like Topsy, Luce had to keep control of it, and as the studies came in and it became more and more obvious that the magazine was going to cost a staggering sum to produce, Luce's involvement increased. One thing he was not happy with were the various proposals that had grown out of Ingersoll's "Notes on a Picture Magazine." So Luce went home one night and wrote what would become perhaps the most famous and oft-quoted magazine prospectus in history. It was dated June 8, 1936, and Ingersoll sent it around the building. It began:

To see life; to see the world, to eyewitness great events; to watch the faces of the poor and the gestures of the proud; to see strange things—machines, armies, multitudes, shadows in the jungle and on the moon; to see man's work—his paintings, towers and discoveries, to see things thousands of miles away, things hidden behind walls and within

*The memo, dated May 1936, is in the Time Inc. Archives. Except for the earlier Experimental Department proposals and dummies (which Ingersoll was perhaps the only Time Inc. executive to endorse), this is the earliest proposal for a picture magazine in all the frenzy of memo and prospectus writing leading up to the publication of *Life* in November of 1936. And until Luce's prospectus was finally approved as the official presentation, Ingersoll's memo was the basis for most discussions of the new magazine. For example, in July Ingersoll talked to the company's production people about the evolution of "PICTURES" and sent his "Notes on a Picture Magazine" in a follow-up memo to top executives. Curiously, these "notes" are not mentioned in any of the versions of *Life*'s origins printed to date.

rooms, things dangerous to come to; the women that men love and many children; to see and to take pleasure in seeing; to see and be amazed; to see and be instructed.

Thus to see, and to be shown, is now the will and new expectancy of half mankind.

To see, and to show, is the mission now undertaken by a new kind of publication, THE SHOW BOOK OF THE WORLD, hereinafter described.

There have been several versions of how *Life* was finally chosen as the name for the "Show Book," and Ingersoll remembers distinctly his contribution. He was sitting at Luce's desk, going over a draft of the prospectus while Luce was on the phone. After reading the opening paragraph quoted above, he circled the third word in the first line, tossed it across the desk, and said, "That's your name." But the name, of course, belonged to another magazine, although everyone knew the magazine was in financial trouble and could probably be bought. Ingersoll knew this better than anyone because his uncle George was executor for the estate of *Life*'s founder.*

Ingersoll asked all Time Inc. executives to comment on the prospectus. He also thought it was time to caution staffers to be a little less enthusiastic about the project, at least with outsiders: "That Time Inc. has been experimenting with a new magazine is no secret within the organization (and less of a secret outside than we would like). *Please* gossip about this in the Chrysler Building. Keep mum about it outside." And while it is true that Luce was now increasing his role in developing the "Show Book," the memoranda in the Time Inc. Archives written in the summer of 1936, help us to see how Ingersoll came to regard the "Show Book" as his baby. One memo about decisions still to be reached shows that Ingersoll, Longwell, and John Martin were responsible for the "final size" of the magazine; Ingersoll and Longwell had to prepare the "revised layout formula"; "sample layouts for advertising pages" were to be developed by Ingersoll, Martin, and Longwell; Ingersoll, Prentice, and Laura Hobson were charged with planning a "series of advertising announcements"; Ingersoll and Cornelius DuBois were to consider the advisability of hiring new promotion personnel; Ingersoll was to work out with Hobson her division of time on promotion ventures; Ingersoll and the Luces (Henry and his son Sheldon, who was to be the business manager) were responsible for a series of house ads about the new magazine to be run in *Time*.

Ingersoll was also involved in the design. In July he had lunch with an art director of Condé Nast, who said there was no one designer who could do for "Show Book" what Tom Cleland had done for *Fortune*. He endorsed Ingersoll and Luce's approach, which was to commission three or four designers to submit ideas. This suggestion had angered Cleland (who was also upset that his former girl friend, Eleanor Treacy, was going to marry Eric Hodgins), and Ingersoll was in the middle of that one too. He finally pacified Cleland by listening to his ideas and paying him a three-thousand-dollar consultancy fee—and he and the designer remained friends for years.

*Time Inc. bought the title for ninety-two thousand dollars, and it was Ingersoll who negotiated the deal.

His own feeling about the early layouts can be seen in a memo he wrote Luce, in which he said they gave him a "sinking feeling": "I felt we just did not have a magazine. The pictures excited me all over again but the layouts confused and bewildered. They yelled at me. I didn't know where to begin, return or where to end. My eyes wouldn't focus. Although some spreads composed, the majority didn't. It seemed to me we had the same old thing over again. Nothing distinctive. Just the sort of a new venture I would expect to spring up on the newsstands."

Ingersoll was also the company spokesman on the subject of a new publication. When *Business Week* announced in August that Time Inc. was planning a picture magazine, the article analyzed the impact the magazine might have on wire-service photos and on existing publications, such as the *Saturday Evening Post, Collier's*, and *Liberty*, and predicted that the newspapers would not "let Henry Luce or anybody else muscle in on the Sunday rotogravure section." Ingersoll wrote the company response, stating that Time Inc. had no intention of "muscling in" on the Sunday supplements, that, in fact, they hoped newspapers would devote even more space to photographs in their pages.

As the summer wore on, Luce became increasingly involved in the editorial planning for the new magazine. But Ingersoll was also very much concerned with editorial and photographic development. Margaret Bourke-White said, "I remember the excitement with which Ralph Ingersoll took me to '21' and told me [about the new picture magazine]. . . . it was mid-afternoon and '21' was almost empty and very quiet and we sat in a corner and both talked our heads off for the rest of the day." And one "R.McA.I." memo told the staff that a new department, to be called "Change," was being considered for "Show Book," and invited contributions; the memo stressed that the search was primarily for "fundamental" changes, but suggested a wide variety of stories that might be considered.

Obviously, the most important editorial decision was the choice of a managing editor, and Ingersoll played a role in that too. Clare Luce insists her husband had led her to believe she was being considered for the job, and Ingersoll confirms this. After the honeymooners had returned from Havana, there had been hints from Luce that he "could persuade her to take the job." But Ingersoll had strong feelings about Clare Luce as editor. "I knew I wasn't about to second Clare's nomination," he says, "because a revived *Vanity Fair* wasn't my idea of what my picture magazine was all about. So I finally came up with the right way to put it to Harry and it was the right way because it involved telling him only truth.

"What I told Harry was 'Look! Clare's a *very*, very talented woman—but she's your wife. There are only two ways you can use her to forward the success of a magazine that belongs to you: as your full partner, i.e., as its co-boss; or as its star contributor. You can't make her managing editor because a managing editor is only a hired hand, half way up the executive ladder. It wouldn't be fair to her; she's too important for that job and people would wonder why she isn't up in your office, in charge with you. And if she does not want the chores involved in being co-boss—play up the teaser that she'll have fun writing for it."

Ingersoll does not know whether his arguments persuaded Luce or not, but he recalls that the idea of making his wife managing editor "seemed to depress him." Clare, however, insists that when they went to their famous dinner at Voisin, which Ingersoll says was a "gang-up on Harry" (staged to revive what Ingersoll sensed was a lagging interest on Luce's part in the picture magazine), Luce had hinted that Ingersoll was going to offer her a job.*

The dinner, in Ingersoll's version, was devoted mostly to trying to convince Luce that since his return from Havana he had not been devoting enough time to the magazines, and that commuting to and from Stamford on a nine-to-five schedule was not adequate. The main reason, he says, for Clare's being present was to convince her that the feeling was widespread and that she should cooperate in the let's-get-Harry-back-in-the-operation movement. Ingersoll recalls Clare "getting whiter and tighter-lipped as the evening wore on and, finally, when she could stand it no longer," she demanded a hearing: "I have been listening very carefully to these men," Ingersoll says she told her husband. "Harry, has it ever occurred to you that you have surrounded yourself with incompetents?" Then she left the restaurant alone, leaving the group, including an embarrassed husband, sitting in awkward silence.

Mrs. Luce genuinely believed she had been the moving force responsible for keeping her husband interested in the picture magazine, and it is therefore understandable that she considered herself a plausible candidate for the job of managing editor. It is also understandable that she would see Ingersoll as the one who stood in her way, and more important, that she was disappointed in her husband. Loudon Wainwright reports that when she talked alone with Luce later that night, she asked him, "Well, what do you say to that?"

And Luce replied, "Well, you know it would be an impossible situation considering the way they feel."

"Now I'll tell you," said Mrs. Luce, "as long as you and I are married, I will *never* put foot in your office† or ever intervene in any way whatsoever with

*Almost everyone accepts that Luce said this to Clare and that she expected the job offer, which seems to substantiate, as much as any single incident, the role Ingersoll played in the evolution of *Life*. If Henry Luce was calling all the shots and pushing through the magazine, why did he simply not go to dinner and announce to all concerned that his wife was being made managing editor of his magazine? Instead, it appeared as if Luce were leaving it up to Ingersoll, and furthermore, he appears to have concurred with everything that transpired that evening, even Ingersoll's plea that he must come off his "perpetual honeymoon" and return to the office.

At the same time, there is no doubt that Ingersoll was not the only one opposed to Mrs. Luce's joining the staff. A former Time Inc. employee who knew the situation well says, "There was not a chance that Clare Luce would be allowed to put her little toe in the affairs of Time Inc. no matter what Harry said."

†Although Mrs. Luce maintained that she never set foot in the Time Inc. offices after this incident, it is not exactly the truth. Luce's assistant in the later 1930s says that Clare had an office next to Luce's and that, in fact, Mrs. Luce would try to persuade Time Incers to work for her on projects she had been assigned. Most declined, and one who came to work for Luce says he made it absolutely clear to Luce from the beginning: "Harry, I work for you—and *not* Clare."

your magazines. . . . There's something very wrong with a guy [Ingersoll] that would do that to a man who has just been married and with no proof of any kind that I have been a drag on you."

Why Luce did not come to Clare's defense and why he appeared at least to be siding with Ingersoll is not clear. We can only speculate, with Mrs. Luce, that an angry defense by her husband "would further strengthen their position that it was all [her] conniving because [she] wanted to edit the magazine." Or, with Wainwright, that perhaps Luce felt Ingersoll was right, and decided on the spot that he had to drop the idea of his wife's working at Time Inc. as an editor and also that he did have to "work much harder on the new magazine." There is also the possibility, as Wainwright suggests, that "Luce really didn't want his wife on the new magazine, didn't dare say so in those honeymoon days and was relieved and ready to use Ingersoll's opposition to his own ends." This last is Ingersoll's interpretation—and others'. One ex-Time Incer who agrees says, "Harry could never face an emotional problem."

Whatever the explanation, the result of that very unpleasant evening was that Henry Luce did become more active in the company; Clare Luce developed an understandable hatred for Ralph Ingersoll which she carried with her into her last years; and Clare Luce did not become the managing editor of *Life*.*

A fourth outcome of the incident was that by September of 1936 Luce had decided "that for an unstated term of months or years," as he put it in a memo, Henry R. Luce would be the managing editor of the picture magazine. The alternate managing editor (and obviously in line to succeed Luce) would be John Martin, who had been managing editor of *Time*. Dan Longwell was designated picture editor. Martin, however, quickly demonstrated that although he was a great editor, he was not a collaborator; not only did he clash with Longwell, he could not get along with Luce. So he was sent back to *Time*, and John Shaw Billings (whom Ingersoll had nominated when he met Luce in Cuba) was made alternate managing editor (eventually to succeed Luce as M.E.). Ingersoll's role was established in a memo he himself wrote to the staff announcing the business organization of the new magazine: "Thus with H. R. Luce's chief concern the editorial contents of *Life*, my job will continue to be all other *Life* operations."

As fall approached, the dummies began coming off the presses, and Ingersoll circulated them throughout the building and in the trade seeking opinions, which he summarized for Luce: "A resume of all outside reaction would sensibly split between layman and professional. Without equivocation, laymen thought Dummy No. 1 swell, were to a man amazed by the 'package for a dime,' interested and excited by the pictures. Without many qualifications, the professionals thought (a) the idea swell, (b) the dummy confused, but—(c) confidence in the future of the magazine unshaken after seeing it." Then he went into a detailed analysis of the reaction and concluded: "An overall criticism would be: too complicated, not sure enough of what it is trying to do."

*Mrs. Luce declined to be interviewed on her or her husband's relationship with Ingersoll or to read this section after it had been completed.

Luce agreed and wrote: "We are now setting out to get the job done." The dummies continued to roll out, gradually improving, and Ingersoll continued putting his thoughts on paper in a marathon ten-installment "Memorandum on *Life*," totaling seventy-four pages, in which he gave Luce some advice on staffing and execution:

I think you have the makings of a swell setup now: Let John Billings managing edit the magazine after you have given him the clearest possible definition of it, getting the pictures in and supervising the whole, complicated, fast-moving scenery.... You and Dan work on the kids hand-in-hand—you concentrating slightly on ideas, Dan on actual picture-getting. But most of all, work on the kids.

I would start with the firm resolve to be tough as hell, with the knowledge that we will have to have as high a turnover on this magazine as *The New Yorker* had twelve years ago. You have had to pick your men too fast, the problems are too new and unsolved, and if you have two or three members of the present staff left after a year you can pat yourself on the back as an inspired picker.

Meanwhile, for the first year or two the easy paternalism of *Time* and *Fortune* will wreck you. Hard work and being a generally competent man does not entitle an individual to a staff editor's job on *Life*. He must make original contributions or he is no use to you. I think the staff must get through its head that we are hunting for hidden talent and that anyone *may* find himself out of his job despite Herculean efforts, for no better reason than we haven't found in him something he never said he had. Crudely but intelligently Ross used to put it "I am firing you because you are not a genius."

Luce was so busy that he did not have time to read the memo, which was just as well. The reference to Harold Ross probably would have irritated him even more than Ingersoll's verbosity because it was about that time that Luce, Ross, Ingersoll, and St. Clair McKelway had their now immortal drunken dinner which ended in a shouting match between Ross and Luce. The dinner had come about as a result of the *New Yorker* profile of Luce that Ross had scheduled to appear in November, when the first issue of *Life* was to be published. The profile was the *New Yorker*'s response to the article on Ross and the *New Yorker*'s staff that Ingersoll had written for *Fortune* two years earlier. Ingersoll says he was suspicious that there would be "a bee in that bouquet," because Ross hated everything about Time Inc.: "its lack of reverence for Fowler's English Usage, its Yale-boys-at-play atmosphere, its glib assumption of omniscience." But Luce, who liked the idea of being profiled, had insisted, so Ingersoll advised, "The fewer facts you give them, the less they'll have to twist to your discomfort." He also insisted to Ross that Time Inc. be given the same courtesy *Fortune* had given the *New Yorker*, that is, that they be shown the piece before it went to press and have the opportunity to comment on the facts. When the galleys finally came in a few weeks before *Life* was scheduled to appear, Ingersoll was enraged. He called McKelway and screamed, "Hearst tactics!"

Luce was even more enraged and arranged a dinner for himself, Ross, Gibbs, and Ingersoll. As Ingersoll recalls, Gibbs "lost his nerve and didn't show. He hid out in some bar and got telephoned flashes from McKelway" (who went in Gibbs's place). It was one long, confused evening, and the several accounts that have come down through the decades differ as to who drank how much and who did or said what to whom. Ingersoll remembers having dinner but could not recall what was served; Swanberg's version, obtained from the participants, including Luce, has it that they did not meet for dinner but met after dinner in Ross's apartment at 22 East Thirty-sixth Street. Ingersoll says, "There was plenty of liquor around and nobody felt like denying himself. Harry, normally the most modest of drinkers, got looped and I had trouble getting him home later." But John Kobler, another chronicler of the evening, said, "Ross broke out a bottle of Scotch. He took none himself, Luce nursed one drink. But McKelway and Ingersoll did not stint themselves. At one point, in their cups, they started for the street to settle matters with their fists. 'I'll take Mac home,' Luce said to Ross. 'You hold McKelway.' But the belligerents subsided." Ingersoll says there was no fight. With apparently everyone drinking, Luce stammering as he does when agitated, and Ross "God damn"-ing through the whole evening, the conversation, says Ingersoll, was hard to follow. But a few memorable lines, mostly Ross's have endured:

• When Luce said there was not a single favorable line in the piece, Ross replied, "That's what you get for being a baby tycoon."
• When Luce said the piece was not constructive, and the facts were wrong, Ross's answer was, "We didn't set out to do a constructive piece. . . . Perhaps [the facts are wrong] but that, after all, is part of the parody of *Time*."
• And Ingersoll's favorite: When Luce, literally purple with rage, said, "But God damn it, Ross, this whole God damn piece is ma—ma—*malicious*," Ross replied, "You've put your finger on it, Luce. I believe in malice."

The article has since become a classic parody and the one quoted most often in Gibbs's obituary. Its most famous sentence, referring to *Time*'s style—"Backward ran sentences until reeled the mind"—has been quoted over and over. The article is, in fact, one long compilation of backward sentences that does make the mind reel. It opens: "Sad-eyed in October, 1936, was middle-sized *Life* President Clair Maxwell as he told newshawks of the sale of the fifty-three-year-old gagmag to *Time*"—and goes on to report the publication of the new *Life*, adding: "Behind this latest, most incomprehensible *Time* enterprise looms as usual ambitious, gimlet-eyed, Baby Tycoon Henry Robinson Luce."

Although the parody of the even then famous *Time* style was brilliant, the piece was truly malicious. James Thurber, commenting on it in his own book, said, "It seems to me that Luce and Ingersoll were justified in resenting the tone of the piece . . . and sometimes its statements." He also said that in the last letter he received from Gibbs, the parodist suggested the piece was "ill-advised."*

*After the profile appeared, Ross wrote Luce a letter saying they felt that the "total effect of the article . . . was enormously favorable" and that he had thrown "out a lot of stuff that would have made the boys' hair stand up." He signed it "Harold Wallace Ross"—"Small man . . . furious . . . mad . . . no taste"—all descriptions that had appeared in Luce publications. Thurber said he could never find a copy of the Ross letter in the *New Yorker* files, but years later a woman sent him a copy saying, "It has been used for 20 years in journalism courses in various colleges and universities around the country."

The last backward sentence in the lampoon was, "Where it [the Lucempire] will end, knows God." We still do not know where the empire will end, but the feud started by Ross and Gibbs ended in 1951, when *Time* printed a very favorable cover story about Thurber—after which the "relationship between the two weeklies became normal and sane," Thurber said.

Annoying as it was, Ingersoll did not let the parody upset him as much as it did Luce, and he finally reached the point where he could shrug it off with a laugh and say that he and Luce really wrote it themselves as a gag. He also knew that a *New Yorker* satire would not hurt them with the audience *Life* was trying to reach. The masses did not read Harold Ross's little book, and as *Life*'s publication day approached, the really big problem Time Inc. faced was not its image but the highly technical question of just what circulation guarantee to give advertisers. A wrong guess here could well bankrupt the company—and it almost did.

Ingersoll always believed *Life*'s potential circulation was in the millions. But Luce continued to urge caution and finally came to a decision, based primarily on a test mailing made in late spring, that the ciruclation, guaranteed for one year, would be 250,000. This meant that no matter how many copies they sold each week, they could only charge advertisers for 250,000. Obviously this figure was too low; a very successful direct-mail subscription campaign brought in 266,000 subscribers before the first issue was even on press.

As deadline day approached, there were the usual problems. The pictures for the first issue did not arrive in New York until twenty-four hours before the time they had to be put on the Twentieth Century Limited for overnight shipment to Chicago. So Ingersoll, with MacLeish (drafted from *Fortune*) writing captions, had to work around the clock doing layouts because Billings and Luce were occupied with other matters. The deadline in Chicago was on a Saturday night, but on Monday Ingersoll was still phoning in changes.

The print order for the first issue was set at 466,600, as Ingersoll stated in a memo to Luce, Larsen, Billings, and Longwell. The first issue was dated November 19, 1936, which was a Monday, but 200,000 copies had gone on sale the previous Thursday morning. The test city was Worcester, which had 475 copies. They sold out in the first hour, and the number of telegrams from newsdealers all over the country indicated that many other cities also sold out immediately. As a result, on that Thursday morning, what Luce already knew would soon be confirmed: They had a huge hit on their hands that would threaten the solvency of the company if it was not properly managed.

Ingersoll was awakened early Thursday in his Fifth Avenue apartment. *Life*'s circulation manager, P. I. Prentice, was calling with the news. He would, he said, keep volume 1, number 1, on the press until further orders, or until the paper ran out, to which Ingersoll replied: "OK, but don't forget that Volume 1, No. 2, has to go on these same presses soon, so take it easy." And he immediately began to worry: How would the company ever recover from "the colossal miscalculation of *Life*'s potential to which Harry's caution had committed us[?]

If the demand was really for millions of copies, where were they to come from? The printing process that R. H. Donnelly had developed for us was unique. To get the fine reproduction at a speed capable of producing even half a million copies a week—their engineers had devised a flash drying process by which the wet-ink-on-shiny-coated-paper was literally burned dry in super-heated tunnels. No other printer was equipped to duplicate the job and Donnelly had converted only enough press units to print what we had asked of him.

"And that was only the beginning. Even if Donnelly could print them, where would the specially processed coated stock for millions of copies come from? Paper mills can't be readapted overnight. And distribution would have to be wholly restructured if we were to meet the fantastic demand there seemed to be. And should we or shouldn't we even try to meet it? In every copy over 250,000 we might sell, we would be giving away our advertising. But if we turned away readers now, would they come back later when we wanted them?"

Ingersoll remembers lingering in his apartment inventorying the problems in his mind. He was, in effect, the publisher of the new magazine as well as general manager of the company—so *Life*'s problems and Time Inc.'s problems were his problems. Once he reached the office, he would have, as he put it, "to keep my head when all about me might be losing theirs in the excitement of it all."

He says he cannot recall whether there was a message from Luce already waiting when he did reach the office, or whether he called shortly after. What he does remember vividly is "coming into [Luce's] huge office, almost, but not quite, starry-eyed—expecting, I imagine, the kind of embrace a world series hero gets from his manager when his home run in the last of the ninth wins the series. For the ball I had hit had gone out of the park and surely I was entitled to one moment of happy hysteria, there alone with Harry! Time enough, then, to face what price the victory and to sit down to hear his wise advice (and God knows I knew I'd need it).

"But if I had been taking my stock before I joined Harry, he had been taking his. There were no preliminaries whatever. Harry's eyes were shining. I was there and what he was saying was for and to me but it was coming out of somewhere so deep in him that I knew I had never been real to him, and was not now. 'Mac, this is very big! I know and you know that *Life* is your baby. But it's mine too. It's actually mine. There comes a time in every man's life when he has to decide whether to take what is his—regardless of how he got it, if it's his. And I've made my decision, Mac. *Life* belongs to me and I'm going to take it from you. And that's only part of what I've decided. You and I know that this is so big that it's going to take all the money we have in reserve and all the earnings of *Time*. It's also going to take men. So I'm going to take whomever I need for *Life*—from the whole organization. And you're going to have to make the money I need from *Time*.

"So that's what I am asking of you: that you take over *Time* and see that it goes on making the money I'll need to spend on *Life*. I am counting on you to understand. This is *so* big!'

"It all happened just like that—that fast, that unambiguously. Of course the words are not the exact ones that Harry used. But the context was writ indelibly. Whole years may leave no memorable impressions but split seconds can be unforgettable!

"Harry had not finished speaking his set piece before my decision had made itself. I heard myself answering: 'Okay, Harry, of course I will. Until you have *Life* in the black—or for five years—whichever comes sooner. And then I am going to leave you.'"

Luce replied, "Thank you, Mac. We'll see. Five years is a long time from now."

That was all there was to it. And Ingersoll says, "I went back to my own office, the publisher of *Time*. Nominally, I remained Time Inc.'s General Manager, but after that morning in November, 'The Weekly Newsmagazine' was my preserve and the *Life* that I had nursed into being was Harry's and I never had anything more to do with it."

And he made his decision while in the elevator of the Chrylser Building, returning to his office: "that I would never again lose myself in the creation of a publication that belonged to someone else—even Harry Luce."

Luce later admitted that he was excited by the publication of *Life*, even when it was losing money: "It was an awful lot more excitement than I ever got out of making money." But it was more than just the excitement that prompted Luce to take *Life* away from Ingersoll and put the number-two man in the company, Larsen, in charge of the publishing side, as he did. If not managed properly, the new magazine would bankrupt the company and Luce himself would be held responsible for that, no matter who was running it. In a few weeks the test city of Worcester would be selling eight thousand copies of *Life* a week, with the dealer asking for twelve thousand. Projected on a national basis, this would have amounted to a circulation of five to six million copies, thus confirming Ingersoll's original concept of "Pictures" as a magazine "for the whole world." The decision was finally made to let the circulation run to 1.5 million and then hold it there until the original ad contracts expired. Meanwhile advertisers were given an unprecedented bargain. Ingersoll says that one Time Inc. executive calculated that an enterprising venture capitalist could have taken a page of *Life* at the prepublication rate, advertised a nonexistent brand of bicarbonate of soda, then, on the strength of the returns he received, could have bought a carload, repackaged it, fulfilled his orders—and he would still have come out with a nice profit.

But if Luce made a mistake in setting the circulation guarantee at a quarter of a million copies, it was also, as Ingersoll says, "a measure of his greatness that he held his hand from slapping me down in the brash venture." He also says that "during the whole process of the creation of *Life*, I was uninitiated in publishing and naive in my approach to it. I was a damned good editor and a reasonably effective editorial executive, totally without credentials as a publisher. But I was possessed with a publishing idea." And forty years later Ingersoll would say: "I was too fascinated with my new role of promoter. . . . 'manipulator' might be closer to what I mean. I sought to create a new publication—to make it happen—by manipulating not only Harry Luce but his whole organization— and I did a very imperfect job of it. It caused the magazine to happen all right, but not the magazine I had dreamed about and seen, ill-defined but shimmering, in the sky. *That* magazine is yet to be created.

"I did have an excuse for myself. The one truth about the creation of a new kind of publication is that no man can see it whole before its birth; it must be evolved in the process of the idea's implementation. Harold Ross had conceived *The New Yorker* but it took years for the skinny and ridiculous Volume I, No. 1 to grow into the magazine that has become a world institution. Harry's own *Time* sprang more nearly whole, but its strength was its unique simplicity. I knew what it had taken to fill out the dream of a 'literature of business' with the outline of a successful *Fortune*. So I was misled into thinking that all that was needed to implement the idea of a new kind of picture magazine was to staff it with men of talent and to leave them alone. This was a total misjudgment. I do not believe that any group can create an original publication. It can only be done by one man—or possibly two if they truly supplement each other as Harry Luce and Brit Hadden did in the creation of *Time*. It will inevitably take a group to implement the creator's idea, but it is he who must recruit the group himself."

His emotional break with Harry Luce was now complete. His ulcers had also returned, and with good reason: 1936 *had* been an epic year. But he came out of it a free man—free from a token marriage, free from his involvement with Lillian Hellman, and free to question the social, economic, and political values of Time Inc. He was also free—or soon would be—to show the world that Ralph McAllister Ingersoll was the best and most compassionate editor and publisher in town. To do that, of course, he would need his own publication.

General Manager and Publisher of Time

8: The Publisher of *Time* Marches Out

Henry Luce may have shown poor judgment in making Ralph Ingersoll general manager of Time Inc.—but it was not his worst decision. An even bigger mistake was making Ingersoll publisher of *Time*. At least he was excited and enthusiastic about becoming general manager, but as publisher of the magazine started by Luce and Hadden, Ingersoll clearly did not have his heart in his job: "I wasn't prepared to command. It wasn't my magazine—it was simply on loan to me from Harry. Nor was I qualified, since I didn't believe in the medium itself."

In March of 1937 Luce finally decided to initiate the system of publishers Ingersoll had planned to propose in 1935: Roy Larsen was designated publisher of *Life*; Eric Hodgins, of *Fortune*, and Ingersoll, of *Time*. Ingersoll also retained the title of general manager, which, as Luce himself conceded, did violate the theory of the scheme; but, he added, they need not be "slaves to an organizational theory." There may, however, have been another reason for retaining a general manager. Apparently Luce was giving some thought to withdrawing from the company.

Ingersoll went immediately into action. His first problem was *Time*'s "image." The *New Yorker* satire had caused considerable comment in the literary and intellectual community, and of course, Gibbs and Ross were not the only ones who hated the *Time* style; virtually every literate reader did. Seven years later Edmund Wilson would articulate a feeling that had been building up since the mid-thirties; "*Time*'s picture of the world," said Wilson, "gives us sometimes simply the effect of schoolboy mentalities in a position to avail themselves of a gigantic research equipment."

Time Inc.'s politics were also under attack. After Dwight Macdonald resigned from *Fortune* in his dispute with Luce over the U.S. Steel article, he wrote a series of articles for the *Nation* in which he called Luce the "great mouthpiece" for the ruling classes of America and said his magazines were moving toward fascism. Ingersoll did not believe that; but he was concerned about *Time*'s coverage of the Spanish civil war. In fact, in August of 1936, several months before he was appointed publisher of *Time*, he had written Laird Goldsborough (*Time*'s foreign news editor) and John Shaw Billings (the managing editor) a blistering memo criticizing the August 24 cover story on General Franco. The story was clearly pro-Franco, but Billings was so enraged by the memo that he countered with a note to Ingersoll that raised the question of whether he had "the capacity to criticize *Time*."

Because of his friendship with MacLeish, the *Fortune* writers, Hemingway, Hellman, and the *New Yorker* crowd, Ingersoll was more attuned to the intellectual community than Luce was and more sensitive to its criticism of *Time*. Not that he approved of the arrogance and preciousness of Ross's magazine either. He did not like the attitude of the *New Yorker* writers who set themselves up to be sensitive, literate young men of good taste who kept themselves aloof from the crowd. But at the same time he was appalled by the prosperous *Time* writers posing as smart-alecky, wisecracking pundits who watched from the sidelines while the world made a fool of itself in its struggle to survive. He decided, however, that before he could change *Time*'s writing he would have to do something about changing its "image." In his first memo to Luce on the subject of *Time*, he said: "We have now grown to the point where a simple success story—'My, my, how those two young Yale boys are getting on!'—is no longer an unmitigated blessing." He also complained of the "arrogance" that pervaded the magazine, and discussed at some length the criticism the intellectual community was leveling at *Time*. He recommended several ways Time Inc. personnel might counteract this criticism and how they might deal with the vexing charge that *Time* was anti-Semitic. Finally, he argued that *Time*'s promotion should begin to stress its "service" (i.e., providing information) rather than its "success."

Aware that one could not separate *Time*'s image from its editorial policies, Ingersoll followed up his memo on public relations with another reflecting his preliminary thinking on the magazine's editorial problems. And this memo—as well as the many to follow—illustrates why Luce valued Ingersoll—for "his talent at stirring things up," as the Time Inc. official history put it.

Ingersoll clearly intended to stir things up. It was time, he wrote, "to admit that there is a discernible grain of truth in the accusation that *Time* is written by well-fattened, insensitive Elis" and in the charges that *"Time*'s editors were well-fed, newly rich Yale boys in whose world labor movements were things to be laughed at, baited, ignored." He also reminded Luce that a year ago he had recommended that *Time* increase its foreign news coverage because it could no longer rely on distilling the foreign press. He also launched the first shot in his campaign to get rid of Goldsborough. Foreign news, he argued, mattered to people now more than ever, and it was essential that *Time* drop its biases and seek the truth.

Then he left for a month's vacation in Lakeville, taking his secretary with him. While preparing to scrape the barnacles off Luce's flagship, he was also getting ready to launch his own communications vessel. At the farm he dictated a sixty-one-page memorandum: "A Discursive Outline of a Proposition to Invent a Daily Newspaper." It began: "The writer's belief in the need for—and the opportunity in—a new *form* of newspaper began with nothing more complicated than the observation that the American newspaper has undergone no important change in design in 50 years and that a more efficient vehicle would be created by the simple application of common sense to a problem which was easily articulated—the problem of getting the news into people's heads."

The only significant innovation in newspaper publishing, he argued, had been the tabloid format introduced in the 1920s. But in the tabloids the pictures had very little relation to the text, and the papers themselves had drifted into sensationalism, in part because of the nature of photojournalism. This "gave the whole movement the unpleasant connotation implied in the new epithet—'tabloid journalism.'"

What Ingersoll proposed was a tabloid newspaper, or what he called "a daily newsmagazine," that would avoid sensationalism and incorporate the new trends in magazine journalism: (1) the classification of news told in stories with a beginning, middle, and end, as in *Time*; (2) the use of good writing, a permanent research staff, and public-opinion samplings, as in *Fortune*; and (3) the marriage of words and photographs, as in *Life*. He also proposed a "Going On About Town" department, as in the *New Yorker*.

Clearly, Ingersoll's gropings toward a "new form of newspaper" had grown out of his magazine experience, and in his "Outline" he asked: Why aren't "newspapers started by young men like Luce and Hadden?" The answer: "Because they take too much money to start. . . . magazines [in 1922 were] traditionally and notoriously (and logically) easy to start on a shoestring."

But Ingersoll claimed that his goal was to reform the American newspaper. This was not, however, his only, nor even his primary, aim. If Luce and the achievements of his company were embodied in the "Outline," so were the ideas of Lillian Hellman, Archibald MacLeish, and Ingersoll's other intellectual friends. "I hasten to set down," he wrote, "the fundamental conception that journalism is more than . . . simply the sale of a news service for profit. And the idea of creating a new paper is only secondly a revolt against the inefficiency of the

U.S. press at its job of telling information and is primarily a revolt against the ideas for which the U.S. press stands—scientific, literary, intellectual and political ideas."

His newspaper would pursue loftier goals—perhaps the loftiest ever proclaimed by a publication in the history of the country: Truth and the idea of a better mankind.

He also devoted several pages to defining the differences between a reactionary and a radical, concluding: "There is no question where I stand in this broad field. I am Radical in believing that people can improve their lot.... I would think any practical man today could be sold the idea of Radicalism simply on the basis of swimming with—understanding—an inevitable tide."

Then came his credo: "We are a group which believes in the existence of Right and Wrong and we believe the Right lies to the Left. But how far? Here, I believe we can be agnostic scientists. I am willing to say frankly I don't know."

And that, he conceded, gives us "an organ of the United Front, not an organ dedicated to putting over the United Front ... but an organization that believes [the Front] was moving in the right direction."

And this was his direction:

Contemporary government: "We would be for it where it conducted an experiment with enough efficiency not to endanger the scientific result; we would be against its reactionary aspects."

Capitalism: "It doesn't exist or, if you like, it exists everywhere." The idea that "U.S. Capitalism must be against Communism is nonsense because in whole sections of our life in this alleged capitalistic country we have no capitalism at all.... We have an open mind about Capitalism.... The question of course is what degree of private property is in the greatest interests of the greatest number— what degree of private property tends to promote the welfare of mankind and its progressive liberation."

Reform: "I would make The Paper revolutionary rather than radical. I would, in the Depression, damn well tell them that they were suckers to bring up families on $12.50-a-week for the great glory of the Corporation. But I don't believe in revolution in this country where we have a toe-hold on democracy and a fighting chance to work it out."

Freedom of the press: We believe in it "from the bottom of our truth-loving soul." But, "to be remembered: Archibald MacLeish's definition of objectivity— 'It is current-day fancy to consider a journalist objective if he hands out slaps and compliments with evenhanded impartiality on both sides of the question. Such an idea is, of course, infantile. Objectivity consists in keeping your eye on the object. Keeping your eye on the object invariably involves describing the object as it is—without regard to the feelings of anyone—and certainly without any attempt to make both sides equally happy or equally mad'"—to which Ingersoll added:

"In fact, the proof of failure to be objective would be the failure of an article to make anyone mad, since no given object appears the same to all people."

The staff: This would be "an expensive, highly trained and talented group of experts . . . experts not only in the subject but also in the art of telling about it."

The target audience: "The lower middle class—which doesn't have to struggle too desperately for a living. . . . The upper 'upper middle class' and the 'upper class' I expect to get free," because "I would expect all my news to be so much more clearly written than that which they now get, even out of their own beloved *N.Y. Times* and *Boston Transcript* that The Paper would be a drink of cool water to them on a hot day."

Then, after a long, detailed discussion of the contents, he concluded his "Outline" with a reminder: "Most of the great newspapers of another day made their names and their reasons-for-being as crusaders. . . . Maybe the formula is good, or basic. Maybe the villain and hero formula is sound editorial technique *and* not indecent morally."

Back in New York, he showed his "Outline" to Luce, who became excited about the project, and they began exploring the idea of Luce's contributing financially to a publishing company that was independent of Time, Inc., but allied with it. With these ideas down on paper, Ingersoll could now return to the problem of reforming Luce's newsmagazine. His critics, such as T. S. Matthews, said that Ingersoll approached his task "in much the same way as would a Roman proconsul who "might have been sent to restore law and order in a disaffected and too independent province." But Ingersoll in his memos and conversations with the staff used a different simile: "If the best airplane motor in the world has run 100 hours, experience has taught the wisdom of giving it what the Department of Commerce calls 'a 100-hour check.'" This means taking the motor apart piece by piece and having each piece examined by specialists. "If a part is sound, it is cleaned and polished and put back into place. If it is unsound, it is replaced." And it was obvious who was going to be making the decision as to which parts should be kept and which replaced. If the staff had been aware of a curious little incident that occurred in mid-May, they really would have been worried; it was not impossible that Ingersoll might become more than a proconsul; he might soon be Caesar himself. On May 19, the night before Luce was to leave for his "second honeymoon" with Clare—this one in Hawaii—Time Inc. employees gave a black-tie stag dinner in his honor at the Blackstone Hotel in Chicago. They rented a private dining room for the occasion, and, says Ingersoll, there was "something in the atmosphere. What Harry said to me that night has stayed with me ever since. The dinner was over. We were in an empty room, disordered tables, the chairs pushed back and Harry was saying come with me—and leading me down empty corridors to his bedroom where there was luggage lying about, half-packed, still open. The door closed behind us and Harry was very tense, tight-lipped, hard-eyed."

This is how Ingersoll, in his unpublished memoirs, recalls the speech he was about to hear: "Mac, what I am going to say to you, no one else knows, not even Clare. There is a time in a man's life when he has to make his decision by himself and I have made mine. I brought you here to tell you that when I go away tomorrow I may never be back!"

Luce took a turn or two around the cluttered room, before he went on. Ingersoll was sitting in an overstuffed chair, and Luce towered over him, glowering down at him, "not warm—cold, angry."

"I am telling you," Luce continued, "because . . . if I do not come back you're the one who will have to explain it . . . as best you can to the directors first, I guess . . . however you like.

"This is my decision, Mac: That my love for Clare means more to me than this company, even though I've built it myself and it's mine. So if I have to choose between them, I will choose Clare."

Ingersoll was staggered. "I remember the stillness of the somber hotel room, and the thoughts that came tumbling through my head. Christ, how can he say such a thing? What conflict can there be left between his life with Clare and his life's work? She is his *wife* now! What gives? And then through that long night he tried to tell me, putting it all together, block by block—in uninterrupted monologue. What was there for me to say? It was not told to me for rebuttal or concurrence or seeking sympathy. Possibly it was not being told me at all; it was being told to himself, wrenched out of a tortured soul to assure it. It *had* to make sense, and be expressible, to be borne; and he was using me to express it to. He was making a confessional of that room in an aging hotel and I was the invisible confessor behind an invisible screen.

"First there came his attempt to explain the crisis he was in and it did not make sense—any sense, and doesn't to me yet. The premise was that in his new life with Clare, in his love for Clare, there was an unrealized component that was worth any sacrifice to fulfill. This was no fault of Clare's; she was everything that a man could desire. But there was an unfulfillment on his part. And it could only be because his commitment was imperfect and must be purified; for if this love that he now felt were not fulfilled then all his life had been for nothing. He had touched faith before and not fulfilled it; not to achieve fulfillment now, in this love that was his greatest faith, meant death to all faith, to his soul.

"So, in total dedication to it, he was now prepared to forsake all other things, past and present, to concentrate totally on breaking through to total oneness with Clare, to total spiritual fulfillment.

"Earlier faiths—and there had been two—had not been fulfilled. The first faith had been in God. He had taken it with him from China and at Hotchkiss it had been challenged. And he had not met the challenge. He had seen that the boys who felt as he felt, truly, were not the 'in' group in this Christian assemblage, and that when a sacred name was invoked in calling them Christers, the term was used derisively. Yet he was not drawn to Christ's defense, but to the company of His critics—the popular and the powerful. It was *their* challenge that he had felt the need to meet, to become one of them, to outdo them. He had given up his faith in God to meet it. He had learned what he really was—'a back-row Christian.' And something went out of him.

"Then the second faith had come—and gone. It had been in words for word's sake, in the meaning that can be wrung from them, by poets and truly great writers, and in the satisfaction that can be realized even by the effort, each according to his talent. And it had gone, too, some time early in the evolution of the weekly newsmagazine, when he had finally to face what he had really long known, that he would never be able to make words sing—as a MacLeish could make them, or even as the most talented of the young writers whose salaries he was paying. Worse, that he would never achieve the satisfaction such men wrung from trying."

And Ingersoll will never forget his conclusion:

"So now, when a new and real and true Faith fills me, I *will* not fail it! I have Faith in love now and I will not lose it."

Then, after a pause:

"I do not know how I'm going to fulfill it but only that I have to and that if it takes all the rest of my life, I will—and to hell with Time Incorporated!"

Ingersoll says he knew Luce would be back, that he would not find what he sought. "But I thought that he would come back in some way changed." Nevertheless, for nearly two months the fate of Time Inc. would depend on whether Henry Luce found fulfillment on the beaches of Hawaii.

It was also about this time that Ingersoll was experiencing a short, curious, and comic flirtation with the Nazis. Through a Wall Street friend, Ingersoll had met a woman who was a friend of Adolf Hitler's and who was doing some intelligence and promotion work for *der Führer* in America. Although she had other duties, her most important function, she had decided, would be to help keep America neutral in the coming conflict in Europe, and to do this she would have to make certain Hitler had a good press. Therefore, she had asked Ingersoll's friend to introduce her to some of the molders of American public opinion.

He had a scheme of his own. And his friend Ralph Ingersoll was one of the first to be brought in on it. As he explained it to Ingersoll: She wants to use you; let's use *her*—to send back some sense to Berlin. If that crazy little bastard doesn't cool off, he'll have us in this war. He'll get himself licked and I don't like the bastard but I'd rather he cool off than hot up *another* war."

Ingersoll liked the idea and thought the game would be fun. But his first meeting with the spy was a shock: Instead of a glamorous femme fatale or even a Berlin tart, the woman he found himself dining with at Voisin was an undistinguished German hausfrau. He was also surprised at the brashness of her candid proposition. "Look, my young friend," she said, "let's not beat about the bush. We are going to take over the world. I'm absolutely convinced of it. Be with us. Now what is it that you want most?"

Ingersoll mumbled something about not wanting anything in particular at the moment, to which she replied, "Nonsense! Every man wants something. That's what life's all about. What is it, with you? Money—I mean *important* money? Women? No, you have women, I think. Power!"

That, she quickly decided (agreeing with most of the upper echelon of Time Inc.), was what Ingersoll wanted: Power!

"You are the General Manager of the Time company—putting out the most influential journals in America. So you do all the work but you are not the one that counts. Nobody ever heard of you! That man Luce gets all the credit. You have to supplant him. That I will arrange."

What she planned to arrange was an interview with Adolf Hitler, which would make Ingersoll "the world's Number 1 journalist," and Hitler's spokesman outside Germany.

Ingersoll and his friend agreed it was a good idea to go along with the charade, and for several months Ingersoll courted the spy, meeting some of her Nazi friends and escorting her down to the docks when the *Bremen* put into port. Then, once they had gained her confidence, they decided on their approach. One night when the three of them were alone Ingersoll's friend said:

"Look, I've known you for a long time and you know I don't horse around. And you know I'm not a dope. Ingersoll and I, *we* do know what the hell makes this country tick. He and I have to tell you, it's all crap, your fellow's wave of the Future. Don't kid me that it's your wave! Nuts! You don't believe in anything. So earn your pay by going back and telling that character that you've cased the joint and it's not the soft touch that his yes men are telling him. If he gets this country on his back—and he's damn near got it there already—he's had it."

"You're right! *I* have no politics," she replied, "that's why I can see it all so clearly! You are old-school Americans, you two; you don't understand the disillusionment in your own country. It is waiting for a leader."

Ingersoll recalls that his friend said something like "bull shit" and suggested that they already had a leader and his name was Roosevelt. They had another martini and continued their argument, but Ingersoll doubts they ever completely persuaded her. She did, however, agree to arrange a secret rendezvous between Hitler and Ingersoll—and Ingersoll was to travel to this meeting on the return flight of the *Hindenburg*, scheduled for early May. Except, of course, that as it was arriving from Germany the dirigible was completely destroyed by fire in Lakehurst, New Jersey. Ingersoll heard the news as he was sitting alone in a New York hotel room, his bags packed and all his good-byes said. He also heard the radio report that among the missing was "Ralph McAllister Ingersoll, publisher of *Time* magazine." The announcer had mistakenly been given the *outgoing* passenger list, so, for the moment at least, Ingersoll was officially dead. He was so shocked that instead of calling the office or home to reassure everyone that he was still alive, he just walked the streets in a daze. His mission to stop Adolf Hitler no longer seemed romantic or amusing, and he decided to abandon it. He did not return to the office for two days, having known, as he has said, "real freedom for a while . . . without past or present engagement with the world around me."

That same spring Ingersoll finally earned his pilot's license and bought a Fairchild 24, which he kept at the small airfield in Canaan, Connecticut. And he had a new girl friend: Laura Hobson, the young woman who had introduced Henry Luce to Clare Brokaw. Theirs must surely be one of the strangest romances in publishing history. There are two records of this affair: one in Laura Hobson's recently published memoirs *Laura Z.** and the other in Ingersoll's unpublished memoirs about his Time-Life and *PM* years, the first version of which was written in the 1950s. The accounts are completely different, and each participant maintains his or her version is correct. Both versions are presented in the following pages, with no effort to determine which one is accurate. For dates and chronology, however, Mrs. Hobson's version must be given the edge because she kept a "datebook" during this period, and such things are generally more reliable than memory.

Hobson says they first met at parties in the early 1930s, when she was still married to Thayer Hobson, and Ingersoll was married to Elizabeth Carden.† Later, after Mrs. Hobson went to work for Time Inc. and they were both divorced, she started having dinner with him. Ingersoll remembers most vividly their first meeting in the office. She told him then that she was making more than Archibald MacLeish, and he could not believe it. Over the next year or so, he says, he saw her around the building and always felt he could detect a glint of willingness in "Laura's engaging eyes." Finally, sometime in 1937, he asked her to join him for dinner at "21," and, according to Ingersoll, it did not take them long to agree on an affair—under conditions, he says, set down by her: "Yes, we would be lovers, but no funny business about love, no messy emotional involvement. And the proprieties would be observed. Everyone would know, of course, but there would be no confirmations for them and in public everything would be discreet." Those were the terms she offered; Ingersoll could take them or leave them. He took them.

There is no mention of terms in Mrs. Hobson's account, although she does concede that she initially approached her relationship with Ingersoll as "an affair"—and not the first one she had had since her divorce. She was, however, concerned about appearances, and she knew everyone would assume that, as a divorced woman, she was sleeping with any man she went out with. In fact, after her divorce her friend Clare Luce had counseled: "The minute you start going out again everybody who sees you with a man will leap to the conclusion that you're having an affair. Just ignore them. Let them guess. Never say a word. Because all the time you'll be happily sleeping with the doorman."

To Mrs. Hobson an affair meant "sex and little more and even I who praise

*New York: Arbor House, 1983.
†Ingersoll does not recall meeting her before she came to work for Time Inc.

sex as one of life's dear, driving forces, know full well that in an affair there was an emptiness that one would soon long to fill. . . . There was nothing of the limited encounter with Mac. . . . To have luncheon with him was to have the fascination of shoptalk and the inside dope about people and problems on all the magazines. He was witty and could be biting and there was plenty to be biting about."

What brought them together intellectually was their liberal dissatisfaction with the increasing tolerance at *Time* magazine for the emerging fascism in Europe, which Hobson, a Jew, and Ingersoll, a violent Hitler-hater, found difficult to endure—and with Luce's increasing conservatism as well.

Ingersoll was now living at the Union Club at Park Avenue and Sixty-ninth, having given up his lavish apartment on Fifth Avenue after great soul-searching about values. The club offered a choice of thirty dishes at breakfast, which could be served in bed, and otherwise solved most of the problems of bachelorhood. Laura had an apartment on Fifth Avenue, and that summer she took a place in Connecticut near Shadow Rock, and the two Luce employees drifted into a sophisticated and warm relationship. She flew with him in his Fairchild, and they spent long weekends and holidays flying on commercial planes to idylls in Jamaica or Colombia or Panama. At home, they played chess or backgammon, enjoyed good food and wine, and talked—mostly about Time Inc., Ingersoll's agonizing relationship with Henry Luce, and the war in Spain.

This highly civilized affair endured for a surprisingly long time. "Each of us," says Ingersoll, "acknowledged and accepted the other's independent life; our relationship was to be conducted as between equals—and it was. We got enormous, and continuing, satisfaction out of each other. We tried, enjoyed and appreciated anything satisfying that occurred to either of us, spontaneously— or after calculation. It had all the breaks. . . . It had been planned so that nothing could go wrong, and nothing did—physically, between us as man and woman. Yet in the end, everything did, leaving only a bitterness (Laura's) and a sense of waste (mine)."

What it lacked, of course, was love on Ingersoll's part. Though not on Laura's—or at least that is the way it appears now. She saw him often at eleven P.M. or one A.M., after they had both had earlier dates; they talked about their other affairs, and once she made him laugh with her remark: "I always swear that now I am single I am going to be absolutely promiscuous. But I just can't seem to live up to it. All that lost opportunity. It makes me mad."

What Mrs. Hobson wanted most was a child. She had been pregnant twice by her first husband, Tom Mount—once before they were married and once after she had learned about another woman in his life—and had had abortions each time. She and Thayer Hobson had tried to have children, and when she could not, she started seeing a gynecologist, Dr. Virgil Damon. She had also submitted an application for adopting a child. After waiting for over a year, she finally received a telegram one night while she and Ingersoll were in Miami after a short vacation in Key West. The Cradle in Evanston, Illinois, had a baby boy ready for her to adopt. So she flew out and adopted Michael Hobson—on February 13, 1937.

Ingersoll knew all about the adoption, of course, and opened a savings account for the new baby. At the time he presumed he was sterile, but that illusion was shattered one night, which Mrs. Hobson vividly remembers—and Ingersoll does not deny. He came to her apartment, visibly pale, tense, and shaken. He had just come from seeing a girl friend who had told him she was pregnant. It had happened on a Yale weekend he had told Laura about earlier. "I could barely listen," she recalls. "The great hook of jealousy lodged in my entrails, yanking, tearing. Pregnant—that thing that happened to everybody else."

They talked a long time about love, marriage, and children, which Ingersoll said he certainly wanted to have if he ever married again. "I had never seen him so unhappy nor so uncertain of himself." She does not remember how they made it through the night, but two days later—December 31, 1937—she made this entry in her datebook. "Dr. Damon—R—Lakeville." She had not been to see a doctor about her infertility for three years, now she wanted to start again.

Three months later, she says, Ralph told her that his girl friend had had an abortion and everything "was okay." And now Dr. Damon was giving her encouragement that she, too, might have a baby—by Ralph. "Hope again," she writes in her memoirs, "renewed hope. Both of our lives were changing, deepening. We both knew that what we were involved with was not only a love affair, but love."*

As Laura indicated in her memoirs, it was an unsettled, unhappy period for Ingersoll, and part of the problem can be traced to the disintegration of his relationship with Luce and his position at Time Inc. When he returned from Chicago and the good-bye dinner for Luce, he said to his fellow executives, "It has been two years since Harry told me that the management's attention to *Time* was three years overdue." He made a number of appointments on the publishing side, then announced that he would work as the assistant managing editor for one week. At the same time he had to prepare for Time Inc.'s annual convention to be held in June at the Hotel Commodore in New York. Luce had reminded Ingersoll that this would be the first convention over which he would preside, and had advised him (1) to apologize for even being there and (2) to lay down the law.

Ingersoll did just that. Using his airplane-motor-with-a-hundred-hours analogy, he announced that his "administration would be aggressive in reconsidering *Time*'s policies and practices." Today, unlike the 1920s, he argued, the news really mattered to people, and in the next five years he planned to make *Time* "the most important news organization in the whole wide world."

Next he turned his attention to writing a new "Prospectus for *Time*—1938–1943," all the while keeping things stirred up as he worked furiously to have

*Ingersoll emphatically denies ever indicating to Laura that he was in love.

significant progress to report when Luce returned from Hawaii in late July. He met the Luces at the airport, and they went to a restaurant—a former speakeasy—on lower Fifth Avenue. Ingersoll waited anxiously for some sign that there had been a change in Luce, some little hint that he had fulfilled himself, that he had found something greater than Time Inc. But nothing had changed. "Clare was briskly anecdotal," he recalls. "Everything had been wonderful. Harry had almost mastered surf-boarding. It was good to be back in civilization. There was no communication with me in Harry's eyes. There was not a vibration in the air; Harry and Clare were just almost-middle-aged married characters and the night in the Blackstone had never happened."

But, Ingersoll adds, he and Clare Luce never communicated again after that night and rarely saw each other. And although Luce indicated nothing specific, it is clear from his actions and memos in the next year and a half that he had made a firm decision: He had come home to run his company and to make sure his firstborn, *Time*, was not too harshly treated. Somehow Ingersoll had missed the signal.

At first there was no real conflict. Luce's priority then was *Life* whose continuing success was costing the company fifty thousand dollars a week. Ingersoll was free to reorganize *Time*'s operation and to change its image by attacking the problem at its heart—the editorial staff. As he wrote Luce:

> The unhappy fact about *Time*'s Editorial Department—dedicated by my prospectus, at least, to the practice and principle of responsible Group Journalism—is that it simply hasn't got what it takes.
>
> *Time* should be a group of at least 10 or 12 brilliant young men—zealots to the religion of keeping people well informed, with boundless curiosity and energy and ingenuity, thoughtful, broad, experienced, specialists. Each should, in the standards of the world we live in, be worth from $15,000 to $25,000 a year. Each should be capable of holding his own in a general editorial discussion aimed at "making the news make sense." Each should be able to represent his department and/or the magazine in the world at large. Each should be able to preach as well as practice an aggressive journalistic doctrine. Each should be excited about life and able to do something with his excitement.
>
> Instead of this group we have, in plain words:
>
> 1) One unstable, highly individualistic M.E. who has, unhappily, never at any time in his career been able even to inspire any group of journalists (excite—yes, inspire with confidence—no). He is also an alcoholic—he is not cured. Alcoholics are never permanently cured. There is no profit playing Pollyanna on this point. His conduct for the last two months has been accurately described as excellent. And with equal accuracy it must be recorded that he missed one whole Monday cold, conducted one Thursday conference after an alcoholic lunch.
>
> 2) Three old Bolsheviks (your term).
>
> 3) Three or four or five writer-editors I would classify as semi-skilled.

Time's writers, he concluded, were not overworked, not lazy, nor were they "sots"; they were just second- or third-rate journalists. He once commented to Roy Larsen that one way to put *Time* out of business would be to produce a sound film of the magazine's Thursday planning conference. "If these are the faces and this is the conversation of the group who keep the 700,000 most intelligent people in this country informed, God save our land."

To save the land, and with Luce's concurrence, Ingersoll completely re-organized *Time*'s editorial department: John Martin was given a year's leave of absence and replaced by a triumvirate of managing editors: Manfred Gottfried, Frank Norris, and T. S. Matthews. The last was a fine stylist who had been writing book reviews, and Ingersoll hoped he would have some influence over other *Time* writers; maybe the Matthews style would replace the *Time* style. But making Matthews an editor was a "misjudgment," Ingersoll says now. Years later, after Matthews had attacked him in an autobiography where he confessed to selling out to *Time*, Ingersoll admitted he did not blame Matthews for hating him because he had been the one who had set him on the road toward selling his soul to a magazine he obviously hated.

Ingersoll also initiated, with Gottfried, a drastic shake-up of the writing staff, adding such talented journalists as Leon Svirsky, Robert Neville, Dana Tasker, Bice Clemow, Winthrop Sargeant, Robert Cantwell, Louis Kronenberger, and John Hersey. Goldsborough remained as foreign editor, but his days were numbered. Ingersoll, aware that one of the most common criticisms of Luce was that he was "aloof," also tried to get to know his staff better. For a while he held staff dinners but finally decided they were "too formal and too far between." So late in 1937, after he had moved to a modest apartment at 19 East Eightieth Street, he issued an invitation to all *Time*'s writers and editors to meet there every Thursday evening at five for drinks and food. "Shop talk would be neither encouraged or barred. Your host guarantees to be on hand from 5 to 7, but will make no commitment beyond that hour. . . . it is your party as well as mine, a by-product of Group Journalism."

The new prospectus was also completed and circulated for comment.* It announced, of course, that *Time* was rededicated to all the principles it had set forth in 1923; denied that there was a "*Time*style," but said that *Time* still believed in telling a story crisply, in pieces with "a beginning, a middle and an end," that it believed in "group journalism as opposed to impressario journalism," and that the group approach, combined with "painstaking responsible research," would enable each department to speak with "final accuracy and authority."

Ingersoll introduced one of his favorite themes: There was, he believed, such a thing as the "Scientific Principle" in life, and here he quoted Charles Darwin: "I have steadily endeavored to keep my mind free, so as to give up any

---

*In its discussion of the new "Prospectus for *Time*—1938–1943," Time Inc.'s official history gives further evidence of its effort to distort Ingersoll's role in these years. The history says that Ingersoll wrote the prospectus while Luce was on vacation (which he did), and that "Ingersoll circulated his prospectus to his colleagues in Luce's absence" (which he did not), clearly implying that Ingersoll was trying to sneak out a new prospectus behind Luce's back, which is nonsense. The covering memo in which Ingersoll asked T. S. Matthews for his comments on the prospectus was dated August 15, 1937 (a month after Luce's return), and in this memo Ingersoll stressed that it was still a draft "for our use only" and that it might or might not be published at later date. He invited criticism, and the memo left little doubt that this was a company project, not an Ingersoll manipulation.

hypothesis, however much beloved, as soon as facts are shown to be opposed to it." Ingersoll thought this approach to life should be applied to journalism, along with the concept of "Fair Play." The prospectus concluded: "The Editors of *Time* make this solemn promise: that should the day ever come when, led by reason and in the light of fact, they decide that any given social doctrine—from Fascism to Anarchy or any in between—is in its judgment more important to the welfare of the American people than the kind of journalism to which we have here dedicated ourselves, *Time* will announce that fact in its own columns and in paid advertisements. Until that time, *Time* serves the old journalistic gods: Accuracy and Fair Play."

One problem with the prospectus was that it came at a time when Luce was undergoing a profound change in his philosophy and editorial thinking; he was moving away from any pretense of objective journalism and arguing that journalists and publications might well be biased. There was little doubt as to his bias; but with Ingersoll running *Time*, and *Life* not especially concerned with politics, the main battleground—at least in 1937—for Luce's swing to the Right was *Fortune*, whose writers and researchers were becoming increasingly unhappy. In a series of memos Luce declared that *Fortune* should clearly announce its bias in favor of private enterprise, and he quoted Thomas Mann, who said that "a magazine . . . intending to deal with the new materialism can have one of two biases: It can be either a great Communist magazine or a great Capitalist magazine."

Obviously, Luce's position made the *Fortune* writers—especially Archibald MacLeish—unhappy, and for a while Luce backed down. But not for long. A few months later he delivered a long address to the Ohio Bankers Association in which he said that Roosevelt had gone too far in his antibusiness policies, and that he (Luce) and his editors were enlisted for life in the war to preserve the freedom of the American economy.

As general manager of his company and publisher of what was still its most important magazine, Ingersoll did not totally disagree with Luce. He knew *Life*, *Time*, and *Fortune* needed corporate advertising, but he also thought you weakened your product, and thereby risked losing your audience, by proclaiming a bias. He thought you could accomplish what Luce wanted through objective journalism based on the scientific principle, which would enable editors and writers to maintain their integrity.

As 1937 came to a close, Luce still believed that Ingersoll was doing the job and that they were a "good team." He did not completely agree with what Ingersoll was doing at *Time*—in fact, much later he would tell Robert Elson that the scientific principle was nonsense. But Luce approved Ingersoll's prospectus and reaffirmed his confidence by taking him out to lunch and offering him one million dollars in Time Inc., stock if he would agree to stay with the company another five years.

One thing that may have influenced Luce's attitude then was that 1937 was turning out to be an excellent year for *Time*: While *Life* was losing a fortune and *Fortune* was going through its intellectual agonies, *Time* had been completely rejuvenated by Ingersoll. Its staff seemed to be happy and was functioning without dissent, and the magazine was on its way to having the best year in its history, with profits of over three million dollars. C. D. Jackson, the company's top executive for public relations, thought *Time* was entering its "golden age."

Things had worked out just as Luce had planned: Ingersoll had reorganized *Time* and was making the money that enabled him to publish *Life*. Ingersoll's leaving would create a huge vacuum in the company just when Luce felt he had to devote all his time and energy to making *Life* profitable. The million in stock he offered Ingersoll was much more than a reward for past services; it was also a dramatic bait designed to keep a much needed executive on the job. But it did not catch the fish. Ingersoll was now totally committed to publishing his own paper and he told Luce so. However, they continued to talk about the project as something into which Luce would put some money and for which he would help Ingersoll raise more.

For most of the 1930s it appeared as if Ralph Ingersoll could do no wrong. But no one can go on forever moving from one dizzying triumph to another, and for Ingersoll 1938 was the year things began to come apart—both personally and professionally. Although there would be a whole new career ahead, national notoriety, best-selling books, heroics in war, a totally satisfying and rewarding love, children, and a multimillion-dollar company of his own—nothing would ever be quite like it was in the fall of 1937, when, at thirty-six, he was probably the most powerful journalist in New York, but was struggling, quite frankly, to move outside the shadow of Henry Luce.

The fight to establish one's own identity in the cutthroat world of big-league publishing was often an ugly one, and to survive one had to play rough. Laura Hobson comments in her memoirs that she knew Ingersoll was hardheaded in business, and that many considered him "ruthless and an egomaniac." She knew all about this side of Ralph Ingersoll but thought she could handle it—until in 1938 an incident occurred that Ingersoll maintains never happened, not at least the way she describes it in her memoirs. Hobson says that she and Ralph had been drawn closer after the pregnancy of the other woman; that Dr. Damon was encouraging her to believe she might have a baby; and that when she missed her period while on a short vacation in Bermuda, she was sure she was pregnant—by Ralph Ingersoll. So she wired him that she was coming home and that she "MIGHT HAVE SOME NEWS."

According to Mrs. Hobson, Ingersoll met her at the airport and she told him the news immediately. "A pride I had never seen seemed to glow in his face," she recalls. "We were headed for New York, but at my news, he turned the car around and we began to drive at random through the summer green countryside of Long Island." They ended up at what Laura thought was an unlikely destination, Jones Beach: "We sat there on the sand and soon we were talking possible names for the baby. If it were a boy, his first son, he would want him to be named Colin Macrae Ingersoll. After his father."

The next day Dr. Damon confirmed the pregnancy, and Mrs. Hobson was rapturously happy; all her earlier "joys and triumphs fell away before this rising, curling breaker in a new ocean of thankful joy." Then, she says, seven days later she received a call from Ingersoll's secretary. He wanted to see her at once. She rushed to his office not sure what to expect, and when she found out she was stunned: "I've been thinking and thinking," he said. "It's simply the worst timing there could be. For this next year, for the next several years, more likely, my whole life has to be devoted to the paper, just to the paper, only the paper. It's impossible for me to fit in getting married, having a baby—I just can't go ahead with it."*

Mrs. Hobson said she could not speak. She hardly remembers leaving the office and going to the ladies room, where she was immediately sick. She also decided that no matter what, she would have the baby. But a month later, while driving on the Merritt Parkway from Greenwich (where she says she moved immediately after Ingersoll's ultimatum) to New York, she suffered a miscarriage. Dr. Damon attended her, and she says, "He must have called Ralph to tell him, for in the afternoon he came, bearing beautiful yellow roses."

Five days after leaving the hospital, Mrs. Hobson decided to see a psychiatrist—Dr. Lawrence Kubie, who soon transferred her to Dr. Raymond Gosselin. "I did not know then that there was anything neurotic about the way I could keep on longing for and being in love with a man who had hurt me or would hurt me again. . . . of course, in due time, I did see him again. . . . [But] I did tell him that I couldn't really have any trust in any future for us unless he too went into analysis, to find out what made him do things that other people so often called ruthless—and he actually did go to a world famous big-shot analyst named Gregory Zilboorg. Perhaps that contributed to my willingness to go on chancing it."

Ingersoll's version of these events is somewhat different: He denies that Mrs. Hobson was ever pregnant by him, but does concede that he decided to see Dr. Zilboorg—and that it was one of the most important events in his life. One day, he says, Mrs. Hobson told him she was seeing a psychiatrist, Dr. Lawrence Kubie. She said she was doubtful how much it might accomplish, and Ingersoll, too, was skeptical. But during the next few months, although Laura's psychoanalysis was never discussed, her comments indicated that she had come around to endorsing the idea. Then, one night when Ingersoll arrived at her apartment, she had the backgammon board out and insisted on playing, although for some time they had abstained from the game because Laura became uncontrollably angry when she lost. When Ingersoll beat her this time, Laura took her defeat in stride. As Ingersoll tells it: "Some profound change had taken place in her highly competitive behavior." He was so impressed that, for the first time, he began to listen seriously to Laura's persuasive arguments in favor of psychoanalysis. He also took stock of his own emotional status—not unmindful

---

*Ingersoll denies all conversations about his fathering the child because he maintains it did not happen.

that the familiar pattern was developing with Laura and that he was moving toward rejection (which was an understatement, if Mrs. Hobson's version of the events is accurate).

Ingersoll decided to have a talk with Dr. Kubie, who in turn gave him a list of three psychiatrists he recommended. Ingersoll understood enough about psychoanalysis to know that if he decided to undertake it, he would be spending a lot of time at the doctor's office, and there was on the list a Dr. Gregory Zilboorg, whose office was at 14 East Seventy-fifth Street, only five blocks from Ingersoll's apartment. So he chose Dr. Zilboorg.

His choice of a psychiatrist was arrived at quite fortuitously, but the circumstances surrounding Ingersoll's analysis are worth noting because, before many years, Gregory Zilboorg would be described by some columnists and writers as an evil Communist Svengali who had masterminded the leftist publication Ingersoll would soon create by bringing together the two men most responsible for its financial support. Gregory Zilboorg had, in fact, been born in Russia and in 1917 had served briefly as a secretary to the minister of labor in Kerensky's government. When Lenin and Trotsky overthrew Kerensky, Zilboorg fled for his life, first to Austria, then to Germany and Holland and eventually to the United States, where he arrived at the age of twenty-eight, penniless but with a great gift for language. By 1926 he had graduated from Columbia University's medical school, having supported himself primarily as a translator. In the ten years following his graduation, he studied psychiatry in New York and Berlin and gradually emerged as an authority on Freudian psychoanalysis. Soon after opening his New York practice, he was analyzing a number of well-known and wealthy people. According to Lillian Hellman, one of his later patients, "he was an old-fashioned socialist who hated inherited wealth as undeserved and many of his patients were people like that."

One of his former patients was a young millionaire named Marshall Field. Zilboorg did have, according to Field's biographer, a profound impact on the wealthy young man, helping him find direction and encouraging him to become involved in, and give "service" to, the welfare of his country. Field's analysis had been completed a year or two before Ingersoll met Zilboorg, and Ingersoll knew nothing of this or of Zilboorg's socialist views before he went to see him. Ingersoll would meet Field a year later, through Field's lawyer who was a partner of Ingersoll's lawyer.

Ingersoll found Zilboorg impressive: "He was a small man with a large head, ornamented with a scraggly, over-sized and drooping mustache and great overhanging eyebrows. His almost bald pate was circled by equally scraggly, overlong black hair. But his eyes were what dominated the whole wild effect. They were dark, and at once warm and intense, and extraordinarily expressive."

In his second session Zilboorg said he thought Ingersoll was, emotionally, a very sick man, and agreed to take him as a patient. It would cost a hundred dollars a week for five years, and he would spend fifty minutes a day in Zilboorg's office, five days a week. In his unpublished memoirs Ingersoll devotes one full

chapter to his psychoanalysis, and it is obvious he came away from the experience
with an understanding of why he behaved as he did and a great respect for both
Zilboorg and the process. "Most of the time," he says, "I recall having to endure
a very great deal of pain; it was not a pleasant process. I suffered a great deal,
not only during the hours I stared up at the ceiling trying to let my thoughts
flow in free association but also in the hours between sessions, when unresolved
conflicts made me writhe in anguish. I have left sessions in which my doctor
had not had a single word to say but in which I recaptured emotions so painful
that I walked out blinded by tears and shaking from head to foot. Often I was
so distraught that I would have to walk it off before I felt calm enough to go
back to the office. But of this whole expensive and extremely uncomfortable
process, I can still say, all these years later, that from no other experience in
my life have I felt so benefited.

"I do not know what would have become of me if I had not gone through
this process of self-analysis with the help of a truly exceptionally able professional. I have a strong suspicion that I would have found some way to destroy
myself. I have a very violent side built into the machinery in which I translate
my emotions into action. By the time I reached analysis—at 37—I had already
established a pattern of overcoming obstacles with a drive of almost frantic
dedication and of achieving precocious successes which, when achieved, I immediately found reasons to destroy. And destroy them I did—in conflicts always
initiated by me and always involving someone whom I cast in a father's or
mother's role."

Zilboorg's telling him at the beginning that he was seriously ill—"much
more ill than you have any idea," as he had put it—scared Ingersoll so much
that during the first year of his analysis it kept him from running away despite
repeated urges to flee. There were times when he recalls lying on the couch
with Zilboorg standing behind him, and pouring out his hatred of the doctor—
or someone. "I would like to cut *your* balls off. . . . You charge too damn much
for these sessions, and you are a damn faker anyway. . . . Did I ever tell you
how much I dislike the furniture you picked out for this room? . . . I am going
to get the hell out of here and stop listening to you."

What was happening, he soon learned, was transference, and after an out-
burst like the one quoted above, Zilboorg would say, "Would you please repeat
what you have just said?" Then: "Does this impress you with the possibility that
the father whom you thought you *loved*, you really then hated—and that he
might have seemed to you, when you were a small child, a menace?"

In *Point of Departure* Ingersoll wrote that he finally had to admit to Dr.
Zilboorg that he had a "good old Oedipus complex," a remark one reviewer
considered insensitive. Ingersoll conceded it was a "sloppy comment, but," he
said, "that is what I did have, and I have long since ceased to be sensitive about
it." Later he added: "I would have sworn on any Bible that I had had no
relationship whatever with my mother, that she simply had not been a part of
my boyhood. The truth was, I had loved her very deeply and felt rejected. I

attributed my failure to win her undivided love to the father who stood blocking my path. Mother belonged to him, not to me. He seemed to wear his conquest of her with arrogance. I would indeed have killed him—my anguished mind revealed so many years later—if I could have found a way. But I could not face the awful truth of my hatred if I had recognized it. So I bottled it up, hid it away, even from my innermost thoughts. Instead of defying him, I made myself into a model of correct behavior, subservient, respectful, fulfilling his slightest command—and emotionally self-castrated."

But he did not remain a model of correct behavior when he went out into the world of men. When he encountered a father figure—such as Ross or Luce—he felt a "demonic need" to challenge and destroy him.

Prior to analysis Ingersoll had taken his confrontations with authoritarian males as "inevitable and innate in adult life." What had brought him to analysis was his confusion about his relationships with women—and there he learned that this was just the other side of the same coin. "From Mother's death onward, I was drawn only—and irresistibly—towards women who were desirable *and* unsatisfactory—seeking the only relationship I was at home with. If they were not innately unsatisfactory, then I would find a way to make them so. Again and again, I sought to recreate Mother for myself. I arranged to love only someone who could not return my love, and then got someone to love me at a time when I could feel no deep response. Then I concluded—on the incontrovertible evidence I had manufactured myself—that the whole experience was inherently unsatisfactory. Anyone with sense would avoid it like a plague."

Mrs. Hobson, to her regret, chose not to avoid it.

Near the end of Zilboorg's life, after he had converted to Catholicism, he confided to Ingersoll that he believed that man simply could not face the whole truth of his nature, and that his denial of truth about himself was a built-in imperative. At the end of five years Zilboorg said he thought Ingersoll was "cured"—meaning that he understood his problem. And Ingersoll says that although from time to time he has since been thrown off emotionally when something reminded him of the intense feelings of his childhood, he was by then no longer their captive; he had them under control.

But in 1938 he was just beginning analysis, and the daily anguish produced by the revelations on the couch contributed to the turmoil of that year. It was also during this period that his relationship with Ernest Hemingway became unpleasant. The break had begun the year before, when MacLeish took Ingersoll out to lunch to meet John Dos Passos and to tell him about a film on the Spanish civil war that MacLeish, Dos Passos, and Hemingway were promoting. It was to be called *The Spanish Earth*, would be shot by a talented young photographer named Joris Ivens, and would be frankly favorable to the Loyalist cause. Hemingway was already in Spain and would help Ivens get started. They wanted Ingersoll to help raise the money and make arrangements for distribution, once the film was ready.

The project began well enough, but then Ingersoll became aware of the tension building between MacLeish and Dos Passos, on the one hand, and between them and Hemingway who had begun to take over the operation in Spain, on the other. MacLeish and Dos Passos were appalled at some of the things the Loyalists did; the execution of two of their friends who had been branded as traitors was especially shocking to them. Hemingway's reaction was: "That's war." And soon word began to filter back that Hemingway was critical of the way MacLeish and Dos Passos were handling the New York end of the operation. Ingersoll was in the middle, acting as a conveyor of messages and trying to remain neutral, but siding with MacLeish, especially when Hemingway started accusing the *Fortune* writer of being a coward.

During this little flap Hemingway also sent Ingersoll a copy of his play *The Fifth Column*, telling him how good it was. "I'm a born playwright," he said, "my dialogue is always good. I think in dialogue. And this is a hell of a plot."

Ingersoll was supposed to find a producer and do some promotion (which Mrs. Hobson says she helped him with), but he could not find a producer and had to return the play to Hemingway, which irritated the author. Then came word that Hemingway was returning to New York with the uncut version of the film *The Spanish Earth* and with Martha Gellhorn, a beautiful writer whom Ingersoll had once rejected as a *Fortune* researcher because he thought her good looks would be disruptive in the office. Hemingway apparently planned to divorce Pauline and marry Martha, which upset both MacLeish and Dos Passos.

MacLeish went to the boat to give Hemingway a piece of his mind. Hemingway and Gellhorn, however, eluded him, turning up at a West Side bar, from which they called Ingersoll and asked him to meet them. Ingersoll says *The Spanish Earth* was a gem but too short for a feature film. He made an effort to distribute it nevertheless, but even with Hemingway's name on it, he could not find a theater chain that would take the film, nor could anyone else. But Gellhorn blamed Ingersoll, who said later, "[she] took a whole morning off to give me the most thorough tongue lashing I can ever remember getting from anybody. I was incompetent, unappreciative (of the sacrifices Ernest had made) and a phoney slob."

Although Ingersoll would see Hemingway again and the writer would eventually do some articles for his "new kind of newspaper," the *Spanish Earth* incident marked the end of their friendship. Whenever they met face to face, Hemingway was pleasant enough, but behind Ingersoll's back he began calling him Ingersnake—which was characteristic of Hemingway, according to Carlos Baker, his biographer. The unpleasant affair also ended the MacLeish-Hemingway friendship, although Ingersoll and MacLeish came out of it with their own relationship undamaged.

With passions in this country running so strong in support of the Spanish Loyalists, it is not surprising that Ingersoll decided it was time he learned more about communism. So, at great risk, he accepted the invitation of some friends to join a study group sponsored by the American Communist party, which met once a week at their apartment in the East Forties. "I was a damn fool," he says, but none of his friends betrayed him. The experience, which lasted a little less than a year, fascinated him. "I came to have a great respect," he says, "for the dedication of several of my tutors. They were laying it on the line—their lives, for many things I believed in then, and still believe in: the humanistic values of racial equality, fair dealing with labor, medicine practiced for patients not profits. That was the content of Communism that attracted most (I might say all) honest American humanists of the thirties—when the C.P. was making it easy with its United Front policy. As usual with my oversimplifying mind, I came out of it all with a handy generality: Little Communists are on the side of the angels; it's the big ones who make the big decisions who are the devils. I came early to the unoriginal conclusion that Marxist Communism was a religion and likened it (as I still do) to Catholicism—or hell-fire Protestantism or Goys-Be-Damned Judaism, for that matter. They own monopolies, the one on how to get to Heaven and the other on how to live here on Earth. To entertain any other faith but theirs is heresy, punishable by damnation—ex-communication leading to starvation (and maybe being murdered), in Communist thinking; to eternal misery in the older monopolies.

"The only genuine, copper-riveted-and-proud-to-be Communists attending my lecture group were the lecturers, who were introduced by pseudonyms with the frank explanation that they had to be because at least one of us was undoubtedly an undercover agent. The rest were, like myself, the most recent of silk stocking recruits. We were, the dozen-odd of us, all *very* genteel and I remember one visiting mentor getting furious because we so often phrased our questions as outsiders: 'How do you people feel about . . . ? What would you do if . . . ?' He was a tough young labor organizer out of the Mid-West and barked that we should be thinking *we*! We new proletarians blushed—and helped ourselves to another Scotch and soda—from our host's handy bar."

Which did not surprise ex-Communist Gregory Zilboorg. Ingersoll says he well remembers his psychiatrist's reaction when he told the doctor he had joined a party study group: "He broke up the session with his roar of laughter: 'You! You . . . they think of you as Party material? You, the totally perfect bourgeois— mind, body and soul! Those simple-minded idiots!'"

When Ingersoll asked Zilboorg to define a "true Communist soul," he responded with a story about two young lovers he had known when he was in a Communist cell in Czarist Russia. They had come to an impasse in an intellectual argument about party doctrine and knew neither could change the other's mind. "So one night," Zilboorg said, "when the young man was making love to the young woman, and actually in the act of penetrating her, she reached under her pillow for the knife she had hidden there and stabbed him in the back, and to death. And all of us understood why she had had to kill him, and how terrible it was for her because she was so deeply in love with him."

Zilboorg sighed.

"So now do you know what a true Communist's soul is made of? No! You will never know because you cannot know. But maybe the story will convince

you that knowledge of the Communist's soul is beyond you." Then he went back
to Ingersoll's analysis, adding that he could never accept a true communist as a
patient. "It would stir up too many savage emotions."

Although Zilboorg was right about the implausibility of Ingersoll's ever
becoming a communist, the reason was not his inherent bourgeis characteristics
but his dedication to journalism. The central issue that divided him from the
Communists was clear: "The intellectual discipline that requires an honest communist to be a dishonest individual—if the Party Line so directs. I came to
believe, and do still believe, without qualification, that individual honesty and
the loyalty demanded by organized communism are totally incompatible. Maybe
a layman could work out a rationalization for himself, but a journalist—never."

When it came time for him to break with the party, Ingersoll, in his fashion,
became quite emotional and wanted to stage a confrontation to make a production
out of his resignation. By then he was well along in his plans for a new kind
of newspaper, and he thought he should "make war" with the party to put them
on notice about where he stood. It was Zilboorg who kept him from making a
fool of himself. "Your friends," he said, "will never understand such a forthright
gesture. To them you will be a Traitor, unequivocally; and a man marked for
destruction from that day on. No! No frankness, no speeches. Simply fade away,
leave them guessing."

Which is exactly what Ingersoll did. And it was just as well. Although a
confrontation with the Communists might have put them on notice as to where
he stood, it also would have publicized the fact that Ralph Ingersoll had been a
member of a Communist party study group for a year, which would not exactly
inspire the VRMs from whom Ingersoll was then seeking money—in large
amounts.

The term *VRM*—for "very rich man"—was one he had learned when, as
a young man, he and his friends were being driven alongside a river in Northern
Italy. Whenever their driver-guide, an Italian, passed an impressive mansion, he
would tip his hat in its direction. After he had done that about five times, Ingersoll
asked why. "Oh," the man said, "that's where a Very Rich Man lives."

Ingersoll's efforts at fund-raising began some time in mid-1938, several
months after he had made his emotional break with Luce by declining the one-
million-dollar stock offer. He asked his brother-in-law, a Boston lawyer, to create
a corporation called Publications Research. Then he decided to start approaching
some VRMs, tipping his hat, to find out how hard it was going to be to raise
the money. One very, very VRM was John Hay "Jock" Whitney, whom everyone
in town knew was fascinated by publishing. And Laura Hobson knew a young
lawyer named John Wharton who was a member of the law firm that represented
Whitney. So she arranged a lunch with Wharton, who was, in fact, the first
person to whom Ingersoll can recall outlining the project he had not yet fully
decided to undertake. "Through what must have been an hour's flight of my
fancy into the creation of a new kind of crusading journalism," Ingersoll says
of his lunch with the slim, quiet young man, "I remember him as so still that I

became unconscious that he was there. And then—it is clear as yesterday—his eyes were alive and he was saying, in that calm, clear gentle, almost effeminate voice: 'I want to do everything I know how to help you succeed. I don't know anything about newspapers. I don't know an awful lot about you. But I believe in what you're trying to do. The only thing I do know anything about is law, and I'm a lawyer, so—Q.E.D., I'm your lawyer.'"

"I don't need a lawyer and I can't afford one," Ingersoll replied.

"You don't pay me anything. I make my living representing a lot of rich guys and they pay me as much money as I can spend. I can afford to do something I want to do, and I want to help you start this newspaper. So let's have no more talk about it. I'm your lawyer—and you'll see that any papers you have to draw up are drawn up by me."

At first Ingersoll thought raising the money would be easy. After his luncheon with Luce in 1937, the two men had had dinner at the Union Club, and Ingersoll had agreed to stay at least another year, or at least until *Life* was out of trouble. Then he would set up his newspaper "across the street" from Luce and his magazine, and they would have fun working together—and together they would form a new press association. But then Luce gradually backed away, which was a crushing blow to Ingersoll, even though he appreciated the problems Luce would have had if he had involved Time Inc. with his newspaper. But, he says, "an investment by HRL would have been an endorsement of me and my ideas—and I could have raised millions over the telephone."

Though backing away from involving himself or Time Inc. in Ingersoll's project, Luce did offer Ingersoll a year's leave of absence—with pay—to develop his idea, feeling sure, Ingersoll is convinced, that without the Time Inc. endorsement he would never raise the money.

Ingersoll then turned to Harry Cushing, the Wall Street friend who had introduced him to Hitler's friend, and who had once tried to sell the *New York Times* to Henry Luce—a deal in which Ingersoll had been very much involved. Cushing started trying to raise the money on Wall Street, while Ingersoll sold his Time Inc. stock, hired a young AP executive, Ed Stanley (at a salary of ten thousand dollars a year, paid out of his own pocket), and set him and Publications Research up in a little rented office on East Forty-second Street, with instructions to begin quietly planning for the newspaper and to make an estimate of how much money they would need. Stanley's first estimate was ten million dollars—which Cushing said frankly would be hard to raise.

No one really knows exactly why Luce began to lose his enthusiasm for the newspaper in late 1938. Ingersoll, however, is convinced the main reason was Clare Luce. On the other hand, the project might simply have been vetoed by other Time Inc. executives whom Luce trusted and who no doubt argued that it would be unwise to involve the company with any publication it did not control. A more likely reason, however, was the gradually increasing journalistic differences between Ingersoll and Luce. Another factor may have been Luce's growing concern over what Ingersoll was doing to *Time* and the magazine's financial position. By the first quarter of 1938 *Life* was not the company's only problem; *Time* was also developing problems. And it was at about this time that Ingersoll suggested to Luce that he appoint an executive vice president "whose sole responsibility is to head this company and who has full authority to speak for you." Luce turned down "that bait," as the official Time Inc. history puts it, thus clearly implying that Ingersoll was bucking for the number-two job, and demonstrating again that Elson's book was curiously loaded against him. By that time Ingersoll had already told Luce that he was leaving the company.

Also, at the beginning of 1938, Luce made official the decision he had probably come to during his second honeymoon: He was ready to take over his company again. In a memo to the staff he announced that he had created a new job for himself: editorial director of *Time*, *Life*, and *Fortune*. "In recent years," he explained, "you have all at various times carried the actual burden of this responsibility without help from me." Ingersoll and Luce were now on a collision course. That Ingersoll had finally cut his emotional and professional ties with Luce, and that Luce no longer intended to share his company with anyone else, may also have been responsible for Ingersoll's increasingly harsh indictment of Luce and Time Inc. in a barrage of memos he wrote during that critical year, 1938.

Luce was, in fact, getting it from all sides. By the summer MacLeish had finally given up and resigned to take a job as curator of the Nieman program at Harvard. In a farewell sermon to Luce he said:

> I wish things had gone differently. . . . I wish you hadn't been so successful as you have been because it is hard to be successful as you have been and still keep your belief in the desperate necessity for fundamental change. I think what you have done is amazing and I give you all credit and honor for it. . . . But . . . you were meant to be a progressive— a pusher-over—a pryer-upper. You would have been very happy, I think, if you could have felt that the New Deal was your affair. Because it was your affair. Maybe I'm wrong. It's presumptuous to guess about another man's happiness but I think you hate being rich. I think you hate being a pal of the people who want you to be their pal. I think you would have liked to write *The People Yes*. I think you have been an honorable journalist. You would have been happier in a fight, though.

People outside the company were also lecturing Time Inc. officials about their magazine's editorial policies and irresponsible journalism, among them were Mrs. Ogden Reid, owner of the *New York Herald-Tribune*, officials of Standard Oil Company, a Catholic publication, the State Department, Harvard faculty members, friends in the Associated Press. And Ingersoll and others reported this to Luce. When a July issue commented on the term *New Deal*, Ingersoll wrote managing editor Manfred Gottfried that when such editorial comments were made he wanted to be consulted. Then he examined the issue, department by department, in a mostly critical analysis. He also wrote a long memo to Luce in which he sought to define what he called "An Editorial Policy for Time Inc."

At the same time Luce let Ingersoll know that more thought and consideration should be given to the Right: "I applaud your insistence on catching up on Labor. But now I think the time has come for a slight change of attitude—to take a deep breath, smile and once again look at the cockeyed world—cockeyed to the left of us as well as to the right of us."

And when *Time* eliminated the department called "Radicals"—radicals, it was decided, would now be included in the general term *liberals*—Luce protested again: "I consider myself a liberal. Perhaps my kind of liberalism is considered far on the right; but certainly I don't want to be lumped with the leftists—and especially not the gutless leftists.... What the hell, are there no more honest radicals left? Are there no more guts left in American leftism?"

Luce was also annoyed by Ingersoll's so-called scientific principle and his insistence on promoting *Time* as a magazine written by experts. But Ingersoll persisted. And the war of the memos continued, as the whole question of "objectivity" in *Time*'s editorial policies, and of what writers who did not agree with them should do about it, kept everyone stirred up. Ingersoll sent Luce a six-page essay labeled "The Articulation and Approval of Editorial Positions, Attitudes, etc. of Time Inc. Publications"; in it he proposed a system for setting and certifying Time Inc. policy. Luce responded by taking thirteen senior executives to dinner at the Union Club to discuss "objectivity" and other matters of concern; then a few weeks later, in a seventeen-page memo to the staff, he wrote: "There is a persistent urge to say that Time is 'unbiased.' That, of course, is nonsense.... You will find an acknowledgment of bias in the first circular." As for dissenters to *Time* policy on the magazine: A few were tolerable, but the majority must be in "fundamental sympathy." He also insisted that *Time* was "liberal."

Ingersoll responded with a six-page "Reaction to Your Memorandum" raising the critical questions:

A. Is one Time Inc. policy the policy of all Time Inc. activities?
B. Who determines this policy?
C. Once stated, must all conform personally? "No, you say, but 75 percent must."
    But if they don't what then? Are you in danger of being accused of—of actually conducting a Hitler plebiscite, calling upon people to agree under pain of not being allowed to work here?...
D. Must all confirm this policy *in their work*?

He also argued that until these points were clarified (and he questioned whether such an edict should ever be put in writing), Luce's position would remain ambiguous.

One reason for this concern about Time Inc.'s editorial policy and who would be obligated to adhere to it was that 1938 was the year the company negotiated its first contract with the Newspaper Guild. The Communists were also active in the company and had their own underground company newspaper, *High Time*, which viewed most Time Inc. executives, including Ingersoll, as capitalist lackeys. Ingersoll did not, of course, have anything to do with the

Time Inc. Communists. The negotiations dragged on for most of 1938 and were marked by naiveté on both sides. "The weekly meetings were often hilarious," he said. For example, Ingersoll himself, thinking he was proposing a "company union," announced that management favored a "closed Shop." "You would have thought," he commented, "I had blasphemed the Virgin Mary at a Eucharistic Congress." There was not very much tension, however, because Time Incers were generally well paid.

The guild contract and editorial policy were not, however, the main problems confronting the company that year. The real crisis was *Time*'s financial situation (on top of *Life*'s continuing losses), and the tension was not improved when Ingersoll passed on to his circulation manager P.I. Prentice a casual remark of Luce's. "There's nothing wrong with *Time* that can't be fixed up by a good circulation letter." This annoyed Prentice, who outdid Ingersoll and Luce with a sixty-two-page memorandum to Ingersoll, in which he said *Time*'s real problems were (1) the competition for both circulation and advertising from *Life* and (2) *Time*'s inept editorial product. Luce may or may not have seen the Prentice blast, but a month later Ingersoll condensed it into a forty-page memo of his own to Luce, with which, he said, he intended to get Luce mad. It is unlikely that anyone would have written such an indictment of Luce and the management of Time Inc. if he planned on a career with that company. And it was as curious as it was harsh. Ingersoll acknowledged the competition of *Life*, though he thought the depression of 1938 was also a factor. But the main reason *Time* was in trouble, he argued, was that the long-range management policies of Time Inc. (read Henry Luce) had finally caught up with them: They had gone on year after year assuming that *Time*'s circulation and advertising revenue would automatically increase every year, and before the firstborn (*Time*) had ever had a chance to grow to maturity, the company had exhausted its energies in a frantic expansion program that saw the creation of *Fortune*, "The March of Time," and *Life*. "It might have been sounder business," he argued, "for *Time*'s proprietors to have minded their knitting and used their wits to move *Time* forward to an unquestioned Number One position in the magazine world." A rather strange indictment coming from the man who boasted of his role in making *Fortune* a success and in creating *Life*.

Ingersoll agreed, in part, with Prentice's indictment of *Time*'s editorial content: "If ever the returns were in on the failure of a major department, the returns are in on *Time*'s Foreign News. . . . I hold the Foreign News Department responsible [for *Time*'s circulation lag]. People do not buy hundreds of thousands of copies of writings of a tired, tired Jesuit." He recommended that Goldsborough be given a year's leave of absence to travel in Europe, "the only stipulation being that he stay no longer than 24 hours in any capital city."

It took Luce almost two weeks to cool off after receiving this blast, and then he came back with a fifteen-page defense of his policies, past and present. As for *Time*'s problems, he said, "I picked the best man [Ingersoll, of course] I could find to give it his full attention and from the moment he took charge, he was permitted . . . to spend vastly more money on *Time*, editorially and other-wise, than had ever been spent before." Luce said he had been aware that *Time* had become dull and sloppy, and the real reason for that was his neglect. But, he went on to say, "that is one mistake I shall never make again." Hence he agreed that *Life* was one distraction too many. But he was also clearly saying that, despite the free hand and unlimited money he had given Ingersoll, his publisher had not done the job. It was also apparent that Ingersoll's criticism of Time Inc.'s expansion stung him, and he would not accept the indictment: "Ours is a series of radical pioneering adventures, none of them a failure, all of them in some way great successes . . . all of them regarded by various groups of dis-criminating people as outstanding, important contributions to the journalism of these great days. . . . There must be something more, Horatio, than is mentioned in your philosophy."

Horatio's days were now numbered; it was just a matter, you might say, of *Time*. Luce agreed to remove Goldsborough, but he also decided to take over as *Time*'s managing editor for two issues to see for himself what the editorial problems were. And, as Elson put it, "he concluded at the end of the two sessions that whatever was wrong with *Time* was rooted less in the managing editor than in the publisher." After editing the two issues, Luce wrote another long memo, which finally ended up in his desk drawer. It was mostly directed at Ingersoll, and Elson quoted it extensively in his official history. One problem, said Luce, was that he conceived a "publisher" as being pretty much on "the vulgar money-making side of things. And in view of the fact that Ingersoll is considerable of a journalist, maybe this is psychologically wrong. But I should like to think not. . . . If I give Ingersoll a job I would prefer to have less of, it is partly because I have had so damned much of it and not because I think it lacks imaginative values."

Perhaps the last straw came at the end of the year, when *Time*'s editors were picking the "Man of the Year." The Man for 1938 had, of course, to be Adolph Hitler, who was threatening to overrun Europe. But what arrived on Ingersoll's desk was a glamorized portrait of *der Führer*, right arm raised in a "*Sieg heil*" salute that made him look the embodiment of leadership. "Where the hell did they get such a portrait?" Ingersoll fumed. "From Goebbels?" He was totally appalled. "That afternoon on Gregory Zilboorg's couch," he says, "I could talk of nothing else. What to do about this unsubtle identification of the magazine of which I am the publisher with 'The Wave of the Future' which revolts me so?"

Zilboorg had a suggestion. If there was time to replace the offensive cover, he knew just the man to draw a new one—a fine artist, anti-Nazi, but not a German. He was an Austrian, both an aristocrat and a Catholic, and no man to be called a red. His name was Rudolph Charles von Ripper. Overnight von Ripper drew a portrait of Hitler in pen and ink (so a quick linecut could be made of it), but in this version the setting left no doubt about how he had made the news that led *Time* to choose him. The background was a catherine wheel on which naked bodies were bound, tortured, and broken. Down in front, accompanying the torture on an organ, was *Time*'s Man of the Year.

Ingersoll did not hold a conference about this cover. He simply scrapped thousands of dollars' worth of four-color printed covers and put through his black-and-white substitute. Luce played no part in the decision, but when he saw the cover, after the issue was already on its way to the newsstands, his secretary, Corinne Thrasher, was on the phone, fast: "Get up here pronto, Mr. I.—pronto."

When Ingersoll arrived in Luce's office, the offending issue lay at the center of his desk, everything else pushed impatiently to one side. "He was standing over it," Ingersoll recalls.

"'Who did this?'

"'I did.'

"'*You* did?'

"Luce's face was white; the blood seemed to have been drained even from his lips.

"'Have you any idea what you've done? A basic tradition destroyed... everything I've built... in one gesture.'" Then Luce paused, actually trembling with rage.

"It was beyond any words that could be exchanged between us," says Ingersoll. "I said nothing, he said no more; we simply stood there, eyes fixed on each other."

Then, abruptly, Luce said, "Spilt milk," and it was over.

Ingersoll left the room, and, he says, he and Luce never discussed editorial matters again. "Harry was right, to have been so shaken," Ingersoll says, "by my taking an open editorial position on the cover of *Time*. The essence of *Time*'s plausibility was its pose of impartiality in public matters and I had blown the cover (no pun intended). But Harry never intended not to take sides in handling news, so from the very beginning he must have been in torture! If *Time* revealed his prejudices, it would lose its plausibility. Yet his basic convictions were very strong and to be objective in areas they touched seemed a betrayal to him. This was the conflict in Harry Luce that he never was to resolve—and the source of his corruption as a journalist who could suppress truths, and even print lies knowingly (as in his defense of Chiang's China) in the service of prejudices that *Time* could never admit to.

"But on that spilt milk morning in 1938, the world was still young and neither Harry nor I ever brought up the issue again. I doubt if either of us understood them, then—I know I didn't."

The Hitler cover incident did have one lasting effect. From then on, *Time*'s cover artists were encouraged to add background to their portraits to suggest why their Men (or Women) were selected that year. And Ingersoll made another significant contribution to *Time*'s cover during his last year as publisher. The cover had not changed since its first issue in 1923, so he brought in the former *Fortune* art director Eleanor Treacy, who was then free-lancing, to give it a new look, which is generally the look it has today. He also insisted that cover stories be researched as thoroughly as *Fortune*'s articles were.

By the beginning of 1939 Ingersoll had made his final, emotional break with Luce, although they were the only two people in Time Inc. who knew Ingersoll would soon be leaving. He could not leave, of course, until his commitment was fulfilled, and it was in February when Luce received his now historic telegram from *Life* general manager C. D. Jackson, while Luce was on a brief vacation in South Carolina: "LIFE IN BLACK FOR JANUARY." Ingersoll was free to leave. But he was hesitant to break his financial ties until he felt more confident about raising the money he needed for his own publication. John Wharton had still not arranged a meeting with Jock Whitney, and Harry Cushing had reported that Wall Street did not look promising as a source. The financial house he worked for, Ladenberg and Thalman, had canvassed the financial markets and reported that ten million was "blue sky money."

Ingersoll said, all right, try for five million, but Cushing reported back that this, too, was blue sky money. "Why?" Ingersoll asked.

"Your projections are too iffy," Cushing replied. "Besides, have you ever heard of something called the Securities and Exchange Commission? The New Deal and your friend Franklin Delano Roosevelt have made a project such as yours almost impossible to start. Ten years ago I could have gotten you your money in ten minutes on the telephone. Now there isn't a house down town that will touch underwriting a new venture. You were born twenty years too late, son."

So, Ingersoll says, "that put it squarely up to me and I made my decision." When Luce returned from South Carolina, Ingersoll would tell his boss that he was ready for the promised sabbatical. He would raise the money himself! As Wolcott Gibbs would later put it, he was ready "for the apocalypse."

His first move was to send two memos to the staff of *Time* foreshadowing, but not announcing, his departure. "My assignment as the publisher of *Time*," he said, "was to put this magazine's house in order after the cyclone of *Life* had whizzed through the back yard and taken off half the living room and kitchen. The period of reorganization was . . . ended with my 1938 year-end report to the President."

The Time Inc. official history gives a somewhat different account of Ingersoll's departure: "One morning, Ingersoll brought up the subject [of his newspaper] again [and] Luce abruptly . . . suggested that Ingersoll should henceforth devote his whole time to the newspaper." Luce, it would appear from this, abruptly asked Ingersoll to leave. At least one former Time Inc. executive supports this version of the story. He was in Luce's outer office the morning Ingersoll had his farewell conversation with Luce. After Ingersoll left, the man was summoned into Luce's office, and, as he says, "Harry said, 'Well, I've just fired Mac Ingersoll.'"

Ingersoll denies this, and a memorandum in the Time, Inc., Archives supports him. He and Luce had discussed Ingersoll's eventual departure for months.

But it did come as a shock to the staff, though not necessarily as a disappointment. T. S. Matthews in his own book called it a "defection," which was surprising. Reading his book you would expect Matthews to have applauded Ingersoll's breaking away from the magazine they both hated.*

From discussions with people who were there, and from the memoirs of those who have criticized his years at Time Inc. it seems clear, however, that Ingersoll's poor reputation among Luce's lieutenants can be blamed, at least in part, on Luce himself. Ingersoll was, admittedly, a loner, abrasive, ambitious, and egocentric, all unattractive qualities not likely to win friends. He also had an annoying habit, according to one former Time, Inc., executive, of trying to take credit for things he did not do. And because he was essentially an editor, when he was appointed publisher he could not resist interfering with the editorial side of the operation, which publishers—especially at Time Inc.—were not supposed to do (unless, of course, they were Henry Luce).

But Ingersoll was also probably the most talented of all the journalists in the building—including Luce himself—which made him both attractive and valuable to Luce, and which led to Ingersoll's rapid rise in the company. This, in turn, inevitably inspired jealousy. Two of the most serious charges ex-Time Incers have leveled at Ingersoll are (1) that he tried to undercut Roy Larsen, and (2) that he was devious and secretive, the most oft-cited evidence being that in his last year and a half at the company he was preparing to launch his own newspaper, "on the sly," as one ex-staffer put it. Some even thought he had been fired because Luce "discovered" he was working on his newspaper while he was supposed to be publishing *Time*.

These are unfair charges. Ingersoll had recommended to Luce that Larsen be made general manager, and Luce had rejected the idea. In fact, the executive who said Luce had told him that he had "fired" Ingersoll concedes Luce might have used the word (even though Ingersoll had resigned) to help compensate for what he had done in 1935 by promoting Ingersoll over Larsen. And although a few Time Incers knew about Ingersoll's newspaper in 1938—and they were mostly the ones he was lining up as future employees—he did, for obvious

---

*Matthews' charge that Ingersoll had "defected" from *Time* also surprised Ingersoll, and he was hurt and offended by Matthews's general attack on him in *Name and Address*. Characteristically, to let off steam, he wrote Matthews a long letter responding to his book, then never mailed it. As he said in the letter, Matthews had failed to perceive that "I hated *Time*'s *Time*ishness as much as you did . . . I was trying to remold it nearer to my heart's desire, and in a hell of a hurry . . . all the while hating it and not respecting it and wanting to get the hell out." Calling Matthews "one of my better picks" as a back-of-the-book editor, he went on to say that Matthews had developed into just another *Time* writer; and after commenting on what he thought was Matthews's misstatement of facts in his book, Ingersoll concluded: "Once a *Time*-writer always a *Time*-writer."

Ingersoll did the same thing when Eric Hodgins attacked him in a review of the Time Inc. official history in the *New Yorker* magazine. (Hodgins was also highly critical of Ingersoll's office politicking in his own memoir, *Trolley to the Moon*.) When Ingersoll read the Hodgins review, he was obviously deeply hurt. Hodgins accused both Ingersoll and Matthews of taking their just rewards and repaying "Luce with subsequent calumny." Ingersoll replied, in another unmailed letter, that this was some gratitude coming from a man whom he had helped pull through a messy suicide attempt that could have ruined Hodgins's career at Time Inc. Furthermore, he did not owe Luce anything. "I left him at least $50,000,000 richer for my efforts [by making *Fortune* a success and by starting *Life*]. So who was in debt to whom?"

reasons, attempt to keep it a secret. But Luce knew all along what he was doing, and had even reached the point where, according to Elson, he was becoming tired of hearing about it.

One of the most significant comments made about Ingersoll at the time of his departure appeared in the diary of John Shaw Billings: "He blew his own horn in the most outrageous way. What a conceited egoist. He's been a snake-in-the-grass in this organization for years and yet, funny thing, he's the only fellow in the company that Luce really seems to want to be 'palsy-walsy' with." And considering the confidence Luce had placed in Ingersoll, how much responsibility he had given him, how well Ingersoll had performed, and the personal friendship Luce had displayed, it is intriguing to speculate what it was that contributed most to Luce's eventually turning against his trusted friend. There would have been several reasons:

• Clare Luce, with some justification, continued passionately to dislike Ingersoll, and her passion was no doubt reinforced both by a subsequent attack on her in *PM* and by the 1948 publication of the novel *The Great Ones*, whose main characters Ingersoll insists he did not model on the Luces, though everyone else thought he did.
• *The Great Ones* alone would have been enough to infuriate Luce, and many think that its publication was the critical turning point in Luce's relationship with his journalistic colleague.
• With Ingersoll gone, the executives at Time Inc. no doubt kept up their criticism of him; Luce certainly continued to hear ugly things about Ingersoll's machin-ations—and quite likely would eventually learn that Ingersoll was a member of a Communist party study group while also publisher of *Time*.
• Finally, Ingersoll's persistent criticism of *Life* and *Time* could not help but irritate Luce. Even before he left Time Inc. Ingersoll in memos to Luce was stating, "*Life* is an intellectual and artistic failure." And after he left the company, and especially during the decade when *Time* became a virtual house organ for the Republican National Committee in general and the presidency of Dwight D. Eisenhower in particular, Ingersoll continually attacked the magazine. In 1964 *Fact* magazine devoted a whole issue to articles by prominent Americans (in-cluding many former Time Inc. employees) accusing *Time* of dishonest jour-nalism. The lead piece, and by far the most effective indictment, was by Ingersoll, who wrote: "The way to sell a successful lie is to include enough truth in it to make it believable—and *Time* is the most successful liar of our times."

Ingersoll was right in telling Hodgins in his unmailed letter that he was not in debt to Luce when he left Time Inc.—and therefore felt free to criticize Luce and his publications. Luce, on the other hand, was certainly in debt to him— for making *Fortune* a success, for running the company during Luce's emotional divorce and remarriage, for providing the force that created *Life*, for beginning the long overdue rejuvenation of *Time*, and, in the realm of less tangible con-tributions, for stirring things up and keeping the company on its toes. At least one Time Inc. executive—Pierre Prentice—says Luce made a big mistake in letting Ingersoll get away. "Harry Luce was a different person without you around," he told Ingersoll at a lunch years later (and he confirmed this in a recent telephone interview).

In assessing Luce, Ingersoll (as did others including John Hersey) saw him as two persons: the humble, energetic, exciting journalist he first met in the 1930s and the powerful spokesman for corporate America who emerged after he married Clare Brokaw and became rich and powerful. "He was for me a superior character in a Greek tragedy," Ingersoll wrote Hodgins, "despite the best of intentions, he was doomed from birth to create evil."

Ingersoll was truly fond of Henry Luce the journalist of the 1930s and perhaps best summed up his feelings in the obituary he wrote for the *Washington Post* in March of 1967. In it he even forgave Luce for printing lies in his magazines: "Henry believed himself implicitly—and believed in himself. And since he always acted consistently with this belief that made him a most honest fellow. He saw life in very simple and characteristically heroic terms. Once upon a time, in his early days, he believed in himself so purely that he was even humble. He believed in words and he was in those days humble towards men who could write them as he knew he never could. He got over that when getting so rich confused him, but in a long life, on balance so constructive, that's forgivable.

"The important imprint Henry Robinson Luce left was the imprint of his faith in words that communicate . . . in the basic, total, inherent worthwhileness of dedicating one's life to words. . . . The world's a little short of faith these days. It's poorer this night that Harry Luce has left us, whether you loved or hated him. And I guess I'm one who loves him still for the times that faith was a shining thing, untarnished by the smog that makes the air of financial success so hard to breathe."

*With two unidentified executives at a typical publishing
cocktail party, where, likely as not, Ingersoll is discussing
"a new kind of newspaper"*

9: Financing the Apocalypse

In a memorandum dated April 3, 1939, announcing to his staff that Ralph
Ingersoll was leaving the company, Henry Luce stressed that "neither Time Inc.
nor any executive of Time Inc. has any responsibility financially or otherwise
for Ingersoll's proposed paper." But the first thing Ingersoll did when he left
Luce was to move Publications Research into rented offices on the sixth floor
of the new Time-Life Building in Rockefeller Center, a move that helped per-
petuate the rumors during the planning stages of *PM* that it was financed by
Time Inc. There were also rumors that the new paper was really the mouthpiece
of the Communist party. Among the people thought to be involved in the preparation of an early dummy were Dashiell Hammett and Lillian Hellman, and
Ingersoll himself was rumored to have been the organizer of a Communist party
study group under the auspices of the "cultural Commissar" of the Communist
party in America. Gilmor did, in fact, loan twenty-five thousand dollars to the
early financing of Publications Research. Since late 1938, in a room at the Plaza,
Hammett had been secretly interviewing prospective contributors for a new liberal
newspaper, and Hellman had been working on the dummy issue. Ingersoll, of
course, had his prospectus, which he was continually rewriting as his project

developed.* But he also needed a dummy to show the VRMs, and he wanted the writing in his first experimental publication to be outstanding. It was, and no wonder: Contributors included Leland Stowe, George Fielding Eliot, Charles Wertenbaker, Dorothy Parker, Oscar Levant, Dashiell Hammett, Heywood Broun, Lillian Hellman, and Elizabeth Hawes. Half its space was devoted to art and photographs (contributed by Margaret Bourke-White), and several pages were printed in four colors. Tom Cleland, who had designed *Fortune*, developed a thirty-two page tabloid with a page size slightly larger than that of the *New York Daily News*. Most of the writers remained anonymous because they were working for other publications, but Ingersoll had a nucleus of a "family," who became identified with him and whom he bombarded with memos. The family included: Bourke-White, Cleland, Harry Cushing, Gilmor, Hammett, Hawes, Hellman, John R. Mench, an advertising man, Ed Stanley, Donald Stewart (a CPA), and John Wharton.

Cushing and Wharton, his financial advisers, were still insisting that because of S.E.C. regulations, he would have a hard time raising even three million dollars. So Ingersoll and Stanley set down to work out the absolute minimum they thought it would take to start publishing, after which the paper might catch on and support itself. "If we can get the paper on the street for a million and a half, that is my irreducible minimum," Ingersoll said. "If I can get that, I'll take it. It'll buy only one turn at bat, in the ninth inning of a losing game, with two out and two strikes on me. But I'll at least have one crack at the ball."

He felt he needed a circulation of only two hundred thousand to break even, which hardly put him in competition with even the weakest of New York's daily papers.† He also decided that if his idea was not good enough to attract $1.5 million in support of it, then he did not have anything anyway.

The next problem was dealing with the Securities and Exchange Commission, and while the dummy was being prepared, Ingersoll went down to Washington to call on Commissioner James Landis in person. Landis had contributed some articles to *Fortune* in the early 1930s, so Ingersoll had an entrée. It was now early summer. Landis was not too busy, and Ingersoll was ushered into his office. He wasted little time telling the commissioner what he wanted, and complained that S.E.C. regulations made it impossible to raise money for any new venture, to which Landis replied, bristling, "Who told you that nonsense?"

"Highly responsible bankers and attorneys on Wall Street," Ingersoll replied. "I'll be glad to name them if you'd like."

"I don't care who the hell they are; they're all alike," Landis snapped back. "They're full of crap. What they told you is just anti-New Deal propaganda.

---

*The *PM* prospectus would eventually become one of the most widely quoted and discussed documents in the history of American journalism—primarily because it articulated every newspaperman's dream of a newspaper. It is reprinted in full in appendix 1.

†In 1939 circulations of Manhattan's daily papers were: *Daily News*, 1,800,000; *Daily Mirror*, 750,000; *Evening Journal*, 600,000; *Times*, 500,000; *World Telegram*, over 400,000; *Herald-Tribune*, 400,000; *Evening Sun*, 300,000; *Evening Post*, 250,000.

Our regulations don't stop any man's starting a legitimate business."

"OK," Ingersoll said. "If they've got it wrong—and they're the best counsel I can hire—you tell me what's right."

"What do you mean?"

"I mean you tell me how I can raise a million and a half dollars without being put in jail. The newspaper I want to finance doesn't exist. The venture is experimental. I just believe in it, that's all. I can't even tell a prospective investor what its operating costs will be—let alone how many people may buy it."

Commissioner Landis was obviously irritated, but Ingersoll went on. "If what you say is true and the New Deal is not against new private enterprise, you tell me the steps I must take to do it legally. Tell me in detail."

Much to Ingersoll's surprise, that is precisely what Landis did. For an hour he told him how to raise the money, while Ingersoll took notes, which he read back to Landis to make sure he had it right. In brief, this was his advice:

First, Ingersoll should put on paper everything he could think of about what he wanted to do, what he guessed it might cost, and how he would spend the money. Most important, put it in his own words. Second, solicit the capital himself, employing no agents and paying no commissions for introductions or even bringing in the money itself. Third, solicit the capital in big chunks. Do *not* take small contributions, even if offered. Name a minimum of $25,000 to $50,000 an investor—or better, $100,000. The legal presumption should be that anyone investing that much money can look after himself. Fourth, solicit only individuals able to lose $100,000 without being hurt.

It was good advice and Ingersoll was eager to return to New York to start fund-raising. But first he wanted to see President Roosevelt. When Ingersoll was editor of *Fortune*, he ran a number of articles about and by members of Roosevelt's administration that must have impressed FDR, because Ingersoll had no trouble gaining an audience with the president. FDR was enthusiastic about the plans for a new kind of newspaper, which was not surprising. After the 1936 election, during which most of the country's newspapers had viciously opposed him, the president had become as critical of the nation's press as Ingersoll was. Not only did Roosevelt like the ideas Ingersoll presented, but he chatted on for an hour—while his secretary held his phone calls—making suggestions about what ought to be in the paper (suggestions Ingersoll ignored).

Back in New York, Ingersoll set January 15, 1940, as the deadline for raising the $1.5 million from fifteen Very Rich Men (or Women). If he did not have it by then, he would give up. And he must have thought raising the money was going to be a cinch because the first hundred thousand came with deceptive ease. One day he was having a drink at the bar in the Plaza Hotel when he met a friend who was lunching with Marian Rosenwald Stern, heir to the Sears, Roebuck fortune. His friend, a young lady, asked Ingersoll to join them. During the meal Ingersoll could not restrain himself from talking about his venture, which he described with his usual infectious enthusiasm. Marian Stern thought it was exciting, and said she would like to invest. "Of course, there's a man you'll have to satisfy who checks these things for me," she added, "but I'm absolutely sure you can count on me."

Ingersoll frankly doubted it, but much to his surprise, the man he had to see, Nathan Levin, head of the Rosenwald Family Association, came through—primarily, says Levin, because Marian Stern had already made up her mind. Also, Ingersoll had decided that no commitment would be binding until he had raised the entire $1.5 million; Levin had no trouble approving the investment.

Having raised a hundred thousand dollars as the result of one casual luncheon meeting, Ingersoll was encouraged. But he was still being urged to abandon his plan by two men whose counsel he could not ignore: Colin Ingersoll and Gregory Zilboorg. His father lived near Ingersoll's Shadow Rock Farm in Lakeville, and they saw each other often on the weekends. On one occasion his father invited him over for a solemn talk, and his counsel went something like this:

"You got to the top of the ladder and I'm proud of you, boy. But now I have to tell you that I believe you've been carried away by the successes you've had and that you may be destroying yourself, leaving Mr. Luce now. I've lived longer than you have; I've seen men whom I've respected overreach themselves. I've seen good men lose fortunes and be broken by it. What will happen to you if you can't raise the money?

"I know you are out on a limb and that it hurts your pride to think of turning back. But it's not too late. You said to me that Mr. Luce wanted you back! Go, boy, go!"

His father had urged him from childhood never to be a quitter. "I knew," Ingersoll says, "he had come hard by this decision to reverse himself, to save the boy he still loved from what he saw as inevitable disaster. He had studied my financial plan with meticulous care and had been just close enough to rich men to know their reaction to speculative projects more promising than mine."

But Ingersoll insisted he was going through with his plans, and although he was saddened by his father's lack of confidence, he was not surprised. Zilboorg's position was something else. "It really shook me," Ingersoll says. "Zilboorg understood me inside out, as father never did. He also really understood what I was attempting and could appraise it more realistically than my father, because he himself moved in the very world which I was assaulting, the big time money world. He had as patients several of the names that were on my project list; he would know my chances with them far better than I. And I had total confidence both in his judgment and in his exercising it in my best interests as a human being. My very soul was under his microscope.

"I had come to his chambers, as normally, expecting to relax on his couch and free associate. But that morning he had sat me down across his desk from him, saying that he wanted, this day, to talk to me more as friend than as doctor to patient although, I must understand, the advice he was going to give me would be consistent with what he would also prescribe as my psychiatrist."

Zilboorg said that however fascinating a plaything Ingersoll might make his project, the rich men whose backing he sought would not, in the end, come through. "So I would be stranded," Ingersoll recalls his saying, "at the end of my year of trying, high, dry and wrung out, with only a crawl on my knees back to Luce left of my career. And, speaking now as both friend and physician, it was not his opinion that I could, as a person, survive that experience. Death was one thing to face bravely but it was not death I was facing; it was mutilation, the crushing of my psychological structure; it would be permanently crippling.

"It's not too late," Zilboorg continued. "You are important to Luce; you have scared him—that you might be able to make it without him—but you've not scared him badly yet. He is still sure you are not going to get the money you need and that you'll be back, a more realistic and humbler man for your whirl at challenging him. Right now, he will enjoy being gracious about reinstating you. But not later. He is already learning to do without you and if you stay away much longer he will get his satisfaction in making an object lesson of your desertion by humiliating you. So go back to him now, in good grace, still walking straight.

"You wish to overcome Luce, to demonstrate that in his own area you are a greater publisher than he. And at the same time you have an unconscious need to fail in the overcoming, to die of your own hand for it. The suicidal component in your drive can arrange for you to defeat yourself."

Ingersoll said later that this was the low point of his sabbatical year. He had too much faith in his psychiatrist to ignore him, but Ingersoll refused to follow Zilboorg's advice. "A year before," he says, "I know that after listening to either my father or Zilboorg I would at least have re-reasoned my position. But that summer, something had finally happened inside me and I knew that I belonged to myself and nobody else and that if that self was to prove inadequate then that was that! It didn't matter, I had no choice. I think this is the point of no return in any man's undertaking. Until he's crossed it, he is still a hostage to somebody or something."

When his dummy was ready, he ordered two hundred copies printed. Then, not too long after his session with Zilboorg, he received a phone call from Washington that made it appear, for a while at least, that his psychiatrist was all wrong about rich men and their money. Ingersoll began to wonder if he was in a dream. The call summoned him down to the office of Tommy Corcoran, President Roosevelt's bright, cocky troubleshooter. Roosevelt had mentioned Ingersoll's project to Corcoran and asked him to look into it. Corcoran had apparently done a thorough job of it because when Ingersoll walked into his office, the president's assistant seemed to know everything about Ingersoll, who recalls Corcoran's first remark: "Ingersoll," he said, "you've got to get used to me. I'm this kind of a guy: If I were driving along in a car and I came to a desert I had to cross—and there on the edge of the desert was the last gas station for a hundred miles—and I knew my tank was almost empty, why, goddam it, I'd keep right on going by that gas station. And you know why? Just because I like the feel of the wind in my whiskers."

Then Corcoran got down to business with his usual directness: "The President likes your newspaper idea. He wants to help raise the money. It's not really a problem. How much do you think you need?"

"Ten million dollars," Ingersoll replied, deciding quickly that he might as well go for the full amount.

"Fine," Tommy answered complacently. "Now, we've been thinking over who ought to put this money up for you—and I think we've got just the fellow. Have you ever heard of Edward Noble?"

"No."

"But you have heard of Life Savers?"

"Life Savers?"

"Sure—candy Life Savers—the ones with the holes in them. That's Edward J. Noble."

"Now I remember," Ingersoll said. "He's Assistant Secretary for Aviation or something like that."

"Of Commerce," Corcoran replied, screwing up his mobile face to give Ingersoll a clear picture of a man who had become rich selling candy, who had given money to the New Deal and been paid off with a minor post! "You go see Noble," Corcoran continued. "He'll fuss but he'll like your idea and he can afford it. Then he'll get scared and will want someone to reassure him. You leave that part to me. When the right time comes, if we have to, we'll get the boss himself to give him the word. You just go see him and play it straight. He'll be useful to you, too; he knows a lot about merchandising—Lifesavers."

Ingersoll returned to New York in search of Edward J. Noble, the Lifesaver king, finally tracking him down at his summer place on one of the Thousand Islands in the gulf of Saint Lawrence. Noble invited him up for a weekend, and soon Ingersoll was flying over the Catskill's in his little Fairchild 24, having decided that the best way to impress Noble and his guests would be to arrive in his own plane, long scarf blowing in the wind. The first evening, joined by Noble's brother and partner Robert P. Noble, they excused themselves from the other guests to talk about the newspaper. Edward Noble seemed only mildly interested in the project—until Ingersoll put the dummy in front of him. Then he caught fire.

"The package," he exclaimed. "The package—in color—you've *got* it."

The brother, who was not a New Dealer, had been listening somewhat skeptically. But now he also began to show a change of attitude. "You don't really understand what you have, Ingersoll," Edward Noble said. "It could be great. In our business it's the packaging. How do you think a simple little piece of sugar candy got to make thirty million dollars? Oh, the hole, too. But that was really started when the price of sugar went up and we had to save on costs. Just think of what a newspaper would do to its competition, with its pictures in color like these, with the front page in color to stand out from all the other papers on the newsstand!"

Ingersoll returned to New York truly excited. "After the Thousand Islands," he says, "came meetings in Washington and New York and at Noble's house somewhere in Westchester. And at each meeting the partnership became more tangible. Between meetings there was Tommy [Corcoran] on the telephone— suddenly, at any hour—to tell me everything was all right. It was the month of August. September would begin the busy fall; we wanted to have it all signed up with Noble before Labor Day. The Boss was described as very pleased."

While Ingersoll was working on Ed Noble, another significant development was taking place: Corcoran had also introduced him to a former Scripps-Howard editor named Nelson Poynter, who had convinced both Corcoran and Ed Stanley, in earlier conversations, that many of his ideas about publishing coincided with Ingersoll's. Poynter had been business manager of the *Washington News* tabloid and had also worked on Scripps-Howard papers in Columbus, Ohio, and Ko- komo, Indiana, where he had become convinced you could publish a profitable newspaper by dropping certain conventional newspaper features, classifying the news, and eliminating advertising. He argued that a small-circulation paper would probably not be able to get advertising anyway, so why not eliminate it and make a virtue of the fact that your paper does not have to cater to advertisers in its editorial pages. He had prepared a prospectus for a paper embodying his ideas and had shown it to Tommy Corcoran when the president's aide was in Saint Petersburg, where Poynter was editor of the *Saint Petersburg Times*. Cor- coran saw the similarity in what Poynter and Ingersoll were trying to do, and brought the two men together in August of 1939—while Noble was trying to make up his mind. The two men took to each other immediately. Ingersoll was especially looking for someone who would take over the business side of the operation, not only because he was spending all his time on promotion and editorial planning, but because he felt that the editorial product was the only thing that really mattered. "It is my arrogance," he wrote Poynter, "to believe that if we have this, all other problems are secondary and soluble." By mid- August Poynter had joined the nucleus family as general manager, and shortly thereafter Ingersoll wrote a memo to his embryo staff: "We are going into business without advertising," he announced to them. The new paper would instead publish a four-page editorial section digesting the advertising news appearing in other New York newspapers—an idea resulting directly from Poynter's expe- rience in Kokomo.

Meanwhile, Edward Noble's brother Robert had lost interest in the project. "Oil wells are more fun than newspapers" was Robert's decision, according to his brother. But Edward was still interested *if* there were at least nine others involved. So Ingersoll decided to lower his goal again—to the original $1.5 million—and set out to convince Noble of the advantages of being the sole financial backer. At the same time, Noble was disturbed at what he was hearing about Ingersoll: that he was a charming but impractical fellow, a "creative genius" with little respect for earnings statements. There was also gossip that Ingersoll had been fired by the *New Yorker*. So Ingersoll asked Ross to spike these rumors, which the *New Yorker* editor effectively did, at the same time offering to put ten- to forty-thousand dollars into the project if it was needed. Ingersoll also suggested to Corcoran that Noble talk to Henry Luce; then he wrote Luce, informing him that a deal was near, that he would probably be hearing from Noble, and asking him to please tell the potential investor that he (Ingersoll) was "a nasty penny pincher at heart."

Luce responded rather generously with a nice letter praising Mac Ingersoll and his ideas, but stressing that Time Inc. was not in any way involved in his project. In a separate letter—which confirms that in August of 1939 he still felt very close to his former general manager—Luce said he was endorsing Ingersoll's project out of friendship: "you have been a close personal friend of mine."

With Luce's endorsement and Poynter (who reassured Noble that the bottom line would not be ignored) a member of the family, Noble agreed by the end of August to put up the full $1.5 million for the project—provided he was given half ownership, which Corcoran urged Ingersoll to do: "Let him write his own contract. He'll be happier about it and you'll have everything you want."

Ingersoll had no objection and told Noble he preferred it that way and wanted Noble to be an active partner in the production and merchandising of the paper.

On August 29, 1939, Noble was in Washington, staying at the Hay Adams House. At Corcoran's suggestion, Ingersoll went down and moved into the Carlton Hotel, across and down Sixteenth Street. He was alone, with no bankers or attorneys. He did not have long to wait. Corcoran himself delivered the papers drawn up by Noble's attorneys. Ingersoll says he cannot remember a single condition Noble imposed. There were lots of them, however, because the papers went on and on for paragraphs. But Noble's reservations turned out to be so trivial they made Corcoran and Ingersoll laugh. "He's got a half dozen lawyers across the street," Corcoran said. "He's just fussing, the way I knew he would. But it'll be all right. He's got the word."

By August 31 the papers had made several trips back and forth across Sixteenth Street, with Ingersoll endorsing every change with one word: "Fine." The dinner hour came and went with Ingersoll sitting by the telephone. At eleven P.M. the telephone rang. It was Corcoran: "Everything is agreed, everything buttoned up, everybody was happy. You can get drunk now—but not so drunk that you can't sign the papers about noon tomorrow after the lawyers have them retyped. Ed will sign them and I'll bring them around. Congratulations; you're a newspaper publisher now."

Ingersoll did not get drunk. He just collapsed into bed, exhausted and numb.

The next morning at about six thirty the phone rang; it was Corcoran again. He had been up all night. "Have you heard what's happened?" he asked. Ingersoll said, "No." Corcoran went on: "At midnight last night Hitler invaded Poland. We've been too busy here for me to call you before."

"What will that mean to Noble?" Ingersoll asked.

"If I know your friend, it will mean that you won't hear from him today."

Corcoran was right. Noble could not even bring himself to break the news to Ingersoll personally. He simply sent a message to say that in view of the unsettled world conditions, he did not feel he could go into such a speculative venture at this time. Ingersoll was crushed—not just because he had been let down, but because the negotiations with Noble had cost him two months of valuable time.

Ingersoll still had Marian Stern's hundred thousand dollars, and then suddenly Cushing came up with another hundred thousand from an investment banker in the firm of Ladenberg and Thalman. His name was Howard Bonbright.

Poynter was also talking about putting in a hundred thousand of his own. But they were still a long way from the rock-bottom figure of $1.5 million, so Ingersoll set about raising money again, using S.E.C. Commissioner Landis's technique—only now he had Poynter's help. Sometimes they would call on a potential backer together, sometimes separately. Poynter was also given the assignment of going back to Noble and persuading him to become part of the group by putting up at least a hundred thousand. And Noble's return to the fold looked promising—until suddenly there was a new problem. In mid-September Ingersoll decided the time had come to define his relationship with Poynter, so he wrote his general manager a long curious letter saying, among other things, he had heard from the "Scripps-Howard people" and "the Cowles boys," Poynter's two previous bosses, that he was overconfident and overambitious. Ingersoll was also irritated by a proposal Poynter had written describing their project as being "run by Ingersoll and Poynter. He wanted it clearly understood that Poynter's only responsibility was a "limited authority over the business operations" and that Poynter was not in line to be either publisher or editor of the new publication. If, however, the newspaper was a success and a similar publication was launched in another city, Poynter would have first crack at publishing it.

Poynter responded "Touché," conceding he had said in a letter that Ingersoll and Poynter were running things. He apologized and stated that he still had a clear idea of their respective, complementary roles, as discussed one night at the Yale Club: "the editorial genius [Ingersoll] and the hard-boiled penny pincher [Poynter]." But he was clearly stunned by Ingersoll's paying attention to "the gossip in the trade" and said that he, too, had picked up some gossip about Ingersoll: to wit, "that you are erratic, hard to work for, get involved with trivia, too literary and academic to edit a newspaper, ruthless, self-centered and selfish, subject to the last man seen." He also said: "You have been too free with promises to make men rich. You have a certain lack of sense of reality. The whole atmosphere in Publications Research Inc. was one of lack of reality, a certain Alice-in-Wonderland playing store, and spending their future riches, hiring future treasurers before a good managing editor. I thought my role was to bring some reality to this charming scene. I was wrong."

Although he earnestly wanted to "see this newspaper started"—"it is important to America"—there was, he concluded, "nothing for me to do but withdraw."

And with Poynter went Noble, who still had some misgivings about Ingersoll's sense of reality. But despite their differences, Ingersoll and Poynter kept in touch. Ingersoll later awarded him two hundred shares of common stock for his contribution, and he continued to give Poynter full credit for persuading him not to take advertising in the newspaper. Poynter shifted his attention to developing a similar paper in Chicago, but nothing ever came of the project. Meanwhile, Ingersoll also had a falling-out with Ed Stanley, who went on a leave of absence in October and was completely out of the family by December. The break with Stanley occurred over the publication of the first sample newspaper, which Ingersoll felt was too slick and impractical. Stanley claimed he was merely trying to carry out Ingersoll's ideas, and one observer said that when they did not work out, Ingersoll put the blame on Stanley.

One thing both Poynter and Ingersoll had agreed on was the necessity of improving Ingersoll's sixty-page prospectus. It needed trimming and sharpening by a professional—and the best copywriter in the country was a young millionaire named William Benton. Ingersoll had played bridge with Benton at Yale and remembered his boast that he intended to make a million dollars by the time he was thirty, a boast he had fulfilled through the advertising agency he formed in partnership with Chester Bowles. Benton was now retired form advertising and working with Robert Hutchins, as vice president of the University of Chicago. Ingersoll had not seen Benton since college, but Laura Hobson, who had come to know him when they both worked for George Batten in the early 1920s, and had kept in touch, set up a meeting between the two men.

Benton was immediately impressed with Ingersoll's ideas and enthusiasm. When Ingersoll asked him to read the long prospectus, he agreed, taking it with him on the train to Southport, Connecticut, where he was spending some time. His reaction was mixed: Where it talked about editorial content and format, the prospectus was, in the words of Benton's biographer, "eloquent and electric with new ideas." But he felt it would not convince a prospective investor that the newspaper was a good risk. He wrote Ingersoll a seven-page, single-spaced typewritten letter offering his suggestions. Two days later Hobson and Ingersoll arranged another meeting and persuaded Benton to boil down the prospectus to a more compact proposal stressing not only Ingersoll's achievements and editorial ideas but the paper's economic potential.

Benton thought the prospectus lacked a proper promotional buildup of Ingersoll and his achievements—which Ingersoll, despite his egocentric self-confidence, found it difficult to write. Furthermore, because Time Inc. practiced anonymous journalism, Ingersoll was virtually unknown. So Ingersoll wrote another letter to Luce, asking permission not only to promote his achievements at Time Inc. in the new prospectus but to include a paragraph signed by Henry Luce that would applaud what Ingersoll was trying to do. "I am persuaded," Ingersoll said, obviously embarrassed at having to make such a request, "that I have so effectively practiced anonymous group journalism for so many years that damn few people know anything about me."

Luce consented, and Benton agreed to write the new prospectus. After meeting again with Hobson and Ingersoll, he went home and dictated a twenty-eight-page proposal that came to be known as the "Blue Book" because Ingersoll put it between light blue paper covers. It was entitled "A Financial Proposal" and was designed to assure prospective investors that the primary purpose of the newspaper was "to make money for its owners." Although it would be a crusading paper, its crusade would be to revolutionize the newspaper business. It would use color lavishly, and at least half of its pages would be devoted to photographs; the other half would be printed in easy-to-read nine-point type printed on better paper than its competitors. The pages would be well designed, with large, snappy headlines. Stories would run continuously (would not be "continued on page 20") and would be written by good, well-paid writers. It would be smaller than most tabloids *and stapled* like a magazine. It would, in fact, appear and read like a large daily magazine—with no advertising.

Purchasers of the $1.5 million preferred stock would also be given half the common stock. The other half (a thousand shares of which were given to Benton for writing the Blue Book) would be reserved for Ingersoll and his chief assistants. The preferred stock would be retired annually with one-third of the net earnings. No dividend would be paid to management until the original preferred stockholders had been fully repaid.

The most important point made by the new prospectus was that Ralph Ingersoll would have full control; half the Blue Book was devoted to promoting Ingersoll and his idea. The approved quote from Henry Luce set the tone:

> What you have in mind . . . may prove to be of great importance in the history of American journalism and in the life of the nation. . . . all omens are favorable, for you have obviously demonstrated unusual talents in the journalistic field.

The Blue Book concluded with several paragraphs from Ingersoll's original prospectus, including the seemingly immortal:

> We are against people who push other people around in this country or abroad. We are against fraud and deceit and greed and cruelty and we shall expose their practitioners. We respect intelligence, honesty and sound accomplishment, religious tolerance. We propose to crusade for those who seek constructively to improve the way men live together.

The most optimistic statement in the Blue Book was its closing sentence: "We are prepared to publish ninety days after the completion of our financing."

With a revised four-color dummy designed by Cleland and written by some of the best journalists in New York and the financial proposal prepared by William Benton, Ingersoll believed he now had a promotion package that would convince anyone that his newspaper might be the greatest thing since the Gutenberg Bible. But although Marion Stern came in for another hundred thousand dollars, he soon found that his first three hundred thousand was the easiest. With his new package it was not difficult to interest people in the project, but getting them to sign the papers was a different matter. "I got to be kind of a traveling act," says Ingersoll. "I flew to Detroit and some automobile people I'd never met before gave me lunch. To a man, they seemed fascinated—but I didn't get anyone to sign. In Philadelphia, a promoter named Wasserman put on a dinner for it must have been twenty or thirty. They listened spellbound, but nothing happened. On Wall Street, there were a dozen eligibles who had been exposed to my story. Each asked that he be kept on my list as an active prospect, he just wanted a little more time to think."

Through Wharton he finally met Jock Whitney, showed him the dummy and the prospectus, and heard that Whitney had told friends that Ingersoll's project "breathed fiery hope into the journalistic picture." The millionaire was impressed. As Whitney's biographer said, Ingersoll "had impeccable breeding. Moreover, the basic philosophy of his paper . . . was to 'be against people who push other people around.' Whitney didn't like pushy people either." But Whitney, like so many others, wanted a little more time to "think it over," although he virtually assured Ingersoll that he wanted to invest. In fact, Ingersoll decided that Whitney was waiting to be the *last* investor, the one to put it over the top, like the state delegation at a political convention that waits to cast the deciding vote for a presidential candidate.

Ingersoll, however, could not afford to wait. He was also getting a little impatient with the dilettantes and playboys who kept dropping by his office in the Time-Life Building to tell him how exciting his ideas were. One handsome young explorer, who had sold photographs to *Fortune* when Ingersoll was editor, dropped by and, during the course of a rather vague conversation, hinted that a friend of his, a young man named Huntington Hartford III, might be interested in working for the new paper. "Which Hartford was that?" Ingersoll asked the explorer, who was shocked by his ignorance.

Huntington was the only son of Princess Pigniatelli, and an heir to the Atlantic and Pacific Tea Company fortune. Ingersoll himself was surprised that he had not recognized the name because, having initiated the first major story on the Hartford family in *Fortune*, he was an admirer of A&P and an authority on its founders. The young explorer explained that the Hartford family was worried about twenty-two-year-old Huntington, because he was recently divorced and did not exactly know what to do with himself. He had once remarked that he would like to be a reporter, so it was only natural for his mother to consider buying him a newspaper. An adviser had suggested that it would be a lot easier to let someone like Ralph Ingersoll start one for him, using Hartford money, of course. A few days later Huntington himself dropped by the office, "a slim, good-looking boy, immaculately dressed, shy and somewhat ill at ease," Ingersoll recalls. The boy found it awkward asking Ingersoll for a job, and Ingersoll said he was a long way from hiring anybody and, in fact, was still trying to raise money to get started.

"Oh," said Huntington, "I'd be interested in that too."

"Some other time," Ingersoll's replied, feeling it totally unrealistic to be talking investments with such an inexperienced youth. Only a Hartford financial adviser could talk seriously about money.

So young Hartford departed, and Ingersoll decided he was more weary than ever of the Very Rich, another subject on which he was becoming an authority. "The first essential in soliciting money in large amounts is never to tip the hat," Ingersoll says, recalling his guide in Northern Italy. "It's not that the hat should be kept clamped on one's head, either. It's just that you should never meet in circumstances which indicate the tipping of anything except a waiter. Preferably, you find yourself at lunch introduced by a mutual friend."

Ingersoll had been to many such lunches, and he was learning enough about raising money to write a book on the subject, which he seriously contemplated: "There is no use talking to a VRM about making an investment unless you know or stumble on the fact that a motive already exists for his committing himself. The motive—the emotional motive—is the thing to look for. You have to remind yourself that he is beyond making a profit for the sake of supporting himself or buying something he wants. But even if he is beyond the profit motive and is really only interested in amusing himself, if he is an American he will probably want assurance that there will be a profit eventually, not because he needs or wants it, but because if he doesn't get it, his friends will make fun of him."

An inventory of motives, says Ingersoll, would be infinite, just as an inventory of emotions would be. "With Marion Stern, the motive was genuine good will. I suspect she was doing what she thought would please her father: using his money to help a young man starting a business she thought would be useful—in the field of public information." On the other hand, banker Howard Bonbright had put in "venture capital" hoping to make a little more money.

But the most important thing Ingersoll learned was that when a Very Rich Man says yes, it doesn't really mean a thing. You still must be approved by his FWD—or financial watchdog, "a professional son-of-a-bitch," says Ingersoll. "Every VRM has to have one so he can get as excited as he likes at the lunch table and all he has to do is somewhere throw in the phrase: 'Of course, you'll check the figures with so-and-so.'"

As the weeks raced by, Ingersoll's list of prospective investors grew longer— genuine prospects either waiting for the decisions of their FWDs or just "thinking it over."

One man on his list was a Wall Streeter named John Loeb, partner in the investment firm of Carl Loeb & Rhoades. Loeb had, in fact, responded to a letter by suggesting that Ingersoll drop by his office. Ingersoll was stretched out on his couch about eleven A.M. on a hot September day and thinking about a long, cool drink and the Caribbean salad his cook, Elizabeth, was preparing for him. It was at that moment, he says, "that I happened to think of how Zilboorg had described the workings of my unconscious mind. It will arrange your thoughts, he'd explained, so that there will always be a logical reason for its getting its way. I was going to call Loeb—but I had come to a logical conclusion not to— today. It will be cooler later; I can do a better job some other time. Is that a suicidal instinct manipulating me? Suddenly I know it is because I am no longer drowsy and I have begun to perspire violently. I'm afraid. Of what? Of picking up that phone to call Loeb. Because he won't be there, because if he is he'll turn me away? No! Because he *may* be there, may listen to you, may even. . . . I picked up the phone, Loeb was in his office. He invited me to come down— on the next subway—and, when I got there that amazing young banker not only heard me out but signed his name on a paper committing him to the investment of $100,000—then and there!"

Ingersoll insists that was the day he knew that although he still might fail, he would survive. He would not destroy himself as Zilboorg had predicted. It was also the day the fund-raising began to move. With a partner in Loeb & Rhoades on the team, two ultraconservatives came in: Deering Howe of the Deering tractor family, and Garrard B. Winston, a former undersecretary of the treasury and a lawyer in the firm of Sherman & Sterling—each for a hundred thousand dollars. Elinor Gimbel, a cousin of the department store Gimbel, was next; she committed herself to one unit, half of which she put up herself, while soliciting the other half from a friend. Ingersoll now had seven hundred thousand dollars. Then came the most important of all his backers, the one he knew least about and had never expected to land. It is an interesting story.

One night Ingersoll was alone in his apartment fixing a scotch and soda when the telephone rang. He answered it, and a voice said, "This is Louis Weiss talking. You don't know me, but I'm a partner of John Wharton. Whatever you're doing, stay where you are until I can get there." Then he hung up.

Although Ingersoll did not know Weiss, he knew quite a bit about him and recalled the conversation he had with Wharton, when Wharton volunteered to be his lawyer. "One of these days, Mac," Wharton said, "someone will tell you that Marshall Field is a client of our office. I want to tell you first, so that you won't think you have an entrée to Field, because you haven't. Louis Weiss and I have a deal; Field is *his* client and none of the rest of us is allowed to have anything to do with him.

"I can't even introduce you to Louis Weiss—because he doesn't want to meet you. He says he understands you're just one of Harry Luce's fat boys and you and your kind are not up his alley. Don't misunderstand me," the lawyer went on. "Louis Weiss is a wonderful fellow but he is not interested in making money. He's a reformer, a do-gooder. Most of his work with Field, actually, is advising Field on his philanthropies."

Ingersoll did not know then that Field's life had been changed through psychoanalysis and that his doctor had been Dr. Gregory Zilboorg. Nor did he know that Field had become a philanthropist. And even if he had known, he would not have approached Field, because, he says, "no investor was ever solicited by me with the bait that our intention was philanthropic—or even that I hoped to reform anything except the practice of daily journalism."

Ten minutes after his mysterious late-evening phone call, Louis Weiss appeared at Ingersoll's door. Ingersoll recalls him as "a slim rather untidy man with very bright and intelligent eyes and the gentlest of smiles. He spoke in a soft voice that was well modulated and often had the quality of suppressed excitement. He spoke also with his eyes, which characteristically responded to one's questions before he answered them."

Once in Ingersoll's apartment, Weiss plunged directly into his subject— which was that he had only just that evening read the prospectus for Ingersoll's paper, which Wharton had had in his office for months. He was very excited. Such a newspaper could be of great significance. "He spoke," says Ingersoll, "in the largest of terms, sitting on a stool on one side of the bar while I leaned across it from the other, trying to gather what this was all about. He came finally to why he'd said he had had to rush over to see me at once, immediately, without any delay. It was because he had decided that my project was so important it *had* to be the exception to his rule that he never brought any man or any project to his client Field."

Ingersoll was instructed to say nothing of this to anyone—not even to Weiss's partner Wharton—and to take no one else's money until he had met with Field. "I want to pick my time," said Weiss. "Marshall is not an easy man. I mean, it's not easy to be sure of his attention. I *must* be sure when I bring you together."

And he added, "Of course, now that Field is in the picture, Cohen, Cole, Weiss and Wharton will continue to represent you, but I will be your attorney instead of John."

"No, no"—as he saw Ingersoll's eyebrows rise. "Don't get excited about that. This is between John and me. We understand each other perfectly. You have nothing to do with this decision."

It was over a month before Ingersoll heard from Weiss again, and his main concern during this period was that Zilboorg might mention to Field that he knew him, and that he would tell Field, "Ingersoll is crazy."

When Ingersoll finally heard from Weiss again, it was in another cryptic phone call: "Meet me at Seventy-first and Park Avenue at four thirty this afternoon—with your prospectus and dummy. We're seeing Field."

Ingersoll and Weiss went up to Field's apartment together, and Field shook hands with Ingersoll apologetically. "Marshall Field's expression was often apologetic," says Ingersoll. "His eyes were gentle and shy and his smile usually diffident. At this first meeting, looking at his watch, he said, 'I'm really dreadfully sorry. I couldn't be sorrier, Louis. I did say I'd meet the children and I actually shouldn't have said I'd see your friend Ingersoll at all because I've got to go in a very few minutes.'"

As Field's biographer, Stephen Becker, described the meeting: "Field nodded now and then, and even yawned politely a couple of times. Ingersoll was sure Field was bored; he raised his voice a bit, spoke faster, compressed his arguments. Field looked at his watch—he carried it in his trousers pocket; it was the kind that snaps in and out of a flat rectangular leather case—and Ingersoll went on almost by reflex, the enthusiasm draining slowly from his voice. Field stood up; so did Ingersoll, still talking."

Ingersoll, recalling the meeting, says, "I could not remember a single individual whose reaction was as negative as Marshall's. His glance at the dummy was perfunctory. Clearly he was thinking about something else—and I was wasting my time. But Field didn't waste much of his. He gave the dummy back to me, shook hands, backed nervously through the lobby to the elevator where his man waited with his hat and coat. 'Ingersoll,' he said in that shy, gentle voice as the elevator door opened. 'I can't really take this on you know. And I'd hate for you to be under some kind of misapprehension; two hundred thousand dollars is absolutely all I can put into it.' Then, the coat was on, Field was in the elevator and the door closed. I turned to Louis Weiss in bewilderment, my expression asking, 'Now what the hell was that all about?'"

"That's exactly the way I wanted it to happen," Weiss said serenely. "You now have two hundred thousand dollars. It won't disappear."

And it did not. Ingersoll put Field in for two units—numbers 8 and 9—not really caring that Field showed so little interest. In fact, Ingersoll had been misled. Field's biographer explains: "Ingersoll's impression of Field's lack of interest—a first impression shared by others—was doubtless reinforced by an odd habit. . . . He yawned a lot. When he felt like yawning, he yawned. He might be having a marvelous time, but when is system called for oxygen, he supplied it. Whether this was simply a slight nervousness or a bizarre sequel to the early rheumatic fever, it was dismaying to casual friends, who were often alert to his slightest reaction, and disconcerting to closer friends."

Despite his surprising success with Marshall Field, the highlight of Ingersoll's fund-raising year was still to come—preceded by a slightly bizarre interlude with Huntington Hartford III. This began with the appearance of H. C. North, representing the Hartford family and the A&P fortune. Young Huntington, it seemed, still wanted to be a reporter. North, whom Ingersoll had compared in his *Fortune* article to Henry Ford's chief operator, Harry Bennett, was accompanied by an assistant, and they were both friendly, amused—and tough. They minced no words:

"Any problem of a Hartford is a problem of ours. Young Huntington has interested himself in you, so we've been doing some checking. I hope it hasn't bothered you to be shadowed," North said, as both A&P men laughed cautiously. "We don't give a damn about your private life; we just felt we had to know all about you. We're here to tell you that it's OK. We don't give a damn how much money you lose, as long as it's respectable—and if you can keep him in a job for a year we'll bless hell out of you. We'll also continue to keep a eye on you," the other man added.

"But you've got one more job," North continued. "The princess wants to see you. She's going to ask you to dinner."

Ingersoll's reaction was, for the first time, to take Hartford seriously. But not too seriously, and his obvious misgivings inspired North and his friend to shift gears to some supersalesmanship: If everything proved all right with the princess, Ingersoll could stop worrying about money. Hell, all he was trying to raise was—how much was it anyway—one million, two million? It would be worth a lot more than that to the Hartford family if Ingersoll succeeded in taking Huntington III off the street. "And he's a hell of a nice kid, too, and won't cause you any trouble."

Ingersoll asked if they had gone over his financial figures as well as his personal life. "Sure" was the answer. "But wait until you get by the princess. If Huntington does take things over, we'll put figure people to work in there who can do a real job for you."

The next day Ingersoll repeated this conversation to Cushing, expressing his misgivings. Cushing said, "Don't be nuts. What makes a Hartford million look any different from any other?" Ingersoll had to agree—and when the call came from the princess with an invitation to dinner, he accepted.

Princess Pigniatelli was living in a modest duplex apartment just off Fifth Avenue in the Seventies. When Ingersoll arrived, he found they were dining *en famille*—just the princess, her son, and Ingersoll. The conversation during dinner was casual and halting. In the presence of his mother, Huntington had nothing much to say, and the princess herself seemed interested only in seeing how much she could read of Ingersoll's character with the aid of an intense and continuous stare. When the last course was removed from the table, she dismissed her son with a gesture that seemed to be sending him up to bed.

"As soon as Huntington was gone," Ingersoll says, "the princess's attitude changed abruptly. With a nod and a smile, she suddenly assumed everything was settled between us and launched into an embarrassingly intimate analysis of what she considered her son's character and how I was to look after him when he became my ward."

As for the financial situation, the princess dismissed that with a snap of the fingers. "We'll take care of your paper. I just wanted to be sure that Huntington would have someone I approved of keeping an eye on him. You have no idea what it will mean to me if being a reporter will really interest him. You won't let him be out too late or get into any kind of trouble, will you? You know it's very difficult because he's such a nice boy. I can see that you're the kind of man who really understands all the trouble people could get him in." Then she dismissed Ingersoll as imperiously as she had dismissed her son. "It was so nice of you to come to dinner with me. I must say good night to you now."

That was the last time Ingersoll ever saw Princess Pigniatelli. The next day North informed him that he had passed the test, which prompted a council of war at the Publications Research offices. As much as Ingersoll respected the A&P, and friendly as the Hartford family seemed, the last thing he wanted was for his newspaper to be financed as a journalism school for a rich playboy. Ingersoll finally gave North his decision: "Yes," Huntington could have a job as a cub reporter at the minimum salary for at least one year, and "No," Ingersoll would not accept a sum of money so large it would give the Hartford family a disproportionate share of the stock. All they could purchase was one unit—a hundred thousand dollars.

Ingersoll now had ten supporters—one million dollars, with only half a million to go. The financial community was well represented, but what he needed was a publishing professional, someone whose faith would convince everyone that what was being said about Ralph Ingersoll was true: He *was* a publishing and editorial genius. Ingersoll did not have far to search. Harry Scherman was the founder and owner of the Book-of-the-Month Club and was recognized around town as an authority not only on the public's taste but also on the business of publishing. After a painstakingly thorough investigation of Ingersoll and his proposal, Scherman signed up as number eleven.

About the time Scherman came aboard, Ingersoll, acting on a whim, called Philip Wrigley, the chewing gum manufacturer, and asked him for an appointment. Then he flew out to Chicago and met with Wrigley at his home, catching him in a gay mood. Wrigley did not even want to see the financial prospectus. He simply said, "It sounds like fun. You can have fifty thousand dollars of my money—and I don't care whether you lose it, which you probably will." Another man who came in for fifty thousand was Benton's former partner Chester Bowles, who was still running their advertising firm and was restless to break into something else. He had wanted to leave advertising when Benton did, but found that it would have wrecked the agency, so he stayed on, biding his time, watching for something that would have more purpose, more meaning. As a colleague said then, "One gets the impression—sharply from Mr. Benton, more moderately from Mr. Bowles—that each looks upon his advertising career as his last orgy before joining Alcoholics Anonymous." Both men, of course, went on to distinguished careers in public service, and Ingersoll's paper seemed, at the time, a good way to start.

With more than one million dollars pledged by a variety of men who either knew what they were doing or were known to have FWDs to make sure they were not being foolish, Ingersoll assumed he would have very little trouble raising the rest, even though time was preciously short. Autumn was passing into wintry November. Then, "all of a sudden," Ingersoll says, "and with no warning, my whole promotional machine came to a halt. Within a matter of weeks—almost of days—the prospects who seemed hottest cooled, doors stopped opening, telephones stopped ringing. A few of those I'd felt closest to said no without explanation; most just drifted away into vagueness. And it was gradually borne in on me that something I didn't know about had happened to my prospects—some malevolent word was out."

As November drifted toward December, his staff in the Time-Life Building was frantic. In a matter of weeks all the contracts signed would expire if the full $1.5 million was not pledged. "The only way I had to meet the crisis," says Ingersoll, "was to try to patch together the last $400,000 by accepting commitments from people who couldn't afford them—people who had become enthusiastic rooters but did not stand up to Commissioner Landis's specifications."

Beside the list of committed stockholders tacked on his wall, Ingersoll had another list of twenty or thirty individuals, each of whom had given him assurance of their interest; the only remaining question was the size of their investment. But the big money men in this group had suddenly become mute, as had many of the smaller investors, most of whom, in Ingersoll's opinion, could not afford anything near a hundred thousand dollars. "Maybe, by adding up five people with $10,000 and pretending they were one with $50,000," he said, "I could patch together a few contributors—and then we would be saved by Jock Whitney. But even stretching the patchwork further and further, by the middle of December I could not see the gap closed. The logical candidate to concentrate on became Jock Whitney."

Whitney, however, was among the mute, and considering his continued interest in the paper, his silence was "the most sudden and the most mysterious," Ingersoll says. "Even Wharton could not explain his new evasiveness. The investor who was only waiting to be the man whose money put us over the top, simply faded away into thin air."

Then, one day, sitting in his office, pondering what had gone wrong, Ingersoll received a mysterious phone call. It was from Laura Hobson. She said she did not want to talk over the phone but had something very important to show him and wanted him to meet her immediately at Central Park, at Sixtieth Street and Fifth Avenue.

Ingersoll went down to Rockefeller Plaza, hailed a cab, and within minutes was in Central Park talking to Laura, who had a large bulky envelope under her arm. It contained a dummy of something called *Newsdaily*, which had been set in type by a printer on the West Side of Manhattan. The proofs had been billed to, and sent to, Time Inc. where someone, either by accident or, more likely, by design, had delivered them to Laura. She felt compelled to show them to Ingersoll.*

Ingersoll was stunned! Someone at Time Inc., he decided, was apparently planning—or at least considering—the publication of a daily newspaper similar to his. "It took no more than a glance at a batch of these proofs to see that, whatever other ideas were behind *Newsdaily*, both concept and format had been lifted whole from my *Newspaper*. *Newsdaily*'s news was seen to be broken into departments, headings for which were either paraphrases or, in some cases, literal copies of my dummies."

Ingersoll did not know what to think. He did know that before he left Time Inc., Charles Stillman, the treasurer, had been highly enthusiastic about Ingersoll's project, which he said would be "worth millions if done right."† He was in favor of Time Inc.'s doing it—provided it was tried first in a small city. Ingersoll also knew that Stillman believed the new publication should be published by Time Inc. and so urged Luce not to let Ingersoll leave. A project of the magnitude of *Newsdaily* could not be undertaken unless someone in the top echelon of the company not only knew about it but had approved it. But who?

*Mrs. Hobson does not recall the incident.
†Charles Stillman declined to be interviewed on any aspect of Ingersoll's career at Time Inc.

He did not think Luce was behind it. That was not in character. Luce might know about it; or one of his lieutenants might be experimenting with a publication that Luce knew nothing about.

Ingersoll thanked Laura and went back to his office pondering his problem. Whatever was going on, he knew that if the word was out around town that Time Inc. was considering the publication of a paper similar to his, it would explain why his sources of money were drying up. He had still not answered all his questions when the time came for his afternoon appointment with Dr. Zilboorg, and he decided to discuss the situation with the psychiatrist. "Analysts are not supposed to give that kind of advice," Ingersoll says, "but Gregory was no ordinary analyst. He knew as much about Henry Luce as if he had been a patient too. After all, I had been free associating about Harry on his couch for over a year."

Zilboorg agreed it was not in Luce's character to play a leading role in this operation. "But we both agreed it was in Clare's," says Ingersoll. "And she would have found ready allies amongst the men who had so bitterly resented Harry's promoting me over them and my arrogant overriding of their opposition to the *Life* project."

In the end Ingersoll concluded that this was exactly what had happened. Under Clare's initiative and probably with Luce's awareness, he decided, a secret task force had been set up within Time Inc. to publish a paper similar to Ingersoll's, first in Hartford, Connecticut, and, if it was successful, later in New York. Someone loyal to Ingersoll had put a set of dummies on Laura Hobson's desk, figuring that she would show them to Ingersoll.

What should he do now? Zilboorg suggested an answer: Ingersoll should confront Luce and make it a matter of conscience so that Luce would have no choice, consistent with his character, but to stand up to Clare. It had to be done carefully, because if Luce felt even the slightest reproach, he would defend the whole undertaking rather than repudiate it.

So the next morning, "at 11 sharp," Ingersoll called Luce and, with his heart pounding, spoke the words he and Zilboorg had agreed on—and which he had carefully written out on a piece of paper: "Harry, I've just learned something that I know you would want to know. So I am passing it on to you. Some people are billing Time Inc. for the work they are doing on the dummy of a newspaper to compete with mine."

There was silence on the other end of the line, a long silence. Then finally Luce said, "Thank you, Mac, it won't happen again."

The rumors that Time Inc. was experimenting with a new kind of newspaper were never heard again. But Ingersoll still could not persuade Jock Whitney to make his commitment, and Whitney's reluctance seemed to be having an effect on the other fence sitters. Again it was Zilboorg who suggested the reason. One day he interrupted Ingersoll's free association to ask: "Didn't I read in Winchell's column that Jock and Clare Luce were—how did Winchell put it—an item?"

The next day Ingersoll asked Whitney to break a luncheon date and meet him at the Louis XIV restaurant in Rockefeller Plaza. The conversation was casual, but again, Ingersoll's speech had been carefully rehearsed. "You know, of course, that some people at Time Inc. have been playing with the idea of beating me out with a newspaper. I talked to Harry about it and he told me that it's all off. That's all I really know about it, Jock—that Harry tells me that they've dropped it."

Then, jokingly, he added, "Of course, Clare was the one who gave those old pals of mine their comfort. She must have had a lot of fun. My buddies are still going on with it, backing a tryout in Hartford. She may even be putting some of her own money in it now—she *may*, I don't really know."

With that, according to Ingersoll, Whitney pushed his chair back, sprang to his feet in his excitement, and said, "So that's why she's been. . . . Ingersoll, that phony. . . . No, never as open as that! That wonderful, beautiful. . . . "

Then Whitney sat down mumbling something about having dinner the night before with Clare Luce. He would say no more, but within twenty-four hours Jock Whitney's lawyer was making an issue of the fact that Ingersoll would not let his client take the rest of the stock in the new venture as originally promised. Ingersoll limited his share to a hundred thousand dollars.

What prompted Whitney's curious reaction to Ingersoll's remark may never be known. Mrs. Luce denies any knowledge of Time Inc.'s having been involved with *Newsdaily* and says she had nothing to do with it herself. There is no mention of the project or any implication of an affair with Mrs. Luce in Whitney's biography, and his biographer, E. J. Kahn, said, when asked about it, "This is the first I ever heard of it."

As the story eventually emerged, there were enough Time Inc. people— and at the very highest level—involved in the evolution of *Newsdaily* to warrant Ingersoll's suspicions, and if Whitney had heard from any source about another newspaper in the planning stage, or if Mrs. Luce had given him even the slightest hint that Time Inc. was involved, that would have been enough to explain Whitney's reaction. Here is what apparently happened:

In the early 1930s Bice Clemow, a young University of Washington graduate who had edited the school paper and was working for the Wenatchee (Washington) *Daily World*, had an idea for a daily newspaper that would repackage and departmentalize the news. The editorial page would be eliminated, and boxed editorials, usually but not always written by the reporter who worked on the assignment, would appear at the end of major stories. Later Clemow came to New York to work first for *Editor and Publisher*, then as a photo editor for the Associated Press, where he also met Ed Stanley. His work at the Associated Press and with Stanley inspired an interest in photos, and when *Life* came out he became excited about adding photographs to his paper, which he had decided to call *Newsdaily*. At first, he was going to publish his paper in Olympia, Washington. But after he started working in New York, he considered several other cities as potential sites for the paper.

In 1936, when Ingersoll was publisher of *Time*, Clemow applied for a job at Time Inc. and after reading a story he had submitted, Ingersoll took him out to lunch. Clemow recalls the meeting vividly: "Ingersoll said, 'Your piece is full of clichés, but you know what you're writing about.' He offered me a job. I was making eighty-five dollars a week at the time, and he said, 'Would ten thousand a year be enough to start?' Was it! I liked Ingersoll. He was a very exciting human being. I remember once, he took *Time*'s editors and writers to dinner at the Union Club and we all got sloshed and then, after dinner, Ingersoll got up and made a little speech. He said the board of directors had just met and decided there had to be budget cuts because advertising was down. But he was still putting us all in for a raise. That really impressed me. I knew I was working for a guy and a company that put writers first."

In late 1937, about the time Ingersoll was beginning to think seriously about his newspaper, Clemow began to plan for *Newsdaily* and received encouragement and free assistance from several printing and paper companies, and from Time Inc. At *Time* Clemow had been assigned to write the "Press" section. This was an area in which Luce was especially interested, and he would ask Clemow to go along whenever he was having lunch with a top press executive — meetings that he hoped would lead to a story. Through these meetings Clemow got to know Luce quite well. At Luce's suggestion, his special assistant, Allen Grover, put Clemow in touch with William Griffin, chairman of the board of Time Inc. and executor of the James Cox Brady estate. Griffin was impressed by Clemow's ideas, and apparently he was ready to put as much as twenty-five thousand dollars of the Brady estate money into *Newsdaily*. Roy Larsen also became interested in the project and sent Clemow to see Chester Bowles, who eventually put in twenty-five hundred dollars as an investment for his son.

Clemow left *Time* in 1938 to develop his paper, which he now planned to publish in Trenton, Harrisburg, New Haven, Worcester, Danbury or Hartford. And Time Inc. continued to be helpful, sending him promising young writers. When he was ready to plan his format, Allen Grover said, "You need a good designer," and recruited Eleanor Treacy, the former *Fortune* art director who was now Mrs. Eric Hodgins and living in Connecticut where she did free-lance work. She designed the paper, "mostly as a favor to Allen Grover," says Clemow. And because she used the Composing Room, a local job type shop, both for the work she did for *Fortune* and the typesetting for the *Newsdaily* dummies, "by accident," says Clemow, "one of our proofs of a consumer column, which we had innovated, went to Laura Hobson." Hobson does not remember the incident. But Treacy does, and she recalls that "Laura was furious." She also remembers Ingersoll being angry, and Clemow said he'd heard Ingersoll was going around saying "He stole the sonofabitch [*Newsdaily*] from me."

Although various top executives at Time Inc. were obviously assisting and encouraging Clemow, he insists that there was never any talk, or suggestion, of Clare Luce or Whitney — or Larsen or Time Inc. or Luce himself — putting any money into *Newsdaily*. Eventually, William Griffin also decided against putting Brady estate money into the venture. "The total Griffin contribution," says

Clemow, "was ten dollars — for a charter subscription. All the money for *Newsdaily* was raised here," he says — meaning by Clemow and his friends in Hartford. The paper finally appeared March 1, 1939, and was published for three and a half months before Clemow's money ran out — shortly before *PM* was launched — and he had to give it up. Clemow knew about *PM* all along, of course, but never thought that he was in competition with Ingersoll. His paper consisted of sixteen pages and never had a circulation over its first day's high of twenty-five thousand. He planned to make another effort when he had raised more money, but the war intervened and he went to work for the War Production Board. His web press, which had produced the first offset daily in America, ended up in Caracas, Venezuela, printing army maps. Today Clemow's company, Imprint, specializes in design and typography and owns a number of weekly newspapers in the Hartford area.

Although Ingersoll might have overreacted to the galleys Hobson had given him, there was clearly some justification for his feeling that *Newsdaily* might have been a Time Inc.–sponsored project. And Whitney's strange reaction to Ingersoll's telling him that Luce said he would put a stop to it seemed to substantiate these suspicions.

At any rate, when the word went around that Ralph Ingersoll's project, supported by some of the wealthiest and most astute men in the country, was "over the top," the dam broke. As Ingersoll describes the scene: "My eight-by-eight cubbyhole in the corner of Publications Research's office, with me on one side, with my feet on the desk, and Ginny Schoales [his assistant] on the other, answering the telephone. Between us stands an open bottle of whiskey. It takes a double shot of bourbon to calm the nerves now. Each time Ginny hangs up the telephone, it rings again — and each time it rings it is a call from another whose name had been scratched off the prospect list. Half of those who turned us down have changed their minds and now want in. Finally not even Ginny's crisp contralto 'No' will get rid of them; they begin coming to the door, *demanding* that we take their money."

It quickly became apparent that Ingersoll could now refinance and raise a lot more than his minimum $1.5 million. "The financial tide had more than turned," he says, "it was a sudden flood. While we were preparing to put to sea in a rowboat, we found ourselves in water that would have floated the battleship we needed." He estimated that he could easily have raised five million dollars after Jock Whitney came in — and, as he says, "with less effort and less tact and diplomacy than it took me to turn it down. I cannot even say, in my own defense, that I was too suddenly exuberant — or too stupid — even to think of it. I thought about it as long and as hard as I knew how, for it was the advice of everyone around me. I turned the suggestion down because each subscriber to a hundred thousand dollars of stock now owned one-fifteenth of the capital's share; if I were to take in the Johnny-come-latelies' money, the interest of those who had been most loyal would be diluted. I felt as if I would be selling them out before they'd had a run for their money."

So, instead of diluting the original stockholders' share by accepting more money, Ingersoll decided to limit the total amount to $1.5 million, but at the last minute he did some reshuffling in an effort to place the stock in the strongest hands and weed out people—columnist Dorothy Thompson, for example—who had come in because they were dedicated to the idea, but could not really afford to risk the money.*

And on January 10, 1940, the day they struck oil, as Ingersoll put it, Laura Hobson filched the two lists of firm and potential backers from his desk and returned them to him framed. They hung in his various offices for years. The money was in, and for a week every meal was a victory celebration with someone. But perhaps the most significant dinner invitation came from Henry Luce, who was put on the phone, stuttering, by his secretary, Corinne Thrasher: "Mac, I've just heard; it's wonderful! I can-can't tell you how ha-a-happy I am for you. I wa-wa-want to see you; I want to talk to you—right now."

The two publishers went separately and secretly from their respective offices in the Time-Life Building to a dimly lit little room that was neither a bar nor a restaurant. Luce was overflowing with sheer enthusiasm and gulped his first drink. As Ingersoll recalls: "Suddenly in the limelight, I was the embarrassed, silent one with the silly grin; Harry was the burbler, the piler-on of words, conveying a master's approval of his prize pupil. And then Harry's brain began to work: to come up through his excitement with hard thoughts, turned out from hard experiences clearly remembered. He had something that was very important to him to say to me and he was saying it, no longer burbling, not even stuttering now."

"Mac," Luce said, "your raising your money brings it all back to me. I lived through just exactly what's happened to you. That was the year I had to do what you've had to do—and done: drop everything to raise the money to do what you really want to do.

"And because of that I am the only man qualified to tell you the trouble which only I know you are in. And only I can tell you what to do about it . . . and how to save yourself.

"Can you take that on faith, Mac?"

Ingersoll says that he first said something like "I don't know." "But," he adds, "I did know. I knew exactly what he meant, instinctively and instantaneously. Less than a year before, I had been an honest man, totally engaged in making a reality of concepts in which I honestly believed. The day I ceased that unfinished effort to go forth to raise money for it was the day on which I had turned myself into something quite different: a promoter. As a promoter, I strove to remain an honest man but to promote a creative idea while it is still in the

*The final list of supporters was: Mrs. Marian Rosenwald Stern, $200,000; Howard Bonbright, $100,000; John Loeb, $100,000; Deering Howe, $100,000; Garrard B. Winston, $100,000; Elinor Gimbel, $50,000; Marshall Field, $200,000; Huntington Hartford III, $100,000; Harry Scherman, $100,000; Dwight Deere Wiman, $50,000; John H. Whitney, $100,000; William and Lessing Rosenwald, $100,000; Philip Wrigley, $50,000; Ira J. Williams, $50,000; Chester Bowles, $50,000; Lincoln Schuster, $50,000.

process of creation is to live in contradiction. What's being promoted must be frozen to be packaged for promotion. The creative process, the evolution, comes to a full stop when it has to be hawked. An automobile salesman's mind, for example, must be closed to the possibility of improving the car he offers. He cannot be thinking of the design of next year's car while he's persuading you to buy this year's. The difference between the psychological attitude of the creator and the promoter is profound."

During most of his sabbatical year Ingersoll had been a promoter, and he knew that Luce was trying to tell him that being a promoter does something to the craftsman's soul. He did not, he told Luce, have to take what Luce wanted to tell him on faith; he knew what Luce was talking about.

"OK, Mac, OK." Luce said. "This is what you must do and do it right now. That's why I had to see you right away, before you could let this moment pass. It won't come again.

"Take all the money and put it in a bank. Then tell your stockholders that there won't be any newspaper for a year.

"They'll scream and scream. You promised! We counted on. . . . You can't do this to us. . . .

"But you do it. You're in the driver's seat, Mac. You have their money and you're the boss of it now."

Ingersoll sat, spellbound.

"I say wait a year," Luce continued, "because it will take you the first few months of it to get the taste of what you've been going through out of your mouth. Then another few getting back to your trade of thinking as a publisher. And that will leave you only a short half year to choose the right men for the right jobs. Then maybe you will have a fighting chance of pulling it off, of making your paper what *you* think it should be.

"If you don't do as I tell you, you'll be licked before you start. Your stockholders will rush you into starting publication before you've got your breath back.

"And I am the only man who can save you because you may listen to me. Everybody else is going to tell you how wonderful you are because you've pulled off the money raising. But I tell you that that success can be dangerous. You've got to give yourself the time to get over it!"

Ingersoll heard Luce out: "His sincerity was beyond question." And he was not the only one urging caution. Ingersoll's father and Zilboorg were still advising him to give up the project, even though the contracts were signed. They did not think he had enough money to start a new publication, and believed he should go back with Luce while he still had the chance. But after thinking it over for a few days, Ingersoll decided to go ahead—another decision he would question later, as he did his decision not to raise more money when he'd had the chance. "I do not know why I did not act on Harry's unanswerable logic. He had spoken the truth, and spoke it with love in his heart. He had hard knowledge in his head but mine, I guess, was still fuzzy with just what he had warned me of: the intoxicating fumes of success as a promoter. I remember contemplating his proposition very seriously but I ended by giving in to my stockholders' impatience, and my own.

"I was a silly fellow."

So he plunged on too hastily and with too little money. Later he would recall that the closeness of war was a factor. "I had persuaded myself that a new newspaper's chances of success would be much greater in a time when violent news was being made. It seemed to me that this would be particularly true for a newspaper without advertising—for war might hurt retail business but it inevitably boomed circulation."

Also, by now his hatred of Adolf Hitler had become an obsession. And it is likely that, if only subconsciously, Ralph Ingersoll thought his newspaper would help persuade a basically isolationist America that its destiny was to defeat Nazi Germany. Besides, the way to stop being a promoter was to start publishing and editing—and the best way to do that was with a deadline. To wait would mean another year of spinning his wheels—and, inevitably, more promoting.

Some of the PM *stockholders in Ingersoll's office in Brooklyn: (Back row, l. to r.) John Loeb, Chester Bowles, Harry Scherman, Eleanor Gimbel, Marshall Field, unidentified, Jock Whitney, Ralph Ingersoll. (Front row, l. to r.) William Benton, Harry Cushing, Nathan Levin, Louis Weiss, Marion Rosenwald Stern (later Mrs. Max Ascoli), Harold Linder, partner in Loeb & Rhoades; Garrard B. Winston, member of law firm Shearman and Sterling*

This photo of the harassed editor hung on many a PM *wall*

10: The Truly Impossible Dream

Ralph Ingersoll says one would have thought that after working twenty years for other people and finally achieving his own publication, he would have found the launching period of his newspaper the most exhilarating time of his life. But it was hardly that. In fact, the only memory he has of the five months during which *PM* was staffed and organized for publication is that of helpless frustration. "No publication I ever worked for," he says, "seemed to belong less to me. The first organization that I had brought into being myself was suddenly not mine."

It was, in fact, no one's property. It seemed already to belong to newspaper legend—the most idealistic, truth-seeking, crusading, literate, and eye-catching newspaper ever published. The trouble was that it did not exist and never would. Ingersoll, however, was committed to creating it out of nothing more than his endless memoranda and his knowledge of magazines. He did, of course, have $1.5 million and the enthusiastic support of virtually all the working reporters in the country. But it was not enough.

On January 20, 1940, Ingersoll met with his stockholders in the living room of his apartment on East Eightieth Street. The purpose of that meeting was to organize a new company, to be called the Newspaper *PM*. Ingersoll sat at a large table in front of the assembled stockholders, "pleased and embarrassed," he recalls, "flanked by attorneys Weiss and Wharton, with piles of papers and typewritten agenda in front of them. I was not the only one who was embarrassed, because few of my stockholders knew one another. They were dressed up strangers, all smiling at me and making it clear they thought I was wonderful and about to do wonderful things, [and] Harry Luce was right; their only concern was for action."

And action they would get, in the most frantic, confused, and overpublicized publication launching in the history of the country. After a week on the beach in Nassau Ingersoll returned to New York and put together a nucleus staff, which included: George Lyon, an experienced editor out of work because his Buffalo Scripps-Howard paper had been sold out from under him, as managing editor; Bill Baumrucker, a young genius with presses who had been lured away from the New York *Daily News*, as production manager; and William Benton, as promotion manager. Benton, having considered investing in *PM*, finally elected to remain the paper's most active noninvesting friend. He told Ingersoll: "I've decided that what you're trying to do is the most important thing that's happening in the country. But I couldn't come in with you before without compromising the University. So I've asked Bob [Hutchins] for a leave of absence." Benton picked as his circulation manager an experienced Hearst executive named Harry Feldman.

The staff began to work in the small Publications Research offices while Ingersoll looked for new quarters. And he quickly learned that production, distribution, and staffing of the new publication would be a much bigger problem than he had anticipated. It was not until two weeks before publication date that Ingersoll was able to devote full time to what he did best—editing. He was spread alarmingly thin, and furthermore, it became increasingly clear that he lacked one of the ingredients essential to the successful management of a large, complex organization: an ability to delegate responsibility to others. After twenty years Ingersoll finally had his own publication, and he wanted to keep control of every detail, on both the publishing and editorial sides of the operation. As one man who helped start *PM* has said: "The boss was imaginative, eager, but not an executive and never hired a top executive. . . . I have always thought that perhaps unconsciously, Ralph hired rather inadequate newsmen for his top ones because he wanted to control everything." Another colleague was impressed by Ingersoll's fervent desire to show Henry Luce what he could do in order "to get even with Luce for some reason."

Ingersoll, himself, was not unaware of the criticism, and in 1946, when he wrote the long "History of *PM*" for the paper, he said of those early days: "Having overcome a succession of apparently insuperable odds in getting the money to start his paper, Ingersoll then proceeded to make a series of apparently irretrievable mistakes in launching it."

One of the biggest mistakes made in the launching of *PM* was not entirely his fault. That mistake was Bill Benton's enthusiastic promotion of an idea that sold itself, which left the wiser PR veterans in New York shaking their heads and saying: "They're promoting themselves out of business." Ingersoll, of course, had welcomed Benton aboard and encouraged him: "I wanted to get promotion out of my system once and for all, and here was the one man I was confident could do the job."

And he did. Ingersoll says that in the beginning, it had been his "pious plan to bring *PM* out with just as little fanfare as possible." His promotion budget was pennies "compared to the budget with which a new cake of soap is promoted." The *PM* promotion was built around a remark made by one of the early New Dealers: "Give me the three best columnists to plug it and I'll make any idea into a law in six months." After the columnists had read the *PM* prospectus, most of them considered any item about the new paper hot news, and they printed it. Soon local reporters were also caught up in the excitement, and every newspaper and magazine published in New York was running items about *PM*, until finally *Time* carried a story about the *PM* prepublication furor. "Even out of hiring a staff he got publicity," commented *Time*, referring to the competition Ingersoll arranged with the Museum of Modern Art in which $1,750 was put up to attract artists who could report news with their drawings. And, of course, every story had something to say about the editor and publisher.

Ingersoll had also given thought to using a Time Inc. promotion gimmick: the sale of charter subscriptions, promoted by mail before publication. "The first issue of any publication is its worst," said Ingersoll. "It's much easier to sell the idea of a publication than it is the publication itself." In newspaper publishing, he thought, this idea could be married to the old established American convention (everywhere except in New York City) of home delivery. Consequently, when stockholder Harry Scherman, director of the Book-of-the-Month Club and one of the country's leading practitioners of direct mail, volunteered to try a mailing, Ingersoll was enthusiastic. The letter was a classic of its kind. It called *PM* a "historic event," devoted several paragraphs to Ingersoll and his achievements, said the editorial staff had been called "the most brilliant . . . ever gathered together by one newspaper," explained why it would not take advertising and how it would keep women readers informed with news about store bargains. In short, it would be "UTTERLY DIFFERENT" and "THE EASIEST TO READ NEWSPAPER EVER PUBLISHED."

The mailing, which included an Ingersoll Memo to his staff,* a refinement of the now famous Ingersoll prospectus,† pulled a response of over twenty percent! A return of two percent is considered good for most mailings, so Scherman was naturally excited and convinced Ingersoll that by spending $300,000 on a direct-mail campaign he would be assured of 150,000 charter subscribers.

*See appendix 2.
†See appendix 1.

Since *PM* needed only 200,000 readers to break even, everyone agreed this would be a smart way to spend approximately one-fifth of Ingersoll's bankroll.

The naming of *PM* is the subject of some confusion, and Ingersoll himself does not recall much about it—except that he remembers leaning toward *PM* because it suggested an afternoon newspaper, which would not compete with the *Daily News* (although it was eventually decided that the paper would appear on the stands all day in three editions). The *New Yorker* ran an interesting "Comment" in May of 1940 giving one version of the christening, and it is as good as any. In Ingersoll's prospectus he called his paper a "newspaper," and Cleland, in the first dummy, used that word on the masthead. Ingersoll liked it, and that was the name for some time. Then, "one night, in a bar," as the *New Yorker* described it, "Lillian Hellman told a group of friends that she thought the name ought to be *PM*. Mr. [Leonard] Lyons somehow got this mixed up, and announced in his column that it *was PM*. So many outsiders came to using the name that when it came to make the formal announcements, Mr. Ingersoll just thought, 'what the hell!'"

Although Ingersoll was not quite sure about what to call his paper, or whether it should be a morning or evening paper, one thing everyone was agreed on was that it would be read (mornings or evenings) by subway riders. So Ingersoll was delighted when he heard that designer Norman Bel Geddes had come up with what he thought was the perfect format for a newspaper to be read by a city of straphangers. At a demonstration for *PM*'s stockholders and staff in his office, Bel Geddes unveiled his invention: a newspaper designed like an accordion, printed on thirty-two feet of uncut newsprint! It could, indeed, be read by someone holding a strap with one hand. He had even designed a special press with a circular cylinder thirty-two feet in circumference. "It's two stories high," said Bel Geddes, "but if you put it in the window of your building—the way the old *Herald* press used to be on Thirty-fourth Street—people will come from all over just to look at it." *PM*'s stockholders were impressed, and Baumrucker, *PM*'s press expert, believed the press could be built. But Ingersoll had a horrible thought—and asked Bel Geddes if he could pick up his paper. When Bel Geddes handed it to him, Ingersoll took the first page in one hand and the last page in the other—the way a person would normally open a book—and out onto the floor spilled thirty-two feet of newspaper. It did not take much imagination to realize the chaos this would create in a subway at rush hour. The group silently put on their hats and left the office, almost as if on cue.

They decided to stick with the conventional, if smaller, tabloid format, but they also wanted to use a new printing process that had worked for magazines but had never been used for printing newspapers at high speed. It involved an ingenious method of printing with hot ink applied by heated type to water-cooled paper. The result was a printed page of a quality comparable to its equivalent in a magazine, but for weeks Ingersoll had to work with the production manager replacing broken parts.

The real crisis, however, was in the area of circulation, as it was there that

Joseph Medill Patterson, the publisher of the *Daily News,* had decided to declare war. One day he had his circulation manager, Ivan Annenberg, tell New York's forty-two hundred city and suburban newsstand dealers that if they sold *PM,* the *Daily News,* with its two-million circulation, would be sold elsewhere. Late that night an angry, frustrated Ingersoll stormed down to the Fifth Avenue apartment of Mayor Fiorello La Guardia, who knew all about Ingersoll and *PM.* The doorman was so startled, he took Ingersoll up unannounced. When the mayor opened the door, Ingersoll burst in, shouting, "Up until this week I thought you were the mayor of this goddamn city."

"I am," the mayor protested.

"The hell you are. You can't even run the newsstands you license. I bet you know damned well right now that Patterson has issued orders that they cannot display my paper. You're not the mayor of this city, Joe Patterson is."

The mayor was furious, but he finally decided he did not want to get his newsstand dealers in trouble with the most powerful publisher in the city. He had a compromise solution: "Get yourself some kind of gadget which you can put papers on—and I'll see that you have a right to put one up alongside every stand in town. And if anyone knocks one over, they're going to have me and my police department on their neck. I'm not going to let anybody turn this town into a Chicago."

The result was the little metal racks on which *PM* was sold. They cost thousands of dollars and solved the problem only for the four thousand city newsstands. La Guardia had no influence over the two hundred suburban news-stands. So Ingersoll called Patterson and requested a meeting. In Patterson's office, which was strewn with souvenir bats and balls for a baseball contest the *News* was running, Ingersoll demanded to know why he was being so tough. "Ingersoll," said Patterson, pacing back and forth behind his desk, swinging one of the baseball bats, "everybody in town thinks you're a damned fool and that you don't know anything about the newspaper business. They don't think *PM*'s got a chance. Well, son, that's exactly what they said about me when I came into town twenty years ago. So look at where I am now and look at where they are. So maybe you'll blow it, maybe you won't. But I ain't going to take a chance on it."

When Ingersoll protested that he had expected Patterson would be the one man in town rooting for him, the publisher replied, "You know, Ingersoll, I'm not sure I wouldn't get a kick out of seeing you come through. But that doesn't mean I'm not going to give you a little bit of a hazing before you get there. If you're man enough to take it, more power to you. It's all a kind of game, isn't it?"

So Ingersoll and *PM* had to play Patterson's game and hire home-delivery trucks for suburbia, which cost still more money.

With funds beginning to run out and the stockholders getting nervous, Ingersoll decided to approach the one investor he knew least, Marshall Field. Field, shy as always, said, "I think you'd be surprised to find how much like everyone else I am," and when they had lunch, he proceeded to demonstrate the point by grumbling over the waitress's refusal to let him substitute pie for the ice cream on the "businessman's lunch" menu. But Ingersoll liked Field and was reassured by the fact that he showed not the slightest inclination to make policy suggestions. When Ingersoll asked what had attracted him to *PM*, Field said it was partly Weiss's enthusiasm and partly his irritation with the *New York Times* and the *Herald-Tribune*, whose financial interests, he felt, dictated much of the material they published. The more he saw of *PM* and Ingersoll, he said, the more he was impressed with their intellectual honesty. He was not inclined, however, to put more money in at that stage and did not, in fact, impress Ingersoll as being particularly interested in the new publication.

It was Ingersoll's plan to have enough editors and writers assembled at least two months before publication to enable him to start publishing dummy issues and work out all the bugs before Volume 1, Number 1. He had finally found an office for the editorial staff: the top floor of a three-story brick building at Sixth Avenue and Pacific Street in Brooklyn, next to A. G. Spalding & Brothers, makers of athletic equipment, and less than a mile from their press which they rented from the *Brooklyn Eagle*. Most of the interviewing and hiring was done by managing editor George Lyon. But Ingersoll, who was now working a sixteen-hour day, seven days a week, living on Benzedrine, and keeping three secretaries busy typing his memos, did manage to interview a few candidates. Those interviews were memorable experiences, and James Wechsler, then a young writer working for the *Nation*, recalls his well. He had gone over to Brooklyn, full of excitement and anticipation at the idea of working for the paper he had heard so much about. And meeting Ingersoll, he says, "I became even more enamored of his idea and instantly devoted to the man. He was sitting in his shirtsleeves when I came in; a big, informal man in his early forties, with a quick, quizzical smile, a prematurely bald head and a self-confident jaunty manner. Not until one looked closely were the dark circles under his eyes noticeable. He seemed full of energy and ideas in a disarmingly unpretentious way; he walked with the plodding purposeful tread of a bear who knew where he is going, head always tilted in front of him, as if unable to restrain its eagerness to get to its destination." Wechsler was offered a job—as an assistant to labor editor Leo Huberman.

Ingersoll had planned to hire the most talented editorial staff in the history of the newspaper business, and he should have been able to do so because *PM*'s prepublication publicity eventually attracted over ten thousand job applications. In 1949 a questionnaire was sent to former *PM* staffers to find out what had made them want to work for the paper, and a majority of those who were hired before publication date said they did so because they had, as one staffer put it, "always dreamed of a paper like the one Ingersoll promised." The "paper had the cachet," said Louis Kronenberger, "of being something you'd kick yourself for having missed."

George Lyon hired as his assistant managing editors two Scripps-Howard associates: John P. Lewis from Buffalo and Elmer Roessner from the New York *World-Telegram*. The original editorial staff, as one study of *PM* has shown, was largely recruited from three main sources:

1. Nonprofessional intellectuals: This group included Elizabeth Hawes, in charge of the "News for Living" department; author of a best-selling book, *Fashion Is Spinach*, and at one time the manager of a very exclusive dressmaking shop; her sister, Charlotte Adams, author of *All the Comforts* and a housewife who had been a trustee of a progressive school as well as a department store clerk; Leane Zugsmith (wife of Carl Randau), a contributor to the first *PM* dummy and the author of six novels; Dalton Trumbo, a screenwriter and novelist; and Leo Huberman, a professor.

2. Nonintellectual professionals: Among them were Ben Robertson, formerly with the New York *Herald-Tribune*; William McCleary of the AP Associated Press, who brought in a large A.P. group; Lowell Leake from the *Washington Post*; Wesley Price from the *World-Telegram*; Duncan Aikman, a *Springfield Republican* alumnus who had also written for the *New York Times Magazine*; and Ken Crawford from the *New York Post*. Ingersoll asked Mayor La Guardia to suggest a City Hall reporter, and he picked William Vogel of the *Herald-Tribune*. Joseph Cummiskey was brought down from Buffalo; Tom Meany, considered the best baseball writer in town, was hired away from the *World-Telegram* as was Carl Randau. Julian Fromer, who had worked for Lyon in Buffalo; Ken Stewart from the *New York Times*; Bill Ryan, former city editor at the *New York American*; Rae Weimer from Scripps-Howard; and Alexander Uhl of the Associated Press were also hired. Hodding Carter, editor and publisher of the *Delta Democrat-Times* (Mississippi), also worked briefly for Ingersoll before deciding that *PM*, the big city, and working for someone else were not for him.

3. Professional intellectuals: Robert Neville, Louis Kronenberger, John McManus, Charles Tudor, and Willar Wiender of *Fortune*, all came over to *PM* from Time Inc. Others in this category included: George Wyall, who had worked for the *New Yorker*, free-lance writer John Kobel, Tom Davin from Random House, Tom Pettey from the Will Hays Office, James Wechsler from the *Nation*, and William Walton from the Associated Press.

Most of these editors and writers came to *PM* for less money than they were making or could have made elsewhere, but there were many New York newspapermen who did not think much of the staff. As one critic put it, "*PM* is short on an absolute necessity: news-getters. Even in selecting journalists, *PM* has been attracted mostly to re-write and office men. After all the advance advertising, *PM* sums up as a daily, pro-Soviet hybrid of *Time* and *Life* with overtones of *The New Yorker*—all publications on which Mr. Ingersoll has worked."

There was some truth in this indictment. Ingersoll was trying to translate magazine journalism into newspaper journalism with a staff that had too few

professional newspaper men and women, and that from the start was competi-
tively divided between professionals and nonprofessionals.

There were also too many Communist sympathizers, the direct result of
Ingersoll's own attraction to Communist ideas and his naïveté about the dedication
of the True Believers. He had dropped out of his Communist study group when
he found he could not follow the party line, but he was still sympathetic to the
cause of the poor, the oppressed, and the laboring man as, of course, the Communists were. And to put the Communist party "on notice" as to where he stood,
he sent word through the leader of his former study group that he wanted to
meet privately with Earl Browder, the head of the American Communist party.
Browder was very friendly, Ingersoll recalls, but he made it clear that he did
not approve of Ingersoll's plan for a newspaper. What Browder advocated was
a militant championship of the labor movement. "I told him," says Ingersoll,
"that while *PM* most emphatically would not be a Communist paper (or a Democratic or Republican) I would like the Communist point of view represented
because I considered it an important factor in contemporary politics." He backed
up this statement by asking Browder to send down a Communist reporter of his
choice to work on the paper "with the clear understanding," says Ingersoll, "his
influence would be limited to the expression of [the party's] opinion *in council*."
Browder did recommend a young man who came to work for Ingersoll for a
few weeks, then quit, saying, "Obviously I cannot be objective." Earlier Ingersoll
himself had had to jettison Daniel Gilmor (who had loaned some money to
Publications Research) because he insisted that *PM* adhere to the party line.

The relationship between *PM* and the Communists was a problem from the
beginning, when Dashiell Hammett was screening applications and interviewing
writers in his Plaza Hotel suite. Although Hammett never actually hired anyone
for *PM*, he and the writers associated with him (many of whom contributed to
the first dummy)—Dorothy Parker, Donald Ogden Stewart, Heywood Broun,
Lillian Hellman—had, at one time or another, been connected with Communist
front organizations. And there were people in New York who kept track of such
things. In the summer of 1939, after the signing of the Hitler-Stalin Pact, the
better-known Communists who had been on the fringes of the *PM* crowd disappeared, but there were still rumors that "Moscow gold" was financing the
operation. These rumors were silenced the following January when Ingersoll
announced his stockholders.

Ingersoll knew his policy of *not* hiring anyone who had been known to
oppose trade unions and racial and religious tolerance was taken by the Communists as an invitation to infiltrate. To discourage this, he told his staff, on
April 18, "we will not hire anyone who in our opinion puts politics ahead of
journalism—who is more interested in putting over a political point of view
than in seeking the truth."

After publication, the rumors started again. Eugene Lyons and Benjamin
Stalberg published articles in the *American Mercury* and the *Saturday Evening*

Post, respectively, citing the number of known Communists or "fellow travelers" working for *PM*—as many as sixteen by one count. How, they asked, had this many "Reds" managed to infiltrate the staff: Was it through Ingersoll's naïveté, or had he welcomed them aboard?

The answer was somewhere in between. Ingersoll would never have rejected an editor or a reporter because at one time or another he had been associated with a Communist front organization. His criterion was simply that the editor or writer be an objective journalist. Job applicants knew this, and it was not hard in an interview to convince George Lyon, who did most of the hiring of reporters, or Ingersoll, who hired the editors, that they were objective journalists first and political activists second. But several *PM* staffers had at one time worked for organizations that were either directly connected with the Communists or at least openly sympathetic to their objectives.

Of course, what Eugene Lyons, Benjamin Stalberg, and the others who were quick to label *PM* a Communist front organization failed to mention was that many of the people said to have worked for Communist front organizations were not really Stalinists and, especially after the Hitler-Stalin Pact, did not advocate ties with Moscow. Many, in fact, had already broken with the Communists. Young Wechsler for example: He had been an activist with the Young Communist League but had made his break and now looked forward to working for *PM* because he presumed it would be free from the political feuding inherent in most Communist organizations. But from the start, he says, "*PM* was an ideological battlefield reminiscent of the Student Union, and often the adults seemed to be getting younger all the time." At first the battle was between the Stalinists, the crypto-Stalinists, and the anti-Stalinists; then the feuding settled down to an all-out war between the Communists and anti-Communists, which, in the opinion of Ingersoll (and others), is what eventually ruined *PM*.

But as publication day approached, and the dummy issues did not seem to improve, the Communists were not the problem. The real enemies were exaggerated expectations, confusion, and inexperience. Most of the seventeen people Elizabeth Hawes hired for the "News for Living" section had never seen the inside of a newspaper office, and her own journalism experience was limited. Assistant managing editor John P. Lewis had to work with her for several days to get her department functioning. "*PM* was started by people who knew nothing about newspapers," says one of the original executives. "The newspapermen placed in authority to start were incompetent to do anything but old school newspaper work. Newspaper people fought nonnewspaper people instead of trying to teach them routines. The nonnewspaper people were snotty to newspaper people. This kind of stupidity, all well-intentioned, could doubtless be traced through every department. It arose out of Ingersoll's personal character."

How much Ingersoll was responsible for the early confusion is debatable. But he knew he had problems. Two weeks before publication he wrote his staff:

It is no secret that the major part of my time and energy for the past few weeks has had to go into problems of promoting and distributing *PM*—and the work of being chief executive. . . . Today I came back into the Editorial Department full time and have just read the last three papers you have gotten out.

Physically, you are rapidly achieving orderliness and *PM* has already a professional quality. Editorially, it is a dull paper, humorless, without life or sparkle, and its personality—what it thinks and believes in—is as obscure as *The New York Times*.

By now, the word-of-mouth promotion and the newspaper stories had been supplemented by two-page ads in such publications as the *New Yorker* and the *New York Herald-Tribune* announcing "a new and different kind of daily newspaper." *PM*'s promoters were still advertising the fact that the paper was "against people who push other people around." And there was genuine excitement in the air. Less than a month before publication President Roosevelt wrote Ingersoll:

Dear Ralph,

This is to welcome *PM* to the New York and to the American scene. Your interesting prospectus leads me to believe that you are about to add a notable chapter to the history of our free press.

It is more important than ever in these fast-moving times that the people be fully, reliably and quickly informed about the march and counter-march of significant events. They should get all the available facts and get them straight.

As you know, I have been critical at times of a part of the daily press. Too often the news of this part of the press has been colored because of front office prejudice or "business" reasons.

Your proposal to sustain your enterprise simply by merchandising information, with the public as your only customer, appeals to me as a new and promising formula for freedom of the press.

As P day approached, the staff was so frazzled and the fatigue, so obvious that, according to one early staffer, "Ralph Ingersoll posted a memo saying that any staff member who was still able to go to bed with his wife would be fired." And Ingersoll's own personal life had suffered during these frantic months. As Laura Hobson found out, it was no time to be having an affair with Ralph Ingersoll. And, again, there are two distinctly different versions of what happened. A few months after beginning her psychoanalysis, Mrs. Hobson was again seeing Ingersoll, although it continued to be an on-again, off-again affair, with Mrs. Hobson more than once writing Ingersoll to say the relationship was "*finis*." They would, nevertheless, soon be intimate again, and in August of 1939, just before Ingersoll went to Washington hoping to close the Noble deal, he and Mrs. Hobson spent two weeks together in Bermuda. When they came back to New York, they were, in her words, "engaged to be married, officially publicly, ring-on-the-finger engaged."

In the Ingersoll-Hobson affair engagement was, however, in the eye of the beholder: Ingersoll maintains it was not really a pledge to marry but a "pretend engagement" initiated by Mrs. Hobson because there was now too much talk around town about them and it was hurting her reputation. He says he consented to this arrangement and, to add public credibility to the deception, gave her the small gold ring with a diamond in it that he had once given Arny—the woman who had raised him—to whom he had often jokingly remarked: "Stick with me and you'll be wearing diamonds." Mrs. Hobson insists, however, that the engagement was for real, and that Ingersoll's father and stepmother threw a big engagement party in Lakeville (which Ingersoll says his father never would have done, because it was out of character and the conservative New Englander would never have approved of his engagement to a New York career girl). She says Tante gave her a mink coat as an engagement present, specifically so she would have something nice to wear when she went to the White House with Ralph, who was meeting with the president to discuss *PM*.

Mrs. Hobson also says her engagement to Ingersoll created a crisis in her career. She had progressed dramatically at Time Inc. to become the first woman to be included in the executive profit-sharing plan, which gave her a total annual income of thirty-one thousand dollars. Gradually, however, their differing politics had begun to create a gulf between her and Luce, and, when her engagement to Ingersoll became known, she felt she should leave. Ingersoll and Time Inc. were innovators, and although she did not consider *PM* a competing publication, she nonetheless felt uncomfortable attending senior staff meetings in which she was privy to both their innovations. Besides, to put it mildly, many top executives at Time Inc. did not like Ingersoll, which made her position even more uncomfortable. They both remembered the story of Clare Luce and *Life* and did not talk about a top job for Mrs. Hobson on the new paper. Still, she was hopeful, though, as she later said, "the only place he could think of for [her] was a labor column at a salary of $75-a-week. But, of course, that might change before pub day. Only it didn't."

Nevertheless, she resigned from Time Inc., apparently (judging from her memoirs) still hoping something would work out on *PM*. But it did not. In fact, by then she and Ingersoll were fighting so much that the engagement—real or pretend—was doomed. Mrs. Hobson claims that the principal reason for the growing tension was politics: That Ingersoll persisted in his trust of Stalin even after the Hitler-Stalin Pact. If this is true, it could not have been for long; Ingersoll and *PM* were openly critical of the Russian accord with the world's number-one enemy. But Mrs. Hobson insists that too often she found herself at parties with people like Lillian Hellman and Dashiell Hammett and that Ingersoll invariably sided with them—and she did not. She recalls getting mad one night, after a party and a late-night argument, and throwing a shoe at him when he said, "You don't trust Stalin. I do."

The arguments continued, and Mrs. Hobson says she finally concluded that this time it was all over between them. Then she became ill with a breast abscess and went into the hospital. When she came out, she went to Hollywood to visit Sinclair Lewis and, eighteen days before *PM* was published, wrote Ingersoll explaining why she knew they had broken for good. And this time, she says, "the *Finis* remained *Finis* forever."

Now Ingersoll's version: At some point, as their relationship deteriorated, they had one final confrontation, in which she said: "It's gone too far. I don't love you; in fact, I hate you. But *everyone's* taken it for granted for too long. So now you've *got* to marry me."

Ingersoll says he replied: "But we've never been in love and I don't want to get married again—to anyone. And for Christ's sake, we are both still in analysis and neither of us has any right to make important emotional commitments."

On one point they both agreed: Mrs. Hobson went into the hospital after their break.

They did not see each other or communicate for over a year, but they did remain *indirectly* in touch. Ingersoll recalls one comic interlude: While he was on the couch in his psychiatrist's office Mrs. Hobson's psychiatrist called Zilboorg, and the two eminent doctors began screaming at each other about what the other was doing to his patient.

Mrs. Hobson's psychiatrist had a right to be concerned about his patient. One friend, who played chess with her regularly during this period, said the experience was horribly traumatic and she found it almost impossible to concentrate on her game.

But even in her distress she dated other men, and before long she became pregnant by a man she chose not to name. And there was the "craving" that would not go away: "I wanted Ralph Ingersoll to know that I was pregnant and that I was going to *have* this baby." She did, however, have one problem, and that was money, which, she decided, also gave her a good reason for calling Ingersoll. So she asked him to her apartment, saying that she had something important to tell him, and he came. They exchanged comments about the war news—Hitler had just invaded Russia—and then she stated her well-rehearsed request: Would he lend her some money for the baby she was going to have? *PM* had been in existence a year by this time, and she knew it was not doing well financially. But, as she concedes, "I was certainly not saintly enough to be sorry for whatever he was feeling about his paper, nor hypocrite enough to think I ought to be." She also says she knew he was probably in no financial position to help, and she was right. He was broke then and did not offer to help, though as he recalls it, her request then was not so much to help her finance the child as to marry her.

A few weeks later Mrs. Hobson (who did have and raise the child) suddenly had an idea for her first novel, which grew out of a personal experience: The efforts of a Jewish doctor in Europe to obtain American visas to help his family escape the Nazis. There was also to be a young girl in the novel named Vee, who, Mrs. Hobson says, she modeled on herself. The American hero was a man named Jason Crown, an ambitious radio tycoon who would stop at nothing to achieve his objectives. She tried, she says, to model him on three men: her father, her brother, and Ralph Ingersoll. But years later she conceded that "what came out was a sort of sludge that might look like a symbol of spite or malice about Ralph Ingersoll." And that was the way many reviewers approached *The Trespassers*.

It is a brutal portrait, with Crown's only redeeming feature being his belief that he wants power to improve the world—specifically, to fight Adolf Hitler and the growth of fascism. There are similarities between Crown and Ingersoll: the passionate need to have his media outlet, a willingness to run over people who stand in his way, his hatred of Hitler, and his unerring belief in the rightness of any cause he adopts.

How does one explain the relationship between Hobson and Ingersoll, and why are their accounts of it so different? An attempt to ascertain the complete truth at this late date would be fruitless. But clearly it was an intensely emotional affair between two people who concede that at that time they were highly neurotic and experiencing a very difficult period in their lives. Mrs. Hobson makes no apologies for her actions; she says she was neurotic and in love, and could not have the man she wanted. Ingersoll, in the draft of an unpublished book he wrote in 1970, has said: "I'd never fallen in love with her . . . and I ran out on a commitment I had never made."

More recently, after Mrs. Hobson's memoirs were published, he said, "I never took any of her writings about me seriously." He is, however, quite candid about the person he was in 1940, at the age of thirty-nine: "I was developing . . . I was a nasty-child-man, so full of a swelling ego which I did not understand that I could barely sense anyone else's needs . . . and was wholly sure of every judgment I made."

* * *

As publication date for *PM* approached, Ingersoll had so little time to devote to the dummy issues that Kronenberger had to write one of Ingersoll's signed contributions. And as they came down to the wire, Kronenberger said, it was, in fact, bedlam in Brooklyn, "with nothing but brand new inmates, all of them rather frantic and everything about them still unfamiliar. . . . Instead of legmen phoning the office, they were seated in it phoning their wives; instead of rushing out to cover a disaster, reporters simply rewrote the wire services"—except that they did not have the one they needed most, the Associated Press. So *PM* had to settle for the United Press, which had inadequate New York coverage and no photo service.

Publication day—June 18, 1940—arrived with a dark omen: smoke from a fire in the city room. Big red engines shrieked to a stop in the street below, and helmeted, rubber-coated firemen burst into the room. But, "according to my memory," says Ingersoll, "not a single man or woman of the 30 or 40 at work there rose from their seats, only a few even deigned to look up."

The prepublication excitement had created such curiosity about the paper that the first delivery trucks to go out were literally mobbed. The five-cents-a-copy tabloid was going for twenty-five to thirty cents, and before the day was over 450,000 copies had been sold. "You'd have thought we put a $20 bill in every paper," said Harry Feldman. But in the excitement the 150,000 charter subscribers, which *PM* had spent $300,000 to acquire, were totally ignored. Worse, no one even realized it at the time!

Everyone knew they would not keep up their 450,000 first-day circulation, but they needed only 200,000 sales to stay in the black. Ten days after publication they were still selling more than 200,000 a day, and Ingersoll knew they still had their charter subscribers in the bank. For almost two weeks it looked as if Ingersoll had pulled it off—a new kind of newspaper that was both a commercial and a journalistic success. On the tenth day Ingersoll experienced his one moment of sheer ecstasy. In his office, with Weiss present, he let go, literally kicking his feet in the air and roaring with laughter: "We've done it, we've done it." Weiss left the office convinced that Ingersoll was headed for a breakdown.

And, indeed, his exhilaration did not last long. Two weeks later, he says, "it seemed as if it would have taken a $20 bill in every paper to persuade people to read *PM*. It was a turkey." As he would later assess the first weeks: "The cocky inference had been clear enough. The editors of *PM* were going to knock 'em dead. They were going to show the rest of the newspaper staffs in New York how good a paper could be when its reporters, photographers and editors were given their heads. Out of such phrases as 'a new kind of newspaper' and 'a daily picture magazine' the public conjured up something superlative and when they didn't get it they were disgusted."

Having read all the assessments of *PM*, having heard all the comments (such as Harold Ross's classic: "*PM* is gotten out by a bunch of young fogies"), and looking back through the first issues, one still finds it hard to understand why *PM* was not immediately successful in newspaper history. It was a notable chapter as President Roosevelt said in his congratulatory letter, and still is. The first page had a touch of color in the logo, big, eye-catching headlines, and a large, intriguing photograph. Inside, the layouts were clean and attractive, featuring excellent photographs and numerous drawings printed on good paper. The writing was usually superior to that which appeared in most papers in the country, and the tabloid's innovations were truly unique in 1940. It covered labor (by Leo Huberman and James Wechsler), the press (by Hodding Carter), radio (by John T. McManus), and movies (by Cecilia Ager) as they had never been covered before. The sports section, edited by Joe Cummiskey and featuring Tom Meany and Tom O'Reilly, was superb and, with the living section, was perhaps *PM*'s most enduring achievement. In fact, the living section under Elizabeth Hawes and the consumer news were not equalled, in most papers, until the 1970s, by which time, incidentally, most of *PM*'s innovations had become common practice in the newspaper business.

The front-page headline of *PM*'s first issue on June 18, 1940, proclaimed: "HITLER ARRIVES IN MUNICH TO MEET MUSSOLINI" (to discuss the fall of France). And almost every issue for the next several weeks announced significant war news on its first page. But instead of helping *PM* get launched, as

There was such a demand for the first issue of PM (BELOW LEFT) published on June 18, 1940, that the trucks carrying them (ABOVE) were mobbed when they went out onto the streets. Nevertheless, the paper was bankrupt after three months and Marshall Field (with Ingersoll, right) bought out the other stockholders at 20 cents on the dollar.

Ingersoll had hoped, the war was perhaps a detriment. As Ingersoll said in his first editorial, "*PM* starts off at the most critical moment in the history of the modern world. The news is too big, too terrible to seem for a second like a break for a newspaper coming into being. Instead, it dwarfs us. It pitches us, without preparation, into the midst of horror. It means that we, who wanted time to grow, shall have no youth—shall be gray-haired from birth."

Events and the problems of getting out a newspaper with a new staff did seem to overwhelm him, and within the first month Ingersoll knew something had to be done. "*PM* was physically confused," he said, "because the editors still didn't know how to put it together." It was spiritually confused because too many things had happened to them in too short a time—and because they were wholly preoccupied with getting to press at all. They were out of touch with the world about which they were writing in their paper. And *PM* was dull, Ingersoll says, "because while there were bright and sparkling writers on the paper, there were too few of them—and the editors were too harassed to make the others better than they were. Most of *PM*'s staff had grown up on papers which needed only reasonably literate writing to keep them in business. They made their money selling advertising space, not writing."

But Ingersoll had still not given up his dream. And now, with the circulation dropping every day and with the carping and sniping coming at him from all sides, he decided to devote full time to achieving his goal—a newspaper that read like a magazine. Traditionally, stories in a newspaper have begun with a lead paragraph that is supposed to tell who, what, when, where, and why, after which the facts of the story are set forth in order of diminishing importance. The reason for this is simple: If space dictates that the story be chopped off at the end, what is left will still give the essential facts. "But I wanted my stories told as writers would tell them," Ingersoll says. "I wanted to return to the classical form of beginning, middle and end. Moreover, I was confident that it could be done—and was even commercially practical because Time Inc. had made fifty million dollars rewriting newspaper stories into miniature compositions and giving them new dimensions."

Ingersoll thought he would have time—before circulation dropped below the two-hundred-thousand mark—to make *PM* the exciting paper he had been dreaming of for years. So he began firing, hiring, and shifting people around, hoping to come up with the right combination. Within the first three months, seventy-five members of the staff left the paper, most fired by Ingersoll—which not only produced a bad case of employment jitters among the staff, but started his prolonged war with the Newspaper Guild, which will be discussed later. This first wave of reorganization was, however, not successful, and Ingersoll began to fear the worst: that maybe you could not produce a newspaper the same way you did a magazine. *PM* was loaded with talent in those early days, but there was simply not enough to go around. Ingersoll had seen Ross hire and fire ten men to come up with the one he wanted, and he knew that, on a magazine if you could count on six to ten inspired, capable assistants, you could do the job.

"If *PM* had been a weekly," Ingersoll says, "it would have been no problem. But *PM* wasn't. Every week there were not one but six issues to be conceived, researched, written, edited and fitted together. Never having successfully done it, I have no absolute answer, but in my opinion, to create a newspaper even approximately fulfilling *PM*'s prospectus would take not five or ten exceptional, superior writers and editors, but no less than fifty really first-class craftsmen— and we never came even within shooting distance of getting that many together at one time."

But he kept trying, and *PM*'s bylines during its first years include a remarkable number of names that would become familiar in journalism or the arts: Jerome Weidman, Albert Deutsch, George Reedy, John Kobler, Ken Crawford, James Wechsler, Frank Sullivan, Selwyn James, Ben Robertson, Penn Kimball, Leonard Engle, Gerald Sykes, William Walton, Weldon James, Cecilia Ager, Sidney Margolius, Erskine Caldwell, Maurice Hindus, I. F. Stone, Jimmy Cannon, Frank Hewlett, H. R. Knickerbocker, Leo Hershfield, Theodor Seuss Geisel (Dr. Seuss), Carl Rose, Max Lerner.

It was also during this period of trying to make one last effort to achieve his dream that he met the man who would eventually join his father, Ross, Luce, and Zilboorg as a shaper of his destiny. One evening his secretary told him he had had a visit from a tall, unusual gentleman who said his name was Charles

PM *staff meeting: (l. to r.) managing editor John Lewis; editor Ralph Ingersoll; Sunday editor Bill McCleary; business manager Lowell Leake; national affairs editor Eugene Lyons; and two unidentified staffers*

Marsh. Marsh wanted to see Ingersoll that night at the Hotel Pierre, where he was staying—no matter what time Ingersoll quit work! It was two A.M. when he left the office that night, but he decided to call on the mysterious stranger, despite the late hour. When the door of Marsh's penthouse opened, Ingersoll, who was six two, was surprised to find himself looking up at a giant of a man with sharp blue eyes, who was dressed in an embroidered Chinese gown. "Who are you?" the man said, glowering down on Ingersoll.

"My name is Ralph Ingersoll and you bullied my secretary into ordering me here."

Marsh said, "Oh, come in a second," and Ingersoll entered the suite. All over the floor were charts and figures. Marsh pointed to them and said: "I'm taking apart the DuPont Company and I don't want to be bothered now. But you're the one who started that paper *PM* and I wanted to tell you what a fine thing you're doing. You will fail, of course, but while you're in business, I'll try to help you and will feed your editors stuff worth printing. Now get out of here because I'm busy."

Ingersoll did not see Marsh again until after Pearl Harbor, but this singular man would eventually play a significant role in his life. And although a little premature, his assessment of *PM* was correct. A few weeks after Ingersoll made his determined effort to bring *PM* to editorial life, the circulation had dropped below the 200,000 break-even point, although Ingersoll still thought he had his 150,000 charter subscribers to cushion the fall. So one day he called in Benton and asked him how the charters were doing: "Have we lost any yet; if so, how many?"

"My God," replied Benton, "I don't know. Let's send for Harry Feldman." But Feldman didn't know either—and what happened next was the most shocking and perplexing incident in all the confusion and chaos of *PM*'s first six months. "There are many parts of *PM*'s story," Ingersoll said years later, "that people find unbelievable. But the fact is, this I don't believe myself. I didn't believe it at the time and I don't believe it now. It absolutely positively could not have happened. But, dammit, it did!"

This is the story: By publication date the logistics for home delivery to the charter subscribers had been arranged. But on P day, when the trucks left the plant, they were literally mobbed and people were offering a quarter and fifty cents for the paper. The trucks came back, reloaded, and went out again, only to have their papers sold before they reached their destination. This went on for a few weeks before the paper finally began to arrive at the suburban newsstands from which they were to be delivered to a home address. But by now the charter subscribers, who were supposed to have been given preferential treatment, were angry and had started to drift away. In the excitement of those first few weeks they had been forgotten, and Feldman had never reported it to Benton.

Ingersoll did not panic. "It's over now," he told Feldman and Benton, "but there's a way out. We still have in our files the names of a hundred and fifty thousand people who once loved us. We've done 'em dirt. OK. So we go right back to them and admit it—with a letter I'll sit down now and write—telling them what boobs we've been and how ashamed of ourselves we are, asking them to give us one more chance. Then we'll give them the paper free every day for a month—and I'll bet we'll keep two-thirds of them."

But the next morning, when they arrived in Brooklyn, the subscription cards were gone. A few were later discovered in a trash basket. Someone had dumped all one hundred and fifty thousand of them in the trash! It could have been one of the many inexperienced clerks, but the theory around *PM* at the time was that someone working for one of the New York dailies had infiltrated the plant and, looking for ways to sabotage the operation, had thrown out the cards. But this was never proved.

When he was finally satisfied that nothing could ever be done to retrieve the lost subscribers, Ingersoll went to his office, sat down with a paper and pencil, and looked at his figures. The bottom line was that if circulation flattened out (at just below two hundred thousand) and all went well (which you could not count on) they would be bankrupt in six months.

But Ingersoll still did not give up. His psychiatrist once said that if Ingersoll was in a losing battle surrounded by deserting troops, he would make a speech, fully expecting the deserters to follow him in a charge against the enemy's strongest position. The reason was his irrational, emotional confidence in himself—"a confidence so great," says Ingersoll, "that I have always, in my good moments, seen no obstacle too great to overcome to reach any objective."

Besides, in those early days he was fighting so many battles on so many fronts that he hardly had time to face the reality of a possible defeat. And his troops did not desert him; they were right in the thick of the fight—only as often as not, they were fighting each other. In fact, when one looks back on it and asks how so many talented people could fail to put out a good newspaper, the most consistent explanation is that the controversies and turmoil stirred up by Ingersoll in his attempt to carry out *PM*'s professed goals created so much tension that it made the task of getting out a daily paper (especially with *PM*'s bright but temperamental staff) virtually impossible.

From the start *PM* inspired and invited controversy, much of it due to Ingersoll's stated intention to oppose people who pushed other people around. *PM*'s first issue appeared on a Tuesday, and within twenty-four hours the Reverend Edward Curran (the Eastern ally of the Reverend Charles Coughlin, who supported the pro-Fascist Christian Front) denounced it as licentious. The following Sunday he attacked *PM* from his pulpit and encouraged his congregation to run the paper out of town. The subject of his sermon was a series of photographs of Gypsy Rose Lee doing her thing at the New York World's Fair—none of the four photographs published in *PM*, it must be said, revealed as much of Miss Lee's body as one would normally see in an ad for lingerie. So Ingersoll went around to see Father Curran personally, and was accused of setting up the headquarters of an atheistic, pro-British, Moscow-inspired propaganda mill. Other pulpits in Brooklyn began to pick up the chant, as did Father Coughlin's mag-

azine, *Social Justice*, published weekly in Detroit. After a while Ingersoll decided
to pay a call on the bishop of New York, the Most Reverend Francis Spellman,
whom he had met while at *Fortune*. When he asked the bishop if he could do
anything to quiet Father Curran, Spellman shook his head and said, "You have
my sympathy. These kinds of priests are a great embarrassment to the Church
and I know how you feel. But," he continued with great sadness and seeming
helplessness, "I cannot issue orders. We are not a military organization." Then
his eyes began to sparkle. "'Tis not a thing you should be concerning yourself
with. It will disappear. That we've learned."

So Ingersoll dropped the subject, asked the bishop to read a copy of *PM*,
and eventually established a close relationship with him, which he maintained
with regular visits to the three-story stone house on Madison Avenue, behind
Saint Patrick's Cathedral. But the opposition from the Christian Fronters never
disappeared, and Ingersoll would eventually have a dramatic confrontation with
Father Coughlin.

The Christian Front was, in fact, only one of the many groups aligning
themselves against *PM*. The next attack came from the militant anticommunists.
They began circulating an unsigned handbill throughout New York newspaper
offices which said: "Although card holding Party members are in the minority
at *PM*, they control some vital desks and otherwise are in positions to doctor
the copy to suit." The circular also included a list of twenty-four *PM* staffers
described as either members of the Communist party (CP) or party sympathizers
(S).

When the handbill reached Ingersoll's desk, he was both enraged and appalled. He did not know most of the staffers named well enough to have an
opinion on their politics, but he felt completely confident that the ones he did
know—Robert Neville, Louis Kronenberger, and Margaret Bourke-White—were
objective journalists, and they were listed as sympathizers. He thought the attack
was scurrilous, and his first reaction was typical. Without consulting anyone on
the staff except Dashiell Hammett, who was still reading all copy, Ingersoll
decided to devote the entire "Press" section to a story headed "Volunteer Ge-
stapo." It contained photos of all twenty-four of the staffers named, a copy of
the handbill, and a signed editorial denouncing the accusations and inviting the
Federal Bureau of Investigation to come up and investigate *PM*.

Hammett, however, did not think it was a good idea, and left the office
that night believing he had talked Ingersoll out of it. But when he got home,
the phone rang and it was Ingersoll announcing that he had decided to run it
anyway. Then he paused and said, "Incidentally, Dash, things are pretty hot
down here right now on this Red issue. Maybe you'd better stay away from the
shop for a month or so until it cools off."

That, Hammett recalled later, ended his association with *PM*.

When Ingersoll's somewhat naive feature was published on July 12, it
created a furor—not only around town but in the *PM* offices as well. "It made
me mad," said Ken Stewart—described as an "(S)"—as it did most of the men

and women listed. When he saw Ingersoll that morning, Stewart told him that although he was not ashamed of the company the list put him in, he did think it highly unfair and dangerous to the interests of those involved to dignify and circulate an underhanded, anonymous attack without first determining its source and giving the men and women named a chance to speak for themselves.

Ingersoll was sympathetic and said this was his way of smoking out the attack. It is also quite likely he was aware the F.B.I. was already investigating him and *PM*. (The F.B.I. files on Ingersoll, now available under the Freedom of Information Act, contain a copy of Ingersoll's controversial piece and his invitation to be investigated.) A ten-page single-spaced memorandum to the director, dated June 22, 1940, discusses in detail Ingersoll and his backers and concludes that Ingersoll was probably not a Communist, although he responded to some of the Communists' ideas and associated with Communist sympathizers and some known Communists. One report described him as "an adventurer on the make who is willing to take any road necessary to his success." Another quoted one man as saying Ingersoll was "a genius as a publisher." But Ingersoll's piece in *PM* prompted a formal investigation of the individuals cited in his article, and the files contain evidence that J. Edgar Hoover himself sent letters and memos to the F.B.I. office in New York with suggestions concerning the *PM* investigation. There is, however, no evidence that the F.B.I. ever considered *PM* to be anything other than what it was: a random collection of predominantly liberal newspaper men and women of varying political persuasions and sympathetic to the labor movement and other causes also supported by the Communists in the 1940s. "Ingersoll's policy was not actually Communist," said a 1960 assessment in the bureau's files, "but on frequent occasions he wrote bizarre defenses of projects which were helpful to the Communists."

The intensity of his staff's reaction surprised Ingersoll and prompted him to think it was just possible that there might have been more truth in the exposé than he had suspected. However, Ken Stewart, who later did a study of *PM*, said the list was eventually exposed as phony. The same month, the *New Leader* published a piece by Victor Riesel, titled "Million Dollar Daily Follows CP Line," which added a few more names to the list of *PM* staffers known to be Communists.

Although Ingersoll was not disturbed by the attacks of the anti-Communists and the rumors, he was well aware that his stockholders were. And he knew they would be even more disturbed when the *American Mercury* piece by Eugene Lyons appeared in the August 1940 issue. So he decided to meet their concern with his usual weapon. He wrote a long editorial in *PM* answering charges that it was a Communist front, and then elaborated on this in his thirteen-page confidential "Memorandum to the Stockholders: Rumors of Radicalism on *PM*." He reminded his financial backers of his first conversation with most of them, and of his reply when they had asked him about rumors that certain leftists and even Communists were working on the dummy: "You mustn't worry about them. They are writers and may or may not work for the paper and will never control the policy. If you are going to worry about such things, you must worry about me because I consider myself an aggressively liberal fellow. I think this country is a swell place, but I don't think it is nearly good enough: Right-minded men can and must do something about it, each in his own trade. My trade is journalism. The paper I get out will not be neutral on the issues of the day. It will be aggressively liberal."

He went on to explain the origins and history of the charges of Communism on *PM*. The first question, Ingersoll said, was why there should be all the "mystery" about *PM*'s politics and so many rumors about its "radicalism," given that he had conceded that he was aggressively liberal: "Why does the charge of some mysterious brand of radicalism continue to buzz irritatingly around *PM*'s head? Why isn't it just taken for granted—like, say the *Post*'s politics—and left at that?"

The explanation, he thought, began with the mystery surrounding the origins of *PM*—a mystery that was both intentional and necessary. In the planning stage, when he had set up Ed Stanley to do the basic research plan for *PM*, the operation had to be secret and hence mysterious because he had promised Henry Luce to make every effort not to "compromise Time Inc.'s reputation" with his activities. At that time he was still publisher of *Time and* a stockholder in the company. Then, when he left the company to begin raising money and developing the dummy, he brought in his old friends Lillian Hellman and Dashiell Hammett to work with writers. And he also became briefly involved with a young radical named Daniel Gilmor, whom he eventually rejected as a financial backer. Hellman and Hammett, both known for their left-wing sympathies, recruited a number of writers—some of whom were also left-wing—and this operation had to remain secret because most of the writers were working for other publications and might have been fired if it had been known they were helping Ralph Ingersoll. This enshrouded the operation in more mystery, and by now the rumors abounded and speculation about who was behind the new publication covered a broad field, from William Hearst and Henry Luce, to the Republican and/or Democratic national committees, to Moscow. Although the secrecy was necessary, said Ingersoll, he nonetheless found it irritating, because frankly he would have preferred to have it known that Ralph Ingersoll was behind all the excitement.

He conceded that Hammett had worked out of the Plaza Hotel—not in a "palatial suite" financed by well-heeled backers, as Lyons implied, but out of his own hotel room. And although he was scouting prospective writers, most of the people he interviewed were never hired, and even if they had been, what difference would it make? Then he cited Dorothy Parker—whose left-wing sympathies were well-known—as a perfect example of the "high gossip value" of certain names. Parker had come up again and again in connection with *PM*, he explained, "yet beyond having written and been paid for a theater review in the first dummy and a couple of book reviews since publication, she has never been on the staff and I have never talked with her about the paper. I wish I knew her better. I am a great admirer of her writing. My acquaintance dates back to

The New Yorker days when she was already a famous writer and I was a cub reporter. Any time Miss Parker will write a review for *PM* I will publish it. But the idea that she has ever been an important influence on *PM* is silly."

He also pointed to another situation, one that would increasingly plague him. He had two men on his staff who were prominent members of the Newspaper Guild: Carl Randau, president of the New York chapter of the guild and a desk editor in *PM*'s foreign news department, and Ken Crawford, president of the national guild organization and chief of his Washington bureau. Randau was the leader of the Left faction in the guild, and Crawford a leader of the Right faction, and yet in all the accusations leveled at *PM*, said Ingersoll, you never heard Crawford's politics mentioned, nor was it ever suggested that he might be influencing policy at *PM*. It was always Randau and his politics that were suspicious. And no one had ever attacked the six senior editors, who really made the policy, while the politics of the head of the research department, who had nothing to say about policy, was always mentioned.

In short, said Ingersoll, the intent of the rumors was to discredit *PM* and the attacks were coming from three sources, all desiring to see *PM* disappear: (1) the Christian Front; (2) the Red-baiting Left—ex-Communists and professional anti-Communists who, said Ingersoll, hated Communist sympathizers even more than they hated Communists—were mostly sincere but must invariably be discredited by their bitterness and carelessness with the facts, and (3) the circulation departments of other newspapers; certain rumors had been traced specifically to Roy Howard, publisher of the *World-Telegram*.

Ingersoll did concede that there might be a Communist cell on *PM*, just as there had been a cell on the *New York Times* and at Time Inc. He then went into a long discussion of what he called "the Communist Party line"—what it is, how you define it, how it is disseminated, and, finally, what a "Communist sympathizer is": "If what is meant by Communist sympathizer is a man who sympathizes with *some* part but not all of the Communist Party line, then I would be willing to state unequivocally that I have not knowingly hired a man who is not a Communist sympathizer. What *PM* is not—what no member of *PM*'s staff, to the best of my knowledge, is—is an organizational member of the Party, taking orders from 14th St (or Moscow), putting politics ahead of journalism and ahead of the welfare of this organization. I am now several times on record as saying that if I catch one such at work doctoring *PM* dishonestly I will put him out on his ear as fast as I can throw him."

The Communist issue had clearly become a problem, and Ingersoll was on the defensive. It would get worse, but just then—in the summer of 1940—Ingersoll and the stockholders had a much more serious problem. By August circulation had sunk to thirty-one thousand, and the company was headed for bankruptcy. As the financial situation continued to worsen, two stockholders, Jock Whitney and Lincoln Schuster, decided to call on Ingersoll to deliver a strong dose of constructive criticism and see what might be done to rescue the paper. Schuster went up to Ingersoll's office while Whitney waited outside in a limousine. When Schuster returned after ten minutes, Whitney asked, "How did you make out?" Schuster replied, "Make out, hell! I didn't get a word in edge-wise. The trouble with Ingersoll is that failure has gone to his head!"—a remark that was picked up in a column by Clifton Fadiman and widely circulated around town.

Ingersoll, of course, knew what was happening, and knew, too, that some-thing had to be done. At first he considered a barnstorming tour: He would go to each of his stockholders to apprise them of the situation and elicit further monetary support. But he no longer had the heart for it; his promotion days were over; so he finally had his lawyers break the bad news to the stockholders and find out how many of them would be agreeable to refinancing. Word came back that three—Hartford, Whitney, and Field—would consider it.

Ingersoll then went to lunch with Field to discuss the situation and learned that the multimillionaire was interested in buying out all the stockholders and putting up the money to keep the paper going. Ingersoll said he did not want to work for anyone—even the benevolent Field—but if he would put up the money, Ingersoll would "work like hell for *PM*." The implication was clear: He would keep going if he had complete freedom to run the paper as if it were his. And Field agreed, although he added one qualification: The paper had to become self-supporting. "You're not the Philharmonic Orchestra, which always will have to have patrons. But as long as you see a prospect of success, I'll continue to finance you."

Shortly thereafter, when a small group of the stockholders met informally to discuss *PM*'s rapidly deteriorating situation, Field made an offer to buy the others out for twenty cents on the dollar—provided all would sell and do it quickly. There was some bickering and one stockholder suggested they all give a little more financial help to tide the paper over while they worked out a new editorial policy. To this suggestion, Field responded with a remark that summed up his attitude for virtually the entire eight years of his association with *PM*: "I'm sorry. I'm not supporting a newspaper, I'm supporting an idea. It wouldn't be fair." Then Hartford and Whitney accepted his offer, and it was agreed that a formal meeting would be held.

The stockholders' meeting was scheduled for September 12, 1940, at the Elbow Room, a semiprivate club in the mid-Fifties, just west of Madison Avenue. Ingersoll hired a lawyer, Harry Root Stern, to represent him, thus relieving Field's lawyer, Louis Weiss, of any conflict of interest. He picked the Elbow Room for sentimental reasons: It was at this plush restaurant, says Ingersoll, "that I first had confided my plan for a new kind of newspaper to John Wharton."

Of the eighteen stockholders, only a handful showed up in person. The rest were represented by lawyers. Hartford, Whitney, and Field were considered "friendly" to Ingersoll; Deering Howe and Garrard Winston were "hostile" and favored dumping him. The others were still dazed at the turn events had taken, and had not made up their minds. After cocktails were offered, Ingersoll made a brief speech: "You all know why I've asked you here. Copies of our current figures are at everyone's place. Projecting our current losses, we should be able to publish for six weeks more—but no longer. I'm putting it up to you to decide what you wish to do about this—and will cooperate with any plan that seems reasonable—or remove myself without further discussion."

He sat down and no one said anything. There did not seem much point in small talk. Then Weiss got up and said Marshall Field was prepared to make an offer on a take-it-or-leave-it basis—but if it was rejected he would consider any other reasonable plan proposed. The offer was to buy out all the other stock-holders for twenty cents on the dollar—period. Ingersoll thinks the attorneys for Winston and Howe said their clients would like more time, and he said he would be glad to grant anyone more time, but there were only six weeks left before bankruptcy. Whitney, who was present, then got up and said he thought Field's offer was fair (Ingersoll had learned earlier that Whitney also had wanted to buy out the others but had deferred to Field). Harry Scherman, also present, said he thought there should be some provision for paying back the remaining eighty cents if *PM* should become profitable, but Weiss said he was not authorized to discuss other provisions. So a motion was made to vote on Field's offer, and it was accepted by a majority. The common stock, of which Ingersoll held half, was invalidated, which meant, as Ingersoll put it, "the company I'd spent five years putting together so that it would be mine, all mine, was wiped out—and with the company that replaced it, I never even had a contract."

Although a couple of the stockholders were unhappy and threatened a lawsuit (which never materialized), most felt Field had done a gentlemanly thing, as one of them put it. "I think we were all lucky to get through the whole mess without more embarrassment than we had," said William Benton, who had no part in the Field takeover but believed Field had bailed them all out. "We should build him a memorial."

* * *

It had been over four years since Ingersoll had drifted in the rowboat off Tavern Island, shaken his fist at Lillian Hellman, and sworn that he would show her and her friends and Henry Luce and everyone else what he could do as editor and publisher of his own publication. Almost every hour since then he had spent dreaming and planning his new kind of newspaper. For one night, in August of 1939, he thought he had found someone to back him with $1.5 million. But when Noble withdrew, he did the impossible: He went out and raised $1.5 million from virtual strangers, on the strength of his ideas, his enthusiasm, and his reputation. On June 18, 1940, he launched perhaps the most exciting newspaper in the history of journalism, and he was the editor and sole owner. It was the impossible dream—and it lasted less than three months.

11: Ingersoll Declares War

Ingersoll had had his one turn at bat, and although he had not hit a home run, neither did he strike out. It was more like an intentional pass; *PM* was still in business and he was still the boss. He had also found that it was almost impossible to get out a daily paper when you were continually preoccupied with financial problems. In truth, says Ingersoll, "I was fed up with the lawyers and balance sheets and I wanted to get the taste of all that out of my mouth and get back to my trade which was reporting and editing."

Marshall Field had promised to give him a free hand. For the most part he kept his word, and Ingersoll was too excited about his first assignment to pay much attention to Charles Cushing, a personal friend whom Field had asked Ingersoll, as a special favor, to hire. For some time Ingersoll had wanted to go to England and with the Battle of Britain raging in the air over London, he believed the moment was right. "Ever since Churchill and Bevin had taken over the leading jobs in the British Government, I had come increasingly to feel that the British might yet undo the man I saw as World Enemy Number One—Adolf Hitler. And yet, like most of us, I was full of doubts. I felt I had to go and see for myself before I could have any real confidence in my opinion and judgment.

If the British were not really fighting, if there was any possibility of the war suddenly ending in a British version of Vichy or if the struggle against Hitler was hopeless—then I wanted to know it and change my policy before it was too late."

Hitler might not have known it, but one of his most dedicated enemies was preparing for war. As Ingersoll put it in what the *New Yorker* would call its "all-time favorite" *Who's Who* entry: "Flew to Great Britain to cover war personally, Fall 1940."

Ingersoll was in London two weeks, during which time he interviewed Winston Churchill, Edward R. Murrow, Ernest Bevin, Claude Cockburn, and numerous other prominent men and women holding out against Hitler. He spent several nights in air-raid shelters; gave two radio broadcasts to the United States over the Mutual network; and returned with what the *Washington Post* called "an amazing bundle of facts, figures, anecdotes and personal observations ... a brilliant journalistic achievement." And Field learned, as Luce had, that when Ingersoll goes out on an assignment, you get your money's worth. Every issue of *PM*, from November 18, 1940, through December 9, 1940, carried a major story filed by Ingersoll from Britain, running anywhere from two to six pages and rating front-page headlines, some of which even made news:

U.S. PLANES OUTCLASSED BY BOTH GERMANS AND BRITISH

and the one that led off the series:

HITLER HAD LONDON IN SEPTEMBER
But When He Lost 200 Planes a Day
He Couldn't Take It

Ingersoll's reports naturally created a sensation in a country already caught up in the war through Edward R. Murrow's nightly reports from London. They also produced a dramatic circulation increase of fifty thousand during the course of their run. Simon and Schuster grabbed the pages almost as they came out of Ingersoll's typewriter and in three weeks rushed *Report on England* into print. Several reviewers commented that his reporting was better than his judgments, but almost every critic agreed with Ralph Thompson whose review in the *New York Times* called *Report on England* "the most informative quick reporting job we have had since the war began." And Walter Millis in the *Herald-Tribune* said that despite the perhaps exaggerated claims about the plight of Britain on September 15 and the poor condition of American planes, "everyone is now talking about the decisive air victory won in mid-September, as they were not until the Ingersoll articles appeared. People are no longer recklessly talking about the unassailable superiority of American planes, as they were before."

They were also talking about Ingersoll's emergence as a star reporter, which had been overlooked when he was turning out his brilliant articles anonymously for Henry Luce and *Fortune*. In the *Saturday Review of Literature* Frederick

Lawrence described Ingersoll's "revised conception of the technique of reporting": subjective, but vivid and alive.

But most important, Ingersoll had come back with the answer to the question
that had motivated his trip to London: The British were ready to fight to the
finish. And Ingersoll planned to enlist *PM* on their side.

The week after the Republican National Convention Ingersoll had flown
out to Denver to meet Wendell Willkie; Mitch Davenport, who had succeeded
Ingersoll as managing editor of *Fortune*, was working for Willkie and had
arranged the meeting. "I was charmed by Willkie," Ingersoll said after he had
met him, "convinced as I had not been of his sincerity. But I felt that his
inexperience would be no match for the Old Guard in the Republican Party."

To no one's surprise, Ingersoll put *PM* behind Roosevelt "150 percent,"
which he let FDR know through Ken Crawford. Ingersoll was in Lisbon when
Roosevelt was reelected in 1940, but he cabled his congratulations; and when
he returned from his London trip, he had a twenty-minute interview with the
president during which he reported on how the British were taking the bombing,
and reaffirmed his impression that the British people were united behind Churchill
in the war against Hitler. In "open letters" to the president Ingersoll had defended
Roosevelt's fight against the Fascists, particularly his efforts to arouse support
for the lend-lease legislation in Congress. He would later send Roosevelt advance
copies of the edition in which he declared war on the Fascists. Roosevelt responded with his support and sent Ingersoll a congratulatory telegram on *PM*'s
first anniversary.

It was little wonder that FDR supported *PM* and Ingersoll. It was the only
major metropolitan paper that stood behind his efforts to arouse the American
people to take seriously the Nazi threat. And Roosevelt must have appreciated
Ingersoll's unqualified support during that curious period in American intellectual
history when the American Right and the Communist Left maintained their
uneasy alliance, as a result of the Hitler-Stalin Pact.

But before Ingersoll could enlist *PM* in the war effort, he had to put his
own troops in order. There was still too much internal bickering and tension,
too many square pegs in round holes. On December 15 he wrote a "taking stock"
memorandum to the staff in which he said that after returning to the office he
had read through the back issues and come to an "overwhelming conclusion:
The people getting out this paper don't know what they're doing."

God knows why the public has had what patience it's had with us. One moment
we're grim and factual; another we're silly and kittenish. One moment we put truth and
facts above everything else. Another moment we apparently don't care where the facts
fall as long as we put over a socio-political point of view. One minute we are very self-
consciously limiting ourselves to facts; next moment we mix facts and opinions hopelessly
in the same piece. Our writers don't know whether they are writing editorials, features,
or inventing new language forms. . . . Confusion about objectives, mistrust and suspicion
within the staff, piled on top of a certain natural amount of incompetence incidental to
starting anything new and the personality that emerges from a month's copies of *PM* is

so bewildering that most people have given up the effort to understand. Why should they have tried to understand us? We're not married to them. We're courting them.

To achieve a consistent personality and bring some necessary economies to the operation, Ingersoll would, he realized, have to make some staff changes, and he found firing difficult, even when a staffer was incompetent. But it had to be done, and it involved him almost immediately in another war—this one with the New York Newspaper Guild, which was dominated by Communists and fellow travelers. *PM* had signed its contract on August 9, and it was considered a good one by the guild. But the guild was concerned with more than just fair treatment for its employees: It was also intent on promoting the party line, stifling Red-baiting, and getting as many party members and fellow travelers as possible hired.

One of the editors Ingersoll decided to fire in his reorganization was labor editor Leo Huberman. The guild immediately stepped in and protested the dismissal, and the result was a running battle that went on for months and became one of the most celebrated personnel cases in the history of New York journalism. And with good reason: The Huberman case went right to the core of the problem that plagued *PM* its entire life and made it virtually impossible to achieve the kind of successful start Ingersoll had hoped for.

In 1940 the American Communist party was in an impossible situation. In the 1930s, when almost all liberals in the country shared the same general goals as the Communists, it had had no trouble recruiting members, as well as legions of sympathizers and fellow travelers. But when Russia signed its pact with Germany, and when Hitler began the open bombing of London, American liberals, progressives, fellow travelers, and many party members deserted, leaving only those who were willing to adhere strictly to the party line set in Moscow. They were immediately isolated and came into open conflict not only with the Right but with the Left and the rank and file of the labor movement, which, of course, they tried to infiltrate and dominate.

In practical terms, the conflict soon focused on the question of strikes, especially in plants that were essential to the war effort. While the Communists could not openly support Hitler, they could support strikes in munitions plants and otherwise side with the isolationists, who were also intent on keeping America out of the war. This was a clever maneuver. Many of the strikes were not justified, and in some cases, where the unions were dominated or influenced by Communist party members, they were initiated primarily to hamper the war effort.

This situation put Ingersoll and *PM* in an awkward position and had a direct bearing on the celebrated Huberman case. One of *PM*'s claims to distinction was that it was the first newspaper to devote a full department and staff to labor news. Huberman, the editor, though not a party member, was obviously a fellow traveler. He had four assistants, three of whom were sympathetic to the Communist position. The fourth, and number-two man in the department, was James

Wechsler, who had once been a member of the Young Communist League but had since broken with the party to become a dedicated anti-Communist.

Wechsler soon found himself isolated in the labor department, and his break with Huberman came in the rather strange case of John L. Lewis's endorsement of a presidential candidate in the 1940 election. Lewis, who was essentially an isolationist and hated Roosevelt, had indicated he might be neutral during the election—thus upholding Huberman's and the Communists' position that both Roosevelt and Willkie were lackeys of the munitions makers and industrialists who wanted war. Ken Crawford wrote a column from Washington implying that Lewis would endorse Willkie. In an adjoining column Huberman wrote: "I do not believe John L. Lewis will endorse Wendell Willkie on Friday."

Two days later Wechsler learned from Jim Carey, secretary of the Congress of Industrial Organizations, that Lewis would endorse Willkie, and when his story appeared in the paper, Huberman preceded it with a piece of his own. Wechsler, he said, was misinformed. When Lewis finally did endorse Willkie, Huberman wrote: "John L. Lewis was wrong," and Wechsler says he had always thought Huberman believed it was he rather than Lewis who betrayed him.

Huberman continued his pro-Communist bias in reporting the labor news until finally, on December 2, 1940, Ingersoll fired him—"for the frankly stated reason," he has said, "that I considered his emotional involvement with a single faction of the labor movement so intense that he could not write or edit objectively." Ingersoll maintains that Huberman agreed with this, but within two hours of his firing, the guild disputed the action and launched defense proceedings that dragged on well into 1941.

Huberman's main defense was a memo Ingersoll had written to his stockholders in August saying that *PM*'s labor department had received many compliments and was "probably the only department which gives clear evidence of knowing what it's about." But Ingersoll now maintained not only that Huberman failed to live up to *PM*'s standards of writing, editing, and management, but that his political beliefs made it impossible for him to follow the policies that Ingersoll felt he had a right to impose: "If I do not follow my judgment but print instead what someone else likes (and I don't) I am a fraud as an editor." In recent months, he said, he and Huberman had come to disagree on basic editorial policy: "We were in complete harmony on *PM*'s policy of aggressive anti-Fascism, but I had come to feel that this policy was best advanced by aggressive support for England in its war with the Fascist countries, concurrently with aggressive improvement of Labor's position in the U.S.—not merely defense of the status quo in Labor, but a continuance of the improvement of Labor's position in this country."

Ingersoll insists that he liked Huberman, and the notes from guild meetings show that he was unusually considerate of Huberman's welfare and concerned that dismissal not hurt his career. But he believed the issue was simple: "the right of the paper arbitrarily to judge the competency of a senior departmental editor and writer by the editor's own standards."

The guild replied that it could not "admit the unquestioned right of a publisher to fire employees as he pleases." And as the case dragged on, it created dissension among the staff which was not relieved when Ingersoll appointed Wechsler head of the labor department. By now Wechsler was one of the leaders in the movement to remove the Communists from power in the guild, and he did not think Ingersoll was really serious in his anticommunism. He thought that Ingersoll was trying to revive the Popular Front long after it was dead, and that despite his advocacy of total war against the Fascists, Ingersoll was too sympathetic to Communist-dominated strikes. When a strike occurred, Ingersoll generally made a great show of assigning a *PM* task force to study the merits of the union's demands, and if they were found valid, *PM* would go all out in support, usually in long, persuasive editorials written by Ingersoll himself. Wechsler and the anti-Communists, however, thought it was naive to think that a Communist-controlled union would have any motive other than a desire to support Moscow's political objectives, which at the time were to restrain America's war efforts. They thought Ingersoll's support of the strikes was inspired solely by his desire to placate the fellow travelers on the staff and in the guild and to avoid any sign of Red-baiting on *PM*.

Ingersoll, on the other hand, said Wechsler had it all wrong, which he maintained was characteristic of the dedicated anti-Communists. And in this instance it is hard not to side with Ingersoll. It is unlikely that Wechsler would have been put in charge of the labor department had Ingersoll been pro-Communist. Ingersoll's antifascism was even more intense than Wechsler's anticommunism, and it is hard to imagine Ingersoll, during this period, willingly doing anything to aid the Fascist cause. Whenever there was a strike in a defense plant, Ingersoll seemed quite clearly to be in a dilemma, torn between supporting the strikers when they had legitimate demands and opposing the strike if it appeared to be hurting the war effort. Wechsler builds his case mostly on the strike of the New York Transit Workers Union, maintaining that Ingersoll's show of neutrality and his dedicating *PM* to determining the merits of the strike were phony. In his opinion, the strike had obviously been ordered in Moscow to hamper America's war effort.

With *PM* beset by constant bickering, it was inevitable that the conflict would become public. Ingersoll and his paper were attacked almost simultaneously by the Establishment press (for being pro-Communist) and by the Communist press (for being anti-Communist). The *Saturday Evening Post* published an article by Benjamin Stalberg titled "Muddled Millions," which included Jock Whitney and Marshall Field among what Stolberg called "Capitalist Angels of Left-Wing Propaganda." The writer stressed that neither Field nor Whitney nor any of the other capitalists who had financed *PM* could "possibly be called a Communist or fellow traveler," but Ingersoll was clearly one. He charged that in 1937, while Ingersoll was the publisher, *Time* magazine followed the party line. Stolberg went on to two dozen or so *PM* staffers who, he said, were Communists or fellow travelers. The article maintained that only after Field took over the paper did Ingersoll fire the majority of his staff and print an editorial unequivocally announcing his anticommunism.

At about the same time the *Daily Worker* and the *New Masses* fired their shots, using the Huberman case, Ingersoll's hiring and firing practices in general, and his alleged Red-baiting and warmongering to accuse him of being, as Ingersoll put it, "a Fascist son of a bitch." Ingersoll responded in his usual fashion—head-on. In a long memorandum to his staff he said it was not coincidental that the Communists began attacking him from the moment he declared *PM*'s open support of Roosevelt and his aggressive pro-British, anti-Fascist foreign policy; the intensity and emotion in the Communist attacks resulted from their waking up to the fact that, despite his liberal persuasions, he was not a Communist and never had been. And in editorials in *PM* he said that he had at one time endorsed the "United Front against Fascism," but it was the Communists, not the liberals like himself, who had deserted the front—after the Russian pact with the Nazis. Communists were "self-appointed Messiahs with a very hard and doctrinaire religion to which they seek to convert." But he also said, "Most of the things the Communists fight for in this country I believe in: civil liberties, collective bargaining, housing reform, socialized medicine." And that, of course, was the problem. How do you fight for things you believe in without being labeled a Communist, when the Communists are fighting for the very same things?

"I had an early ambition," he said, "that *PM* as an independent liberal, anti-Fascist paper, might be the first journal with a sane and unhysterical approach to the problem of 'the Communist in national affairs.' I wanted *PM*'s Labor Page to find out about allegations of Communist influence in trade unionism. . . . I wanted *PM*'s National News section to prove or disprove the reckless and malicious everyday charges of Communism in the Government. . . . Then when *PM* came out, the paper itself caught it in the neck, with every red-baiter and reactionary seeing his chance to attack a new pro-Labor journal before it could establish itself."

But, as a good journalist who knew he had a hot issue going, Ingersoll pledged *PM* to continue the fight against Fascism and for reform in America, regardless of what the Communists did. He also said that *PM* would not hesitate to expose someone as a Communist if he thought it was relevant to do so, no matter how loud and long the Communists cried "civil liberties" and "Red-baiting."

The case of Leo Huberman was seen by the guild and the pro-Communists as a perfect example of Red-baiting, but Ingersoll persisted. Huberman was finally reinstated and permitted to resign with a cash settlement. At the same time Ingersoll fired almost a dozen writers for reasons of economy or for incompetence, and the guild fought every dismissal. They said he had a right to move staffers from departments in which their work was unsatisfactory, but he could not fire them. Ingersoll responded by sending the writer Julian Fromer and several others home, saying he would mail them their checks until their contracts ran out but he did not want them to come to the office. This prompted the guild to denounce Ingersoll for a new, evil antilabor practice they called "Fromerization," which came to be defined around New York bars as "hanging by paycheck until dead."

Meanwhile, Field's friend Charles Cushing, who was gradually gaining power at the paper, commissioned a management-study group to survey the efficiency of *PM*. Although Ingersoll did not endorse the idea, he sent a memo to the staff saying it would do no harm. In March of 1941 the group issued a report in which it described chaotic conditions in the editorial department, and recommended cutting the weekly editorial payroll by thirty-five hundred dollars and appointing a managing editor, with whom Ingersoll would have to deal, to run the paper. "In few cases," said the report, "is the old adage of a corporation being the elongated shadow of one man more applicable than in the case of *PM*. There is just no question that Mr. Ingersoll dominates, controls and influences every employee in the Editorial Department. Writers do not think 'how should I write this article' but 'how would Mr. Ingersoll write this article?' The most commonly mentioned objective on the part of all writers was to interpret the viewpoint of Mr. Ingersoll and the second most common was the admission that they did not know what it is."

Virginia Schoales, Ingersoll's assistant, says, however, that the man who did the interviewing for the report did not document his conclusions. "He was fooled and tricked," said Miss Schoales, "and incredibly stupid about judging people. He indiscriminately chose people to give him advice."

Although the interviewer may have been stupid, most people who have commented on *PM*'s first two years agree that, for better or worse, the paper was the shadow of one man. As Robert Lasch wrote in his "*PM* Post Mortem" published in the *Atlantic Monthly* in 1948: "During the crucial two years of its life, *PM* was Ingersoll and Ingersoll was *PM*. In its flight from the evil influence of advertisers, in its admirable struggle to escape one-man domination by a publisher, *PM* delivered itself to the one-man domination of Ingersoll. Had Ingersoll been the kind of editor who could submerge his personality in a corporate identity, this might have worked. But *PM* never had a chance to be his lengthened shadow. It became instead the stage on which he continued an intellectual strip tease."

Many veterans of *PM* have agreed. "The Center of *PM*," said Louis Kronenberger, "was certainly Ingersoll. But he was a movable center, omnipresent in one sense, frequently absent in another, the two being interrelated." And, in the opinion of many, this resulted in more problems than achievements. William McClearey said that all of *PM*'s troubles boiled down to one word: "Ingersoll." The other problems could have been solved, he thought, but Ingersoll's emotional, unpredictable personality created a situation in which it was impossible to work.

Ingersoll was aware of his critics, both on and off the paper, but he mostly ignored them, attributing the sniping to the usual grumbling you get when one man steps out in front and tries to overcome tradition and break new ground. And in his effort to bring *PM* to life, he went looking for journalists to do special features for the paper—journalists who cost more money but who were not controlled by the guild, and with whom, incidentally, he did not mind sharing bylines. Ingersoll, in fact, was always quick to give anyone on his staff full credit for a good story or feature. Some of the people he hired were well-known at the time, others were talented young men who were just getting started. James Thurber wrote a twice-weekly column, "If You Ask Me," from September of 1940 to July of 1941; Ben Hecht also wrote the column "1001 Afternoons in New York." Hecht had spent an evening drinking with Sherwood Anderson who was about to depart for South America, and in his account of that meeting he wrote that Anderson was "a man leaving not a country but life," and that he was like "a wearied animal going off to an unfamiliar place to die." The morning this column appeared, it was preceded by a box announcing that Anderson had died on shipboard bound for Brazil. Ernest Hemingway was hired to do two reports on the war in the Far East, and spent four months in Asia for the second report. Theodor Geisell, who later created the Dr. Seuss children's books, did three cartoons a week for *PM* until he joined the army in 1942. Dr. Benjamin Spock was hired to do a series on baby and child care, which followed a baby named Lois from birth through infancy. The series began Dr. Spock's career as the man who raised America's postwar generation with his book *Baby and Child Care*.

These features, however, sometimes went almost unnoticed in the turmoil that seemed always to rage around *PM*. By late 1940 the charges of radicalism had become so hostile that Ingersoll had to take an open position against the Communists. But even this did not reduce the attacks from the Catholic church, Wall Street, the Establishment, the Communists, the anti-Communists, the Fascists, and the Bund. He was threatened with personal violence, and during one strike a group of militant Communists appeared at Madison Square Garden chanting "Ingersoll is better dead." A *PM* photographer was beaten up by the Bund. The Communist cell in *PM* was thought to have conspired to hand the paper over to the Kremlin. The U.S. Army included *PM* on its list of dangerous publications, despite, or perhaps because of, its all-out support of war against Hitler.

Its followers were often ridiculed by friends for reading the "hysterical," "hyperthyroid," "pinko" "Uptown *Daily Worker*." And Ingersoll concedes that while his primary goal had always been to reform the newspaper business, *PM*, from its first day, had been a crusader "for liberal causes." But the paper, as Kronenberger said, "had become not just an advocate of causes, but something of a cause itself." During most of 1941 it continued to be one of the main battlegrounds in the country for pro-Communists and anti-Communists. And for those caught in the middle and not inclined to take sides, as Hodding Carter was, the Communists especially could be an insufferable bore: "Their dull, positive oratory . . . ordered a man to declare himself either on the side of the

Fascists, which included us in the South, or of the angels whose wings often glowed an unheavenly pink." However, as Carter concluded in his book *Where Main Street Meets the River*, which provides one of the best assessments of the early *PM*, it was not the Communists, mismanagement, or interoffice jealousies that did *PM* in so much as the "dreary, humorless, consecrated insistence upon conformity to a fixed and condescending liberalism." And he quoted comedian Henry Morgan's remark that a *PM* story always began: "My name is Minnie Moscowitz and I live on Flatbush Avenue, Brooklyn, and I think it's a shame . . ."

Meanwhile, *PM* was also doing its share of what has come to be known as "investigative reporting," usually supporting its articles with large, dramatic photographs. It exposed the German "Tourist Office" as the front for a Nazi spy ring; it exposed the sale of rotten chickens in the New York poultry market; it correctly predicted a Nazi plot to blow up the Hercules Power company plant in New Jersey; it proved that buying houses on the installment plan cheated the poor; it exposed price-fixing laws; it dramatized New York's worn-out school buses; it exposed a Negro "slave market" in which domestics were hired on the streets at substandard wages; it carried a full report on government hearings about what was wrong with the insurance business; it began stories that led to the investigation of Jersey City's mayor Frank Hague. It exposed Standard Oil's sale of oil to the Nazis and revealed that John L. Lewis hired gunmen to coerce workers who backed FDR and the New Deal.

Of course, most of its big stories brought out the wounded, who cried "*PM* is Red." There were stories and Ingersoll editorials denouncing Charles Lindbergh as pro-Fascist and anti-Semitic and calling on him to resign his commission in the air corps reserve; the story exposing Henry Ford's anti-Semitism and a series of articles on comparative shopping and high-priced merchandise—together with the paper's general opposition to advertising, which implied it was corrupting—aroused the enmity of the business community. The right-wing press, which did not really need a reason, was aroused to special fury by a series that exposed what *PM* called "the Fascist lines of Hearst and the *Daily News*." But what seemed to disturb most people was *PM*'s continuing call to arms, its constant hammering away at the fact that Hitler was the enemy and that America must sooner or later go to war to stop him. People agreed, but it made them uncomfortable. They really were not ready to go to war.

But Ingersoll was. When the Allies began suffering serious reverses in the Balkans, the Mediterranean, and North Africa, Ingersoll decided the time had come for *PM* to take its stand. On April 21, 1941, he wrote an editorial in support of arming American convoys to Great Britain, and he planned another series of major features declaring *PM*'s open support of the Allies in their war with the Fascists. "I recognized," he said, "that others might not feel the way I do—that . . . we have no choice but to stand against the armed expansion of Fascism, even if that stand leads to our starting to fight Hitler before he puts us in a spot in which we have to fight."

So on April 23 he called an unusual meeting in which, as Wechsler later put it, "Ingersoll informed the staff that *PM* was about to go to war." And, as predicted, there was resistance. One staffer rose to say he was a religious man and could only join in this effort if he was convinced that the war against Hitler was a just war—and he would have to consult with his spiritual advisers before he made up his mind. Ingersoll understood and accepted this position and, as he put it, "made it clear that those who could not in good conscience go along or were confused about whether they should or should not—would, for the duration of this crisis, be given what I called 'noncombatant work'—assignments unrelated to the war."

PM's ammunition, of course, was words and photographs, and their first shots were fired two days later in fifteen pages of anti-Fascist features announced by a front-page headline in huge block letters: "FASCISTS ARE WINNING: WHAT ARE WE GOING TO DO ABOUT IT?" In the lead editorial Ingersoll announced, "The total war, which the Fascists promised the world, has begun." And *PM* was ready. "If only war will destroy the threat of the expansive force of Fascism, then war it will be. *PM* believes there are things worth fighting for. *PM* believes America is worth fighting for [and] that our future as free citizens ruled by consent of the governed, depends on our decisive, unequivocal action against all forms of Fascism. . . . Adolf Hitler has made academic the question of whether this policy 'leads to war' or stops at some mysterious boundary far beyond making guns to kill Fascists, but just short of shooting them. . . . People of America, to be confused now is to be lost. . . . This is the fateful Spring of 1941. Our time has come."

The files in the Roosevelt Library at Hyde Park reveal the close relationship between Roosevelt and Ingersoll during this period and throughout the war. A month after Ingersoll had declared war, President Roosevelt proclaimed a state of national emergency and announced that American ships and planes would shoot to defend the freedom of the seas. *PM* devoted fifteen pages to the president's speech, and Ingersoll responded with an editorial: "It's done," he wrote. "We're in it."

While Ingersoll was writing his pro-war editorials in the spring of 1941, Bobbs-Merrill was setting them in print for another Ingersoll book—this one entitled *America Is Worth Fighting For*. It was published simultaneously with General Hugh S. Johnson's *Hell-Bent for War*, and for most reviewers, the two books, taken together, summed up the views of the interventionists and the isolationists. As the *Indianapolis News* put it: "Both men write vigorously, each has an array of data that is impressive. Each is certain that he has the only answer. Neither is a sensationalist. Their arguments are sincere for their thoughts are embedded in strong convictions." And it concluded: "Both books are arresting and challenging, for the editor of *PM* is as vivid and violent as the syndicated columnist."

Ingersoll preceded his arguments with a rather dramatic statement: "The spring of 1941 is a time that history has made famous before it has happened"— which suggests that either there would be a dramatic turning point, such as the

Not only did Ingersoll's trips to London and Moscow establish his credentials as a war correspondent, but his reports in PM (ABOVE) helped increase circulation by as much as 50,000 copies. (RIGHT) When President Roosevelt gave a speech in May of 1941 proclaiming a state of national emergency, Ingersoll decided the time had come to declare war, eight months before Pearl Harbor.

United States' entry into the war, or, perhaps, that his own declaration of war was dramatic enough to assure the spring of 1941's place in history. Most reviewers presented their arguments in a straightforward manner, suggesting that the debate was a standoff or, at least, that their paper did not want to get involved. But a few could not resist taking a shot or two at the controversial Ingersoll: "*America Is Worth Fighting For* is a striking example of how to ruin a good cause," said Nicholas Roosevelt in the New York *Herald-Tribune*; and Harry Hansen in the New York *World-Telegram* said he was pleased to note that Ingersoll said the world press had never brought its followers the news more ably. "This is quite a concession," said Hansen, "from the man who, about a year ago, was telling us how sick the newspapers were and how he had found an elixir."

By the summer of 1941 the sides were clearly drawn: Great Britain and Ralph Ingersoll, with open support from President Roosevelt, were locked in a fight-to-the-finish war with Adolf Hitler. Then suddenly Hitler broke his pact with Stalin and invaded Russia. This was tremendous news for Ingersoll. Not only did he now have the Red Army on his side, but the United Front could be revived. The Communists could openly support intervention. Until the end of the year *PM*'s enemies were narrowed to the pro-Fascists and the anti-Communists; then after Pearl Harbor, the pro-Fascists would go underground.

The German invasion came on Saturday night–Sunday morning, June 21 and 22. Ingersoll was in Lakeville when managing editor Lewis reached him. They decided to put out an extra for Sunday and managed to recruit twenty to thirty staffers, who assembled in Brooklyn between eleven P.M. and two A.M. to prepare a thirty-two-page special edition. They had practically no information on Russia and little help from the wire services who could not make contact with their reporters in Moscow. But *PM*'s editors managed to fill the thirty-two pages, and Ingersoll's lead editorial set the tone: "This is the time," he wrote, "to keep as cool as the news and the temperature permits, to watch what happens and to remember that your President foresaw it many months ago when he warned you that this was a *total* war. The sudden scrapping of the world's most momentous pact is one of the things total war means. What it might mean to the U.S.A. before it is over could be just as dramatic—if we ever let anything happen to Great Britain or we take our eye—for one single moment—off our enemy, Hitler. It will not end until he is destroyed."

At the end of the week reports from the front indicated the Germans had encircled hundreds of thousands of Red Army troops between Minsk and the border. But the America wire services were still getting precious little news from their own reporters in Russia. "Moscow is calm" was about all the American press could report for certain. Ingersoll knew that sheer numbers would not worry Germany's military leaders. Furthermore, the Red Army had been humiliated in Finland, so, in Ingersoll's view, the fate of the war seemed to depend on two things: (1) the morale of the Russian people and their ability to withstand the shock that had destroyed the French, and (2) the ability of Russia's industry to keep the Red Army supplied with weapons, ammunition, and food. And

Ingersoll decided there was only one way to be certain of what was happening. He would have to go to Moscow—"to see for myself," he said.

On the Friday after the German invasion, Ingersoll went to Washington to talk with the Russian ambassador, Constantin Oumansky, and to get permission to travel to Moscow to report on the war for *PM*—which, Ingersoll reminded the ambassador, did not share the prejudice against Russia held by most U.S. papers.

Oumansky, a small, lively, intense man, had once been a newspaper correspondent. Ingersoll had met him earlier while making the rounds of the embassies in Washington to establish diplomatic contacts for *PM*. Oumansky had been very friendly then. But now, Ingersoll learned, the official Russian position was that Ingersoll and *PM* were no friends of the Communists. His violent attack on Stalin's accommodation with the world's number-one enemy, Adolf Hitler, had taken its toll. Wall Street, the Catholic church, and the professional anti-Communists may have thought that Ingersoll and *PM* were pro-Communist, but the Communist leadership most certainly did not. After Ingersoll had made his case for burying the hatchet and uniting to rid the world of Hitler, Oumansky leaned over his desk and, waving his right hand, said, "Mr. Ingersoll, if I were to make a list of all the references to the Soviet Union in *PM* which have outraged me—it would take *three* days to read it."

Ingersoll has a hard time controlling his thoughts when he is angry, and Oumansky was making him hot under the collar. He was about to launch into one of his Hitler-is-the-enemy-of-civilization lectures when the ambassador said, "Stop. I would like to speak before you. I would like to make a suggestion . . . that we let bygones be bygones. I agree that you hate Hitler. I will go further and say that I admire your paper for its courage in sticking to its principles in the face of all attacks. . . . You and I will not talk again of the past. Now what would you like me to do?"

"It was," Ingersoll recalled, "the most extraordinary change of a person in a short conversation I can ever remember." And he answered Oumansky immediately: "I want to go to Moscow and there I want two privileges—to be sent to the front and to have a visit with Mr. Stalin."

Oumansky slapped his hand on his desk. "It is done. You must go very quickly. There is not a minute to lose. How soon can you get to Chungking?" There would be a plane to meet Ingersoll, the ambassador said.

It took him about a month to get organized, and on July 17 he left San Francisco to circumnavigate the globe by air, boat, and train. It took him ninety-eight days, "beating Nellie Bly by almost four weeks," Wolcott Gibbs wrote later, "and Magellan by a good two and a half years." Because he was afraid customs officials and censors might confiscate it, he did not keep a diary, but made notes on scraps of paper and the backs of envelopes and depended on the tape recorder in his brain to recall what he had seen and heard—which, as always, it did.

There was little doubt that what America wanted most in the summer of

1941 was news about its new allies, Joseph Stalin and the Soviet Union. For years Russia had been virtually a closed society, and after Stalin allied his country with Hitler, communications between Russia and America were almost non-existent. Now, suddenly, the country many Americans had feared even more than Germany was our friend, and people were forced to agree with Senator Claude Pepper that "when you're in a fight, you're not squeamish about who pitches in to help you win."

Ingersoll was not squeamish. He welcomed Russia's entry into the war and immediately became a booster for the Red Army and for the Russians, a people of grit and determination. His trip to Moscow was, indeed, dramatic, and he made it even more so by stressing that he was in a race with the Germans. By the time he arrived, the Germans were less than 150 miles away and Luftwaffe planes were over the city.

In addition to wanting to interview Stalin and report to his readers on Russia, Ingersoll had a mission: to persuade Stalin to allow more coverage of the Soviet Union in order to promote greater understanding between that country and the United States. His interview with Stalin was something of an anticlimax because he was not allowed to quote the Soviet leader. But his impressions of the man were vivid, and he came away convinced of Stalin's strength and his dedication to the defeat of Hitler. He felt, as President Roosevelt did, that Stalin could be trusted. He also believed that the Russian people and their leaders were dedicated to the defeat of Hitler. The purges of the 1930s had been brutal, but one result was to eliminate the Pétains and the Lavals, who had contributed to the collapse of France. The Russians had put in power mostly young people who knew no system other than communism and who were convinced it was the wave of the future. Ingersoll joked that the hardest thing to find in Russia was a Communist, because in a country of 160 million people, only 2 million were party members. But for the duration, at least, he could detect no opposition to the government.

In Russia Ingersoll himself was news: He made a broadcast to the Russian people and wrote at least two articles for the *Moscow News* about his impressions (all favorable, naturally) of the Russians at war. His trip was also making news at home. Stories of Ingersoll's exploits and brashness always made good copy, and the columnists were following the trip closely. Walter Winchell told how Ingersoll had complained to Steve Early, the White House press secretary, that the Russians were holding up his passport. Early's reply: "What! And they want us to give them a hundred million dollars worth of machinery." Leonard Lyons reported that when Ingersoll told Stalin that the U.S. press wanted permission to visit the front, and that the Americans were just as brave as Russian reporters, Stalin said, "Don't let them tell you about their being at the front. No Russian correspondent is within 100 miles of the front." And Mollie Panter-Downes, in the *New Yorker*, reported the story of a brush the British ambassador to Moscow Sir Stafford Cripps had with Ingersoll. Ingersoll was trying to persuade Cripps to use his influence to help Ingersoll obtain an interview with Stalin (at a time when it appeared the Russian bureaucracy would prevent Ingersoll's promised audience with the Soviet leader). He argued with Cripps that he was not just an ordinary reporter, the kind who was always hanging around the Foreign Office seeking an interview with Stalin. "After all, who are they?" Ingersoll asked. "Never heard of any of them before in my life."

"For that matter," Cripps replied in his best diplomatic monotone, "I never heard of you before in my life."

The *New Yorker*, in fact, never seemed to tire of Ingersoll stories, and his straightforward, man-in-the-street reporting was a natural target for the magazine's arched-eyebrow commentary. One "Talk of the Town" reporter wrote that while he was waiting to see the new Russian consulate at 7 East Sixty-first Street, he thumbed through the *Moscow News* and noted an article, "Impressions of Moscow," with a "familiar by-line, that of Ralph Ingersoll." He quoted Ingersoll's description of the Russian people as being "fresh and young and strong" and "obviously very well organized," then commented that when he looked up from the tabloid, he was distracted by a Russian secretary in a sweater "who passed through the hall looking awfully fresh and young and strong and obviously well organized."

Ingersoll returned to New York on October 17 and immediately went to Washington to report to Roosevelt on his trip and to find out, as he put it, "what had been going on in the Pacific since I had traveled through the war areas there." He had been told repeatedly in the Pacific that the Japanese attack would come by December 15. He had visited Pearl Harbor and talked with General Walter Short. "The USSR is our only natural ally against Japan," said Short, who had fought against the Communists in 1921, "and we have been foolish to take chances with Soviet friendship. We were tied up with a bunch of crooks in Vladivostok in 1921. The White generals we were supporting were all gangsters. We are going to have to fight Japan and we need Russia's help."

Pearl Harbor "looks very vulnerable to me," Ingersoll commented in his notes; but he was assured by everyone he talked to that the Japanese bases were too far away to pose a threat to U.S. naval bases. Now, in Washington, he was assured that the United States was ready, and that "there would be no Oriental Munich."

Ingersoll returned to New York and began to write an account of his trip. The result was a series of widely quoted articles for *PM*, which began on October 27 and continued every day for over a month. He also rushed off to Harper Brothers the manuscript for a book, dedicated to Marshall and Ruth Field, that would be published the following spring under the title *Action on All Fronts*. It was another journalistic coup, and by that time Ralph Ingersoll had become perhaps the most celebrated—and satirized—reporter in America.

Ingersoll's style of reporting was very simple: He recorded faithfully, and in as much detail as space would permit, everything he had seen and heard. And he was capable of *total* reporting. "Ralph could walk into a room," said one person who worked with him closely for years, "and later tell you in minute detail everything that was in the room, every piece of furniture, describe everyone and recount, almost word-for-word, everything that was said." He also had the editor's instinct for what makes a good story and what people want to know about a new place or situation. He was, himself, intensely curious and assumed that if he wanted to know more about something or somebody his readers would too. And he was invariably right, although he generally piled on more detail than some of his more sensitive readers felt necessary. And too often he tended to give significance to or dramatize the obvious.

The result was a sort of breathless prose that seemed to come out of a tape recorder and camera all at once, as if you, the reader, were with him moment by moment, hour by hour, day by day. But it was also, as Wolcott Gibbs pointed out, dangerously close to a parody of itself, "combining the more diabolic features of Evelyn Waugh and Mrs. Humphry Ward." As a result, it was easy and fun to spoof, and near the end of the Around-the-World reports appearing in *PM* William Attwood did a beautiful satire in the *New Yorker* titled "Alf Stringersoll Reports in Brooklyn." It recounts a journey taken by Stringersoll, the editor of *AM*, into the borough of Brooklyn, where he reported on everything he saw, felt, and heard in his seventy-two hours there. Clearly Ralph Ingersoll had arrived. When the *New Yorker* devotes its precious space to satirizing you, you have become a celebrity. In fact, for some time staffers had been trying to persuade Ross to do a profile of Ingersoll, but he had always replied, "the time to do a story on a billy goat is not when he is in the middle of leaping from one mountain peak to another, but when he has landed safely on the other side." *PM* and its controversial founder had now landed, and at the end of 1941, despite the magazine's general distaste for writing anything about alumni, the *New Yorker* was ready for a profile of Ingersoll.

Ingersoll had returned from his trips with his mind made up about the international situation. To wit: The Japanese were not a serious threat, despite their successes in the Far East; yet as early as November 11, he warned his readers that America was not preparing for war, and asked, "How would you like to have Japan take a crack at us in the Pacific?"

Less than a month later the Japanese took the crack, and Ingersoll was not surprised—except at the daring they showed in launching an attack from over a thousand miles away. He had long been among those in America who felt it was just a matter of time before Japan struck somewhere, and he had been arguing that if the British, Chinese, Russians, and Americans had attacked Japan simultaneously in the fall of 1941, Japan would have been defeated in six months. He maintained that every military expert he talked to in China and Russia had agreed.

After Pearl Harbor Ingersoll was, for a few weeks, somewhat out of focus, as the Communists had been when they had suddenly to reverse their foreign policy position after the Nazi attack on the Soviet Union. Wechsler recalls that in the days after Pearl Harbor "Ingersoll walked about the city room in a kind of vacant trance" and finally "confessed at a staff meeting that he was no longer certain of the paper's excuse for existence. Its mission was accomplished. The nation was at war."

Ingersoll concedes that he had become caught up in the war for most of 1941 and had turned the paper into a crusading daily pamphlet. He was deflated after Pearl Harbor, but he had no regrets. And he did not have to rethink his position very long before he decided what *PM*'s new mission would be. A week after Pearl Harbor he assembled his troops and put this proposition to them: "What can each of you do in your work on *PM* to help this country win the war? How can we use the paper, not simply to tell the news—but to arouse America from its everyday life, to channel all America's energies into winning a quick victory?"

The new crusade: to flush out right-wing subversion, profascism, and to prod American businessmen into abandoning a business-as-usual approach to the war. America was in perhaps the greatest crisis of its history.

And so was *PM*. A second financial crisis was threatening the paper's ability to help FDR win the war. Ingersoll's reports from England, Russia, and the other fronts, and the war news in general, had helped *PM* pull its circulation up from a historic low of 31,000 in August of 1940, to over 90,000 by the end of 1941. But that was still 150,000 short of the figure they now estimated was necessary to keep the publication operating in the black. Field still insisted he was not supporting a charity; but with wartime prices driving up the cost of printing, and with the Newspaper Guild making it difficult to economize by cutting the staff, *PM* was losing $25,000 a day. Even Field found that expensive, but he was still reluctant to give up the dream of an independent newspaper. Ingersoll conferred with his backer and persuaded Field to give him 60 days from January 1—one last chance to raise circulation while, at the same time, cutting costs. Field was skeptical but agreed.

Ingersoll was, as usual, confident. The nation was at war, and newspapers generally do well in a war. The first move in his new crusade was to go after American companies that were not showing the proper enthusiasm for the war. In this fight Ingersoll had an untiring lieutenant in a young reporter who had been on the staff about a year. His name was I. F. Stone and, like Wechsler, he had worked on the *Nation*. But unlike Wechsler, who had been transferred to the Washington bureau, he agreed that Hitler was the real enemy, and that if a labor union or anyone else took a position similar to that of the Communists, it did not automatically make the holder of that position either a fellow traveler or a dupe. As early as November 1941 Stone broke a big story about the amount of U.S. oil flowing into Franco's Spain and on to Hitler, which resulted in the halting of U.S. oil shipments to Franco. After Pearl Harbor Stone launched a series of reports on the arms programs, which cited numerous incidents of a business-as-usual approach to arms production and led to the creation of the War Production Board.

Then on February 10, 1942, came one of *PM*'s most memorable stories.

For some time the paper had a young reporter named Edmund Scott working on the French liner *Normandie*, which was tied up at a pier in the North River. His assignment was to look for possibilities of sabotage, and he found so much flammable material placed at various points around the ship that even an incompetent arsonist would have had no trouble destroying it. *PM* did not report the story because it would have been a blueprint for sabotage. But when the liner did catch fire on February 9, the paper rushed into print with an eye-catching page-one headline stating that the French liner could easily have been sabotaged, and the accompanying story documented its charges with Scott's findings. The navy launched an investigation, and Scott was called to Washington to testify.

Scott's story alerted the public to the possibilities of sabotage, and *PM* launched a series of articles attempting to uncover subversion and expose pro-Fascist sympathizers wherever they might be found—which seemed to be almost everywhere, including the Catholic church and the right-wing press. By early spring open warfare existed between Ingersoll and the Christian Front, especially Father Coughlin and his followers in the Catholic church. The pope had made his peace with Mussolini, and loyal church members in this country continued to follow the Holy Writ, even after Pearl Harbor.

The sixty-day trial period imposed by Marshall Field came to an end in March 1942, and *PM* appeared, at that time, to have turned the corner. By the following May the paper had added 77,000 in new circulation; its unit cost had been reduced, and its deficit was down thirty-seven percent. For a few months it looked as if Ingersoll's dream might come true. He no longer owned his paper, but it seemed on the way to becoming a success—if Marshall Field's interest and money held out. Furthermore, *PM* was being treated with new respect, and Ingersoll had emerged from the anonymity that marked his years with Henry Luce.

In April his book *Action on All Fronts* was published, and with the country at war and *PM* itself making news almost every day, it was naturally a widely read and much-discussed best-seller. Wolcott Gibbs, who at the time was working on his profile of Ingersoll, wrote a few kind words for the dust jacket: "It is really quite a book. . . . I knew that Ingersoll was a first-rate reporter, but did not know before how much of a writer he was. . . . The description of the bombing of Chungking, for instance, is about as graphic and eloquent as anything I have read about this war."

Although every reviewer agreed with Gibbs that Ingersoll's reporting was "as good as any to come out of the war," many of them also questioned his "masterminding," as the *New Yorker* phrased it. But not President Roosevelt. Ingersoll argued that the real key to the war was American production. If the outpouring from the arsenal of democracy, he said, were to be divided and spread over all the fronts on which we were fighting the Axis, we would have to increase our efforts at least fivefold and perhaps replace with American forces the European armies now in the field. But there was another way, which was "to recognize the strengths and limitations of our position and, taking command, direct the war from its true focal point, Franklin Delano Roosevelt's desk in Washington, D.C."

It is easy to see why the man in the Oval Office kept sending him those "Dear Ralph" letters, one of which was proudly displayed on his office wall. It is also easy to understand why FDR's door was always open to Ingersoll and why the president's men felt Ingersoll was the man of the hour. And, of course, Ingersoll's name popped up in the columns regularly, including Mrs. Roosevelt's "My Day," in which she paid him one of his most memorable tributes: "I wonder if *PM* is becoming to you as interesting a paper as I find it? There is barely a day when some article in it is not worth reading from beginning to end."

It was through Mrs. Roosevelt, in fact, that Ingersoll came to confront one of the most perplexing situations in his career as an editor—and the story provides an amusing and curious sidelight to the war. "One day," as Ingersoll tells it, "I got a message, personally delivered by a mutual friend, that Mrs. Roosevelt wanted to see me to discuss a highly personal problem which was of great concern to her." When he arrived at the White House, the First Lady received him downstairs. "[She] led me immediately to the second floor sitting room where she unburdened herself at once. She had sent for me, she said, because she knew of my loyalty to her husband and she felt that, with my newspaper's resources, I was in an unique position to help her to protect him. And then she outlined, in her precise silvery voice, what was concerning her.

"It was truly appalling: it was no less than a belief that there was a plot afoot to take over the government of the United States by military coup d'état. She named the plotters: four or five generals, two in the Air Force—then still technically a part of the army—backed by civilian millionaires, whose names I knew and associated with Texas.

"The plot itself was to take over by either arresting or assassinating—preferably by arresting to avoid his martyrdom—the President himself and then issuing the necessary orders from the White House itself, in the name of the self-appointed Committee of Crisis. This country would then instantaneously be converted from the Democratic to Fascist form of government in the name of the crisis."

Ingersoll says that he thinks he asked the First Lady who else knew about the plot, but that he does not recall her exact answer: "It seems to me that she said she was hesitant to take her fears through official channels because once she began thinking such thoughts as had been aroused by the 'information' she had received, one commenced doubting even those closest—which was why she had turned to me, trustworthy personally and politically, but an outsider. Once I had the information which she had already given me, she was sure that I could, with my resources as a publisher, do more with it, with better security, than she."

Ingersoll was in a quandary. What should he do? "What I did in the end," he says, "was the most sensible thing I could have done, even if it was the least dramatic. I decided to ask . . . Franklin D. Roosevelt himself what I should do, what *he* would like me to do. His wife had made it clear that *she* had not consulted him, lest it too deeply distract him.

"So I asked for an appointment, and got on the calendar within not too many days, and there I was in the familiar half-round room, sitting at the side of the President's desk and him beaming as usual:

"'I talked with Mrs. Roosevelt last week, Mr. President, and she is very much concerned . . . about your safety . . . about persons who may be conspiring to do you harm—to do the country harm."

The president asked Ingersoll to tell him the whole story. Then he tilted his head back and let forth that "great laugh," as Ingersoll describes it.

"Ralph," he said when he had stopped laughing. "Ralph, you should *always* listen to a woman. You were quite right to listen. But you don't *always* take a woman seriously. My wife's a wonderful woman, but you don't *always* take her seriously."

"And that's all I ever did," Ingersoll concludes, "about Eleanor Roosevelt's fear of a plot to take over the government by capture of her husband . . . except to worry like hell now and then lest I had taken the wrong Roosevelt seriously."

Not since 1937, when he was the apple of Henry Luce's eye and turned down a one-million-dollar stock offer to stay with Time Inc., had Ingersoll ridden so high. *PM* was looking good. Ingersoll's fanatic anti-Hitler crusade had been redeemed by America's entry into the war, and he himself was finally recognized as one of America's foremost journalists.

Ingersoll had obviously arrived—and was ready for the ultimate celebrity accolade, a profile in the *New Yorker*, and the profile, which appeared in the first two weeks of May 1942, was surprisingly gentle. Maybe it was the war or the fact that the *New Yorker* staff naturally sided with *PM* in most of its struggles, but along the way Wolcott Gibbs had become an Ingersoll fan. Gibbs saw Ingersoll in 1942 as a latter-day Saul of Tarsus, "who," he wrote, "somewhere on the wild road to Damascus was accosted by the Spirit and straight away became St. Paul the Apostle." Ralph McAllister Ingersoll, the grandnephew of Ward McAllister, a Yaleman and an ornament of Luce's capitalistic press, had become Ralph Ingersoll, a devoted follower of FDR and editor of Marshall Field's *PM*, "a journal of salvation." The conversion, Gibbs noted with awe, had taken place in the offices of Time Inc., "where such miracles are neither frequent, nor particularly encouraged."

He described the new apostle for truth and justice as looking like any other six-foot-two Yaleman of his vintage, in his button-down shirts, striped ties, and double-breasted suits of the distinguished shapelessness for which Brooks Brothers is noted. "He walks with a sort of brisk shamble and in general he has an air of having been rather loosely and casually assembled. His eyes protrude a little and so does his lower lip in a modified Hapsburg pout. His skin is pale, with a yellowish tinge, in memory of old sunburns. His usual expression is one of intense and distant concentration, as if he were perpetually looking for the right words for a rather difficult idea, and, indeed, such expressions as 'I tried to understand,' 'I tried to get the picture,' and 'I tried to make sense out of him' figure largely in his conversation. His hair is thin and recently he shaved off a mustache which was once notably dashing and profuse." Because of the hours he devotes to his job, Gibbs observed, he "breakfasts late and lunches on two dry martinis, a cup of black coffee, and a chain of cigarets."

Gibbs devoted several columns to explaining the paradox of how such an obvious product of America's corporate establishment could be thought by so many to be a pinko, and went on to record the extent to which he was also *persona non grata* to the Communists; there was, Gibbs concluded, considerable substance and justification to Ingersoll's own vision of himself as a crusading journalist. After quoting Ingersoll as saying that in a world that was cynical and corrupt, *PM* refused to resign itself to corruption and fraud, Gibbs remarked: "This is not a dream confined exclusively to the dreamer. There are a lot of people who think that Ingersoll is hot on the trail of salvation, if not already in charge of it, and others who feel that he is gifted far beyond most editors in the business."

Although Gibbs made some unflattering comments about Ingersoll's egotism, crusading fervor, and lack of humor, there was, running throughout the profile, an underlying tone of restrained applause. It was as if Gibbs were speaking for all the wits and intellectuals who sat on the sidelines with their devastatingly witty remarks and brilliantly analytical pieces while this man, although perhaps somewhat egocentric and naive, had the courage to take on everyone's enemies: the Fascists, the Socialists, the Communists, Big Business, Wall Street, the right-wing press, even the Catholic church. And when *PM*'s second anniversary came around in June, congratulatory letters poured into the office, and the paper printed two pages of extracts from them. And who could blame it? *PM* had quite a few distinguished fans: President and Mrs. Roosevelt; Vice President Henry Wallace; Senators Lister Hill and Harry Truman; cabinet members Harold Ickes, Frank Knox, and Frances Perkins; the outgoing governor of New York Herbert Lehman and his soon-to-be-elected successor Thomas E. Dewey; and an assortment of prominent citizens, including Louis Adamic, Jack Benny, Eddie Cantor, Elmer Davis, Joseph E. Davies, Melvyn Douglas, Albert Einstein, J. Edgar Hoover, Robert Sherwood, Thomas Mann, Al Smith, Wendell Willkie, and Raymond Gram Swing.

But if *PM* and Ingersoll had collected a blue-ribbon fan club, they had their enemies too. And most of them, as he would soon find out, thought Ralph Ingersoll should be in the army fighting the war he had been promoting for so long.

Since his breakup with Laura Hobson, Ingersoll had had very little time to devote to women. But after he returned from his around-the-world trip in the fall of 1941, he met Geraldine Morris, who was married to William Morris, the theatrical agent. Ingersoll says he asked Mrs. Morris to marry him, but she did not want to divorce her husband.

He was still supporting Tommy, from whom he was divorced (and who, in the summer of 1942, was facing a serious operation on her lung), as well as his invalided former governess, Arny. He was forty-one years old, and the proprietor of a large organization; and President Roosevelt had personally requested that he stay out of the army to help the president, through *PM*, maintain support for the war and fight his enemies. Nevertheless, in June of 1942, Ingersoll received notice to report to Draft Board 44 in New York; he had been classified 1-A and faced induction. The notice put him in a genuine dilemma. On the one hand, ever since 1917, when, as he put it, he was "cheated out of my war," he had been a frustrated war hero. "I had a real case of the kind of boyish patriotic fever that was rampant in 1917," he says. And after his trips to London and Moscow, where he saw what Nazi bombers were doing to open cities, he "wanted personally to squirt lead into a Messerschmitt or drop a bomb on Berlin," as he would write his draft board. The prose was vintage Ingersoll, but the sentiment was genuine. "The day after Pearl Harbor, I knew I wanted more than anything else to get in on the show."

At the same time he was wedded to his job as editor of *PM*. Although Charles Cushing was becoming increasingly critical, Ingersoll was in complete control of his paper. He loved the power it gave him and the outlet it provided for his compulsive urge to write. Furthermore, he truly felt that he could do more for his country as a journalist than as a private in the army. He had been commissioned to serve as an engineer in the reserve, but he had not practiced that profession since 1924. On the other hand, he believed in the democratic process for drafting men into the armed forces and did not feel anyone should be given special dispensation.

There was, however, one thing that troubled him. He had heard reports that his draft board was prejudiced and, in a sense, stacked against *PM*. Most New York draft boards contained a Protestant, a Jew, and a Catholic. Number 44, however, was made up of a Protestant and two Catholics, and both, he had heard, were followers of Father Coughlin and the right-wing Christian Front. By the summer of 1942, *PM*'s two-year fight with the Christian Front had come to a rather dramatic confrontation. Father Coughlin, the Roman Catholic priest who had cofounded, with Gerald L. K. Smith, the right-wing National Union for Social Justice, had been preaching his political gospel from Detroit in radio broadcasts that reached more than thirty-two million people through more than forty stations and in his magazine *Social Justice*. *PM* organized a huge write-in campaign, and as a result twenty-five hundred cards were sent to the Justice Department urging that Coughlin be put off the air and *Social Justice* banned from the mails. Ingersoll had also planned a march on Washington, but Ken Crawford persuaded mutual friends in the New Deal to talk Ingersoll out of it. Ingersoll critics, such as Wechsler, saw his attempt to censor *Social Justice* as being no different from right-wing efforts to ban the *New Masses*, whose right to publish *PM* had defended. Ingersoll argued, however, that *Social Justice* and Coughlin were supporting the enemy in a shooting war, and he published in *PM* Abraham Lincoln's 1863 message to Erastus Corning, in which the president argued that in times of crisis it might become necessary to "suspend" the Constitution. "Must I shoot a simpleminded soldier who deserts," wrote Lincoln, "while I must not touch a hair of a wily agitator who induces him to desert?"

Ingersoll and *PM* argued that Coughlin was a wily agitator who was arousing his followers to oppose their leader in war, President Roosevelt, whom he had called, among other things, "a great liar and betrayer."

Ingersoll did cancel the march on Washington, and it was the church that forced Coughlin off the air. He was also removed as editor of *Social Justice*. And when Ingersoll went to his first draft hearing, the questions put to him by the board convinced him beyond any doubt that at least two of the members were prejudiced against him. The decision to classify him 1-A was, he believed, essentially a counterattack on *PM* for its war against the Christian Front. The questions: "Don't you think it would be a fitting climax to *PM*'s career to have it end with your being inducted?" and "Wouldn't your competitors laugh if *PM* went out of business as a result of your being inducted?" When Ingersoll replied, "They'd howl with delight," the draft broad broke up in laughter.

Meanwhile, the drafting of Ralph Ingersoll was escalating into a national issue. Marshall Field, without consulting Ingersoll, appealed to his friend, General Lewis B. Hershey, head of the Selective Service System, to exempt Ingersoll. At the same time four hundred *PM* staffers signed a letter to FDR requesting that the president exempt their editor. When he heard about these efforts, Ingersoll wired the president to ignore both Field and his *PM* supporters: "PLEASE BELIEVE ME I SPECIFICALLY WAIVED MY RIGHT TO APPEAL AND ASKED ALL CONCERNED THAT MY DECISION BE RESPECTED. I BELIEVE IN DEMOCRATIC PROCESS OF SELECTIVE SERVICE AND WOULD FIGHT TO DEFEND IT."

Then Ingersoll was attacked on another flank. The previous fall Marshall Field had founded the liberal *Chicago Sun*, which was to be an antidote to the right-wing *Chicago Tribune*, published by Colonel Bertie McCormick. McCormick had attacked Field in his paper, and Field had refused to reply. Now McCormick turned his attention to Ingersoll, calling him a coward and a disgrace to his profession. McCormick's cousin Cissy Patterson, owner of the *Washington Herald*, supported the attack, as did Congressman John Rankin of Mississippi and other ultraconservatives, such as the columnist who wrote in the *Dispatch* (Columbus, Ohio): "In view of his recorded belligerency, one might have expected to see [Ingersoll] heading the line at his home town recruiting station on Monday, December 8, 1941."

But Ingersoll had his defenders too, and not just the hundreds of *PM* staffers who would soon be carrying placards in front of Draft Board 44: the New York *Herald-Tribune*; Raymond Gram Swing; the author Philip Wylie; and Lin Yüt'ang who, like many others, came forward to argue that *PM* was "worth a division of home guards."

Ingersoll had resigned himself to entering the service and went to Washington to talk with Felix Frankfurter, for he wanted to find out from the president's adviser which branch of the army would be mostly likely to go into action first—he wanted to join that one. And while in Washington he had dinner with Charles Marsh, the enigmatic Texas millionaire who had summoned him to his New York hotel suite one night in the early days of *PM*. The two men—so similar in their enthusiasms, energy, intelligence, and pro-New Deal politics—had become good friends. Marsh enjoyed helping young men he admired, and had given many—including Lyndon Johnson—a boost in their careers. He was living now in Washington, where he liked to play a quiet, behind-the-scenes role in government. The dinner at Marsh's house in Georgetown developed into a conversation lasting well into the early hours of the morning, during which they both agreed that Ingersoll should not let the draft board defer him, even if Marshall Field was successful in his efforts. But Marsh argued that it was essential for Ingersoll to expose Draft Board 44's prejudice and what it was trying to do to *PM*.

As a result, Ingersoll went back to New York and wrote a six-thousand-word letter to his draft board, which he also published in *PM*, accompanied by a front-page headline, of a size suitable for announcing the fall of France: "RALPH INGERSOLL VS. DRAFT BOARD NO. 44." In it Ingersoll accused the draft board of being prejudiced, explained why, and said that "even Justices of the Supreme Court of the United States disqualify themselves when [there is] possibility of a prejudice." He said that he had not asked for, nor would he accept, Marshall Field's request for deferral; that he would waive his right to claim his two dependents, that he had no objection to serving in the army, but that he genuinely felt he could serve his country better by continuing as editor of *PM*. He was not requesting deferral, only that his case be heard by another, unprejudiced, draft board.

The request was denied, and the board met again and confirmed his 1-A classification. By now the Ingersoll case was a *cause célèbre*, and in making it a front-page story, he had seriously damaged his reputation. Many people simply did not understand that Ingersoll genuinely had no objection to serving in the army but felt compelled to launch a typically Ingersollian counterattack against prejudice and his attackers. He was now on the front pages of most of the country's newspapers; magazines, from *Editor and Publisher* to *Time* and *Newsweek*, followed the man and the case, as did editorials and radio broadcasts; and people with signs for and against Ingersoll were picketing the White House and his draft board.* The issue had now escalated beyond the personal—"Ralph Ingersoll the draft dodger"—to the broader question: Are newspaper editors and reporters essential to the war effort?

It was finally resolved that they were, but only after Ingersoll himself quietly showed up one morning to be first in line at the induction center on Whitehall

---

*The case also inspired a movie, *Over 12*, starring Alexander Knox, who plays an editor who joins the army when he does not have to—so that he will be worthy to write about the postwar world. Irene Dunne plays the editor's wife. *Time* magazine, in its review, paid tribute to Ingersoll's catalytic role.

Street. As he walked deliberately, and unnoticed by fellow inductees, through the line the radio blared: "INGERSOLL HAS ENLISTED."

At Governors Island a young medical lieutenant, who was also a *PM* fan, happily reported that Ingersoll had a spot on his lung and could not be inducted unless he could prove the condition had been arrested. Ironically, Ingersoll would easily have gone back to *PM* exonerated, but he chose not to. "The whole idea was repugnant to me," he said later. "The noisy public arguments with the baring of breast and soul involved, had truly nauseated me. I couldn't go back."

He remembered an X ray taken in the 1930s for the Metropolitan Insurance Company, which had passed him as a preferred risk. He had his doctor track down the X ray and took it to the army doctor as proof that the spot had been there since the 1930s and that the TB had been arrested. He was finally in-ducted—but not before he wrote one last letter for publication in *PM*. It was dated July 24, 1942, and was addressed to Marshall Field and his colleagues on the paper:

"I never considered myself indispensable to *PM*," he wrote. "But when I faced Local Draft Board No. 44, I am proud to say that I became indispensable for a few brief weeks—as the symbol of the *PM* which a majority of the board would have liked to silence. And *PM* became the symbol of a free press." He went on to explain why he now felt compelled to fight the board, and to say he felt confident that he had won the fight and he knew *PM* would continue it.

As a farewell memento, *PM* artist Leo Hershfield made a large scroll, which was signed by the entire staff. At the top it read:

PUSH 'EM AROUND RALPH

By 1942 Ingersoll had achieved his dream: to create a new kind of newspaper that was against people who push other people around. Now he was about to achieve another dream just as intense, if less publicized: to go off to fight a war whose cause was just. And he hoped to return a hero.

Ingersoll chose to make his fight with the draft board front page news, which he later came to regret

Sergeant, 1942

12: Lying to Hitler

Given his instinct for challenging superiors, and his talent for alienating colleagues, one would have thought that before the war was over, the energetic,
ambitious Ralph Ingersoll would have alienated the entire U.S. Army organization and perhaps, even, been shot in the back by one of his own men. But
that was not the case. In the course of his rapid and impressive rise through the
ranks, he managed not only to avoid alienating and irritating those around him
but to end up with quite a few friends. One of them, Wentworth Eldredge, who
served with him in the Fortitude program, thought the reason might have been
that the war brought out the "noble" part of Ralph Ingersoll—perhaps for the
only time in his life. Ingersoll, in his unpublished memoirs, has a more prosaic
explanation and gives the credit to Dr. Gregory Zilboorg: "The first adventure
into which I was thrown after my analysis," he said, "was a career as a soldier.
Here again began a familiar scenario. I rose rapidly—from buck private to
lieutenant colonel on the General Staff. But had I followed my pre-analysis
pattern, just as soon as this change in my status brought me into conflict with
my first solid father image—and an army multiplies father images as in a mirror
maze—I would have turned on him and surely have ended my war court-martialed

for insubordination. Instead, for the first time in my life I found myself able to master a relationship with authority. Instead of making my superiors enemies, I made them into friends"—and they were still friends twenty years later.

For a civilian solider, Ingersoll did, in fact, have a remarkable military career and, superb journalist that he is, came home with as good a collection of war stories as you will ever hear. During his conversation with Felix Frankfurter in Washington, he had learned that Roosevelt had created the Engineer Amphibian Command (E.A.C.), already headquartered on Cape Cod where it was staging a mock assault on the beaches of France. He had also learned that if he enlisted (which was another reason he did not wait to be drafted) he could request assignment with the E.A.C., take his basic training at Camp Edwards, and come out a sergeant. He also felt certain he would be assigned to the E.A.C.: Not only was he an engineer, but as Frankfurter had informed him, the E.A.C. was looking for men with aircraft pilot licenses, which Ingersoll still had. Two weeks after his enlistment Ingersoll reported to the army's reception center at Camp Upton, Long Island. And one man who helped process him says he still remembers "the electric excitement that spread through Camp Upton when a new private amassed the near-perfect score of 158 out of a possible 163 in the army general classification IQ test." The next day Ingersoll reported for basic training at Camp Edwards on Cape Cod.

And, as usual, he immediately became the center of a commotion, the number-one topic of conversation in the barracks. He was still making news, so reporters had followed him to camp. Edwards's commander Brigadier General Daniel Noce barred the press and had his men report back every move the private made. But Ingersoll was ready for anything Noce and his top sergeants could dish out: "If I was to be put in my place as a potential prima donna by being assigned to picking up cigarette butts from the parade ground, I would make myself the best damn cigarette-butt-picker-upper in the whole damned army."

If there were any doubts that Camp Edwards had a celebrity on its hands, they were dispelled a couple of weeks after his enlistment. One man in Ingersoll's platoon had come down with the measles, so the platoon was isolated from the rest of the company and ordered to conduct maneuvers by itself. Ingersoll was lying in the middle of a field when a lieutenant blew his whistle and yelled, "At rest—stay in place." Ingersoll looked around and saw two jeeps full of brass approaching the lieutenant. They conferred, then the officers reentered their jeeps and drove toward Ingersoll. When they reached him, a full colonel with a medical insignia said, "Get in, Ingersoll." The jeep returned to Ingersoll's barracks and pulled up to an outdoor telephone, which another medical officer was spraying with disinfectant. The obviously annoyed colonel motioned Ingersoll to the phone. The screaming voice on the other end belonged to Mayor Fiorello La Guardia, who had written a column for *PM* and was now a friend of Ingersoll's. "Ralph Ingersoll?" the mayor yelled. "It's really you? Those goddamn sons of bitches. They can't do this. I told the goddamned commander that! He actually tried to tell me you were quarantined. What in hell's going on?"

Ingersoll explained, and then La Guardia came to the point: "Ingersoll, it's all arranged. I'll have you out of there in twenty-four hours. We've had a meeting and everyone agrees. They can't keep you in the army because we're running you for governor of the state—on the Liberal ticket!"

Ingersoll was first "dumbfounded,' then "appalled," and it took him several minutes to respond. But he finally managed to assure the mayor that he did not want to get out of the army, that he was doing what he wanted.

Basic training was an exhilarating and satisfying experience for the former editor, and he was gratified to learn that in the physical training he could compete with men twenty years younger. He and most of his officers were astonished to find that his final rifle score was the highest in the platoon. His first eleven shots were bull's eyes, and he says, "I would have gone on making bull's eyes if I hadn't got score fever and grown so tense I had to take the rifle down from my shoulder." The old soldier who was scoring for him was also excited and made him more nervous by saying, "Now, all you have to do is keep calm." Years later, when the soldier was arrested in Boston for drunkenness, he remembered Ingersoll and gave the judge his name as a reference. The judge called Ingersoll (collect) to see if he recalled the incident, and Ingersoll said, "I most certainly do."

Near the end of his basic training he began to develop something of a philosophy of war and soldiering, which he would later outline in one of his books: "We had been soldiers now for a month. That's long enough to know how tough it is for a soft civilian to march even five miles with nothing but a rifle on his shoulders and no pack, how uncomfortable it is to sleep on a hard and narrow cot. It is long enough, too, to know that, man for man, in the field, soldiers who could walk not five but twenty miles and to whom a cot was not a hardship but a luxury, would have very little difficulty killing us.

"The military phrase for a soldier's mission is quite explicit. It is to impose one's will on the enemy. At the end of a month in the army we knew—and it was quite a startling bit of new knowledge—how weak we were, how easy it would be in a showdown for anyone to impose his will on us. If we were not yet disciplined, we already knew the value of discipline—for already we had been lost on marches, we had mock-fired in mock skirmishes on those who were supposed to be our friends. We knew, all the big talk aside, how we stank.

"We also knew, fresh in the morning, marching in solid columns, swinging out from camp with our new M-1's on our shoulders, just how tough an army that was good could be."

A week after the bizarre incident with Mayor La Guardia, Ingersoll was yanked out of maneuvers again by a jeepful of brass and taken this time to see General Noce. The general explained that he would have summoned Ingersoll earlier but had first been compelled to find out everything about him because he had created such a commotion in camp. Noce said he had learned what he wanted to know; he fully appreciated Ingersoll's reasons for enlisting and understood the controversy it aroused. He also felt Ingersoll could serve his country best as an officer, and he wanted to reissue his Reserved Officers' Training Corps commission, originally conferred in 1918, if Ingersoll did not object.

Ingersoll was delighted, but, as it turned out, commissioning him was not that easy. The application for the notorious Ralph Ingersoll's commission was bucked all the way up the line, with officer after officer refusing to stick his neck out, until it finally landed on the desk of the secretary of war, Henry Stimson, and there a note from Frankfurter helped produce the necessary signature.

It was apparent to everyone in camp that First Lieutenant Ingersoll was an eager beaver. But General Noce wanted to know whether he could actually do anything. So Ingersoll's first assignment, a rush job, was to develop a first-aid manual for an amphibian corps. Ingersoll published it within a few weeks, and later General Noce told him, "What impressed me was that a man who had been such a big shot could still do a job of real work."

The manual was a real job of work, which is what anyone would have expected from an editor who had been instrumental in the development or production of five major American publications. Up to that time there had not existed in the U.S. military any basic manual prescribing policies and procedures for launching an amphibious assault. Assembling a staff of twenty to thirty specialists, Ingersoll and his "publishing house" produced a half dozen manuals that drew heavily on the *Fortune* and *Life* technique of giving as much instruction as possible in photographs, drawings, and charts.

Impressed with his ability to articulate plans and programs, Noce decided to make Ingersoll his public-relations officer. "That was precisely what I did not want to have happen to me," says Ingersoll, "but by this time I'd learned enough about the army to find out how to get out of an assignment I didn't like. I doubt if it's a secret in any military establishment that the way to con your way to a promotion is to make it sound so important that you have to have an assistant. Then, if you want, you can maneuver him into replacing you."

Ingersoll convinced Noce not only that his command was failing to get the publicity it deserved but that the whole damn army was being eclipsed by the publication attention given to the navy and the marines. Ingersoll says he did not realize at the time that he had touched one of the army's most sensitive nerves. With a little research, he discovered that one reason for the marines' favorable press was that they had a public-relations specialist—called a "combat correspondent"—attached to every unit. Why couldn't the army do that? Ingersoll asked Noce.

Noce thought it was a great idea, and asked Ingersoll to fly with him to Washington. Together they would try to convince the army that such a program was needed. They failed, but in the process Ingersoll convinced Noce that he had not joined the army to become a P.R. man, and that if Noce assigned him a junior officer, Ingersoll would train him before going on to a new assignment.

Noce agreed, and Naval Lieutenant Mortimer Howland Cobb became Ingersoll's assistant. Although Ingersoll would know him only briefly, Cobb would come to play a significant role in his life.

Cobb, a gangling young man, was six feet two with carrot-colored hair. On his enlistment form, he had listed yachting as his avocation, so he had been assigned to the amphibian corps. "Morty was a character to me," says Ingersoll, "from the day he beamed into my shack of an office, so grateful for having been rescued from messy things like diesel engines and landing craft." Cobb immediately attached himself to Ingersoll, who soon learned that Cobb's wife, Elaine, was a researcher on *Life* and that, in fact, she had worked for Time Inc. while Ingersoll was still there. With Ingersoll's permission, Cobb invited Elaine up for a weekend and insisted that his boss join them for dinner on the night of her arrival.

The dinner was a strange one, with Cobb acting as emcee and mediating the conversation between his bride and his boss. Ingersoll was, after all, the intruder, so tactfully he announced his departure for camp, as soon as he could. When he arose to shake hands and then made his way to the door, he was surprised to find Cobb at his side.

"Morty, you—what the hell?"

"Oh, I've told Elaine I'll try to get back to see her tomorrow. I'm going with you, sir."

Nor could Ingersoll persuade him otherwise.

So they drove back in silence and never referred to that curious night during their brief service together at Camp Edwards. Ingersoll did not see Elaine again until after the war was over in Europe.

Meanwhile, there were disturbing rumors going around camp that Admiral Ernest J. King had persuaded President Roosevelt to transfer the E.A.C. to the navy. When Noce finally confirmed the rumors, he was furious. He knew Ingersoll had met Roosevelt, so he called him in. "Is there any way," he asked his assistant, "you can get to the president and ask him to reconsider? They simply can't put together overnight the experienced organization we've built here."

Ingersoll frankly did not think he could gain an audience with the president now that he was no longer editor of *PM*. But he also knew you did not say no to General Noce. As he made his way out of Noce's office, Ingersoll's approach to Roosevelt was already taking shape in his mind. He knew Harry Hopkins would put a memo on the president's desk, and it would be read. He also knew the memo had to be short and to the point. So he wrote a persuasive one-page letter, which has long since been lost. But the first words Ingersoll still remembered years later: "We have no enemies who are not separated from us by a body of water that we must cross to meet them. We have *in existence* a highly trained organization that can land assault troops anywhere. It would be an immense waste of skills and training and effort to break it up and begin all over again."

He ended the letter with the question: "Would you reconsider the decision to abolish the Engineer Amphibian Command?"

In Washington Hopkins read the letter, agreed with what Noce had said in it, and put it on FDR's desk. The president was persuaded by Ingersoll's logic but also, as a navy man himself, he was receptive to Admiral King's arguments that carrying men and supplies across water was the navy's job. So he came up with a typical Roosevelt solution: The navy would take over responsibility for the landings in Europe, but the E.A.C. would be responsible for supporting General Douglas MacArthur's island-hopping in the Pacific.

Noce was not happy, but he knew it was the best he would get out of Washington. Within hours of Ingersoll's return he was on a plane headed for Australia to find out if MacArthur could use the landing fleet he had been building at Camp Edwards. "Hell, I can use anything that floats," MacArthur is reported to have told Noce.

After he returned to Edwards, and while the E.A.C. was being dismantled for shipment to the Pacific, Noce decided to go to North Africa to see what he could learn from the American army's first landings under fire. He took Ingersoll along as his right-hand man in charge of articulating and putting on paper anything that might be of value to his troops. And while Noce was conferring with the army brass in Algiers, Ingersoll persuaded the general to let him visit the front, near Tunis, where the American First Army was still fighting the Axis powers. He had been in the army almost a year now, and he still had not seen any fighting. Noce reluctantly agreed, and the moment Ingersoll had been awaiting for over twenty years was about to arrive. He would know, at last, how he would react under fire.

When he reached the front, Ingersoll managed to get himself attached to Colonel William Darby's Rangers, D Company. And if one hung around headquarters, he learned, it was not difficult to get a sense of when the company was getting ready to go into action. The tension that preceded one particular meeting clearly suggested battle, and Ingersoll blocked the path of a colonel as he emerged from the session, and persuaded the officer to let him go along with the attack group.

Ingersoll had stumbled into the battle for North Africa just after Gafsa had been taken by the First Division, which was still fighting General Rommel's troops; this time around el Guettar. The Germans were concentrated in a mountain fortress to which there seemed to be only two entrances—across an open plain or through a narrow, heavily fortified canyon. Both appeared impregnable. But there was also a third approach: Specially trained troops could go around to the left of the canyon and attack the troops defending it from behind. They would have to travel at night along five miles of mountain paths and, at one point, scale a twelve-foot cliff. A difficult enough task for men carrying rations and M-1 rifles, but Company D also carried .30-caliber machine guns and mortars.

To Ingersoll, the most important thing about el Guettar was finding out how he would react to battle. "I was afraid of being afraid," he said. He was also afraid of breaking down physically, "like an old ball player or prizefighter and being left behind by the younger men."

All these thoughts were going through his head, when suddenly the regiment captain stuck his head in the tent where Ingersoll was waiting with the other officers: "Hurry it up," he shouted. "Let's take off. They want us out ahead of the column. In another half hour, the roads will be full." For the rest of the night Ingersoll did not have much time to worry about being afraid, and he came through his first battle physically and mentally sound, conducting himself with honor and distinction and demonstrating remarkable stamina for a forty-two-year-old ex-editor who for most of his life had avoided any exercise more strenuous than swinging a golf club.

Either General Rommel was unaware of a possible approach around his flank or he did not think a sizable attack force could make the journey — at night and quietly enough to prevent its being detected by his sentries. But Darby's combat team did, and came up on the rear of the Germans at el Guettar, recording a decisive victory that contributed to Rommel's defeat in North Africa. (Ingersoll tells the story of the battle, and the role he played in it, in his book *The Battle Is the Payoff*.) He was proud of what he did, but could not help recalling the story about the private in Stonewall Jackson's army. The old soldier was sore and hungry and miserable and barely able to keep up with the column, when Jackson rode up beside him: "You all right, soldier?" The soldier trudged along in silence for a moment, then said, "I'm all right, General. But God damn my soul if I ever love another country."

Ingersoll was ordered back to Algiers before the Battle of el Guettar was over. When he arrived, General Noce told him that General Frank Andrews, head of the American command in Europe, had been killed, and that he was being replaced by Noce's friend General Jacob Devers. Devers had asked Noce to become his G-3 (Plans and Operations Officer) and Noce, in turn, wanted Ingersoll to go along as his own aide. It was an especially exciting prospect, because Churchill and Roosevelt had recently met in Washington and decided that the British and Americans would begin immediately to plan for an invasion of northwest Europe from the British Isles. Headquarters for this invasion would be in London. "I don't know exactly when we'll get our orders," Noce told Ingersoll, "but you've got a lot of leave coming. So take off and just wait for a telegram from me."

Ingersoll took off for New York with, as he put it, "the memories and sensations of the first battle I'd been in still churning my insides," and he had a nagging compulsion to get as much of it down on paper as he could. He also wanted to see how *PM* was doing in his absence, and of course, he missed his girl friend, Geraldine Morris.

PM, which had been totally dominated by Ingersoll during his two years as editor, was now being run by a triumvirate. John P. Lewis had succeeded George Lyon as managing editor before Ingersoll enlisted, and he had now taken

THE BATTLE
IS THE PAY-OFF

CAPTAIN
RALPH INGERSOLL

Because of his World War I reserve commission, it did not take Private First Class Ingersoll long to become a rather young-looking but 41-year-old lieutenant (ABOVE, LEFT). After amphibious training, he volunteered to go on a mission with Darby's Rangers to North Africa, which produced one of the war's first best-sellers. By the time the book (ABOVE, RIGHT) appeared, the author had been promoted. (BELOW) Lieutenant Ingersoll (left) talks with Sergeant Phil Stern after the battle of el Guettar

over most of Ingersoll's day-to-day editorial functions. The editorial page was being run by a young man named Max Lerner, who was teaching philosophy at Williams College when Ingersoll interviewed him. As Lerner recalls it, after reading his sample pieces, Ingersoll told him, "You'll never be a journalist." The business side of the operation was headed by Lowell Leake, one of the original managing editors. After a short tour of duty in the government, Leake had returned, just before Ingersoll's departure, to become an assistant to Ingersoll in budget control. Now he was feuding with the editorial side of the paper.

Another person playing an important role in the operation of the paper was Ginny Schoales, Ingersoll's personal assistant. And it did not take Ingersoll many lunches and drinks with Ginny, Lewis, and others on the staff to find out that things had not changed much. The Communist-dominated Newspaper Guild and the anti-Communists (led by James Wechsler and Ken Crawford, with support from Harold Lavine, an ex-Hearst reporter, and Arnold Beichman, who had worked for David Dubinsky at the International Ladies' Garment Workers Union) were still trying to outmaneuver one another for control. The breach between Crawford and Lewis was widening, and Crawford would soon be in open conflict over his reporting on North Africa, a dispute which would lead to his resignation. Lewis was trying to carry on "in the Ingersoll tradition," as Wechsler put it, but seemed to lean toward the anti-Communists. After Ingersoll left, "the men who were known to be anti-Communist achieved a preponderance of control of the major departments" of *PM*, says Wechsler. But like Ingersoll, Lewis also tried to avoid a head-on collision between the two groups.

The atmosphere had become so tense that by the time of the third anniversary party, in June of 1943, many staffers stayed away just to avoid the unpleasantness. And of course, there were the usual editorial problems, as summed up in this memo Lewis sent to Crawford in Washington early in 1943: "It's becoming increasingly apparent that we are losing all element of surprise in the paper. Ingersoll used to get highly excited about whatever happened to be in his mind at the time, and it was damn good because he forced us into getting excited, too. It's not so important whether the excitement is about important or trivial things just so we do have the human quality of getting hot and bothered and not taking everything deadpan."

In short, *PM* was still championing its special causes with a consistency that led one of its critics to describe its editorial credo as "Man Bites Underdog." But, as one observer noted, the paper had become "much more subdued under the editorship of John P. Lewis. . . . Lewis shared most of Ingersoll's political beliefs, but he was a more easy-going personality and less inclined to send himself or the paper on enthusiastic wild goose chases."

By the spring of 1943 Ingersoll was too obsessed with the urge to write about men in battle (a compulsion which had been with him since his *Kirmayer Echo* days) to become involved in the affairs of a paper which no longer belonged to him, and to which, deep down, he felt he might never return. He had no idea when his orders would come from General Noce, so after clearing his project with army public relations and getting an enthusiastic response from Harcourt Brace, the publishers, Ingersoll began work on an account of his service with the First Army's Engineer Corps and Darby's rangers. He started dictating to Millie Hollander, his secretary at *PM*, in his hotel room, but when his orders did not come, Marshall Field invited him to move into the paneled library of his Park Avenue apartment. It took Ingersoll an estimated one hundred hours of dictating to finish the book, and within hours of Millie's typing the last page he received his orders to report to General Noce at the American military head-quarters in London. He left all the details to his agents, Ingersoll (Tommy, his former wife) and Brennan, and did not hear anything about the book until late that year, when he was proud and delighted to learn that *The Battle Is the Payoff* by Captain (a promotion came through that summer, causing some frantic last-minute changes in the dust jacket) Ralph Ingersoll was in the bookstores and had become one of the war's first big best-sellers.

The book was picked by the Book-of-the-Month Club as its November selection, and the *Infantry Journal* (whose editor called it the Number One book of the war" in his *New York Times* review) published large sections from it in its November 1943 issue and made arrangements for a special armed-forces edition to be sold in its army PXs. Ingersoll gave the rights to the book to the U.S. Army, which, in turn, let him have a one-half-cent royalty on every copy sold. He made several thousand dollars on the trade edition but ended up with just enough money to pay his back taxes.

It is impossible to find one indictment of either the book or its controversial author in any of the reviews. This time Ingersoll had impressed everyone with his reporting, and it was obviously bad form to say anything unkind about a man who had risked his life to tell American boys and their parents what they were getting into. It is indeed a remarkable book, one, in fact, that reminded I. F. Stone of *The Red Badge of Courage*. The book was dedicated to Geraldine Morris. In his brief foreword General Noce said: "It may be rather strong reading for some, but it must be remembered that a battle is not a game of ping pong."

In his own introduction Ingersoll recounted his basic training and how he had ceased being a journalist to become "one four-millionth or one seven-millionth or one eight-millionth part of the Army of the United States— for the duration." Most reviewers insisted, however, that Ingersoll was still essentially a journalist and that his account of modern warfare in *The Battle Is the Payoff* was reporting at its finest.

One of the most striking aspects of the response to *Battle* is that Ralph Ingersoll, the controversial "celebrity" who had irritated so many people as editor of *PM*, especially in his highly publicized enlistment, was forgiven for his past transgressions. "The whole book has practically nothing to do with Ralph Ingersoll the personality," said P. R. Knauth in the *Saturday Review*. "From start to finish, he is only a vehicle carrying the reader through the vast, complex, intensely human machinery of an army moving into battle. . . . He is the best salesman of that Army, the best teacher of its workings that we have had in

World War II. And in that anonymity Ralph Ingersoll has done his best work yet as a reporter." Walter Millis, in the *Weekly Book Review*, concurred: "The Ralph Ingersoll who founded and edited *PM*—the crusading journalist and social trend finder inclined to get tangled up in his own big ideas—appears briefly in the introduction and concluding 20 pages. Through all the rest, it is Captain Ingersoll speaking, giving a remarkably detailed and vividly observed account of just what he saw and heard, did and felt in the course of one day of battle in Tunisia. It is a brilliant piece of straight, evocative reporting and any one with any interest in our combat soldiers or in the mechanics of the new American Army in battle action can't help reading it with avidity."

The army agreed that *Battle* was an excellent primer for the modern soldier and used it extensively in its training programs. And obviously the book provided a healthy boost to a continuing public career: Every soldier who arrived in London after November of 1943 had heard of Captain Ralph Ingersoll, the best-selling author. In the concluding pages of *The Battle Is the Payoff* Ingersoll says he disagreed with those who said after the defeat of the Germans in North Africa that the war would be over soon—maybe as early as December, but certainly some time in the following year. He argues that Hitler and Goebbels had such a grip on German public opinion that they would be able to hold out until they were defeated in a major battle as close to Berlin as Waterloo was to Paris. He also felt that hundreds of thousands of Americans would have to be trained and sent to England for an invasion of Europe. He believed that the Nazis would have to be defeated before we crushed the Japanese in the Far East, but that after the defeat of Germany the fall of Japan would be inevitable. Most of his prognostications proved correct.

* * *

When he arrived at Allied Headquarters in Grosvenor Square, London, he found his duties involved nothing more than staying close to General Noce and out of trouble. He did neither, wasting little time in becoming Ingersoll the Celebrity again. One evening he was walking down a side street off Grosvenor Square, headed for a genteel British "Officers Only" Club, when he spotted a pretty girl on the other side of the street. The girl smiled, and Captain Ingersoll, forgetting that automobiles drive on the "wrong" side of the street in London, immediately crossed over, was hit by a taxicab and hurled into the air. He regained consciousness in Middlesex Hospital where he heard a solemn old British doctor telling a group of medical students crowded around Ingersoll: "We have here the case of a man whose skull may or may not have been fractured. So we keep him absolutely flat on a hard surface until we find out—with X rays."

For several days thereafter a young lady took X rays, until Ingersoll was sure he had a rare and very serious kind of skull fracture. Finally another young lady, a reporter from the *Daily Express* who had recognized Ingersoll's name on the casualty list, appeared in his room to prop him up (contrary to regulations governing the treatment of skull fractures) and take his picture. When it appeared in the paper the next day, General Noce, who was relieved to find that his aide was not AWOL, came storming into the hospital to demand the return of his captain. But the British doctor refused to give him up, none of the X rays had come out, and he still did not know whether his patient's skull was fractured.

So once again Ingersoll was in the news—in the kind of story that helped Londoners take their minds off the war: British army medicos had the famous Captain Ralph Ingersoll in their custody and refused to give him up to the American army medical corps. And in the week that it took to resolve this jurisdictional dispute, the patient suddenly contracted a "case of screaming heebie-jeebies." He was overcome with an unreasoning fear and spent days and nights in a cold sweat—pure terror. He did not know what to do, so he started writing long letters to Zilboorg, hoping he could work off his mysterious anguish by free-associating through the mails and across the Atlantic.

Unfortunately, the letters were included in the papers Zilboorg destroyed before he died, but Ingersoll says that the simple act of writing those letters served to alleviate his anxiety. And Zilboorg said that for many years he used the letters in one of his lectures on self-analysis by a patient suffering from shock. He responded to Ingersoll only once: "What you've been going through is quite normal. The trauma which you experienced simply shook up the neuroses you had come to understand in analysis. But, writing me, you got through to them and they'll go back in their box." And they did, even before the U.S. Army managed to recover one of its more illustrious officers.

Ingersoll spent his recovery period at the Hampshire home of Tommy's cousins, Carrie and Gerald Constable-Maxwell. Wing Commander Maxwell, perhaps the only pilot to see combat in two world wars, had been a special hero of Ingersoll's ever since he had first learned that the wing commander had been in four separate airplane duels with the famous Red Baron, and that neither had put a bullet in the other's plane. There was also a postscript to the story of Ingersoll's near-fractured skull: When he returned to duty, General Noce ordered him never to call or see the girl who had lured him into his collision with the taxicab. The girl's mother was threatening to sue the U.S. Army because one of its officers had caused her daughter to have a nervous breakdown—a condition allegedly brought on by the shock of having witnessed Captain Ingersoll's body tossed in the air by a taxicab.

Not long after this incident the American headquarters was entrusted with the supersecret British plan for Operation Overlord—the invasion of Europe. It was July 1943, and the crossing of the channel was supposed to take place within a year. "It was a beautiful thing to look at," Ingersoll recalls: "a volume of 113 legal-size pages with 10 accompanying maps." But it contained so many *if*s— "if the wind were not too strong, if the tide was just right"—that many American officers were appalled because, if approved as written, "it would be easy," said Ingersoll, "to bring about a situation in which it could *not* be executed." After reading that one of the *if*s was "if the Germans had no more than twelve reserve divisions in northwest Europe," Joseph Stalin—always skeptical of British plans for invading the Continent—reportedly said: "So what if there are thirteen?"

There also appeared to be no provision for building the required landing craft in time, and the whole question of command disturbed the headquarters staff. They were certain the supreme command would be an American, but they also knew the army, navy, and tactical air force commanders would be British. General Devers and his staff had already seen enough of British officers (who seemed to specialize in developing reasons why something could *not* be done) to feel that with them in command there would never be an invasion.

But what bothered Ingersoll most about Overlord was its dependence on the element of surprise. "To think its preparations could be disguised," he told Noce in a memorandum, "would be to assume one could camouflage an elephant by painting its tail white." Oddly enough, within a few weeks Ingersoll himself would be helping to paint the elephant's tail.

One morning, not long after he had written his reaction to Overlord, Ingersoll was summoned by General Noce. "Ralph," said the general, "Jakie [Devers] has just gotten a silly request from down the street. The Limeys are up to something they call very hush-hush. They want a 'very special' personal representative to go out to some damn castle and be told what they are going to do. Get yourself a car and go see what it's all about."

An hour or so later Ingersoll arrived at a picture-book British castle on a remote hillside outside London for his first personal encounter with the British concern for form and procedure, which would irritate him during the entire war. When he showed the sentry at the gate his orders from General Devers, the British military policeman said, "Sorry, sir, our orders are that only red tabs are to be admitted."

In British military parlance *red tab* means full colonel, and Ingersoll was still a captain. Ingersoll had the M.P. call an officer, and the officer was even more adamant: No one below the level of colonel could be admitted. After a heated phone conversation between General Noce and someone inside the castle, Captain Ingersoll was finally admitted, although his chilly reception remained proof that his rank was not acceptable.

At this first meeting Ingersoll learned only that the British were planning a highly organized and most secret undertaking to conceal Overlord's real objective. Ingersoll was instructed to convey this to the American commander of the European theater of operations and told he would be given directives in the future, which the American forces were to follow—in secret and without question! The immediate objectives were not to be revealed at any level below that of the commanding general and his immediate staff.

Ingersoll was promoted to major (a rank he always disliked), put in charge of the special plans section of General Noce's G-3 branch, and issued orders that enabled him to go anywhere, anytime, in the European theater. At first the section consisted solely of Ingersoll and a sergeant typist, but Noce soon discovered that he needed someone with more clout to deal with the British and

American brass. So a West Point graduate, Colonel William Harris, was added to the staff, and because he outranked Ingersoll, he was the nominal chief of section, although Ingersoll continued to run it. He was also joined by a young Dartmouth professor, Captain Wentworth Eldredge, who had been working on a history of the Eighth Air Force. Eldredge was assigned the intelligence aspects of the cover plan. When, later on, Ingersoll decided he needed someone experienced in landings, he was given Lieutenant Colonel Clare Beck, who had distinguished himself as a battalion commander with the first infantry in North Africa.

Ingersoll's opposite number on the British side was Lieutenant Colonel David Strangeways, who was eventually made chairman of what was called the "hard-core" cover-plan committee, consisting of Strangeways, Ingersoll, and representatives of the British navy and air force. Various specialists were added to the committee as needed, and by September of 1943 the group was meeting regularly. Ingersoll continued to voice his skepticism. Embellishing his elephant theme somewhat in a memorandum to the committee, he likened an attempt to conceal such a huge undertaking as Overlord to "putting a hooped skirt and ruffled pants on an elephant to make it look like a crinoline girl." He went on to say, "I propose adding one real and one imaginary elephant. The imaginary elephant takes a little more doing. . . . The Pas de Calais is the enemy's most strongly fortified channel position. He would take a threat [there] seriously only if it became obvious to him that we are preparing an enormous force for the crossing. I do not believe two or three divisions would possibly scare him." Ingersoll proposed that instead of trying to conceal Overlord, the Allies use the Dunkirk evacuation fleet to mount a gigantic phantom invasion involving what would appear to be at least a hundred thousand men presumably destined for Calais. And he presented his plan in a dramatic manner that clearly impressed the British. "Suppose the Prime Minister called to Number 10 Downing Street the commanding officers of the Home Guard and made a speech to them. He would begin by saying that in England's time of need they had saved the country. And now he was about to offer them a role in the historic retribution, the invasion of Europe. He was going to put to them the task of re-assembling and moving the Dunkirk fleet to the southeast of England, where they would prepare to ferry two million men to France. With that many men involved you could not keep the planned invasion a secret, but what this dummy fleet of Dunkirk veterans would be preparing for was an invasion of Europe at Calais—not Normandy, which the OVERLORD plan called for."

By the end of November the British had begun to move toward the American approach, and on the twenty-fifth, at Norfolk House, they presented the committee with what the notes from the meeting termed "a modification of an earlier proposal." It called for "a diversion in the Pas de Calais area," which would place "principal reliance . . . on radio counter-measures, display of dummy landing craft and . . . the release of information by what is known as 'special means.'"

Although Ingersoll was at first skeptical of deception efforts in general, he was quickly converted. As Sefton Delmer writes in *The Counterfeit Spy*, a study of espionage and deception in the European war: "For Ingersoll it was love at first sight. He became one of the foremost American exponents of the art of deception." Ingersoll, the creative editor who was always brimming with ideas for stories and articles, had no trouble retooling his imagination for the business of deception. Even his severest critics from civilian life would have said he was a genius at deviousness, and his colleagues in the army agreed that he was good at it. "Any problem, he would just think a bit and come out with something," says Eldredge. "This was damn irritating for a college professor. He was always three moves ahead of you. I'd say: 'Shut up for a moment and let me think.' But I'll say one thing; he was out to win this war for the United States."

They also agreed that he was smarter than anyone else in the special plans section but was deceptive himself. "Ingersoll was the trickiest, most elusive person I've ever dealt with," said Eldredge. "I've never met anyone who was such a bright guy who was such a goddamned liar. He'd say anything to get what he wanted."

And lying to Adolf Hitler was no trick at all for Ingersoll. His biggest lie, he thinks, was the creation of the phantom First Army, positioned on the coast of England and across from Calais, whose false radio broadcasts and dummy installations and equipment convinced the Germans it was real and poised for an invasion.

In building their dummy armies, the British used wooden guns and tanks, meticulously put together by carpenters and painted so that from the distance of a few yards it was impossible to tell them from the real thing. "Watching them being put together," Ingersoll says, "it amused me to think of them as toys and thinking of them as toys put an idea into my head: Why couldn't they be manufactured as such—as inflatable toys? Why not make heavy rubber ones which could be blown up by compressed air?"

Ingersoll had seen enough rubber toys to know that they could be just as realistic as the handmade wooden dummies, and also they could be mass-produced, which would save precious manpower. He conferred with General Noce about his idea, and within two days he was on a plane to Washington to sell his idea to the Pentagon. A meeting was set up with rubber manufacturing experts, and Ingersoll says it took him only two hours to convince the brass and the production experts that his idea for "life-size rubber toys of war" was feasible.

While at the Pentagon, he also talked with a number of officers involved in the planning for Overlord. He was amazed to find out how little they knew about what was going on in London, and how much trouble they were having with the navy about increasing the production of landing craft. Donald Nelson, chief of the War Production Board, had, only the month before, doubled the order for landing craft, but the navy was still resisting because the British had told them it was not necessary.

Ingersoll's conversations at the Pentagon disturbed him so much that he decided to schedule a meeting with Harry Hopkins at the White House. He made sure Hopkins understood that he was talking as an old prewar friend, and that he was not acting in an official capacity, nor was he in any way representing his commanding officers. "As far as I am aware," he says, "General Devers never knew of this conversation." First he told Hopkins about the need for more landing craft, stressing that there was very little time for building them. According to Ingersoll, Hopkins "seemed astonished" and said that as long as he could remember, there always seemed to be a bottleneck in landing craft. He promised to look into it.

Then Ingersoll told him that the American commander of the European theater was frustrated because the coming invasion had not yet been placed under anyone's command. "Hopkins's first reaction," says Ingersoll, "was to ask how the Americans in the European Theater really felt abut the chances of Overlord's success anyway. I said that the headquarters I was in felt that the difficulties were magnified by our Allies and overrated. Devers and his generals were sure the invasion would work. I said that to Americans studying the problems, it seemed as if our Allies' looking for trouble was intentional—part, perhaps, of an organized effort to discredit or discourage the idea of invading."

Ingersoll indicated that he spoke as a reporter, not as a military expert or a diplomat. As he saw it, at the next high-level conference the British would offer to trade the Americans the job of supreme commander of the invasion in return for the three field commands: the army, navy, and air force. The supreme commander would be at such a high level that he would have little impact on strategy in the field. The British field commanders would insist on having the American forces under their command, and when they were, the Americans would be merged with the British. Ingersoll argued that the American army was good enough to fight under its own command, and that since, in the end, it was plain that the American forces would be many times the size of the British forces, it was neither militarily nor politically reasonable that it should be asked to fight under foreign command, however brilliant.

Hopkins agreed and said that an American commander would be named soon. In his opinion, the only man qualified for the job was General George Marshall. He strongly implied that Marshall would be the commander, and that no matter who served under him, Marshall would really be in command of the invasion.

Ingersoll left Hopkins's office satisfied and reassured. Six weeks later, at Teheran, Roosevelt and Churchill named General Dwight D. Eisenhower supreme commander of all forces in Europe. The three field commanders named were British: Field Marshal Bernard Law Montgomery (army), Admiral Sir Bertram Ramsey (navy), and Air Marshal Sir Trafford Leigh Mallory (tactical air force). The strategic air force was under an American, General Henry "Hap" Arnold. Deception was also discussed at Teheran; and it was there that Churchill said, "In war-time, truth is so precious that she should always be attended by a bodyguard of lies."

Within two weeks of his return to London Ingersoll learned from Noce that his rubber tanks, guns, and trucks were already in production. They came in a package easily handled by one man; a few men could inflate and assemble a hundred tanks, guns, and trucks. Then one real tank would make tracks for the enemy's spies to discover. But the deception went further: Once the toy battalions were in place, they were organized into field units with army names and numbers, which sent out radio transmissions using, for example, Texas telegraphers if the unit was supposed to be from Texas. An expert signal monitor can distinguish different "accents" and "dialects" in a wireless transmission. The roads leading into and out of the phoney encampments were also widened to look like two-lane roads and then camouflaged (with just enough showing) to let aerial reconnaissance planes know they were still there. Later, Ingersoll's team made recordings which, at night, were used to simulate the starting of engines, complete with backfires, and the clanking movement of trucks and tanks and heavy equipment. This technique was especially effective later in France, as was the practice of sending soldiers into local bars with their well-known division insignias torn off their shoulders, leaving a carefully retained outline for enemy agents to identify.

Despite the ingenuity of Ingersoll's deceptions, later studies showed that, at least until the troops reached the Continent, they had little impact. The reasons were that by 1943 the Germans were doing relatively little monitoring of radio traffic, preferring to rely on other means of intelligence. They were also doing very little aerial reconnaissance because the Royal Air Force controlled the skies over Britain. And most important, they were doing very little spying in England because British intelligence had captured most of the German spies and so controlled their intelligence.

It was the controlled spies, however, who won the national battle. As a postwar study of the deception plan by R. F. Hesketh—one of the participants— revealed, although the radio and physical techniques were almost one hundred percent successful in fooling the Germans, they did not really know enough about them to be convinced. But what little they did know was confirmed by the controlled, double-agent spies—especially two, code-named Garbo and Brutus.

How Ingersoll's task force viewed its work was summed up in the official report signed by Harris, Ingersoll, and Eldredge in 1945:

During the summer of 1943, the undersigned officers entered deception operations in the United Kingdom with grave misgivings as to their value. By the fall of '43, in fact, their mood was so critical that they successfully destroyed the first Cover plan proposed for Operation OVERLORD—by means of a staff study prepared for General Devers.

By the completion of the various FORTITUDE deception operations (which covered the assault landings in Europe), the undersigned were completely convinced of the effectiveness of strategic deception as an offensive weapon. The FORTITUDE operations had the dual mission of achieving surprise in the invasion (by concealing the time and target area) and of rendering a decisive number of enemy divisions ineffective *following* the establishment of the initial beachhead—by pinning them away from the battle area for a minimum of thirty days. These large objectives were achieved.

It is the final appreciation of the undersigned that Cover and Deception is a weapon of very great value. It is doubtful if another can be named which can do the enemy more damage with the expenditure of less personnel and materiel resources.

For most of his time in London, Ingersoll's office was in the Grosvenor Square headquarters of the American army's European theater of operations. He was at the center of London's wartime social life, and he, like the British, did not let the bombings or the preparations for an invasion of the Continent curb his fun. Ingersoll probably saw every show that played in London while he was stationed at Grosvenor Square, which was an easy walk to Piccadilly, even in a blackout.

During this period he met many attractive women in London and was still involved with Geraldine Morris, for whom he was trying to find a job in London. (One letter from Tommy said: "I went to dinner a while back and the main topic of conversation was how to get Jerry to England. I thought this might amuse you.") But he was unable to make an emotional commitment, and through most of his London amours, Ingersoll's usual tape-recorder memory failed him. "Only the background music is clear. The intensity of my preoccupation with playing soldier." One of his female companions during this period was a German Jewess he met while she was selling tickets at a broker's stall in Claridge's. He took her out to dinner and was impressed by her ability to mimic every British accent he had ever heard. But despite the fact that she was from a prosperous family, she had one little problem—kleptomania. After she lost her ticket-selling job (for taking money from the till, Ingersoll later learned) she moved in with him. It amused him to see her sneaking a few pounds from his pockets when he would gladly have given her the money, but he was never involved with her emotionally and knew the relationship would end when headquarters moved to Europe. Later, while he was in France, he received an indignant letter from her father: She was in prison but would be paroled before her child was born, and what was he—Ingersoll—going to do about the child?

Ingersoll flew back to London to confirm what he knew: that in the last months before he left England, during which time his girl friend must have become pregnant, she had been seeing several officers. He also learned that she had been arrested for stealing the pocketbook of a young lady attending a party in her flat. One of Ingersoll's friends put him in touch with Scotland Yard, which confirmed the story. "We have quite a thick file on the young lady," one crisp young officer told Ingersoll. "We are sorry you've been disturbed, sir. We do not like our allies' officers victimized. The fact that she was pregnant did not come out until after she was arrested. To be safe, sir, if I were you I would get myself a legal chap to keep me clear." Ingersoll said he did not know a legal chap and was in town on two days' leave "from the front."

"I don't know whether it's quite in order for me to do so, sir, but I can recommend a man who can handle it all neatly," replied the Yard man. And he did. Years later, when Ingersoll was in New York, he was visited by a young man who announced that he was the illegitimate son of Ingersoll's girl friend. She had married a man of some substance, who raised the boy as his own and sent him to a British university where he met an American and married her. He had never known who his real father was, but his mother had told him something about Ingersoll and he had come to New York to find out who he was. In Ingersoll's opinion, the young man did not look much like him or his wartime girl friend, and he could give the young man no help in his search. What moved him most, however, was the news that, for no apparent reason, the boy's mother had committed suicide.

When he was not living with a mistress, Ingersoll shared quarters with General Noce at 48 Grosvenor Square, and during this period he came to know his commander as a wise and ingenious officer. He also, gradually and to his surprise, gained tremendous respect for the U.S. Army. Its basic structure, he discovered, "was practical and soundly conceived to make the best of its inherent liabilities—the vanities, the ambitions and laziness, the meanness and the cruelties, that plague all mankind. Dan Noce was not the only professional soldier who was to demonstrate to me how effective our World War II army could be, but he was the first."

Noce and Ingersoll had the whole second floor of number 48. Noce occupied a bedroom overlooking the square, and Ingersoll and the general's aide, Jimmy Smith, shared a bedroom overlooking the courtyard in the rear. The floor above was occupied by an archbishop who was sophisticated enough not to be surprised by some of the wartime shenanigans that went on below. They had more than the comforts of home and were attended by an aging butler named Blackburn. He was incredibly inefficient, and after "a series of gaucheries, including trying to serve the archbishop when hopelessly drunk on the latter's champagne," says Ingersoll, Smith called him in and growled, "Blackburn, you're just no damn good."

The butler looked Smith squarely in the eye and responded, "Yes, sir, never was, sir."

Although Ingersoll was impressed with the American army, he at times had reservations about our political leaders. At one point a party of eight senators, accompanied by twenty-four aides, descended on headquarters for two weeks. Each senator was assigned one of Noce's top aides, and the group was given a pool of twenty secretaries along with a calligrapher to write their personal letters to the constituents at home to whom they reported on the London front. Each senator gave his military aide a shopping list several pages long, stressing such items as Irish lace and cashmere sweaters. When the junketing senators visited an army hospital whose staff had spent a week scrubbing it for them, they lingered so long over lunch that there was only time for a whirlwind tour, during which Ingersoll's senator (James M. Mead of New York) went from door to door, hastily poking his head in each room to say, "Any of you boys from New

York? We're proud of you and I'll be writing your good mothers and telling them so."

On another occasion a full infantry division waited all night in the rain to stage a mock battle, but the senators failed to show up. The division commander was so mad that he came all the way to London to express his rage to General Devers, who sympathized but could do nothing about it. The climax of the junket came the last night: When Senator Styles Bridges returned to his hotel room, he was startled to find that he was locked out and feminine giggles were coming from within. Fearing for his reputation in New Hampshire and Washington, he panicked and called the hotel manager in a purple rage, demanding that the woman be ejected and punished. When the door was opened, the room was empty—and Bridges demanded an "official investigation." The army never got around to it, but an unofficial investigation made by Ingersoll and others revealed that, indeed, there had been a woman in the senator's room—the guest of the colonel who piloted him back to the United States.

Obviously, Ingersoll the teller of stories would come home with more than his share, but they were not all so amusing as the one concerning the senators. For example, one day he read an intelligence report about a new bombing technique the Germans were about to try, in which the lead planes would drop a series of magnesium markers, culminating in a very bright red flare indicating the target. When he heard the sirens the next night, Ingersoll went out in the alley next to where he was staying, which happened to be across the street from First U.S. Army Group headquarters. He was fascinated as he watched the raid develop, with the Germans using the new tactics reported in the intelligence summary. "It was like seeing a play one had just finished reading," he says. But then, suddenly, he realized that he was in the play: A beautiful red flare, which Ingersoll thought must be the target marker, appeared almost directly overhead. FUSAG itself was the target, which, if nothing else, confirmed that the Germans were still taken in by Fortitude, because FUSAG had no troops, no mission, and, as far as anyone could see, no future.

Then there was the time Noce ordered Ingersoll to see how the navy was training its landing craft crews. Ingersoll located the young navy officer in charge, a disgruntled former submarine commander. He told Ingersoll that formal exercises were to start the next week on an East Coast beach, so Ingersoll and his assistant, Lieutenant Colonel Clare Beck, went out to watch them.

"The beach we were directed to," Ingersoll wrote years later, "was a sandy crescent with four- or five-foot waves breaking rhythmically as they rolled in: Fair test for beginners, we agreed, as we established ourselves at one end of the crescent on a bluff overlooking the whole stretch of sand and sea. Through binoculars, we watched a file of thirty-six LCTs come abreast, a mile away, and wheel like well-trained cavalry into a perfect line to charge the shore.... What bothered me was that the vessels of the oncoming fleet were only a single boat length apart. Off shore, the sea was not breaking, and they seemed to me so close to each other that they undulated in rhythm. I was appalled, for I knew that in each and every one of them there were five men in a buttoned-down tank. Their motors would already be warming up. . . .

"To beach a heavily-loaded landing craft safely, there are two rules that cannot be broken. One is that your craft must be at absolute right angles to the beach and the other is that when you feel your vessel lifted by the last wave, before it breaks, you *don't* cut your motor; you gun it hard, so that it speeds up with the wave. But had these green Naval-trained coxswains been taught them?

"On and on they came. Now only seconds were left before the moment of truth.

"It was with total and stunning horror that Clare and I watched and together saw the coxswain of the craft on the farthest flank slip back, and we both knew what was about to happen. The first craft broached, its bow swinging towards its neighbor on the left and *its* coxswain swung *his* boat away, broaching *it*. And then, in turn, each successive craft in the once perfect alignment swung its neighbor broadside to the crashing surf—to be capsized! In seconds, all thirty-six of them were turned upside down, with four- or five-foot waves breaking over their bottoms! . . .

"The report I turned in to Dan was as savage and vicious as the freshness of the experience could make it. And when he'd read it and cross-questioned Clare and me, Noce's anger was a near match to ours. So I'm sure our message was well passed on. But we were the Army and all we'd lost were thirty-six tanks and 180 replaceable personnel. The landing craft were under the Navy's command. The young admiral from the submarine service was not relieved."

Another Ingersoll story could also have ended in tragedy. The air force was trying to convince the general that its tactical bombing was now so accurate that it could lay down a barrage a hundred yards in from of an advancing infantry. So Noce said, "OK, show me," and a demonstration was set up with the target a little more than a hundred yards offshore. A bleacherful of brass was assembled to watch the show from the beach. The air force planes came in, swooped low, and dropped their bombs not about a hundred yards in front of the target—*but right on the grandstand*! Fortunately, Noce had had the good sense to order that the bombs be made of bags of flour, so the red faces of the air force generals were mostly camouflaged white.

But it was yet another incident that gave Ingersoll his most vivid scare of the war, and probably his closest scrape with death. He had to attend a meeting in Portsmouth for which he commandeered an L-5, a small, low-powered, two-seat, high-wing monoplane used for artillery spotting and running errands. A young sergeant pilot flew him down in two hours, he attended the meeting and was on the way back shortly after noon. It had started out a sunny day, but some clouds were coming in. Still, everything was relaxed as the sergeant pilot flew home by the "iron compass," the railroad tracks easily visible through the clouds. Ingersoll had been studying the map when he looked up to notice that they had left the iron compass and were in a cloud bank. For the first time Ingersoll looked over his pilot's shoulder to see that they did not have the proper instruments for flying in the clouds. And before long, says Ingersoll, "with no horizon to steer by and no instruments to warn him, my pilot had dropped one wing lower and lower. I had just caught it on the compass—which was all there was to warn that we were now circling—when he caught it too. He dropped the opposite wing and the nose at the same time and, terrified, jammed open the throttle to give himself more power. We yawed awkwardly—and popped clean over onto our backs, upside down! The canned K-rations were flying everywhere, and we were now hanging by our seat belts with the blood pounding into our heads and eyes."

Ingersoll did not even know the name of the pilot, who was now, he was certain, taking him to their doom. "We had probably been airborne half an hour by then. We had no idea where we were—or way of finding out."

The pilot finally managed to get them right side up again; they began to climb, and then Ingersoll knew he had to get to work.

"I can't remember exactly when it became clear to me that, stick or no stick, I had to find some way to take charge of what was going on. In the early days, when you learned to fly, you were taught that if you ever feel panic coming on, take your hands and feet off the controls and let the plane fly itself. There is, in light planes, a little handle in the roof of the cockpit which adjusts the tail's angle of attack; the plane will lose or gain altitude as you turn it.

"So my problem was not how to maneuver the plane but how to handle the pilot. The young man in front of me was already in panic and close to the far edge of it. No use hitting him on the head—the K-rations were already doing that, as spin followed spin. So I took on his neck. I started by massaging it with both hands, and, stretching forward till my mouth communicated directly into one of his ears, lullabyed, 'Easy, boy, easy.' Then: 'Let go that stick—just let it go and take your feet off the rudder bar. She'll come out of it herself. Believe me, boy, believe me!' If he did, I could reach up to the stabilizer's handle and take a turn on it myself.

"It was a long, slow process, but finally it worked! After we had stalled a few more times, twice coming out with the plane flying upside down, with us hanging from our belts, I began to get through to him.

"By my wristwatch, this went on for over an hour—or approximately ten years, four months and three days!

"But the thing I remembered is that as we spent more and more time horizontal, the altimeter was going up, closer and closer to two thousand." Scanning the solid grey in which I was conducting my psychotherapy, I saw at last a patch of it darker than the rest. It seemed about 45° off our course and just *above* it. We must have been on our back again. But one of my hands quit its massaging and took a hard hold on my boy's neck, and the other pointed him to the dark patch. I yelled in his ear: 'There! Go there!' . . . The patch grew darker and larger and was now below us. Then, within minutes, we were no longer in the cloud but under it, looking down on a cleared hilltop of solid ground! I shouted, 'Pancake it!'—and he did, managing his last stall only a few feet above a strip of deserted moorland. A stalled L-5 landed at the ridiculous speed of less than thirty miles an hour. We did not even break its landing gear, bumping to a stop."

* * *

Most of the officers in the American headquarters assumed and hoped that General Devers would end up commanding the invasion. But after one night in the fall of 1943, they were taking bets that it would be somebody else—presumably Marshall. Devers had been given the thumbs-down, Ingersoll was sure, when he had his first meeting with Churchill. It was at a dinner, and everyone knew that Devers was being viewed by the prime minister as the possible American commander of the invasion who, of course, had to have the P.M.'s endorsement. Noce and Devers spent the afternoon discussing how Devers should conduct himself in the Great Man's presence. Then that night Noce sat vigil at headquarters, while Ingersoll and Jimmy Smith waited at 48 Grosvenor. It was at least two A.M. when General Noce came in with the report: "I never saw him, before or after, so euphoric," says Ingersoll. Then Noce told the story, as later recounted by Ingersoll: "The P.M. had seated Devers on his right. Then the P.M. ignored his other guests to beam his whole personality on Devers. There had been no military talk until after the champagne and a succession of brandies. Jakie had kept his impatience magnificently under control, and Dan said he was relaxed and alert, waiting for his host to get around to the subject of the war.

"When its turn finally came, the P.M. began with a comment on the invasion of Sicily and from that beginning he went on a long and rambling dissertation on impending victories of the allies—in Southern Europe. Then, came the climax. The P.M.'s voice came up to address the table as a whole: 'Every landing a victory. Headlines of victories, victories, victories.' And, chubby fist pounding on that table, 'Headlines of victories are what we need, Gentlemen.'

"It was in the silence that followed, Dan told us, that Jakie Devers showed his real quality as the man of character that he was, the true American Commanding Officer. When the table recovered from his pounding, Churchill had turned to Devers and added, 'And what is your opinion of *that*, General?' To which Jakie had replied, after a moment of respectful silence, 'Mr. Prime Minister, I think one squad of soldiers across the Channel will mean more to the world than all the headlines of victories put together.'"

Noce may have been euphoric, but Ingersoll was appalled. He knew this remark had killed any chance of Devers's being appointed invasion commander. A few months later, when Eisenhower was made supreme commander, Devers was transferred to the Mediterranean, taking Noce with him, and his headquarters staff was dissolved. Before leaving London, Devers introduced Ingersoll to General Omar Bradley and convinced the general that Ingersoll was doing a good job. So Ingersoll's special plans section was transferred to Bradley's staff. Then, almost immediately, he was detached, and was one of six American officers assigned to serve as observers on the staff of the British general Montgomery. Their assignment was to familiarize themselves with Montgomery's operation so that when the American troops under Montgomery reverted to American command, there would be a handful of American officers who could help make the transition. So in March of 1944 Ingersoll moved to Portsmouth, where his unit set up tents on the lawns of a lovely country estate known as Southwick Park.

The British were quick to remind Ingersoll and the rest of the American contingent that they were there as observers, not participants. "General Montgomery has asked me to tell you that he is very glad you are here," said Monty's chief of staff, setting the ground rules. "He would like you to understand that this is not an *Anglo-American* headquarters. This is a *British* headquarters."

This no-nonsense attitude did not disturb Ingersoll, who was, in any case, getting a little tired of what he called the usual sweet, sticky British approach. It also sounded as if Monty and the British really meant business. In January the field marshal had postponed the invasion date one month, to the end of May. This had been disturbing news because after June the tides and the weather would become unfavorable and the invasion would have to be put off until the following year. There could be no more delays. But after only a month with Monty's staff, Ingersoll was convinced that the invasion was on track; that, in fact, there was not much Monty or anyone else could do to derail it. "By April," he says, "Overlord's momentum was too great to be stopped."

Everyone in London knew the casualties would be high when they hit the beaches of France. "I wasn't as courageous as I might have been," said Ingersoll's top aide, Major Eldredge. "I didn't want to go in and have my ass shot off." And Clare Beck, who had seen some action, did his best to convince Ingersoll that he, too, should wait until a beachhead had been established. "You think you are going to see something thrilling—but you're not. I've been through a landing [in Africa] and there is no sense to it. You only see blown-up tanks and abandoned vehicles and men being hit that you can't help."

But Ingersoll could not be dissuaded from going with the invasion forces, despite the fact that he knew well in advance of D day where the Americans were headed and what their chances were. The three assault divisions of the American army were to land on two beaches on either side of the elbow joint from which the Cherbourg peninsula points toward England. The one on the left, as you faced it, had the code name Omaha; the one on the right was Utah. "And considering the hard realities," says Ingersoll, "after the decision had set itself somewhere inside me, I saw very well that it could be close to suicidal. The original estimates for the Utah landing were around fifty percent. Those for Omaha were only slightly less. And I had no solid faith that either would succeed."

Despite the risk, Ingersoll knew he had to go. In the first place, his personal war against Hitler probably would not have been satisfied with anything less than a landing under fire from Fortress Europa; in the second, as a journalist, he could not resist being in on such an historic event, and of course, having written one best-selling book about the war, he was already planning another. But there was another factor: For six months he had had an ugly sore on his back which he had self-diagnosed as cancer. He did not report it to the army medicos because he knew he would be sent home for an operation if his diagnosis were correct. So Ingersoll considered himself quite likely expendable: "I would be thumbing my nose at the Nazis if they succeeded in killing me before the cancer did."

As D day approached, Ingersoll had several opportunities to go along in a combat capacity. He had become good friends with a young West Point graduate named Paul Thompson, who had worked for Noce, then had been made brigadier general and put in command of the First Amphibian Brigade, which was assigned to land the First Division at Omaha. Thompson offered to take Ingersoll as his second in command, even though he was only a major. "After Camp Edwards," he told Ingersoll, "my hunch is that you know more about landing craft than I do. Think it over."

While he thought it over, Ingersoll had another, even more tempting offer— from an officer he did not know. Colonel Edson Raff was also an academy graduate, attached to the Eighty-second Airborne Division, which was to drop at dawn on D day. He was a "gung-ho character," says Ingersoll, straight out of fiction, who had served in Africa and was known to be a nut on the subject of parachuting. "Raff had set up a waterborne task force which was to land sixteen tanks and crews with the first assault waves on Utah. Their mission would be to streak through to the Eighty-second, which was to drop eight or ten miles inland, just west of a town called Saint-Mère-Église. 'I've only got the captains of the tanks to back me up,' Raff told me. 'Want to come along as my second in command? You'd have to take over if I got hit, but I don't expect to. Think it over.'"

Ingersoll considered both offers and decided to go with Raff. He had done his soul-searching and come to the conclusion that the arguments for being in on D day outweighed arguments for going later with his unit, which was surely the more sensible decision. "I did not think there was any honorable way I could avoid fighting Hitler. I had worked on plans that none of us were sure would work and I was calling my own bluff to see if they would work."

As the invasion approached, the tension continued to mount, but not without some comic relief. The landing craft Ingersoll would be riding in had only room for the commander's jeep, but Ingersoll figured he could cram in a motorcycle for his own personal transportation, once ashore. The problem was that he did not know how to operate one. So he began teaching himself by riding a motor-cyle around General Montgomery's palace quarters in Portsmouth. One day the handlebar throttle stuck, and he could not make the machine slow down: "Faster and faster, I bumped through field after field, concentrating on making it through the openings between them. In fact I was so concentrated that when my rebellious steed finally bucked me off and skidded away on its side, I was totally unaware of where I'd landed."

But in a moment a chorus of feminine screams revealed that he had landed in the middle of a bevvy of sunbathing British WACs who were "naked as jaybirds," Ingersoll fondly recalls. Then standing over him, with both hands on her hips, was a stern-faced petty officer, fully dressed in WAC uniform. Looking down on Ingersoll, she said, "And what in 'ell do you think *that* trick will get you, Yank?"

All the trick got him was a quick look at a platoon of naked feminine rear ends, and one of his last London war stories. A few weeks later, on the afternoon of June 3, 1944, Major Ingersoll arrived at a loading ramp in Dartmouth. For the invasion, Raff's task force was attached to the Fourth Infantry Division, which Ingersoll finally located. He entered a shed, from the rear of which they were loading tanks into a 105-foot landing craft. A grinning colonel was sitting at a table in front of an open box of Purple Hearts. To amuse the troops, he was running his hands through them and tossing them in the air. Soon Colonel Raff appeared and, standing by a table spread with assorted weapons, he said to Ingersoll, "Pick the one you are handiest with." Ingersoll had no trouble selecting an M-1 rifle, the weapon with which he had so impressed everyone at Camp Edwards.

Behind the table in one corner sat a row of WACs handing out bundles of crisp new hundred-franc notes, cartons of cigarettes, cans of soup (which had an ingenious heating device that produced hot soup in minutes), and all the candy bars you could stuff into your pockets. "Nothing too good," Ingersoll recalls, "for the boys who were waiting to get the Purple Hearts."

Lieutenant Colonel, 1945

13: Invading Fortress Europa

We stood on the deck which roofed the little cabin and all we could see through the black was the flicker of gun flashes along the shore and the twinkle of the shells bursting far up in the sky, soundlessly.* The wind came across the water and slapped the waves up against the flat side of the LCT [Landing Craft Tank] *and the air was full of the mist from them. The noise of the wind was constant. There was no room left in the air for any other noise; the noise of the wind and the water—and the low throbbing from the Diesels underneath us—filled it full.*

The first Fort [Flying Fortress, an American bomber] *to catch fire carried a torch through the rippling sparkle of the shells breaking, drawing a long trailing line across the sky, flat and straight. Now it curved gently down, dropping, bending the line it drew; it turned down still more steeply until it balanced a trail of flame almost straight up and down.*

In the light of the explosion the plane made when it struck the ground, we

---

*The italicized passages are condensed from Ingersoll's book *Top Secret*, written immediately after the war was over in Europe. Not only do they illustrate his tape-recorder ability for almost total recall, but they constitute a dramatic account of one man's reaction to going into battle and what it was like on Utah beach on the morning of June 6, 1944.

saw France for the first time. . . . It did not last long and after it was gone, there was again only the fitful flashing of the ack-ack batteries on the shore and the shells bursting on their evenly set fuses, all at one altitude.

There were no lights on the 105-foot landing craft just ahead of us or on the one whose nose wobbled and teetered only a few yards behind where we stood on the stern above the pilot house. We were hardly moving now and it was 0430 hours on the morning of the sixth of June.

The second and third Forts came down, each flaming like the first. They arched down, dropped, exploded. When the bombs fell from the Forts still up there, they tore open great chunks of blackness and lit the horizon in jagged pattern of angry bursts of color. But none were as beautiful or as awful as the explosions the Forts made when they hit.

We were very, very cold and I could not tell whether the cold came from within or without. We had been on the landing craft for three days and two nights and fear had come in so many different forms we were very bored with it and not even curious about its symptoms now. The first day when we thought we were really under way we talked about it and were interested in the fact that it made our throats dry and sometimes glazed over one's consciousness until one saw a man speaking and did not hear him. Moreover, I thought that fear— just fear all by itself, fear with nothing that could be done about it—made most of the men sleepy. They huddled in corners or stretched out under the tanks, and slept and slept as if to run away from the reality that everything that could be done had been done and there was now nothing to do but sit and be carried to where death was waiting.

A little lieutenant from Brooklyn, whose platoon of engineers were going overside to take out the underwater obstacles, had a waking fantasy. He used to lean on the rail next to me and say, "You don't suppose there has been an armistice and nobody has told us, do you? Gee, it would be funny if it were all over and we didn't know it, wouldn't it?" Every few hours you would see him kicking this idea around with someone. He liked it and his face lit up when he talked about it and it gave him comfort.

Most of the tankers didn't talk at all. They were very polite with each other about little things, like trying to find a place to rig a tarpaulin to keep off the spray and the intermittent rain. They gathered around one of the little aluminum stoves that tank crews are issued and helped someone make coffee in a big tin or heat up some of the ten-in-one rations. . . .

We had that night to ourselves to go all over it again, and I think that was what let the fear in. You could count on your fingers the things that could happen to you and nothing could be done about any of them. There were the E-Boats that had sunk our landing craft on maneuvers the month before, no further from the English shore than where we lay at anchor. There were the submarines we had our reasons for believing the Hun might risk in the Channel if he knew this was the real thing. There were the mines. Most of all, on a crossing like ours, there was the air. No cover could wholly seal the air over the Channel and the long lines of landing craft would be bobbing ducks in a shooting gallery. Six knots we made in convoy; if we ran for it, our craft could do eight.

It was somewhere along about here that one began to get bored thinking about what it would be like. . . .

Edson Raff is a quiet fellow and nothing seemed to bother him until the stragglers from the airborne operation came back. We had, of course, the precise plans for the landing of the airborne division we were to join. The great fleet of aircraft that carried them was to fly over to the north of our course and, circling after the drop, should have come back directly overhead—or at least should have crossed our path flying low enough for us to feel the vibration of their flight. At three o'clock, I think it was, the first one passed us. One C-47 aircraft went by all alone, mast high and jerking through the air, trying to see down to where the water way and yet not strike the waves.

After the first plane, there came a flight of two more and then another—then nothing.

"They're gone," said Edson.

"Who's gone?" I said.

"I mean they're done for," he said. "Something's happened to them. There should have been hundreds—in formation—if they dropped right. Now they're scattered. It didn't come off."

We stood and looked into the night.

"What do we do now, Boss?" I said.

Edson grunted. "We can go on to where they were supposed to have dropped."

A dozen more planes came out of the night and sped over us in ragged formation, ducking and dodging like the others. Then no more at all came. . . .

From the deck of the LCT, when France was only a few hundred yards away you could still make no sense out of how it was going there. The men on the beach were little black figures against the white sand. Amongst them the sand spouted up in little geysers and the black figures seemed to be dancing about these geysers. Now and then a tiny vehicle would pop out of one of half a dozen landing craft that had beached up ahead of us—pop out and then move very slowly through the geysers and stop entirely or climb up over a dune and disappear. We were one of a very long line of LCTs, all dirty white in the morning sun. We were bow to stern in a straight line moving very, very slowly. The landing points were already jammed up and it was not noon yet. . . .

For a little while, coming in, we had heard the dull vibration of battlewagons firing but now our own tanks in the hold below us were warming their motors and our ears were packed with the sound of them. Seen but not heard through this din, strange topsy-turvy things were going on around us. A little landing craft full of men, running alongside of us, raised itself gently in the air and with the majesty of slow motion yawed over until it was quite upside down and its open mouth, still filled with men, bit into the water and sank until only a thin line of its keel showed. The geysers that had shown on the beach as we watched, marched out to meet us. Tall plumes of white and gray water rose and fell. A little boat came toward us bobbing out from the beach and passed directly below where we stood. We looked down and saw the hurt men lying there on the bottom—some twisting, some just lying. The two landing craft ahead of us were in now and there was a little stretch of open water between us and shore. The young skipper said, "Here we go now," and the battered old LCT seemed to pick itself up and reach for the land. As we came closer, the men around the geysers of sand on the beach seemed to be playing with them. They ran about amongst them and threw themselves down on the ground and wiggled and twisted. One man, just before we touched, stood right next to a geyser and spun twice around with his arms thrown out.

All these things we saw from the deck as in a trance. When a second boat further to the right of us lifted into the air and capsized, the water around it boiled and spurted. The whole experience of the night, the big Forts flaming and crashing, the horizon burning with the cold flames of the battleships' broadsides, the wild wind and water—all these things blended into a single experience.....

When we grounded and the ramp went down, the moment of child-like wonder was past. From then on it was intensely prosaic. The Colonel and I had one jeep between us, an armored jeep with a sheet of quarter-inch steel instead of a windshield and a .50-caliber machine gun on a pedestal just behind the two front seats. We had a driver and a gunner. We did not want to trust ourselves to the jeep going in, so we tied it on to be pulled ashore by the last tank off, and the Colonel rode on the back of the first tank while I climbed up on the back of the last—the one with the jeep in tow. This was in case something happened to one of us. We had a place marked on the map just inside the first ridge of dunes where we would meet with the tanks from the other landing craft. Our platoon of mechanized cavalry and the glider infantry who were to ride the tanks were to meet us there, too.

The skipper had done a good job for us in landing.... Our nose was in directly opposite a cut in the dunes where a roadway went through. Majestically each of the first five of our tanks dropped its nose down the ramp, waded and waddled across water and beach, upended over the dunes and was out of sight. Halfway over the beach my sixth tank, jerking the jeep behind it, took it into its head to pause and think things over. Sitting on top of it, while it was still on the ramp, I had made a quick appraisal of the beach ahead. Most of the sand geysers were from what I thought must be mortar fire. The mortar shells were dropping short, to the left of where we wanted to go. They did not seem worth more than a mental note that if they came closer one should drop on the far side of the tank. Just about the time the tank stopped, somewhere up in the foothills they changed their range and the shells began going long, reaching over us.

The next thing I knew I was bounced off my vibrating steel perch by the blast of something and I was in the sand back near the jeep that was in tow. One of the men in the jeep, I saw, had been hurt by whatever knocked me off, but it was only a bloody scratch, and the three of us fell to wrestling with the tow-rope to get the jeep loose. When we got it loose I sent it ahead to the Colonel and began to pound on the metal sides of the tank to try to get the driver to pay some attention to me.

We were stopped smack in the only roadway ashore and the whole invasion seemed to be piling up behind us or swirling out of the ruts to follow the jeep around and thus get past us. Men were running clumsily through the sand, swaying from side to side from the awkwardness of their footing and from the gear they carried. All of us had big flat rubber inner-tube-like preservers around us under our arms.

My damn driver couldn't hear me from inside the tank. The tank was buttoned up. There was no way to talk into it. The mortars dropped long and dropped short, each spinning the sand into the air and breaking the air itself open with sharp concussion. Then there was suddenly that fast high note that later on I knew was the shell from an 88—but only knew it later on because when you have heard one close, you don't have to think or remember ever again. You will always be on your face flat before you have time to recognize anything, so instant is the connection between that sound and a reaction to get out of its way. It must have gone a long way past for I don't remember feeling it hit.

There followed a nightmarish five minutes while first I got up and pounded on the tank and then I dived back into the sand as that flick of sound came again. Men were not running past now. Everything was still on the beach around me, everyone flat. I could only think that as long as my tank was there, that gun would keep on firing until it hit it. I climbed up on the front of the tank and pounded on the bullet-proof glass in the driver's slot. Reluctantly, the hatch came up next to me and a head in a football helmet rose from it. I roared into its ear, "Get the hell off this beach." The head disappeared, the hatch closed and finally, finally, finally we began to move again.

We went up over the dune. In the shelter of the sea side of the dune there was a long row of men scrabbling in the sand to make themselves foxholes. I sat, majestic, on the top of the tank but I could not direct it. It waddled along in the tracks in front of it, then the driver turned sharply and went down the inshore edge of the dune.

There were no geysers of sand here. Off to my left were the still waters of the inland lake which I had thought so much about. The water lay calm and peaceful. Beyond, the sloping hillsides were a rich green, with fringes of trees between the fields and woods along the skyline. A mile or two away, that lone steeple I'd seen from the sea rose higher than the trees.

A hundred yards down the beach we came abruptly on the other tanks. Their lids were up and their crews out of them, tearing off the big air scoops that stuck up like bustles on their behinds. The scoops were part of their water-proofing gear. The colonel and the captain of the tank company and several of the sergeants were standing about grinning.

When I slid off to join them, my driver friend spun his tank at right angles,

rolling one tread over a five-gallon can of machine oil which one of the other
tanks had unloaded there. It sprayed me head to foot with black oil. The oil
dripped off my ears and my nose and everybody laughed. We felt very fine to
be ashore in the sunlight. There had been nothing to it.

* * *

Utah beach was a long, narrow stretch of land, beyond which the Germans had
made a lake about two miles wide but shallow enough for infantrymen to wade
across. There was one road through the lake, but the invasion planners had
assumed it would be either destroyed or fortified with barbed wire and mines.
There was also a bluff (part of the old French Maginot Line) where the Germans
had guns capable of smothering the beach with shrapnel. But, as Ingersoll said,
there was nothing to coming ashore on Utah—for three reasons: (1) The two
days of bad weather that had forced the invasion fleet to stay at sea had also
covered it with a blanket of clouds, preventing German reconnaissance planes
from seeing how large the fleet was. As a result, the landing came as a complete
surprise and met little resistance. (2) The preinvasion bombing of the guns on
the Maginot Line had missed the German gun emplacements by at least a quarter
of a mile, but the explosions and concussions apparently panicked the crews
who fled, leaving the guns intact and thousands of rounds of unused ammunition
stacked next to them. (3) The road over the shallow lake was in perfect condition
and unfortified. The Germans must have kept it open for the local population,
or so they could deliver ammunition to their pillboxes on the beach.

As a result, Raff's tank battalion came out of the landing craft and raced
over the road across the lake without a shot being fired. Then Raff and Ingersoll
headed inland, with a small reconnaissance party under the command of an
enthusiastic young officer, who said to the tankers, "Do you realize this is the
first scout car to have penetrated Fortress Europa?"—a thought that must have
pleased Adolf Hitler's number-one enemy, Ralph Ingersoll, who also happened
to be a first-rate journalist.*

By nightfall Raff's group had reached a hill held by a German infantry
battalion. They met a few Eighty-second Airborne gliders coming in for landings
under fire, but they had not yet linked up with General Matthew Ridgway's
command post. So Raff put his tanks in a circle, "like the wagon train in a wild
west movie," says Ingersoll, and stationed glider pilots (who had presumably
slept on cots the night before) on guard. About midnight everyone tried to get
some rest. Ingersoll dropped his canvas roll in a ditch. "I was asleep on it before
I could get it unrolled. Then someone was kicking the hell out of me and it was
a whole four hours later and D plus 1 had begun."

On D + 1 Ingersoll's first assignment was to try to organize the glider pilots

*The five days Ingersoll spent on the beach at Normandy are described in detail in *Top Secret*,
and like the account of his D-day crossing of the Channel, it is recommended reading for anyone
interested in the invasion of Europe or examples of excellent war reporting.

into a combat group to help Raff's men take the hill held by the German battalion. Most of the pilots insisted they did not know how to handle an M-1 and had been told to return to England as soon as they landed their gliders. Brandishing his .45, Ingersoll ordered them to join the fight against the Germans, but within a few hours the young captain leading the assault on the hill reported that most of the pilots had disappeared and he did not have enough men left to rout the Germans.

By this time Ingersoll had corralled more pilots, and he sent them out with the captain, who reported back about noon that he had managed to put an .88 mm out of commission, but the Germans still held the hill. He had only about twelve pilots left of the more than seventy Ingersoll had commandeered. But now Ingersoll had a new problem: Raff had made radio contact with General Ridgway's headquarters, which was only about three miles away and was surrounded by Germans and low on ammunition and medical supplies. Raff and his tanks were planning to break through the German lines surrounding Ridgway. They were still attached to the Fourth Division, whose commander had the right to keep Raff and his tanks if he felt his need was greater, but when Raff told him about Ridgway's plight, the general's reaction was, "Look here, I've got a crazy battle on my hands and I'm fighting in three directions right now and I don't know what I'm up against or what's going on." After a pause he said, "But you pull out of here and I'll put something in to take your place. See if you can't find some way around the town and in to Ridgway."

So Raff and his tanks went to help Ridgway, and Ingersoll and a couple of men were sent back to the beach to scrounge up some ammunition, medical supplies, and a couple of trucks in which to carry them. Ingersoll completed this mission under fire from German pillboxes up the beach and headed back with two loaded trucks. He had traveled only a mile or so inland by the time it was dark, so he parked his small convoy on a hillside and bedded down for the night. When the alarm clock in his head went off, "I woke with an eerily silent dawn breaking," he says. "And that was when it happened. What I recall of its beginning were the two steps I took to look down at the sleeping boys, faces upturned, relaxed in the slumber of babes. It happened in the seconds I stood looking down at their innocence, knowing I would have to awaken them to a harsh reality. Suddenly the whole world stopped and I felt I knew everything in it. I did feel and I did know and I was totally at peace in my soul. As I had never been before nor have been wholly since. . . . I was experiencing total serenity, in a total understanding of the wholeness and delicacy of life itself.

"There is still in me the awareness that I had been granted a miracle—and the knowledge I had at the time of how fleeting it would be. These were my children, lying there, and I did not want to waken them or to break the spell. . . . then I finally stirred them. I felt a very deep sadness inside me. The spell had passed."

The next morning Ingersoll and his boys caught up with the rear of Raff's columns, the breakthrough was made, and the ammunition and medical supplies were delivered to the men who needed them. When Ingersoll made contact with Raff in Ridgway's headquarters, he learned that the general was in touch with only about one-fourth of his division and presumed the rest was lost or scattered too far over the countryside to be of much help.*

With Raff, his tanks, and Ridgway linked up, Ingersoll's D-day assignment was over, and he prepared to look for Bradley's tactical headquarters, then find transportation back to England. His special plans section was still playing a crucial part in the war, convincing Hitler that a large American army under General Patton remained in England preparing for the main assault on Fortress Europa at Calais. As a result, Hitler was holding the German Fifteenth Army in the north, despite the fact that his generals, trying to hold off the attack at Normandy, desperately needed help. It was not until July, and after General Patton's Third Army landed at Normandy, that Hitler finally decided the threat to Calais was a hoax and sent the Fifteenth Army south. By then it was too late. The Allies were established at Normandy and could not be pushed back into the sea.

Well before that, however, Ingersoll was convinced that Hitler's days were numbered. The conviction came at Ridgway's headquarters during a moment when the command post was under fire from a German .88 and Ingersoll was diving for cover. When the screaming of the shells had stopped, Ingersoll looked up from his hedgerow and saw that every officer but one had disappeared into their foxholes; General Ridgway, bareheaded, stood looking down at his officers. Then he said quietly, "I *thought* they were ranging on that radio [that is, firing the .88 in the direction of the radio]. You know, I think we ought to tell them to move it. They might get hurt over there."

Ingersoll was impressed: "Cut off, dwindling in strength, not knowing what next, there was a tension there that could have been snapped by the enemy's locating the CP [Command Post]—where all the wounded and the prisoners were, and the commanding General and his staff, and his communications. One flicker of indecision and that whole tenuous thing you write about as morale would have broken like a glass dropped on stone. It was obviously a crazy thing for the commanding general to do—to stand there without even a helmet on and let the .88 fire break around his head. But it was one of the things he had to do and Ridgway did it with grace and dignity—and great courage.

"The .88 kept on firing; its bursts were now long, now short. After a few more shells, it was obvious that its gunners did not really know where we were but were simply ranging around looking for us. The dangerous moment was past. The show went on.

"I thought to myself, we are here to stay. OVERLORD is going to work."

With Hitler's defeat now in the capable hands of men like General Ridgway, Colonel Raff, and their troops, Ingersoll headed for home. But he would still

---

*Ridgway was wrong. Within a week most of his division had been located. His troops had not been very far from headquarters, but their radios had been smashed and they were out of touch.

have more invasion stories to tell his grandchildren—and the thousands of readers
he presumed his book would have, if he ever got to write it. He found Bradley's
tactical headquarters on D + 4, but as a major who had not graduated from West
Point, he did not have enough clout to get a seat on a plane headed for England.
Then, on D + 6, he ran into his West Point colonel Billy Harris, and together
they began looking for a ride. The first place they tried was an airfield the Allies
had built on a bluff overlooking Omaha beach. Out at the end of an improved
runway was a Flying Fort, ready to take off. Its passengers, Ingersoll and Harris
sooned learned, would include General Eisenhower and Prime Minister Churchill, who had been attending their first conference in France. It turned out that
the pilot was a classmate of Harris's from the academy, and he agreed to put
them both in an unoccupied forward gun pit as stowaways. The illustrious
passengers returned about an hour before sunset, and as the plane took off,
Ingersoll had one of his real scares of the invasion: The Fort had reached the
end of the runway on the cliff overlooking Omaha and *was still not airborne*!
"Well, we would be in good company when we piled up," Ingersoll remembers
thinking, and one can only wonder if the romanticist who was convinced he was
dying of cancer, did not, for one brief moment, relish the *PM* headline proclaiming "EISENHOWER, CHURCHILL, AND INGERSOLL KILLED IN
PLANE CRASH LEAVING NORMANDY."

But Ingersoll had underestimated Harris's classmate and, describing what
happened next, he says: "The Fort's wheels started up exactly at the second they
went off the runway—and down its nose dipped at a sharp enough angle to pick
up the lift it needed to keep us in the air, only just above the breaking waves.
It was a brilliant maneuver."

They had hardly recovered from this scare when they had another. The pilot
was headed for an offshore island, which Ingersoll and Harris knew to be held
by the Germans and fortified with an antiaircraft battery. But apparently the pilot
did not know this. And again Ingersoll's dramatic twist of mind could not help
but create a good story: "I can't remember whether it was Billy or I who pulled
the trouser legs above our heads to get the pilot to put his head down to where
we could gesture and point to the island which was dead on course. 'No, no,
no—enemy held!' God bless aviators' quick reactions. The pilot got the message
and the plane banked 90° just as the first antiaircraft shell broke in the air ahead
of us, where we had been headed. Had the coincidence of Billy Harris' and my
hitchhiking on that plane saved the war? Neither of us will ever know, but *we*
thought so."

The Fort landed at an airport in the country near London, and Ingersoll and
Harris took a commuter train into town. Ingersoll had given up his flat, so he
decided to spend the night at Claridge's where he had been staying just before
the invasion. When he appeared in the uniform he had been wearing for ten
days, covered with dirt and dried diesel fuel, the doorman on duty, without
blinking an eye, said, "Good evening, sir, good to see you back." And inside,
before he could even ask for a room, the receptionist behind the desk said, "I'm

afraid we have no suite vacant, sir. I have only a double to take you to, but I hope you'll find it comfortable."

Ingersoll was now certain there would always be an England.

Back in special plans, Ingersoll had an excited and envious audience, although he confessed that he deserved a reprimand, and got one from Bradley for risking the future and efficiency of his section. But he had learned more about men at war. "In an invasion of hostile shores," he says, "cowards are conspicuous for their absence. The very obvious reason is that it is *all* too scary, and there is no place to run away to—except back into the ocean. If it is too much for a few, and they try to lie down or dig in, they are up again in a few moments, because whatever it is that is ahead of them, it can't be any worse than where they are.

"In the courage department, I know only this: that your throat may be catching with fear when you go into action but the minute you are being shot at you have no emotional reactions whatever. At least I had none. You are a non-human, unmoved by the death and mutilation around you and totally concentrated on whatever action your survival seems to depend. You are not angry and you are not brave; you are inhuman and without feeling.

"Later—much later—you may remember how lucky you were to have survived intact, and shake all over. But you do not recall feeling anything at the time of truth."

Soon after his return to London, Ingersoll's special plans section was transported across the Channel in British speedboats and landed at one of the artificial harbors the British had constructed after the invasion. They were now part of the headquarters of Bradley's very real Twelfth Army, although Ingersoll was still serving with Montgomery's staff as the principal American representative in the deception program. Ingersoll thought that once the Germans realized they had been deceived at Calais, the deception program would be abandoned. He had had invitations to transfer to Colonel Beck's First Infantry or General Ridgway's Eighty-second Airborne but had come to the conclusion that he did not like being shot at and that he had made much more of a contribution in the deception program and as a staff officer than in the field.

So it was a pleasant surprise when one day, soon after he had settled into his tent in the American sector and was pondering which assignment to take, Colonel Strangeways came across the line from the British sector and asked him, literally, to go for a walk in the woods. Strangeways told him that the deception program was to be continued, and asked whether Ingersoll was still interested in being part of it. If he accepted, there would be two conditions: (1) He could *never* reveal or write about his role in the deception program, and (2) he could never again engage in personal combat with the enemy. It was a basic assumption of the British that the Germans would extract information from any captured soldier.

Ingersoll agreed to the conditions, and then, for the first time, he was told about Ultra—one of the main reasons he would not be permitted to go into combat, where he might be captured. In his new capacity, he would be one of the few officers permitted entrance to the small shack where the daily Ultra traffic, decoded from the German radios, was read. Ultra not only could break the German code but unscrambled it so fast that the information could be made available to commanders in the field minutes after it was received.

So, as the battle for Europe began, Ingersoll became an Ultra, in the military parlance of the day. At the same time he was privy to the Most Secret messages that came across from the British, and had access to information about Bradley's plans and operations. He also had orders in his pocket giving him the freedom to travel anywhere on the front or behind it. It was, in an Ingersoll understatement, "a journalistic dream"—and he would put it to good use.

Soon after Ingersoll was approached by Strangeways, General Montgomery came into disfavor with Eisenhower for his failure to take Caen, and General Bradley took his place as commander of the Allied troops in Europe. Ingersoll and his special plans unit returned to Bradley's headquarters. Shortly thereafter the Allies liberated Paris, incidentally providing Ingersoll with enough war stories to fill one whole chapter of his unpublished memoirs. Most of the officers who served with him agreed with Eldredge "that Ingersoll was great fun to be with." To offset the dullness of army life, they set up what Eldredge calls the "Rigors of War Department." Every night Ingersoll would make the martinis, and was usually in charge of ferreting out the girls as well.

With Paris liberated, Bradley sent Patton streaking across the south of France and asked Ingersoll to see if his special plans section could keep the Germans from finding out that his command's southern flank was thus left undefended. Ingersoll said that he could. "We can put a whole corps just south of it, sir. All I will need is a company of infantry with real guns—to keep infiltrators out of the areas where we'll be setting up."

Ingersoll caught up with Patton's headquarters after only an hour's drive. "He was resplendent as ever," says Ingersoll, "complete with pearl-handled pistols and polished boots."

After the salutes Patton said, "At ease, Major, sit down and we'll talk. I got the message that you were coming to save me." Despite the caustic remark, Patton was friendly and made some constructive suggestions about Ingersoll's plans for fooling the Germans into thinking he had left a division behind to cover Bradley's southern flank. Then, as he was about to leave, Ingersoll witnessed a classic "Georgie Patton performance." As Ingersoll tells this story, they were both suddenly startled by a loud voice in the courtyard where Patton's trailer command post was set up. "A buttoned-down armor-encased vehicle was rocketing through the trees to roll up a few feet in front of us. Coming to a full stop, the hatch in its roof opened and there appeared the head and shoulders of a young American lieutenant colonel. Half out of the vehicle, he turned back with a solicitous gesture, obviously giving assistance to someone behind him. Then, scrambling out to get footholds on the ladder down the vehicle's side, he again reached back to give a hand-up—guess who he was bringing to Georgie Patton's for dinner?—no less than a live German general, resplendent in the bemedaled uniform he had chosen for his surrender. He was actually tidying the gold braid on his outfit as his captor gently assisted him to the ground.

"My mouth was still open when Georgie's first bellow shook my ears, 'Stop kissing that Kraut bastard's ass! Who do you think he is? Jesus Christ? Kick his God-damned ass over here and kick it fast.'

"By this time, the poor Kraut brass, an under-sized specimen, was trembling as he staggered the few feet he had to cross to the trailer's balcony. From there, Georgie Patton was looking down on him, legs wide apart, arms akimbo and face a snarl. . . . The quaking representative of the Third Reich was doing what he could to hold himself in attention. He was pale and visibly shaken. At which point, Georgie's tirade ended as abruptly as it began.

"Suddenly, abruptly, and without transitional gestures or remarks, Patton's whole personality seemed to change. His body relaxed, his arms dropped to his side, and he took a step past me to hold out his hand to the 'Kraut bastard' to the latter's (and my) total confusion. He actually helped his tottering prisoner up the caravan steps, pumped his hand warmly and half turned to introduce *me* to him. I hadn't ever expected to shake a Nazi general's hand, during or after the war, but I had no choice then. Patton put his hand on the man's shoulder and said, 'Come, come—relax. We're both professional soldiers. We just happen to be in different corners and you just lost a round.'

"And over his shoulder, towards the caravan's interior, 'Sergeant! Get the general whatever he wants to drink.' And to the general: 'Sit down and rest a spell; there's no reason we shouldn't make some comradely conversation before you have to go.'"

When Patton was gone, Ingersoll and his battalion of radio operators and sound recorders went into action, setting up their rubber division in the woods. He never saw documented proof that this deception worked, but the Germans did not attack Bradley's flank as they could have done. The company of riflemen Patton had promised never showed up, and Ingersoll's battalion had to protect itself from infiltrators with its own rifles and the assistance of the FiFis, as the French called their underground. When his company commander asked, "Where is that damned company of infantrymen you promised me?" Ingersoll finally got the answer from Patton's liaison officer: "The general says to tell Ingersoll that his boy scouts would have learned more about what a real war is like if they had been shot at."

Both Montgomery and Bradley thought the war could be ended quickly, before winter set in, but the British plan called for invading Germany through the lowlands of Holland and across the Hamburg plains, striking directly at Berlin, in hopes of preventing the northern coast of Germany and its capital from falling into Russian hands. The Americans favored an attack through what was called the Frankfurt corridor, where they felt the Germans were weakest. There were not enough supplies, trucks, or gasoline to launch both attacks simultaneously, so in August, according to Ingersoll, Eisenhower split the supplies and transportation between the two generals. And, in Ingersoll's view, "he diverted just enough to break Bradley's momentum without solving Montgomery's problem." He also believed that if Eisenhower had not been so "wishy washy" and had backed either Montgomery *or* Bradley in the fall of 1944, the war would have been over by Christmas. Instead, he hesitated, then backed Montgomery when it was too late, and Montgomery was defeated at the Battle of Arnheim. This caused a lull in the fighting, with the Americans and British regrouping for a final assault in the spring and the Germans, presumably, preparing for a last-ditch defense of the fatherland.

During this lull Ingersoll went along with Bradley's headquarters as the Twelfth Army command moved slowly northeast, finally, in late October, ending up in Luxembourg. Ingersoll went into an army hospital for the removal of the sore on his back, which did prove to be malignant but was not fatal. There was also another personal development when, suddenly, the vivacious and witty Geraldine Morris, looking more beautiful than ever in her UNRA uniform, turned up in Luxembourg and announced that she was now divorced and free to marry Ingersoll. Despite all his efforts to help Geraldine get to London, he had been unsuccessful; she had found the UNRA job on her own initiative. They had corresponded while Ingersoll was in London, and it was obvious from her letters that Geraldine felt strongly about him. In one, written just after the publication of Laura Hobson's novel *The Trespassers*, Geraldine declared that she still loved him—even if everything Laura said about him in her book was true.

Ingersoll, although he had once tried to persuade Geraldine to marry him, was strangely unresponsive when she arrived in Luxembourg. "I was amazed to find myself totally without reaction. As a human being in my life, I suddenly realized with clarity, she simply did not exist. I tried to tell her, with a simplicity that startled me, that I'd become a man so totally involved in the war to which I had committed myself that I was absolutely without feelings of any kind in my heart—towards anybody. As I said this, I knew that I was revealing something that I had not known about myself until that moment. I felt very cold and alone."

Geraldine was sympathetic and understanding: war, she realized, did such things to people, and after it was all over, maybe he would regain his feelings as a human being, and possibly his feelings for her. But they were never close again. "I think Ralph lacks the human quotient" she said, "and could not get along with people, especially women. I would rather not talk about him."

In 1944 Ingersoll could not disagree with Mrs. Morris. "I *was* then, pure and simply, as I never had been before or have been since, a man without human feelings." Ingersoll blamed his reaction on the war and especially the position he was in at the time—as an observer and recorder of one of the most dreadful slaughters in human history. And he says he remembers "thinking about this in the months that followed and feeling that the only honor left me came from my dishonorable trade as a deceiver. At least the con artist's job is to hoodwink the enemy instead of slugging it out with him. It does save lives."

With Bradley's armies stalled (in part because they had outrun their gasoline supplies and in part because of the weather) and strung out along a line running roughly from Antwerp through Aachen and down through Luxembourg, it was the Germans' turn to mount a surprise. Bradley realized he did not have enough men and equipment to remain strong all along this front, and he chose the area around the Ardennes forest to be his weakest point, a "calculated risk," as Bradley later put it. He continued to get reports from his intelligence officers telling him that he had nothing to worry about, that most of the troops in the German lines consisted of home guard and seventeen-year-old kids who would not be ready to fight until spring. With a lull in the fighting, and with a reporter's desire to learn as much about the progress of the war and the decision-making process as he could, Ingersoll had asked for, and been given, permission to sit in on the meetings of Bradley's G-2 (intelligence) officers. This led to a curious incident, which Ingersoll thought might someday put him before a congressional investigation committee. In the middle of December Bradley's G-2 officers were so convinced of the weakness in the German lines in the Ardennes that they were urging him to attack, arguing that one platoon of tanks could knife through the lines like butter. But Bradley refused to move. Finally, at one frustrating meeting, a G-2 officer complained, "How can we get it through the boss's head? Dammit, we're all writing militarese. Can't someone put it in purple prose?"

Another officer suggested they give the job to Ingersoll, the professional writer.

So Ingersoll wrote the next G-2 "Enemy's Capabilities" assessment in his "purple prose"—and the assessment was the last one given to Bradley before the Germans surprised everyone with their breakthrough in the Ardennes, leading to the Battle of the Bulge. By blacking out for the first and last time all radio messages discussing their intentions to move a whole army from the Hamburg plains to the Ardennes—and with the help of the weather, which restricted reconnaissance—the Germans took Bradley by surprise. "It was a shock I can hardly forget," Ingersoll recalls, "turning up a little late at the morning briefing on December 16 to hear a white-faced roomful of my fellow officers being told that a major panzer attack had broken our front lines wide open—about thirty miles from where we stood." Knowing how the American political system worked, and aware that the last, reassuring intelligence report to Bradley *before* the Battle of the Bulge and the isolation of Bastogne was in his prose, Ingersoll was sure he would be the one to testify in Washington and would possibly even become the scapegoat. But, in fact, he need not have worried; he learned later that both Eisenhower's and Montgomery's staffs had been given the same appraisal of the situation by their own intelligence officers—if in a somewhat less lurid style.

The Germans were moving so fast that within a few days they had completely surrounded the American garrison at Bastogne. Bradley then called a meeting of his general officers to which Ingersoll was also summoned. The general had decided to pull Patton's Third Army out of the line and send it to the relief of Bastogne—at night and across icy roads! The meeting was intense, and "it was just as I arrived," says Ingersoll, "that a radio telephone call came through from Bastogne itself. Bradley had the besieged commander there on the line to ask him if he felt he could not hold out until we could break through to him. Patton was present, too. He was striding up and down the room, not the cocky man I remembered, but one with lines of grim concern etched on his face."

When he signed off with Bastogne, Bradley spoke to the assembled officers: "The Third Army is to start coming North tonight. There is no way the movement can be accomplished without all its radios talking in the clear—and the vehicles will have to use their headlights. Is there anything you and your people," Bradley continued, looking at Ingersoll, "can think of to throw the Germans off—about where they are going to strike?"

Ingersoll, with all eyes in the room on him, replied, "Yes, sir. We can do . . . something."

After a moment of silence Bradley said, "Then do it"—and turned away.

His idea had come to him, Ingersoll said, as a flash: If they could not keep Patton's movement quiet, the next best thing would be to flood the airwaves with so many messages about so many different maneuvers that the Germans would not have time to sort them all out and decide which ones indicated where Patton was really going to attack.

Within hours of what Ingersoll calls his "cheeky yes, sir" to Bradley, his transmitters were on the air from dozens of different locations—and this bit of trickery, Ingersoll learned, did work. When the first Third Army troops arrived at Bastogne, the German command was completely confused about where the rest of Patton's army might attack. This was Ingersoll's last experience in deception, and its success was probably responsible for Bradley's awarding him the Legion of Merit and promoting him to lieutenant colonel.

Ingersoll remained on the fringes of the fighting during the Battle of the Bulge, although he did make one quick flight to London to pick up a half ton of aerial photographs of the German rear lines. On the trip he was grounded in Belgium and had to make the rest of the trip in a three-quarter-ton truck, driving mostly at night, blacked out and over icy roads. He also made several trips to Bastogne after it was relieved, always filing information in the back of his mind for future writing.

Pulling Patton out of the line, and sending the Third Army to the relief of Bastogne, stunned the Germans and marked the turning point in the Battle of the Bulge. This, however, did not prevent General Montgomery from claiming credit for the victory, and he held a controversial press conference (which, many years later, he admitted was a mistake) to make sure the world would have his version of what happened. During the battle Eisenhower had temporarily placed the American First and Ninth armies under Montgomery's command, and now Ingersoll and others on Bradley's staff were convinced that Montgomery's press conference was primarily intended to force Ike to let the First and Ninth armies remain with him. Ingersoll, who had access to the British cables, now felt he had come "to know more about our Allies politico-military situation than our enemy's." The British, he was convinced, had decided that to keep power in the postwar world they would need victories—which General Montgomery had not been doing a very good job of supplying. So, after Montgomery's press conference, Ingersoll launched a furious campaign to warn Bradley of the clear and present danger of a British power play.

It did not take much to convince Bradley that Montgomery was challenging him. He was furious over the field marshal's press conference and refused to hear any suggestion that the American First and Ninth armies might remain permanently under British command, which would, in effect, make Montgomery the primary field commander in Europe. So Bradley phoned Ike, expressed his dissatisfaction, and said that neither he nor Patton would serve under Montgomery.

But neither Ingersoll nor Chet Hanson, Bradley's chief aide, believed the phone call to Ike was enough. Ingersoll says he convinced Hanson that the only way to save Bradley's command was to hold a press conference, countering Montgomery's in which Bradley would explain what had *really* happened in the Battle of the Bulge—that is, that his daring had saved the day, as well as Montgomery's flanks.

Eisenhower had issued orders that press conferences about the progress of the war were to emanate only from Supreme Command Headquarters, now located in Paris. Bradley's command was stationed in Luxembourg; and everyone knew that because of the politics involved, Eisenhower would not permit him to contradict Montgomery's version of the battle. Ingersoll asked Hanson to arrange for a fifteen-minute interview, in which he would persuade Bradley to hold a press conference. Bradley agreed to hear Ingersoll's arguments, setting the stage for what Ingersoll calls perhaps his most important contribution to the war in Europe. The two men sat in armchairs in Bradley's office; the general was tired and depressed. For nearly fifteen minutes Ingersoll presented his case, articulating with as much persuasion as possible what he thought would happen if Montgomery's version of the Battle of the Bulge were allowed to stand on the record. He concluded with the comment: "I believe I know what I am talking about, General. Unless you can let the world know what the real situation is, the First and Ninth armies will remain under Montgomery's command."

By the end of Ingersoll's speech, Bradley was pacing the room, and when he replied it was as if he were speaking to himself: "But I can't do it. The army is my life, Ingersoll. A direct order is a direct order and I cannot break it." Then he paused and looked straight at Ingersoll: "But those are American soldiers we are talking about. I do not believe he is a competent general. I have no right to commit so many sons of American mothers to his judgment. . . . I know you are right, but this is a decision I have to make myself. Can you get it through your head how hard a one it is for me to make?"

"I believe I do, General," Ingersoll replied, "but I don't believe Ike has the guts to tell the truth." Nor did he believe President Roosevelt or General George Marshall would let him.

After another pause Bradley said, "Tell Chet to get the press up here to-morrow morning—without informing Paris."

The next day Bradley held his press conference and read a statement written by Hanson and Ingersoll, telling what had actually happened in the Battle of the Bulge. He added comments of his own and used a map to help explain the situation. During the press conference Ingersoll remained out of sight at the back of the room, not wanting to be questioned by any of his former colleagues. When it was over, Bradley asked if there were any final questions. "Some damn fool," as Ingersoll describes him, "got to his feet to challenge Bradley. 'But there are still German troops in the pocket; what will they do now?' At which Omar broke out his famous grin reserved for when things had been going well: 'Yes, there are a few that haven't been able to get out yet. What will they do? Oh, they'll rattle the bars of their cage.'"

Eisenhower's headquarters remained silent, and, as Bradley has said, "We heard no more from those quarters about Monty being the hero of the Bulge and the British press clamor to nominate him land commander abruptly ceased."

Ingersoll did not talk again with the general during the war, but he was personally convinced it was General Bradley who played the most important role in the defeat of Adolf Hitler. As for Omar the man, Ingersoll says, "I could set down the names of at least one hundred of his officers (besides myself) who, if the choice had been put to them starkly, might unhesitatingly have chosen to give up their lives to save his. Omar Bradley had that capacity of inspiring a combination of admiration and love.... When he was away from Headquarters the young officers were almost frightened; when he came back, even though they only saw him striding through the hall, everything was all right again, father had come home. The breakthrough would be held and the Germans beaten; Omar would know what to do. I never heard him say a harsh word to anyone."

Most of the rest of the war Ingersoll spent in the map room, Ultra cubicle, and intelligence offices, storing material for the book now definitely taking shape in his mind. And he began to see the war as a sporting exercise approached differently by the participants: for the Americans it was much like a football game; for the British, a cricket match; and for the Russians, a chess game. The Germans, he says, "lost the war because war wasn't a game of any kind to them. They took war *too* seriously."

Ingersoll recalls being rather cynical about war as the games moved toward their inevitable conclusion: "Coming out of the unworldly preoccupation of the map room and running head on into the realities of why we were at war ... was a huge experience." And one of his most moving experiences came near the end, when a platoon of tanks took a small city named Landsberg. He had heard that there was a Nazi concentration camp there, and out of sheer curiosity he went to see what it was like: "I came back chastened and shaken." The sight reinforced his belief that stopping the Fascist idea was "a reason really good enough to die for." And he was reminded again of his intense hatred of Adolf Hitler, the man who had disrupted his life and turned him into an unfeeling human being.

When the American troops finally met the Russians in Germany, their lower-echelon officers had several dinner meetings featuring mountains of food and gallons of vodka, which the Americans countered with bourbon and gin. The Russians then introduced entertainment, and the escalation of rank and ceremony continued, with the Americans finally throwing in George Patton and his pearl-handled pistols; the general sent the Russians home as impressed as they were drunk. The next dinner would be Marshal Georgy Zhukov's show and then it would be Bradley's turn, and as everyone at headquarters knew, it would have to be a production. So Ingersoll was ordered to produce a program for Bradley's dinner. The objective, Ingersoll knew, was not just to provide an evening of entertainment, but to impress upon the Russian commander and Premier Joseph Stalin, who would surely hear about the show, the competence of the U.S. Army, the unique national character of the American people—their vitality, strength, and resourcefulness—the high standard of living enjoyed by Americans, *and* that our defeat of the Wehrmacht on the western front was no mere accident or by-product of Russian gallantry on the eastern front.

Ingersoll had a week to prepare his plan, which he called "Imagination's Finest Hour." The menu—to be prepared by Major Jack Kriendler of "21," whom Ingersoll knew to be somewhere in Europe—was to consist of a variety of regional dishes from Florida, Iowa, Maine, Kansas City, California, and New England, with coffee from New Orleans, all preceded by very dry martinis— only three to an officer because he wanted them sober for the big show. The music would be by Benny Goodman in a program dedicated to Glenn Miller, who had been killed during the war. The skits would be written in New York by Harold Ross and his *New Yorker* wits and performed by GIs and Red Cross girls. The dancing would be American jitterbugging by the troops and the Red Cross girls, and the musical finale would be provided by the Rockettes, flown over from New York.

Then Bradley would step forward to make a few toasts and announce the finale: an enactment of the storming of the German west wall—complete with pillboxes and tank traps—by American assault troops. The dinner was to be held on the bluff overlooking a river, on the other side of which would be a duplication of the west wall. There would be shelling and dive-bombing of the wall before the troops crossed the river in boats to storm ashore, hurling grenades and firing flamethrowers, which would produce a spectacular orange light in the approaching twilight, when the show was to be staged.

For a while the entire headquarters staff was talking with excitement and anticipation about the plan, and Bradley is reported to have chuckled when he read it. But then he said, "Tell Ingersoll we haven't finished *this* war yet—and we ought to before we start another."

What actually happened at the dinner was an exchange of gifts and the usual drinking and merriment.

V-E day—May 8, 1945—Ingersoll spent with a somber group of fellow headquarters officers praying in a little chapel near Berlin. And in the confusing days after the armistice, he was in and out of a number of assignments, turning down one tempting offer to stay in Paris for a year to write the army's history of the war in Europe.

When the point system was announced, Ingersoll had more than enough to request his return to the States, and he was immediately put to work in the deepest recesses of the Pentagon writing the story of the deception plan he had worked on in Europe. When he was done, he felt it was "the best and most comprehensive piece I'd ever gotten on paper"—which made it all the more discouraging when he learned, years later, that the document had been lost.

When he arrived in New York after completing the Pentagon assignment, he could not find any place to stay, but Sherman Billingsley of the Stork Club found him a room at the Hotel Lexington. Then Ingersoll did the first thing any soldier on leave does when he arrives in town: He settled down at the telephone with his little black book, trying to line up a date. But first, he decided, he must call to thank Elaine Cobb, whom he had met at that curious dinner at Camp Edwards, for sending him reviews of *The Battle Is the Payoff*. The phone call produced his best war story ever—"the only true miracle of the whole business," he says. When he could not reach Elaine at her Time Inc. office, he became irritated and began calling repeatedly, leaving messages for her to call him back. Finally, at around five P.M., she returned his calls, and although he had not said anything about going out to dinner, she said she was busy that night, but invited him to come around for a drink at her apartment, which was only a few blocks from his hotel. He went, and when she opened the door, the miracle happened! "We stood there both speechless and knew that we were totally and irrevocably in love. Almost total strangers to each other, we simply stepped forward and embraced without a single spoken word."

Several hours later one of them—Ingersoll cannot remember which—said, "My God, we've got to tell Morty."

In the summer of 1945 Captain Mortimer Howland Cobb was commanding a sub chaser in the Gulf of Mexico. Ingersoll had not seen or heard from him since their brief days together at Camp Edwards in 1942, although he still remembered Cobb as a "strange man." And apparently he had not changed. Using his clout as a lieutenant colonel and telling the officer of the day at the Pensacola Naval Base that this was an Emergency Priority Call 1, Ingersoll was able to reach Captain Cobb on board his ship. Soon a voice on the other end said, "This is Captain Cobb, Colonel."

"Morty, I've got through to tell you that Elaine and I are in love with each other. We will marry each other as soon as I can arrange it."

There were thirty seconds of silence, and then Cobb's voice came through loud and clear enough to be audible to Elaine, whose head was next to Ingersoll's:

"Bully! I am so happy for you both," he said, adding graciously, "You can't know how happy you've made me!"

After a few minutes' conversation with Elaine, Cobb then said he had a favor to ask of the colonel, and Ingersoll took the phone, eager to do anything he could to help the cooperative husband: "Yes, Morty?"

"Colonel, could you use your connections in Washington to help me get the command I want—a troopship in the Pacific?"

Ingersoll said he would try, and, in fact, one of the last things he did before leaving the service himself was to obtain for Cobb the command of the ship he wanted.

Ingersoll had decided long before he returned to the States that he wanted to get out of the service as soon as possible so as to be free of army censors when he wrote his book. He felt that finishing off the Japanese would be a routine matter and, besides, he did not have the same emotional commitment to the defeat of Emperor Hirohito as he did to the defeat of Adolf Hitler. His age (forty-four) and tour of duty in Europe gave him enough points for a discharge, but when he went down to Washington to wind up his military career, there was a problem. An admiral in the Pacific, whose name he has forgotten, wanted Ingersoll to serve on his public-relations staff, and the request had been granted by the army. Ingersoll was crushed when a sergeant in the Pentagon told him the news, but when he saw Ingersoll's reaction, he said, "Don't worry, Colonel, we'll find a way to handle it."

And they did. Ingersoll's discharge papers were prepared, and the orders transferring him to the Pacific were delayed so that both would be waiting, on the same morning, on the desk of the Pentagon general who had to approve them. The general always arrived at ten thirty sharp. At ten o'clock that particular morning Ingersoll's cooperative sergeant walked through the general's office and slipped Ingersoll's Pacific orders into the outgoing basket. The general signed Ingersoll's discharge, and he was on his way to New York before the active-duty orders were ever discovered.

So Ralph Ingersoll's personal fight with fascism was over. He was one of the first Americans to declare war on Adolf Hitler; he stayed the course to V-E day and played a significant role in his defeat, probably getting as near the top of the army command as any civilian could while at the same time seeing his share of action. He came out of the war with seven Bronze Stars (signifying action in a war zone) and an Arrowhead (for going over with the troops on D day). Although in his opinion the war, more than any single thing, prevented him from making his newspaper a success, he had no regrets. As he said many years later, "If I had not been in the army, I would never have met the mother of my two sons. I can never regret that. I suppose the strangest part is that I do not really regret any of my experiences as an amateur soldier. I am horrified by what one of my sons went through in Viet Nam but 'my war' bore no resemblance to the one he got entangled in. I can still think of mine as an honest one and remain proud that I engaged in it. We did fight Evil and cast out Devils, even though I doubt if many of us ever thought of it in those terms.

   "But mainly I think it is the feeling of being united with one's fellow men in a common effort that binds veterans—of any war. . . . I am glad it was won— and that I was in it."

The colonel and his lady (Elaine) share a soda

The 1946 Ingersoll Christmas card

14: The Taming of Ralph Ingersoll

When Elaine Keiffer Cobb met Ralph Ingersoll at Camp Edwards in 1942, she was working on the staff of *Life*, and although the corridors of Time Inc. were full of Ingersoll haters, she was not one of them, despite the fact that she was also a friend of Clare Luce. For Elaine it was obviously a case of love at first sight, intensified by a dash of what appears to be pure hero worship, the extent of which can be seen in her own writings. In a piece written for the *Sarah Lawrence Alumnae Review* after their marriage, she said: "Ralph Ingersoll, editor, writer, soldier and U.S. Citizen has spent many of his 46 years trying to make a 'better system.'" Later, in a letter to her housekeeper, Nellie, she wrote: "Mr. Ingersoll is one of the great men of our times." And although Ingersoll may have impressed some as being primarily out for number one, to Elaine he was a dedicated humanitarian: "You've lived such a wonderful life," she wrote him, "all of it unselfish and all of it for others."

Ingersoll argues that Elaine proved his psychoanalysis had been successful; now, at least, he was able to fall in love with the right woman for him. He came back from the war a very eligible bachelor with many former girl friends to choose from: "Bent as I was on falling in love, one would have said I was ripe for a fall, for an impulsive decision. Yet the woman I fell in love with, intensely and naturally, fell in love with me—and became the mother of my two sons. I had with her a totally happy experience."

People who knew Elaine remember her as a very big woman, who seemed to tower above the guests at the parties she covered for *"Life* Goes to a Party," which became her regular beat at the magazine. She was very bright, alert, and vivacious, and she loved parties, four or five of which she had to attend every week. This led some of her colleagues to feel she and Ingersoll were an unlikely couple. "Here was Ralph," said one, "who was immersed in causes. He was a reformer. He didn't give a damn about some party in Southampton. To me, they were a superb example of opposites attracting one another."

With Cobb giving no indication that he would resist, and with the blessings of her parents (who apparently were never too fond of her first husband), Elaine was anxious for a divorce and remarriage. The problem was how, with wartime restrictions on transportation and gas, they would get to Reno. Elaine had a friend in government who promised her two tickets on a commercial airline. When the promise fell through, Ingersoll faced perhaps the greatest challenge of his wartime years. And the man who had, with considerable help, defeated the Wehrmacht, went into action: He called Marshall Field's wife, Ruthie, and reduced her to tears with his story of true love denied its ultimate reward at the altar. She ordered one of the many Field automobiles, which were being stored on blocks in their garage on Long Island, to be made ready; and the drivers of *PM*'s trucks, who had gasoline ration stamps for delivering their papers, chipped in to give Ingersoll enough stamps for two transcontinental trips.

So Ralph and Elaine drove to Nevada and spent six weeks fulfilling Nevada residency requirements at a cottage on Lake Tahoe, where he dictated the first draft of his book about the war—and Elaine had the first and only emotional crisis in their marriage. They had hardly settled into their cottage on the lake, when there was a phone call that clearly disturbed her. "It was Morty," she said as she hung up. "He's on his way to San Francisco to pick up the ship you got him and the plane is stopping in Reno around midnight. He wants us to meet him."

Ingersoll was appalled and could tell from the look on Elaine's face that she was distressed—enough perhaps, if Cobb pulled a scene at the airport, to prevent her from going through with the marriage. Ingersoll tells the story of the night they drove to the Reno airport to meet Cobb: "Out of the darkness of the sky came the DC-3 and up to the floodlights it taxied noisily. As its engines sputtered into silence, its door opened and its lone deplaning passenger stepped out, Captain Mortimer Howland Cobb in a crisply pressed and spotless uniform. Elaine stepped hesitantly forward—while I hung discreetly back a few yards to one side."

Then, said Ingersoll, Cobb drew himself to his full height, marched past Elaine, and saluted: "I just wanted to thank you for everything you've done for me—sir," he said. Out of the corner of his eye, he saw Elaine and turned to grin at her. Later Ingersoll would comment, "I never really knew Mortimer Cobb but I doubt if he had even the remotest idea of how good a job he'd made of setting two people free."

They were married on August 9, 1945, at Lake Tahoe, and one of the first people Elaine informed was Clare Luce. "I know you used to know Ralph well," she wrote Clare, "and he has a lot of feeling about the old days with you and Harry—and is a great admirer of your courage and character." Ingersoll had, of course, not always been so admiring of Clare, but he went along with Elaine's friendship, saying that he considered Clare a "natural force, evoking no emotion. You couldn't hate Clare for being Clare anymore than you could hate a hurricane for being a hurricane."

Hurricane Clare remembered Elaine as a "very delightful girl" but was surprised that such a sweet, unsophisticated woman would appeal to Ralph. She said that she and her husband did not see much of the Ingersolls, "because Ralph was not very friendly toward either me or my husband." She had no comment on the marriage, except to refer to Elaine as "long suffering."

Laura Hobson's reaction was somewhat more emotional. She was in Hollywood flirting with a screenwriting career when she read in the papers about the marriage. She immediately had a "bout of depression" and, as she recalls it in her memoirs, "was suddenly inundated with memories of the years when I had loved him and overwhelmed with guilt at being ignoble enough to be jealous." After reading Mrs. Hobson's memoirs, published in 1983, Clare Luce commented, "Poor Laura, I think she's still in love with Ralph."

For their honeymoon, Ingersoll and Elaine went to California where the San Francisco press reported on the glamorous couple and interviewed Ingersoll, who suggested total surrender by the Japanese and said the United States would not go to war with Russia. Then they returned to Shadow Rock Farm, and Ingersoll was once again a hot item for the press: The editor of *PM* was said to be one of the army officers Congress would be looking at in their investigation of rapid promotions in the armed forces; *Life* reported the wedding with a picture of Ingersoll in his army uniform and Elaine, who, they said, had married "*PM*'s leftist editor"; the *Hollywood Reporter* quoted Ingersoll as saying Marshall Field would soon publish another edition of *PM* on the West Coast and in many other cities; Danton Walker's syndicated "Broadway" column said: "There'll be a drastic clean up in *PM*'s personnel when Col. Ralph Ingersoll returns. And in another column Walker predicted that Ingersoll would run for Congress on the Democratic ticket in New York's Fifth District. The *New Yorker* reported that he was back in Connecticut, would not return to *PM* until he had rewritten his book, and quoted him as saying: "I read 15 newspapers a day and write notes to my managing editor. I'm trying to find out what the hell's going on in the States." As for *PM*, he predicted that in five years its circulation "will be clearing millions."

Settled at Shadow Rock, Ingersoll and Elaine were ecstatically happy, and they both began to gain weight. "A chubby aproned lady," as Lillian Ross

described Elaine in her *New Yorker* "Talk" piece, told Ross she had gained
fourteen pounds in as many days. Ingersoll was deep in the second draft of his
book, and the advance notices appearing in the *New Yorker* and elsewhere were
already giving indications that it would be more typically Ingersoll than his
previous book about the war: "People have the idea Patton was the most important
general. Fact is, all Patton's victories were based on Bradley's strategy. Omar
deserves having that known. That doesn't mean Patton wasn't a good general.
Patton was nuts, but he was a wonderful general."

But Patton was not the only general Ingersoll would put in the shadows of
the spotlight he intended to focus on Bradley. General Eisenhower and Field
Marshal Montgomery would also be portrayed as mere mortals, who were
fumbling and ineffective during most of the war. Ingersoll happened to be in
Washington the day Eisenhower flew back from Europe, and he was amazed:
"I found the whole city was excited by his homecoming. It was the first time I
had ever thought of him as our nation's idol. How ignorant we had all been in
Europe and how ignorant the American people were, about what had really gone
on there and who deserved what laurels."

Ingersoll would try to correct the impression that it was Eisenhower, Montgomery, and Patton who had won the war, and he would give the credit where
it was due—to General Bradley. But, he said, "the one thing I made certain
was that when the book was published, Omar Bradley could honestly say he
had never known that I was writing one and had never seen a word of it before
publication." A half dozen senior officers of the Twelfth Army Group read the
manuscript, but they all kept Ingersoll's secret, aware of how much it would
hurt Bradley if Eisenhower could accuse him of having any knowledge of the
book. They also concurred with Ingersoll's view of what had happened between
the top command posts in Europe, although Ingersoll obviously saw things from
Bradley's point of view, as did, naturally, the Twelfth Army Group officers who
reviewed his manuscript. One of his colleagues, however, did not agree with
Ingersoll's thesis that the British were manipulating the Americans, and that the
Russians could be trusted. Although Ingersoll does not recall this, Wentworth
Eldredge says that at one time he was going to coauthor the book about the war,
but told Ingersoll, after seeing an outline, "Ralph, it wasn't like this. I don't
like it." He did, however, agree with Ingersoll's appraisal of Bradley's role and
Montgomery's failings, and his contention that undue credit was given to the
supreme commander. "Eisenhower we called the chiseler," he says. "Twelfth
Army Group hated Eisenhower. If we could have killed him we would have."

Ingersoll's case for his general was simple: "It was observing Omar Bradley
in Command that made me understand, for the first time, that there really are
. . . truly great Generals. . . . I used the word genius cautiously, but I do believe
that it can be applied to a man whose judgments prove consistently right when
elementary common sense told me that it was impossible that they could be,
given the problems confronting the man making them. . . . There will never be

another like him because there can never be another war like the Second World War."

Ingersoll placed the book with Harcourt Brace, the publisher of *The Battle Is the Payoff*, which annoyed Marshall Field who had just bought Simon and Schuster and felt his house should have first option on it. As Ingersoll explains it, "I did not want Marshall to think that he owned me." Harcourt Brace decided on the title *Top Secret*, although Ingersoll wanted to call it "High-Level Horseshit," which he says, is "what junior officers at headquarters called orders they didn't like that were handed down for them to execute." Also, the real top secret project he had worked on—the deception program—could not be mentioned in the book because of his promise to the British never to reveal its existence. Working at a furious pace from dawn to dusk, often dictating to three stenographers at a rate of ten thousand words a day, Ingersoll completed the book before the end of the year, turned it in to Harcourt Brace, and waited for the furor he knew would result when it was published in the spring.

* * *

With his book finished, Ingersoll could no longer put off returning to *PM*. He had tried to forget the paper when he went into the army, in part because his memories of it were so unpleasant, and in part because he was convinced he would probably never return. But after he survived Normandy and his cancer operation, the occasional copies of the paper and the periodic reports from Ginny Schoales that came in the mail could not help but remind him that someday he would have to return to his new kind of newspaper. "I was scareder of the idea of going back," he says, "than of the German army. The whole memory of *PM* was distasteful and revolting."

So as the European war came to an end in the spring of 1945 and Ingersoll's discharge from the army was more than a dream, he began to make "a hobby," as he put it, of reexamining *PM*, and he came to two firm conclusions: (1) The paper was a complete failure; and (2) the failure was one hundred percent his fault. While acknowledging that he had failed to raise enough money and had allowed an inadequate staff to be hired, he felt also that he was "responsible solely and simply for failure to meet the combined challenges of those who wanted *PM* to be what they wanted rather than what I conceived." The new kind of newspaper was to have been a crusade, all right—but "a crusade not for any political or social reform, but simply against the stupidity, the lack of imagination and ingenuity—and the occasional venality—of the Big Business American newspaper of the twentieth century."

The real problem narrowed down, he felt, to the question of who was boss. He had foreseen the challenge from capital and felt he had met that, but he had failed to see the challenge from labor: "I lacked the courage of my convictions that I and I alone was qualified to hire and fire my own newspaper's staff."

When the Newspaper Guild challenged his right to fire anyone he wanted, he should have "stopped the show . . . and said NO. Bargain on wages and hours? Until hell freezes over. Bargain on my right to fire and hire . . . until I have a staff that I believe is capable of carrying out my ideas? Not for a single minute!" But, he said, he simply lacked the moral courage to commit his loyal employees to a life-or-death showdown—although he decided in Europe that he would have won it. He also believed that, morally, he was wrong not to commit his staff to a showdown with the guild because their lives would have been hurt less if he had lost the battle and been forced to shut down *PM*.

As he prepared to return in January of 1946, he knew what he had to do: He had to start over, regain control of his paper and hire the kind of people he felt capable of turning out the paper he wanted *PM* to be. Certainly, in his opinion, the triumvirate of Lewis, Lerner, and Leake were not publishing that kind of paper. And Field must have agreed because he urged Ingersoll to return.

Even before he appeared at the new *PM* offices at 21 Hudson Street, Ingersoll had begun meeting with some of his staff at his apartment, and it did not take him long to discover that regaining control of the paper and eliminating the still existing conflict between the pro-Communists and the anti-Communists was not to be easy. For one thing. he had returned home "officially a hero," as he put it. "You weren't supposed to talk straight to a hero—to tell him the Facts of Life, which were that the world had been going right on around in his absence . . . and that, whatever they said about his right to his old job back, 'things had changed.'" At the weekly meetings with his staff he was given hints that while he was away, there had been disloyalty, especially from Lewis and Leake. And what, he wondered, was the significance of Max Lerner's having been made a director of the company? Lerner was, after all, Lewis's man, not his. When Ingersoll began making inquiries about Lerner, the word got out that he felt Lerner was trying to take over the paper, which made Lerner feel he had to reassure Ingersoll (as he did at dinner one night) that he had no ambitions whatsoever beyond his present job as editorial page editor.

In one meeting with John P. Lewis, Ingersoll was "bewildered" by the managing editor's theory of journalism as practiced at *PM*—that is, that truth was best arrived at by balancing the pro-Communist and the anti-Communists on the staff. Lewis was amazed, says Ingersoll, when he announced his intention to have a showdown with the union and to let them know who was running *PM*. Lewis was afraid that the firing and hiring Ingersoll contemplated would involve them in another fight with the guild, and he was obviously disturbed at the thought of disrupting what he now considered a smooth-running machine— although he did agree with Ingersoll that the product would be better.

Ingersoll, in fact, thought the paper was dreadful, and one of the first things he did in January was to write Field two long letters defining the problem and suggesting alternative solutions. "The paper has turned into a reasonably competent and reliable, if somewhat dull and monotonous, special pleader," he said. "It has almost entirely abandoned its efforts to be a complete newspaper. And its headlines, its feature writers and the play it gives the material that comes to it, all confirm the opinion that it makes its living nowadays pamphleteering, chiefly for racial and religious tolerance, with some interest to the consumer on the side [and] against a general background of sympathy for the underprivileged."

When Ingersoll had first come back, Field had reported that the paper was finally "in the black." But it was quickly apparent that *PM*'s solvency was primarily due to wartime price controls, and as soon as they were lifted, the paper started losing money—as much as five thousand to six thousand dollars a week by March. Ingersoll believed they had two courses: either improve quality in an effort to publish the kind of newspaper Ingersoll originally had in mind or cut back the staff and the operation dramatically to produce what would, in effect, to be a self-supporting crusading pamphlet for *PM*'s loyal, hard-core readers. Ingersoll, of course, favored the first alternative but conceded that it would cost a lot more money.

The discussions with Field and Lewis in the first weeks after his return revolved around several points:

1. Ingersoll felt the time had come to hire the Associated Press wire, which would enable the paper to broaden its news coverage. He thought that the *Chicago Sun* bureau was doing a good job covering Washington, and that by using the *Sun* material and the Associated Press, they could cut back their own Washington office substantially.

2. He wanted to hire a number of new reporters and feature writers, paying them a least $15,000 a year, and he began quietly to talk with candidates, although his early conversations were discouraging. When he approached Paul Thompson, the young colonel he had met in the army, Thompson told him he had offers from Time Inc. (for $18,000) and *Reader's Digest* (for $25,000). Ingersoll advised him to go with DeWitt Wallace at the *Digest*. And Archibald MacLeish, although writing that he was honored by an invitation to join Ingersoll on *PM*—because "you and I have always been able to work together with complete understanding"—declined because he felt working for *PM* would be so demanding it would not leave time for his own writing.

3. And there was the question of *PM*'s editorial policy. Although Ingersoll came back from the war regretting that *PM* had become a crusading pamphlet, he himself did not intend to give up crusading. In his discussions with Lewis, and in one long memo, Ingersoll reminded his managing editor that *PM* had gained its early momentum and retained its hard-core loyalists because it had been a "free newspaper willing to slug it out for the people . . . and our franchise is still in old-fashioned crusading journalism."* The new crusades would be *against* the "warmakers and warmongers"; *for* the United Nations (providing it did its job and did not revert to "discredited diplomatic doubletalk"); *for* keeping prices down; *against* unplanned production; *for* decent housing; *for* developing

---

*Because the memorandum contains probably the best summation of Ingersoll's postwar journalistic, economic, and political philosophy, extracts from it are reprinted as appendix 3.

atomic energy in the people's interest; and, perhaps most significant, *for* merging the best of "parliamentary capitalism" and "socialization," which was what he was convinced the American people wanted—and what he, personally, wanted.

On the weekend of March 2 and 3, at Field's house at Lloyd's Neck on Long Island, Field and Ingersoll went over his plans for a revitalized *PM*. As Ingersoll noted in the diary he kept during this period: "Marshall and I had for the first time an honest difference of opinion on an important subject"—that is, sale of advertising. Field said quite frankly he wanted to see it in *PM*. In "as friendly a way as possible," Ingersoll says, he told Field "the paper was certainly his, even if I had created it, and I felt I should bow out" if he insisted on taking advertising now. Field listened carefully to Ingersoll's plans for *PM* and his estimate that it would take another $300,000 to $400,000 and a year and a half to fulfill them. Field finally agreed to go along with Ingersoll, *if* he did not rule out the possibility of someday selling advertising and if the new capital would be spent on improving the paper and not on promoting it. He also wanted Ingersoll to present his plan to *PM*'s board, which, according to attorney Louis Weiss, Field viewed as a sort of town meeting where all conflicting points of view could be heard.

The board met on Tuesday and endorsed continuation, for the time being, of the policy of not taking advertising, but it passed a number of directives that left everyone confused as to how much it was willing to spend to put Ingersoll's plans into effect. "After sweating over the directives reached by the Board in the last five minutes of play," Lewis wrote Ingersoll, ". . . when you strip off the unessentials . . . you find a strange contradiction . . . we have elected, first, to retrench until it hurts and then, on top of that, we have decided on generous expansion." Lewis was also convinced that if they cut back the Washington office and claimed "economy," as they were planning to do, they would be asking for trouble from the Newspaper Guild.

That point did not worry Ingersoll. But he, too, was confused by the board's action, so he scheduled a meeting with Field's attorney Weiss to see what his interpretation was. If Weiss felt the board was not behind Field, Ingersoll said he would bow out. "Like Winston Churchill, I am not here to preside over the liquidation of this undertaking."

Weiss thought the question of taking advertising was definitely dead for the moment, but he, too, was confused as to how much the board felt could be spent in the future. Weiss agreed that Ingersoll could interpret the directives any way he wished and that "it would be silly to talk in terms of specific figures." The net result appeared to be that Field had given him a green light and the board had given him an amber one. Ingersoll decided to proceed until it turned red.

So Ingersoll took the first step in his reorganization—and Lewis was right: It again made *PM* the center of a controversial internal struggle that went public and raised anew the old anti-Communist and pro-Communist feud. In late March Ingersoll called Wechsler to New York for a dinner and told him that they were losing $5,000 to $6,000 a week, that the board had decided to make some personnel cuts, and that one of the first places cut would be the Washington bureau, which Ingersoll wanted to reduce from eight to five, eliminating Elizabeth Donahue, Milton Murray, and John Moutoux. Wechsler said that he did not approve of the cuts and that Ingersoll was trying to force him to quit. But when Ingersoll accused Wechsler of calling him a liar, Wechsler apologized and said he would carry out the orders. Ingersoll also agreed to help the three employees find work, which in the end he was unable to do. At another dinner meeting in New York Wechsler refused to do the firing, and in an ugly confrontation he suggested that Ingersoll fire, instead, I. F. Stone and Alex Uhl, two *PM* staffers he did not admire. Ingersoll did not fire Wechsler but removed him as head of the Washington bureau. Then he sent Howard Alloway, acting as a management representative, to Washington to tell the three employees they could remain with *PM* if they transferred to New York, without a reduction in pay. They refused, and Ingersoll fired them. The guild, as expected, protested, and the case went to an arbitrator, Judge Edmund Morgan. But now the flap had escalated into the biggest public fight in *PM*'s stormy history. Donahue, Murray, and Moutoux told reporters they were fired because Ingersoll had decided to rid the staff of anyone who was not pro-Communist. And the anti-Communists went to work on *PM* and its editor—mostly in the pages of the *New Leader*, which was well established as their principal voice. When Ingersoll wrote an editorial defending Russian foreign policy and stating his oft-repeated credo that he did not think the Russians wanted war, Alfred Baker Lewis said Ingersoll was either naive or a fellow traveler, but more likely "a little of both. Ferdinand Lundberg called him "the dark genius of *PM*" but said, "*PM* is a phoney and a dangerous phoney" because it continued to endorse Russian foreign policy.

In June Judge Morgan upheld Ingersoll's firing of the three reporters. Wechsler and all but one member of the Washington bureau resigned in protest, issuing a statement blaming the whole thing on Ingersoll's efforts to clean the anti-Communists out of the Washington office. "Although not himself a Communist," the statement said, "he has continuously yielded to Communist pressure and has denounced as factionists those staff members who have tried to keep the party line out of the paper."

Shortly thereafter the *New Leader* came out with still another attack on Ingersoll and *PM* by a writer who used the pen name Karl Collins. Collins gave a long, anti-Communist view of the history of *PM*, in which he told of the early days of the paper when, he said, Ingersoll openly catered to the Communists. He also said that when Ingersoll left and Lewis took charge, the tide changed. "Under Lewis," said Collins, "three well known anti-Communists were assigned executive positions—Harold Lavine became assistant managing editor, Arnold Beichman was city editor and James Wechsler was appointed national editor. When Kenneth Crawford, whose realistic reports from abroad had been tampered with, quit in disgust as Washington Bureau Chief, Wechsler also was given that post."

This last sentence was a nice touch for, as Ken Stewart later pointed out in his study of *PM*, the anonymous "Collins" was Ken Crawford, also head of the Washington chapter of the guild, which had led the protest against *PM*'s firing of the three Washington reporters. Crawford/Collins concluded his article by saying that the "grip of the Stalinists [on *PM*] is stronger than ever" and citing a number of staffers he said were fellow travelers. It was 1941 all over again.

Ingersoll, of course, knew what he was getting into when he took on the Washington office, and was convinced the whole thing was a power play by the anti-Communists. He says that when Wechsler returned from the army, he had warned him that he felt the Washington bureau needed to be improved. Wechsler did not seem to disagree. And during his first weeks back in the office, Ingersoll kept firing memos to Wechsler, indicating his displeasure with the bureau. "Get the old bean working, Jimmy. Kick that staff of yours in the ass and get them more interested in writing for *PM* than in whatever it is [i.e., promoting the anti-Communits line] that interests them now and leaves their writing empty and dull."

Ingersoll says that at first Wechsler did not protest when he was told of plans to cut the Washington bureau. Then suddenly and quite deliberately, he changed his position. The anti-Communists had lost their power when Wechsler and Lavine were called into the army, and according to Ingersoll, "Wechsler became so bitter that he accused John [P. Lewis] of plotting against him in allowing Selective Service to draft Lavine and himself. This accusation Wechsler made personally to me. That during my absence Wechsler spoke openly to his associates of his ambition to take over the paper from John is known to me from a first-hand source." Now, Ingersoll had decided, "the remnants of Wechsler's ambition remain. . . . It is common knowledge in Washington—knowledge spread by Wechsler himself—that his group, as well as the Communists, seeks to influence *PM* by means of pitting me against Max [Lerner] or John against me."

Whether Wechsler's ambitions were more personal than ideological will probably never be known, but there can be little doubt that he viewed the 1946 dispute in the same way as the other professional anti-Communists who were sounding off against *PM* in the *New Leader*. In his book *The Age of Suspicion*, published nine years later, Wechsler said that Ingersoll went down to Washington one day, took him to lunch at the Carlton, and lectured him about loyalty and Red-baiting. "I almost felt as if I were being called upon to sign a non-anti-Communist affidavit." And he said Lewis told him that Ingersoll was obsessed with his political insubordination, that he felt the Communists were no longer a problem at *PM*, but the real menace was a "socialist conspiracy" of anti-Communists intent on seizing control of the paper.

With Wechsler gone, Ingersoll believed that threat had been removed. It was announced that for the time being the Washington office would be under the direction of its national editor, Frank Bear, and its stories would be filed by Gordon Cole (the one Washington hand who still remained), I. F. Stone, Alex

Uhl, and the *Sun* and Associated Press bureaus. The firings and the controversy they generated remained in the press for weeks. The anti-Communists continued their attacks on Ingersoll, although Ken Stewart, Louis Kronenberger, and other staffers stated flatly that they did not agree with the statement issued by Wechsler and those who resigned with him. Sports editor Tom O'Reilly said, "If it happens that Ralph Ingersoll is the star of this paper that is all right with me. I'll hitch the Shay O'Reilly to a star any day." And Tom O'Connor, winner of a Broun Memorial Award, said, "This whole affair reminds me of Gulliver in Lilliput— only Swift's little men never thought of trying to kill the great big guy with sour grapes."

But others on the staff were not so sure they wanted to hitch their wagons to a man who had in only four short months managed to revive the old wars of 1941. The board of directors and some of the men close to Field were getting nervous. Business manager Leake sent a long memo to Field, enclosed the Collins article, and said there was much truth in it. He also said he knew the "communist" Newspaper Guild had a "plan" to take over editorial control of *PM*.

And once again, as in 1941, Ingersoll was catching it from both sides. When he wrote in a *PM* editorial that he felt certain there would not be a war soon, the *Daily Worker* attacked him and said that of course there would be a war because "the evidence of war preparations is far beyond the stage of talk." And at the same time he was the center of another controversy resulting from his interpretation of the war in Europe as expressed in his book *Top Secret*, now in the bookstores and being serialized in *PM*.

Ingersoll knew *Top Secret* would cause a controversy, and in fact, he had considered not writing it because he was aware that his criticism of the British would appear unpatriotic to those who thought the already developing Cold War with the Russians justified Allied solidarity, even if it meant glossing over the unpleasant aspects of our relationship with Britain during the war. Ingersoll argued that the British had fought a political war in Europe, putting self-interest ahead of military decisions. At the same time he said that Russia was not intent on dominating the world and did not want war. Gradually, he believed, her "extremism would subside and [she] would move to the Right as we were moving to the Left"—and the two countries might find common ground.

Over the years Ingersoll gradually came to change his mind about the Russians, and finally he would tell one correspondent, "I've long since run out of tolerance for the 'Russian experiment.'" But in 1946 Great Britain was the villain, and Russia was not to be feared. He was still swayed by what he had seen in Russia during his dramatic 1941 visit and by the emotional fact that Russia had been our ally and had contributed far more, in his opinion, to the defeat of Hitler than the British had. Part of the problem was Montgomery, who, he felt, was a fraud as an officer and as a person, an arrogant bore who managed to alienate everyone—the British and the Americans alike. He also criticized Churchill for persisting as long as he did in urging that Germany be attacked through Italy and the "soft underbelly of Europe" rather than across the Channel

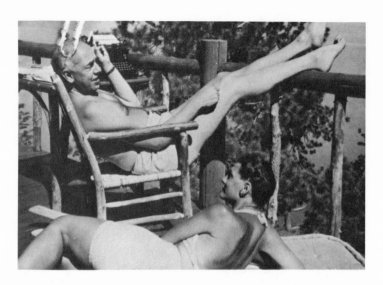

In an old photograph (ABOVE), marred by a paper-clip mark on Ingersoll's head, he is discussing his controversial book, Top Secret, *at Lake Tahoe in 1945 with a secretary Elaine hired to work on the book. It was published almost simultaneously with Captain Harry C. Butcher's* My Three Years with Eisenhower *and the two books, which presented contrasting views of Ike, were often discussed together in the press. (BELOW, LEFT) Ingersoll and Elaine attend the Broadway opening of a Cary Grant movie*

and through France, as the Americans preferred. Eisenhower he viewed as a chairman of the board, picked over Marshall primarily for his ability to compromise; his selection was part of the British master plan to put a pliable American in charge of the whole Overlord operation so that the British themselves would have command of the land, air, and sea.

Considering the extent to which Ingersoll's views differed from the prevailing conventional wisdom, and that he voiced them in the immediate aftermath of the war and at the beginning of the Cold War with Russia, it is, in fact, remarkable just how many people appeared to agree with him, or at least appeared to think he made a good case. Bruce Catton wrote him that it was one of the most important books he had read: not only because it gave a new picture of the war but because it was a "guide post" for formulating postwar policies. Herb Caen, the San Francisco columist, wrote: "Congratulations. . . . As one who had a small opportunity to witness some of the shenanigans you have so superbly reported, I can fully appreciate the many and telling points you make." Ralph Bates wrote in the *Nation*: "Make no mistake about it, Mr. Ingersoll has written one of the most brilliant and provocative books about the war that has yet appeared." Josephus Daniels wrote him: "I'm glad you told the real story"; and Assistant Secretary of War Stuart Symington wrote: "I am primarily annoyed at you for sending me that book because I cannot stop reading it."

Probably the most rewarding applause came from the military. The *Infantry Journal*, in a review by an anonymous officer, "G.V.," said that there were some distortions, but they were to be forgiven because of the author's desire to show that General Bradley was the greatest leader of the European theater, a claim with which G.V. agreed completely. "If at times his feelings appear to distort the facts, I think the reader can simply realize that this was how it looked from Colonel Ingersoll's corner. . . . It is my opinion that every man who has the slightest interest in what happened in the European Theater from 1943 to 1945 will read [*Top Secret*] with the closest attention." And in a letter Bennett Cerf called it "the most exciting book I have read this year." He also told Ingersoll that he had recently visited an admiral at the submarine base in New London who had said, "I could have written every word of that book myself." Cerf added that if you knew the admiral, "that is the God damnedest compliment an author has received in the 20th century." The admiral was in fact only one of dozens of military men who praised the book. Most of them could not say so in public, but they wrote, phoned, or visited Ingersoll to tell him what they thought and to add examples from their own experience to support his views about Bradley, Patton, Montgomery, and Eisenhower.

And they all agreed with Elmer Davis, who said: "You've written one hell of a book, which is going to start one hell of an argument," which it did— although it is interesting to note that none of Ingersoll's American critics disagreed with his appraisal of Bradley, Patton, or Montgomery, and all agreed that Bradley had been overlooked by the public and in their excitement over Ike. But most of the reviewers could not accept Ingersoll's criticism of Eisenhower or, more important, his trust in the Russians and his obvious distrust of our allies, the British. Charles Poore, in the *New York Times*, called it "the most unbalanced, vigorous—and readable—battle piece of the year"; Arthur M. Schlesinger, Jr., said Ingersoll should not have treated the issues he raised "with a glibness even a *PM* editor might be ashamed of"; *Time* called it an "earnest shrill World War II history as interpreted by the editor of Manhattan's earnest shrill daily tabloid, *PM*"; and the *Yale Review* said that as history and an account of high strategy, "it is worse than useless." Edgar Ansel Mowrer said "it could become the most destructive and harmful book of the past 10 years" for poisoning the American people against their British allies; and Mark Watson, the *Baltimore Sun*'s military writer, wrote in the *Saturday Review*: "Most of us who know how superbly General Ike did his unprecedented and enormous job, remain eternally strong for Ike and grateful that his services to his country are not yet over." In other words, the presidential boom for Ike had already begun, and it is not surprising that most of those writing for Establishment publications did not want to hear criticism of their hero.

A great many reviewers, of course, chose the "both sides of the issue" approach, suggesting they did not have the knowledge to dispute Ingersoll and begging off with the comment that the armchair generals would be arguing for years about who had won what battle in World War II. One approach was to review *Top Secret* along with the book by Eisenhower's aide, Captain Harry C. Butcher (*My Three Years with Eisenhower*), simply pointing out their contrasting views. In *Book Week* William Sloane seemed to speak for those who could not quite make up their mind: "This is a book of strong words, of highly flavored and colored opinions and of intense personal convictions. Its author is not the man to pull punches, even when there is nobody else in the ring with him, and most of the time there is a whole crowd in there. It deserves a very wide reading, not alone because it is exciting and fresh in its approach, but also because it sounds as though its author were right a good part of the time."

Perhaps the most authoritative and thoughtful criticism came in a long article by Charles H. Taylor in the *Atlantic*. Taylor, a Harvard professor, had been in the historical branch of G-2, took part in the Normandy and French campaigns, was attached to First Army Headquarters staff, and wrote the War Department study *Omaha Beachhead*. His *Atlantic* piece was called "The Errors of Ralph Ingersoll"; in it he attempted to discredit *Top Secret* by pointing out a number of factual errors while agreeing with Ingersoll's fundamental point that, as Taylor put it, "General Bradley is *the* great field general of the war in Europe."

Because of Taylor's credentials, Ingersoll could not ignore him, so he wrote a rebuttal, which *Atlantic* editor Edward Weeks called a "star piece . . . controversy at its best," and printed in a piece titled "The Integrity of *Top Secret*."

Ingersoll began by saying "there is nothing so reassuring to an author of a book which touches on history as to have a Professor go to work on it with a microscope, looking for factual flaws, misplaced minutiae, and have him come up with an unqualified endorsement of one of the author's main themes" (that is, that Bradley was the great general of the war). "It feels good," Ingersoll went on, "to one who entered the campaign in Europe by the landing craft route on D-Day to find that even the men who stayed in headquarters and rustled the papers came to this same conclusion."

Having established his beachhead, Ingersoll then went inland to counter-attack Taylor's charges that *Top Secret* was full of factual errors and therefore could not be taken seriously. Ingersoll said that when he wrote *Top Secret*, he had only an "intimate knowledge of the strategy tactics and personalities of the campaign gained from a little over two years of seven-days-a-week-work with the men who were making, commanding and executing the plans." It was a masterful counterattack and vintage Ingersoll. But the battle over *Top Secret* was not being waged on the book review pages alone; it also spilled over into the news columns both in America and, as might have been expected, in Britain. Although Churchill would not comment, a spokesman for the prime minister was quoted in the *London Daily Sketch* as discrediting Ingersoll's claim that Churchill and Roosevelt had had a serious falling out over the strategy for occupying Berlin: it was, he said, "utter tosh." Eisenhower also declined to comment, although he was reported to have said that Ingersoll had a torch to carry, and that he wondered how he could be so authoritative on a subject he knew so little about. Averell Harriman, the American ambassador to Britain, said at a dinner that the American writer who had recently published a book about the war offended "every sense of good taste." Then Sir Alan Herbert, a member of Parliament, rose to propose a toast to "a great new comic writer . . . his name is Ralph Ingersoll and his rank must be something like air field marshal of the fleet."

But Ingersoll was ready, as always, with a counterattack. "Intemperate comments about *Top Secret* that have reached me from overseas were made by interested parties who obviously have not read the book — so far as I know, only one copy of *Top Secret* has been sent to England." And responding to Harriman's comment, he said: "It is an ambassador's job to say things which he thinks will please his host and I note in the dispatch that Field Marshal Viscount Montgomery was sitting a few feet from him. And if I am as bad a reporter as Sir Alan Herbert seems to suggest, I don't know where that leaves the scores of professional officers who have beaten a path to my door to tell me how accurate they found the story and to add details and confirmation. These officers, of course, cannot make speeches at public banquets."

Nearly forty years is enough time for the dust to settle and today we can say a number of things about *Top Secret*:

1. It is still one of the most readable and compelling books about the war. Even Ingersoll's severest critics agreed that it was well written and that General Bradley did deserve more credit than he had received.

2. Without any doubt, it was written in the emotional aftermath of the war, when Ingersoll (and most of the officers in Bradley's headquarters) still felt

strongly about Montgomery's shortcomings, the lack of appreciation for Bradley, and Eisenhower's wishy-washiness in dealing with the British commander. As several reviewers pointed out, the book clearly reflected the irritation any staff in the field felt for the headquarters staff removed from the fighting.

3. In the final analysis, on the question of top-level strategy for Overlord and the fighting in Europe, Ingersoll was probably closer to the truth than his 1946 critics. There *were* tension and hard feelings in the high command, although subsequent memoirs and histories have demonstrated that Eisenhower played a greater role in the battles than Ingersoll gave him credit for, and that he was just as impatient and angry with Montgomery as was Bradley's headquarters. It has also been established that the British fought a political war, which Ingersoll never really objected to but which he also thought should be pointed out to the American people. The weakest sections are those dealing with Russian foreign policy. They simply do not stand the test of time, and it is hard not to agree with Edward Earle, who said in his *New York Times* review that the last chapters, in which Ingersoll presents his personal views on foreign policy, could have been omitted.

Top Secret was published in the midst of Ingersoll's struggle to convince Marshall Field that he could remake *PM* into the newspaper he had originally conceived. Its attacks on America's hero, Eisenhower, and our ally, Great Britain, and its defense of Russia, combined with the renewed charges that Ingersoll and *PM* were Communist fellow travelers, gave additional ammunition to the growing number of men who were trying to discredit him. Field, an Anglophile, could not help being persuaded that there was some truth to what Ingersoll's detractors were saying. Then, in June of 1946, his controversial editor gave him more cause for dissatisfaction. Ingersoll was convinced that the best way to raise circulation and money was through a direct appeal to *PM*'s loyal readers. He wrote a special "History of *PM*," a twelve-page brochure scheduled to appear in the June 18 issue, at the same time that *Top Secret* was running in installments.

During this period Field was in Chicago taking care of the *Sun*, which had problems of its own. A copy of the "History" arrived, cold, on his desk, with a letter from Ingersoll explaining that he would have flown out personally except that Elaine was about to give birth to their first child and he thought he would have to go to the hospital at any moment.

Field was not satisfied with Ingersoll's excuse for not consulting him about the "History," which was a long, highly personalized story of *PM*, told in an "exuberant, hair-down style," as John Tebbel, one of Field's biographers, describes it. And in the opinion of many, including Field, it was in bad taste and read as if *PM* was a one-man show, the one man, of course, being Ralph Ingersoll. Tebbel reports that the men around Field had never seen him so upset, although he managed to regain his composure when he called Ingersoll. "Ralph," he said, "I'd like to see that brochure held up, at least temporarily." When Ingersoll told him it was too late—twenty thousand copies had already been printed—"there was a long telephonic argument," says Tebbel. "Field, at first cold and angry, grew more reasonable and at last he suggested a compromise. His strong sense of fair play compelled him to give Ingersoll one more chance to see if the 'no advertising' principle could be salvaged and agreed to the publication of the brochure." Then Field turned to the men present during the conversation and said, "At least they can't say I didn't give them a chance."

Ingersoll agrees that Field was "mad as hell," and also that the promotion stunt did not work. Using the heroic journalistic story of *PM* as told in the "History," its readers were supposed to go out as missionaries among the readers of conventional newspapers and proselytize potential converts to the new religion of "honest journalism," uncorrupted by advertising business interests. At the same time Ingersoll announced six major changes for the paper: a revised front page; more total pages; enlarged sports staff and coverage; more pictures; increased emphasis on local news; and the addition of the Associated Press service. But the promotion did not work, and neither did the announced improvements. Field had given Ingersoll his chance, and he had failed.

By fall it was obvious that Field had given up on Ingersoll and had made up his mind to take advertising. And there can be little doubt that he was persuaded in part by what he and some of his staff considered *PM*'s impact on the *Chicago Sun*. The *Sun* was not bringing in enough advertising, and many of the people on Field's staff were convinced that the controversial *PM* with its nonadvertising policy was the main reason for this. One day in late October Field asked Ingersoll to come to his apartment. Ingersoll was prepared for the meeting—with another plan for reorganizing *PM*. He opened the conversation by saying, "My first step will be to get out of my contract with the newspaper guild which deprives me of the right to hire and fire. This, of course, will mean a strike—but I'm prepared for it."

Field interrupted: "The name of Marshall Field can never be associated with a strike."

Ingersoll shrugged his shoulders, aware that the show was over. Then Field told Ingersoll that his advisers were positive that *PM* could be put in the black instantly by selling advertising. "That gives me a perfect excuse for resigning," Ingersoll replied, "which I hereby do."

"I'm glad you said that," Field replied, "because if you hadn't, I would have had to tell you that I don't think you're the man for this new policy." As Ingersoll puts it: "I resigned one sentence before I would have been fired."

So Ingersoll wrote a letter of resignation stating that "no advertising in *PM* had been woven into the fabric of his conception of the paper," and that he remained convinced that "there should be at least one mass newspaper in this country supported solely by its readers." A week later he called a meeting of his staff, gave them copies of his letter to Field, and sat on his desk to deliver what he called "Not a Farewell Address." Many in the room were crying. "The one thing that's really important to me," said Ingersoll, "is that you all understand that had I known any other way in which I could serve *PM* better than by resigning, I would have taken it."

Ingersoll did not ask for severance pay, but when Gregory Zilboorg heard the circumstances surrounding his resignation, he was enraged. "They shall not castrate Ingersoll on a cross of advertising" became his slogan, and he launched a campaign to see that Ingersoll, who had by now spent all his earnings from *Top Secret*, was taken care of. The result was a two-year contract, with an annual stipend of twenty thousand dollars, to write for Field a monthly critique of *PM*'s editorial policy.

Although advertising was the focal point of Ingersoll's differences with Field, the conflict obviously went much deeper. Ingersoll did not think *PM* was very good in 1946, and wanted to spend more money immediately to make it the paper he had always dreamed of. Field was tired of deficits and wanted to make the paper self-supporting, which he felt could not be done without advertising. Also, by now Field's real interest was no doubt the *Sun*, which was his paper—rather than *PM*, which had once again become clearly identified with Ingersoll. Said Ingersoll: "Marshall Field had torn up the 'gentleman's agreement.' Whatever spell I had had on him was gone—and had been gone, I suspect, since the day I went in the service."

The two men parted on friendly terms, but the fact is that Ingersoll did not think highly of his patron, and down through the years his dislike of Field intensified. In 1949, when Ken Stewart interviewed Ingersoll for a study of *PM* commissioned by Field, he found that "a bitterness toward Marshall Field ran through the whole conversation. At one point [Ingersoll] called him a 'horse's ass' and repeatedly said he was not to be trusted." As Ingersoll told another interviewer years later, he had felt betrayed. "Obviously Marshall was a dupe, handled by other people. He was a damned fool."

Ingersoll's resignation was, of course, a big story in the press, and laments and condolences poured in. E. B. White wrote: "I don't feel as strongly as you about the ad-vs.-no-ad thing, but . . . I am always stimulated by the sight of somebody hanging on to a principle (like a thrown rider to the bridle)." And the *New Yorker* commented in a "Talk" piece: "We have often wondered why it is so difficult to publish such a paper [supported solely by its readers]. One of the odd things about advertising . . . is that the public rather counts on it. We found that out during the war, when we sent an edition overseas with no ads. The boys complained that they were being shortchanged."

Although *PM* was still alive and would presumably be around for some time, a great many editorial writers agreed with *Time* that Ingersoll's departure and the lifting of the ban on advertising marked the end of an experiment: "Ingersoll was out; advertising was in"—which, as the *Washington Post* editorialized, brought "real disappointment to many newspapermen who entertained high hopes for its interesting journalistic experiment." Tom O'Reilly, the *PM* sports columnist, was more to the point in his letter of "congratulations" to Ingersoll: "[Ingersoll's] plan for *PM* was and still is the most magnificent ever presented in modern journalism. . . . All of my life I have heard newspapermen belly-ache about what a great paper they would get out if they didn't have to handle so many sacred cows from the advertising world. They said they wanted to be fearless. They even believed it. But the unvarnished truth is that their greed will always interfere with their fearlessness."

But, as Ingersoll predicted, opening *PM*'s pages to advertising did not solve its problems, and to him the reasons were clear enough: "*PM* has so little to offer the reader for his five cents ... and the heart of this is lack of talent," he wrote Field in one of his monthly reports.

Two years after Ingersoll's resignation, Field turned the paper over to two men: Bartley Crum who had worked for John Francis Neylan, the lawyer who helped Ingersoll get his Hearst story for *Fortune* in 1935, and Joseph Barnes, a *New York Herald-Tribune* correspondent. They changed the name to the *Star* and ran it for another six months as a liberal tabloid, putting a lot of their own money into it, but the advertising still did not appear. In 1949, the *Star* folded; the presses were sold to a newspaper in Pennsylvania and the building was eventually bought by Ted Thackrey, who used it to house his own tabloid, the *New York Compass*, which never had anything to do with *PM*, although legend says it was the successor to the *Star*.

Ralph Ingersoll's dream of a new and different kind of newspaper lasted only eight years—but it lives on in journalism schools and in the biographies and memoirs of the men and women who were associated with it. For years its alumni got together to reminisce about the "good old days" when Huntington Hartford, who would arrive at work in his chauffeur-driven Cadillac, was assigned to cover a Communist rally; when Ralph Ingersoll was battling Wall Street, the Communist party, Adolf Hitler, and the Catholic church; and when *PM* reporters were poised to expose everything and everyone, from poultry processors to Charles Lindbergh and Father Coughlin. "It was kind of the happiest time of my life," said cartoonist Charles E. Martin at one of the reunions. But it was not a happy time for Ingersoll, who was too emotionally caught up in the many battles he was waging. "I was too busy to be either happy or unhappy," Ingersoll recalls. "All I remember is violent action—just to keep it alive."

Why did *PM* die? Over the years there have been many assessments of the newspaper, by ex-*PM* staffers, Nieman fellows, journalism professors—and, of course, by Ingersoll himself. In the 1949 study done for Marshall Field, Blair Clark came to the conclusion that Ingersoll's unbusinesslike approach to publishing played a significant part in *PM*'s early financial failure. For the same study, Ken Stewart sent questionnaires to two hundred former employees, and the majority of those replying said editorial mismanagement, bad business management, and biased news were the paper's principal faults. Only twenty percent faulted Ingersoll's "personal journalism," but it was among the most vivid of their memories. "Ingersoll was responsible for the paper's failure," said one; "Ralph Ingersoll," said another, "was a complete crusader intent upon saving the world his own way, but he knew nothing of what was inside any other single human being."

But Ingersoll also had his defenders: "In my book Ralph Ingersoll was the smartest guy we ever had in the joint," said one ex-staffer. "It was surprising to find so many fellows who realized that *PM* was washed up the moment Ingersoll went off to war."

To anyone reading back over the early issues before July of 1942, *PM* appears as a classic example of personal journalism, which bothered many people. "Never before," said a 1941 *New Yorker* "Talk" piece, "has a daily newspaper been so closely identified with its editor. . . . Everywhere, in fact, the reader is able to observe the workings of a single brain, turning over as publicly as a sample motor at the Automobile Show. All this is very novel and interesting but now and then we have an uncomfortable moment, a vague touch of embarrassment. It is almost too intimate, like reading somebody else's mail."

PM, of course, was written and edited for people who liked reading other people's mail, not for *New Yorker* editors; but this kind of personal journalism could be annoying, even to those who agreed with *PM* on the issues. *PM*'s failure cannot, however, be blamed on one man—or, obviously, it would have succeeded during Ingersoll's war years or after he had quit. It had many faults, and the serious studies made of them list these as being among the most significant: It was not a complete newspaper; it reached newsstands later than its competitors, with older news; the staff did not have enough professionals; the war between the pro-Communists and the anti-Communists seriously disrupted the staff; it was erratic—even in the things it did well.

Ingersoll thought the primary problem was lack of money, which prevented him from hiring the talent he believed he needed to turn out the kind of paper he envisioned. But there was also the intangible mystique of *PM*. "It was that mystique," says Ingersoll, "that drew uninvited passionate friends—and unexpected enemies, even more passionately dedicated to its destruction. The only thing I am clear about now is my own innocence of the forces I had trapped." But in 1966 he said, "If I had to start a paper today, I'd so the same damn thing as I did with *PM*."

PM may have failed financially, but there are many people today who do not feel it failed editorially. I. F. Stone, an alumnus who continued the *PM* tradition for years, writing his *Weekly* in Washington, said it was a "gallant defeat, which is more glorious than a victory because it was something original, courageous and different."

My own assessment is that Ingersoll was trying to do the impossible in 1940—that is, to publish a newspaper by magazine standards. There was just not enough talent around at the time to do that on a daily basis; and after the war, when there was more talent, it was too expensive and he did not have the money. In the final analysis, *PM*'s success rests on its impact on the newspaper profession. "*PM* shook up the conventional American press," says Clayton Fritchey, columnist, former editor, and astute observer of the newspaper business. "Editors began to take a second look at what they were doing. Also, *PM* came at a time when the press was overwhelmingly conservative—anti-New Deal, anti-Roosevelt and isolationist, although most reporters and some editorial writers were liberal. But *PM* shook them up by coming out openly for the New Deal and early for intervention in Europe."

Ingersoll brought the American newspaper screaming and kicking into the twentieth century, forcing it to compete with the magazine press which was pioneering new techniques in reporting, writing, layouts, art, and photography. Newspapers, as a matter of course, now cover labor, radio, the press, and consumer news, although even today, according to a Ph.D. thesis done by Patrick Mahoney for the University of Michigan, consumer news coverage in the press does not compare to *PM*'s forty years ago. Ingersoll, in his own phrase, "made things happen." He did not create the *New Yorker, Fortune,* or *Life,* but in each case he was a catalyst—the one who made things happen, which led to their success. He did create *PM,* and in doing so, he made things happen to the American newspaper. And although *PM* did not survive, neither has *Life. Fortune* is not the magazine it was in the 1930s—and many people think the *New Yorker* is not the magazine it was under Harold Ross. Publishing is essentially an

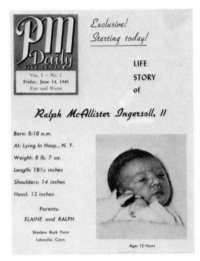

After he left PM, *Ingersoll was very happy living the life of the gentleman author with Elaine at Shadow Rock. And they were excited about the birth of their first son, whose arrival was announced with typical Ingersollian flair*

ephemeral business, and Ingersoll's lasting impact on it has probably been as significant as that of any journalist in the twentieth century.

* * *

Although Ingersoll would have preferred to stay with *PM* and see it become the paper he had dreamed of, his final parting with Field and the paper "was a relief," he says. Staffers had noticed him displaying a restlessness at his desk, and anyone close to him knew he still had that deep urge to write, which had been with him since his youth. If he was ever going to establish himself as an author, now was the time to do it. *Top Secret* had brought him back into the literary world and reminded everyone of his earlier war books. At the same time he was very happy living at Shadow Rock with Elaine. Their first son, Ralph II, had been born during the final crisis at *PM* and Ingersoll was looking forward to the life of a gentleman author, surrounded by a growing family and the hills of Connecticut.

Meanwhile, as a "controversial author," he was also in demand as a speaker, and during much of the winter of 1946–47 he toured the lecture circuit appearing on the radio and in town hall debates, in which he was invariably on the side that favored maintaining price controls and giving Russia a chance to prove that she was not out to conquer the world. In a debate with James Reston on U.S. policy toward Russia, he said he did not know what our policy was, but if it was "to work up a holy war against Russia," then he was against it: "I am for dealing with the Russians for what they are—a sovereign nation which was allied to us in the great and victorious war recently fought. We had two principal allies in that war—Russia and Great Britain. I'm for treating them both with evenhanded fairness, standing on all our rights and giving them theirs."

In January of 1947 Poland was scheduled to hold an election, and the big question being debated in the press then was: Would the elections be free—was Poland a Communist state, or was it "independent" as the Big Four had agreed it should be? The American press took the position that Poland was a Communist state, and reported all events in that country as if it were a satellite of the Soviet Union—an assumption with which Ingersoll disagreed. So he arranged with *PM* to cover the elections for the paper, and for a magazine called *Reader's Scope* he would write a 3,500-word article on press coverage in Poland. The result was a typical Ingersoll confrontation with the Establishment. In mid-January he flew to Warsaw and spent a frantic week during which he met and dined with pro-Communist and anti-Communist Polish officials; he met with the American ambassador and made contact with someone at the British embassy whom he had known in the army; he had dinner at the British embassy; he attended all the press conferences; he met and talked with all the American and some of the British press reporters; and he devoured everything he could find to read about Poland. It was another quick study by the man who seven years earlier had told

Americans more than they had ever known about London and the Battle of Britain.

The American press in Warsaw in 1947 consisted of five correspondents: Larry Allen for the Associated Press; Ruth Lloyd for the United Press; Sidney Gruson for the *New York Times*; Mrs. Sidney Gruson for *Time*; and Marguerite Higgins for the *New York Herald-Tribune*. Each one represented publications that assumed Poland was a police state and the elections had been rigged in favor of the coalition government of Communists and Socialists that was elected. Ingersoll, however, reported for *PM* that this black-and-white picture was inaccurate. "This is a highly complicated situation which cannot easily be analyzed in brief news dispatches." Poland was not a police state: "It is a really new kind of state in which honest men of many parties are honestly trying to make Poland livable again." He conceded that "without exception, every man, woman and child dislikes Russia personally"—but only the "lunatic fringe" did not agree that because of her history and geography, Poland had no choice but to be a friend of Russia and to have a foreign policy identical with Russia's and a government acceptable to Russia. In short, after the death of millions of Russians in World War II, Russia had no intention of permitting a truly "independent" Poland on her western frontier, across which Germany, perhaps someday in alliance with the capitalist countries, would invade her again.

He also reported that the five representatives of the American press, when talking in private and to friends, agreed that although the Socialists in the new government would probably be absorbed someday by the Communists, the present government was the best thing for Poland, and it was unrealistic to think that Russia would ever permit a truly democratic Poland on her frontier. As for the elections, he conceded they were not fair by American standards, but he argued that they were not as bad as some of our worst state and local elections. He also said that everyone he talked with privately in the various embassies disagreed with the view of Poland and the elections that was reported by the press. And why was the truth not being reported in America? For the simple reason that American papers and magazines—and especially *Time*—chose to ignore what their correspondents sent them, and printed their own version of events instead. The correspondents were not happy about this but, for various reasons, accepted it and chose to continue the charade.

Ingersoll's continuing tolerance of Russian foreign policy and his criticism of the way the press covered Poland further estranged him from his American colleagues. *Time* described him as a "flimflamboyant" ex-editor, left of leftish *PM*, and oversimplified his reports in characteristic *Time* style, making him appear an idiot. Dorothy Thompson, who had also covered the elections for the *New York Post*, was equally critical. Upon their return, Thompson and Ingersoll engaged in a debate for CBS's "People's Platform," about which Dwight Cook, the moderator, said, "It's very hard to believe you've both visited the same country." The transcript is difficult to follow because of frequent "interruptions" and the many points at which both were reported to be speaking simultaneously, but it is clear that Ingersoll wanted to give the Polish Socialist party a chance to work out an accommodation with Russia, and Miss Thompson was sure it would not work.

In the long run, Miss Thompson was proved right, and Ingersoll's defense of Russian foreign policy would eventually become an embarrassment. Although no one, except perhaps a few hard-core anti-Communists, believed he was a Communist or lacking in patriotism, his persistent defense of the Russians made him suspect in the eyes of some and naive in the view of many. By 1947 it had become inconceivable that Ralph Ingersoll could find a job in the media compatible with his experience and ability.

But then, in 1947 he did not really care. He still wanted to write; the problem was, What would he write about? He had become so firmly typed as a left-wing radical that it would be difficult for him to find a publisher for a book on current events; but he had an idea for a novel about ambition and success, subjects on which he was something of an expert. By the time he flew to Poland to cover the elections, he had signed a contract with Harcourt Brace.

In the late winter and spring of 1947, in the prime of life at the age of forty-six, Ralph Ingersoll's personal life could not have been better. He was happier than he had ever been, and very possibly ever would be again. He and Elaine had an apartment in Manhattan, but they spent most of their time at Shadow Rock, where Ingersoll was becoming increasingly preoccupied with Elaine, his baby son, Ralph II, and the life of the gentleman farmer–author. Reporters coming up to the farm would be regaled with stories about his maple-sugar trees; his Guernsey cow Honesty; his homemade, completely stocked delicatessen; the "pocket baskets" Elaine was making and selling to Best's and Altman's (for a handsome profit); or his latest purchase at a country auction. They were less likely to hear about his political philosophy or his opinions on who won the war.

Despite this bucolic life, when he settled down to write, it was the old Ingersoll—filling fifteen strategically located ashtrays with cigarette butts; drinking the thirty cups of coffee a day that Elaine was constantly preparing for him; dictating, sometimes ten thousand words a day, while lying on his back and looking out a picture window at a swamp full of birds and animals. "He sometimes uses field glasses for a better view," said Elaine, "dictating all the while with his back to one of his long suffering secretaries."

Which may explain why the novel would emerge as one of the strangest works of fiction ever to be published. *The Great Ones* was about the careers, love affair, and marriage of Sturges Strong, an ambitious, ruthless, conservative magazine publisher, and Letia Long, actress, dress designer, artist, author—and all-around bitch. In fact, says Ingersoll, to come up with just the right blend, he modeled Letia on three women he had known, of varying degrees of bitchiness. One of them, he concedes, might have been Clare Luce, "but, if so, it was unintentional. There are no portraits in it." Strong, he insists, was never intended to be Harry Luce, but rather a prototype of the typical New York executive of the 1930s. "I put a lot of myself into him—for better or worse he is an invention." And to emphasize that Sturges and Letia are inventions, he brought Clare and Henry Luce into the novel as sort of fictional cameos—along with many other prominent celebrities of the day. As Elaine, excited about the book her husband had finished by late December, wrote her friend Clare Luce: "You, President Roosevelt, Bergdorf Goodman and just about any other famous name of our time flip through the pages, for Ralph's fabulous characters live in a very real world. . . . Everyone who has read it so far is mad about it and predicts a terrific future for it."

But there was trouble ahead, and Ralph sensed it: "I knew damn well the book wouldn't write," he says, "and should have been torn up and started all over again. But my wife and my publisher were *mad* for it. *Mad* for it! And so were the movies. And Elaine thought Clare would take as a joke any resemblance to the publisher's wife. Clare is a super phenomenon, too, she'll love it."

But, Ingersoll says now, "I regard my publishing *The Great Ones* as a catastrophic mistake. I'm sure if I had not been rushed into print, I would have rewritten it and made Sturges an inventor instead of a publisher. I chose to write about publishing because I was sure I could write it accurately, which I did; the plot is much too close to what actually happened," which, no doubt, helps explain why, once he started writing it, the book had "taken off on its own."

Before *The Great Ones* was ever published, the New York columnists knew there was a bombshell of a book on the way, and Walter Winchell in the *Mirror* and Danton Walker in the *News* pointed out the similarity between Henry and Clare Luce and the characters Sturges and Letia. Ingersoll quickly wrote Winchell and Walker denying that the book was patterned on anyone specific; he argued that because the Luces themselves, as well as Time Inc. appear in the book, Sturges and Letia could not be the Luces. Then he sent Luce copies of his letters, denying again that the book was about him and apologizing for the speculation in the press.

But Ingersoll did protest too much, and with one exception, no one accepted his denial that his fictional the *great ones* were Henry and Clare Luce. That one exception, however, was interesting; Celia Sugerman, a former archivist at Time Inc., believed that Sturges was actually based on Ingersoll. And there is justification for this observation: Sturges frequents Miss Swift's massage parlor, as did Ingersoll; Sturges also wrote one last article for his magazine *Facts*, and the subject was William Randolph Hearst—just as Ingersoll had written his last article for *Fortune* on Hearst; and coming back from California, where he had researched the Hearst article, Sturges is forced down in Albuquerque, where he meets Letia for the first time. Surprisingly, despite their respective successes, neither has heard of the other, and they fall immediately in love—almost exactly as it had happened with Ingersoll and Lillian Hellman in 1935. And many of the beliefs, attributes, and characteristics that Sturges shares with Henry Luce are the very ones the fictional publisher shares with Ingersoll. And, of course, there are the continual references in the novel to the real Henry and Clare—and to Ingersoll: When Sturges falls in love with Letia, he has lunch with Ralph Ingersoll and they have a long discussion about the Luces and why Harry had never made Clare an editor in his organization. Then he confides to Ralph that he has fallen in love with a women (Letia) "even more beautiful than Clare Luce and even more talented."

If the portraits had been complimentary, the media might have yawned and focused solely on the novel as a novel, which would have given them enough to talk about. The trouble with *The Great Ones* is not that it was thought to be a *roman à clef* of questionable taste, but that it was simply a poorly conceived and badly executed novel. Elaine, in one of her letters to Clare, said her husband was experimenting with a "new way to write fiction," which resulted in a novel that reads like a very long *Fortune* piece. It goes on, page after page, in magazine-style narrative, unrelieved by either anecdotes or quotes. For a novel, there is very little dialogue between its characters, which is just as well because what dialogue there is sounds artificial.

The book did have its supporters, however, beginning with the reader at Harcourt Brace, who described it as "extremely readable, a brilliantly realized, thought-out, well-constructed satire—important reading." Tommy, who was back in Saranac, wrote that everyone she had talked to thought it was a "howling success," with comments ranging from "It's a great book, reminds one of *The Fountainhead*," to "I had to put it down at the end of each chapter to get my breath." (She signed her note "Best to Elaine and to you and love to the baby," which suggests that any wounds from the divorce thirteen years earlier had healed.) Arthur Gouldin, writing for the *Toledo Blade*, said: "*The Great Ones* seems to me to be a promise of good novels to come from Ingersoll if—and that *if* rests on my memory of Ingersoll's emotional reporting of the Battle of Britain—he will wed the emotion to an authentic picture of life. . . . Then he will have written a novel worthy of the name." In the *New Republic* Penn Kimball, a *PM* staffer, thought it "an interesting document" that would cause a "flutter"; Ingersoll, Kimball predicted, "may end up as the John P. Marquand of New York and Reno." The great majority, however, thought that, as a novelist, reporter Ingersoll was a disaster. To Charles Rolo, writing in the *Atlantic*, it was "not a novel, but a dossier—ream upon ream of factual reporting with just enough imaginative transposition to put it on the fiction list and elude the laws of libel." Merle Miller, in the *Saturday Review*, said, "*The Great Ones* is the work of a reporter, not a novelist." *Newsweek* thought it was a "perfect example of how not to write a novel . . . a combination of obit and telegraph report." Harry Hansen, in the New York *World-Telegram*, was surprised that there was not "the usual disclaimer that all this is imaginary"; it was, he thought, "one of the meanest jobs in print." And Jacques Barzun, reviewing the novel for *Harper's*, carried the reporter-as-novelist criticism to the ultimate: "The hero's first love affair in college reads like an Associated Press dispatch in several installments."

All the reviewers, friend and foe alike, predicted *The Great Ones* would create a sensation, and it did, with most of the reaction centering on what they thought was an undisguised and perhaps tasteless attack by Ingersoll on his old friend and former boss, Henry Luce. Orville Prescott, in the *New York Times*, thought the origins of the book might go back to *The Trespassers*, in which Laura Hobson, a former employee of Time Inc. and a good friend of Clare and Henry Luce, published her presumed attack on Ingersoll; this, in Prescott's view, had led Ingersoll to feel that when it came to the fictional treatment of controversial characters "no holds are barred." The *New Yorker* did not think much of the novel and said that "as an example of broken field running through the libel laws, it stands a good chance of being re-issued indefinitely." In her column, Dorothy Kilgallen reported that "Clare Booth and Henry Luce are collaborating on a play about Ralph Ingersoll" (which was funny, but not true); and Walter Winchell reported a Chicago bookseller as commenting that the book "reads like a post mortem on a friendship"—which it was. If Henry Luce, after Ingersoll's attacks in *PM* (and out) on the integrity of *Time* magazine and Clare Luce (who always considered Ingersoll the man who had prevented her from becoming editor of *Life*), had retained any feeling of friendship for the former Time Inc. editor, it was gone now. Significantly, a twelve-page feature in the twenty-fifth anniversary issue of *Time*, which appeared during this period, failed to mention Ralph Ingersoll or that he had been publisher of *Time* and vice president and general manager of Time Inc. Ingersoll heard from several sources that Clare was countering the novel by telling friends at cocktail parties that his bitterness resulted from his being a frustrated would-be lover and that she was responsible for killing MGM's interest in the novel by threatening to keep reviews of MGM movies out of *Time* and *Life* if that studio ever made the movie. Mrs. Luce, of course, denies this, and MGM does not have a file on *The Great Ones* or on Ingersoll. But Ingersoll's notes at the time indicate that MGM and other studios showed definite interest in *The Great Ones* and that discussions with one agency reached the point of considering actresses to play Letia. The gossip columns also reported that several studios were excited about the possibility of a movie based on *The Great Ones* but felt that, in the long run, they could not touch it for fear of offending Time Inc. The fact is, a movie was never made, although the story line, as Ingersoll concedes, hews so close to what actually happened to Luce during his courtship of and marriage to Clare, and during the publication of *Life*, that, properly done, *The Great Ones* could readily have resulted in a version of *Citizen Kane*, this one the story of a magazine publisher.

The publication of *The Great Ones* was not only a disaster for Ingersoll, but a crushing disappointment. He had genuinely wanted to spend the rest of his life as an author, and secretly he had hoped to develop as a writer of fiction. In 1947 he sold to *Good Housekeeping* a short story ("Afternoon in a Brownstone Front") based on an anecdote he had heard in the 1920s, and he had hoped *The Great Ones* would establish him as a novelist. Now the seemingly inexhaustible Ingersoll confidence was shaken. But he had one great source of strength, and that was Elaine. She still had undying faith in her hero, and when he lapsed into periods of doubt and depression, she would bring him out of them with her conviction that he could do anything he set out to do—even write a great novel. She also had borne him a son, whom he loved, and was about to give birth to another. It was to be a caesarean delivery, which meant she could pick the date. After long consideration she finally decided on April 1, which would at least, she reasoned, make it easy for his wife to remember his birthday. Just before she was to give birth, she wrote a curious letter to the housekeeper, Nellie, telling her that if she had not come to work for them, Ralph's latest book would not have been published—"and his books are more than just books. They are great contributions to our world and our way of living." She thanked Nellie for everything she had done, and urged her to stay with Ralph and help him if anything happened to her.

The day before Elaine was scheduled to have the baby, Ingersoll took her to Lenox Hill Hospital in New York, then went down to Wilmington, Delaware, for a Book and Author Luncheon devoted to *The Great Ones*. Ingersoll told the guests about the imminent birth of his second child, and one columnist reported: "No one at the meeting will forget the cheerfulness of Mr. Ingersoll and all applauded when he departed for the train connection."

Jonathan Ingersoll VIII was born on April 1, 1948; Elaine had insisted on the name after hearing that there were seven Jonathans in the Ingersoll family tree. Although the birth had been by caesarean section, there were no surgical problems and Ingersoll spent an hour with Elaine, saw his new son, then went back to their apartment on Seventy-second Street, jubilant. After a quick nap and a few telephone calls to spread the word, he returned to the hospital "for my first warning of trouble brewing," he says in an unpublished autobiographical sketch. "The only doctor on hand was a young intern who remarked that there seemed to be some discomfort. He was a supercilious young man who put my first rocket up with the comment: 'Your wife seems to have a low threshold of pain.'" Ingersoll ran down the hall to a telephone and called the gynecologist, who appeared at the hospital within half an hour. "I simply can't understand it" was his first comment to Ingersoll, which put him on the phone again, calling every specialist and diagnostician he could find. Tests were hastily taken, and they showed something was wrong with the blood. The white corpuscles were soaring, and Elaine required a transfusion. Ingersoll was permitted to see her, and she roused herself, half sitting up, to ask, "What the hell is going on? Doesn't anybody know what's wrong with me?"

They knew very little, only that her liver seemed to have gone into an almost spontaneous disintegration. Ingersoll went down the hall to sit with her parents, who had now arrived. It was around eight P.M. when Elaine's gynecologist backed out of her room, beckoning Ingersoll to come. He ran down the hall, and as he entered the room the doctor said, "She has only a few more minutes to live."

Seconds later, with Ingersoll helplessly looking over her, Elaine died. That night he found a letter she had carried into the hospital. It began: "Darling: I love you so terribly much and I want you always to be your happiest. I don't know how I can make you happy when I'm not around to do it with things and gestures and words and by loving you and making love to you—but this is to try."

She concluded: "to be your wife and bear your children is the greatest honor any woman can have—to think less than this would make one unworthy of you."

15: Making Money, Spending It, and Making More

It is difficult to imagine how stunned and depressed Elaine's death left Ingersoll. He was forty-seven years old, a writer who no longer had the will to write, and if and when he did, his future as a novelist looked bleak. Even his reputation as a writer of nonfiction had been shaken by the publication of *Top Secret* and his open support of Russia. And because his experience at *PM* had convinced some that he was a Communist and others that, although he might be a great reporter and editor, he was incapable of running an organization, his chances of finding a responsible job in journalism were slim. He had effectively cut his ties with the U.S. Army by criticizing General Eisenhower in *Top Secret*. He also had two motherless babies to raise, no money with which to do it, and no idea how to earn it. Most important, his confidence was gone: "With Elaine," he said, "failure in anything was inconceivable; without her, success in anything was just as unimaginable. . . . As a functioning personality, I was destroyed."

He had taken Jonathan home and was still trying to find out what had happened to Elaine, when he was hit by another loss: Eight days after Elaine's death his father died. He was truly alone. He was not close to his sisters, and except for his college pal, Louis Bishop, he had virtually no friends. In fact, after his enlistment in the army in 1942, the only person who went to visit him at Camp Edwards was Charles Marsh, the eccentric millionaire he had met while at *PM*. Marsh also sent him a telegram when Elaine died. It said simply: "WHEN YOUR SPIRIT MOVES YOU MY WAY YOU WILL FIND ME AT 6 EAST 92 ST BETWEEN APRIL 15TH and 25TH. I SHALL COME ANYWHERE YOU SAY."

By now Marsh and Claudia Haines, his secretary, were close enough to Ingersoll to know the extent to which he would be shattered by Elaine's death. Another person who must have sensed it was John P. Lewis, the managing editor of *PM* and one of the triumvirate Ingersoll always believed had turned Field against him. The day after Elaine's death, Ingersoll says, Lewis burst into his apartment on Seventy-second Street, fell on his knees crying, told him how sorry he was to hear about Elaine, and apologized for his role in the plot to discredit Ingersoll on the paper.

Though never completely sure what killed Elaine, the doctors diagnosed it as a rare blood condition that she had had for at least a year and that would probably have killed her even if she had survived the birth of Jonathan. The actual cause of death was a burst blood vessel in her brain. Dr. Zilboorg had another explanation: That she suffered from a deep guilt in her happiness with Ingersoll—a guilt that tapped buried emotions involving her childhood relations with her father. There could be no way of confirming Zilboorg's analysis, but Ingersoll has always been convinced that Elaine had had a premonition of death when she went into the hospital, which was reflected in the letters she wrote to him and to Nellie, the housekeeper.

Ingersoll was now totally devoid of will or ambition and had come to the conclusion that if there was any purpose in his life it was "to somehow care for the byproducts of three years of fulfillment." But how? Of course, he did not just want a job—any job. He wanted to lead the good life he had always led and to raise his children with enough money to give them some freedom in choosing a career.

The idea of money—big money—had always fascinated him. On the *New Yorker* he had ridiculed the rich; on *Fortune* he had analyzed wealthy industrialists and successful companies and had attempted to show how it was done. Making money, in his view, was usually accomplished by inferior people, and it was easy to do, once you knew how. In *The Great Ones* he reported how Letia "had decided to build a new life around finding out how money was made in this good capitalistic world. . . . She would begin at the bottom to find out how rich people got rich in the first place."

Now Ingersoll decided he would do the same. And if he was half as smart as he thought he was, he could, as he put it, "knock it over with my eyes closed." But, unlike Letia, he planned to start at the top. He made a list of ten people he knew, all of them men "to whom money seemed to cling." The rich always needed lieutenants they could trust to help them make money, and he decided he would go to one of them and offer to be the lieutenant—but instead of asking for money, he would request knowledge, the knowledge that would enable him to make money himself.

He also decided that the person who agreed to teach him how to make money would also have to like him, and he felt this meant he, in turn, would have to like his teacher, because people generally do not like someone they sense does not like them. That excluded most of the men on the list, and the rest were eliminated because they were relatives or people to whom he felt he was too close—Charles Marsh, for example. Eliminating Marsh reminded him that he had not responded to Marsh's telegram, so one Sunday morning in April Ingersoll went to his Ninety-second Street apartment. The room was full of people who had dropped by to bid farewell to Marsh, who was sailing for Europe the next day.

"I just stopped by to thank you for the telegram you sent," Ingersoll said to Marsh when he had a chance. "I am grateful for your thoughtfulness, but I don't need help," which was not exactly the truth.

Marsh said nothing, then, with a dramatic flair that surpassed even Ingersoll's, he turned to a friend who happened to be in the apartment: "Give Ingersoll his ticket." Ingersoll was handed an envelope, which, when he opened it, revealed a ticket for an A-deck cabin on the *Saturnia*, sailing for Genoa at midnight the following evening. "I'm taking Claudia to see Europe again. That's your ticket to come with us, at least as far as Genoa."

Although Marsh would eventually marry Claudia, Ingersoll has always

Shortly after Ingersoll made this publicity photo (LEFT) for the publication of his novel, The Great Ones, *in 1948, he and Charles Marsh, right, formed the RJ Company to enable Ingersoll to make the money he would need to raise and educate his children.*

assumed Marsh had purchased the extra ticket so he would have a second cabin, which would protect Claudia's reputation. He offered this ticket to Ingersoll in such a way as to mystify all those who were in the room.

Ingersoll thanked him but said, "It's impossible, of course."

"Put it in your pocket. You'll either be on board or you won't," said Marsh. Then he changed the subject and did not mention the ticket again that afternoon.

The following night, after hastily arranging to have Elaine's mother take care of the children, Ingersoll was on the boat. Six weeks later he returned to America from a trip that marked another turning point in his career. "I had been a dead man, emotionally, that weekend when it all began. By the time I was on the plane for home, I was alive again. It was Charles, of course, who had made it happen. . . . The changes he wrought in our relationship—in me—seemed the result of improvised gestures, without premeditation, method or even perceptible logic. Never 'a long conversation'—at least about *my* life. It was just that being in his orbit somehow stimulated or renewed a will to live again."

The most significant thing to happen on the trip was Ingersoll's reversal of his decision not to ask Marsh to help him. "Somewhere in the South Atlantic," Ingersoll recalls, "a week or so out of New York and on deck together alone, I got around to saying bluntly: 'Charles, will you teach me how to make money?'"

Marsh laughed, then said, "It can't be taught." But then he began to speculate. "I won't teach you, but maybe you can learn. You want to make the money you need to bring up Elaine's children. All right. We'll make a partnership. It will be fifty-fifty. If you can pick it up—well, then, you've picked it up. But it's going to be hard, because there's so much of the engineer in you. You'll have to find out that two and two don't make four—they make zero or six or sixty. A dollar can be a lot of different things. . . . If you are able to get inside you that all the while the people you are dealing with are talking figures, what they are really being moved by are emotions—greed and generosity, hate and love. They wouldn't be talking to you at all about buying or selling or trading unless they were moved by their own emotions. And their emotions toward you—in the beginning are probably the smallest factor."

This is a condensation of Ingersoll's first conversation with Marsh, which must have lasted a couple of hours. At the time when he flew home, he already knew he had met the man who was going to help him earn the money he would need to raise and educate his children. Claudia confirms that Marsh genuinely wanted to help Ingersoll; but it was not charity. Marsh had neglected his own personal fortune during the war and wanted to make a little more to achieve his goal of leaving his Public Welfare Foundation with a fifty-million-dollar endowment.

Ingersoll's problem was how to raise enough money (which Marsh had agreed to match) to form a company with adequate operating capital. Then he had a windfall. By the time Marsh returned from Europe, Ingersoll had learned that he had substantial capital to invest: $100,000 which Elaine had left in a trust fund for the children; $50,000 which Elaine's parents had set up as a trust fund for her, and which Ingersoll, to his surprise, had inherited; and $100,000 which his father had left in a trust fund for him to invest for his widow and which, when she died, was to be split among Ingersoll and his two sisters. He told Marsh he would put in the $50,000 he had inherited from Elaine. Marsh matched this with a bond, collateralized by one of the several newspapers he owned, which was probably worth more than $50,000 but was not negotiable. As Ingersoll says, "Charles had already begun my education; $50,000 cash plus $50,000 in unsalable bonds do not add up to $100,000 of liquid capital. And in character, he left me to find that out for myself—by talking a banker in New York into taking the bond as collateral for 80 percent of face value—which, believe it or not, I did."

At the time they formed the partnership, Marsh asked Ingersoll, "Now, before we begin to do business, how much money do you want to make?"

Ingersoll asked why that made a difference. "Because money is corrupting," Marsh replied. "When you've made what you want, you will find yourself wanting just a little more—it will be so easy to get. And when you have that, the wanting of still more will be a tug twice as strong. You may be corrupted beyond help—like Jesse Jones. Worth a hundred million and in his nineties, he boasted to me that he had just swindled a man out of ten million more."

Marsh then insisted that Ingersoll take a piece of paper and write down how much he wanted to make. Ingersoll thought $100,000 would assure his children's future, but when Marsh saw the figure, he laughed: "You haven't brought up any children so you don't know how much they cost." He changed the figure to $500,000, then said, "Now sign it—and I'll put it away to remind you when you're ready to go out of business."

So late in the summer of 1948, only a few months after Elaine's death, when Ingersoll's world appeared to have totally collapsed, he began a new life— as an entrepreneur with the goal of making enough money to raise and educate his children. Marsh dictated the terms of the partnership to Claudia in his Ninety-second Street apartment: fifty-fifty in and fifty-fifty out, to be dissolved when either party desired. And he suggested the enterprise be called the R. J. Company, after Ralph II and Jonathan, the two babies it was meant to support.

The country was about to lose one of its most creative and innovative journalists. Although Ralph Ingersoll would go on eventually to become part owner and manager of several small and medium-sized newspapers, he would take very little interest in their editorial content unless he was forced to. And when he did, he would go to considerable effort not to change the nature and character of the established paper. Ralph Ingersoll was no longer interested in reforming the newspaper business. He still wanted to give the communities in which he invested a good newspaper, but his primary goal was to make money, not journalism history.

Now that his children's financial future seemed assured, all they needed was a mother—and by the end of November he had taken care of that too. Although Ingersoll had enjoyed his bachelorhood when he was living in New

In 1948 Ingersoll married Mary Hill Doolittle (ABOVE, AT WEDDING) in part because he was impressed with her three young children, Patricia, Jerry, and Bill, Jr. (BELOW)

York and moving around in the publishing world, being stuck in the country with a family to raise was something else: "It's a horrifying experience," he says, "being an eligible bachelor with two small children and supposed to have big bucks, which I didn't. Women I hardly knew would knock on the door of my house in Lakeville and come in to spend the night. The nurse I had hired to help me bring up the children was literally terrified."

To educate his children, Ingersoll had started the Shadow Rock Play Group, a private school in Lakeville, open to local neighborhood children and run by Claudia Haines's daughter. One day he was on top of his station wagon taking photographs of the school, when suddenly a tall, beautiful blonde appeared below him. He scrambled down, and Mary Hill "Sue" Doolittle introduced herself. It developed that they had a mutual friend named Alice Jane Fairfield, who was playing Cupid. Sue had recently been divorced by William Doolittle, headmaster of the Indian Mountain School, and was now the "notorious lady" of northwest Connecticut. Alice Fairfield defended Sue and helped convince Ingersoll he should marry her. But what really persuaded Ingersoll that Sue would make him a good wife was her three children, Patricia (fourteen), Jerry (fifteen), and Bill junior (twelve). He looked them over carefully and came to the conclusion that anyone who could raise such fine children would certainly be a good mother to his sons. He and Sue were married on Thanksgiving Day, 1948, less than seven months after Elaine died, but with Ingersoll convinced that she approved. The marriage, however, was a disaster—"the worst mistake of my life," says Ingersoll.

They honeymooned in Florida and Argentina, then returned to Shadow Rock, which Sue soon found intolerable because Elaine had lived there. She also found it difficult to be in the same town as her ex-husband, although it did not bother Ingersoll. The divorce decree specified that the Doolittle children were in the custody of their mother, and when Ingersoll learned that Doolittle was permitted to see his children only on specified occasions, he went up to the Indian Mountain School and barged into Doolittle's office. The arrangement, he said, was nonsense: "You can see your children any damn time you want."

Ingersoll and Doolittle eventually became good friends, but Sue still wanted to leave. So reluctantly and unhappily, Ingersoll sold his beloved Shadow Rock Farm to the mystery writer Georges Simenon, and they moved to Doylestown, Pennsylvania. The R. J. Company also bought an office-apartment at 9 East Sixty-second Street in New York, and for a year the Ingersolls divided their time between the city and Bucks County.

At first the marriage seemed to work, and the stepchildren remember the good times when Ingersoll and Sue, with her "crazy kind of energy," had a lot of fun together. But gradually the tensions began to appear. He traveled a great deal on R. J. Company business, and eventually other women came into his life. Sue was often left alone on the farm, although they both spent considerable time in their New York apartment. But most important, she did not get along with Ingersoll's young boys, especially Ralph II.

In addition, Ingersoll was a disappointment as a father, at least to his own children. When he was not on the road or in New York, he seemed to show more interest in the Doolittle children because they were older and hence more interesting to him. Bill junior remembers that when his mother first married Ingersoll, his new stepfather won him over by coming into his room one day with an armful of miniature tanks, which he had somehow smuggled out of Germany. He became very close to Ingersoll, who was, Bill junior says, "somebody to play games with and somebody who was extremely loyal. He was somebody I could turn to at times of crisis to really fix things. I could count on him always."

By contrast, Ralph II and Jonathan do not recall being close to their father when they were growing up. "My father, I really didn't know," Jonathan says about his childhood. "He was away working so much and I really didn't feel I had a relationship with him." And young Ralph says: "From the age of nine on, I was never home. I was either in a boarding school or working on one of the papers. My father was coming and going so much I hardly ever saw him. I developed surrogate fathers—Chet Spooner, Seymour Schneidman. Seymour taught me to dance."

One thing the Doolittle boys remember is that their stepfather insisted on quiet when he wanted to write. And when they were still living in Lakeville, they could not go near the swimming pool during writing hours because it was near Ingersoll's office. After his marriage to Sue Ingersoll revived his desire to write, his first effort was a biography of Eva Perón. He had done some research on the wife of Juan Perón and had taken copious notes when he was honeymooning in Argentina. He also had a ten-thousand-dollar advance for the biography from Harcourt Brace. But he says he was only half serious about the project, which he finally abandoned, eventually returning the advance to the publisher. His next effort was a novel, *Wine of Violence*, a World War II romance set in London and France, which was actually based on his love affair with Elaine. His literary approach to love and war was obviously influenced by Hemingway, but unfortunately *Wine of Violence*, which was published in 1951, did not do for World War II (or American literature) what *A Farewell to Arms* had done for World War I, despite the fact that Ingersoll's recounting of the mood and battles of the war in Europe was moving and authentic. "*Wine of Violence* is a lively, at times mildly moving and always readable book," said the *Times*. But most readers would agree with the reviewer's conclusion: "As a novelist, Mr. Ingersoll is still a fine war correspondent." It was Ingersoll's last published novel, but not his last attempt to write fiction.

With *Wine of Violence* out of his system, Ingersoll was able, for a while at least, to devote full time to the R. J. Company, and it was obvious from the first that the partnership of Marsh and Ingersoll had been made in business heaven. They were a perfect team, perhaps even surpassing the 1930s team of Luce and Ingersoll. No one who has been interviewed about the relationship between these two unusually bright and energetic men can recall their ever having a fight or a disagreement; and their correspondence reflects nothing but mutual confidence and respect. Perhaps this cooperative atmosphere was the result of Ingersoll's psychoanalysis, in which, he maintains, Gregory Zilboorg helped relieve him of the urge to destroy anyone who appeared to be a father image. Or perhaps Charles Marsh was the only man he ever met—except, perhaps, for Omar Bradley—whom Ingersoll believed to be smarter than he was. "He was far and away the most interesting man I have ever known," Ingersoll concedes, "with the most brilliant mind and the greatest potential as a human being."

Ingersoll was not the only one impressed by Marsh. Seymour Schneidman, who later became Ingersoll's bookkeeper and business partner, said, "[He] was one of the geniuses of the world, one of the most brilliant men I have ever known." And Lyndon Johnson always considered Marsh one of his mentors: The story goes that Marsh was the first person Johnson visited after his return to Washington from Dallas and the assassination of John F. Kennedy.

Marsh's appraisal of himself was pragmatic: "I am a wholesaler. Most people are retailers." He seemed, however, genuinely more interested in helping others than in enriching himself. His Public Welfare Foundation, to which he eventually left most of his fortune, was and is still devoted, in his words, to "the Greater Good of the greatest number." If he did not consider himself God, he did have a rather lofty view of his approach to the Greatest Good: "I am an eagle who floats in purposeless patterns—very, very high in the sky—until my eye catches a tiny object on the ground and I drop down in a single swoop to light squarely on it." And he was always looking for something new: "I wipe the slate that is my mind clean every night and begin with a clean one."

Many people have commented on the similarity between Ingersoll and Marsh—their quick intelligence, humanitarian liberalism, restless energy, volatile emotion, and an impetuosity that would prompt them, on the spur of the moment, to jump in one of their cars and drive to Oklahoma or Texas or South Carolina to look at a newspaper they were thinking about buying, or to Middletown, New York, to watch a harness race. They both loved to tell a story and did not hesitate to embellish the truth to improve it, usually with Marsh's disclaimer: "But in the main, it's true." They were also alternately outspoken or silent, depending on their mood. As Claudia says of her husband: "He never hesitated to express himself and he'd give you hell if he thought you were being stupid. . . . He was very peculiar because sometimes he'd just sit down and talk and be perfectly marvelous, but if he didn't feel like doing that, he'd be indifferent and not say much of anything."

When Marsh did talk, he usually mesmerized his audience. Once, in Hartford, he lectured a group of bankers on the newspaper business and afterwards one of them told Ingersoll, "All I want is to spend four days just listening to that man—that's the most extraordinary speech I ever heard."

Marsh's effect on Ingersoll was obvious to anyone who was around the two men, and Ingersoll made no effort to hide his admiration for his business mentor. Marsh, in fact, was the only man who ever inspired Ingersoll to biography. One day, when they were riding across Texas, Ingersoll said to him, "Charles, I've got to knock off and try to get you on paper some day." Marsh yelled, "Stop the car." And when Ingersoll pulled over to the side of the road, Marsh leaped out, ordered Ingersoll to follow, then came around and looked him straight in the eye. "Ralph," he said, "if you ever write one word about me, you will neither speak with me or ever see me again."

Years later, after Marsh's death, Ingersoll did start a biography of his business partner, and his admiration, fondness, and respect are apparent in the eight chapters of the unfinished manuscript. On one page he says simply: "I loved him." As Ingersoll describes Marsh, he was built like Lincoln, tall and gangly, but instead of Lincoln's craggy features, he had a head equally beautiful in its classical ugliness but quite different. "It is the head of a Mediterranean Semite— skull flawlessly shaped, great strength and size, a nose set between those inconsistent eyes and with a classically clean cut jaw." He was a Mediterranean Semite in his tastes too. Marsh loved lace, jewels, fine rugs—and bargaining for them. "He bought thousands of dollars worth of them just to give them away," says Ingersoll. "Paradoxically, he was totally without interest in possessing them himself."

Marsh was convinced that people did not live age chronologically. "When we were both in our sixties," says Ingersoll, "he told me that he estimated his age at around seven or eight hundred—and that I was still far from full grown, hardly more than five or six hundred"—a polite way, perhaps, of reminding Ingersoll of the emotional immaturity others have noticed in him. It was characteristic of Marsh to want always to appear to dominate those around him. One ex-*PM* staffer recalls visiting him: "I remember the morning," he says, "because Ingersoll was waiting outside in the hall, pacing up and down, as the old fox entertained me with tales of his prowess. And Marsh told me, a young stranger, that Ingersoll was at his beck and call: 'See the great Ingersoll out there? He'll do anything I tell him to because he wants the money and he's making a lot.'"

They were making money, which should have surprised no one. But what was surprising was that they enjoyed it so much. "They had great fun," says one who remembers the two men working together. "They had nothing but laughs. Jesus, it was funny to be with those men. There was just an electricity in the air when they were together."

The first venture undertaken by Marsh and Ingersoll was the backing of a mutual friend, Carol Janeway, in a small china-making business, primarily because Marsh wanted to help rehabilitate her. But Miss Janeway would not be rehabilitated, and after the R. J. Company took its losses, Marsh said, "Fine. Every business should begin with a failure."

The second venture—the buying and leasing of a press to a young newspaper publisher in Lawton, Oklahoma—was more profitable. Ingersoll played a major role in this coup, and it gave him his first real understanding of how money is made. But more important—to Marsh—the venture fulfilled all the essentials a business deal had to have to justify its usefulness in society: "The young publisher has a press he couldn't afford to buy, the banker is pleased with himself for having made his tiny profit, and Lawton, Oklahoma, has a better paper." And, of course, the company now had a net income of $1,000 a year made with OPM—"other people's money." A few years later, when the publisher bought the press, it had a $5,000 profit.

One of the principal reasons why Marsh invited Ingersoll to go into business with him was his desire to expand his newspaper holdings. He owned a number of papers in the Southwest and three in the East—in Clearwater, Florida; Martinsville, Virginia; and Middletown, New York. He wanted to add papers in the East, especially around Washington, D.C., and thought Ingersoll, who lived in the East and shared some of his ideas about newspapers, was "the natural person to do some traveling and investigating."

With Marsh directing the use of OPM, and Ingersoll enthusiastically carrying out orders, the R. J. Company prospered during the next four years, not only in the acquisition of small newspapers but in Texas oil, New York real estate, and stock market speculations. For Ingersoll, however, their most important venture by far was a complicated transaction in which Marsh transferred his eighty-percent ownership of the *Middletown Times-Herald* (New York) to the R. J. Company.

Another complicated deal was the one that enabled Ingersoll and Sue to become farmers on a large estate near Warrenton, Virginia. About the time Ingersoll and Sue were moving to Bucks County, Pennsylvania, Marsh acquired title to a large farm near his own estate in Virginia. It was a strange deal in which Marsh's wife, Alice, from whom he was separated but not divorced, had purchased for Marsh's younger brother a farm of Civil War vintage to give to Alice's sister as a wedding present. The price was sixteen thousand dollars. Charles's brother, who had just struck it rich in a Texas oil deal engineered by Charles, gave Alice a check for that amount, which she used to buy the estate after the title had been certified. The next day Charles's brother came to New York to visit him and dropped dead in his room in the St. Regis Hotel. Ingersoll and Sue happened to be at Marsh's apartment when he received a phone call from Alice asking him if the check was still valid, despite his brother's death. Marsh assured her that it was. And the farm was purchased in Marsh's name.

About a year later, when Sue had become bored in Bucks County, Alice was visited by Marsh's late brother's son and his bride-to-be. During the course of the visit the nephew asked, "By the way, Aunt Alice, what was the check for that my father gave you the day he died?" Alice explained about the farm, and the nephew said, "Maybe the place is mine, then"—and asked to see it. Alice took him over, and the bride-to-be looked around and then said, "Oh, we don't want that old house, but let's have those lovely boxwoods sent to us."

Marsh's reaction to all this was to sell the house immediately, before his nephew changed his mind, and the logical buyer was Ingersoll who was bored with commuting to New York and had a wife who was even more bored with his absences. Ingersoll still wanted to be a gentleman farmer and thought it would be wise to be closer to Marsh and to Washington, where the R. J. Company now owned forty-eight percent of the *Alexandria Gazette* (which it would later sell). So he took Sue down to see the farm, and "her reaction was instantaneous," he says. "At last, I'd found something that could really engage her; restoring and furnishing Castleton House."

Ingersoll leased Castleton in May of 1951 from the R. J. Company, which bought it from Marsh. But he did not move down to Virginia until the spring of 1952, just about the time Marsh decided to dissolve the R. J. Company. In 1952 the company was worth a little over a million dollars, which, divided by two, gave Ingersoll the half million Marsh had thought Ingersoll would need to raise and educate his children. Besides, Marsh's health was failing, so in the summer of 1952 he wrote Seymour Schneidman that he wanted to liquidate R. J., explaining that both he and Ingersoll were "looking forward to spending more and more time in Virginia at our respective residences—myself because of age and Ralph because he wishes to write in proper surroundings."

Schneidman had been Elaine's accountant, and after her marriage to Ingersoll he took over Ingersoll's tax accounting on *Top Secret*. Later he became the R. J. Company's accountant, and he would remain with Ingersoll for the next thirty years, eventually becoming his partner in various ventures and playing a critical role in the building and disposition of Ingersoll's own financial empire. Dividing the R. J. Company in 1952 was easy: the *Middletown Times-Herald* was worth approximately $500,000, so Marsh agreed to let Ingersoll have it (and Castleton), while he took the rest of the company, which consisted mostly of minority stock holdings in the Gannett newspaper company. The deal was very attractive to Ingersoll because the *Times-Herald* was then a monopoly

Castleton House—near Culpepper, where Ingersoll tried briefly to become a Virginia gentleman in the 1950s.

newspaper. Run by Charles Koons, the paper was producing an annual income of over $100,000—which was not a bad return on Ingersoll's original investment of $50,000.

At this point Ralph Ingersoll looked like a business genius and was so carried away with his success that he began to outline a book to be titled "How to Make Money" (it was never completed). His own skepticism about just how well he was going to handle his newly gained wealth is reflected in the introduction: "I haven't had my dollars, say half a million of them, long enough to convince the objective part of me that I will keep them. . . . My previous record is against it. . . . Clearly, I am not emotionally adjusted to give it all away, to say the hell with it, it's only a game and the game is over because I've won."

What he really wanted most was to settle into the comfortable life of the Virginia gentleman and devote his time to farming and writing. Sue, meanwhile, was doing very well in the poultry business and had become a well-known figure around the Virginia suburbs of Washington, where she went door-to-door in her station wagon selling her eggs to the wives of Pentagon generals.

She was not, however, doing very well in her marriage. She had gradually begun to develop emotional problems and was eventually diagnosed as psychotic. As a result, she became a difficult and unpredictable mother, not only to Ralph's two young children but to her own as well. As the tensions mounted she and Ralph became formally estranged; Ingersoll's female friends made her jealous, which increased the tension between her and Ralph's children.

As long as there was income from the Middletown paper, and the going was good, the Ingersolls managed to maintain their marriage. But the death of Charles Koons in late 1952 upset their precarious tranquility. Ingersoll had to spend more time in Middletown helping to train Helen Mauro, the *Times-Herald*'s office manager, to run the paper while he looked for a new publisher.

Ingersoll guessed that with Koons's death there would be renewed outside interest in the Middletown situation, and he was right: By the end of the year he had received a number of offers to buy the *Times-Herald*, and there were rumors of other publishers coming in to start a competing paper. But Ingersoll exuded confidence and at one stockholder's meeting said he was not alarmed: "The histories of these raids on established positions are monotonously similar." He went on to describe how the competitors come in, buy shiny new equipment, spend a lot of money, only to find that the community can support only one paper. Then "the proprietor of the established property will be offered the choice of buying out the assets of the competitor or plugging along until it drowns in its own red ink. How long this cycle takes to complete itself depends entirely on how well-heeled are the backers of the new paper. If they are both rich and stubborn, the contest will go on for a long time. . . . But the contest always comes out in favor of the established paper because the ultimate decision is with the readers of both papers and the tradition of the established paper is too strong."

Ingersoll's prescience was, in fact, uncanny. Within four years his prophesy came true, and the results were almost as he had predicted—almost, but not quite.

Ingersoll's immediate reaction was to abandon the good life of the Virginia gentleman and move to Middletown. But Sue would not leave Castleton. So Ingersoll had to make frequent trips to New York, which meant leaving Sue alone and spending more time with Koons's assistant, Helen Mauro. Mauro was, at first, somewhat awed by Ingersoll. He radiated confidence and charm and seemed to "know it all." He had total recall of meetings and events and was a superb "money man," meaning he was good at finding sources from which to borrow money and at charming the bankers into letting him have it. A 1953 letter reveals Mauro congratulating him for his finesse in handling one of these deals; she says, too, how much she would like to have the opportunity to help him with a book.

Gradually, as Ingersoll spent more and more time in Middletown, he and Helen became intimate. Ingersoll says, "It was a very practical business on both sides. Helen knew I was unhappy with Sue. OK. She made me happy enough to take Sue, whom she admired and was not jealous of. Life settled down to my coming to Middletown regularly to see Helen very much 'on business.'" Sue, of course, learned of the relationship. She did not seem to be jealous at first, but eventually a psychiatrist told her she was harboring a deep resentment and needed therapy.

At the same time Mauro, while charmed by Ingersoll personally and still respecting his financial manipulations, came gradually to question his ability as a manager. "He's very poor with unions," she says, "because he's always pro-labor." She also complained that he continually took too much money out of the company—for his cows, his yacht, his way of life—which prevented the paper from maintaining adequate operating reserves. "I hope you will make a New Year's resolution," she wrote him near the end of 1954, "to get down to work and earn some money so that we have a reserve for meeting emergencies. . . . If not, you can start looking for someone to take over from me. I don't mind being Mrs. *Times-Herald* but being both Mr. and Mrs. *Times-Herald* without any help from you and without any operating reserves is getting me down."

Mauro, however, did not quit, though Ingersoll continued to take money out of the paper. "I remember one time," she says, "he came up and told me he wanted twenty thousand dollars. I looked at him and told him he couldn't have it. I thought he was going to hit me. And he leaned across the desk and said: 'It's my money,' and I said: 'If you hit me, there's a police department across the street.'"

In Ingersoll's defense, he had at that time had little experience of running a small paper and did not want any part of it. One problem was that despite his skill at engineering "deals," he was never really interested in money, except in so far as it allowed him to lead the good life, have the freedom to write, and, during this period, maintain the Castleton farm. He had gone extensively into the cattle business—a proper occupation for a Virginia gentleman, which he found interesting as well. And, of course, this life of modest luxury proved to people that while he might have failed at *PM*, he had succeeded in life. He believed he had the right to take out of the *Times-Herald* money he had earned.

From time to time there were rumors around Middletown that Ralph Ingersoll was a Communist and that his paper *PM* had been Communist. This would give Helen Mauro a headache for a while, but it was not hard to convince people that any paper that carried Westbrook Pegler (as the *Times-Herald* did) could not be Red. The fact is, it made little difference whether Ingersoll was a Communist or not because he had nothing to do with running the paper. All Ingersoll wanted was the money; and in late 1955 he was complaining to Helen that he needed "to get back to writing for six months" without having to worry about money problems.

The truth is, things were not going well at Castleton. Ingersoll had never really recovered from the loss of Elaine. He wrote about his feelings one Christmas in an autobiographical sketch: "'Tis the night after Christmas and here sits Santa. Santa of Castleton. . . . This is a self-portrait of Santa. Santa by Santa, aged 53. . . . Yesterday he felt like Hell. Christmas has got out of hand. . . . For four years, up to this year, he could blame it on his new wife and children. . . . "No satisfaction at all in blaming it on them this year. Everything went smoothly. . . . If Christmas meant more debts, they weren't as large—and there was more money around with which to Peter and Paul them. It showed shabby to get angry because Sue had been brought up to fill the stockings weeks ahead and slip them into the children's room after they fell asleep—instead of simply hanging them in Father and Mother's room to be found filled on the dawn's first visit.

"The trouble was not with the family. It was with Santa. . . . Christmas comes when it has to, but it shouldn't come to Santa when he's writing a book about himself. It takes him back, it takes him back."

The book referred to was an effort "to put the fantastic story of *PM* on paper," as he had put it to Simon Michael Bessie, an editor at Harper Brothers. But when he had written about seventy thousand words, Bessie told him that Cass Canfield "thought the idea as dead as *PM*."

So he abandoned that project and was casting about for his next subject when he received a letter from John McCallum, a new editor at Harcourt Brace, who wanted to come to Castleton to meet him. The meeting produced a contract with a $2,000 advance for a five-volume autobiography. The first volume was supposed to be ready in the spring of 1956, but it was slow going. There were simply too many problems—at Castleton and then in Middletown. Sue was fighting more with young Ralph, who was by then, according to Helen Mauro, "the apple of his father's eye." But Sue said quite openly that she hated him. Another point of tension developed in 1956, when Sue, against Ingersoll's wishes, decided to adopt a baby boy. The baby was christened Stephen Brooks Ingersoll, and Sue would not let Ingersoll have anything to do with him, a state of affairs that did not particularly upset Ingersoll. In addition, his farming was turning sour: "I'm sure of only one thing," he wrote Schneidman, "that I know less now than when I started. I am not even sure I am enjoying it."

Then, sometime in mid-1956, Ingersoll heard that Jacob Kaplan had sold his company, which produced Welch's grape juice, and decided to move into Middletown to start a competing newspaper. Ingersoll had met Kaplan years earlier when Marsh still owned the *Times-Herald* and Kaplan tried to buy it. Marsh had treated Kaplan rather arrogantly, told him how much Middletown was making annually, and offered to sell the paper at an outrageously high price. Now Kaplan was back, attempting to start a new paper.

At first Ingersoll did not take his competition seriously. "Enter the Ingersoll ego," he says. "I did not think [Kaplan's] boys could break my monopoly." When he was asked by Nathan Levin (whom he knew from *PM* days when Levin represented the Rosenwald family) if he would meet with Kaplan, Ingersoll said sure: "I have no good news to give Kaplan—only that if he [comes into] Middletown, I would give him one hell of a bloody nose." Ingersoll also told Levin he had been assured there would be "a united hostile front against Kaplan coming into New York State—with no holds barred."

Kaplan was not frightened, however, and went ahead with his plan to compete with Ingersoll in Middletown—why, no one is quite sure. Some thought he wanted to establish a paper sympathetic to liberal Jewish ideas in a conservative, anti-Semitic community; others speculated that with Ingersoll absent, draining money from the operation, and thought by many in the community to be a Communist, Kaplan believed the *Times-Herald* was vulnerable. Kaplan said at the time that his plan was to start a morning tabloid, to be called the *Record*, which would be printed by the new photo-offset process. And if this new process was as revolutionary as he thought it might be, he could go around the country starting new papers on photo-offset presses and run the existing papers out of business.

Middletown was picked, he said, because studies convinced him the town needed another newspaper, because he had been given a promise of advertising support, and because the prospects for the future growth of Middletown were excellent enough to support two papers. Kaplan, who had also owned and operated Hearn's department store in New York, had established a tax-free foundation, and, according to *Editor and Publisher*, his Middletown newspaper was being financed by the foundation, which made it even more difficult for Ingersoll to compete. As Kaplan says today: "I had two bright young journalists I wanted to back and I thought we could start a paper for a half-million dollars. We tried to pick a town that had a miserable paper and Ingersoll's paper in Middletown was one of the worst in the country."

Whatever the motives, Kaplan came in and Ingersoll prepared for a fight. He had the backing of most New England publishers, and a broker, Vincent Manno, told him, "If you ever sell out to Kaplan—or give him one single dollar for his property—you'll be underwriting blackmail and have every publisher in the country against you for life."

The fight with Kaplan in Middletown dragged on for three years and was given continuing coverage by *Editor and Publisher*, which considered it a struggle of historic significance. Could a publisher with big money, which he was ready and willing to lose, come into a community and spend the established paper into bankruptcy by forcing it to compete with the interloper? It was a tactic the big food chains and oil companies had used to force small grocery stores and gas stations out of business, and now it was being tried in the newspaper business.

Ingersoll did everything he could to compete with Kaplan, but according to Helen Mauro it was too late. He had taken too much out of the company, and it did not have the reserves to match Kaplan's. Ingersoll's first move was to write Kaplan proposing a cooperative venture in a neighboring area, but Kaplan declined. Tom Braden, the author, publisher, and TV commentator, made an offer to buy the *Times-Herald*, but Ingersoll declined. The rumors began to spread that he could not afford to compete with Kaplan and would be forced to sell out to him. Ingersoll conceded that Kaplan's competition had forced him to spend money on new equipment and that he had lost some advertising to Kaplan, but he told his staff, "We are not selling out. Nuts to such rumors." He put an investigator to work looking into Kaplan's past, but the information he gained did not help. He stopped taking a salary from the paper and began to cut operating costs as much as possible.

For the first six months after Kaplan announced his decision to come in, Ingersoll remained in Virginia, working on his autobiography, confident that Helen Mauro and her staff could handle the situation. Rumors kept drifting back to Castleton that Kaplan was boasting he could wear Ingersoll down, that he was "Standard Oil" and Ingersoll just a little gas station. He knew Ingersoll's resources "to the penny," Kaplan said, so was certain he could not afford to compete. It would not have been hard to ascertain Ingersoll's resources because they were minimal and draining fast. By early 1957 he had had to sell his yacht, give up the good life in Virginia, and move up to Middletown to take over. He rented a small apartment in Goshen, New York (about ten miles from Middletown), a move he did not regret. Although he had not formally separated from Sue, life with her had become virtually intolerable and the crisis in Middletown enabled him to make a plausible withdrawal. Sue refused to move to New York, although she did visit him there.

The crisis also meant that he had to give up his writing, at least temporarily. When he had finished the first volume of his autobiography in 1956, Harcourt Brace said they liked it but wanted him to cut it in some places and carry it through the *New Yorker* years. His editor, John McCallum, also reported that one of their young editors had said, "The book keeps setting my teeth on edge." This reaction, McCallum explained, had to do with Ingersoll's annoying habit of suddenly inserting personal asides, usually corny, which disturbed the narrative and suggested that he did not have confidence in his story and was somewhat embarrassed by what he was writing. It was a valid criticism about a fault

Ingersoll never successfully overcame in his memoirs—published or unpublished.

Before he went to Goshen, Ingersoll rewrote the first volume of the autobiography, following his publisher's suggestions. Then, several months later and while he was up to his neck in the Middletown fight, McCallum wrote him a long letter saying that although he was satisfied with the book in general, he had several complaints, especially about the *New Yorker* section, which, he said, was not "exceedingly good autobiography or even exceedingly good writing. You have thrown chronology and structure and narrative out of the window" —again, a valid criticism of Ingersoll's autobiographical efforts. He does not stick to chronology in his narrative, and his memoirs invariably come out as a collection of disjointed "stories," often concluded with a corny comment, such as "Thus endeth the story of my affair with Lillian Hellman." McCallum also thought the book needed a theme.

Ingersoll was furious. He said he should have had the publisher's response in the fall, before he had packed up and moved to Goshen; and as for the theme, he wrote, "the nearest theme I found was that I didn't really know who or what I was and was writing this book to see if I could find some club. . . . If that's dopey, it's true. Your famous men who write piously about the influences that make them great are—I have concluded—talking through their hats." He also said: "I cannot tear up the ms. and start over again. I have gone back to work full time, seven days and nights a week in Middletown. . . . When this struggle is determined (either way) I will be back to writing. Not before."

The first three or four months in Middletown he spent, as he told one magazine writer, "learning what was to me a new trade—for I have personally never administered an operation of this size . . . a very different thing from a 200,000 circulation newspaper in New York or a . . . national magazine."

Ingersoll did not alter the Middletown operation dramatically. He still tried to give his local people maximum authority and made no effort to reform the *Times-Herald* or to introduce innovations, as he had done on *PM*. Instead, he adhered to the time-honored formula of the small-town newspaper—local news gathered by local reporters, local editorials written by local editorial writers, national world news, as well as background and feature stories supplied by the Associated Press and the United Press, additional features and comics bought from the syndicates. It was Kaplan who supplied the innovations with his tabloid format, emphasis on photographs, and short news stories. And, of course, the new offset press—which Ingersoll concedes he was slow to appreciate.

Although Ingersoll never lost money during this period and his circulation actually increased, Kaplan did take advertising revenue away from the *Times-Herald*, and the *Record*'s circulation increased in the outlying areas, a situation Ingersoll countered by buying the *Port Jarvis Union-Gazette*. By mid-July he was writing Marsh to give him a full report and outline his "overall plan." That plan, he said, was to drive through July and August for circulation "and to back up both my rate increase and financing efforts necessary for the purchase of a new press to replace an obsolete press and a new building to house the new press. If successful, I will go ahead this Fall with the building—in the meantime seeing what I can do to cut back editorial costs once we have our circulation objective. Knock, knock on wood. All this presumes that Kaplan will still be here but I gamble (1) that he will not improve his second running position and (2) that he will eventually tire and quit and move elsewhere. If I lose these gambles, I am cooked."

By the end of the year the situation had become critical. But something else had developed that would mark a significant turning point in Ingersoll's life. Seymour Schneidman had found another paper for him—the *Pawtucket Times* (Rhode Island). In addition to advising Marsh and Ingersoll on their financial affairs, Schneidman was the accountant for Mark Goodson and William Todman, inventors and producers of several successful television game shows— the best-known of which, at that time, was "What's My Line." As Goodson recalls it, one of their shows had just gone off the air, leaving them with a defunct company that had accumulated a lot of cash. That money would have to be reinvested in a hurry or else it would be taxed. Goodson and Todman had in the past put most of their excess money into "little pieces of real estate." But Schneidman (who was both impressed by Ingersoll's reputation and ability as a newspaperman and convinced he was fighting a losing battle against Kaplan in Middletown) suggested to them that they meet with Ingersoll and talk about buying the *Pawtucket Times*, which he knew was available. Goodson and Todman would put up fifty percent of the money, while Ingersoll, Schneidman, and some of his clients would put up the other fifty percent. Ingersoll would be paid for operating the paper and Ingersoll and Schneidman would get a small share of stock for their services, in addition to whatever stock they purchased. This deal not only relieved Ingersoll's personal financial problem but provided the structure for a rather unusual and complex newspaper "empire" that today produces a gross revenue of over two hundred million dollars a year.

Ingersoll met with Goodson and Todman in New York, and the first problem was that Goodson had never heard of Pawtucket or the *Times*. Furthermore, he wondered why anyone would want to own a paper that had to compete with the *Providence Journal*. But Ingersoll convinced him that this was the essence of the local newspaper business: that despite the existence of a big, well-known neighboring paper, people still looked to their hometown papers as the only place they could find coverage of local events and local advertising. Goodson was impressed also by Ingersoll himself: "That was the first time," he recalls, "that I learned about his connections with Henry Luce and *Fortune* and Ross and the *New Yorker*. I did know him as the editor of *PM* and I thought: 'Oh, here's this fellow that ran *PM* and he's probably a superliberal. How will he be in the hard-nosed business of running a local paper to make money? Of course, it turned out that his liberalness never interfered with his being a tough businessman. He was a very hard-nosed guy with dollars and cents. He was also very self-confident, highly articulate, slightly dramatic, a theatrical fellow. Extremely optimistic. And that optimism especially impressed Goodson who says he tends to be skeptical, "always waiting for the next earthquake to happen."

They agreed to buy the paper jointly. Most of the $3 million asking price was advanced by local bankers, and the remaining $700,000 was put up in cash with Goodson and Todman contributing half of that amount and Schneidman, Ingersoll, and a couple of Schneidman's clients contributing the remaining half. To finance his share, Ingersoll used the money he held in trust for Ralph II and Jonathan.

One problem in the beginning was that some of the bankers were convinced Ralph Ingersoll was a Communist. To reassure them, he made a special trip to Pawtucket to show them his entry in *Who's Who*. The next problem was the suspicion among Pawtucket residents that their paper was being taken over by some sort of New York mafia group. "We went up there for the closing," says Goodson, "and in walked these men from the bank. There was nobody in there under ninety years of age. They were wearing their original suits. We walked in there with Schneidman smoking a cigar, Todman and Chick Vincent [an investor] wearing camel-hair coats, and me in one of my fancy New York Dunhill suits. Ralph had on conservative New England-style clothes. But the youth and slickness of this group surprised the bankers. I thought, at first, they were going to change their minds. They demanded a certified check, which we had, and they would not hand over their piece of paper until we handed them ours." At lunch there were at least twelve, and Goodson says, "It was cold up there and we had twelve coats. So I gave the hatcheck girl two dollars and a shocked New Englander said, 'You want to spoil them?' I said, Well, I thought for twelve coats that wasn't too much, and another banker said, 'Oh, don't do that. You'll come up here and just destroy everything.' They were very conservative."

The bankers finally agreed to the sale, however, and Ingersoll went back to coping with his Middletown crisis, although he now had overall responsibility for management of the Pawtucket paper as well, for which he received a salary of twenty-five thousand dollars a year.

In Middletown there were signs that Kaplan was beginning to chafe at his losses, which were estimated to be as high as twenty thousand dollars a month. A meeting was arranged for Kaplan and Ingersoll. It took place in New York at the Oak Room of the Plaza, where Kaplan offered to buy Ingersoll out, hire him as vice president and director, and give him twenty-five percent of the stock with the right to draw cash against it. Ingersoll said he would think it over. Then he arranged another meeting through the go-between, Harry Madden, telling Madden to report back to Kaplan that he did not want to be part of any operation in which he was not "in the driver's seat," but that as he thought a merger would be mutually advantageous, he was prepared to make Kaplan the same offer he (Kaplan) had made him.

They met again at the Oak Room to discuss Ingersoll's counterproposal. When Kaplan read the memo Ingersoll had prepared, he was incredulous and waved it violently as he spoke: "I don't believe a word of this, it's just a trading move." Ingersoll replied that if Kaplan did not believe it, there was nothing more to talk about. According to Ingersoll, Kaplan then launched into a lengthy monologue during which he was alternately disturbed, visibly so, then calm and reasonable. At one point he yelled, "Ingersoll, who the hell do you think you are? You never did a damned thing in your whole life"—by which he meant that Ingersoll was a failure because he had not retained any equity in the publications for which he had worked. "This did not seem so much personal hostility," Ingersoll says, "but an argument that Kaplan really believed should influence me. If I would recognize that I was a hired hand by nature, he was prepared to show me that he was the best employer I could imagine."

Ingersoll occasionally intervened to defend himself, and after about an hour of Kaplan's monologue he managed to get the floor to make his case: which was that he was the best man to give Middletown the paper it deserved and could support handsomely, if the two competing papers were merged.

Nothing came of the meeting, so the "war in Middletown," as the press had begun to describe it, dragged on, with Kaplan spending more and more and Ingersoll enjoying it less and less. At the same time his relationship with Sue was deteriorating, and her hostility to the Ingersoll children was becoming unbearable. By this time young Ralph II was spending most of his time in private schools, but when he was home, Sue made his life miserable, and at one point, young Ralph says, she tried to kill him. By early 1959 Ingersoll's emotional state was so disturbed that he thought he ought to see Dr. Gregory Zilboorg again. His affair with Helen Mauro was over, although she was still loyal to Ingersoll, but even more doubtful of his ability to manage any property he owned. "When he hitches his wagon to a star," she said, "and is responsible to somebody else, because of an ingrained honesty, he has better judgment in running an operation than he does running it for himself." To confirm this impression, she pointed to *PM*, his Castleton farm operation and the *Times-Herald*. "You couldn't reason with him when it came down to certain things as far as business was concerned."

Mrs. Mauro was also disturbed by the effects his battle with Kaplan and his distressing personal life seemed to be having on her boss. He was drinking more and often talked of suicide; when they drove around New York City, he would point out all the tall buildings from which numerous friends had jumped. Sue would come up to see him in Goshen or New York City, then she became catatonic and have to be carried upstairs or driven back to Virginia. Or else she would call him from Castleton and berate him in long, hysterical conversations about everything from an electrical problem to his extramarital affairs.

The last years of Ingersoll's marriage to Sue Doolittle are indeed tragic and depressing to report. And accounts of the relationship are conflicting. One who knew them both very well said, "Sue was kind of pathetic. I don't think she was very bright, and she just didn't fit." Another said, "She really was a number-one nuisance. She just wasn't right. There was definitely something wrong with the woman." Her emotional problems were also testified to by her sons, Jerry and Bill. They both carry scars from their childhood, and Bill finally became completely estranged from his mother: "I never saw her for the last ten years of her life." Ingersoll's younger son, Jonathan, has no complaints about his step-mother, but Ralph II remembers only that she hated him and they fought most of the time. Another person who knew them said, "I liked Sue. I think she got a dirty rotten break . . . one reason Ralph married her was for her money."

That charge plagued Ingersoll all during the declining years of his marriage to Sue. She did have about a hundred thousand dollars in an inherited trust fund, which, he says, he invested and doubled for her. But she also spent money recklessly, says Ingersoll, "all the time claiming: 'It's my money I'm spending.' She spent her money several times over," he adds, but when his back was to the wall in Middletown, he put the last thirty-five thousand dollars of Sue's money into the company. It is debatable, however, who married whom "for the money." Long before they were divorced, says Sue's former husband, but at a time when they were talking of a separation, Sue had indicated she wanted a divorce to marry someone with money. In fact, says Doolittle, "most of the problems in our marriage concerned money."

Meanwhile, Tommy, Ingersoll's first wife, was asking him to increase her alimony from five thousand to ten thousand dollars a year, and Ingersoll was seeking comfort from Millicent Matland, Elaine's younger sister whose husband had been killed in the highly publicized collision of two airliners over the Grand Canyon in 1956. Ingersoll was obviously very attracted to Mrs. Matland, but she declined to marry him.

By the summer of 1959 both Schneidman and Zilboorg were advising Ingersoll to leave Middletown. His paper, however, would show a profit for the year (even though it lost thirty-five hundred dollars in June), and Ingersoll did not want to give in to Kaplan. The press was following the "war" closely now. *Newsweek* said: "Whatever the outcome of the struggle, the remarkable and encouraging fact is that at a time when newspapers are dying or merging . . . today Middletown has two good newspapers with a [total] circulation of more than 30,000."

Ingersoll met with David Bernstein, Kaplan's public-relations manager, who had been installed as editor and publisher of the *Record*. They agreed the war could not go on; Middletown could not support two papers. Bernstein acknowl-edged that the *Record* was losing money, but said it did not matter because Kaplan's pride was involved and Kaplan did not like to lose. Ingersoll said he didn't either, and he intended to stick it out—for five years if necessary.

But that was not the truth. Ingersoll was ready to sell and had already been approached by James Ottaway, who owned a number of papers in New York and Pennsylvania. At the same time Schneidman had located another paper, the *Elizabeth Journal* (New Jersey), which could be bought from the Robert Crane family for $2.25 million. Ingersoll's ego made it difficult for him to sell out to Ottaway and he was firmly convinced he had licked Kaplan, a belief that was confirmed by two financial surveys of the *Times-Herald* Ottaway had made, which showed the paper was a sound investment. But Ingersoll also knew that Kaplan would never give in as long as he was running the *Times-Herald*, and he did not have the stomach to fight him any longer. He assessed their rivalry as the meanest kind of fight, with no political principles involved. They were both liberals who supported Democrats nationally and Republicans locally, and usually seconded each other's proposals in town meetings.

So, on a Friday in November of 1959, Ingersoll sold the *Times-Herald* to Ottaway, took the hundred thousand dollars he had left after paying off his debts, and invested it, along with Goodson, Todman, and Schneidman in the purchase of the *Elizabeth Journal*. Ingersoll took over the paper and began to run it on the following Monday. Now Ingersoll had definitely come out of retirement; he was running two newspapers and looking for more. From that time until his gradual retirement in the mid-1970s, he was in the business of newspaper management—and he did extremely well, despite his record at *PM* and the *Times-Herald*, and despite the feeling of Mauro and others that he was a poor operator, although a good administrator. Years later, he met Kaplan at a cocktail party and told him, "I want to thank you for one thing—for making me get off my ass and back to my trade."

Within a year of the sale of Ingersoll's Middletown paper, Ottaway bought the *Record* from Kaplan and folded the 109-year-old *Times-Herald*; Middletown became a one-paper town again. Kaplan shifted his operation to Binghamton and eventually lost interest in the newspaper business. Today, however, he says, "It was a big mistake to sell the Middletown paper. But it had cost too much to start; we thought we could do it for a half million and we spent two million on it." Ingersoll's feelings about the affair are reflected in a letter he wrote to a friend a year later: "No one, I think, who has ever had his heart in a competition is free from a little feeling of guilt when he turns the job of finishing the fight over to somebody else—however reasonable and profitable the move. The cold fact is that I could have stayed in Middletown—at a cost of the few more years of active life left me—'and for Christ's sake,' I told myself, 'what for?' It had turned into the kind of fight one gets into in one's early youth when somebody in a bar calls you a son of a bitch and you feel you have to defend your honor."

The situation in Elizabeth was much more to his liking. In the first place, the *Journal* was a monopoly paper with a circulation of fifty-two thousand. "A paper this size is ideal," he told a *Newsweek* reporter. "It's big enough so you can produce a good paper and not be pushed around by advertisers." It had always been a money-maker, and Ingersoll saw ways to make it more profitable. When Ingersoll took over, the staff was fearful that he would leave the operation in the hands of its former owner, Robert Crane, who was also editor and publisher. But he quickly became dissatisfied with Crane's management and took over the publishing side of the paper himself. Crane continued as editor, but eventually Ingersoll started an editorial column of his own—"Off My Chest." The editorials, however, were signed, and he made it clear that the opinions expressed therein were his own and that he was not speaking as the editorial voice of the *Journal*.

Josephine Novella, who worked for Crane and eventually became Ingersoll's personal secretary and assistant—a job she continued to hold for more than twenty years—recalls her first impression of him: "In the beginning I was apprehensive because I had never worked for anyone like him. He was an extraordinary person, a marvelous administrator, who knew what he was doing. He would come in in the morning and go through his mail in maybe a half hour; he read a letter and decided immediately what had to be done about it. His letters were fascinating, just as though he was talking to someone, very down-to-earth. When the paper did not change, people were relieved."

At first it did not appear that the partnership with Goodson and Todman would last, because the television producers were skeptical about Ingersoll's management ability. The focal point of the conflict was the *Pawtucket Times*. Allen Kander, the original broker, tried, with some success, to convince Goodson and Todman that Ingersoll was detrimental to the paper. Schneidman assured them otherwise and pointed out that one of the banks had the right to recall its loan if Ingersoll did not manage the paper. So Ingersoll remained, and Goodson and Todman were eventually convinced that he was essential to the operation.

As soon as the *Journal* was functioning under his management, Ingersoll became interested in the Trenton, New Jersey, *Trentonian*, and we began negotiating with its publisher, Edmund Goodrich. But they would go out to lunch, agree on a price, and then nothing would happen. Goodrich went to Las Vegas every winter, so in February of 1961 Ingersoll decided to bring the deal to a head. He took a plane to Vegas and spent several days with Goodrich, mostly at the gaming tables. They never talked about the *Trentonian*. Finally Ingersoll gave up and was ready to leave; at the airport Goodrich said, "I've got to have one million fifty-five thousand dollars for the paper!"*

"You've got it," Ingersoll said, convinced it was worth much more. He, Schneidman, and friends of Schneidman's put up twenty-five percent of the down payment; Goodson and Todman put up twenty-five percent, and they borrowed the rest. Goodrich wanted to retire, but Ingersoll insisted that, as part of the deal, he stay on and run it for five years. Goodrich agreed, and the *Trentonian* prospered, gaining about two thousand new readers a year for several years.

The purchase was completed in May of 1961, and the following month the same group bought the *Delaware County Daily Times*, published in Chester, Pennsylvania—another complex transaction, with Goodson and Todman owning ninety percent; Schneidman, five percent; and Ingersoll, five percent. Ingersoll also had a firm contract to manage the paper, for which he was paid a salary.

Despite his expanding newspaper operations, Ingersoll once more found time to write. In 1960 he had settled down to rework his autobiography for Harcourt Brace. When it was delivered, they were still disappointed but published

---

*Goodrich had paid $55,000 for the paper originally and confessed to Schneidman years later that he had arrived at this figure because he wanted to make a profit of $1 million.

it anyway in the fall of 1961 under the title *Point of Departure*. The reviews were generally favorable, although a few, such as the one in *Newsweek*, found it "disappointingly mediocre." But the *Library Journal* said it "recaptured the spirit of that innocent optimism which animated America and Americans until the advent of the Great Depression"; the *Herald-Tribune* thought Ingersoll's style "gives it charm"; the *(London) Times* said Ingersoll was "not a writer of the class of the late James Thurber" but commented that he made Harold Ross "more intelligible and more attractive"; and William Horn, in the *San Francisco Chronicle*, lamented that the memoirs ended with Ingersoll's leaving the *New Yorker*. The best, he said, was yet to come.

The title, *Point of Departure*, was carefully selected by Ingersoll. This was, it was meant to suggest, just the beginning. Still to come were the *Time-Life* years with Luce, the "fabulous" story of *PM*, the war years, and then his life as a successful manager of small newspapers. Ingersoll started work on the next volume in the fall of 1961—although by this time it was his personal life, not the newspapers, that made it difficult for him to write.

In the winter of 1961 he had his final fight with Sue, who threatened him with a knife and demanded that he take his children and leave Castleton at once. He had been living most of the time in New York and commuting to Elizabeth. Now he bought a house in Red Bank, New Jersey, halfway between Trenton and Elizabeth and on the Navesink River, which he thought would provide Ralph and Jonathan a place for a boat when they were home from school. Sue kept Castleton, and Ingersoll gave financial support. Although he saw her from time to time and they did correspond, the break was final and would end in divorce.

Once again Ralph Ingersoll was at a low point in his life; he felt he had never really regained his capacity to love or show emotion after Elaine's death and the three-year fight in Middletown had taken its toll. The new papers provided an income, but they did not really interest him. His ambition, still, was to write, although the reviews of *Point of Departure* had not been particularly encouraging. The fact is that as Ingersoll grew older, he began to lose that white-heat edge to his writing that had made his reporting so compelling. The personal style of his autobiographies was a little too coy and cute to please most of his readers or his editors.

He still had his family, though, and rereading his voluminous correspondence of the 1950s and 1960s, one sees how much he loved his stepchildren and his two sons and how proud he was of them. He may not have given his sons all the love and attention they needed, but he was an extremely loyal father who did everything in his power to help them. In 1961, when he separated from Sue, young Ralph was fifteen and Jonathan thirteen. Ralph was studious and intellectual and rapidly growing taller than his father. Johno, as they called Jonathan, was stockier, very handsome and sociable, and had ambitions to be a football player. Young Ralph showed signs of wanting to be a writer and had already worked on one of his father and Charles Marsh's newspapers, although he had also indicated to his father that he felt newspaper work was not intellectually challenging. Jonathan, on the other hand, showed little interest in journalism. Stepsons Jerry and Bill junior had already gone into journalism: Jerry was writing a satiric column for the *Washington Post*; Bill junior, after working for his stepfather on the *Trentonian*, was a reporter for the *Boston Globe* and would eventually own a paper in Saranac Lake, New York. Patricia had married, divorced, attended the University of Michigan where she studied mathematics, and was happily remarried. The stepchildren felt that, while their stepfather could sometimes be emotional and unpredictable, and had a "hair-trigger temper," he was loyal, concerned about their well-being, and caring. Bill junior vividly remembers one period when his stepfather came to his aid—while he was at Harvard and, inexplicably, in a deep depression. "I thought I was going crazy," Doolittle says. "He came up to Middletown where I was working that summer and we went out to lunch. It took him about half an hour before he said, 'There's something wrong, Bill. What is it?' I hadn't said anything to him. We started talking. I think he saved my life that day. I think I was getting extremely suicidal. He recognized it and nobody else recognized it. He said, 'I'm going to get you some help'—and he did."

As he entered his sixties Ingersoll began to put on weight; he developed a puffy, gray look, and to many who knew him during this period, he appeared to be very bored. He had also become a card-carrying member of the Establishment, accepting an invitation to become a director of the Central Home Trust Company in Elizabeth and delivering the commencement address at the Union County Junior College. He was writing steadily, but the book about his years with Luce was not going well. Socially, he was a bachelor much in demand, with hostesses sometimes boasting that they had invited the famous Ralph Ingersoll for dinner, then wondering afterwards why he was reputed to be such an exciting character. Thelma Bradford, widow of the artist Francis Scott Bradford, remembers meeting Ingersoll at the house of a mutual friend, Paul Tishman. "He was gray-faced, bored and very fat." The hostess said to her in an aside, "I really can't understand all the fuss about Ralph Ingersoll, he never utters a word."

But Thelma, called Toby by almost everyone, and Ingersoll discovered they had many mutual friends, including Millicent Matland, whom Ralph was still attracted to, although she gave him little encouragement. He and Toby went out together occasionally, and then one night, as Toby tells the story, "Ralph called me to go to an opening at the Huntington Hartford Museum. We had a big dinner, and fancy too, and all evening long I was depressed and could see that Ralph was depressed too. And, as we were leaving, he said, 'I should take you to a nightclub to dance, but I just can't tonight.'

"That bothered me. And so the next morning I called his office in New Jersey, and said, 'How are you? Are you OK?' And by noon I had two dozen yellow roses.

"He said would I have lunch. And I said, 'I can't. I'm going to Spain.'

"That was my first intimation that there was somebody hiding under that face."

Ingersoll asked Toby to call him when she returned from Spain, and she did. They continued seeing each other, but neither was very interested in getting married: Toby, because she had just been through ten years of watching her husband die slowly from a heart ailment and then cancer; Ralph, because he still suffered from the lingering aftermath of the loss of Elaine and the unpleasantness of what he felt was a big mistake in marrying Sue. "I was totally convinced," he says, "I would never have a whole emotion again. Knowing Toby convinced me I could. It accumulated. It was not a case of love at first sight."

They began to see more and more of each other, and then, one day, Ingersoll went to Cornwall Bridge in Connecticut to advise Toby about her property. Earlier, when she had spent a year in Italy, she had lent her house to friends. Vandals had broken in, started a fire in one of the bedrooms, and the center of the house was gutted (and, tragically, most of Bradford's paintings destroyed). She wanted Ralph to help her decide whether to rebuild the old house or start a new one. "Tear it down," he said, "and marry me!"

She took his advice on both counts, and in 1964 Thelma Bradford and Ingersoll were married in the Tishmans' apartment on Sutton Place South, in New York City. And, of course, people picking up Sue's immediate reaction were quick to say, "He married her for her real estate."

Honorary Doctor of Humane Letters, Boston University, 1980

16: One Last Controversy

When he married Thelma Bradford, Ralph Ingersoll was sixty-three years old and she was several years younger. Soon he was writing friends: "It took a long time to find the right wife again and I often wonder what entitles me to be so fortunate as I am."

Instead of rebuilding the Bradford house on the Housatonic, they built a new one, and Ingersoll could contemplate the coming years with a devoted younger wife, two children, and three stepchildren, who remained close to him—closer, in fact, than they were to their own parents. His generation was beginning to die or drift into retirement, thinking as often of the past as of the present. "Probably, we should form a survivors' club group," wrote E. B. White, "with an annual meeting and high dues. Perhaps you can throw out an extra wing on that house you are building to hold us. I shouldn't think it would have to be very large. The *New Yorker*, by the way, just celebrated its 40th—as you doubtless observed in the papers. God must watch over it—forty years, fifty-two issues a year.... Yours, down memory lane—Andy."

In 1965 they moved into the new house, which, having risen from ashes, was christened appropriately. "The Phoenix is a joy," Ingersoll wrote his step-daughter. He was still dependent primarily on his income; and although he had been in a deep depression when he married Toby, he soon came out of it. "Ralph has very blue eyes," says Toby, "and I can always tell when he is unhappy. They turn cold gray." Now his eyes were blue most of the time, "and he was terribly witty during this period. He was having the time of his life." Ingersoll was beginning what he would later tell Toby was the happiest twenty years of his life. "For the first time, I'm not driven."

He also had the time and inclination to do the kinds of things a man of achievement and affairs does as he enters the downside of his career: At Toby's urging, he sat for a portrait by the Philadelphia artist Franklin Watkins; he donated his papers to Boston University, picking that library because the chief of special collections, Dr. Howard Gotlieb, was interested in all the Ingersoll family papers, not just Ralph's, and because they were beginning to take up considerable space. There was also an honorary degree for the donor. The couple took long trips abroad: "We would go to Tahiti on a weekend," says Toby. After moving into the Phoenix in 1965, they traveled by boat through the Greek islands, and the following summer they went back to Europe for what Ingersoll called "the longest holiday I've taken for almost 20 years." The winter was spent in Antigua, where they stayed with some friends, the Larry Hammonds, and visited the Archibald MacLeishes. Afterwards they decided to buy a winter home in the Caribbean.

Ingersoll was also writing long letters to his family and friends boasting of the achievements of his sons and stepchildren. The Doolittles, Bill junior, Jerry, and Patricia, were young adults now, on their own and progressing in their chosen walks of life: Bill by then had become owner and publisher of the *Adirondack Daily Enterprise* in Saranac Lake; Jerry had joined the U.S. Information Agency and was stationed in Casablanca (later he would be transferred to Laos); and Patricia had a Ph.D. in mathematics and her husband, Fred Shure, was teaching plasma physics at the University of Michigan. Young Ralph and Jonathan were growing up, too, despite a father who loved his sons but was not very good at raising children. "Ralph loves helping young people," says Toby, "but he is not a father. He is a man for a woman. He could never sustain an interest in a small child."

Ingersoll always felt guilty about entrusting his two sons (whom he considered a "present" from Elaine) to Sue Doolittle, and Jonathan once said to him, "Why didn't you have enough sense to get a nice, fat nanny?" Toby tried to fill the gap, but it was not easy, and at the time she married Ingersoll, it was really too late. Ralph junior was eighteen and Jonathan, sixteen. There were also the usual teenage problems and revolt. Jonathan's rebellion had reached the point where he was calling himself Ian, rather than his given name, and when he was preparing to enter his senior year at the Salisbury School, he suddenly announced that he was going to finish his education in Europe, as his brother had. His father said "No dice," so Ian disappeared for over a month, putting his parents "in a state." When they finally heard of him it was to learn that he had enlisted in the army, was in basic training at Camp Gordon, Georgia, and intent on joining the paratroopers. Ingersoll immediately wrote his friend Clare Beck, now a general stationed in Honolulu, asking him to "keep an eye on [Ian] in the army—without his knowing that I'm doing any such thing." He stressed that he was not opposed to an army career and had no objection to his son's going into combat, but he felt Ian was exceptional and it would be to the army's advantage to see that he completed his high-school education and become a candidate for officers training school. Beck said he would see what he could do.

Meanwhile, Ian was doing very well on his own. Although he had not completed high school, he was admitted to the officer candidate school at Fort Benning, came out a lieutenant, and was sent to Vietnam. Put in charge of a paratroop platoon, he went into combat, despite his father's efforts to keep him out. Ian was opposed to the war and felt it had been a mistake to join the army. But he knew he had to see it through, although he spent most of the war trying to keep himself and his platoon alive. He made his men read *Catch-22*. When he was discharged in 1968, he had earned two Bronze Stars, three Purple Hearts, and eight lesser medals, all, he says, for pulling other people out of trouble. When he came out of the army, he changed his name legally to Ian Macrae Ingersoll, married the daughter of General Beck, and went home for a short visit with his parents.

Young Ralph's rebellion was more subtle and gradual but, in the long run, more emphatic and dramatic. He, too, failed to finish prep school. He was expelled from Groton for "attitude," which sent his father into a fury of letter-writing: to the headmaster (protesting the way the matter was handled), to young Ralph (telling him what was wrong with him). And he wrote to various friends, trying to help his son gain admission to the International School in Geneva—which he did after Clayton Fritchey (press secretary to the U.S. ambassador to the United Nations, Adlai Stevenson) and Roger Tubby (the ambassador to the U.S. Mission in Geneva) wrote letters stating that young Ralph came from a brilliant family and seemed "to have inherited some of the talents of his father," as Fritchey phrased it.

After graduating from the International School, he enrolled in the University of Grenoble, France, for a year. Then he returned to this country to attend New York University as a premed student, although his father wrote one friend, "I really doubt his ending up in medicine; he's a born newspaper character." While at N.Y.U., Ralph II met and married an attractive young German girl named Ursula Daiber. Unfortunately, his father and Toby were not able to get along with the new Mrs. Ingersoll, and the groundwork was laid for a simmering interfamily feud that intensified over the years. Young Ralph decided not to go into medicine. He graduated from N.Y.U. with a degree in chemistry, then proceeded to dissipate part of his inheritance from his mother in the stock market.

The problems and frictions that marked the first years of Ingersoll's marriage to Toby were probably no greater than those experienced by any family with teenagers, and perhaps not as traumatic as one might have expected in the circumstances. And Ingersoll spent quite a bit of his time traveling and in New York. "I tried to retire 10 years ago," he told a reporter, referring to his retreat to Castleton and his attempt to become a gentleman farmer-author, "but it didn't take." He was still primarily interested in writing, and the summer they went to Greece, he wrote a long series on the Greek islands for his papers. He also covered the Cassius Clay–Floyd Patterson fight in Las Vegas for the *Trentonian*, and when Henry Luce died, he wrote a remembrance for the *Washington Post*, conceding to friends that Luce's death marked "kind of an end of an era for me."

In 1967, when he was on his way to visit his stepson Jerry in Morocco, war broke out between the Arabs and the Israelis. The war-horse reporter responded to the bell and tried to get to the action, but it was too late, although he did do one piece for his papers, which concluded: "It must have been a curious war, indeed. I am sorry that I missed it." In fact, he had to fly back to London to find out who had won the Six-Day War.

When he had time, he was also working on "High Time," his book about the Luce years, which was not going well. Harcourt Brace rejected it, so he put it aside for a while, then dictated another draft to a new secretary. When it was completed, he found that the secretary was partially deaf and, because she did not want to say anything about it, had made up what she could not hear of Ingersoll's dictation. When Ingersoll discovered what had happened, he was so discouraged he put the manuscript aside for several years.

His newspaper management business, however, was doing very well—too well, in fact. By the fall of 1967 he had gone "kind of nuts," as he told one friend, and bought nine more newspapers for his management group. This contributed to the return of his ulcer, and when it perforated, he had two-thirds of his stomach removed. After the operation he felt better than he had done at any time in the last twenty years, but it gave him a tremendous scare, because he was convinced he had cancer that would prove terminal on the operating table, as it had for his old friend Charles Wertenbaker. His anxiety was relieved only by overhearing a conversation between interns—"otherwise I would never have been quite sure."

The ongoing partnership between the former editor of *PM* and the two television game show producers (who owned fifty percent of the company; the rest being owned by Ingersoll, Schneidman, and several of Schneidman's clients) was a curious one—and not without friction. Ingersoll made it clear to Goodson and Todman that they were in the partnership for one thing—investment. "He didn't want us to mingle too much in the newspaper business and get our names involved," says Goodson. "He wanted the Ingersoll name on those papers. And this annoyed us. I would meet people and they would say; 'What do you do besides television?' And I would say, 'Oh, we're involved in some newspapers.' And they would say, 'Oh. And where is that?' 'Well, we've got papers in Pawtucket and Fall River.' The guy would say, 'I thought those are Ingersoll papers.' I would say, 'We're involved.' 'To what extent?' 'Well, between Bill and myself, we own anywhere from fifty to eighty to ninety percent of the papers.' 'You do! We didn't know that.' "

Every now and then this sort of thing would "get to me," says Goodson, and he would tell his partner, "Ralph, I want more recognition." Ingersoll would reply, "Listen, what do you want—to make money or have recognition? This is not your area."

Occasionally, Ingersoll had the urge to own a newspaper completely, but when he arranged to buy one, Goodson and Todman were annoyed. "We're furnishing the bulk of the money for this operation," Goodson would say to Ingersoll, "and we're jealous of your time. I don't think you have any right to buy papers without us." So, in the early days, Ingersoll owned only one paper outright: the *Claremont Daily Eagle* (New Hampshire). And he decided to take all his capital out of General Publications, although he did have small shares of stock in most of the papers as a result of his management contracts. He now had responsibility for the management of seventeen papers (including eight weeklies). "I give myself the British title of managing director," he told one interviewer; and much of his time was spent looking for new papers for Goodson and Todman to buy, putting together the deals, then convincing the owners of the papers and the banks that Ralph Ingersoll was the best possible journalist in the country to manage the paper.

Every deal was different, but the typical "consultation contract" signed by Ingersoll called for him to take responsibility for, and to advise on the management of, the paper. He did not have to produce results, but he was given five percent of the increased profits. He was also usually given five percent of the paper's stock and an annual consultancy fee of twenty-five thousand dollars. And although he had the responsibility, Chet Spooner, manager of the Pawtucket paper, was number-two man and chief operating officer in Ingersoll's General Publications Company. A contract could be canceled with ninety days' notice.

After the early conflict over the management of the *Pawtucket Times*, the Ingersoll-Goodson-Todman partnership flourished, and despite the television producers' periodic desire for more recognition, the friction was held to a minimum— the principal reason, of course, being that under Ingersoll's management the papers made money. And as the money came in, more papers were bought, which made even more money. It was a nice deal for all the investors, even if the people Goodson and Todman met at cocktail parties treated them as television game show producers rather than newspaper publishers. It was also a nice deal for Ingersoll, who knew the newspaper business, no longer wanted to reform it, and was content to give a community a good newspaper, which would also make enough money to give him the freedom to write and travel. Ingersoll was good at what he did, and although most of his associates thought he was better at putting the "empire" together than he was at administering it, his company made money—and lots of it.

There was no particular Ingersoll "formula" for the acquisition and running of a newspaper. A small or medium-size paper usually did not come on the market until an owner died and taxes forced a sale, or when children or grand-children had inherited a paper, could not agree on who should run it, or how, and the paper was not producing the money they had come to expect. "The most important single fact I learned from Charles Marsh about buying newspapers," Ingersoll says, "was that the key to success was understanding the emotional relationship involved. Every single newspaper I ever bought or tried to buy eventually put me in possession of enough material for a solid novel, none of which was ever written."

His reports, Schneidman and Goodson agree, were superb and as readable as a novel. He was also adept at negotiations. "Ralph used to romance these old folks," says Goodson. "They would seem very resistant to some smart-ass tele-vision producer with his game shows. . . . He also didn't want the unions running around thinking they're dealing with Goodson and Todman, the rich television producers. . . . At least, Ralph used to tell us that, to keep us out."

The key to the success of the operation was Ingersoll's reputation, and everyone involved knew it. "And number two," says Schneidman, "his person-ality. He spoke in a very low-key way, no high pressure." In other words, the man who had convinced some of the wealthiest people in the country in 1939 that he was going to create a "new kind of newspaper" had not lost his touch. Only now he had a different message. "When newspaper people sell a paper," says Schneidman, "the family may have owned it for eighty or a hundred years. And they don't want anything upset. They knew that if Ralph bought the paper, he wouldn't change anything one iota. He would run it the same way; he would make economies and change the administrative end, but he wouldn't change the flavor of the paper. It was kind of a monument the people were selling and Ralph would convince them it would not be torn down. And if the people who worked for the paper were any good, he would not fire them. He had that reputation and people knew it."

The ideal property to buy, of course, was a monopoly paper in a small or medium-size town with a good economic base. And the worse the paper was doing, the better. If the paper was losing money or barely making a profit, the price would be lower. Ingersoll knew he would soon have the paper making more money—in some cases, *much* more. The papers Goodson, Todman, In-gersoll, and Schneidman bought after their acquisition of *Delaware County Daily Times* in 1961 include six Philadelphia suburban papers; the *Pottstown Mercury* (Pennsylvania); the *Daily Freeman* (New York); the *Fall River Herald News* (Massachusetts); and the *Milford Citizen* (Connecticut). In most cases Goodson would own forty-five percent of a paper; Todman, forty-five percent; Ingersoll, five percent; and Schneidman, five percent. In addition, Ingersoll had a contract to manage, for a fee, each new paper.

It was obviously impossible for one man to run seventeen newspapers spread over the eastern seaboard, and Ingersoll's method of operation was simple: Pick good men and give them their head. If you do not feel they are doing a good job, fire them. But do not interfere in day-to-day editorial matters. He was not really interested in the editorial operation of a small-town newspaper, although from time to time he could not resist using his newspapers to promote special causes—such as the energy crisis, which was the subject of an alarming book published in 1972, entitled *The Limits of Growth*, by The Club of Rome, which Ingersoll had condensed and offered to his papers. Generally, however, he just set the broad policies, then turned their execution over to Spooner, who was assuming increasing responsibility for daily management of General Publications.

Ingersoll, obviously, was approaching a time in his life when he would normally pass responsibilities along to his sons, if they had an interest in, or aptitude for his business. In the 1970s one did; but the other did not, and furthermore, he had broken with his father. In the late 1960s Ian, with his new wife, and Ralph II, with his wife and new baby, were sharing a house in Connecticut, which Ingersoll had originally rented for a secretary and which had been lent them for the winter. Ralph II thought the land had been "given" to him. Ian was just there temporarily after his discharge from the army, but young Ralph was building a house on nearby property owned by his father, which he thought had been given to him. Suddenly, one day in October of 1969, Ingersoll summoned both boys to his office in Cornwall Bridge and told them to be off his property in twenty-four hours. "We have never to this day," says Ralph II, "discovered what prompted him to do that. To his credit, he later reimbursed me for the out-of-pocket costs of the house under construction."

Ingersoll says the move was directed mostly at young Ralph. There was continuing friction between the Ingersolls and young Ralph's wife; in addition, the Ingersolls felt young Ralph still had enough of his inheritance to support his family and was taking advantage of Ingersoll himself. Both boys were of course, stunned. And it was several years before Ian could reestablish any kind of relationship with his father.

Ian's wife had a miscarriage, and his marriage ended in divorce. After drifting for a while, he returned to Cornwall, Connecticut, and, using his inheritance, bought, with Ralph II, for twenty-five thousand dollars a ninety-acre mountaintop on which he built a house with his own hands. Later Ralph II sold Ian his share of the property. Ian married again and became a cabinetmaker, eventually establishing a profitable business producing imitation Shaker furniture. But years after the break with his father, Ingersoll was writing friends that Ian was "still a cut out from society": "He avoids us. We 'don't understand.'"

Young Ralph, on the other hand, tried to heal the break with his father. While at N.Y.U., he had worked as a reporter on a number of Ingersoll publications, and he had become quite friendly with, and clearly impressed, Chet Spooner, the company's chief operating officer. After his bad experience in the stock market, and a modestly profitable real-estate investment in Hillsdale, New York, young Ingersoll was wondering what to do next, when Spooner convinced him to come back into the newspaper business. He knew he would have to make peace with his father, but the break between his wife and his parents was virtually irremediable, so he arranged to meet his father on what Ingersoll calls "neutral ground," at the Under Mountain Inn, just north of Lakeville. He told his father that he wanted a reconciliation, and that if they were going to establish any kind of relationship it would have to be through something they could do alone, without their wives' involvement—like fly casting or working together. He asked his father to teach him the newspaper trade.

Ingersoll agreed with his son: "The best way we could keep a relationship is not to let our wives get near each other." He would teach his son the business—on one condition: "You go anywhere and do anything I tell you for two years. After three years, you're totally free and under no obligation whatsoever."

At that time, says Ingersoll, he did not intend to do anything more than "train him for two years and then send him to another company." There was never any thought of grooming his son to replace him. There are, he says, five disciplines in the newspaper business: advertising, production, business management, circulation, and editorial. He felt young Ralph should be proficient in all before he considered himself "educated" in his trade. He also wanted to show him that life for a young newspaperman and his family would not be easy, and to emphasize this he at first decided to send his son to work for two years on a small paper in western Texas. But Spooner, who had become very close to young Ralph, intervened and convinced Ingersoll to apprentice with him, Spooner.

Ingersoll agreed, and young Ralph went to work on the *Pottstown Mercury*, where he intended first to learn the sales side of the business. Spooner picked the Pottstown paper because its publisher, Ellis Rietzel, had a solid background in the business side of publishing, which young Ingersoll felt he needed more experience in. But at least one member of the family thought young Ralph's working for his father was a mistake. "He should have gone to work for an archrival," says Ian, "and worked his way up." Instead young Ralph's first assignment was selling advertising for the *Mercury*, and one of the first people he met there was a young reporter named Tom Geyer. "There was a certain amount of apprehension," says Geyer, "about having the son of the manager of the Ingersoll group working on the paper, but young Ralph was incredibly good at what he set out to do. I was enormously impressed, as I think everyone is who meets him for the first time." Geyer, who was also chairman of the paper's Newspaper Guild unit (which young Ingersoll joined and later became president of) eventually became good friends with the boss's son and recalls his saying at the time that he was attending a "school for publishers." His ambition, however, was not to take over his father's company, but to "learn the business so he could go into it on his own."

After they had worked on the *Mercury* together for nearly two years, Geyer decided to try city life and moved to Boston and a job on a trade paper. Young Ingersoll was transferred to a more advanced course in his special school—as assistant publisher of the *Daily Freeman* in Kingston, New York. Then in 1973 Spooner had a stroke. He was obviously going to be incapacitated for some time and very likely would never function again at full speed. Ingersoll's first choice to replace Spooner was Dean Krenz, former publisher of the *Trentonian*, at the time a special assistant to Ingersoll and "heir apparent" to Spooner. But Spooner argued that young Ingersoll was a very promising publisher and should be given the job. So Ingersoll asked his son if he wanted to run the company jointly with Krenz. Young Ingersoll said no but made a counteroffer, which Spooner endorsed: "I don't think Chet will ever be active again," he told his father. "He and I will collaborate. Then you will have the best of both worlds—his judgment and my energy to carry out his decisions."

This was not unlike the arrangement Ingersoll had had with Charles Marsh in the 1950s, and that had worked very well. So Krenz was appointed publisher of the *Elizabeth Journal*, and young Ralph was made chief operating officer of the company. Ingersoll told his stockholders, "I don't believe in nepotism and I'm not putting him in because he's my son. I'm putting him in because he's the best candidate I can think of to work with Spooner." And Ingersoll sincerely believed this. He had always had a high regard for young Ralph's intelligence and ability and was impressed by the work he had done for the company.

Ingersoll was still concerned, however, about his son's youth and inexperience. So after he announced that Ralph II would become Spooner's right-hand man, he wrote all his publishers that if they had any grievances, they could come directly to him. Young Ingersoll says he discussed this with Richard Treat, publisher of the *Daily Freeman* and an old navy man, who told him you could not run a ship that way; he would have to let everyone in the company know who was boss. "So I told each of the publishers that I had no objection to Pa's letter, but if they did go to him, they had better be prepared to work for and with him—and that would be all right, if Pa agreed. But if he did not agree, they were in trouble. A couple tried it and Pa did not want to work with them and they were out of a job."

Young Ralph also says that after he took over, he discovered something that surprised him: "I thought my father had set up an organization. But it became obvious soon that he did not have a good system. In fact, I finally realized that he never really wanted to run a newspaper group. And I cannot fault my father for not doing something that he did not really want to do. By 1975 I had set up what I consider a real operating team."

The year 1975 was a significant one for the company. In the first place, a strain developed between the Ingersolls and Goodson and Todman over the sale of the *Elizabeth Journal*, which was the flagship paper. Although Ingersoll had sold his share in the paper to Goodson and Todman in the 1960s, he still used its Elizabeth office as his base headquarters and considered it one of his best papers. Goodson had been told at a cocktail party that he could get $6 million for the *Journal*, and was intrigued with the idea of finding out just how much one of his papers was worth. The Ingersolls and Schneidman tried to dissuade Goodson from selling the *Journal*, but the more they argued, the more it seemed to Goodson that "there might be vinegar in those vintage bottles after all," as Goodson's son-in-law told young Ingersoll. They finally sold it for $13.9.

Young Ralph believed that Goodson had made a very serious mistake in selling the *Elizabeth Journal* when and how he did. He went to his father and said he would not continue to operate under the kind of arrangement that permitted Goodson to sell a profitable paper. He felt his father had been an "angel of major proportions in making money for a company that gave him no long-range guarantee of security," and he did not want to commit his life to that kind of arrangement or ask others to do it. So he proposed that all new contracts (and as many of the existing ones as possible), instead of being cancelable on ninety days' notice, be valid for a period of at least fifteen years, and that they give Ingersoll a higher percentage of any increased profits. But most important, the contracts would remain in effect if the paper was sold without Ingersoll's consent, as the *Journal* had been. At this time young Ingersoll had a substantial job offer from another publishing company, and both his father and Goodson knew that he was prepared to leave if his proposals were not accepted.

Ingersoll and Goodson eventually agreed to the proposed arrangements. But this required the formation of a new company. So General Publications was liquidated and a Connecticut partnership called Ingersoll Publications was formed. In Connecticut a partnership must consist of at least three partners, so Richard Treat, publisher of the *Kingston Daily Freeman*, was brought in, made a general partner, and given a two-percent share; Ralph senior and Ralph II each held a forty-nine-percent share. It was also agreed that $150,000 a year would go directly to Ralph senior; the rest would be split among the partners, according to their holdings in the partnership.

Ingersoll senior has a clear recollection of his feelings about the reorganization. He says he was bored with the papers and wanted out. He felt that Ralph II was capable of managing them—but capable men had fallen on their faces before, and he wished to protect himself until he was certain his son could succeed. So he drew individual contracts with companies owning profitable newspapers which, in aggregate, would yield a monthly income which would be based on individual corporate obligations, regardless of who owned the papers so that if they were sold by Ingersoll Publications the sale would not affect his income. Then he arranged to sell his interest in *The Trentonian*, giving the younger Ingersoll twenty years to pay for the stock, with payments beginning in 1983. Ralph senior also sold his share of the *Claremont Daily Eagle* to Ralph II.

He then agreed to the formation of a partnership in which, he says, in effect, he gave his son fifty percent and retained fifty percent for himself. He insists it was his intention to sell his son his fifty-percent interest on the same terms as those on which he later sold him the interest in the New Jersey paper, once he was assured of his son's survival. This he attests to by the fact that he never again took any action involving any of the papers he had managed.

His son sees the reorganization somewhat differently. "What he did," says young Ingersoll, "was surrender his General Publications contracts in exchange for a guaranteed one hundred fifty thousand dollars a year and forty-nine percent of whatever we could make with the company. After that, we made millions and he also got more stock in some deals."

The new company was a sweet deal for everyone, and gradually young Ingersoll became identified as the driving force in Ingersoll Publications, and achieved a reputation as a tough, ambitious, but successful publisher. And the senior Ingersoll, with a minimum of work, which enabled him to devote most of his time to his writing, had a substantial income (by 1982 it would amount to over a million dollars a year) and reestablished his credentials as a successful publisher, which pleased the man who, since 1940, had carried an aura of failure as a result of his *PM* experience.

Ingersoll's approach to publishing was a curious one. He was not motivated by the ambition that drives many newspaper publishers—that is, the desire to build a communications outlet that would give him power and influence in a community and/or the nation. Ingersoll did enjoy the status newspaper ownership endows, but what he wanted most was the money the newspapers produced—which gave him the freedom to do the things he wanted to do. He maintains that he has never really been interested in money *per se*, and this is true. However, the one thing that BIG money can buy—freedom—is very important to him. So, if he is not interested in money, he is terribly interested in the freedom money can buy—which, in the end, can amount to the same thing. "Except for powerful cars," says Toby, "he has no interest in buying things for himself. But he has a great interest in fancy restaurants and clubs." Helen Mauro, who worked with Ingersoll in Middletown and Trenton, says, "He may not be interested in money, but he sure knew how to spend it."

It should also be stressed that the things Ingersoll wanted money for included some worthy professional goals. He devoted a good part of the 1960s and 1970s to looking for a young man who could create, as one want ad put it, "a press whose sole interest is in seeking out, writing interestingly and printing readably the news on which Americans are dependent on making our decisions on how to govern ourselves. . . . In the above, the word *sole* is underlined to distinguish the undertaking in mind from any existing newspaper establishment, the bulk of whose income is derived from selling its space to hucksters—necessarily because the establishment's profits depend on that formula and the success of a newspaper is defined by its profitability."

Despite all the money he was making from the sale of advertising in the newspapers he managed, he still yearned for the newspaperman's dream—the completely independent publication supported solely by its subscriptions and newsstand sales. But the right person to run this publication was hard to find: "For some 10 years, now," he said in a 1972 ad, "I've been extending this invitation without turning up a single prospect."

Still, what he wanted most was to write. But despite the successes of his wartime books, he was never able to establish himself as an author, which meant returning to his "trade," as he called it—which generated the money he needed to maintain the good life and continue his efforts to write. And as the money coming in from the newspapers accumulated, he had a brilliant idea, which served both ends. In the winter of 1968–69 the Ingersolls visited Tahiti and acquired "a rather bad case of instant intoxication with the islands." For the following year, he decided, it would be nice to organize a two-month cruise of the islands of the South Pacific to absorb background for a novel that was forming in his mind.

The novel, which he called "Unicorn," is a futuristic, science-fiction story which predates the current "star wars" concept by several years. It centers on a "mad scientist," who, in the process of working for the government on a top secret project in the South Pacific, develops an electrical ray that can destroy any target in the world. At the same time the group working on the little atoll of Unicorn makes a scientific "breakthrough," which enables them to surround Unicorn with a "bubble of impenetrability." Not even a guided missile can penetrate the protective screen around their island, but they can eliminate any place on the planet, including Moscow and Washington. In short, they control the world.

But what can they do with their power? That, of course, is the novel, and one of the first things Ingersoll planned to have them do is to secede from the United States and set up a self-sustaining small nation, which would then impose its will on the superpowers. Their objective, more or less, would be to disarm the world and help its inhabitants return to the simple life of the Polynesians. Ingersoll was very enthusiastic about his story and went so far as to arrange a lunch with his friend Clayton Fritchey to learn just how small, would-be country goes about seceding from an established empire. He also wanted to visit the South Pacific to get a feeling for the islands, the people, and the life they lead.

Toby's friend Dr. Harry Shapiro was head of the Anthropology Department of the American Museum of Natural History in New York. Shapiro introduced them to the president of the museum, Gardiner Stout, and Ingersoll proposed that, as a gift to the museum, he would finance an expedition to the South Seas, which would be under Ingersoll's direction ("a boat can have only one skipper," he and Stout agreed) but with objectives proposed by the museum. Stout thought it was a fine idea, and Ingersoll began to organize things with his usual energy and dedication.

At first he thought the trip would cost thirty thousand dollars (the eventual price tag was eighty-five thousand), but as a "gift" to the museum it would be tax deductible. When Ingersoll mentioned his own literary plans, however, Stout raised the possibility of a conflict of interest, so Ingersoll said, "The show is my contribution and if the U.S. doesn't think it is of scientific value, that's my hard luck."

To make the voyage, he rented the *Aleta II*, a 165-foot yacht built for Colonel Jacob Ruppert, the beer manufacturer. After his death it passed through the hands of several millionaires and had been used during World War II as a subchaser. The scientific purpose of the expedition was, in the broadest sense, to study the culture of a people who had lived an established, unchanging life for centuries, in part because they occupied areas just rich enough in resources to sustain life, but not rich enough to inspire anyone to exploit them. More specific objectives were to explore Rapa Island for clues about the prehistoric migration of people down through Polynesia and eventually into New Zealand. Dr. Shapiro wanted to study the racial and biological origins of the Polynesians and the genetic differences that might have resulted from their isolation.

But after the trip to Polynesia in 1970, Ingersoll decided to "scrap" "Unicorn"'s beginnings because, as he wrote his publisher, the two months in the South Pacific "changed too many of my assumptions about life there." But he never did finish the novel, primarily because the ending presented practical and philosophical problems he could not resolve. Toby remembers the day he gave up: They were in Tobago and she asked him why he was quitting. "Here am I, an old man," he answered, "and it's finally come home to me. There's no fixing up the world. Human beings will have to fix it themselves. How am I going to end this book? I'm an optimist."

The ongoing autobiography was also having problems. In 1968 Robert Elson's official history of Time Inc. was published, and Elson's treatment of Ingersoll made him so angry he decided he had to reply. He went back to "High Time," rewrote it, eliminating all the mistakes contributed by his deaf secretary, gave it a new title ("Years with Luce"), and, just before flying off to Tahiti, he put it in the hands of Marshall Best, a friend and editor at Viking Press. When he returned, he and Best went over the manuscript again, but it was rejected by Thomas Guinzberg, the president of Viking. The main problem was Ingersoll's treatment of Laura Hobson, a friend of Guinzberg's. Best said Guinzberg had shown it to Mrs. Hobson and that she was furious—which is not hard to understand.

When "Years with Luce" was rejected by Viking, Ingersoll went into another depression. He was, says Toby, emotionally unprepared to have a book turned down again. But there would be more rejections. After he came out of his depression, he wrote a book about his army experience, "Time Out for a War," which was also rejected, as was a book about *PM*, which he tried to revive. And he never did find a publisher for the Luce book.

Considering that Ingersoll had one of the most significant and fascinating careers in American journalism and was a best-selling author, his failure to find a publisher for his memoir of the years following his *New Yorker* experience is curious. One reason for the rejections was skepticism on the part of publishers that anyone would remember *PM* or care about Ingersoll's contribution to *Fortune* and *Life*; another was his account of relationships with people still very much alive and active. And it was not just a question of libel. Ingersoll has a tape-recorder memory and does not hesitate to put down on paper anything he can recall. Of course, as most people do, he tends to recall events in a way that minimizes his own faults and mistakes. And to make a better story, he is not above stretching the truth a little, always adhering to Marsh's dictum: "In the main it's true." But it was not so much that he did not tell the truth in his memoirs; more often the problem resulted from his being *too* truthful. A tape-recorded version of events is very effective in reporting a war, describing conditions in a foreign country, or explaining the structure of a big corporation. But it is not the best way to handle human relationships, especially with living people. There are no rules. It is a matter of taste and judgment, and Ingersoll often cannot tell when he has gone too far.

But perhaps the main reason he could not find a publisher for his memoirs was the execution. Ingersoll's prose style, perfect for reporting, does not lend itself to the personal writing necessary for successful autobiography. And his tendency to cuteness and archaic phrasing, which increased in later years, is even harder to accept when he is writing uncomplimentary things about other people. Also, he is the first to concede that his lack of interest in human relationships is one reason for his failure as a novelist—and it very likely contributed as well to his inability to write personal memoirs.

The rejection of his autobiographical books by various publishers was a genuine blow to Ingersoll, not only because he still hoped to establish himself as a successful author but because he wanted to tell the full story of *PM*, his relationship with Luce (especially during the launching of *Life*), and, to a lesser extent, his experiences during the war (which he rightly considered significant). The official Time Inc. history, plus a number of memoirs by ex-Time Inc'ers—most notably T. S. Matthews and Eric Hodgins—had presented a picture of Ingersoll's years with Luce that Ingersoll, with considerable justification, felt was distorted. No one, however modest (which Ingersoll is not), cherishes the idea of fading out with his achievements unrecognized and unrecorded. He wanted to set the record straight.

Although his efforts to write books were not succeeding, Ingersoll still had his newspapers as an outlet for his writing. From time to time he would do a special piece, although he continued to resist the temptation to use his papers to promote his causes. "The papers I operate today," he wrote one friend in the late 1960s, "are not what we are calling 'crusading organs.'" But when his old World War II friend General Noce began criticizing the media coverage of the war in Vietnam, Ingersoll rose to the press's defense, although he did concede that there were always some biased reporters: "I hold it equally true that the main body of American reportage is both honest and reasonably objective. It is simply not a tenable position that all American reporters are in conspiracy against the truth. . . . Telling the truth, whether it hurts or soothes, is the proper function of a free press in a free Democracy."

As did most liberals, Ingersoll opposed the Vietnam War, and one fact-finding expedition took him to Laos in 1971 for an interview with Prince Souvanna Phouma and a report on that country's effort to stay out of the conflict in Southeast Asia. He liked Phouma, who, he said, was "tough, intelligent, and no fool." As for Laos: "Its logical illogic is way beyond Lewis Carroll," he said.

"Here is a wonderland in which nobody tells anything as it is, a wonderland of non-facts that kill cripple and displace whole peoples—all in the name of 'goodwill.'"

Politically, of course, Ingersoll was still what the conservative press called leftist, although by 1970 he had long given up on the Russian experiment. The Communists in Russia, as far as he was concerned, were just another bunch of power seekers out to exploit the people for their own gain. They were different from the Fascists, however, in that they were invariably on the right side of the issues. In Third World countries the Communists usually managed to back programs and causes that the liberals also supported—although the liberals generally favored achieving their goals by democratic vote rather than armed revolution.

After World War II Ingersoll consistently supported liberal Democrats, with varying enthusiasm. And in a few campaigns he was on the fringe of presidential politics: In 1956 he wrote position papers for Estes Kefauver; in 1968 he supported Senator Eugene McCarthy; and in 1971, during the primaries in Connecticut, he gave a fund-raiser for Senator George McGovern. When the senator, much to Ingersoll's surprise, won the nomination in 1972, he attempted to enlist his papers on the side of McGovern—and against Richard Nixon. This brought him into direct conflict with Goodson, who, although a dove and a liberal supporter of Senator McCarthy, was seriously concerned about McGovern's economic policies—as were a great many liberal Democrats. They finally agreed the papers should support whomever they wanted (most supported Nixon), and Ingersoll began writing position papers for McGovern. Then, in September of 1972, he sent what he called a "Free Speech for McGovern" to the *New York Times*. The speech explained why he supported McGovern, then said: "I am spitting mad at McGovern and his people for their ineptness in presenting their case for his replacing Nixon as our President. I want him to come out fighting, with the flashing blade of truths so cutting as to shatter Nixon's shield of synthetic half truths. Why can't George McGovern come out with a rousing counterattack, such as . . ."

The speech said all the things liberals, such as Mary McGrory and Anthony Lewis, were complaining McGovern was not saying. The *Times* printed a digested version of it and then ran an editorial disagreeing with the liberals who said McGovern's caution was killing his campaign. The problem, said the *Times*, was the nature of his primary campaign, which was "guaranteed to lose the election."

Ingersoll was annoyed that the *Times* had cut the speech without saying anything to him about it or giving him a chance to make the cuts himself (which is standard practice when writers of Ingersoll's stature are involved). But it also gave him an excuse to send the full speech to all his own papers, pointing out to each that by publishing it, the *Times* had made the speech a national story. He still gave them the option of printing it or ignoring it; many, but not all, printed it.

Meanwhile, McGovern was impressed by the *Times* piece. He wrote

Ingersoll that it said exactly what he thought he had been saying during the campaign. Also he asked him to do some more speech writing for him: "I would rather see you spitting mad at Nixon than at me."

Ingersoll replied that he would be delighted to be a McGovern speech writer, but he insisted that he have at least one uninterrupted private session with the candidate to discuss what he thought would be a counterattack on Nixon— preferably to be delivered on prime time television. McGovern agreed to meet him in Hartford, and Ingersoll wrote a major address, incorporating much of the *New York Times* "speech." By the time of their meeting, however, "someone had cut my throat," Ingersoll says, "and they had decided they didn't want me in the campaign, that I would be a liability. Maybe I would have been." Veterans of the McGovern campaign vaguely recall the incident but do not remember who, if anyone, cut Ingersoll's throat.

By election eve Ingersoll knew Nixon would be reelected in a landslide, and in a long editorial, which he did not send to his papers, he lamented America's loss of idealism, and the decision to pick an amoral pragmatist to lead her. "Right this moment," he wrote, "I think we are tired of ourselves—and particularly of the idealist in us. So we are not merely content, but actually eager to put ourselves in service to a President whose administration stands for our acceptance of the inequalities among us."

Although he made every effort to give his editors and publishers their independence, he still could not resist the urge to write and comment on current events. But as he approached his mid-seventies, with the Ingersoll name now virtually unknown among the new generation of readers, and with the sharpness of his writing declining, the sad truth was that his papers were the only outlet he had left. So, in October of 1974, he devised a scheme that enabled him to write—but did not *impose* his views on the readers of the newspapers he managed. A signed column was sent to his editors, who were not obliged to use it. Some did, but most did not.

The column was a mixture of his views on current events, his personal philosophy, and old stories about his journalism days. They were interesting but not very well written, and, as in his memoirs, he often used an annoying personal style, which few of his editors were inclined to alter. As do most columnists, he kept an eye on the presidency ("When a man has authority bestowed upon him, he becomes much better or much worse than he ever thought he could be. Being President does not seem to have made any changes in Gerald Ford") and the other on the Russians ("Communism in Russia would eventually collapse of its own weight, a mammoth dinosaur"). He supported Jimmy Carter lukewarmly, worried about the military-industrial complex and the energy crisis, and told many stories about Ross, the *New Yorker*, Henry Luce, and *PM*. He also would discourse occasionally on the newspaper business. One column, in particular, was significant not only for its commentary on the newspaper "chains" that were beginning to dominate the American print media but for the commentator himself. The views it expressed came from the man who, a generation earlier, had pub-

Ingersoll (SIPPING COFFEE ABOVE) was in Casablanca in 1967 visiting his stepson, Jerry Doolittle, who was with the USIA. Thelma Ingersoll is at Ingersoll's right; the young lady is Khadija El Fekkak, an airport hostess. (BELOW) Ingersoll, seated and looking up at the candidate, hosts a fund-raiser for George McGovern during the 1972 Democratic primary.

lished what many still believe to be the most ideally conceived newspaper ever printed in America.

Responding to a reader who had asked what he thought of the larger and larger combinations of once individually owned newspapers, he wrote:

Well, after a long life in the vicinity of the printed word, I'd say it was inevitable but not necessarily bad.

The secret that newspapers could make money for their owners was well kept for many generations but had eventually to be exposed. Once that fact seeped through to bankers and investors, it was only a question of time before capital, which acquired them not for their editorial value but for their capacity to make money, took over. And since the capital involved is considerable it was only a question of a little more time before the acquisitive ones turned to the public for more than their papers generated.

But curiously enough the greed motif involved was quite a bright lining of silver as well as a dark gold center. The silver lining is that money making is basically amoral. The acquirer of a newspaper for the sole purpose of making money is primarily interested in its cost of production and its revenue from advertising. He is not particularly interested in what his editors print, provided it interests people enough to buy it.

It takes the investor a while to see that this and this alone is what creates the earning power of "the property." If he is intelligent enough—almost a foregone conclusion—he soon realizes that his editorial people know more about this than he. He gives them vastly more freedom in what to print than the former family ownership did.

By the early 1970s Ralph Ingersoll was certainly giving his papers freedom, and not just because he believed that is what an absentee publisher should do. Tom Geyer, who had returned to the company as editor of the *Claremont Daily Eagle* (New Hampshire), and who is now president of the company, recalls conversations with the senior Ingersoll, which gave him the impression that "the great passions of his life were Time Inc. and *PM* and he never quite felt the excitement for the small-town daily newspaper business. He didn't want to grow enormously large," Geyer added. "He often mentioned to me, after I got to know him, that he thought our interest in business *per se* was perhaps even unseemly, that we were too interested in money."

Ingersoll Publications is, in fact, interested in making money, and Geyer and Ralph II do not deny it. Young Ingersoll also admires Rupert Murdoch, the controversial Australian publisher who has had publicized fights involving the acquisition and running of the *New York Post*, *The Times* (of London), and the *Chicago Sun Times*, for what he terms Murdoch's seemingly insatiable curiosity about the interests and aspirations of the majority of his readers.

But there are also those who say that Ingersoll Publications' profits have been, in some cases at least, at the expense of improved journalism. As Loreen Ghiglione writes (in *The Buying and Selling of America's Newspapers*) at the conclusion of a study he did of Ingersoll's acquisition of the *North Adams* (Mass.) *Transcript*: "Whatever can be said for the management, however, the *Transcript* pushes too hard for greater profitability, and, in the process, sacrifices journalistic quality."

But disagreement over the way the company was being managed was not what produced the final controversy in the controversial life of Ralph Ingersoll. It was, rather, a personal conflict with his oldest son, which is difficult and sad to report.

For a while, after the company was reorganized in 1975, the partnership seemed to be working, although the relationship and nature of the conflict is often misunderstood. "I never worked for my father," says young Ralph. "I would have liked to, but I worked for Chet—and I'm proud of it." Ingersoll had given Spooner virtually a free hand, and he gave the same freedom to his son. And there are differences in their approach to newspaper publishing. Young Ingersoll says quite simply, "There are five disciplines in the newspaper business—and we disagree on one or more points in every discipline. He never looked at a paper from the reader's point of view. What I look at are story count, circulation, text use, organization, stagnant circulation." He also insists that he has a better appreciation of the local communities where the company owns papers because he has worked in so many of them and knows what interests the people. "I have a bar-stool understanding of them," he says.

Young Ingersoll's critics disagree, but an assessment of Ingersoll Publications as it operates today is outside the scope of this biography. Someday, no doubt, someone will tell young Ingersoll's story, but, as Harold Ross said about his father, "you don't write a profile of a goat trying to jump from one mountain peak to another. You wait until you know whether he made it or not." At present it looks as if young Ingersoll will make it, and he is disarmingly frank in answering his critics. To the charge that Ingersoll Publications squeezes its papers for money, he says, "I think there is some truth to it; we do push for profits and there is no bones about it." But he argues that they do not do this at the expense of giving the community a good newspaper. One barometer of how likely it is that a newsroom will excel is generally considered to be the percentage of revenue the paper commits to editorial expense and the national average is slightly under nine percent. Ingersoll says his papers average thirteen percent, the reasons being (1) that most of his papers are in the low-revenue East and Midwest, which means that to achieve the kind of editorial operation they want they have to spend a greater percentage of their revenue, and (2) that their production efficiency allows them to put more cash into their editorial departments. He also admits he charges top dollar for advertising—"We may rue that decision sometime in this century," he concedes. But family-owned newspapers, in his opinion, generally charge too little for their advertising space because the publisher has to go to the Rotary meetings and listen to the businessmen gripe. When there is absentee ownership of a paper, the local publisher can blame it on "that bastard in Lakeville." The man they blame, in this case, is Tom Geyer.

As for Murdoch, Ingersoll and his aides do not deny their admiration for the controversial Australian publisher. After young Ingersoll made a sudden decision in 1981 to convert the *Delaware County Daily Times* in Pennsylvania from a "typical Gannett paper," as its publisher H. L. C. Schwartz called it, to a racy tabloid, Schwartz said, "Ralph is an admirer of Rupert Murdoch and I think everybody here likes the *New York Post*." Geyer says of Ingersoll's admiration for Murdoch: "I think he recognizes Murdoch as one of the very few other smart thoughtful people working in the newspaper business who is willing to look at reality for what it is." (The *Columbia Journalism Review*, however, says, "The *New York Post* is no longer merely a journalistic problem. It is a social problem, a force for evil.")

Young Ingersoll does concede there is "some truth" to charges that the transition during the "takeover" of a local newspaper can be rough on the staff: "When we buy a paper at market prices, we have to earn a certain rate of return on sales in order to service debt. Cutting staff in an overstaffed property is one direct way of increasing the operating cash flow necessary to service acquisition debt. Ingersoll says he has to cut somewhere, and the people they try to retain are the most efficient and capable people, which in some (but not all) cases means letting senior people go. As for the question of interference, he and Geyer prefer to call it education, but he does concede that his editors and publishers receive constant guidance from Lakeville, for the obvious reason that he feels he and Geyer know more about modern newspaper publishing techniques than the editors and publishers who come with the papers they buy. "Of the five newspaper publishing disciplines," says Ingersoll, "a publisher will have no doubt come up through one of them and is probably weak in the other four. You can do what my father did and throw them in the water and see if they can swim. And often you lose your man. Or you can yell at them or bully them, which sometimes works with the right person." What young Ingersoll prefers is to teach them—the Ingersoll Way. But he insists that there is never any effort to interfere with editorial policy by dictating whom the paper should support in local and national elections or what positions it should take on local or national issues. They do require that editorials be locally written, not purchased from syndicates, and prefer that the editorials be confined to local issues. Young Ingersoll feels his greatest impact on the editorial operation of his newspapers (and the thing that gives him the most trouble with his editors) is his insistence that they hire more copy and desk editors and specialized, part-time correspondents and fewer full-time reporters. His editors do not like this because good in-house editors are hard to find today, when every young journalist wants to be an investigative reporter.

Young Ingersoll argues that the papers he manages are better today than when his father was in charge, and he points to the two Pulitzer Prizes (in Trenton and Pottstown) their papers have won. Geyer concurs: "From the time I entered the company, there was no evidence that the Senior Ingersoll took a serious and sustained interest in the journalistic quality of his papers when he was in charge of them. He didn't involve himself enough to have any influence over them." Geyer also maintains that young Ingersoll came out of his school for publishing imbued with his father's journalistic philosophy: "That you don't impose your identity on the paper to the point where employees think they work for Ralph Ingersoll instead of the local publisher."

But he also says, "I'm not sure it would be fair to say he maintains [this philosophy] and, interestingly enough, if it is not maintained now, it's probably because of me, not because of Ralph junior. Enormous changes began to take place in newspapering over the last ten years. The automation of typesetting, the elimination of seventy-five to eighty percent of all composing-room work and competition from new kinds of publications—shoppers, free newspapers, direct mail. It became necessary to launch what is really a vast reeducation program with publishers and department heads about how to manage a newspaper. Young Ralph began that and did it extremely successfully. But I wouldn't call it 'interference.' It's obviously a question of semantics. We track much more what goes on in the papers and we ask the publishers to explain why certain things are happening. We suggest in much more detail what we think they ought to do about it."

So the "reeducation" of the publishers and editors who work for Ingersoll Publications progresses under the general direction of Ralph Ingersoll II and the specific guidance of President Tom Geyer, who has definite views about the editorial function of his operation: "It isn't economically absolutely necessary to worry about the editorial quality of a small-town newspaper because it doesn't make a lot of difference, frankly. Some groups operate on the principle that all they really have to publish in a small town are the obituaries, the marriages, and the classified ads. . . . We provide in small towns a luxury service. We provide a density of coverage of local people and their activities that no metro paper does. We provide more column inches of local news per citizen than the *New York Times*. . . . The most profitable newspaper group that operates in this country is the Thomson newspapers. . . . They publish in basically the same kind of markets we do, but spend approximately half as much in their newsrooms as we do on comparable papers; they know they can get away with that. We could make more money out of our papers if we did the same thing."

On one point there can be no debate: Under young Ingersoll the company has made more money every year. In 1979 *Fortune* listed his father among the "Private Rich," worth $75 to $100 million. This was incorrect, of course, because the estimate assumed that Ingersoll owned most of the stock in the newspapers he managed, which is not the case. But he was wealthy, and his son was making him wealthier. Between 1974 and 1983 he quadrupled revenues, which by 1983 were approximately $140 million.

Advertising Age listed Ingersoll Publications a couple of years ago among the top hundred media companies in the country, and Ingersoll II talks about a company someday with a market value of $1 billion and revenue of $400 to $500 million a year. "You reach a critical mass at some point in this business," he says, "when several options open up—to buy a big competing newspaper (like the *Houston Post*) or start something new, but mainly put your time and energy into anything you want"—and here, in the last analysis, he sounds like his father, who wanted money to give himself the freedom to write and to live the way the rich live. Young Ralph says, "I don't want to write, because I don't have anything to say. . . . What I would like to do is tackle bigger problems." But his father is still driving him, in a way: "I think in the back of Ralph's mind," says Geyer, "is the thought he would like to go back and do what his father did, in some form or other, something new and revolutionary—and do it under circumstances where he has enough capital to do the job right."

In the early 1980s the young Ralph appeared to be on the way to amassing the capital that would enable him to emulate his father. (An achievement, he says, that came about because he stopped counting on either his father or Mark Goodson, or any of the original stockholders, and by trading on his track record persuaded several major banks and a group of pension funds to back him.) Rather dramatically, however, he was also on a collision course with the founder of the company that was going to give him that capital. But it was not over the operation of the company. "He was successful from the beginning," Ingersoll says of his son, and there were times when he was quite clearly the proud father, "bursting his buttons," as one observer put it, when young Ralph did well at a stockholder's meeting. Another former employee reports that on more than one occasion the senior Ingersoll told him, "Young Ralph, in many areas is more skillful and has more ability than I do."

As for young Ingersoll's management of the newspapers: "I was totally disinterested," says his father. "My concern was that he would overexpand too rapidly." Then, gradually, as his son gained tighter and tighter control of the company, came the final break. But even so, the senior Ingersoll says, "It was not his taking over the company that bothered me, it was the elaborate, unnecessary conspiracy he arranged." At first, he says, his son would consult with him and go into "all kinds of decisions. It was a gradual process, over the years, of taking on things without consulting me. I'd find out about it later. I'd ask him about it and then reproach him and I'd get an endless flow of words explaining what he had done. I never considered replacing him because there wasn't anyone else around. Ian was totally disinterested. There were lots of people who could have handled the job, but they weren't in my organization. I would never have put an ad in *Editor and Publisher*. . . . I'm in favor of promoting within the organization."

Young Ingersoll and others connected with the company today do not, of course, agree that young Ingersoll took the company from his father by force and he argues that operating companies it manages are better capitalized today than when he took over. He also says his father had no objection to bringing in outsiders, and cites Dean Krenz and Bill Sweetland, whom, he says, his father brought into the company over Spooner's objection. As for the real reason he was not replaced: "Other stockholders realized that my father was spending much of his time outside the country, and they had come to depend on me to mind the store. If he had had control of the voting stock of the companies we managed, then I might have been tossed out as abruptly as I had been asked off his Cornwall land in 1969."

Ingersoll insists that one method his son used to gain control was to make it impossible for anyone in the company to have an independent relationship with him. His son denies this, although when he first took over the company from Spooner, he made it quite clear to employees whom they were working for. One young man caught up in the conflict gave a rather moving account of his dilemma in a letter to Toby Ingersoll. He had been brought into the company by Ralph senior and became friends with the Ingersolls. But the situation at the company eventually reached the point where he said he could no longer continue the friendship. At dinner one night with Ralph II, the subject of this young man's friendship with the senior Ingersolls came up and, much to his surprise, Ralph II became quite emotional and said he would prefer that the man not continue his friendship with his father and stepmother. The young man, in explaining to the senior Ingersolls why he could no longer be friends, said he knew they were aware of young Ralph's concern about loyalty and stressed that the reason he had chosen to side with him was not because of the money but because Ralph II had been so supportive of him during his career. He also said that management work had turned the creative part of his brain to oatmeal. But he stayed on with the company in a management capacity and has done very well.

Another man caught in the middle was Schneidman, the company's certified public accountant. He says he still loves Ralph senior and calls him "a compassionate, wonderful human being." "Ralph senior was a creator," he says, "an artist, a writer who never worried about money. He knew he could always make a good living. His philosophy about money was not like his young son's. He wants to build a nest egg for his wife and kids. He's a hard-nosed businessman, interested in the bottom line like any good businessman would be."

Gradually—according to Schneidman, Geyer, young Ingersoll, and others— the elder Ingersoll became more difficult to deal with. Ingersoll had always managed to avoid the physical-fitness craze that hit this country in the late 1970s ("I stick my head out of the door, take one long breath, and get back in as quickly as possible," he told one friend, describing his attitude toward exercise). He also consumed his share of alcohol and cigars, becoming increasingly short of breath. By the mid-1970s he had developed emphysema, an irreversible condition that would eventually affect his heart. And as he grew older and his health deteriorated he became more difficult to work with; young Ingersoll found it easier to ignore his father. "He began to sulk [which Ingersoll denies] when he was not consulted," he says. "I decided it was better not to ask him, rather than consult him and then not do it his way."

After Ingersoll learned about his emphysema and was convinced he would never again recover his full strength and energy, he went into another prolonged depression. He had finally given up on his autobiographies but was still enjoying his columns—until he came to realize that they were being used less and less.

*   *   *

In 1979 he stopped writing his column and left the fate of the world to others. But he was psychologically incapable of just fading away to Grenada, sitting in the warm Caribbean sun and reading the *Wall Streel Journal*. In fact, wherever he went, Ingersoll managed to find trouble—even in the Caribbean. In 1980 there was a Communist revolution on his little island, and Ingersoll recalls that this marked the first time he really became unhappy with his son the publisher. The revolution came early one morning. "I was asleep and he roused me. He had already chartered a boat and I was yanked out of bed and led down to the dock. The first thing I knew, I was on the boat getting off the island," said the man who had covered the London blitz in 1940, tried to beat the Germans to Moscow in 1941, and invaded Hitler's Fortress Europa on June 6, 1944. "Then I found out it had not been the chaos it was supposed to have been. So within a few days I went back." But he did not stay long and soon moved his winter residence to Saint Croix.

Ingersoll did not think there was anything to be afraid of, and more important, he did not think newspapermen should run away from a story, especially in a war or revolution. Young Ingersoll, however, did not see it that way: "Pa went quite voluntarily and seemed to enjoy the sail. He accused me of running away from a story, but I had been on the street and I knew men had been killed and I did not want to be a white man in a black Communist revolution. I was not in Grenada to cover the revolution."

The people associated with the company today do not agree that young Ingersoll took the business away from his father. They say that the senior Ingersoll, as he became less interested in the small newspapers, withdrew from the company, and the son did what anyone would have done—he ran it his way. They also think there was nothing wrong with what he did; rather, they point to the record and say that young Ingersoll is one of the smartest young men in the business. Goodson thinks that he is a very capable and successful publisher, and that the friction between him and his father is simply an ancient problem, which goes back to the Greek and Shakespearean plays. "So often, the king doesn't want to get off the throne," he says. "I have a son who works for my company. I want him to be successful, but every once in a while I want to push him back slightly. In the old days the son would actually plot to have the father knocked off. So there is that kind of robbery—understandably. However, I don't think I ever sensed any real pushing on young Ralph's part to get his dad out. I have the sense that maybe he resents that the young son doesn't need him any more in the enterprise."

Others think that the basic cause of the conflict between Ingersoll and his son is the tension between the two wives, and that Toby Ingersoll is really in command of her husband. Whatever the reasons, by the early 1980s their partnership was on a collision course, and although Ingersoll did not hide the tension from others, he did nothing to change it. The collision finally came in the winter of 1981 when Ingersoll was seriously ill in Saint Croix. At young Ralph's insistence, Ingersoll was flown to Miami, where he and Toby were met at the airport by young Ralph and Schneidman. All Ingersoll remembers is that he woke up in a Miami hospital, suffering from a pulmonary collapse and temporary liver and kidney failure produced by his medicine. He was angry about his son's insistence that he be flown to Miami (which young Ralph and others say saved his life). Ingersoll had said many times that he wanted to die peacefully when his time came and did not want to be put on machines. "I knew that when I took him from Saint Croix forcefully and to a hospital in Miami," says his son, "I was, in effect, putting him on machines against his express wishes."

When Ingersoll was released from the hospital, the doctors said that he could not return to Saint Croix without risking his life; that he had to be near a major hospital for further treatment of his liver and kidney ailments. So Ingersoll remained in Miami for the winter, living in a rented condominium and continuing the quarrel with his son. He asked for company reports, but he says his son would not give them to him. His son says he always was given the reports he wanted, and seldom commented on them.

Ingersoll now says that the conflict resulting from his illness was the beginning of his distrust of his son. While recuperating in the Miami condominium, he wrote a letter to young Ralph: When he returned to Connecticut in the spring, he wanted to discuss the financial situation of Ingersoll Publications because he was considering retirement and a breakup of the partnership. "I took the letter to Seymour [Schneidman]," says young Ingersoll, "and he said this is ridiculous. There would be no way to calculate the value of the company. No one knows what the future will hold. The only thing I can tell you is that your father is much better off in partnership with you than out."

So young Ingersoll wrote his father. The idea of his retirement, he said, "makes no sense to me," and even if it did, "I don't know how a fair price could be bargained."

Ingersoll replied: "I do not bargain with my son, we will discuss it quietly when I come home."

Although young Ingersoll had rejected his father's overture, the letter did cause some consternation within the company. Murray Schwartz, a full partner and a lawyer, pointed out that if Ralph II were to die *before* his father, his father would have a "majority in interest" in the partnership and would therefore be free to expel any of the minority partners. "Since they, and I," says young Ralph, "believed that Toby's will and my father's were indistinguishable, my own passing would have meant Toby's *de facto* control of Ingersoll Publications. This had never occurred to us before because . . . everyone had assumed that I would survive my father."

When Ingersoll returned to Connecticut in the spring of 1982, his son sent him the draft of an agreement for Ingersoll's resignation, "the terms to be negotiated," he says. And if this could not be arranged, they would have to find some way to deal with the problem of what would happen to the company if Ingersoll should outlive his son. "I was looking for a dialogue," said young Ingersoll.

He then went to Cornwall Bridge to discuss the situation, telling his father quite frankly that his partners would not remain with the company if anything happened to him.

Ingersoll said that the partners would have nothing to fear if he took over the company, and that he did not want to change the partnership agreement. Young Ingersoll went back to Schneidman, who also tried to persuade Ingersoll to do something to resolve the situation. But Ingersoll would not agree to resign or to change the partnership so that the partners would have equal control of the company in the event of young Ingersoll's death. So young Ingersoll says his father forced the other partners to vote him out, and he asked Schneidman to recommend a settlement. It was agreed that they would double Ingersoll's guaranteed annual income of $150,000 and also guarantee Toby $150,000 a year for life if she outlived her husband. They also agreed to liquidate Ingersoll's capital account—totaling $600,000.

The terms of the partnership specifically stated that a majority of partners could vote any partner out of the company. At that time the partnership consisted of Ingersoll (with forty-eight-percent ownership), young Ralph (also with forty-eight percent), and Tom Geyer, Murray Schwartz, James Plugh, and Roy Cockburn, all men who had been brought into the partnership by young Ingersoll. They each held one percent. Ingersoll told his father that if he did not accept the resignation agreement, the partners were prepared to vote him out.

Ingersoll knew they had the power and would do it, so he accepted the retirement agreement and resigned. But because his total income from the partnership in 1981 had been over a million dollars, he did not think the settlement was fair. "One hundred and fifty thousand of what I get a year I contracted for with each individual paper before I gave Ralph fifty percent of the company," he says (all of which Ralph II denies). "That sum was given to me for my lifetime as retirement pay and . . . Ralph had nothing whatever to do with that. . . . So the settlement Ralph made for my half of the company was a hundred fifty thousand a year, not three hundred thousand . . . and half the company was worth a hell of a lot more."

What really irritated him—and, he says, the reason why young Ralph's action came as a "total and shocking surprise"—was his son's "so ungraciously grabbing the whole thing when [Ralph senior] was in the process of giving it to him." But he insists, still, that it was not how his son operated the company, or his taking it over, that bothered him, but the way he did it.

Young Ingersoll insists the settlement was "economically fair"; but it was, he says, "spiritually unfair for me to have to ask my father out of the partnership." He does concede that it was a "tough" thing to do, but "not unethical or illegal." He says his father would have had a far greater income if he had remained a partner, and argues that it was difficult to estimate the worth of the company. "If we had a stock arrangement it might have been possible to make a different settlement," he says, "but in a partnership you are either a partner or not a partner. And my father simply would not talk about it. He wanted no change."

Ingersoll now says he is relieved that the newspapers and his son are out of his life. Mutual friends and acquaintances have made some attempts to bring about a reconciliation, but they have been unsuccessful, and father and son are virtually not speaking to each other. So Ralph Ingersoll left the newspaper business the way he entered it—in a blaze of controversy. And just to let the trade and friends know that he was not fading out gracefully, he put this curious notice in both *Editor & Publisher* and the *Lakeville Journal*:

NOT ASSOCIATED

Ralph Ingersoll, Sr., informed *Editor & Publisher* that he is no longer associated with Ingersoll Publications Co. The company, which operates as a confederation, has long-term agreements with each newspaper company to provide specialized business advice. Ralph Ingersoll II, his son, is now chairman and chief executive officer of each publishing company and a senior partner of Ingersoll Publications. The younger Ingersoll has bought out his father's interest in the publishing company.

* * *

It is a sad story to have to report, but it is not an uncommon one. The *Wall Street Journal* regularly publishes articles on the problems presented by a son succeeding the father in a business, and Ian, in fact, remembers a *Journal* piece on this subject that triggered half-joking conversations: "How come, Ralph, you're working this company into shape and keeping your father on the payroll at two hundred thousand a year, or whatever? Why don't you just fire him?"

More than a generation gap separated Ralph Ingersoll and his son. Ralph senior was a journalist in the grand tradition, "a world-class player," said one of the editors who was drawn into Ingersoll Publications out of respect for "the old man": As a young journalist, Ingersoll had burned with a desire to enlist truth, as he saw it, on the side of improving the world and "against people who push other people around." These are crusading instincts with which one is born—some would say cursed—and they are often derided as naive and ideal- istic. Sometimes, in some people, they appear that way, but fortunately crusaders come along in every generation. Such instincts cannot be taught in journalism schools or business schools—or even the special "school for publishers" that Ingersoll set up for his son. As Goodson has suggested, there are elements of Greek tragedy in the break between Ralph Ingersoll and his son over the man- agement of their company—a break that saddens many people who know them. But not all. In Laura Hobson's 1943 novel about Jason Crown, modeled at least in part on the Ralph Ingersoll of *Time-Life* and *PM*, a character says of Crown, "someday, somewhere, somebody is going to pay him back for the way he's smashed around him all his life." Certainly, there are those who would agree that Ralph Ingersoll had it coming to him, and who would feel it only fitting

Ingersoll's sons: (ABOVE, LEFT) Ian in his furniture shop in West Cornwall, Connecticut; (ABOVE, RIGHT) Ralph II in front of his company office in Lakeville, Connecticut

Ingersoll's stepchildren: (BELOW, RIGHT) Jerry Doolittle; (BELOW, LEFT) Bill Doolittle, Jr.; (LEFT) Patricia Doolittle Shure

that he was paid back by his own son. There are those close to Ingersoll, in fact, who say that as a young man Ingersoll was very much like his son emotionally, and that a confrontation was inevitable.

Ironically, in recent years Ingersoll and his son Ian have resolved their differences and are now closer than at any other time in their lives. Ingersoll is also extremely close to his stepchildren and continues to lead the good life in Connecticut and Saint Martin (in the French West Indies), where they bought a house in January 1985. But as he said in the closing pages of *Point of Departure*: "It still is now, as it was in the beginning, a toss up to me whether life is more fun to live or to write about." When asked whether he regretted any of his decisions—giving up a million dollars in Time Inc. stock to start *PM*, leaving *PM* to go into the army, abandoning writing to concentrate on making money— he replied, "Except for the time I wasted after the war moaning over what happened to *PM*, I have no regrets about anything I ever did. I would do it all over again."

Then he paused and added, "But I do wish I was a better writer." At eighty-four he no longer writes, but he continues to take an intense interest in the news, and although he walks with a cane, he still takes a vigorous half-hour swim every day. And he feels he has a right to say that after marrying the widow of Francis Scott Bradford, he "lived happily ever after."

But the last word, perhaps, is best left to his wife, Toby. One day when Ingersoll was eighty-three and not in good health, they were talking, and he said, "I have been giving serious thought as to whether you are better off with me or without me—and I have decided you are better off with me."

To which Toby replied, "And who do you think you are, God?" Later she said, "But I do think he's frustrated because he didn't change the world."

Ralph and Toby Ingersoll in 1982 on the patio of their home
in Cornwall Bridge, Connecticut

Appendix 1

A Proposition to Create a New Newspaper
(Fourth Draft)

The Proposition. On the one hand: there exists in all men, but particularly in men of intelligence and education, an inordinate desire to know what is going on in the world today. This desire is not satisfied by the existing daily press.

On the other hand, there exists today all the facilities necessary to produce a daily paper which would satisfy this curiosity. They simply wait to be organized into a profit-making venture.

There are available, for instance:

A large number of American writers of distinction whose talents are not now engaged in journalism, but who are moved by the prospect of using their art to tell the most significant and exciting story of all: the story of the times we live in.

An enormous number of trained journalists, the excellence of whose work you do not recognize because of the limitations of the papers they write for now. They are accurate reporters, skillful rewrite men and honest critics. They want only encouragement, education and direction to produce a paper of real discernment. An alert, intelligent, knowing paper that will be both exciting and satisfying to read.

A world of technicians and specialists who currently smart for the violence done the reporting of their specialties. To a man, they are available to help make news, in their respective fields, make sense before it is printed. For they, too, are men who love truth.

A generation's experience making the world's news at once sensible and salable in media other than the daily press. Specifically the experience of the editors of such eminently successful magazines as the *New Yorker, Fortune* and *Time.* Each of these groups have made important contributions to contemporary journalism. The daily press has made little use of what they have found out about the problem of "keeping intelligent people well informed." (The quote is from *Time*'s Prospectus.)

A generation's experience in developing an entirely new medium for the conveying of information from one mind to another: the reproduced picture. The daily press has made only fragmentary use of this medium which has been developed most successfully in other fields: the magazine (*Life* and its imitators) and the moving picture.

A generation's development of the art of printing, which has resulted in enormous technological improvements not currently being made use of by the daily press. Included in the phrase "the art of printing" is the manufacture of paper and the art of engraving, as well as the actual methods of reproducing in black and white, and in color.

* * *

All these raw materials are at hand. It is proposed to organize them into a coherent, profit-making enterprise and thus to create and publish an original daily news journal. To satisfy man's desire to know what is going on in his world each day.

> *The Purpose* of this newspaper is to keep its readers intelligently and entertainingly and truthfully informed on what has happened in the world in the last twenty-four hours.

The History. The ideas contained in this Prospectus have been germinating for fifteen years. Active work to reduce them to writing was begun two years ago (in April, 1937). The present organization, Publications Research, Inc., was set up in October, 1938, and an office opened for the purpose of proving these ideas in the practical world of printers, paper manufacturers, specialists in newspaper circulation and advertising, etc.—and of reducing them to working costs.

At the same time all of these ideas were discussed and further developed with all kinds of possible collaborators—writers, reporters, editors, researchers, laymen, production experts, etc., etc. The project is now prepared to the point of actual practice with an actual staff. No flaws have been found either in the basic proposition or in the practical dollars and cents figures.

What has been decided.

The atmosphere of this undertaking has been the atmosphere of first pure, and then applied, science. That is, the proposition of a new newspaper was attacked first as an abstract problem in how to get twenty-four hours of news onto paper and into the heads of a large group of readers, starting simply with an inventory of available means (men, paper, machines and ideas) and attempting to keep a completely open mind until the logic of the situation made its own decision as to the best solution of any given problem (such as size, format, printing process, editorial approach to any given classification of news, etc., etc.). Many decisions remain to be made, in particular those which can only sensibly be arrived at in actual working experiment.

But among the basic decisions made so far, are:

1. That the paper shall be an afternoon paper in New York City. . . . for reasons having to do with the current competitive situation in Metropolitan New York.

2. That it shall sell for 5¢ retail. . . . because it will be worth it. It will look and feel like five cents worth to begin with. But, more importantly, it will contain fifty cents worth of writing by any fair comparison with existing competition. (An analogy, not altogether exact but still apt: a weakly magazine called the *Saturday Evening Post* cost 5¢ [and] found considerable difficulty selling itself at that price. An original, modernly

reproduced magazine called *Life* was started, priced itself at 10¢, could not supply the demand.)

3. That its paper, its reproduction and the original way it will be put together for its readers' convenience will be a sharp improvement over any contemporary daily paper. Printing process: a new combination of gravure and letterpress. Nearest existing exhibit: the magazine section of the *New York Times*. But even this is misleading since it lacks reproduced colors, neither paper nor ink will be the same etc.

4. That it shall be very slightly larger than the most successful paper in the U.S., the *New York Daily News*. It will also be slightly different in shape.

5. That it shall expect a circulation, at the end of its first year, of 250,000

. . . . the *New York Times* (daily) 493,024, (Sunday) 744,727; the *News* (daily) 1,783,341, (Sunday) 3,122,720.

6. That its ultimate circulation may reach 5,000,000.

* * *

The case for a new newspaper rests on the fact that the best present-day newspaper— say the *New York Times*—highly organized as it is, mechanically marvellous to the layman and staffed with many men of brilliance, nevertheless fails—for reasons which are beyond its control—to give you each day the clear, cogent, exciting and amusing picture of the news to which you are entitled.

The reasons why the best existing newspapers fail to keep you well-informed may be inventoried:

1. *Ownership*—Newspaper ownership today is by men of property rather than by journalists. These men of property simply do not understand journalism, therefore can hardly be expected to improve its practice.

2. *Capital Investment*—in mechanical equipment and real estate. Which means the management has, by the nature of its problem, to be conservative and reactionary, i.e., to eschew change, initiative, innovation and, instead, to respect the operating status quo.

The perfect parallel is the U.S. railroad, whose management, by the nature of its responsibility, could not and did not pioneer such successful methods of transportation as the pipeline, the truck, the bus, the airplane, or even the streamline train. (The ideology and technique of the streamline train [were] complete in 1920 or before, but their application was held back a generation by the nature of railroad finance and management.)

3. Dependence on Advertising. A million words have been written on the baleful influence of advertising on journalism. The case is much confused by amateur critics, politicians and cranks. But no honest, competent newspaperman will deny that the pressure generated by the existing advertising operation in daily journalism works consistently and without interruption against the interest of the reader. It works so efficiently, in fact, that publishers and editors and writers censor themselves 100 times for every once their advertisers censor them. This is the unconscious self-censorship by managements which are too intelligent ever to forget on which side their bread is buttered. It is an important reason why your newspaper is not able to tell you what's going on.

4. *Writing Talent*. A newspaper is, after all, only a blank sheet of paper on which words (and pictures) are printed (just as a play is an empty stage on which actors appear and speak lines). All it has to sell is its words and how they are put together. It takes exceptional talent to put words together well. The newspapers have forgotten that. Which is curious, because the publishers of magazines and books, the producers of plays and motion pictures continue to get rich all around them through the exploitation of talented writers.

The reason why there is shortage of talent in newswriting is involved with ownership and capital load; it was apparently found that writing costs could be cut by the introduction of an easily learned formula for newswriting. A formula which any twelve year old could learn. But whatever the explanation, it is an academic issue. What is really important to us is the situation as it is today: the great world newsgathering organization which it has taken three generations to create is manned by $25 to $100 a week young men and old hacks, worked too hard for them either to become well-informed or to improve themselves. A single line of comparison pins this failure home. A really talented writer has these rewards to look forward to:

> *In the advertising world:* ($10,000 to $50,000 a year as a crack copy-
> writer—steady employment and often an interest in profits created.
> *In fiction writing:* as big a plum as $100,000 a year in as silly a pie as
> pulp magazine writing,
> : the whole fiction magazine field from which to take $15,000
> to $50,000 a year,
> : fame and fortune writing the great American novel,
> : fame and fortune writing the great American play,
> : from $500 to $4,000 a week in Hollywood.
> *In non-fiction writing:* $10,000 to $50,000 a year for top magazine article
> manufacturers (like Courtney Riley Cooper),
> : fame and fortune writing biographical books, etc.
> *In straight newswriting:* a really talented writer, as a grade A reporter on
> a big metropolitan paper, may expect to earn $75 a week.

* * *

(The circle completed itself when the newspaper, having forced talent out of its news-columns, had to import it back as columnists—who are used, not to tell you what happened yesterday but as circus performers, aping, prying, gossiping, interpreting the news with violent personal bias as their stock in trade.)

So your newspaper neither really entertains or informs you because the men who write its news are not as talented as the men who entertain you in your books, at your plays and movies, and over your radio.

5. *Restrictions on Writing.* While all the above is true beyond the need of further documentation, it is still only half the story of why writing in the newspapers bores you. There *are* men of talent writing news—particularly amongst the younger men. Hardly a writing name now established in other fields but has at some time worked for a newspaper and been lured away or driven out. The point is that these men are, generally speaking, not allowed to use their talents.

Curse # 1 of newspaper writing: the news story form—the tortuous "tell-all" lead sentence from which facts dribble away to fill space.

Curse # 2: the spiritual degradation of writers writing "the truth," not as they see it, but as the owner or the policy of the paper sees it. (See *Time's* success simply rehashing the newspapers' news with some respect for vigorous, colorful writing and the writer's own viewpoint on what's happened.)

So present-day restrictions on newswriting rob you of the real services of even such talents as are now employed by newspapers.

6. *Failure to recognize "the picture" as a vehicle for conveying information.* The newspaper world is a world of words, however hackneyed. The picture is now used solely as an illustration, an ornament, a supernumerary. Yet for many years the volume and quality of newspictures has been such that they have been available for use in journalism as a *primary* means of conveying information (and two years ago *Life* magazine, which "reads" 12,000 pictures a week, proved it).

The reason for this curious failure to utilize an invaluable tool—large immobile capital investment—is the reactionary nature of newspaper thinking. Newspaper management, down to night city editors—like railroad management, down to superintendents—is a priesthood dedicated to the worship of old gods.

Thus the newspaper of today (with very limited exceptions) denies you the seeing and studying of pictures which will show you what's going on as no words can describe it to you.

By pictures are meant all kinds of visual exhibits: paintings, sketches, diagrams, isometric maps as well as photographs.

7. *Mechanical Limitations*. Intimately bound up with the effect of large capital investment as a cause, and inability to *show* you what's going on in the world as an effect, is the fact that, marvellous as they are to the Sunday visitor, the presses in which newspapers are printed today are obsolete for their purposes. The first tri-motor Ford was a magnificent airplane but the aviation industry would be not unlike the railroad or the newspaper industry if it were still flying them. The uncomplicated fact is that present newspaper press operations can not reproduce:

> 1. The fine screen picture which alone gives it to you to *see* (the present wide-screen-on-bad-paper newspaper cut merely *suggests* its pictures to you),
> 2. color reproduction, day in day out, everyday—not just now and then, on Sundays, in special supplements.

8. *Lack of physical improvement of the package*. Last but perhaps not least: almost everything else on which you lay your hands or rest your eyes today has been physically improved in the last generation—from your hand-set telephone to the can in which your baking soda comes, but not your newspaper. It's still large and cumbersome or small and fat and unwieldy. It still falls apart. Its paper has been cheapened—not made better, more readable, more substantial.

* * *

For all these reasons, we believe that a great opportunity exists: an opportunity to create a journal which will be so much more effective than the best existing newspaper in keeping its readers well-informed—in well-chosen word and with well-reproduced picture—and so much more attractive physically, that it will be not just "another newspaper" but a "new" newspaper in every sense of the word.

We will describe this paper presently but we must first stop to consider something even more important than well-chosen words and finer presses: the larger purpose to which we believe a newspaper should be dedicated.

The larger purpose is the service of the truth. Let us take for granted the world's need for the truth. It is bitterly, tragically apparent—to everyone from millionaire to W.P.A. worker. So what's different in our service of the truth from the service paid by the existing press? The difference is the difference between the service of scientific truth in a dusty 1890 laboratory and in the knowingly equipped laboratories of Cal Tech in 1938. Most newspapermen serve truth and print as much of it as they understand or dare. It is in their understanding and their daring—and in the tools with which they have to work—that they are limited.

The truth has always been, and is now, difficult to arrive at. He is a fool who boasts it is there for the reaching out. It is often by nature too obscure, often too savagely opposed by men. In journalism—which is the pursuit of the truth in man's contemporary society and history—the best in talent and organization, in knowledge and perception, in courage and wisdom, is not so perfect that it should also be asked to carry the burden of obsolete tools, of interests antagonistic to the truth, of famine of knowledge and the talent to digest it.

Our dedication to the service of the truth is not only in words but in actions—in the steps we shall take to remove the obstacles now between you as a reader and a knowledge of the world and what's happening in it and the men who are making it happen. Our attack on the truth will be well trained, well armed. That is all we can promise you.

Whether the truth takes us to the right or to the left we are not concerned. Except in these respects: we are human beings and we are proud of it. We believe in human beings. In the value of all men and in the greatness of some (and the villainy of others). And as human beings we admit to—are proud of—feeling emotions of love and hate.

So we shall hardly be unbiased journalists. We do not, in fact, believe unbiased journalism exists, feeling rather that claims to emotional disinterest are, consciously or unconsciously, fraudulent.

What do we love and what do we hate? Our readers are entitled to that information, freely and frankly given.

We are against people who push other people around, just for the fun of pushing, whether they flourish in this country or abroad. We are against fraud and deceit and greed and cruelty and we will seek to expose their practitioners. We are for people who are kindly and courageous and honest. We respect intelligence, sound accomplishment, open-mindedness, religious tolerance. We do not believe all mankind's problems are soluble in any existing social order, certainly not our own, and we propose to applaud those who seek constructively to improve the way men live together. We are American and we prefer democracy to any other form of government.

In politics, we are scrupulously non-partisan, not because we lack interest, but because we can not help but feel that there is both truth and fiction in every platform, heroes and villains on every ticket and that our function is to tell you what's what and who's who, not to whoop it up for the dear old Donkey or the Grand Old Elephant.

We sincerely believe that these are the values most generally subscribed to by the best Americans. But if they are not, there would be nothing we could do about it, because these are our values and we do not believe men can do honest work on any but their own standards. Thus we intend neither to write "down" nor write "up" to any imagined audience. For better or worse we will be ourselves.

* * *

So, saying all these things, we are prepared to publish, for you as a reader, a new newspaper which will keep you so honestly and entertainingly informed that you will respect and support us—so well, even, that if we are half as good as we think we are you will make us rich. And we say that because we do not believe we can call ourselves a success in this civilization if we cannot persuade you to make us as rich, say, as the men who manufacture your candy Life Savers or who make your double-feature movies.

What guarantees are there that we can do it? Well, we will tell you how we propose to go about it and you will make up your mind on two scores.

1. Have we freed ourselves from the frictions which keep existing newspapers from serving you better?

2. Have we the outlines of a structure which has a reasonable chance of creating a paper which sounds to you as if you would pay 5¢ a day for it?

* * *

Let us go back to our inventory of the reasons why your present newspaper fails either to keep you well-informed or to hold your interest. Of the new newspaper we propose, it can be said that:

1. Its proprietors are, in fact, not promise, journalists.

Fundamental in the set-up of this paper is the control of its policies by its management, by a group of working journalists. This is the sine qua non.

2. It shall own no real estate, no press equipment.

... by resolve, for reasons stated. But also for another very logical reason. Printing processes are subject to technological obsolescence. New and improved (and often cheaper) processes are constantly being perfected. The owner of expensive, still-to-be-amortized-off equipment can not take advantage of such improvements. The contract-buyer of facilities can. He can shop for the best process, the best price.

3. It shall be able to support itself without a line of paid advertising.

It is able to do this for three reasons:

1. Its price of 5¢ per copy, which sharply increases its gross income.
2. Its small size, which cuts down the amount of paper it has to buy.
3. The fact that it will not print all the news it can lay its typewriter on, but will concentrate on doing a bang-up job on the news which it finds most significant, most interesting, most amusing. Words cost money to get, to write, to print. The paper on which they are printed costs more money. This newspaper saves money on the unnecessary, unwanted and useless words it does not print.

Concerning Advertising:

The fact that this paper can support itself ex-advertising is of prime importance to its readers.

In practice it intends to publicize this fact—and then to take advertising after all. But on a very different basis than advertising has ever been taken before:

Essence of this paper's advertising policy: that it puts the interest of the reader ahead of the interest of the advertiser. It serves the buyer (who is also the buyer of the paper) rather than the seller.

It does this under the direction of an Advertising Editor (rather than a Manager or Director) who applies the same standards of truth and accuracy to the acceptance of advertising that the News Editor applies to the acceptance of new copy.

It limits position and size of advertisements, in the interests of the reader.

It apologizes to the reader, in equivalent space, whenever it finds it has inadvertently accepted and published a false or misleading advertising claim. (This is the teeth in its policy.)

It may openly ally itself with consumer groups, may one day maintain its own testing laboratories.

It does these things because it considers truthful advertising a service in the distribution of goods—always providing the tail never wags the dog. The reader's guarantee that this shall not happen lies in the fact that the paper is not dependent on advertising.

4. It is founded on respect for talent.

All its proprietors' success came through respect for talent.

5. It is founded on no restrictions on talent.

Honest men shall work for it and not only their ability with words but their intellectual integrity shall be respected.

What kind of writers will write for it?

In the editors' experience, there are three fields from which to draw:

a) Well-known writers now established as novelists, playwrights, moving picture writers, fiction story and article writers who will work for this paper not primarily because it pays them but because only here can they write honestly what they know and see. Writing honestly is what makes them tick.

b) Young (aged 25–35) newspaper men, at present underpaid and badly treated (as writers). Their abilities are at present known only to their associates because the conditions under which they now work do not permit them to write as well as they know how.

   c)   Young men graduating yearly from Universities (from which most of *Time, Fortune* and the *New Yorker*'s staffs were recruited). These men need training, guiding, practical education. But you can train, guide and educate a real writer whereas you can not teach merely well educated men how to write.

The problem of staffing such a paper as this is solely one of selection. We believe that there are today 100 good men for every job to be filled.

   6. The technique of handling the picture.

The proprietors of this paper have probably done more original work in the adaptation of the picture to journalism than any editors in the trade—Stanley in the development of the Associated Press famed Wire Photo services and others in the creation of *Fortune* and *Life* magazines. They are their own best witnesses on ways and means of using the picture to show you what is happening, to whom it happened and how.

   7 and 8. Mechanical Improvements and The Package.

Not one, but three contract printers are prepared to produce this paper by a combination of gravure printing (for quality of reproduction) and letterpress (for speed in late news). All three have made preliminary estimates which are included in current budgets.

Samples of, and estimates on, improved newsprint have been obtained, and are satisfactory.

The objective is to produce a newspaper, which will look and feel as much better than those of competitors as the new *Life* is physically more attractive than the *Saturday Evening Post*.

Other considerations:

Management, Ex-editorial.

If the truth is difficult to arrive at and requires talent, judgment and character to maintain, so is a balanced budget. As in journalism, so in finance, the best is not so infallible that the next best will do. The proprietors of this paper have no sympathy either with disembodied Promotional Enthusiasm, or with that way of thinking, which holds that the Lord will Provice so long as a man's heart is Pure. This paper, once again, must support itself well and repay its financial backers handsomely or it is not what it appears to be. To serve these ends its financing must be more than adequate and above reproach. Its money is to be made by selling newspapers, not stock. Its assets are to be conserved for the actual cash requirements of its management, not gambled with for the possible, temporary profit of its stockholders.

This is its creed.

   1. Its working management shall control its editorial policies, in perpetuity.

   2. Until it makes its first profit, its management and its staff will expect to make personal sacrifices, in time and money, to insure its success.

But thereafter . . .

   3. Its staff shall be well paid and shall share in its profits above a stated reward to its capital investment.

   4. Its affairs shall be so ordered that there shall be a fair expectancy of breaking even by the end of the first year.

   5. But its capital investment must be adequate to finance it through three years of possible adversity.

   6. It shall at all times have its own independent financial management which shall be responsible to the stockholders, to insure conservative attention to their interests, and to the management, to insure it freedom from financial pressure on the editorial contents as well as freedom from the necessity of compromising on the quality of the product.

Appendix 2

CONFIDENTIAL MEMORANDUM:
Ralph Ingersoll to the Staff of PM
Subject: This paper as of May 14, 1940

PM is a daily newspaper, published in New York City. Vol. I, No. 1, will be dated June 18th. It will sell for 5¢ a copy on the newsstands—daily except Saturday—from around ten in the morning until late in the evening. A Week-End double-size Sunday Edition will sell for 10¢. It carries no advertising. In most metropolitan and suburban areas it will be delivered to homes and offices by carrier. To other points, by mail.

PM is a new kind of newspaper in that it imitates no existing publication. It has grown out of some five years of experimentation which began with a hypothetical question I posed myself: Suppose there were no newspapers in existence whatever, but simply, on the one hand, a great desire and need to know what's going on and, on the other, the raw material, the men, machines, ideas and knowledge of publishing with which that demand might be better satisfied than it is now. How would a reasonable and imaginative group of editors, writers, photographers and artists put these materials together in a daily publication supported directly by its readers—rather than being supported indirectly by its advertisers?

PHYSICAL APPEARANCE

The paper which has emerged from our preliminary experiments is:

1. Thirty-two pages thick, the same number of pages every day, (except for the Sunday Edition which will be sixty-four pages).

2. The pages are approximately eleven by fourteen inches in size—which is slightly smaller than a regular tabloid newspaper—and squarer.

3. The paper stock costs more, is a special grade, dull finish, but firmer and fuller fibred.

4. The pages are stapled together on the press for the reader's convenience, so that they do not fall apart.

5. The printing is by a special process, using a recently developed ink which makes it possible to use finer screen plates for better reproduction of photos and drawings. Another unique feature of this ink is that it doesn't rub off.

6. The type is larger than usual for newspapers (9 pt. Caledonia, on a 10 pt. base), more legible—easier on the eyes than the type found in most magazines.

7. The make-up is 4 columns to a page. The columns are 25% wider than the standard for newspapers. This new kind of typography brings order out of confusion—makes the news easier to get at, easier to read.

8. All stories are printed in full in one page. There are no carryovers from one page to another far back in the paper.

On eight of the thirty-two pages, there is an extra color in addition to black. We will change this color daily—partially to enable our readers to distinguish today's paper from yesterday's, but mainly to lend variety and interest—and to give the artists who draw for the paper a succession of colors in which to work. There will always be one color in addition to black on the front page.

EDITORIAL CONTENTS

First of all, *PM* will be a *complete* paper. From the point of continuity, *PM* will be edited as if no other newspaper were being published. In other words, each issue of *PM* will cover the news between that issue and the last issue of the day before. It will not presume that people have read any other papers. In fact, they will not need to read any other to get all the news that *is* news.

PM will be completely departmentalized, so that those interested in local, national and foreign affairs can find and follow the news they are interested in as easily as a sports fan can follow his sporting news in today"s papers, where the sporting page is always in the same place.

PM will try not to force its departmentalization. As far as the orthodox news report goes, *PM* starts with only five classifications: New York News, News of the Nation, Foreign News, Sports, Financial.

PM will not, as some people seem to think, subdivide New York News, say, into departments on crime, politics, society, Broadway, etc.

FRONT PAGE

PM's front page will start the job of telling people what's happened since yesterday by confining itself to headlines and pictures. The headlines will be accompanied by large numerals referring to the story inside the paper. Headlines will be informal, not tailored to fit the space, and they will be written by the writers of the stories concerned. The pictures will be dramatic. The object of the whole page is to give the reader a thirty-second answer to the question: What's new?

STANDARD NEWS HANDLING

Prominent on the first page of each major department inside the paper will be a box summary written by the department's editor, putting together all the news in his department. The effect should be a three to five minute conversation with the editor, who has been watching the news come in during the last eight hours, to whom the reader has in effect said: "Tell me what's been going on in your field today."

The right hand column of this first page of each department will carry two features each day:

FIRST, there's a column called "For the Record" in which *PM* will print (in paragraphs of not more than fifty words) the serious news its editors think you should have, straight, and without benefit of repetition or elaboration. For example:

> "The War Department signed contracts with five unidentified companies for $50,000,000 worth of bombers and pursuit planes. (Details tomorrow)"

> "Appearing before the Senate Foreign Relations Committee, Dorothy Thompson, *Herald-Tribune* columnist, urged repeal of the neutrality act; Paul Scharrenberg, reading a statement authorized by President William Green of the A.F.L., opposed any change in the act."

> "Representative Cooley, North Carolina Democrat, said the President told him he would not veto a processing tax to raise a 'reasonable amount of money' for farm parity payments."

SECOND, a feature which we are currently calling "File and Forget." Here, in another set of short, terse paragraphs, the editors aim to dispose of those items of news which they feel and imply are not as important as the press agent would have us believe — in fact, we may carry a standing italic note reading something like this: *"The following news came over the wire. We do not consider it important enough to give much space."* Some examples:

> "Jesse James' nephew—Jesse Hall—has been appointed night marshal of Liberty, Mo."

> "Governor Carl E. Bailey of Arkansas said today that his state's delegation to the Democratic National Convention will consider no presidential candidate who had not made clear his attitude toward freight-rate equalization."

> "Mrs. Sara Delano Roosevelt, mother of the President, today unveiled a 36-inch nickel-silver bust of her son at the rear of the Federal Building, off Constitution Mall, at the World's Fair. As she pulled the string, she said, 'It is delightful to unveil this statue of my son.' Then, as the likeness came into view she said. 'Oh, but it's not a statue, it's a bust.'"

With these three simple devices *PM* has given its readers:
1. A quick and informed resume of the news.
2. A record of the serious content of the news.
3. Due notice that the Barrymores have been divorced again, a warehouse has been burned, etc.—covering the reader on news that may occupy twenty or thirty per cent or more of the space in other evening papers.

* * *

The stories left to tell, *PM* will tell at more length—possibly even at greater length than in the standard press.

* * *

PM will carry full coverage of sports. Daily, it will review and comment on movies, theatre, music, art, books—giving more than the usual space to movies. Its financial page will print news for 95% of its readers—rather than for 5% who "play the market." Instead of editorials, a page of letters from the readers is planned. But a single editorial a day may be added.

Thus, *PM* will handle orthodox news—based on the United Press Service for which

PM has contracted—and on the enterprise of its own reporters and correspondents here and abroad.

Unorthodox News

But *PM* considers this only the beginning of its job. *PM* considers the news gathering facilities of the Twentieth Century as one of the modern miracles. But it suspects that the direction of this machinery may have become over a period of years too traditionalized and that the basic concept "What's new?" can be greatly expanded by enterprise and ingenuity.

In addition to the unorthodox treatment of the orthodox news report, *PM* will print:

1. A daily department on news of LABOR, including news of the unemployed and those who work outside the regular economic system in various government projects.

2. A department devoted to the news of the PRESS itself, not only because we think this news interesting to the public, but also because we feel that it's important for the people of a democracy to understand their principal medium of information.

3. So large a department devoted to RADIO that it cannot be compared to any existing treatment—this department including two pages of tables to help the reader find his way through the ether, a daily column called the Listener's Digest which prints excerpts from the most interesting scripts of the last twenty-four hours, news of the commercial success of programs, etc., etc.

News for Living

Now continuing with the recital of *PM*'s contents, we come to what *PM* calls News for Living. This section includes:

1. A digest of news now found in paid advertising in other papers of the *same day*.

2. News on prices and values in food, not currently available anywhere outside the New York Department of Markets.

3. News of what's for sale in the stores of New York not covered in paid advertisements in *any* papers.

4. News bearing on other problems of living, such as Housing, Health, Education, Medicine, etc.

These sections, taken as a whole, will replace the possibly outworn Woman's Page and household features in the standard newspaper. They have grown out of an intensive study of how a newspaper unencumbered by the conflicting influence of advertising might be more helpful to its readers. I look on them as of enormous importance in earning *PM* the loyalty of its readers, testifying as to whose side we are on in the struggle for existence. It's the buyers of goods, not the sellers, for whom we shall be working.

* * *

The basic principle on which *PM* was undertaken was that the paper would have to have enough appeal to enough readers so that it would be supported for itself alone—it would not have to rely on advertising income. Moreover, although I had no philosophical prejudice against advertising as such, I had long felt strongly that, as currently organized, the advertising operation in newspapers worked against the reader in many ways—tending to limit the editors' freedom of action, making the paper cumbersome and inconvenient physically, and constantly distracting the publisher from devising new ways to make his paper more valuable to the reader.

So, once I had found a commercial formula which did away with the need for advertising (a 5¢ price for a small sized but much more carefully compiled and better printed paper) I was sure that its success would be enhanced by selling no advertising at all in it. In this way, people will be convinced from the very beginning that we are getting out a paper entirely in their interest—instead of in the interest of merchants trying to sell them something—and it will keep the minds of the management on the job of pleasing the reader.

But at the same time I recognized that, without advertising, *PM* would be found lacking by some people. Much valuable news of what's for sale in New York is printed nowhere except in the ads; many women buy newspapers simply to read the advertising in them and in order to get the advantage of going without ads we would have to sacrifice their interest.

The obvious solution was to give them the advertising news they want—but not to charge the advertiser for it. Thus, *PM* could have its cake—give its readers the news in the ads—without getting indigestion from eating it.

From this reasoning comes *PM*'s section called "Advertising Digest," the editor of which collects the copy on all advertising to be published in New York within the next few days and, with the aid of his staff, makes a daily selection of two to four illustrated pages of condensed information contained in the advertisements scheduled to appear *that* day in other papers.

To forestall any misunderstandings: This department exercises no critical function. It guarantees no product, underwrites no sale. Its *one* purpose is to read advertisements in the shoppers' interest and to make the news that will be spread out through hundreds of pages in nine daily papers compactly and effectively available in one place. And, by getting this information several days in advance of publication, through the cooperation of the advertising departments of the various stores, *PM* will be able to give its readers the digest of advertising on the same day that the advertisements appear in the other papers. Its staff will canvass the advertising so carefully that to get the same information from the other papers, the New York housewife would probably have to spend her whole day at home reading. In the end it will be cheaper and more fun for her to buy *PM*— and having read *PM* at lunch, she can go downtown and do her thrifty shopping or go to the movies secure in the knowledge that she is passing up no important bargain sale.

OTHER "NEWS FOR LIVING" SECTIONS

The advertising news section is disinterested, non-critical, completely objective. The other sections of News for Living do not claim these things. Each stands for the paper's conception of a better life—a less expensive life with more for your money and more fun in it. This important division of *PM* will be headed by Elizabeth Hawes, noted fashion authority and author.

Biggest News for Living section outside of Advertising News is the Food Page which, published daily, selects from the reports of the Department of Markets and other institutions, the twenty or thirty best buys in foods for the day—then arranges these foods—these particular bargain foods—in two menus. One menu is for a household with a low budget—the other for a medium budget household. A recipe is given for the unusual dishes on each menu, along with comments on preparation and reference to cookbooks. Recipes are given each day for left-overs of the day before.

The department dedicated to Clothes is an aggressive shopper for unadvertised bargains, critical, skeptical and highly personal.

Our Beauty Department will have only one pre-occupation; enhancing the good looks for our readers in the most scientific way, at the lowest possible cost and with the least trouble.

We feel that the Housing Problem in New York is one of trying to buy space, air, light, transportation, recreation facilities at prices the reader can afford. We will print all the useful news we can find on the subject.

The problem of Education—and the broader statement of that problem in terms of the whole Youth Movement—is of vital interest to our readers as parents, teachers, students, or the youthful unemployed. We will try to make the problem clearer, seek solutions with an open mind.

Many of *PM*'s regular features will appeal to children and young people. The radio section will make it easier for them to find their favorite programs. They will like the thirty drawings *PM* will reproduce daily. *PM*'s dramatic two-color maps will make geography and current history more exciting and interesting for them.

The health of our readers interests us—if not as much as it does them, still a lot—and an important part of their News for Living will be vitally concerned with it.

Since we think fun is as vital as part of living as the national political scene or how much your food costs, we will include that as a separate department. We'll try to tell where you can have your fun without overspending your budget.

There is not room for all to appear each day, so these departments will run on alternating schedules, a given department appearing on the same day of every week.

Here, then, in these News for living pages, is a complete new publication aimed at giving several nickels a day worth of information to the family.

PM WILL BE WRITTEN IN WORDS AND PICTURES

PM's choice of words: *PM* will be written in English—as distinct from journalese.

Probably the first words ever said on paper about *PM* declared that it should be written by men and women with a talent for words. Its staff will create its style, giving its columns their own personality.

Meanwhile, I record my respect for these elements in journalistic writing:

1. A due respect for the fact that a story can properly be begun at the beginning, the middle or the end—but that each story should have all three components.

2. A definite interest in the personalities and characters of the people who make the news, as well as in the news itself.

3. An interest in the stage on which news is played. In *PM* the murder will not be committed at 2614 Amsterdam Ave., but "in a six-story red brick tenement on upper Amsterdam Ave. (No. 2614), the ground floor of which is shared by a German delicatessen and a Polish newsdealer."

4. A definite interest in the background and continuity of news—and a similar interest in appraising the future.

5. A definite interest in the significance and meaning of news.

And, perhaps more important than any of the above: A consuming interest in the story value of the news. When *PM* uses a column of its precious space to write a story at length, it must be a story—it must be readable in itself. Implicit in *PM*'s relationship with its readers is the understanding that if *PM* devotes much space to a story, it must be a *good* story.

* * *

The writer of every story in *PM* will be identified. All stories will be signed by initials. Where two men have collaborated—as reporter and rewrite man, for instance—the initials of both will be included. A masthead will list all names so that unfamiliar initials can be identified.

PM WILL BE WRITTEN IN WORDS AND PICTURES

PM's choice of pictures: Over half *PM*'s space will be filled with pictures—because *PM* will use pictures not simply to illustrate stories, but to tell them. Thus, the tabloids notwithstanding, *PM* is actually the first picture paper under the sun.

When *PM*'s news comes into the city room it is stopped at the Managing Editor's desk and a decision is made in collaboration with the departmental editor and the picture editors. The problem: Will the story be told in pictures or in words?

If the story is told in words, it may be accompanied by pictures, but they will serve merely as illustrations.

If the story is told in pictures they will be accompanied by no running text, words being confined to captions. All the incoming news in *PM* will be subject to this process and will come out in the paper with a clear emphasis on either words or pictures. (*PM* is put together with an alteration of word and picture pages to facilitate handling, to make better layouts possible and to improve reproduction.)

PM has made a contract with one of the major picture agencies for its full international picture service. *PM* will also maintain a staff of its own photographers, headed by Margaret Bourke-White, and employing the foremost experts in the country. In addition to this, special editors of *PM* will devote all their time and energy to tapping every possible photographic source, such as the 12,000,000 American camera fans, government bureaus, foreign agencies, etc.

As with stories, pictures will not appear in *PM* simply because we have them in the shop, but each must justify its own space in its interest to the reader. To maintain quality *PM* will draw from a large bank of photographs and will make no bones about the fact that it would rather print a fine, striking picture, only indirectly connected with the news of the day, than a dull spot news wirephoto. For, once more, as with its words so with its pictures: *PM* must not bore the reader.

(*PM* does not believe in horror for horror's sake—but its editors will not deny its readers truth of social importance simply because it's unpleasant.)

There is still another innovation in *PM*'s pictures. After a decision has been made that a story will be told in pictures rather than words, another decision is called for: Whether the picture story should be told in photographs or in drawings. For, to make its picture coverage more flexible, *PM* will maintain two staffs of illustrators: a camera staff and a staff of illustrators-by-hand.

PM'S ART

PM will not maintain a large staff of artists on salary, but has chosen rather to develop a group of journalistically-minded artists—numbering forty or fifty—from whom two or three a day will be chosen to take assignments, each in the field for which he is best qualified. (You may have seen announcements of the competition *PM* sponsored with the Museum of Modern Art—a competition called "The Artist as Reporter.")

With *PM* buying and reproducing three to a dozen black and white and two-color drawings and paintings a day, *PM*'s policy unquestionably constitutes the largest endowment of living art in contemporary times. *PM* decided on this policy to give its readers a more exciting, dramatic, meaningful picture reportage. But that objective accomplished, *PM* is happy to find that leading authorities on art foresee in our success an important revival in contemporary art.

EDITORIAL PURPOSE

We have assembled these fine new instruments for the practice of journalism. Of course the most important question of all is: What are we going to do with them? What is the editorial policy of the paper?

PM is in business to tell as much of the truth as it can find out—because it believes journalism's function in a democracy is to see truth in contemporary life and to print it without fear or favor.

But what kind of truth? No one can inventory all the kinds of truth which the people of a great industrial democracy like ours should know in order to govern themselves better and to get more out of the lives they lead. It is only possible to talk in terms of direction. And the direction in which this paper is going is that which used to be called liberal.

The qualification "used to be called" is added because of the last ten years of growing confusion over what the word liberal means. It certainly includes a philosophy of optimism—that we who live in it can make the world a better place than it is today;

that we should not resign ourselves to injustice and inequality of opportunity, to fraud and corruption, to the cruelty of man to man—any more than the scientist of yesterday should have resigned himself to the fact that yellow fever was thought to be incurable, or the scientist of today to the present fact that trichinosis is incurable. But *PM*'s course will not be charted too narrowly for fear of marking out a path which in the end might lead us away from the truth instead of toward it.

That this paper will be without political affiliations has always been taken for granted—because a politician's platform presumes that he knows the truth and is practicing it. Whereas *PM* admits it does not know the solution for all the ills of mankind. What *PM* believes in is the search—and in the legitimacy of the search: The public's right to know whatever we as journalists believe at the moment it is to the public's interest to know.

Without any question, *PM* will come to have strong feelings for or against this or that candidate in local, state and national elections. These feelings, like those of any other journal, will be reflected in its columns. *PM* belongs to no political party and its positions will be taken on the merits of indivduals and individual situations. What makes *PM* tick is a serious belief in honest journalism as an end in itself—the bringing of the truth to the people so that they may decide for themselves what to do about it.

For an example of this paper's policy:

PM believes in the institution of the trade union. Set against the paternalism in industry of the last century there is not a shadow of doubt but that trade unionism is a more democratic, more effective way of life than paternalism—and that honesty practiced, collective bargaining is in the interest of the whole country. Would *PM* then refrain from exposing a corrupt trade union? Of course not! But what *PM* would be against would be the corruption, not the fact that the men were gathered together in a trade union to bargain with their employer.

That this paper will be against racial intolerance goes without saying—and for once, in this paper, the cause of racial tolerance will be championed without fear of accusation that it is influenced by the race or nationality or creeds of owners, advertisers or political factions.

A very early prospectus of this paper set down:

"We are against people who push other people around, just for the fun of pushing, whether they flourish in this country or abroad. We are against fraud and deceit and greed and cruelty and we will seek to expose their practitioners. We are for people who are kindly and courageous and honest. We respect intelligence, sound accomplishment, open-mindedness, religious tolerance. We do not believe all mankind's problems are now being solved successfully by any existing social order, certainly not our own, and we propose to crusade for those who seek constructively to improve the way men live together. We are Americans and we prefer democracy to any other principle of government."

PM still feels that way.

RALPH INGERSOLL,
Editor and Publisher

Appendix 3

MEMORANDUM: Ralph Ingersoll to John P. Lewis
April 9, 1946

What is there that we can do, that no one else can do—or cares to do? How can we be of most use to the society that supports us—in specific terms?

We are agreed that we want to be a more complete newspaper—and a much more alert and readable one.

We are also agreed that we must respect the American tradition of keeping editorial opinion out of the news columns. In writing news we will be interested in facts first, last and always—and we will save our crusading for (1) the editorial page, (2) "special" articles clearly labeled as such, and (3) the play we give stories, which indicates which we think are important. People have been educated in these three ways to crusade.

We are agreed, then, on making the paper both more complete and more orthodox in its approach to news. We are agreed on this for two reasons: (1) so whoever gets to depend on *PM* won't be penalized by having to buy another paper to get the "rest of the news," and (2) to lessen that kind of reader resistance which is called forth by the strangeness of anything new.

But *the guts of PM*—the thing that will get us that next 100,000 circulation—is not these things. It is the use of our journalistic tools—our people and our sources and our organizations—and above all, our brains and curiosity—to get to the folks facts which it is to their interest to know.

That was the original idea behind the advertisingless, editor-managed newspaperman's newspaper: the observation that the other papers—circumscribed by tradition and business office influence, pushed around by the owner's politics and whims—had forgotten how to fight for the people—to catch the crook, to expose the phony, to call the lie, to show the ulterior motive in the proposed legislation.

. . . where I came in was that—because of the chain newspaper, and because of advertising having become Big, Big, Big Business, and because there were people like Cissy and Joe Patterson, and because Ochs was dead and Sulzberger had taken his place— there was a wide open market—a great and crying need—for a good old-fashioned free newspaper, willing to go out and slug for the people.

I just run over this again to be sure we start from the same place. Our franchise is still in old-fashioned crusading journalism. And now what are we going to use our franchise to crusade about?

I start here: the first thing the American people want is the chance to get back to work in peace. Therefore, I am going to crusade like hell against warmakers and warmongers.

The list of warmakers begins with the people who hate Russia so that they want to go to war with Russia right now quick—and, however they disguise their arguments (which I intend to show up), they would have us go out and die on battlefields or stay home and sweat in factories to remove what is, at best, a remote and abstract threat to their dividends.

Next on the list of warmakers come the professional soldiers and sailors who want to go to war because why shouldn't they—that's their trade—and unfortunately they now have a lot of money to spend, and having recently been deprived of their importance by history they yearn for the good old days when they had navies and armies to command. Or some of them do—however pious their statements that there should never be another war (God forbid, they say under their breaths).

I consider Germany still a threat to peace. It has by no means been proved that Germany cannot rise from the ashes a second time to threaten the world.

I call newspapers that mix political motives with desire to keep circulation steamed up, by screaming war, the warmongers.

The Anglophiles are halfway in between. I don't know how many of them actually want another war, but it is certain that the rulers of the British Empire are now working hard to arouse American aggressions against Russia, making capital of our capitalist fears of Communism—and of our imperial tendencies, to make us jealous. The people who have always followed England's lead, the out and out cheerers of Churchill—I am against.

It goes without saying that people want UN to work—to get in there and do a job of keeping the peace. Therefore, I am for UN. But I am for UN so thoroughly that I have no hesitation at all about demanding a superior performance of the delegates—and the governments they represent—to make it work. I think our job is to jump on UN hard when, instead of acting like the enlightened world government that it must become— handling problems frankly and intelligently—they revert to discredited diplomatic double-talk, and reveal ulterior motives. I think we have a unique opportunity to treat delegates like responsible human beings instead of diplomatic dummies, wired for sound—and to make them real and understandable to people—and to hold them responsible for their acts—for the whole world looks to them and they must not be allowed to let the world down.

Next to securing peace, I would say that Americans want to be able to make a living. There are two ways of keeping them from making a living. One is to keep their wages down; and when this fails, the other is to get prices raised.

At this moment in history, I see nothing in trying to raise top wages—for the resultant instability would more than offset the limited gains for the limited numbers. On the wage front, an important objective seems to me to get the lowest wages up to the level—to help the unorganized to form unions, to get the bottom of the pay brackets up. I have a strong hunch that one third of the nation is still ill-fed and ill-housed—12 years after Roosevelt coined that phrase!

But mainly—in the campaign to help people make a living—I think we've got to fight like hell to keep prices down.

Against us, there is the terrific demand that five years of doing without—and wearing out what we had—have built up. Also, more people have more money than they ever had because of savings from war wages—and higher wages in many industries. . . .

And simultaneously I propose to campaign against the idiocies and selfishness of *un*planned production—the wastage of material into buildings only 1% of the people can afford to buy, into clothes and furniture that only 1% of the people can afford to buy. If you take it as an assumption that it is sinful to waste materials—or to leave them unused for lack of planning their use—you have the basis for a whole succession of attacks which are in the public interest. Let's get this country back to the land of plenty it is supposed to be. (Incidentally, one of the most effective ways to waste the most in the shortest time is to build up a large standing army right after large standing armies have been rendered obsolete by aircraft and atom explosives.)

Decent housing is essential to decent living—and we are millions of houses short in this country—and that's a hell of a note for a country as rich as this. Let us crusade like hell to get something done about it.

So we keep the peace.

So we fight to make people's dollars go further and get them roofs over their heads.

BUT—it is a fact for rejoicing or concern (depending on how you care to look at it) that most of all today the American people, after four years of war anxiety, are just about as interested in having a good time as they are in all of the above. Lots and lots and lots and lots of people have more money to spend than they ever had before and are bent on having a good time with it. And they may be damned fools to spend it on new cars and movies and luxuries they can't afford—and maybe it is all just about to disappear in a devaluation of money—but there certainly is a spending spree on, and a vital part of any statement of what people want is to have fun and to be amused.

Certainly this doesn't go under the heading of crusade. Just as certainly, it is a thing to be recognized in making a paper which is acceptable because it gives the people what they want: a feeling that life is good and let's make the most of it. There is, I think more interest in play for play's sake than there is in work for work's sake. There's interest in work, to make the necessary dollars to pay the bills—but not work for work's sake. The American people are in the market for gaiety—they have been lectured to with wartime propaganda for a long time now. Exactly the same thing happened after the last war that produced the gay and nutty '20s.

Over this gaiety hangs the shadow of the atom bomb—and behind the shadow maybe the sun-rise of atom power, and a new era of higher standards of living based on the intelligent development of that atom power. So, we are continually interested in the atom, and one of our serious crusades will certainly be for its development in the people's interest.

Now about politics.

Broadly, our original dedication to democracy goes double. It is much commented on that The Great Experiment of Soviet Russia is no longer an experiment because it has stood the test of war. So, by God, has The Great American Democracy. Everybody thought this country might fly apart under the pressures of war. Both the Japanese and the Germans were absolutely sure that we were too soft to put up a good fight. And, in the end, the whole world's fate hung on American production—and American production didn't let the world down. And the American armed forces—on land and in the air in Europe, and on the sea and in the air in the Pacific—turned in spectacular and historic performances. And all this was accomplished by a unity of purpose in our democracy.

The moral is optimism and we should spread it. There isn't anything we can't accomplish in this country—and let's go to it.

And now about the politics that elect presidents. I make an assumption that the broad base of popular support on which the New Deal rested was not Franklin Roosevelt, but the historic development of this country. In other words, the need for it, the desire for it, is just as real today as it was when Roosevelt articulated it.

Essentially, the New Deal can be seen as an attempt to preserve the personal freedom and incentives of parliamentary capitalism by adjusting them to take advantage of the enormous gains—in production and security—available from socialization. Socialization is simply the pooling of efforts for the common good. I believe that the merger of the best in both systems is what the Americans want (it's what I personally want). It is what we tried to work out in Roosevelt's ten prewar years: a way to bake our cake as socialists and to eat it as regulated capitalists. And, therefore, I think that if we can take the lead in articulating this we will have popular support.

I have a hunch that despite all the wiseacres, no matter how badly Mr. Truman does—and whether he runs again or not—we are going to come up to the next elections with the Republicans, who control the press, convincing everybody that they are about to win, and then, after the election results are counted, the Democrats will have won by another landslide. Why? Because somebody has got to work this thing out in this country because the people want it. The New Deal element in the Democratic Party is the only group that really understands this duality of motive in the American people—the fact that they want things planned socialistically so that electricity is cheap and there's lots of it, and forests aren't wasted so that there's plenty of wood to build things, etc., etc.—but they also want the rewards divided on a capitalistic basis, however circumscribed—a union strong enough to see that the worker gets his share and the rich kept from becoming too rich by income and inheritance taxes—and monopolies kept vaguely in check by the anti-trust laws.

Sources

By far the most important source for this book has been Ralph Ingersoll himself. He gave me complete access to the papers he had stored in his Cornwall Bridge, Connecticut, house and office, and requested that the extensive collection of papers he had donated to the Boston University Library be made available. He also was completely accessible for interviews, not only long formal ones conducted in his living room overlooking the restless Housatonic, but those short telephone interviews that are invaluable to an author when he has a quick question or a mystery that needs to be resolved. Alice and Robert Yoakum also did several interviews with Ingersoll and his wife, Thelma, and made the interviews available to me. And Ingersoll responded to dozens of questions by mail, from Connecticut as well as from his winter home in Saint Croix, and read every page of the manuscript for inaccuracies. However, it was agreed in advance that Ingersoll's contribution to the project would be limited solely to providing information and facts. The author was free to make his own judgments and, of course, seek other viewpoints and information about the events described herein.

The Ingersoll Papers in the Boston University Memorial Library include extensive correspondence to and from Ingersoll, scrapbooks, diaries, manuscripts of his published books (his unpublished books are still in his own office in Cornwall), published short stories, pounds of memoranda (mostly from his *PM* days), dummies and proposals for "a new kind of newspaper," and a variety of personal memorabilia, ranging from his U.S. Army papers to family histories. The diaries cover only the years 1912, 1915,

1920, 1922, 1923, 1924, and the first half of 1925. There is also an extensive correspondence file in his Cornwall office, which will eventually be given to Boston University.

The papers relating to his *Time-Life* years are still retained by the Time Inc. Archives,
as Ingersoll chose not to take them with him when he left. Permission must be obtained
to use them.

By far the single most valuable written source for this biography is Ingersoll's own
unpublished memoirs. In addition to the first and only published volume (*Point of Departure*) of a planned five-volume autobiography, Ingersoll wrote three unpublished autobiographies as well as a brief biography of his close friend Charles Marsh, which
contains much Ingersoll autobiographical information. The three autobiographies are:
"The Story of PM"; "High Time" (later retitled "Years with Luce"); and "Time Out for
a War." The titles suggest the periods of his life they cover, and as I worked on some
sections of this book, I felt as if I were editing an autobiography rather than writing a
biography.

Some general sources were also helpful: *20th Century Authors; Who's Who in
America; Current Biography*; "A Very Active Type Man" by Wolcott Gibbs, in the *New
Yorker* of May 2 and May 9, 1942, which was especially useful; "Violent Man" by Elaine
Brown Keiffer, in the *Sarah Lawrence Alumnae Review* of February 1947.

Of course, Ingersoll's published books and articles, most of which are rich in autobiographical material, were essential.

* * *

Publications by Ralph Ingersoll

BOOKS

In and Under Mexico. New York: Century Book Company, 1924.
Report on England. New York: Simon and Schuster, 1940.
America Is Worth Fighting For. Indianapolis; New York: Bobbs-Merrill, 1941.
Action on All Fronts. New York: Harper & Brothers, 1942.
The Battle Is the Payoff. New York: Harcourt Brace, 1943.
Top Secret. New York: Harcourt Brace, 1946.
The Great Ones. New York: Harcourt Brace, 1948.
Wine of Violence. New York: Farrar Straus and Young, 1951.
Point of Departure. New York: Harcourt Brace, 1961.

ARTICLES

THE NEW YORKER

For a brief period in 1930, Ingersoll wrote a column on college football under the heading
"Football" and signed "Linesman." The column appeared in the following issues: October
4, 11, and 18 and November 8 and 15, 1930. He also wrote a few "Talk of the Town"
pieces, but they are unsigned and difficult to pinpoint. He does not have a collection of
them. After Ingersoll left the *New Yorker*, Ross published his "New York Childhood,"—
April 14, 1934

FORTUNE

(*Fortune* articles did not carry bylines.)
"A Great Gold Argument." February 1931.
"Australia." August 1931.
"S. Klein." July 1932.
"Gold in Canada." June 1933.
"Empire of Cattle: The King Ranch of Texas." December 1933.

"The New Yorker." August 1934.
"The Communist Party." September 1934.
"The Business of Burlesque." February 1935.
"Hearst." October 1935.

MISCELLANEOUS MAGAZINE ARTICLES
Under pseudonym "Ralph McAllister." "The Air Route to Rome." *Vogue*, March 1923.
"Mexicans 'On The Job.'" *Our World*, August 1923.
Under pseudonym "A. W. Sperry." "Kiss Me Again." *I Confess*. December 14, 1923.
"Tips Within Tips." *Saturday Evening Post*, December 20, 1924.
"Confessions of a Society Girl." *Art Lovers*, February 1925.
"The Magic Disk." *Saturday Evening Post*, April 18, 1925.
Under the pseudonym "Robert Ingerley." "Gene Tunney: Champion DeLuxe." *Liberty*,
May 14, 1927.
"Afternoon in a Brownstone." *Good Houskeeping*, October 1947.
"The Sweet Consequences of Murder," *Coronet*, June 1956.

PM
Ingersoll wrote many signed articles and editorials for *PM* from its first issue in 1940
until he left the newspaper in July of 1942, as well as during his brief return to the paper
from January to September of 1946. His books *Report on England, America Is Worth
Fighting For*, and *Action on All Fronts* were based on material that first appeared in *PM*,
and large sections of *The Battle Is the Payoff* and *Top Secret* appeared in *PM* prior to
their publication.

NEWSPAPER COLUMN
From October 6, 1974, to October 7, 1979, Ingersoll wrote weekly bylined newspaper
columns which appeared in many of the papers he owned or managed.

* * *

Interviews
    Many people who knew Ingersoll at various stages of his life were kind enough to
grant me interviews. They are, in alphabetical order, Mrs. Max Ascoli; Julian Bache;
Dr. Louis Bishop; Blair Clark; Bice Clemow; Jerome Doolittle; William Doolittle; William
Doolittle, Jr.; Wentworth Eldredge; Thomas Geyer; Mark Goodson; Allen Grover; Ian
Ingersoll; Ralph Ingersoll II; Thelma Ingersoll; Jacob Kaplan; Dean Krenz; Max Lerner;
Clare Boothe Luce; Mrs. Claudia Marsh; Millicent Matland; Helen Mauro; Brantz Mayer;
Josephine Novella; James Parton; Seymour Schneidman; Gil Spencer; Lee Stauffer;
I. F. Stone; Donald Warner; Alice and Robert Yoakum.

* * *

Chapter One
    The story of Ingersoll's meeting with Henry Luce in 1937 is recorded by Ingersoll
in "Years with Luce." Additional sources for the chapter include the Wolcott Gibbs two-
part profile of Ingersoll in the *New Yorker* of May 2 and 9, 1942; *Trolley to the Moon*
by Eric Hodgins; *Marshall Field III* by Stephen Becker; *Clare Boothe Luce* by Stephen
Shadegg; *Time Inc.* by Robert Elson; and *Name and Address* by T. S. Matthews.

Chapter Two
    The primary sources for this chapter are Ingersoll's autobiography *Point of Departure*
and the book about his experiences in the mines, *In and Under Mexico*. His papers at

Boston University also contain memorabilia, scrapbooks, files, and autobiographical writings pertaining to his childhood and Yale days. His article "New York Childhood" (*New Yorker*, April 14, 1934) has good material on that period. And "The Air Route to Rome," which appeared in the March 1, 1923, issue of *Vogue*, is a good account of his airplane trip over the Alps. "The Sweet Consequences of Murder," written by Ingersoll for the June 1956 issue of *Coronet*, tells the story of the mining incident in which he almost killed a man.

Chapter Three

The autobiography and Ingersoll's diaries in the Ingersoll Papers at Boston University are the most important sources for this chapter. The Boston collection also includes a file of Ingersoll's contribution to the *New York American* in the 1920s, as well as the reviews of *In and Under Mexico*. A good account of the S.S. *Southern Cross* trip to South America is contained in his *Saturday Evening Post* article of December 20, 1924 "Tips Within Tips." Other Ingersoll articles contributing to this chapter are "Mexicans on the Job," in *Our World* of August 1923; "Kiss Me Again" (under the pseudonym W. Sperry), in *I Confess* of December 14, 1923; "Confessions of a Society Girl," in *Art Lovers* of February 1925; and "Magic Disc," in the *Saturday Evening Post* of March 18, 1925.

Chapter Four

The primary source for the early years of the *New Yorker* is the *Fortune* article of August 1934 written by Ingersoll himself. Ingersoll's diary for 1925 also has some significant entries relevant to Ross and the *New Yorker*, but unfortunately he quit diary keeping forever shortly after joining the *New Yorker* staff. His Boston University papers contain letters and memoranda pertaining to his years with Ross, but the best source for these years is his published autobiography *Point of Departure*. Other writings about the *New Yorker*, which include references to Ingersoll are *Years with Ross* by James Thurber; *Ross, The New Yorker, and Me* by Jane Grant; *Ross and the New Yorker* by Dale Kramer; and *Thurber* by Burton Bernstein. The Wolcott Gibbs *New Yorker* profile also has sections dealing with Ingersoll's years on the magazine.

Chapters Five, Six, Seven, and Eight

Ingersoll's unpublished account of his ten years with Time Inc. went through several drafts and two titles—"High Time" and "Years with Luce." They are, of course, the most important source for the chapters on the *Time-Life-Fortune* period. In addition, his files in the Time Inc. Archives contain invaluable material, as does the first volume of Robert Elson's official history, *Time Inc.* Ingersoll wrote an extensive response to Elson's history (intended for publication but never published) which is among his papers at Cornwall Bridge. Interviews with James Parton, Eleanor Treacy, Brantz Mayer, Allen Grover, and P. I. Prentice (by telephone) were also helpful, as was Robert Elson's response to the first draft of several sections from these chapters. Veronica Keating's interview also shed light on the drafting of the first *PM* prospectus. Books that contributed to this chapter include: *Portrait of Myself* by Margaret Bourke-White; *Trolley to the Moon* by Eric Hodgins; *The Restless James Agee* by G. Moreau; *Discriminations* by Dwight Macdonald; *Name and Address* by T. S. Matthews; *Clare Boothe Luce* by Stephen Shadegg. Loudon Wainwright's article "Life Begins," in the May 1978 *Atlantic* also contains invaluable information on the origins of *Life*, and Wolcott Gibbs's *New Yorker* profile on Ingersoll has illuminating material about his Time Inc. years. Other valuable sources are John Shaw Billings's diaries at the South Caroliniana Library at the University of South Carolina. Finally, Laura Hobson's memoir, *Laura Z.*, is essential for a complete understanding of her friendship with Ingersoll in the 1930s and 1940s.

Chapters Nine, Ten, and Eleven

The most important source for the period that begins with Ingersoll leaving Time Inc., in 1939 to launch *PM* and ends with his enlistment in the army in 1942 is his own unpublished manuscript "The Story of PM." His book about the Luce years also has a section on *PM*. A study of *PM* that Ken Stewart made for Marshall Field, and which is now with Stewart's papers in the library at the University of Wyoming, contains extremely valuable information. And Nelson Poynter's papers in the library at the University of Southern Florida have an extensive file on Poynter's relationship with Ingersoll and *PM*. Gladys Uhl made available to me the *PM* file of her husband, Alex, who was with *PM* during most of its years. The Franklin Delano Roosevelt Library at Hyde Park has files pertaining to Ingersoll and *PM*. The incident concerning Mrs. Roosevelt and the alleged military plot to take over the government is discussed in an Ingersoll memo among his papers at Boston University.

Books that were helpful in preparing these chapters include Ingersoll's books about the war (see the list of his publications above); *No Whippings, No Gold Watches* by Louis Kronenberger; *Where Main Street Meets the River* by Hodding Carter; *The File* by Penn Kimball; *The Age of Suspicion* by James Wechsler; *William Benton* by Sidney Hyman; *Marshall Field* by Stephen Becker; *Jock* by E. J. Kahn; and *The Trespassers* and *Laura Z.* by Laura Hobson. Magazine articles that were consulted include: "The History of *PM*" by Ralph Ingersoll, in *PM*, of June 18, 1946; "The Strange Case of *PM*" by Eugene Lyons, in the *American Mercury* of August 1940; "Muddled Millions" by Benjamin Stalberg, in the *Saturday Evening Post* of February 15, 1949; the Wolcott Gibbs profile of Ingersoll; "*PM* Post-Mortem" by Robert Lasch, in the *Atlantic Monthly* of July 1948. And, of course, Ingersoll's bylined writings in *PM* from June 1940 to July 1942. I also talked with I. F. Stone, Max Lerner, Mrs. Max Ascoli, and others associated in one way or another with *PM*.

Chapters Twelve and Thirteen

Ingersoll's "Time Out for a War" is the primary source for these two chapters. In addition, among the Ingersoll Papers at Boston University are his military file and notes he kept while in Europe. Ingersoll's published books about the war, *The Battle Is the Payoff* and *Top Secret*, contain much autobiographical material. The National Archives has declassified the papers pertaining to the deception plan, and I found that Ingersoll's name frequently appears in them. Wentworth Eldredge, who served with Ingersoll in London, was very helpful and provided me with a copy of the "Report to the Joint Security Control," dated May 25, 1945, in which William Harris, Ingersoll, and Eldredge discuss the deception plan. Other sources are *Counterfeit Spy* by Sefton Delmar; *The Game of Foxes* by Ladislas Farago; *Strategic Military Deception*, edited by Donald Daniel and Katherniene Herbig; *A General's Life* by General Omar Bradley and Clay Blair. The plan for the postwar dinner for General Zhukov was contained in an Ingersoll memo, "Imagination's Finest Hour," in the Boston papers.

Chapter Fourteen

Numerous letters and papers in the Boston collection and Ingersoll's files in Cornwall Bridge are among the sources for this chapter. Also helpful were Elaine Brown Keiffer's article "Violent Man" in the *Sarah Lawrence Alumnae Review*, and Ken Stewart's study of *PM* and his interview with Ingersoll (both with Stewart's papers at the University of Wyoming). Other sources are Ingersoll's unpublished memoirs "Time Out for a War" and "The Story of PM"; "*PM*: An Anniversary Assessment," in the *Columbia Journalism Review* of summer 1965; Patrick Mahoney's Ph.D. thesis for the University of Michigan; *Laura Z.* by Laura Hobson; *Age of Suspicion* by James Wechsler; *The Marshall Fields* by John Tebbel; and *Marshall Field* by Stephen Becker. Boston University also has some original recordings of Ingersoll's radio addresses: The two quoted here were done for WABC New York on September 24, 1946, and KSTP, Saint Paul, Minnesota, on November 14, 1946. The reviews of *Top Secret* and *The Great Ones* are in the Ingersoll Papers, as is his account of Elaine's death, entitled "Piece of an Autobiography." He also kept a daily notebook for a brief period in 1946, and Elaine's letters to her housekeeper, Nellie, and to Ingersoll are in the Ingersoll papers at Cornwall Bridge. I also interviewed the following people for this chapter: Julian Bache; Wentworth Eldredge; Clayton Fritchey; Max Lerner, Clare Boothe Luce, and I. F. Stone.

Chapter Fifteen

Ingersoll started to write a biography of Charles Marsh (which is with his papers at Cornwall Bridge), and although he never completed it, it is an invaluable source for this chapter, as are the extensive files on the R. J. Company and the *Middletown Times Herald*, in the Ingersoll Papers. Ingersoll also wrote two unpublished pieces, "How to Make Money" and "Autobiographical Sketch" (December 26, 1953), which were helpful. Also consulted were *Editor & Publisher* of November 3, 1956, and October 8, 1960; *Newsweek* of November 30, 1946, and *Current Biography* of May 1978. The reviews of *Point of Departure* are in the Ingersoll Papers at Boston University. Interviewed for this chapter were Blaire Clark; Jerome Doolittle; William Doolittle; William Doolittle, Jr.; Mark Goodson; Ian Ingersoll; Ralph Ingersoll II; Thelma Ingersoll; Jacob Kaplan; Claudia Marsh; Millicent Matland; Helen Mauro; and Seymour Schneidman.

Chapter Sixteen

The extensive files on the voyage of the *Aleta II* and the various newspapers Ingersoll purchased are in his papers at Boston University. A scrapbook of Ingersoll's newspaper columns is in his files at Cornwall Bridge. Also consulted for this chapter were the *Columbia Journalism Review* of February 1980; *Prisons and Palaces* by Dorothea Straus; and *The Trespassers* by Laura Hobson. I interviewed Dr. Louis Bishop; Jerome Doolittle; William Doolittle, Jr.; Tom Geyer; Mark Goodson; Ian Ingersoll; Ralph Ingersoll II; Thelma Ingersoll; Dean Krenz; Josephine Novella; Dr. Harry Shapiro; Seymour Schneidman; Gil Spencer; Lee Stauffer; and Donald Warner.

Acknowledgments

I wish to express my gratitude to Ralph and Thelma Ingersoll, who extended every possible courtesy and assistance in this project, from making available to me a large, comfortable studio across the street from their house in Cornwall Bridge, Connecticut, to granting me exclusive use of Ingersoll's papers in his Cornwall Bridge office and at Boston University. Dr. Howard Gotlieb, chief of the special collections at Boston University's Mugar Memorial Library, did everything possible to assist me in my researches, and a special word of thanks is due him and his staff, which includes Chris Burns, Margaret Goostray, Douglas Macdonald, Ted Murphy, Charles Niles, Amy Sheperdson, and Rhona Swartz. Elaine Felsher, director of the Time Inc. Archives, also extended me every courtesy and assistance in researching Ingersoll's years with the Luce publications.

I also wish to thank Alice and Robert Yoakum for their special contributions to this project; Tom Stewart and Judith Kern, my editors at Atheneum; and my brother, David Hoopes, for editorial contributions to the manuscript. Ellen Yoakum and Bonnie Sheldon also were helpful in producing this manuscript. The bulk of the manuscript was typed by Beverly Unsworth, but there were also typing contributions by Rhoda Durkan and Mrs. Marguerite Rhodes. I also want to thank my wife, Cora Hoopes, for editorial assistance and moral support throughout the project.

Many other people granted me interviews, helped in my research, or otherwise provided assistance along the way: Alan Abrams; Kim Arnett; Mrs. Max Ascoli; Julian Bache; Donald Baldwin; James Baughman; Edwin Bayley; Dr. Louis Bishop; Robert

Bliss; Douglass Cater; Emmett D. Chisum; Blair Clark; Bice Clemow; Shelby Coffee; Rob Cowley; Sally DeBelles; Jerome Doolittle; William Doolittle, Sr.; William Doolittle, Jr.; H. Wentworth Eldredge; Robert Elson; Katherine Evans; James W. Fletcher; Clayton Fritchey; Lloyd K. Garrison; Thomas Geyer; Mark Goodson; Gene M. Gressley; Allen Grover; Gordon C. Hamilton; Huntington Hartford III; John Hersey; Serrell Hillman; Laura Z. Hobson; Eleanor Treacy Hodgins; Ian Ingersoll; Ralph Ingersoll II; E. J. Kahn; Veronica Keating; Cary Kenney; Spencer Klaw; Dorothy Knight; William Koshland; Karen Kraft; Max Lerner; Nathan Levin; Clare Boothe Luce; Patrick R. Mahoney; Tom Massie; Helen Mauro; Brantz Mayer; Amy Bess Miller; Lawrence K. Miller; Geraldine Morris; Julian P. Muller; Josephine Novella; James Parton; Steve Polly Greco; Mrs. Nelson Poynter; P. I. Prentice; Don Romine; Orville Rush; Seymour Schneidman; I. F. Stone; Volta Torrey; Gladys Uhl; Loudon Wainwright; Donald Warner; Stanley Weintraub; Ray Wennick; E. B. White; and Dan Wickendon.

Index

Roy Hoopes has been a journalist, author and editor for over thirty years and has worked for Time-Life International, *High Fidelity, The Democratic Digest, The National Geographic, Playboy* and *The Washingtonian*. His articles have appeared in more than forty magazines and newspapers and he has published several books, the most recent being *Cain*, a prize-winning biography of the late American novelist, James M. Cain. Mr. Hoopes has two sons, Spencer and Tom, and with his wife, Cora, divides his time between Rehobeth Beach, Delaware, and Mohican Hills, Maryland.